Acknowledgements

Writers often sound as if they are accepting awards when they pen their acknowledgements, thanking everyone from their Great-Grandpa Cletus to the lady who sells them typewriter ribbons. I don't plan to do that. The folks I plan to mention here did indeed play an important role in the genesis, gestation, and development of this work. They are not listed in order of importance, affection, nor depth of contribution, but roughly chronologically. Certainly, many others have invested time and money and skill in this work. My intent is not to slight, but to spotlight. . . .

My heartfelt thanks go to Neal Knox, formerly of Wolfe Publishing Company, the producer of *Handloader* and *Rifle* magazines. Neal bought my first article, encouraged me to write more, offered helpful criticism and just enough words of approbation to keep me in the traces. Neal is the best editor I ever wrote for.

If it weren't for editor Bob Anderson, this tome would not be in existence. He kept after me to submit the idea for this book; stayed on me to stick with it when my brain bogged down and I needed a prod; and preferred helpful suggestions. This is as much Bob's book as mine.

My wife, Barbara. What can I say? She is hardnosed, encouraging, unyielding, pragmatic, humorous, wise, lovely. Barb had to put up with the dour moods with which I was frequently engulfed after hours at the typewriter; had to invent just the right poke to galvanize me into action when I was mired in a slump; had to step around, over, and sometimes atop mounds of guns, ammunition, research books, manuscript pages. Her kitchen table was often littered with the detritus of creativity. She suffered at least with forebearance, if not complete capitulation. She is quite a lady.

Mike Holloway, friend, hunting partner, motorcycling buddy. Mike was more excited about the prospect of this book than I. For years he has patiently accompanied me to the range for photographic sessions; his handsome profile has appeared in more magazines than I can readily recall. Unsurpassingly supportive, intensely loyal, Mike personifies the word "friendship." He aggrandized this book through faith.

Guns Illustrated editor, Harold Murtz, lured me back into the fold with magazine assignments. Harold is one of those rare fellows who is sensitive to a writer's viewpoint. When he gives you an assignment, he means it. No haggling over money, no telling you how to write the thing, no backing out at the last minute. A pro. This business is not overloaded with them.

Rick Jamison is a long-time friend. A close friend. He is also one of the few gun writers always worth reading. Rick was another who kept after me to write this book. He provided me with advice, and Rick's advice is always carefully considered before being offered. As he is one of the two or three top rifle scribes in this country, only a fool would ignore his opinions. I never do. This book is dotted with hunting anecdotes I got from Rick. You can bank on their validity.

Layne Simpson is another worthy writer. Although I've read and admired Layne's work over the years, I'd never met him until recently. He is a soft-spoken Southern gentleman, a gunner of the first water, modest in the extreme. There is no better writer in this business today, nor any more erudite and honest. Layne provided some hunting tales, photos, some handloading data, and much friendly support.

Bill Lindley is one of the most knowledgeable riflemen I ever met. He is manager of the gun department in a local hardware store. Bill often keeps his thoughts to himself; I'm often present when steely-eyed novice shooters douse him with nonsensical "facts." He never contradicts, just says, "Is that right?" A diplomat, Bill Lindley. Generous to a fault, he made available to me much of the information imparted here.

My brother-in-law, Dale Hawks, helped load ammo for the immense amount of shooting involved in this work. He assisted with the photography, handled some of the shooting chores, in general took care of the fun stuff while I did the work. Nice guy.

One of my newest pals is Linc Davidson, of Euclid, Ohio. Linc not only provided moral buttressing, he assisted my wife in keeping me pecking away at the keys. And he tells everyone he meets to rush out and buy a copy of this book; wouldn't be surprised if he doesn't threaten 'em. My kind of guy.

Within the firearms industry, three men have consistently provided more generous support than all their peers combined. Earl Harrington of Harrington & Richardson has always been there when I needed a friend or a hand. Dick Dietz of Remington has gone to bat for me many times over the years, contributed photographs to this book, and been more than generous with his time and expertise. Tom Hall of Weatherby has not only been one of my staunchest supporters, he provided me with much historical information about the Weatherby line of cartridges.

In the ammunition and reloading-component business, Bob Nosler has been a reliable purveyor of information, product and friendship. Bob lined me up for my first elk hunt. Dave Andrews at Speer has often helped with thorny ballistic difficulties no one else seemed able to rectify. Mike Bussard, formerly of Federal Cartridge Corporation, then Sierra Bullets, now with Fiocchi Ammunition, is a pal of long standing. A great deal of the ammunition expended to provide the charts for this book came courtesy of Mike.

And through it all, for 15 years there has been Roger Barnes. Roger helped make my first article possible by securing a mint condition Winchester Model 71 for me to test and write about. Since then he has assisted in so many ways that to list them would merely embarrass him. He was filled with transparent joy when he learned of this book. His enthusiasm has not banked to this day, God bless him.

Lastly, a very special thanks to Ken Ramage of Lyman. Without Kens assistance, and the presence of the Lyman Reloading Handbook, 46th Ed., this effort would not be complete.

And so can you see that this work is far from mine alone. Whatever flaws you discover, lay the blame at my feet. Should you find any merit, distribute the credit to those above-mentioned. They deserve it. And more.

Contents

POPULAR SPORTING RIFLE CARTRIDGES

by
CLAY HARVEY

DBI BOOKS, INC., Northfield, Illinois

Staff

EDITOR
Robert S.L. Anderson

COVER PHOTOGRAPHY
John Hanusin

PRODUCTION MANAGER
Pamela J. Johnson

PUBLISHER
Sheldon L. Factor

DEDICATION
This book is dedicated to my mother, Leola Atkins Harvey. She can no longer read it, but she can heft it in her hand and feel its good weight. . . .

ISBN 0-910676-74-7

Library of Congress Catalog Card #84-070735

MEDIUM/HEAVY BIG GAME CARTRIDGES

CARTRIDGE SELECTION: SOME CONCLUSIONS

Introduction

THIS BOOK is intended to be entertaining, factual, and reasonably unbiased. All of us—particularly writers—have our own opinions, prejudices, and quirks. While I gave my opinions free reign during the book's construction, I did try to base my conclusions on something other than prejudice and quirks. I like to consider myself a reasonably impartial observer having a modicum of common sense and an open mind. The facts found here are offered as such, although it was and is often difficult if not impossible to be completely certain of such esoterica as cartridge introduction dates, original ballistics, every specific model and variation produced in a certain caliber, and similar historical data.

For example, the 280 Ross is sometimes said to have been introduced in 1910, although other sources give 1906. Which is correct? I know which date I *personally* agree with, but *not* which one is "true."

You will note that I frequently borrowed from other sources, ones I considered to be reliable and reputable unless otherwise stated in the text. I also used many hunting anecdotes other than my own, for which I certainly do not apologize. For one thing, one can hunt only so much; if I relied solely on my own hunting experiences, my opinions (or prejudices) would be quite different from what they are. As an example, I personally feel that the 243 Winchester is adequate for deer only under the most ideal of circumstances and within a much shorter range than used to be thought acceptable. I know many hunters who both agree and disagree, and have killed enough game to be entitled to an opinion. I tried to take the views of each camp into advisement when I wrote of the 243.

Along the same lines, I have never owned a sporter-weight 222 Remington that would group under an inch for five-shots *consistently*. (Another writer I know quite well has owned a half-dozen Triple-Deuce sporters and has had a similar lack of "braggin' accuracy" from all of his.) Therefore, *from my own experience* I'd have to say that the 222 is a mediocre grouper in sporting rifles. I know such is not the case; I've talked to too many reliable, honest gunners not to realize that my experiences with the Deuce are atypical. The 222 will indeed group very, very well in hunting rifles; I *know* it but I can't *prove* it. Not with my rifles at any rate.

One other thing to keep in mind is that this book is not intended to be a reloading manual. For good, hard, pressure-tested load data every handloader should buy and study such handbooks as the Lyman, Hornady, Speer, Nosler, Sierra, and Hodgdon (not necessarily in that order). The loads mentioned in the text and entabulated throughout this book are provided as a guide, to show what worked well (or perhaps not so well) in *my* rifles.

In some instances I have commented, in the text, on excellent accuracy or performance from certain components. These comments reflect *my* experience (and/or the experience of others) and are meant to serve only as a guide post to component selection; the *exact* load data not always appearing in tabular form. Using those comments, the reader is urged to refer to the loading manuals mentioned above for more information pertaining to specific loads utilizing those mentioned components. If you do try any of them, follow the standard practice of starting lower than the listed charge and working up while keeping an eye out for pressure signs.

Please bear in mind that this work is the result of much shooting, reading, discussing, and digging. It was not written off the cuff, but with as much fairplay and clarity as I could muster.

Enjoy.

Popular Sporting Rifle Cartridges

22 HORNET
222 REMINGTON
223 REMINGTON
222 REMINGTON MAGNUM
225 WINCHESTER
224 WEATHERBY MAGNUM
22-250 REMINGTON
220 SWIFT

VARMINT/TARGET

22 Hornet

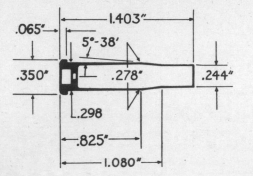

"Assuming a fine gunner, one who knows the limitations of the cartridge relative to ranging ability and striking energy, the Hornet is death on crows, chucks, turkeys and assorted creatures of similar ilk."

WAY BACK in the late 1920s, shooters were hankering for an honest-to-goodness varmint cartridge, one designed specifically for the taking of woodchucks, crows, and suchlike at ridiculously long range. Say a couple of hundred yards. The 30-06 was steadily gaining in popularity, and the new 270 Winchester cartridge was weaning the boys from the more plodding rounds. But both kicked too much for varmint shooting. Savage had their little 22 Hi-Power and the 250-3000, but they were touted as big-game loads. The Hi-Power, originally called the Imp, often displayed accuracy sad enough to make a stevedore weep, especially in the take-down leverguns so popular at the time. The 250-3000 performed okay, downright sensational in solid-frame guns, but it was still a deer rifle. What the fellows longed for was a 22-caliber centerfire that would work in single shot rifles and also feed smoothly through a turnbolt.

G.L. Wotkyns took the 1885-vintage 22 Winchester Center Fire cartridge, an elderly blackpowder number that showed a modest velocity of about 1500 fps and began to experiment. This was not an unprecedented move. In Germany, the 5.6x35R Vierling, based on the same cartridge case, had been achieving some fairly impressive speeds when loaded with jacketed bullets and smokeless powder. Wotkyns decided to go the Germans a step or two better.

Using reamers made for him by George Titherington of Stockdale, California, Wotkyns rechambered a Model 1922 Springfield 22 Long Rifle barrel and stuck it on a BSA Number 12 Martini single shot action. The rifle had been altered to accept centerfire ammunition. In his first experiments, Captain Wotkyns used both the UMC 45-grain Velo-Dog and Neidner 44½-grain bullets. His load was 12.0 grains of the old No. 1204 powder. Since the bullet diameter of the factory 22 WCF was nearly .226-inch, Wotkyns had to neck his brass down to accept the smaller .223-inch diameter slugs. Having no chronograph, he estimated his muzzle velocity by calculating the maximum ordinate at 100 yards, combining that figure with the angle of elevation necessitated at that range and the ballistic coefficient of the Neidner bullet. He came up with between 2400 and 2500 fps. That jibed quite closely with the figures later obtained on a chronograph.

Wotkyns wrote Colonel Townsend Whelen about his testing, and succeeded in interesting the good Colonel in his research. Whelen enlisted the aid of some of his co-workers at the Springfield Armory, including G.A. Woody and A.L. Woodworth. These gentlemen promptly set up their own test rifle, rechambering a Model 1922 Springfield and altering it to handle the 22 WCF case.

Dissatisfied with the Velo-Dog full-jacketed bullets, the Springfield Armory contingent formed their own jacketed slugs using 22 Short cartridge cases (still in the manufacturing process, not spent brass) to form the

Du Pont's IMR 4227, as well as the near-identical H4227, are propellants for the 22 Hornet.

Introduced in the '30s, Winchester's Model 70 in 22 Hornet proved to be a winner with varmint hunters. Unfortunately, many of those now-valuable pre-'64 Hornets were converted to 222 Remington, back in the '50s and early '60s. (The Hornet seen here is in original dress and, with the right loads, will group under an inch at 100 yards.)

jackets and using 22 Long Rifle lead bullets for the cores. The resulting bullets were of semi-spitzer shape, weighed 45 grains, and were .2233-inch in diameter.

Like Wotkyns, they used No. 1204 propellant, but in 11.0-grain doses. Muzzle speeds ran between 2300 and 2400 fps; 10-shot groups measured from ⅞-inch to 1½ inches at 100 yards, fired from a machine rest.

Townsend Whelen and his cohorts ensnared the Hercules Powder Company, not being as happy with No. 1204 powder as they might have been. After much experimentation, Hercules 2400 powder was born. Muzzle velocities with the new propellant made it to an honest 2400 fps. (And now you know where Hercules 2400 got its name.)

By 1930, Winchester had horned in on the act, making up their own test rifle along with an experimental batch of ammunition. They discovered that their new rifle/ammo combination would provide the tightest groups of any cartridge tested to that time. Enthralled and excited by their discovery, Winchester offered the ".22 Winchester Hornet" to the public 2 years before they catalogued a rifle for it.

The prestigious New York firm of Griffin & Howe began advertising custom-built 22 Hornet-Springfield rifles in January of 1931. Most early Hornets were modified Model 1922 Springfields, although Savage became the first firm to offer a factory rifle in this chambering by making the Model 23-D available in August,

Affordable and well made, the Savage 340 bolt-action is still being chambered for 22 Hornet. Many 340 owners report excellent accuracy from these rifles.

Kimber's Model 82 Cascade Hornet is one of the most beautiful rifles ever to hit the market. If you want to know how accurate this rifle can be, you have two choices: 1) to buy one; 2) ask someone who owns one.

While not designed for the benchrest crowd, the Savage 24-V combination (22 Hornet/20-gauge) gun is a dandy package for the hunter. Out to about 100 yards or so, the factory iron sights will do the job; beyond that you'll have to take advantage of the 24V's integral scope base.

1932. Winchester finally entered the market in February of 1933. Savage added the Model 19-H turnbolt and the Stevens "Walnut Hill" single-shot to the growing list of 22 Hornet rifles.

Factory ballistics sheets of the 1940-era showed the Hornet as being available with your choice of a 45- or 46-grain soft or hollow point, respectively. Factory ammo was loaded with 10.2 grains of Hercules 2400; advertised velocities were 2600-2625 fps. Pressures were said to average between 38,000 and 40,000 psi.

During the '30s and '40s, the Hornet became very popular with the varmint-hunting crowd. Turkey hunters didn't ignore it either. The Hornet is still considered to be the premier centerfire turkey cartridge in factory persuasion.

Today, the 22 Hornet is as potent as ever. Winchester continues to make a 45-grain soft point and a 46-grain hollow point, both now listed at 2690 fps at the muzzle. Remington's profferings both weigh 45 grains; otherwise the numbers read the same. Muzzle energy is 723 foot-pounds for the 45-grainers; 200-yard retained energy is 225 fpe with three of the loads, 230 fpe with the Winchester hollow point. That's not a whole lot of punch.

When the 222 Remington came along in 1950, the 22 Hornet's popularity dropped like the price of silver. For the next 2½ decades, it hung on by its teeth. Where earlier such marques as Winchester, Sako, Anschutz, BRNO, Walther, Charles Daly, and BSA had been reamed for the Hornet, only one or two brands remained. The excellent Anschutz stayed around, and I believe the H&R Topper could be had. The others abandoned ship.

Interest picked up in the '70s. Ruger included it in their catalogue, chambered in the No. 3 single shot; Savage offered it in the Model 24; Sako imported the Model 78. In 1982, Kimber of Oregon tooled up for the neglected Hornet. All of a sudden it was business as usual.

A lot of folks aren't aware of it, but the Hornet even served time for Uncle Sam. During WWII and Korea, survival rifles chambered for the cartridge were carried aboard aircraft. In the event of a crash, a downed pilot had along a handy tool for subsistence and self-defense. Ammo provided for the lightweight guns was loaded with a non-expanding bullet, as per the Hague Accords. There was one exception. A soft point loading was issued (for "foraging" purposes), with its container admonishing against its use in combat. Who was kidding whom?

Although perhaps not much as a combat load, the 22 Hornet is generally considered to be adequate fare for woodchuck hunting out to 150 yards or so. Some authorities set the limit at 175 yards, citing the rapid drop past that distance as their reason for trying to stay within that range. Yet other experts feel that the Hornet has what it takes for 200-yard kills, if the wind is calm and a quick-expanding bullet is selected. If we settle on 175 yards or so as the maximum effective range, due to wind drift and retained energy, will the Hornet hold up its end in the requisite accuracy department?

Gunwriter Layne Simpson phoned me while I was typing this chapter. After exchanging insults and swapping tales, he asked me what I had been up to. I told him I was composing the chapter devoted to one of his favorite cartridges, the 22 Hornet. He queried as to what I had said about accuracy. I told him nothing yet.

"If you say it's not accurate, I'll quit writing your articles for you," quipped he.

"What should I say?" Guileless.

"That it'll shoot as well as any other 22 centerfire, given calm conditions, good bullets, and an accurate rifle. I've been considering having a benchrest rifle built, with a 1-in-10 twist, just to show what the cartridge will do with match-grade bullets."

I considered asking him who he was going to get to handle the shooting, but I deferred. Instead I said, "Wind sensitive, is it?"

"You bet. The slightest puff will toss those lightweight bullets around like you wouldn't believe. Almost like a 22 rimfire."

"Can I quote you?"

"I'll have to charge."

"Been nice talking to you." We hung up. I like Layne. Sometimes he tends to get a bit defensive about the Hornet, but he means well.

One of the secrets to accuracy in the Kimber Hornet is the quality of the barrels used. The introduction of the Kimber Hornet literally gave that old but valuable 22 centerfire a new lease on life.

Although a Hornet is not really a 200-yard load except maybe under calm conditions, this is what a little 40-grain bullet will do to a gallon jug of water at that distance.

(Right) Left to right: the factory 22 Hornet, the Hornet Improved and the K-Hornet. The latter round was, many years ago, a popular wildcat; to many it still is.

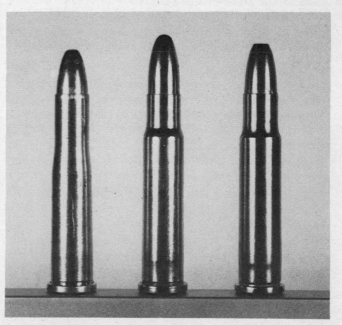

22 Hornet: Varmint/Target

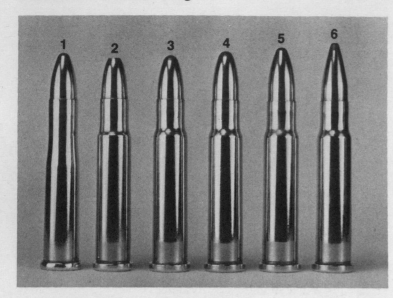

Fireforming the standard 22 Hornet case (1) will increase its capacity by 10 to 12 percent, depending on the density of the powder used. The K-Hornet (2) has a 35-degree shoulder angle as compared to 25 degrees for my improved Hornet (3), no difference in performance between the two. I know because I've owned both. The following 224-diameter bullets are shown seated out for best accuracy in my rifle: 40-grain Sierra (3); 45-grain Sierra (4); 45-grain Speer (5); 45-grain Hornady (6). (Photo and data courtesy Layne Simpson.)

(Right) Although the 45-grain bullets, such as the Sierra soft point at left, are traditional for the small-capacity Hornet, some guns handle the 50-grainers acceptably. Left to right—45 gr. Sierra SP, 50-gr. Speer SP, 50-gr. Remington PL, 50-gr. Nosler SB, 50-gr. Nosler JHP(M).

Regarding the accuracy question, here's what the *NRA Handloader's Guide* has to say:

> The Hornet has the reputation of being somewhat critical when it comes to developing accurate handloads. A common impression is that rifles chambered for the Hornet will change zero readily and for no accountable reason. Actually, there is little justification for this . . . Also, light bullets are used which are sensitive to wind conditions. There is nothing at all about the cartridge itself which would cause it to be any more critical than other cartridges . . .

Let Layne Simpson have the last word, from the July-August, 1983, *Handloader* magazine:

> The Kimber Hornets have barrels with a 14-inch twist, not the long-standard 16-inch, which is good news to turkey hunters who like to use bullets heavier than 45 grains. My Kimber shows just how accurate a good Hornet can be: I have fired 222 groups of five shots each, so far, for an aggregate group of 1.113 inches. That ain't half bad for a rifle fresh out of its box. You think I like the Kimber Hornet? You *know* it!

As Layne mentions, the standard twist rate is 1-in-16 inches, which works all right with bullets of 45 grains or under. Not so good with those of 50 grains and up, particularly if they have a long, tapering ogive. The likely reason this hasn't been changed over the years is that, due to the limited case capacity, velocities fall off quite markedly once bullets heavier than factory-standard are stuffed in the case. Not only will accuracy suffer from the resulting lack of stabilization, but bullet expansion would become very iffy. Stick with the 40- to 45-grain class in the Hornet.

Best powders for the pleasant little cartridge are those with a burning rate similar to Hercules 2400, powders like Winchester 296 and 680, Du Pont IMR 4227, Hodgdon H4227 and H110. Eleven grains of Winchester 680 coupled with the 40-grain Sierra 223 Hornet soft point makes a dandy load, accurate, and with muzzle speeds comparable to the factory-published numbers for the 45-grain slugs. Use 11.5 grains of 680 with the 45 Speer .224-inch diameter soft point for a very accurate load that roughly equals the original 1930 ballistics.

One of Layne's favorite recipes is 11.7 grains of H4227 under the 45-grain Nosler semi-spitzer. In his 1-in-14-twist Kimber, this load averages *less than ½-inch,* and clocks 2762 fps. Now *that* is a good load. Another of his pets consists of the 45-grain Sierra semi-spitzer riding 10.2 grains of Hercules 2400 to 2745 fps. His group average was .42-inch with that load. Remember, that is a light sporter he's shooting! Inaccurate?

And so we leave the 22 Hornet. It is a mild-mannered cartridge, easy on the ear as well as the shoulder. I have read of Hornet rifles that went 10,000 rounds with no decrease in accuracy. You can get about 600 reloads from a pound can of powder. In the right rifles, and under the best conditions, the accuracy exhibited is as good as with any other cartridge. A plethora of rifles is available, and not all of them will set you back a month's salary. Assuming a fine gunner, one who knows the limitations of the cartridge relative to ranging ability and striking energy, the Hornet is death on crows, chucks, turkeys, and assorted creatures of similar ilk. Try it.

22 Hornet

HANDLOAD DATA

Bullet Wt. Grs.	Type	Powder Wt. Grs.	Type	Primer	Case	MV (fps)	ME (fpe)	Rifle/ Bbl. (in.)	Remarks
40	Speer SP	13.0	Win. 680	6½-116	Win.	2891	742	Kmbr. M82/22	Vry. acc.; L. Simpson data
45	Speer SP	11.5	H4227	6½-116	Win.	2715	737	Kmbr. M82/22	Vry. acc.; L. Simpson data
45	Speer SP	**11.7**	H4227	6½-116	Win.	**2762**	**762**	Kmbr. M82/22	Extrmly. acc.; L. Simpson data
45	Hrndy. SP	11.3	Win. 296	6½-116	Win.	2784	775	Kmbr. M82/22	Extrmly. acc.; L. Simpson data
45	Nosler SP	9.3	H110	6½-116	Win.	2564	657	Kmbr. M82/22	Extrmly. acc.; L. Simpson data
45	Speer SP	11.5	Win. 680	Norma	West.	2681	718	Win. M54/24	Extrmly. acc.; K. Waters data
52	Speer JHP	**10.5**	IMR 4227	Rem. 6½	Rem.	**2427**	**680**	Sav. M219/26	Lyman Hndbk., 46th Ed. (Acc. Ld.)

SP—Soft Point; JHP—Jacketed Hollow Point.

FACTORY LOAD DATA

Bullet Wt. Grs.	Type	MV (fps)	ME (fpe)	Rifle/ Bbl. (in.)	Remarks
45	Win. SP	2655	704	Kmbr. M82/22	Accurate; L. Simpson data
45	Rem. SP	2723	740	Kmbr. M82/22	Poor acc.; L. Simpson data
45	Rem. JHP	2689	722	Kmbr. M82/22	Vry. acc.; L. Simpson data
46	Win. JHP	2668	727	Kmbr. M82/22	Vry. acc.; L. Simpson data

SP—Soft Point; JHP—Jacketed Hollow Point.

SPECIFICATIONS

Shell Holders
RCBS: 12
Bonanza: 8
Lyman: 4
Pacific: 3

Bullet Diameter
Jacketed: .223"-.224"

Lengths
Trim: 1.393"
Maximum Case: 1.403"
Maximum Overall: 1.723"

CAUTION:
Loads recommended and suggested herein have been carefully listed, but are intended solely as a guide to readers and neither the publisher nor author accept any responsibility for results of their use. **Maximum loads, listed in bold, should be reduced by 10 percent and worked up to cautiously.**

222 Remington

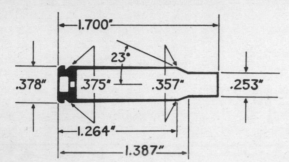

"I fired a group, peered through the spotting scope, rubbed my eyes, looked again, then strolled downrange. The five shots spanned .38-inch, center-to-center . . . "

WHEN the Remington Arms Company introduced the 222 Remington in 1950, it is doubtful that they anticipated their modest little cartridge would virtually establish an empire. Varmint shooters had for years been torn between the mild 22 Hornet and the wild 220 Swift. The 218 Bee was little more potent than the Hornet and not available in such classy rifles as the Winchester Model 70. The 219 Zipper offered ballistics in the same area as the new 222, and had since 1937, but the Zipper was essentially a lever-action cartridge insufficiently precise for long-range work. No help there. Except for such wildcat loads as the 219 Donaldson Wasp, 22 Varminter, and 2R Lovell, the small-bore centerfire buff was out in the cold.

Along came the happy little 222. Overnight it revolutionized the 22 centerfire lineup. The Swift was busy "burning" out barrels and getting bad press. The Zipper was dying, the Bee about buzzed out, and the Hornet was setting few sales records. Not so the 222.

While its ballistics were anything but sensational, its accuracy was. In the '50s the plain-Jane Model 722 Remington was a bell ringer, the perfect vehicle to introduce the pleasures of chuck hunting to those nimrods who did not handload. Groups well under 1 inch at 100 yards, with factory ammunition, were as common as "I like Ike" buttons. Folks weren't used to such. Word got around.

Most every factory of any count has chambered one or another of their models for the Triple-Deuce. In addition to the plethora of turnbolts, Remington made up a few trombone actions to take the round; Ruger offered it in the Number 1 one-shooter; heck, even a semi-automatic has been factory-reamed for the cartridge. I know of no leverguns, but as soon as this hits print I doubtless will.

Accuracy

Is the 222 really as accurate as they say? Will a puppy dog fertilize the carpet! The one 222 I have shot that was not a true precision tool was a Ruger Number 1 that I acquired back in the late 1960s. That handsome, beautifully built piece of craftsmanship would do well to group five shots inside 1½ inches at 100 yards. I swapped it off.

The next Triple Deuce I bought was a Remington 40-XBR, a factory-prepared benchrest rifle. When I settled on a good handload and got used to the gun, it rewarded me with groups that seldom exceeded ½-inch. On one occasion I fired five consecutive five-shot strings that averaged .3203-inch. The best that rifle did was one exceptional five-hole string of .166-inch. Accurate?

Last summer I worked extensively with one of the new Remington Model 7s, a super-lightweight sporter with a barrel slender as a fairy's wand. With choice fodder, that little cream puff would group just over 1 inch.

A bevy of 222s, left to right: Hart-barreled M700-actioned benchrest competition rig, re-chambered pre-'64 Winchester Model 70, a rare Ruger Number 1, Sako L-46, Sako L-461, and a Martini in 222 Rimmed.

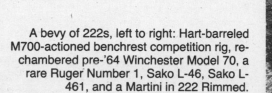

The Remington 788, shown here, was available in 222 for most of its sales life. Accuracy is usually exceptional.

This lightweight Remington Model Seven will group just over 1 inch for five-shots, on the average. Excellent performance from a super-airweight gun.

Remington's 40X series of superbly accurate bench rifles have probably likely been chambered more often in 222 than any other caliber. The author had one that nearly always stayed inside .40-inch.

The Savage 112-V was chambered for 222 as well as other cartridges. Every 112-V the author has fired has been very accurate; the 222 chambering was *very* accurate.

The author's wife is obviously pleased with her group! That's a Sako 222, a rifle long known for superb accuracy when chambered for the "Triple-Deuce."

My most recent acquisition is a Remington Model 788. Untuned, with the factory-bestowed heavy, creepy, trigger pull, that rifle will go into 1.03 inches with Federal factory ammo. And that with less than 40 rounds through the barrel. With a little cleaning up of the barrel channel, some good handloads, and a few more rounds down the chute, I'll bet an oatmeal cookie that 788 will group into .75-inch or less, group after group. Accurate?

Let's see what other writers have to say regarding the 222's accuracy potential. Here's the extremely knowledgeable Jim Carmichel—*Outdoor Life's* in-house expert—from his book, *The Modern Rifle:*

> I bought my first Sako, a 222 with Mannlicher stock, back about 1952. The retail price then was about $125, which in those days was pretty steep, more even than a Model 70 . . . Outfitted with a Lyman 10X Wolverine scope, the trim little rifle would put *ten* rounds inside an inch on any occasion and was light enough to carry over the hills from dawn to dusk.

Jim went on to discuss the 222 Remington's fame as a benchrest competition cartridge, which is considerable. Ten years ago, any time a benchrest tourney was won by a cartridge *other* than the 222 it was an exception to the norm. I'll go out on a limb and say that more benchrest matches have been won with the Triple Deuce than all other cartridges combined. Even today, during the reign of the wildcat 22 PPC, the 222 can hold its own unless the competition is too keen. The 222 Remington is without a doubt the most accurate *factory* cartridge ever produced in this country, and likely anywhere else.

The 222 for Varminting

How about varmint hunting? How does the 222 stack up today against such stiff competitors as the 223 Remington, the 22-250, and the two 6mms? Let's go back to

the beginning. When the 222 had just been freshly minted, C.S. Landis wrote this in the 1951 *Gun Digest:*

> Remington has come out rather recently with . . . a cartridge called the 222 Remington. It is not a 222 caliber at all; the bullet used is a full 224 . . . It is a somewhat overgrown R-2 but with a larger, more costly, rimless case, with a shoulder of about 23 degrees.
>
> The [722-A] seems to have been improved slightly since it first appeared, but it is still 2 to 3½ pounds too light for a perfect woodchuck rifle . . . Even if it were of full weight, and with a good action and fine pull, it would still not be using one of the very best woodchuck cartridges, either of long range, or one of softer report. It is essentially about a 250-yard rifle, if fitted with a first class scope, and you happen to draw a good barrel.

Now how's that for objective reporting? First Mr. Landis chides Remington for referring to the new load as the 222 when it actually took 224 bullets. (Of course, so did the 218 Bee, 220 Swift, et al.) He goes on to compare the 222 to the R2 Lovell, which the Remington cartridge resembles only by having a bullet in one end and a primer in the other. (Note also the reference to

(Above) A light rifle and a fat chuck, one balancing the other for a long trek back to the automobile.

As Dave Coffee illustrates here, a light 222 like this Remington Model Seven will do the job on chucks—providing you keep the shooting range to about 250 yards, or less.

(Right) One advantage any short-action 222 has going for it is that it is easily slung out of the way. The 222, and the guns chambered for it, have long been popular with walking varmint hunters. They make the walking easy and don't weigh down the shooter as he glasses for chucks or crows.

the 222 as being "more costly.") Our author does give Remington credit for improving the Model 722 "slightly," but then goes on to chastise the gun for its lack of *avoir dupois,* and the cartridge for being a middle-of-the-road number, neither hot nor cold nor yet just right. Finally, he grudgingly admits that the Model 722/222 combination will do okay for groundhogs out to 250 yards if you're fortunate enough to get an accurate barrel.

I quoted the above to show that the 222 overcame such yellow journalism to become an immoderate success, and because about the only erudite, nonprejudicial ruling Mr. Landis made was his maximum-range assessment of 250 yards.

Jack O'Conner said of the 222: ". . . it will kill varmints up to the size of jackrabbits and woodchucks as well as any other cartridge to 225-250 yards."

Jim Carmichel has written: "With a little estimating for bullet drop this gives the round an effective range of upwards of 300 yards, and this is about as far as most of us can hope to hit a chuck-sized target anyway."

Frank Barnes, in *Cartridges of the World:* "It is an excellent 200- to 250-yard cartridge for the full range of varmint and small game animals up to, but not including deer."

Looks like Landis was close to being right. If we average O'Conner's 225-250 yardages, Carmichel's 300, and Barnes' 200-250, we'll come up right smack in the middle at 250 yards, plus or minus a millimeter. Let's settle on that.

Now back to our comparisons. The 223 Remington offers another 100 fps over the 222 in factory form, and a 10 percent increase in bullet weight. At 300 yards, the 223 hits 8.5 inches low from a 200-yard zero; the 222 shows a 10-inch drop. Retained energy out at the 300 mark is 443 fpe for the 223, 321 for the Triple Deuce.

The 22-250 dips only about 5½ inches out at 400, and carries in excess of 600 fpe. That's about half the drop and twice the energy of the 222, another class altogether. The 6mm cartridges are simply more of the same.

Bear in mind what Jim Carmichel said about the difficulty of connecting on tiny targets at long distances. He is absolutely correct. Most of us don't *need* a flatter trajectory than the 222 Remington provides, although I do

The single best five-shot group ever fired by the author with factory ammo was shot from a Remington M700-V similar to this one. The string measured .38-inch.

The Savage Model 24-V can be had in 222/20 gauge combination. Makes a great combination for turkey hunting!

believe that the increased punch of something like the 223 is good insurance in case of a peripheral hit on a chuck. Then again, maybe not. It takes real power to nail a poorly-hit groundhog, more than is provided by most of the 222 centerfires.

For what it's worth, my sentiments ally themselves with those of Frank Barnes. I think of the Triple Deuce as a 200-yard cartridge under most circumstances when used by the average gunner. For the superb shot who will not take risky attempts, who avails himself of a sturdy rest, and who knows how to place his shot, the 222 will suffice on varmints to perhaps 250 yards. I'm sure that the cartridge is capable of *hitting* chucks much further than that, but *hitting* is not all we should be concerned with.

The 222, at left, is roughly comparable to the 6mm Remington, right, in trajectory but not in energy or wind-bucking characteristics.

Handloading

Barrel life with the 222 is pretty good. The consensus is that for varmint use, upwards of 5000 or more rounds can be slid down a rifle barrel without totally destroying its accuracy. Benchrest shooters sometimes consider their tubes shot out at 2500 or even less, but they live in a different world from the varmint hunter accuracy-wise. If I shot my 222s a lot, my least concern would be abbreviated barrel life. Not so my 22-250, Swift, or the 6mms.

I like Hercules ReLoder 7 in my 222s, although IMR 4198 is the "traditional" propellant. My Model Seven likes 21.1 grains ReLoder 7 and the 52-grain Sierra match boat-tail, for 3045 fps from its 18½-inch barrel.

In my Remington 40-XBR, 23.5 grains of IMR 4895 and the 52-grain Sierra benchrest bullet is the show pony. Close behind is 21.1 of ReLoder 7 with the defunct 52-grain Remington benchrest bullet. Groups with this latter load average .407-inch.

Fastest load in my Model 7 is a maximum charge of 26.2 grains of Winchester 748 pushing the 52-grain

Speer hollow point to a muzzle speed of nearly 3200 fps in the short barrel, a sizzler indeed. Pressures are okay; in fact, several loading manuals go a ½-grain higher than this. Since accuracy in my rifle is just fine at the 26.2-grain level, I'll stick with that.

The most accurate factory loads in my experience are the Federal 50-grain soft points, on the average. My Model 7 groups the ammo at 1.31 inches, excellent for such a light rifle. The Model 788 Remington goes 1.03 inches.

The swiftest factory-brewed stuff is generally the 50-grain Remington Power-Lokt hollow point. My 788 clocks 3175 fps with that load, which exceeds factory-quoted ballistics substantially, and from a 24-inch barrel. The Federal soft point loading gets 2984 fps in my 18½-inch M7, 3058 fps from the 788.

Incidentally, the tightest five-shot group I ever fired

with factory ammunition was shot with the Frontier 55-grain SX soft point 222 ammunition. A gentleman at the range asked me to testfire his brand new Remington 700 Varmint; he was new to centerfire rifle shooting, and he thought the gun was shooting pretty well. The gun was fresh from the carton and had, I believe, a Redfield variable scope on the bridge. I fired a group, peered through the spotting scope, rubbed my eyes, looked again, then strolled downrange. The five shots spanned .38-inch, center-to-center of the widest shots. Accurate?

As I write this, the 222 Remington is 34 years old. It has been largely supplanted as a competition load by wildcat cartridges designed for that one purpose only.

There can be had from the factories several 22-caliber hotshots that can lick the Triple Deuce coming and going in the varmint fields. However, the 222 sired the cartridge that serves this republic in a defensive role. It was the progenitor of the 222 Magnum, a cartridge that has died in the marketplace, even though it was intended as the 222's replacement. It has lived through the birth and demise of a Winchester offering aimed squarely at it, and still manages to place in the top 15 on the RCBS die-popularity chart.

No factory cartridge is more accurate. Few will do such a thorough job on a chuck or crow with a concomitant lack of recoil and muzzle roar. Good cartridge, the Triple Deuce. Outdated, outdone. But still here.

222 Remington

HANDLOAD DATA

Bullet Wt. Grs.	Type	Powder Wt. Grs.	Type	Primer	Case	MV, (fps)	ME, (fpe)	Rifle/ Bbl. (in.)	Remarks
52	Speer JHP	20.2	IMR 4198	Rem. 7½	Fed.	2963	1014	Rem. M7/18½	Erratic velocity
52	Rem. BR	21.1	ReLod. 7	Rem. 7½	Fed.	3085	1099	Rem. 40-XBR/20	Extremely accurate
52	Sierra JHPBT(M)	21.1	ReLod. 7	Rem. 7½	Rem.	3045	1071	Rem. M7/18½	Fair accuracy
52	Sierra JHPBT(M)	23.4	IMR 4895	Fed. 205	Rem.	2883	960	Rem. M7/18½	Mild
52	Speer JHP	**26.2**	Win. 748	Rem. 7½	Fed.	**3197**	**1180**	Rem. M7/18½	Highest vel. this gun

JHP—Jacketed Hollow Point; BR—Bench Rest; JHPBT(M)—Jacketed Hollow Point Boat-Tail (Match)

FACTORY LOAD DATA

Bullet Wt. Grs.	Type	MV, (fps)	ME, (fpe)	Rifle/ Bbl. (in.)	Remarks
50	Fed. SP	2984	989	Rem. M7/18½	Very accurate
50	Fed. SP	3058	1038	Rem. M788/24	Most acc. ld. in this gun
50	Hrndy. SX	2960	973	Rem. M788/24	Accurate
50	Rem. PL	2956	970	Rem. M7/18½	Good velocity
50	Rem. PL	3175	1119	Rem. M788/24	Very fast
50	Win. SP	2960	973	Rem. M7/18½	Good velocity
55	Fed. FMJ	2842	987	Rem. M788/24	————

SP—Soft Point; SX—Super Explosive; PL—Power Lokt; FMJ—Full Metal Jacket.

SPECIFICATIONS

Shell Holders
RCBS: 10
Bonanza: 6
Lyman: 26
Pacific: 16

Bullet Diameter
Jacketed: .224"
Lengths
Trim: 1.690"
Maximum Case: 1.700"
Maximum Overall: 2.130"

223 Remington

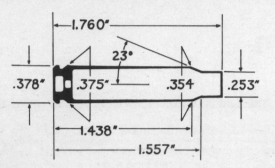

"If you prefer to walk more than 50 feet from your car, if an artificial support draped over the hood of your pickup leaves you cold, if just seeing country and bagging an occasional groundhog is your meat, the 223 is your load."

LIKELY you believe that the 22-250 Remington is the most popular 22 centerfire cartridge in today's market. Wrong. According to the RCBS "Top 30" die popularity chart, the 22-250 is ranked twelfth of all dies sold, including those for handguns. The 223 Remington is in fourth place in total die sales, second in sales of rifle dies only. That means the lackluster 223 is ahead of such favorite deer loads as the 243, 270 Winchester, 308 Winchester, and 30-30. No other varmint round comes close to it, unless you consider the 22-250's placing to be close.

Factory ammo availability reflects quite accurately a cartridge's popularity. The more factories that load it, the more popular it is. I'm not certain just how many overseas outfits produce the 223, but since it is a standard NATO round I suspect the number is considerable. In the United States, Winchester offers three versions of it, Remington catalogs three, so does Federal, and Hornady sells two permutations in their Frontier line. That's 11 different loadings made domestically alone.

In contrast, the 22-250 is offered in one loading by Winchester, two by Remington (the parent company!), and three each by Hornady and Federal. The tally is nine. If such foreign outfits as Squires-Bingham or PMC make the 22-250, I'm not aware of it.

Other hotshot 22s go like this: 222 Remington, nine different iterations; the 220 Swift, three; 225 Winchester, (are you kidding?) one; the 224 Weatherby Mag-

num, two. (As a concession to Layne Simpson, I'll include the 22 Hornet as a "hotshot;" there are four factory loads for it.) Remember, this is for domestic ammunition only; I can't keep up with the imported brands. One week they're here, next week . . .

And you thought the 22-250 was Queen of the May. Don't get me wrong; the 22-250 is very popular and an excellent cartridge. Ballistically, it skunks all factory-loaded 224s except the Swift. If I were restricted to one varmint rifle and had to choose a 22-caliber, I'd probably be forced to pick a 22-250. But only because the Swift is available in so few rifles. And, to be completely honest, if I were restricted to one centerfire varmint rifle, I'd not be very happy with a 22-bore. Better a 243 or 6mm or 250-3000.

But we're discussing the 223. Perhaps you are wondering just why the 223 Remington is such a good seller if the 22-250 is so much better. Who said better? Me? The 22-250 is better at hitting distant objects with a minimum of holdover; and better at making your ears ring. The 22-250 is better at stopping a chuck in its tracks with a hit "around the edges;" and better at making your shoulder sore after a day's shooting in a prairie dog town. The 22-250 is better at depleting your cash reserves when you purchase ammunition, better at burning up powder in hefty doses, better at wearing out barrels, better at keeping holes farther apart on target paper, better at recoiling just enough to cause you to

Factory fodder for the 223 isn't always found in military-type, brown cardboard boxes. Federal offers a 55-grain hollow point boat-tail loading that's ideal for varmints.

The 223 has found a home in the hearts of varmint hunters nationwide. This fat chuck was taken with a new Remington 223 Model Seven.

From left to right, the 222 Remington, 222 Remington Magnum and the 223 Remington. All three are, or have been, popular with the varmint/benchrest crowd. In years past, the 222 got the nod in the popularity poll; today it's the 223. The 222 Remington Magnum has always come in last.

lose sight of your game in the scope's field so you can't spot your bullet's strike and make a correction, better at costing you an arm and a limb when you buy new brass. Who said better?

Varmints

As a varmint round, the 223 has enough for most jobs but not too much. How can you have too much? Try hunting in heavily-populated areas, or on the farm of a dairyman who equates *loud* with dead cattle. You'll

soon see how you can have too much.

Try replacing your rifle barrel after every other season of extensive varminting, instead of once every 4 or 5 years. Try working over a "dog" town with 10 rapid shots, then laying your tender cheek against the barrel. Try having your buddy rush to get off a shot before you can plug up your hearing mechanism. You'll soon see how you can have too much.

Most varmint gunners have great difficulty hitting animals the size of a woodchuck past 250 yards, unless

223 Remington: Varmint/Target

they can pinpoint the *exact* range and shoot from a rock-steady artificial rest. If expensive range finders and toting sandbags turn you on, then the 223 and its ilk may not impress you much. But if you prefer to walk more than 50 feet from your car, if an artificial support draped over the hood of your pickup leaves you cold, if just seeing country and bagging an occasional groundhog is your meat, the 223 is your load. Stay with me.

The 223 yields around 400 fps to the 22-250 when both are loaded to equal pressures in barrels of identical length. The ballistics charts show a greater disparity, but that's because the 223 is loaded a tad on the light side in deference to military firearms. My experience has been that it is no trick to get 3300 fps from a 55-grain bullet in the 223 if you have at least 24 inches of tube to play with. The current *Hornady Handbook* will bear me out.

So what do you lose along with your 400 fps? Well, at

(Right) While the 223 isn't a 400-yard varmint cartridge, it'll do nice work out to 250-300 yards.

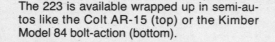

The 223 is available wrapped up in semi-autos like the Colt AR-15 (top) or the Kimber Model 84 bolt-action (bottom).

300 yards your 55-grain Hornady spire point will drop 1.8 inches more if fired from your 223 than if launched out of your pal's 22-250, assuming a 200-yard zero for each. Wow. It will retain about 24 percent less energy when it reaches 300 yards. It will expand a little less explosively. Will the chuck or crow feel the difference? You decide.

If you wanted to cheat, you could load your 223 with the streamlined Nosler 55-grain Solid Base bullet. Then you'd relinquish only 1 inch in trajectory at 300 yards, and a mere 11 percent in energy, assuming your unsuspecting croney stuck with his flat-based Hornady slug. Of course, *he* could load the same bullet and you'd be back where you started, but you see what I mean.

Let's leave the more mundane matters and get back to the considerable popularity enjoyed by the little 223. One of the reasons for its widespread approbation is its

chambering in a bevy of assault rifles. Such ordnance as the Bushmaster, Colt AR-15 and CAR-15, FNC, Heckler & Koch, Ruger Mini-14, Steyr A.U.G., Valmet M82 Bullpup, and probably a few more, are all reamed for the 223. The survivalists go plumb crazy over these paramilitary arms, buy them by the basketful. Sell a bunch of guns, you sell a lot of ammo.

For the varmint chasers, there are the Kimber M84, Krico 600, M-S Safari Arms, Remington Models 7, 700, and 700-V, Savage 340, Sako, Shilen DGA, Smith & Wesson 1500-V and 1500 Mountaineer, Steyr-Mannlicher SL and L, Wichita, Thompson-Center, Ruger Number 1 and 3, and the Remington 40-X series of target guns. Again, I may have missed a few. Sell a bait of rifles to varmint hunters, and you peddle a mess of ammo and brass, not to mention components also used in other calibers.

Even the deer hunters get into the act. In my baili-wick, it is perfectly legal to hunt deer with a 22 center-fire. In fact, one or two oddball counties in my home state *require* a 22 centerfire if you use a rifle at all. (I *said* they were odd.) Two of the most popular deer guns in my locale are the Colt AR-15 and the Ruger Mini-14. I'm not saying I condone such calibers or weaponry for deer hunting, just that those 223-chambered rifles are commonly put to that use in my neck of the woods.

What with the survivalist crowd, the varmint hunters, and the deerslayers all in the act, and all willing to cough up hard cash for their preferences, it takes no seer to deduce why the 223 is high in the public-opinion polls. Couple with that the easy availability of military brass and ammo and you have a combination that's tough to beat.

Accuracy

The 223's inherent accuracy doesn't hurt it either. I have owned three Remington Model 788 turnbolts chambered for the cartridge, a Savage 112-V varmint ri-fle, and a Ruger Mini-14. Only the Ruger failed to pro-

Note the Kimber 84's bolt release at the traditional location. Also note the top of the receiver; it's grooved to accept integral scope bases— a plus for any 223 varmint rig.

vide excellent accuracy. Actually I have little way of knowing what level of accuracy would be appropriate for the Ruger. In my experience, autoloaders generally provide pretty sad accuracy by normal standards. If I compare my Mini-14 to other autos I've fired, it fared not so badly. Groups ran a little over 3¼ inches for an average at 100 yards, and I mean five-shot strings, not three-shotters. The most recent Remington semi-auto I test-fired wouldn't approach that. In fact, no Reming-ton self-shucker that I have worked with or *seen* anyone else work with would equal my Ruger.

The bolt-actions were another matter. My eldest 788, which I received direct from Remington several years ago, is a bell-ringer. With its most precise load—25.5 grains of Hodgdon's H4895 and the 52-grain Sierra boat-tail match—that rifle averaged exactly ⅝-inch for eight, five-shot groups. That's from a sporter! It's the

most accurate sporter-weight rifle I ever fired.

When I heard Remington was deep-sixing the 788 line, I quickly gathered up all the strays I could find. Two are in 223. I sighted one of them in with the same load that does so well in the above mentioned rifle; it printed .83-inch for three strings. The other new acqui-sition has been fired only with factory ammo. Reming-ton's 55-grain soft point has averaged .97-inch so far.

My heavy-barreled rifle is a Savage 112-V, now dis-continued. That gun will stay in .66-inch for 10 five-shot groups with my standby load of 25.5/H4895 and the 52-grain Sierra boat-tail. Incidentally, that load is quite fast in the Savage, clocking 3348 fps. In the 24-inch bar-reled Remington 788 it gets 3302 fps. Using the 53-grain Hornady boat-tail match slug, my Ruger chronographs 3025 fps with the same charge of powder and groups its best.

Handloads

All my 223s like 25.5 grains of the Hodgdon version of 4895. I've used bullets from the 52-grain Sierra match up to the 60-grain Nosler Solid Base with excellent ac-

One of the prettiest 223s to come down the pike is the Kimber Model 84. The Kimber is the first, true, controlled-feed (Mauser extractor/ejector) rifle to be commercially produced in the U.S. since 1963.

curacy and good muzzle speeds. No rifle has ever shown the slightest sign of excessive pressures with that load.

The runner-up load in my Savage again utilizes H4895, this time with a 26.5-grain charge pushing the 50-grain Nosler match hollow point to a lusty 3525 fps while grouping .69-inch. That's one heck of a good load!

Although H4895 is one of my favorites for use in the 223, Winchester 748 functions well in the Savage, at least with some bullets. Pair 26.0 grains of 748 with the 55-grain Speer soft point spitzer and I get a .67-inch group average and 3280 fps. (Olin data shows 26.3 grains of 748 as maximum for the 223 with that bullet weight; my Savage displays no pressure pains.)

My favored factory fodder is either the 55-grain Hor-nady soft point or the 55 Remington Power-Lokt. In the Savage, the Remington stuff groups into a clannish .83-

The author's Savage 112-V in 223 is a superb performer at 100 yards. Five-shot groups run .66-inch.

When loaded in Hornady's Frontier factory ammo, this 55-grain FMJ bullet is the fastest of the factory fodder. It's a great slug to opt for if you're force-feeding a semi-auto or trying to save the hide of a valuable fur bearer.

The proliferation of 224-caliber bullets has always been great. On the far left is the 45-gr. Speer soft point, on the far right the 70-gr. Speer soft point. The slugs in between are some of the offerings from Sierra, Hornady and Nosler. The man reloading the 223 has a wide choice of bullets.

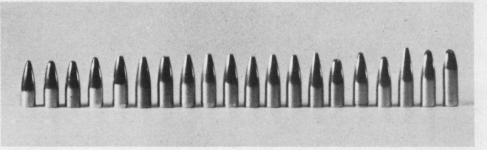

inch aggregate. The 55-grain Hornady prints 1.2 inches in that gun, as does the 55-grain Winchester soft point. In the Ruger Mini-14, the Remington's 55-grain load shows a 4.27-inch average while the Hornady ammo provides 3.60 inches.

For sheer speed, the Hornady 55-grain full-jacketed factory load is tops in my Mini-14, getting 3103 fps. No other load was as fast. Accuracy wasn't bad, either; groups stayed under 4 inches. In the Savage, the same load produced a blistering 3370 fps, but groups were lemon-sized. The Remington Power-Lokt ammo gave 3181 fps in the 112-V, 3186 in the 788, only 2825 fps in the Mini-14 with its 18½-inch tube.

One thing to watch in handloading the 223-chambered self-loader is the pressure-time curve, relative to bullet travel down the barrel. The maximum-acceptable pressure level of the 223 is 52,000 CUP, which is plenty safe in a strong, modern semi-automatic. It is high gas-port pressures that cause problems for reloaders, and ammo manufacturers too, for that matter. Powders with a too-slow burning rate are the culprits. One of the reasons given for the frequent jamming of M-16 rifles during the Viet Nam fracas was excessive gas-port pressures. Since the M-16/AR-15 system feeds expanding gasses directly to the bolt/carrier, it is much more sensitive to variations in port pressures than rifles such as the M-14 and Ruger Mini-14, both of which use a gas piston to manipulate the bolt. The M-16 taps its gas nearer the chamber end of the barrel, when pressures are still rela-

tively high and on the down slope of the pressure curve, rather than after the pressure/time trace has flattened. With gas being bled off at this location, pressures are more apt to be erratic; the variation will have a more direct effect on action cycling due to the direct gas action on the bolt/carrier. Reloaders must take special note of this since slow powders increase gas-port pressure, resulting in more violent working of the action and increased wear and tear on the rifle. Brass will suffer as well, frequently exhibiting such symptoms as excessive stretching, tearing, or deep extractor marks. The moral is to steer clear of the slower powders.

So which ones are the "slower powders" for this size cartridge, you ask? Anything slower than H4895 or Winchester 748 should be avoided like your mother-in-law. In fact, I personally would lean toward such quick-burners as IMR 4198 if I wanted my self-shucker to live as long as possible, particularly if it were one of the AR-15/Armalite variants. The Mini-14 seems bereft of these difficulties, due to its Garand heritage.

You may have noted that I have neglected to retell the story of how the 223 (or more correctly, the 5.56mm NATO) came to be our national defense cartridge. This was no oversight. In the first place, I touch on it in the chapter on the 222 Remington Magnum, to which I'll now refer you; covering the same ground here would be redundant. In the second place, the story is boring unless you happen to be a military buff or historian.

The 223 Remington is an ambiguous cartridge. It is

used for deer, although it's not really adequate under most conditions. It is overlooked by many varmint hunters because it is inferior to the 22-250 on paper, although in the field most fellows will kill as many woodchucks with it as the faster cartridge. (Taking varmints cleanly is a matter of hitting; the 223 is a more "hittable" load than the 22-250.) It is often eschewed by shooters casting about for a super-accurate, semi-serious, club-level benchrest rifle because it is considered less accurate than the 222, which is incorrect unless the gun in question is capable of ¼-minute accuracy. (And the shooter!) The survival crowd likes it because it is widely chambered in guns of their choice, and because of its unlimited supply in military guise, not due to any specific ballistic attributes.

Like the spouse of a famous person, the 223 is not heralded because of its merit, but because of its association. Too bad. It's a fine cartridge.

223 Remington

HANDLOAD DATA

Bullet Wt. Grs.	Type	Powder Wt. Grs.	Type	Primer	Case	MV, (fps)	ME, (fpe)	Rifle Bbl. (in.)	Remarks
50	Nosler JHP(M)	26.5	H4895	Fed. 205	Fron.	3525	1379	Sav. 112-V/26	Extremely accurate
52	Sierra JHPBT(M)	25.5	H4895	Fed. 205	Rem.	3348	1294	Sav. 112-V/26	Most acc. ld. this gun
52	Sierra JHPBT(M)	25.5	H4895	Fed. 205	Fron.	3302	1259	Rem. 788/24	Most acc. ld. this gun
53	Hrndy. JHP(M)	25.5	H4895	Fed. 205	Fed.	3025	1077	Rug. M-14/18½	Most acc. ld. this gun
55	Hrndy. SX	25.5	H4895	Fed. 205	Fron.	3323	1348	Sav. 112-V/26	Extremely acc. and fast
55	Speer SP	26.0	Win. 748	Fed. 205	Rem.	3280	1314	Sav. 112-V/26	Extremely accurate
60	Nosler SB	**25.5**	H4895	Fed. 205	Fron.	**3328**	**1475**	Sav. 112-V/26	Extremely fast; acc.

JHP(M)—Jacketed Hollow Point (Match); JHPBT(M)—Jacketed Hollow Point Boat-Tail (Match); SX—Super Explosive; SP—Soft Point; SB—Solid Base.

FACTORY LOAD DATA

Bullet Wt. Grs.	Type	MV, (fps)	ME, (fpe)	Rifle Bbl. (in.)	Remarks
55	Rem. HPPL	2825	975	Rug. M-14/18½	Fair accuracy
55	Rem. HPPL	3186	1240	Rem. 788/24	Poor accuracy
55	Rem. HPPL	3181	1236	Sav. 112-V/26	Most acc. fact. ld.
55	Hrndy. SP	2839	984	Rug. M-14/18½	Most acc. fact. ld.
55	Hrndy. SP	3210	1259	Sav. 112-V/26	Accurate
55	Hrndy. FMJ	3103	1176	Rug. M-14/18½	Very fast
55	Hrndy. FMJ	3370	1387	Sav. 112-V/26	Very fast and potent
55	Win. SP	2791	951	Rug. M-14/18½	Generally poor load
55	Win. SP	3131	1197	Sav. 112-V/26	Accurate; slow
55	Fed. SP	2994	1094	Rug. M-14/18½	Very good velocity

HPPL—Hollow Point Power Lokt; SP—Soft Point; FMJ—Full Metal Jacket.

SPECIFICATIONS

Shell Holders
RCBS: 10
Bonanza: 6
Lyman: 26
Pacific: 16

Bullet Diameter
Jacketed: .224"

Lengths
Trim: 1.750"
Maximum Case: 1.760"
Maximum Overall: 2.260"

CAUTION:
Loads recommended and suggested herein have been carefully listed, but are intended solely as a guide to readers and neither the publisher nor author accept any responsibility for results of their use.
Maximum loads, listed in bold, should be reduced by 10 percent and worked up to cautiously.

222 Remington Magnum

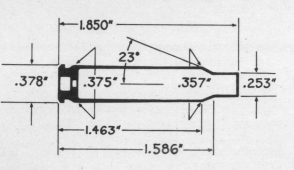

.378" .375" 23° .357" .253"

1.850"

1.463"

1.586"

" . . . if a varmint hunter were limited to one cartridge, he could do much worse than the 222 Magnum."

TO SAY that the 222 Remington Magnum has passed its zenith would be incorrect. It never had a zenith. If it achieves any immortality, it will do so on the strength of one or the other of three notable points. Which are? Stay with me.

First, the 222 Magnum is the case from which the 6x47, a popular benchrest cartridge, is formed. Of late, even the very accurate 6x47 seems to be losing ground to the newer series of benchrest loads. The 222 Mag. may yet sink without a trace.

Second claim to notoriety is that the 222 Remington Magnum is no more a magnum than my wife is Greta Garbo. It is *called* a magnum, but it carries no belted case. It is barely more potent than its parent cartridge, the 222 Remington, and much less so than such high-speed wonders as the 225 Winchester, 22-250 Remington, and 220 Swift, none of which boast a magnum appellation or a belt at their head. Thus, it was and is totally ludicrous to refer to the little cartridge as a magnum.

Finally, the 222 Mag. is totally superfluous for any practical purpose. It is but marginally faster than the 222 and no more accurate. The 223 Remington will do anything the 222 Mag. will do at least as well. The trio of 224 centerfires mentioned above will leave it for dead when it comes to muzzle velocity, energy, wind-bucking characteristics, and trajectory. If you want a really mild round to use in settled communities, there is the 22

Hornet. On game as hardy as coyotes, a 6mm is better than any 22. And so on.

Well, you might ask, if the 222 Magnum is so worthless, why was it introduced? I never said it was worthless. I said it was "superfluous." Redundant. Unneeded. The 222 Mag. can be likened to the Pony Express. At the time of its birth, it seemed like a terrific idea. Within a very short time span, progress had made it obsolete.

In 1953, Uncle Sam was experimenting with a necked-down 30 Carbine case, in search of a 22-caliber battle cartridge. The punch provided by this Lilliputian round was quickly deemed inadequate. Work proceeded with a shortened 222 Remington case. That load, too, was abandoned for lack of power.

Remington raised its hand at the back of the room. Working under contract to the Springfield Armory, they had developed a longer 222-type cartridge. The Army tried it and nixed it; perhaps because it was a little too long for the Armalite rifle Uncle Sam had his eye on. Remington, hoping to recoup some of its investment time, gave the public a shot at it. Since "magnum mania" was just hitting its stride in 1958, Remington encumbered its new cartridge with a title that quickly became a little embarrassing. The 222 Remington Magnum was born.

The Army, determined to find the 222 centerfire of its dreams, turned to both Remington and Winchester

In the old days it was called plain old "Ball-C"—today it's known as "BL-C Lot #2." Shooters who grew up in the '50s and bought Hodgdon's original Ball-C at $1 (or less) a pound, still find top accuracy in that outfit's current BL-C (#2). It's a superb performer in the 222 Remington Magnum.

Although the 222 Remington Magnum is useful in such woodchuck terrain, you must select your shots with care. The chuck hole this shooter is zeroed in on is only about 250 yards away. If he were to try a shot at the sloping hill in the background, he'd be out of luck. It's more than 400 yards distant.

not only for a cartridge, but a rifle to handle it. Winchester sent its engineers into a huddle, slipsticks whirred, and out trundled the 224 Winchester. Remington responded with what at the time was dubbed the 222 Remington Special, soon to be renamed the 223 Remington in its commercial form. (I wish Remington had applied the title to the earlier 222 Magnum. "Special" has a nice ring to it.)

The Winchester and Remington cartridges were quite similar. The Olin offering carried a 53-grain flat-base bullet at a muzzle velocity of 3300 fps. The Bridgeport version kicked a 55-grain boat-tail to 3265 fps. The Winchester load was usable in either rifle; the Remington number would work only in that company's firearm. Both cartridges differed strategically from the 222 Magnum.

The military carried out exhaustive tests on the two

cartridges, including trials under Arctic conditions. Recoil, which was mild (something that had been stipulated), indeed was the primary reason for going to a smaller caliber in the first place. So far, so good.

The bug in the broth was long-range accuracy. At 500 yards (I *said* long range), bullet holes in target paper revealed yawing, the tendency of a bullet to wobble around its long axis. Under Arctic conditions, bullet penetration was inadequate, which may have stemmed from the same problem that was affecting accuracy.

Finally, the gremlin was identified. Due to its relatively short bearing surface, greater length, and long point, the boat-tail bullet was only marginally stabilized in the 1-in-14 twist of the test rifles. There were two fixes: the twist rate could be made steeper to increase gyroscopic stability, or the boat-tail could be eliminated and the nose shortened.

222 Remington Magnum: Varmint/Target

The Armed Forces opted for an increased twist, changing to 1-in-12 in 1963. This simple change improved stability some 37 percent, overcoming the obstacles that had plagued the trials.

The upshot of all this rambling is that while the 222 Remington Magnum was doing its damnedest to gain a public following, Remington was being subsidized by the government to create a cartridge that would outdate it overnight. That cartridge was the 223 Remington. When it appeared on the market in 1964 (near as I can tell), the 223 virtually buried the 7-year-old 222 Mag.

All that is history. Today the 222 Mag. is dead as bobby sox and pedal pushers. It simply hadn't enough to recommend it. Let's see what it did have when it served its time in the sun.

At the time of its introduction, the 222 Magnum had the following published ballistics: 55-grain soft point at 3300 fps. Today those numbers read: 55-grain soft or hollow point at 3240 fps. I have chronographed a batch of each. The Remington Power-Lokt factory load managed only 3024 fps in a 23-inch-barreled Sako; the soft point loading fared better at 3176 fps. Considering that my barrel was shorter than that used by the factory ballistics lab, that latter load was pretty fast.

Good handloads will show around 3485 fps with 50-grain bullets according to the various loading manuals. The 55-grain slugs can be driven to 3370 fps, or so I found by averaging the fastest loads in each current reloading manual. For comparison, I also averaged the data on similar *maximum* safe loads in the 222 Remington. That cartridge will show around 3310 fps with the

50-grain bullets, 3170 fps with the 55s. I used my own data for the 223 Remington because much published information was taken in short-barreled rifles, such as the Colt AR-15. In my testing of 223 rifles, it was no trick to get 3500 fps out of the 50-grain projectiles, and reach 3340 fps with the 55-grain slugs.

Thus, we find that the 222 Magnum outruns the 222 Remington by 200 fps with the heavy bullets, 175 fps with the 50-grain. The 223 and 222 Mag. are neck and neck, as is seemly since their case capacities are close, but I'll concede to the 222 Magnum 30 fps with the 55-grain bullets. I won't give an inch with the 50s.

What does the advantage gained by using the 222 Magnum mean in real terms? Not too much. Zero a 222 at 200 yards, kick along a 50-grain Nosler hollow point to 3300 fps, and we have this: 100 yards, 1.5 inches high; 300 yards, 7.8 inches low; 400 yards, 24.9 inches low. Move the same bullet to 3500 fps in the magnum case, and it looks like this: 100 yards, 1.2 inches high; 300 yards, 6.8 inches low; 400 yards, 21.5 inches low. That's only 1 inch difference in drop at 300 yards, which is a bit far out for these two cartridges anyway; retained energy is well under 500 fpe at that range. Folks claim that the 222 Magnum adds 50 yards to the 222's effective range. Maybe some day one of them will explain to me how.

Handloading

Before you decide I am a confirmed 222 Magnum hater, let me persuade you otherwise. If I owned a perfectly good 222 Magnum, which I don't, and was content to do my varminting at 250 yards or under, I'd

A favorite with many 222/222 Magnum shooters is Du Pont's IMR 4895. Oftentimes accuracy with this propellant (and the right bullet) is outstanding.

While this light barreled Sako 222 Remington Magnum is not in the benchrest class, it's no stinker either. With its best load, this Sako will average 1⅓ inches at 100 yards.

These four bullets are excellent choices for ultimate accuracy in the 222 Magnum. (The excellent Winchester offering is discontinued, but may still be on some dealer's shelves.) From left to right: 52-grain Speer JHP; 53-grain JHP(M); 53-grain Winchester JHP(M) and the 53-grain Hornady JHP(M).

scarcely consider trading it off. On the other hand, if I owned a 222 or 223, I would certainly not swap it for a 222 Magnum. If I had none of the above, a 222 Mag. would not be on my list of desirables. And for the record, I'd choose the 223 over the 222 Remington.

Still, if a varmint hunter were limited to one cartridge, he could do much worse than the 222 Magnum. The 22-250 would be a better rig ballistically, as would the 220 Swift, but both cost more to shoot, belt you a little harder, and are loud enough to make the hens lay golf balls. The 223 is as good as the 222 Magnum from any standpoint, is available in new rifles of a broad variety, and there is an abundance of military brass. Ah, but you've read that the longer neck on the 222 Magnum makes it a better cartridge for reloading.

I'll let Jim Carmichel dispose of that bromide, since he does it so well in *The Modern Rifle:*

> Some talk has been made of the fact that the .223 has a shorter neck than the .222 or the .222 Magnum and for this reason isn't as good for handloading. Why such tales as this get started I'll never understand, but apparently they're made up by a swamp-dwelling ogre with one eye and pimply green skin who only comes out at night.

If you're still convinced of the advantages of long necks, then explain why so many benchrest shooters seat their bullets only far enough into the necks to hold them firmly. I've also heard that a long neck more perfectly aligns the bullet with the chamber, preventing a "cocked" bullet. Right. And I'm Shirley Temple.

Think about it. One of the items most deleterious to precision accuracy is the effect uneven neck tension has on a seated bullet. Competitive benchrest gunners go to great lengths to reduce said effects, turning or reaming case necks to uniform dimensions, checking loaded rounds for bullet "run-out." If anything contributes to a cocked bullet, *it is a long neck.* Assuming a cartridge

has a neck length sufficient to hold a bullet in place, it serves its purpose. It has no other.

Good powders for use in the 222 Magnum are those on the faster side of a medium burning rate. Propellants like IMR 3031 and IMR 4895, such Hodgdon numbers as BL-C(2), H335, H4895, and Winchester 748 are apropos to this case size. The Lyman manual lists many accuracy loads utilizing BL-C(2) in their fabrication. So does Ken Waters in his book of *Pet Loads.*

Ken found that the 52-grain Sierra match hollow point boat-tail proved to be the most accurate load in his Remington Model 722 when coupled with 26.5 grains of BL-C(2). His 26-inch barreled rifle showed a 3253 fps muzzle speed. I tried the same bullet and charge in a Sako I had brief access to; it was the most accurate load fired in that rifle as well. This shows once again that there are indeed "pet" loads that work well in many if not most rifles, despite what you read to the contrary.

Another good load in my Sako was 26.0 grains of IMR 4895 under the 55-grain Speer soft point. Although accuracy was nothing to crow about, the velocity was pretty fair at 3171 fps.

Few rifles have been offered in 222 Remington Magnum. Remington made some Model 722 turnbolts, and a few model 700s are around. The round was offered as late as 1980, I believe, in the Remington 40-X series of target rifles. It is not listed in the 1983 catalog. Sako sold guns so chambered as late as 1979, perhaps later.

There's not much left to say about the 222 Remington Magnum. There wasn't much to begin with. The cartridge is sort of like the homely girl at the school prom; she may have an abundance of hidden virtues, but few that extend to the surface. While you may not mind sitting a spell to talk with her, you wouldn't care to take her home. If you did take her home, you probably wouldn't want to keep her. Yep, the 222 Magnum is just like that.

222 Remington Magnum

HANDLOAD DATA

Bullet Wt. Grs.	Type	Powder Wt. Grs.	Type	Primer	Case	MV (fps)	ME (fpe)	Rifle/ Bbl. (in.)	Remarks
45 Sierra SP		25.0	BL-C (2)	Rem. 7½	Rem.	2958	874	Rem. M700/24	Lyman Hndbk., 46th Ed. (Acc. Ld.)
45 Sierra SP		**28.5**	BL-C (2)	Rem. 7½	Rem.	**3333**	**1110**	Rem. M700/24	Lym. Hndbk., 46th Ed.
50 Sierra SP		**26.5**	IMR 3031	Rem. 7½	Rem.	**3497**	**1357**	Rem. M700/24	Lym. Hndbk., 46th Ed.
52 Sierra JHPBT(M)		26.5	BL-C (2)	RWS	Rem.	3253	1222	Rem. M722/26	Ken Waters acc. load
52 Sierra JHPBT(M)		26.5	BL-C (2)	Rem. 7½	Rem.	3103	1112	Sako/23	Most acc. load Sako
55 Speer SP		26.0	IMR 4895	Fed. 205	Rem.	3171	1228	Sako/23	Mediocre acc., gd. vel.

SP—Soft Point; JHPBT(M)—Jacketed Hollow Point Boat-Tail (Match).

FACTORY LOAD DATA

Bullet Wt. Grs.	Type	MV (fps)	ME (fpe)	Rifle/ Bbl. (in.)	Remarks
55 Rem.	PLHP	3024	1117	Sako/23	Most acc. of factory ammo
55 Rem.	SP	3176	1229	Sako/23	Fastest load tested; acc.

PLHP—Power-Lokt Hollow Point; SP—Soft Point.

SPECIFICATIONS

Shell Holders
RCBS: 10
Bonanza: 6
Lyman: 26
Pacific: 16

Bullet Diameter
Jacketed: .224"

Lengths
Trim: 1.840"
Maximum Case: 1.850"
Maximum Overall: 2.280"

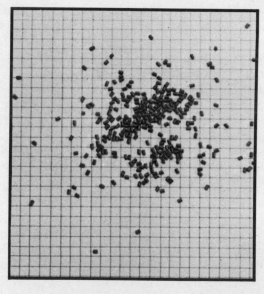

IMR 4895, shown here on a ¹⁄₁₀-inch grid, is a fine choice for the 222 Magnum. It gives both good accuracy and high speeds.

CAUTION:
Loads recommended and suggested herein have been carefully listed, but are intended solely as a guide to readers and neither the publisher nor author accept any responsibility for results of their use. **Maximum loads, listed in bold, should be reduced by 10 percent and worked up to cautiously.**

225 Winchester

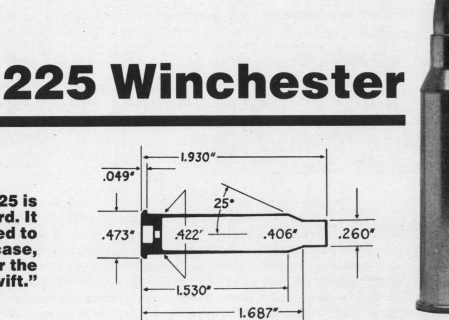

"Physically, the 225 is rather an odd bird. It has what is referred to as a semi-rimmed case, as did its progenitor the 220 Swift."

THE 225 Winchester is said to be one of the most accurate cartridges ever offered to the American shooting public. When paired with the Winchester Model 70, the combined accuracy of factory ammunition and rifle was amazing. In the 20th Edition of *Gun Digest,* Ken Waters wrote in the "Testfire" section:

Early five-shot groups [of a M70-V] at 100 yards ran on the order of 1⅛-1¼" spread, but after tightening the fore-end screw things changed in a hurry. The next six groups in succession [with handloads], measured ¾", ⁹⁄₁₆", ⅝", ⅞", ⁹⁄₁₆", and ⁷⁄₁₆". In 22 groups, this rifle averaged ¹¹⁄₁₆" center-to-center of farthest-apart holes, the largest spread being 1" and the smallest a pretty ⅜"! *Even the 55-gr. Winchester factory loads (Lot 94VG61) averaged ¾".* A 10x Unertl target scope was used for sighting. [Italics mine.]

Admittedly, most of the above loads were handloads. Nonetheless, such accuracy from an out-of-the-box rifle is astounding in my opinion. And when was the last time you had a factory-made untuned rifle group into ¾-inch with factory ammo? I can remember well when it happened to me—never.

Introduced in 1964, along with the much-maligned post-'64 Model 70 Winchester, the 225 was quite similar

In 1964 the 225 Winchester (top), replaced the 220 Swift in Winchester varmint rifles. The Swift was a much faster load, although the 225 is said to be more accurate by some folks.

The 225 (right) came head-to-head with the 22-250 Remington (left), which was introduced about the same time. The 225 lost.

Here are the factory hotshot 22s. From top to bottom: 225 Winchester, 22-250 Rem. and the 220 Swift. The 225 never made the grade.

to the Kilbourn 219 Improved Zipper, circa 1938. I'm not certain if that helped or hindered the popularity of the nascent 22 centerfire, but it's interesting anyway. At this juncture, it should be said that the 225 was and is nowhere near the 220 Swift in ballistic capabilities, but it certainly didn't develop a reputation for blowing rifles to smithereens as had its forebear. For a while, fate, if not actually smiling, at least didn't frown on the struggling-to-please 225 Winchester.

The public on the other hand greeted the little cartridge with a broad yawn. The few shooters I've talked to who tried it have uniformly praised it. In fact, I have never spoken to a person who owned a 225 Model 70 who didn't quickly assault your ear with its virtues. It is known for its tractibility and accuracy. Alas, too few gunners anted up their grocery money; the cartridge languished, then died.

Aside from the disapprobation that accompanied the "improvements" visited upon the Model 70, which alone would have prevented any new cartridge from achieving maximum growth potential, the 225 had to contend with a vicious blow dealt by the boys from Ilion—the 22-250 Remington. The 22-250 was an ancient wildcat originally dreamed up by the late Harvey Donaldson, except for a slight difference in bullet diameter. Jerry Gebby copyrighted the name "Varminter" and bestowed it on the 250-3000 case necked to 224-caliber, which is otherwise known as the 22-250. For many decades the 22-250, or 22 Varminter, had been accumulating disciples, many of whom had tirelessly stumped for its legitimizing by one of the ammo makers. In 1965 such came to pass. The 225 was doomed.

Actually, the 22-250 isn't too much better than the 225 in the velocity sweepstakes. According to the *Speer Reloading Manual Number Ten,* the 225 gets 3641 fps from 50-grain bullets, 3571 fps with the 52-grain hollow point, and 3503 fps with the 55-grain spitzer, all from a 24-inch barreled Model 70. The 22-250 shows 3876 fps with the 50-grainers, 3841 fps from the 52-grain hollow point, and 3826 fps with the 55s, ballistics taken in a 24-inch barreled Model 700 Remington. The difference is about 276 fps throughout those bullet weights. Such an advantage is worth about 1 inch less drop at 300 yards with the 55-grain soft point spitzer, assuming a 200-yard zero. Earthshaking? I don't think so either.

Being a cartridge ideally suited for reloading, it still seems a bit odd that the 225 didn't gain a following of some sort among the more individualistic hull-stuffers. That it failed to do so can be attributed to something besides the 22-250. Right after the 225's introduction, the B.E. Hodgdon Powder Company ran some pressure and velocity tests on various handloads. It was discovered that pressures fluctuated more than is prudent with both IMR 3031 and IMR 4064 when the cartridge was loaded to the upper levels. NRA tests later reported the same phenomena with IMR 4320 and IMR 4895. No reasons for such pressure vacillations were forthcoming.

The *Lyman Reloading Handbook* has this to say in the 45th Edition:

> Velocity readings in [the 225] tend to be very erratic from one gun to the next. Pressures tend to jump around quite a bit. Data taken in one gun will not necessarily be uniform with results in another gun.

With such warnings abounding, it is no wonder handloaders looked to greener, and safer, pastures.

Let me note here that IMR 4350, Hodgdon H380, and Hodgdon BL-C(2) provided excellent pressure/velocity relationships, displaying no erraticism. The current, 46th Lyman Handbook says: "IMR 4320 proved to be the best powder for ballistic uniformity in our lab tests." [!] Sierra's Reloading Manual has this: "IMR 4064 seems to be the best powder for the 225."

And now I trust you are totally confused. I am. Due to the foregoing conflicting data, I plan to stay out of

IMR 4320 is often considered one of the best powders for the 225. The 52-grain Speer HP is often quite accurate in the 225.

the discussion; I will offer no thoughts on powder selection for the 225 Winchester. You're on your own.

Physically, the 225 is rather an odd bird. It has what is referred to as a semi-rimmed case, as did its progenitor the 220 Swift. Since the case headspaces on its shoulder, as do rimless designs, the reasons for its half-hearted rim are: (1) it will work in rifles with the "standard" bolt face, that of the 30-06; or, (2) it was intended by Winchester that it be readily adaptable to single shot rifles, which necessitated a rim for extraction purposes. (Since Winchester had not offered a single shot for many years prior to the genesis of the 225, I discount this last theory, personally.)

According to the NRA publication *Handloading,* typical chamber pressures for the 225 run about 50,000 CUP. The maximum product average of 225 factory ammo should not exceed the 53,200 CUP level. The same book lists the 22-250 at 3,000 CUP higher, which may have more than a little to do with the 22-250's on-paper ballistic advantage.

Actually, neither cartridge has such a surplus of re-

tained energy out at 400 yards to qualify as the premier varmint cartridge. Kick a 55-grain Hornady spire point to 3500 fps in the 225, 3800 fps in the 22-250, and the former shows a 400-yard energy of 457 fpe, the latter 561 fpe. Neither is my idea of what to smack a fat woodchuck with at such extended ranges.

For comparison, the 243 retains more than 900 fpe if an 87-grain spire point is started at 3200 fps. A 90-grain Sierra hollow point leaving the muzzle of a 25-06 at 3400 fps still has 781 fpe of crunch way out at 400 yards, not to mention close to double the bullet weight of the 22-bores. I realize that many chucks are killed each year with such as the 225 and 22-250, some of them at *very* long range. I also wonder how many of them make it to their dens to die a lingering death. My own thoughts are that the 225, 224 Weatherby Magnum, and 22-250 are 300-yard chuck loads. The Swift adds a few yards, perhaps 50. But then maybe not.

On prairie dogs and crows, the problem is *hitting* them at long range; most anything will kill them if you can tag 'em way out yonder. Actually, considering the size of the target, the 222-class of cartridge is about right for crows and such. Recoil is light, so you can see where your bullet strikes for correction, and you can shoot them all day without stocking up on liniment.

And so we see that the 225 Winchester is a potentially accurate load, useful for various varminting chores out to a full 300 yards, more in some folks' opinions. So far as I know, the Savage Model 340 turnbolt and the Model 70 were the only factory-made rifles chambered for the 225; so guns are getting scarce. The day may come when it will be more economically feasible to stash the old 225 as an investment than shoot it. Until then it will serve its owner as one of the best varmint loads available.

I would like to return to the subject of "wild" pressure excursions before closing. In *Handloader* magazine's May-June, 1972, issue, Ken Waters discussed the 225 at length. Ken also noted some pretty scary pressure-related incidents with both 3031 and 4064. Such happenings did not deter his using those propellants, as accuracy was "just too good to miss," especially with 4064. So Ken said he would continue to load 4064, being careful not to exceed a conservative maximum in his 225s.

As with Lyman's lab crew, Ken found no complaints with IMR 4320. He wrote: "IMR 4320, like H4895 doesn't appear given to such wild pressure sweeps [as 3031 and 4064], and yet comes very close to giving as good accuracy."

All this mystery has invoked a keen interest in the 225 as far as I'm concerned. Layne Simpson has a nice, unfired standard-weight Model 70 he bought for tradin' stock. I wonder . . .

224 Weatherby Magnum

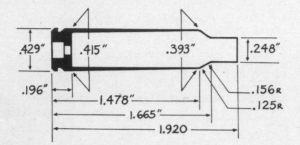

"Accuracy should be no problem. Everything I've read leads me to believe that the Varmintmaster is a very precise shooter."

THE MOST interesting aspects of the 224 Weatherby Magnum have nothing whatever to do with its ballistics, its performance on targets or game, or its popularity. They are esoteric in nature. First, it is the only American, factory-loaded 22 centerfire cartridge that sports a belted case. Secondly, it was the impetus for the dainty Weatherby Varmintmaster action, which was designed to give it a home. (Ironically, the Varmintmaster also came to house the rival 22-250 Remington, and sold much better so chambered.)

Finally, its nomenclature creates some minor confusion. One of our most august and respected handloading tomes labeled the cartridge, "the 224 Weatherby Varmintmaster." As with the 375 Winchester, which more than a few writers have erroneously called the 375 Winchester Big Bore, the *cartridge* has had thrust upon it the name of a *firearm*. The correct title for the little belted cutey is 224 Weatherby Magnum, just as with all the other factory-loaded Weatherby cartridges.

The rifle it is chambered for is the Weatherby Varmintmaster. Referring to it as the 224 Varmintmaster is akin to dubbing Weatherby's belted 30-caliber cartridge the 300 Weatherby Mark V.

If any production rifle other than the Weatherby has been reamed for the round, I've been unable to unearth it. I doubt any will be. Mind you, there is nothing at all wrong with the cartridge; it merely has little to recommend it over its competitors.

The belted case is no advantage, although one authority seems to think it is, saying: "It is a belted case with the advantages of this type of construction. For the handloader it eliminates certain headspace and case-stretch problems and should provide maximum case life." Of course, that's assuming you know how to adjust a full-length sizing die correctly so as not to set the shoulder back and *decrease* case longevity, or use a neck sizer to avoid the problem altogether.

Case capacity is similar to the equally neglected 225

Weatherby's Mark V Varmintmaster is the only rifle commercially chambered for the 224 Weatherby Magnum.

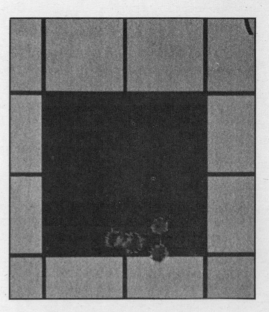

This 5-shot, 100-yard group measures ⅝-inch–it illustrates what a good Weatherby Varmintmaster is capable of.

Winchester, and slightly inferior to the 22-250 Remington. Factory-quoted velocities show a 55-grain spitzer at 3750 fps in the 225, the same bullet weight getting 3680 fps in the 22-250, and again the identical weight starting at 3650 from the 224 Weatherby Magnum.

Actually, the difference is more pronounced than first meets the eye. The Weatherby data are for a 26-inch test barrel; the others are taken in 24-inch barrels. As you can see, the Weatherby round offers no ballistic superiority to others in its class.

Further castigating it are economic factors. The Weatherby Varmintmaster, while an excellent rifle, is roughly twice as expensive at retail as some guns taking the 22-250. You can often find a dealer who is pushing a Brand X or Brand Y 22-250 at a discount because of volume buying, poor sales, or the fact his wife wants a new mink coat. I have seldom seen a Weatherby Mark V rifle offered at a discount.

Weatherby 224 ammunition is imported only by Weatherby and is not cheap. Brass is not plentiful; ammo is harder to come by than 22-250 or 243, or the 303 British for that matter. The cartridge case is not easily formed from other brass; indeed, reforming may be virtually impossible.

Factory loads, when you can locate some, are produced in only two iterations, 50- and 55-grain Pointed Expanding. If a non-handloader owns a light-barreled Varmintmaster 224 and finds that it is a bit picky about its provender, as light sporters frequently are, he is out of luck unless he can scrounge up a custom ammo manufacturer. As I mention elsewhere in this opus, I once owned a lightweight 284 Winchester rifle that refused to shoot either weight of factory-loaded ammo into less than 3 inches at 100 yards. Being a handloader, my straits were not dire. The first load I cobbled up grouped 1.19 inches. Point is, if you want a 224 Weatherby Magnum, better consider spoon-feeding it.

Accuracy should be no problem. Everything I've read leads me to believe that the Varmintmaster is a very precise shooter. Bob Hagel, writing in the November-December, 1979, *Handloader* magazine, said that he often had three-shot strings go well under an inch at 100 yards, and sometimes got five-shot groups to do the same thing. Naturally, that was with the better handloads.

In the "Testfire" section of *Gun Digest* for 1965, Ken Waters reported similar accuracy levels from his sample 224. Weatherby factory ammo in both bullet weights averaged around 1½ inches, which does not make for wallet filing. Switching to Sierra's 53-grain hollow point match bullet and 32.0 grains of IMR 4064, Ken obtained an occasional ½-inch, 100-yard group, with a dependable average of about ¾-inch. From a lightweight rifle, that is *outstanding*. In fact, it is excellent from *any* rifle except a full-fledged target arm.

In the 21st Ed. of *The Weatherby Guide* there is reprinted an article by Dick Eades from a past issue of *Shooting Times* magazine. Dick wrote: "I fired 60 rounds of factory ammo and group sizes remained constant, in the vicinity of an inch; the best one was ⅞-inch."

Three different rifles tested over 15 years by three reputable writers grouped five shots well under an inch from the bench. I'd say that is a pretty good recommendation for both the Varmintmaster and the 224 Magnum cartridge.

Best powders for the handloader are those on the fast side, but not as quick as IMR 4198 or ReLoder 7. *The Weatherby Guide* lists only IMR 3031 with both bullet weights. Bob Hagel backs it up. In the aforementioned *Handloader* article, he wrote: "It doesn't take much load development, however, to find that IMR 3031 is probably the best powder in the 224 for both velocity and accuracy with all bullet weights tried except the 70-grain Speer, where it gives a little less velocity than the slower powders."

Winchester 748, IMR 4064, and Norma 202 also work well in cases of this capacity. Ken Waters' load of 32.0 grains of IMR 4064 and the 53-grain Sierra would be a good place to initiate an accuracy search. Hagel went to 31.5 grains of IMR 4064 with the 52-grain Sierra boat-tail, for 3653 fps, but he didn't list group sizes.

If I were enamored of the little Weatherby Varmintmaster, could afford the price, and could locate a goodly supply of brass or ammo, I'd probably choose the 224 over the 22-250 in that gun. After all, I can buy a 22-250 in almost any other brand and type of rifle; it's nothing if not *common*. But the Weatherby cartridge is nearly as good, likely equally accurate in comparable rifles, and it is unique. If price were an obstacle, or I had no local source of brass or ammunition, or for some reason I didn't like the Varmintmaster rifle, I'd choose a 22-250 or 220 Swift and never look back.

(Below) IMR 3031 is the single best propellant for use in the 224 Weatherby, both for accuracy and velocity with bullets up to 63 grains in weight.

Good 22-caliber bullet choices for the 224 Weatherby Magnum include (left to right): 50-grain Nosler Hollow Point Match; 52-grain Remington Hollow Point Match; 52-grain Sierra Hollow Point Boat-tail Benchrest; 53-grain Sierra Hollow Point Benchrest; 55-grain Hornady Soft Point; 55-grain Speer Soft Point; 60-grain Nosler Solid Base and the 60-grain Hornady Hollow Point.

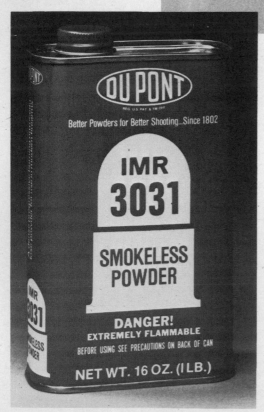

All these powders yield good results in the 224 Weatherby Magnum, but IMR 3031 and IMR 4895 are the most dependable when it comes to accuracy.

224 Weatherby Magnum

HANDLOAD DATA

Bullet Wt. Grs.	Type	Powder Wt. Grs.	Type	Primer	Case	MV (fps)	ME (fpe)	Rifle/ Bbl. (in.)	Remarks
45	Sierra SP	25.0	IMR 4198	Rem. 9½	Wby.	3448	1188	Wby. MKV/26	Lyman Hndbk., 46th Ed. (Acc. Ld.)
45	Sierra SP	**32.0**	IMR 3031	Rem. 9½	Wby.	3984	1586	Wby. MKV/26	Lym. Hndbk., 46th Ed.
45	Hrndy. SP	**36.1**	Win. 760	Fed. 210	Wby.	3600	1295	Wby. MKV/26	Hrndy. Hndbk., 3rd Ed.
50	Sierra SP	**27.5**	IMR 4198	Rem. 9½	Wby.	3708	1527	Wby. MKV/26	Lyman Hndbk., 46th Ed. (Acc. Ld.)
50	Sierra SP	**31.5**	IMR 3031	Rem. 9½	Wby.	3831	1630	Wby. MKV/26	Lym. Hndbk., 46th Ed.
50	Hrndy. SP	**34.5**	H335	Fed. 210	Wby.	3900	1689	Wby. MKV/26	Hrndy. Hndbk., 3rd Ed.
52	Speer JHP	24.0	IMR 4198	Rem. 9½	Wby.	3215	1193	Wby. MKV/26	Lyman Hndbk., 46th Ed. (Acc. Ld.)
52	Speer JHP	**31.0**	IMR 3031	Rem. 9½	Wby.	3773	1644	Wby. MKV/26	Lym. Hndbk., 46th Ed.
55	Rem. PSP	**32.8**	IMR 4064	Rem. 9½	Wby.	3717	1688	Wby. MKV/26	Lyman Hndbk., 46th Ed.; acc.
55	Hrndy. SP	**32.9**	IMR 4064	Fed. 210	Wby.	3700	1672	Wby. MKV/26	Hrndy. Hndbk., 3rd Ed.
60	Hrndy. SP	**32.4**	IMR 4895	Fed. 210	Wby.	3600	1727	Wby. MKV/26	Hrndy. Hndbk., 3rd Ed.

SP—Soft Point; JHP—Jacketed Hollow Point; PSP—Pointed Soft Point.

FACTORY LOAD DATA

Bullet Wt. Grs.	Type	MV (fps)	ME (fpe)	Rifle/ Bbl. (in.)	Remarks
50	Wby. PE	3750	1562	Wby. V.M./26	Fact. ballistics
55	Wby. PE	3650	1627	Wby. V.M./26	Fact. ballistics

PE—Pointed Expanding.

SPECIFICATIONS

Shell Holders
RCBS: 27
Bonanza: 28
Lyman: 3
Pacific: 17

Bullet Diameter
Jacketed: .224"
Lengths
Trim: 1.915"
Maximum Case: 1.925"
Maximum Overall: 2.312"

CAUTION:
Loads recommended and suggested herein have been carefully listed, but are intended solely as a guide to readers and neither the publisher nor author accept any responsibility for results of their use.
Maximum loads, listed in bold, should be reduced by 10 percent and worked up to cautiously.

22-250 Remington

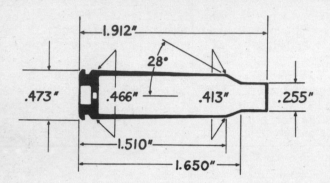

"Everyone I know who uses the 22-250 is happy with it. Nearly every rifle so-chambered gives uncommon accuracy, coupled with a relatively mild report and the merest nudge at the buttplate."

I HAVE never been a devoted fan of the 22-250 Remington. There are no flies on the cartridge, no bitter diatribes have I read; the rifles I have owned have been generally good shooters. But . . . I dunno. No charisma.

The Swift, now there's a charismatic cartridge; folks'll nearly come to blows when discussing the ol' 220. The 222 Remington, a mild, pleasant, incredibly accurate load that will take varmints at normal ranges with alacrity then win a benchrest match on Sunday. Then there's the underdog, the nearly-dead 225 Winchester; everyone pulls for the guy who's had naught but bad breaks from life. I know and respect the 223 Remington, am familiar with its awesome accuracy potential, its availability in a staggering array of firearms for virtually all purposes. The 224 Weatherby Magnum — it's cute, with its tiny little belt, looking just like a real grown-up magnum, and it comes in the petite Varmintmaster I like so much. But the 22-250 . . .

It'll do almost anything that any of the above cartridges will do. It is hot on the Swift's heels in muzzle velocity, so close any difference is academic. In a sporter-weight rifle, it is fully as accurate as most any 222 or 223, and in a varmint gun the difference is certainly not pronounced. The 225 Winchester, despite its poor sales history and reputation for precision accuracy, is just not quite up to the 22-250 in any way I can see. The 224 suffers the disadvantages of its proprietary heritage, and the cost and availability of ammunition works against it, not to mention the fact that it, like the 225, just won't quite measure up to the 22-250 ballistically. So why am I not in love with the 22-250 Remington? Got me.

Rick Jamison is. He has slain more prairie dogs, jackrabbits, and coyotes with his beat-up Remington 788 than I've ever seen. He has written magazine articles to the effect that if you don't own at least one 22-250, you know nothing worth telling about guns. He could be right.

Ed White simply dotes on his 22-250s, of which he has at least four and has owned more. I recently spent some time at the range while Ed was load-testing a pair of his rifles. Every so often I'd sneak a peek at his target frame through my spotting scope. I watched him fire group after group from his Remington 788 into about 5/8-inch, witnessed cluster after cluster from his Ruger M77-Varmint, only one of them exceeding 1/2-inch. These were five-shot strings, fellows, not the excuse-making three-shotters so many guys favor when they want to make a rifle appear accurate. Two things were readily apparent: the 22-250 can really shoot; Ed White can really shoot. Ed used to have a Browning BLR lever-action that would group around 1½ inches; you won't find many leverguns that'll shade that. What we are obviously discussing here is one super-accurate cartridge. So why don't I love it? Got me.

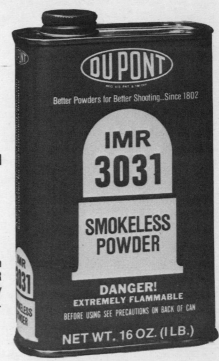

The author's first choice in propellants for the 22-250 is IMR 3031. It provides fine accuracy and high muzzle velocity.

On the left is the parent 250-3000 with the offspring on the right.

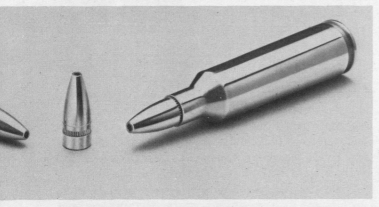

The new Federal "Blitz" in 22-250 is the fastest factory load available in that caliber. The load features a 40-grain bullet that exits the muzzle at a sizzling 4000 fps.

22-250 Ballistics

Let's talk ballistics. I've heard that the 22-250 "shoots plumb flat for ½-mile, then raises up a mite." Well, it doesn't shoot quite *that* flat. Normal velocity levels for the common 55-grain spitzer are around 3700 fps, although I have chronographed one lot of Remington ammunition that reached a whopping 3845 fps in a 24-inch barreled Model 788. Good handloads run in the same neighborhood, with some of the manuals showing as high as 3800-3825 fps from the 55-grainers. Factory ballistic sheets read 3680 fps for the standard-weight slugs, and 4000 fps for the speedy new Federal 40-grain hollow point. Let's agree on 3700 fps as the norm and go from there.

If we boost a 55-grain spitzer flat base such as the Sierra, to 3700 fps at the muzzle, the bullet retains 3308 fps at 100 yards, 2950 fps at 200, 2607 fps at 300 yards, and still has 2277 fps out at 400. Retained energy at 300 yards is 830 fpe, and there is still 633 fpe on tap at the full 400 yards.

In contrast, the 222 Remington, starting the same slug at 3100 fps, has left only 539 fpe at 300 yards, nearly 100 less than the 22-250 shows at *400*. The 223 kicks up another 150 fps or so at the nozzle, thus carries perhaps 600 fpe out at 300 yards, still well abaft of what the 22-250 boasts at 400 yards.

The 220 Swift beats the 22-250 by 100-150 fps in muz-

From left to right: 52-grain Nosler JHP Match; 52-grain Speer JHP; 52-grain Winchester JHPBT Match; 53-grain Winchester JHP Match; 55-grain Hornady SP; 55-grain Speer SP; 60-grain Nosler Solid Base and the 60-grain Hornady JHP. While the Winchester bullets have passed into history, the rest are still available and good performers in the 22-250.

zle speed, and maybe 70 fpe of energy at 400 yards. That's an increase of roughly 10 percent in punch at that extreme range. I'll let you decide if that is significant to you.

The excellent Federal 55-grain boat-tail Premium factory load is listed at 3680 fps at the muzzle. Assuming that it will actually achieve such numbers, the 300-yard energy is 815 fpe, and at 400 yards it is 630 fpe. That's comparable to good handloads.

To wit: the 22-250 shows as much retained velocity at 300 yards as the factory-loaded 22 Hornet has at the muzzle; it carries at 400 yards more energy than the 222, 222 Remington Magnum, and 223 show at 300, and it is a scant 10 percent behind the legendary 220 Swift in energy out at the 400-yard mark.

Back to trajectory. With the above mentioned 55-grain Sierra spitzer starting at 3700 fps, the 22-250, when sighted in for 200 yards, shows this bullet path: 100 yards, .84-inch high; 200 yards, zero; 300 yards, 4.9 inches low; 400 yards, 14.8 inches down. Using a 250-yard zero, the figures would be about 2.8 inches low at 300, 12.5 inches down at 400 yards. That's flat.

The 222 class would exhibit a 400-yard dive of from 21 to 23 inches with a 200-yard zero. The Swift would dip around 13.5 inches, depending on the exact velocity. Thus, the 22-250 drops about 32 percent less than the 222 and its ilk while itself dipping 9½ percent more than the vaunted Swift. Seems like a good trade to me; you accept a moderate increase in ammunition costs, noise pollution, and recoil for a genuine advantage in down-range punch and flatness of bullet flight over the 222 and 223 Remington. On the other hand, you give up only 10 percent in trajectory and 400-yard energy to the 220 Swift while gaining a load that is more readily obtainable, available in a wider variety of factory loads and rifles, and one easier on barrel steel. So why don't I love it? It's getting harder to explain.

My first 22-250 was a fine Ruger M77 heavy barrel. With that wonderful rifle and select, carefully-concocted handloads, I obtained the tightest groups I had encountered up to that time. As I recall, that gun averaged exactly ¾-inch with a load I got from Ken Waters, 32.0 grains of the long-gone Hercules ReLoder 11 un-

As a bench performer, the 22-250 is capable of some mighty fine groups. At 100 yards, five-shot groups of 1 inch or better are not uncommon.

der the always-accurate 52-grain Speer hollow point. My first sub-½-inch cluster came with that Ruger.

The Remington 55-grain soft points grouped amazingly tight, with one five-shot string measuring only .63-inch. Of course the rifle wouldn't average that, but it did stay in ⅞-inch for four, five-shotters. I used that M77 the summer of 1970, then for some inane reason traded it off. Wish I hadn't.

My next 22-250 was a big, heavy, cumbersome Remington 40-XB complete with 27½-inch stainless steel tube, target stock, and superb trigger. Try as I might, that gun would not average under ½-inch. In fact, it clustered five holes below .50-inch on only one occasion. It was, however, consistent. Using from 31.3 to 31.5 grains of IMR 3031 and the 53-grain Hornady match bullet, the big Remington averaged .57-inch, which is not shabby. But larger than I expected. The 40-X went away.

In 1975 I bought one of the ill-fated Colt Sharps, chambered in 22-250. With the 55-grain Federal factory load, that single shot would group 1.79 inches for an average. Not good enough for closet space. Away it went. Considering what those guns are bringing today

As a varmint rifle, the 22-250 fills the bill nicely. Both of these chucks were taken with the Ruger Ultra Light seen here. Note the exit wound on the chuck under the barrel.

Varmints

The first thing I ever saw shot with a 22-250 was a fat starling at 25 yards or so. Tweety disintegrated. Literally. The largest section of remains was the size of a quarter.

Then, for some years, a dry spell. In 1976, Rick Jamison escorted me on my first coyote hunt. Since I was his guest, Rick was looking hard for a yodel-dog. Bumping along in his Bronco, he spied one. Since I was his guest, he slammed on the brakes, jumped out of the truck, propped his lanky carcass across the hood, and shot my coyote. I was still getting out of the vehicle when the report of his rifle slammed my ears.

"Gotta be fast to get the drop on a coyote," said Rick, then trotted off to retrieve his prize. I waited at the Bronco, wondering about the Arizona laws pertaining to justifiable homicide.

Later that day, I made a magnificent shot at a coyote probably 375 yards out. Unfortunately I missed. He took off, running broadside to me. I ran out from behind some brush to get a clear shot at him. In my peripheral vision, I saw Rick wrap himself around a boul-

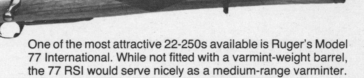

One of the most attractive 22-250s available is Ruger's Model 77 International. While not fitted with a varmint-weight barrel, the 77 RSI would serve nicely as a medium-range varminter.

on the collector's market, I think I erred.

I suspect there have been another two or three 22-250s around my homestead, I just "disremember" them. I've done a fair amount of shooting with my pal Jimmy Michael's Ruger Number 1. It prints around 1 inch almost all the time with a couple of loads. Then there is the Ithaca LSA that lives with my chuck-hunting croney Howard Adams. I chronographed his favorite load one day — a maximum load of 34.5 grains IMR 3031 under the 52-grain Hornady hollow point — at 3720 fps. While doing so, I fired three, five-shot groups; they averaged .96-inch including the fouling shot. Remember, the LSA is a very light sporter. Howard lets me hold his rifle sometimes now, and sort of caress it.

Currently, no 22-250 rifles take up space around my spread. Maybe I need to get one. But which one? At present only these firms offer a 22-250: Browning, Remington, Ruger, Alpine, BSA, Bighorn, Colt-Sauer, Champlin, DuBiel, Krico, M-S Safari Arms, Interarms, Sako, Savage, Shilen, Smith & Wesson, Steyr-Mannlicher, Weatherby, Tikka, Tradewinds, Whitworth, Wichita, and Winchester. With such a limited selection, I should have little trouble.

This particular Ruger No. 1, chambered for 22-250 has accounted for more than its share of varmints. It'll toss 1-inch groups all day. Typical.

22-250 Remington: Varmint/Target

der, solidly supporting his 22-250, and let fly. At my coyote. He dumped him. Three-hundred-seventy-five yards. Running full tilt.

Maybe I could plead insanity, I thought. "Nice shot," I said. Rick grinned and went to pick up the coyote. I stayed up on the mountain, watching the corpse, plotting revenge.

Rick has killed enough coyotes with the 22-250 to sink a coal barge. (He also used it once on a big javelina. His 63-grain Sierra soft point took the pig broadside at 150 yards and decked it on the spot.)

Despite his success on all kinds of animals, Rick tells me that for a come-what-may coyote rifle, he would prefer something a little larger. Like a 243 or 6mm Remington. A coyote, he says, takes a lot of killing, particularly with a shot imperfectly placed. But for a careful hunter who picks his chances conscientiously, the 22-250 is enough gun.

For chucks and crows, it would be hard to imagine a better all-around choice than the 22-250 for the one-gun man. Out to 350 or 400 yards, a good shot should be able to garner his share of chucks under most conditions. One of the 6mms or maybe a 25-06 just might shade the 22-250 under windy conditions, but it would depend on which bullet was used in each. The 22-250 is

One propellant capable of excellent performance in the 22-250 is IMR 4895.

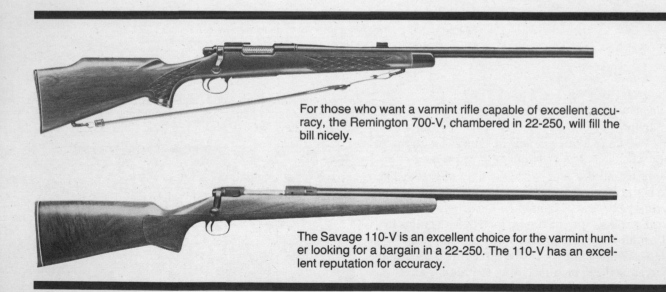

For those who want a varmint rifle capable of excellent accuracy, the Remington 700-V, chambered in 22-250, will fill the bill nicely.

The Savage 110-V is an excellent choice for the varmint hunter looking for a bargain in a 22-250. The 110-V has an excellent reputation for accuracy.

almost a perfect chuck cartridge.

My first choice in propellants for the 22-250 is IMR 3031. I've always received fine accuracy and suitably high muzzle speeds. My second choice would be either IMR or Hodgdon 4895, which is what does the best in Jimmy Michael's Ruger.

Ed White likes 37.0 grains of Hodgdon's H380 under the 52-grain Hornady boat-tail match in his 788 Rem-

ington. Groups to date have averaged .649-inch. The same charge behind the 52-grain Watson match slug showed a .498-inch aggregate in his Ruger M77-V.

Everyone I know who uses the 22-250 is happy with it. Nearly every rifle so-chambered gives uncommon accuracy, coupled with a relatively mild report and the merest nudge at the buttplate. Great varmint round. Popular. Well-liked. Wonder why I don't love it.

22-250 Remington

HANDLOAD DATA

Bullet Wt. Grs.	Type	Powder Wt. Grs.	Type	Primer	Case	MV, (fps)	ME, (fpe)	Rifle/ Bbl. (in.)	Remarks
50	Nosler JHP(M)	35.0	IMR 4895	CCI 200	Fed.	3646	1476	Rem. 788/24	Fair accuracy
52	Hrndy. JHPBT	**34.5**	IMR 3031	8½-120	Win.	**3720**	**1598**	Ithaca LSA/23	Extrmly. acc. and fast
52	Hrndy. JHPBT	**34.5**	IMR 3031	Fed. 210	Nor.	**3716**	**1595**	Ruger No. 1/26	Extremely accurate
52	Speer JHP	35.0	IMR 4895	CCI 200	Fed.	3660	1547	Rem. 788/24	Accurate
52	Hrndy. JHPBT	37.0	H380	Fed. 210M	Rem.	NC*	NC*	Rem. 788/24	Extremely accurate; E. White load
53	Hrndy. JHP(M)	35.7	IMR 4064	CCI 200	Nor.	3510	1450	Ruger No. 1/26	Accurate

*NC — Not Chronographed

JHPBT—Jacketed Hollow Point Boat-Tail; JHP(M)—Jacketed Hollow Point (Match).

FACTORY LOAD DATA

Bullet Wt. Grs.	Type	MV, (fps)	ME, (fpe)	Rifle/ Bbl. (in.)	Remarks
55	Rem. SP	3743	1711	Colt Sharps/28	Fair accuracy; Lot 1
55	Rem. SP	3576	1562	Ruger No. 1/26	Fair accuracy; Lot 2
55	Rem. SP	3845	1806	Rem. 788/24	Accurate; Lot 3
55	Rem. SP	3730	1700	Rem. 788/24	Fair accuracy; Lot 4

SP—Soft Point.

SPECIFICATIONS

Shell Holders
RCBS: 3
Bonanza: 1
Lyman: 2
Pacific: 1

Bullet Diameter
Jacketed: .224″

Lengths
Trim: 1.902″
Maximum Case: 1.912″
Maximum Overall: 2.350″

Federal's Premium line of center-fire ammunition includes offerings in 22-250. It has an excellent reputation for off-the-shelf accuracy.

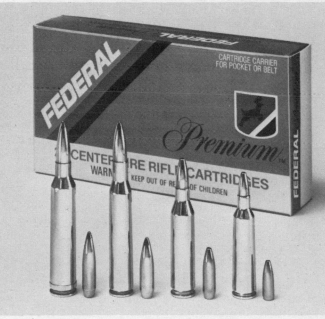

CAUTION:
Loads recommended and suggested herein have been carefully listed, but are intended solely as a guide to readers and neither the publisher nor author accept any responsibility for results of their use. **Maximum loads, listed in bold, should be reduced by 10 percent and worked up to cautiously.**

220 Swift

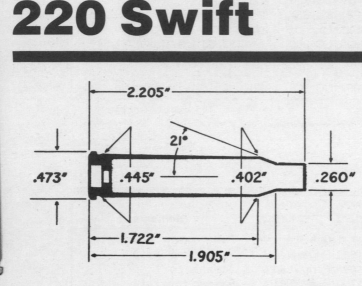

2.205"

21°

.473" .445" .402" .260"

1.722"

1.905"

"When loaded to full throttle, the 220 Swift is an incredibly fine cartridge for its purpose—the taking of varmint-class animals at long range."

WINCHESTER begat the semi-rimmed 220 Swift in 1935, thus initiating a raging controversy that continues to this day. Only the initial Model 54 bolt-action rifle and the subsequent Model 70 were chambered for the Swift in the United States until the 1970s. Ruger added it to their line in 1973; Savage Arms followed suit in 1975. I wrote the Savage Model 112-V up in the November-December, 1975, issue of *Rifle* magazine, and followed in the next issue with a piece including both the Savage and the Ruger M77 heavy-barrel.

Both of my sample rifles—one provided by Savage Arms, the other purchased at retail—were extremely accurate. The 112-V grouped its best load into .625-inch for an average of several five-shot strings.

I mention the foregoing simply to illustrate that the 220 Swift is quite accurate, a condition that has been denied in the press over the years. Not only has the Swift been accused of inaccuracy, but it is often considered picky about its loads, extremely tough on barrel steel, difficult to load down to more pedestrian velocities while retaining a semblance of tight grouping, and prone to unexplainable "pressure excursions" that are apt to blow your wig off. Let's examine some of these bromides to see if they'll make weight.

Light Loads, Barrel Wear and Pressure

We've covered accuracy, so let's turn to that old saw about not being able to down-load the Swift to less bar-

rel-straining speeds. Several of the most accurate loads worked up in my Savage were from 2 to 3 grains below my rifle's maximum-working level. An example is the 52-grain Speer hollow point and 34 grains of IMR 3031, a load that, at 3674 fps, is no barrel burner. It groups five rounds into .625-inch at 100 yards.

Conversely, the Swift works quite well at full throttle. In short, my experience with the 220 indicates that it is amenable to varying charge levels as far as their effects on accuracy are concerned.

Next we have the barrel-wear tenet. Folks used to speculate that the Swift would wear out a nickel-steel barrel in 1,000 rounds or less. Actually, what happened was that Swift bores became badly metal-fouled due to improper or infrequent cleaning, perhaps aggravated by softer bullet jackets than we have today. This caused a dreadful decrease in accuracy and occasioned much gnashing of teeth. Modern paste-type bore cleaners such as J-B compound have alleviated this complaint, but nasty rumors still plague the cartridge.

And now to the pressure-excursion dictum. To that charge there may be a kernel of truth. My first experience with "blown" primers—an instance where a case head expands so much that the primer falls out of its pocket when the case is extracted—came via the Savage Swift. I have since experienced the uncomfortable phenomena with several other cartridges, but the 220 broke me in.

Never overload! The Swift churns up some pretty good pressures, so don't experiment. Stick to reliable load data and start light, looking for pressure signs as you work up. Note the *greatly* enlarged primer pocket and heavily cratered primer.

The throat on the author's Ruger 77V is slightly shallower than that on his Savage 112-V in the same chambering. By simply reversing a bullet of proper caliber, and placing it into the neck of a sized/unprimed empty case (and chambering it) you can determine the throat depth on your own Swift.

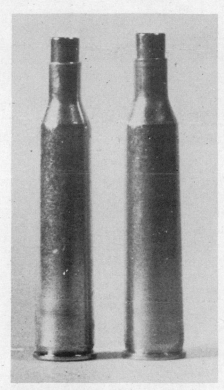

There's an old saw that goes, "Swift barrels are worn out before they get to 1000 rounds." Here's proof that "old saws" don't always work. This 5-shot group, rounds No. 999 through 1003, measures .625-inch. Enough said.

Two of the escapades came with a load of 37.3 grains of IMR 4064 and a 53-grain match hollow point. I checked my case necks; they were neither too long nor too thick. I pulled bullets and reweighed powder charges. No luck there. Bullets were of normal diameter; brass was once-fired; the moon was in its first quarter. My Ruger had digested an even stiffer charge of IMR 4064 with the identical bullet (from the same box); I was at a loss. My buddy Rick Jamison suggested I check the throat of the Savage. I did; it was even longer than the Ruger's.

Clutching at straws, I slugged the bore of the 112-V. Aha! It miked .223-inch, which is a little undersized. Not much, just a thousandth of an inch, but it was the first abnormality I had discovered. I talked it over with Rick. I talked it over with Neal Knox. None of us was convinced that the slightly skinny bore of the Savage was to blame for the too-high pressures. I'm still not, 8 years later. Neal appended to my magazine article the following: "Since bullets used by handloaders will often vary by as much as .001-inch from different makers, I would be surprised if a .001-inch undersize barrel—assuming Clay's slugging and miking were accurate—were to cause as much of a pressure difference as he noted." Amen.

In every instance, and with every propellant, my Savage showed excessive-pressure signs when published maximums were approached to within 3 or 4 grains with

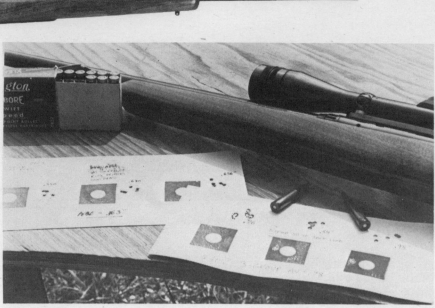

(Above) Many shooters have found the Ruger 77V in 220 Swift to be a sub-minute performer. A rifle like this is ideal for the serious varmint hunter. The author's 77V regularly turns in groups running .75-inch.

(Right) The author's Savage Model 112-V, chambered for the Swift, is capable of turning in some impressive groups. The targets to the left were fired with handloads; the targets to the right were fired with Norma factory ammo using a 50-grain soft point bullet. The average for three, 5-shot groups with the factory fodder was .78-inch—excellent accuracy.

a suitable propellant. Assuming this to be the result of a too-tight bore, I expected velocities of my milder-than-published handloads to run higher than identical loads fired in a normal-sized barrel. Not so; my chronograph read off instrumental speeds that closely matched those found in loading manuals using loads of the same charge level. Additionally, my chronograph testing of factory ammunition closely jibed with results published by independent testers.

In the book *Principles and Practice of Loading Ammunition,* by Earl Naramore, the author surmises that there is no direct relationship between velocity and pressure. If he is correct, that might explain why my undersized barrel produced normal velocities at abnormal pressures. It might be hypothesized that normal published velocities, at maximum levels, are out of reach in my 112-V. If so, how can one explain that factory loads showed normal, high muzzle speeds in the Savage without any manifestations of extremely high pressures?

The upshot of all this is that while I'm not certain that the Swift is cantankerous to load for, I can't prove it isn't either. My experiences with the Savage, and that of erudite shooters who have used the Swift before me, cannot be ignored. Neither are they an unequivocal indictment of the 220 Swift. They are merely a friendly warning sign.

Bear in mind that I had no problems whatever with my Ruger M77 Varmint, and I loaded some pretty warm ammunition for that rifle. There *were* some anomalies with the Savage that I still can't explain except by putting them down as normal rifle-to-rifle variations.

The primary lesson I learned from my relationship with the Swift is to watch case length carefully, turn or ream fired case necks if I find thay have become too

thick to accept a bullet easily, to approach maximum published charge levels with a jaundiced eye.

Performance

The Swift's claim to fame is its varminting ability. Indeed, it is known as the King of Varminters, a title it emphatically deserves. Take an accurate 220 stoked with gilt-edged handloads boosted to full power, find the range with acceptable accuracy, allow for drop, draw a bead on your target, and let fly. If the wind is down, your hold good, and the distance to the target ¼-mile or less, you'll likely score with laser-like precision and convincing devastation.

The Swift is no slouch even when the breezes blow. Assuming a 55-grain spitzer boat-tail, such as the Nosler Solid Base, starting at 3800 fps, the wind drift at 400 yards in a 10mph crosswind would be 14.8 inches. Not bad. A heavy-loaded 243 Winchester can drive an 85-grain Nosler Solid Base to 3300 fps, showing a 13.0-inch drift at the 400-yard line. A 1.8-inch advantage is no advantage at all at 400 yards, so pay no attention to the guys who insist that the 6mm's completely outclass the Swift on windy days.

A bursting-at-the-seams 25-06 handload can push a 100-grain Nosler Solid Base to 3400 fps; wind drift is an even 11 inches out at 400 yards. Go to the 117-grain Sierra pointed flat base—definitely not a varmint slug—and you get 13.4 inches of sideways motion. No improvement there. Hike a super-streamlined 130-grain Sierra boat-tail spitzer to 3000 fps in a 270, about all the muzzle velocity you'll get in normal barrel lengths, and the drift is still 12.7 inches, four football fields away. Yep, the Swift will hold its own in any company where wind-initiated movement is concerned.

From the bench, at 100 yards, Harvey's Savage Model 112-V can turn in groups of ⅝-inch using handloads. Scope is a Lyman 10x.

In the "good old days" every major cartridge house offered loaded Swift ammo. Today, only Norma and Frontier can supply you with the real thing, unprimed brass still being available from Winchester.

How about trajectory? Hell, the Swift is the original *flat-shooting* cartridge. Zip a Nosler 55-grain Solid Base along at 3800 fps and the trajectory looks like this: .7-inch high at 100 yards, 0 at 200, 4.5 inches low at 300 yards, and only 13.8 inches down at 400. Take a look at the above-mentioned 243 hotshot: 1.1 inches up at 100, 0 at 200 yards, 5.7 down at 300, and 16.8 inches below the mark at 400 yards. In my opinion, 3 inches less drop at 400 yards is more important than a 1.8-inch edge in wind drift. Also in my opinion, the 220 Swift is a better varmint cartridge than the 243 for animals under 20 pounds in weight under any condition.

The Swift is no big game cartridge, although a slew of the bigger beasts have succumbed to a dose of lead poison courtesy of one of those speedy little bullets. Harry Goodwin, a local whitetail hunter of repute, has taken several with a Ruger M77 with nary a failure. However, Harry is a fine shot and knows his deer anatomy. He slips the bullet in where it'll do the most good. He doesn't recommend the practice for anyone else, and neither do I. I merely offer his experience as an indication of what the Swift can do under expert guidance.

For predator calling, a light sporter-weight Swift, such as the standard model Ruger M77, would be the berries. At ranges up to 250 or 300 yards, the Swift has plenty of killing punch for varmints of coyote size. Past that distance, I would opt for something with a tad more bullet weight like the 243 or 6mm Remington. Still, Rick Jamison has slain a garageful of yodel dogs with a 22-250, which is less potent than the 220, and he has killed some way out yonder.

For extremely long-range gunning of crows or prairie dogs, and I'd consider anything past 300 yards to be very long range on such critters, the Swift is as good as you can get. Period. Not only is there nothing better, there is nothing quite its equal. The 22-250 is great, but it falls short of the 220 by 100-150 fps when both are loaded up to snuff. In addition, the 22-250 is not one whit more accurate. The 6mm's are fine but not quite as accurate as the 220 on the average, and they kick a lot more. The 25-06 is more of the same, although a 25-06 with good bullets in a super-accurate rifle can give the most accurate of Swifts a run for its money. (I've never understood just why the 25-06 is so accurate. It burns a hatful of powder, wears a barrel out as if it were made of soap instead of steel, and it lays into your shoulder with authority. Despite all this, the dang things'll *shoot!*)

Favorite Loads

When it comes to powder selection, my favorite Swift handloads revolve around IMR 4064 and 3031. Bullets include the 50-grain Nosler match hollow point, the 52-grain Speer hollow point and the 55-grain Nosler Solid Base.

The best load in the Savage 112-V features the 52-grain Speer HP and 34.0 grains of IMR 3031; groups run ⅝-inch for an average and the velocity is just under 3700 fps. My Ruger No. 1-V prefers the same load.

The top factory load I've tested is the Norma 50-grain. It clocked 4028 fps in the 112-V and printed a .78-inch average of three, 5-shot strings. I haven't tried it in the Ruger M77 but I did fire some in a Ruger Number 1-B. One lot of ammo grouped into 1.24 inches for three,

5-shot groups clocking 4013 fps while doing so. A second lot produced a crummy 2.28-inch group average and was slower to boot at 3971 fps. I also plan to give the Frontier factory loads a more thorough try in the future, but haven't had a chance to date. Currently, only Frontier and Norma manufacture Swift ammunition, with Winchester peddling virgin brass.

When loaded to full throttle, the 220 Swift is an incredibly fine cartridge for its purpose—the taking of varmint-class animals at long range. For ranges under 300 yards, there are better cartridges, ones that caress the innards of a rifle barrel more lovingly and belt your shoulder less brutally. For predators the size of coyotes and bobcats, there are also more suitable loads, ones that smack the target with a tad more authority. But for varmint hunting come-what-may, for close distances and long, for vermin of all shapes and sizes, nothing beats the Swift. Long live the King.

220 Swift

HANDLOAD DATA

Bullet Wt. Grs. Type	Powder Wt. Grs. Type	Primer	Case	MV (fps)	ME (fpe)	Rifle/ Bbl. (in.)	Remarks
50 Nosler SB	34.0 IMR 3031	Fed. 210M	Nor.	3640	1471	Savage 112-V/26	Fair accuracy
50 Nosler SB	34.0 IMR 3031	Fed. 210	Nor.	3610	1447	Ruger No. 1-V/26	Most acc. ld. this gun
52 Speer JHP	34.0 IMR 3031	Fed. 210M	Nor.	3674	1559	Savage 112-V/26	Most acc. ld. this gun
52 Speer JHP	34.0 IMR 3031	Fed. 210	Nor.	3575	1476	Ruger No. 1-V/26	Accurate
52 Speer JHP	34.0 IMR 3031	Fed. 210M	Win.	3526	1436	Ruger 77V/26	Very accurate
53 Win. JHP(M)	35.0 IMR 4064	CCI BR-2	Nor.	3591	1518	Savage 112-V/26	Accurate
55 Speer FMJ	35.0 IMR 4064	CCI BR-2	Win.	3495	1492	Ruger 77V/26	Mild
55 Nosler SB	35.0 IMR 4064	CCI BR-2	Win.	3516	1501	Savage 112-V/26	Fair accuracy
55 Sierra SPBT	37.6 IMR 4064	CCI 200	Nor.	3569	1553	Ruger No. 1-V/26	Fair accuracy

SB—Solid Base; JHP—Jacketed Hollow Point; FMJ—Full Metal Jacket; JHP(M)—Jacketed Hollow Point (Match); SPBT—Soft Point Boat-Tail.

FACTORY LOAD DATA

Bullet Wt. Grs. Type	MV (fps)	ME (fpe)	Rifle/ Bbl. (in.)	Remarks
50 Norma SP	4028	1802	Savage 112-V/26	Extremely acc. and fast
50 Norma SP (Lot 1)	4013	1788	Ruger No. 1-B/26	Extremely acc. and fast
50 Norma SP (Lot 1)	4048	1820	Ruger No. 1-V/26	Very accurate
50 Norma SP (Lot 2)	3971	1750	Ruger No. 1-B/26	Slower, less accurate
50 Norma SP (Lot 2)	3885	1677	Ruger No. 1-V/26	Slower, less accurate
55 Fron. SP	3490	1485	Ruger No. 1-V/26	Fair accuracy
60 Fron. JHP	3538	1665	Ruger No. 1-V/26	Fair accuracy

SP—Soft Point; JHP—Jacketed Hollow Point.

SPECIFICATIONS

Shell Holders
RCBS: 11
Bonanza: 7
Lyman: 5
Pacific: 4

Bullet Diameter
Jacketed: .224″

Lengths
Trim: 2.195″
Maximum Case: 2.205″
Maximum Overall: 2.680″

CAUTION:
Loads recommended and suggested herein have been carefully listed, but are intended solely as a guide to readers and neither the publisher nor author accept any responsibility for results of their use.
Maximum loads, listed in bold, should be reduced by 10 percent and worked up to cautiously.

Popular Sporting Rifle Cartridges

243 WINCHESTER
6mm REMINGTON
240 WEATHERBY MAGNUM
250-3000 SAVAGE
257 ROBERTS
25-06 REMINGTON
257 WEATHERBY MAGNUM

VARMINT/DEER

243 Winchester

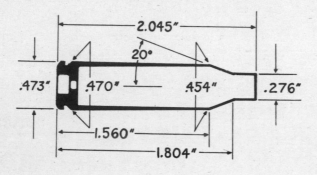

2.045"
20°
.473" .470" .454" .276"
1.560"
1.804"

"The 243 is renowned for its accuracy. I used to hold the opinion that the reputation was overdone. No more. I know the 243 to be accurate in the right rifle, sometimes astoundingly so."

THE 243 Winchester saw its genesis in 1955 when it was introduced in that firm's Model 70 bolt-action and Model 88 levergun. It was an overnight success. Ballyhooed as the perfect combination cartridge for varmint and deer, and factory loaded with bullets suitable for either pursuit, virtually every sporting-rifle manufacturer in the free world tooled up for the sizzling new round. Its burgeoning popularity inundated the popular 257 Roberts and the antideluvian 250-3000, long rivals for the same crown.

Not only did the 243 bury the aforementioned 25s, it also trounced Remington's equally nascent 244, at least at the box office. Ballistically, the two newcomers were as alike as a pair of turnips, so it was the rapid rise of the one and the rampant uninterest in the other that provided much grist for the gun writers' mill during the past 28 years. Let's go over the ground once more for those of you who just came in.

Warren Page, former shooting editor of *Field & Stream,* was said to have instigated the 243 by forming a wildcat cartridge from the 308 Winchester case. Page dubbed his offspring the 240 Page Souper Pooper and pressured Winchester to legitimize the load. They did so after a fashion, modifying the case to their own idea of ballistic efficiency and ease of manufacture. At about the same time, the folks at Ilion were busy gestating a cartridge identical in bullet diameter, quite different in parent case, that became the 244 Remington. The pair

toed the line; Winchester won. Why?

Some writers advance the theory that the 244's languid rifling twist of one turn in 12 inches did it in. The 243 was designed for barrels having a twist rate of 1-in-10 inches, better to stabilize the longer 100-grain bullets meant for big game. Word got around that the 243 would plop all its heavy bullets into tight little clusters while the slow-twist 244 keyholed its slugs all over the target. Maybe. Maybe not. Tests have been run to support both contentions. It doesn't matter, anyway. A stout 90-grain bullet, *as initially offered by Remington,* was adequate for any game the 243 was good for with its 100-grain load. That's why Remington offered the cartridge with two bullet weights in the first place. They merely opted for different weights than Winchester. No, ballistic considerations didn't decide the battle.

What really hurt the 244 was Winchester's Model 70. Remington's vehicle for their new offering was the inexpensive Model 722, a rifle as plain as your Aunt Mildred. New Haven tucked their new cartridge into as nice a sporting bolt-action as America has produced, and in no less than four permutations. Available were the Standard Model, the Featherweight, a varmint rig, and a target rifle. Something for everyone.

The 722 Remington was accurate enough, priced right, and available. It was also long in the barrel, low-dollar in execution, and heavy. It became obvious to anyone with an eye for observation that the Ilion crew

The author's favorite deer load consists of a maximum load of 46 grains of Norma MRP, 100-grain Nosler Solid Base spitzers and Federal No. 215 Magnum primers.

The late Warren Page, former shooting editor for *Field & Stream,* is said to have been responsible for the birth of the 243 Winchester. The cartridge that started it all, the "240 Page Souper Pooper" is seen here—it's a 6mm wildcat based on the 308 Winchester case. Note the length of the neck.

viewed their new 244 as a *varmint*/deer load, whereas the Winchester contingent thought of the 243 more as a *deer*/varmint cartridge. Shooters agreed. Light, 243 sporters were gobbled up like Reese's Pieces at a cub scout picnic; heavy, homely 244's gathered cobwebs in dealers' racks. A classic case of the silk purse versus the sow's ear. The 244 languished.

Incidentally, it is widely held that the 243 was the first 6mm cartridge. Wrong. In the late 1800s, Winchester produced a straight-pull bolt-action for the U.S. Navy chambered for a round known as the 6mm Lee Navy. In Europe, such cartridges as the 6x57 Mauser, 244 Halger Magnum, 240 Apex, and numerous others held sway. The 24-bore wasn't new in 1955, just revived, gussied up, and advertised.

And such advertising! The 243 was loudly touted as being ample for pushing an 80-grain varmint bullet to 3500 fps while getting 3070 fps from the 100-grain deer load. What was less loudly proclaimed was the 26-inch barrel necessary to achieve such lofty numbers if they were, in fact, achieved outside of a ballistics lab. Hunters took in these figures, went glassy-eyed and fell into a swoon. And thus did the more pedestrian 25 calibers get dirt tossed on their graves.

Then came the day of the inexpensive chronograph. Every gun writer worth his salt had one, used it to clock a few sample rounds, mused over the unexpected results and renounced the 243 as a flaccid shell of its re-

puted self. Current ballistic tables are more candid. And conservative. The 243 is now listed at about 3350 fps with 80-grain bullets, 2960 fps for 100-grain bullets, fired from a 24-inch pressure barrel. (Some ammo brands actually equal or exceed these numbers.)

During the time since the Eisenhower administration, the 243 has become enormously popular. It usually manages to place in the top five or six centerfire rifle cartridges in ammunition sales, and RCBS has carried it in their top 10 listing of reloading die sales since 1976. (I have no data on earlier years.) That's the top 10 in *total* die sales, handgun cartridges included. Among rifle cartridges alone, the 243 was either second or third for 5 years running, only recently dropping to sixth place.

Despite the 243's legion of fans and its universal approbation, a few warts have come to light. One of the most prevalent is an increasing reputation for excessive barrel wear. Considering the years of bad press generated by the 220 Swift, I'll bet Winchester is gnashing its corporate teeth at this arrant turn of events. As with the Swift, things are not so bad as they're made out. Sure, the 243 is tough on barrels; any small-bore, high-intensity, large-capacity cartridge is. There are other cartridges that are worse. Big deal. Most shooters don't fire enough rounds to burn a barrel out in a lifetime. If they do, they can crate the gun and pack it off to its maker for a new one at the cost of one steel-belted radial tire.

243 Winchester: Varmint/Deer

More serious is the allegation that some 243-caliber rifles have come apart at the seams for no apparent reason. That *is* alarming. But is it true? Perhaps. One Winchester magnate confided in me his theory regarding these rare but not unheard of mishaps. As he told it, there are three contributing factors: the "high" maximum-working chamber pressures (52,000 c.u.p.), the length of the 100-grain game bullet and, if present, barrel erosion ahead of the chamber's throat. What happens, he hypothesized, is this: The force of a detonating primer kicks the bullet out of the case mouth before the powder charge is ignited; the bullet's long bearing surface causes it to snag in the eroded throat section of a much-fired rifle; the powder ignites; burning gasses catch the bullet mired in the eroded throat; things start to break. The problem seems not to arise in new, or

(Above) The most consistent accuracy the author has received from a 243 factory load, in several rifles, came from the 80-grain Federal soft point (left). The 100-grain Norma FMJ beside it is the fastest 243 heavy-bullet load the author has chronographed.

(Left) The most accurate 243 the author ever tested was this Remington Model 788. It would average under ¾-inch with its pet load. Scope is a 6x Redfield Low Profile.

nearly new, barrels or with varmint-weight projectiles. SAAMI, cognizant of the situation, is rumored to be advocating a modest reduction in working pressures to alleviate the problem.

Some of the ammo makers have indeed cut back. The Hornady ballistic lab ran some tests for me a few years back. Fired from the Hornady P and V barrel, Norma's 100-grain soft point showed the highest average pressure of 51,400 c.u.p., just under the wire. Federal's 100-grain soft point gave 48,440 c.u.p. and more than 200 fps less muzzle speed. The Winchester 100-grain soft point showed 46,440 and an even lower muzzle velocity. In short, you don't get high speeds without concomitant pressures.

In my chronograph tests of a Savage Model 111 with 22-inch barrel, the fastest big game load was the Norma 100-grain soft point at 3096 fps. Speediest from a domestic maker was the 100-grain Hornady soft point "Frontier" loading at 2948. Remington, Winchester, and Federal lagged behind by a wide margin, although the Federal soft point nearly cracked 2900. One lot of Winchester ammo clocked only 2698 fps; I discounted that batch as a fluke.

Most of the varmint loads put up by the factories ran a comparable amount aft of listed speeds. Closest to published data in my tests was the 80-grain Winchester soft point, averaging 3346 in the Savage Model 111 and 3352 in a crisp new Remington Model 788, both with 22-inch barrels. The Remington and Federal 80-grain loads brought up the drag, neither achieving 3200 fps.

What about handloads? Can the reloader hope to reach those figures listed by the factories, or even those actually realized with factory ammunition? Absolutely. It's no real trick to punch a 70-grain varmint or match bullet out of a 22-inch tube at 3500 fps, and do it with first-rate accuracy. The "seventy-fives" will reach 3450 fps, or better, and the "eighties" about 3400 fps. The 85-grain bullet group can reach 3300-plus fps with several powders, and the 90-grain Speer will go to 3150 fps in some rifles (although 3100 fps is a more reasonable expectation). The heavy 100-grain deer slayers can be pushed to 3000 fps easily, 3050 fps occasionally, with some powders and at least 22 inches of barrel. The 105-grain Speer spitzer is good for about 2950 fps in most rifles, although I had one long-throated Ruger Number 1 22-inch sporter that would reach 3100!

That's about it for alleged negatives. To recap, a 243 can be a bit pressure-sensitive, particularly if it has digested a lot of ammo; it's more erosive to barrel steel than is economically ideal; it frequently fails to achieve

On the bags is a Savage Model 99-A lever gun, scoped by Redfield. Beside it on the bench is an old Ruger Model 77 bolt-action. The Ruger would group under 1½ inches at 100 yards from a benchrest.

This is the Model 70 Varmint tested by the author and mentioned in the text. The rifle averaged under 1 inch from 100 yards with several loads. Heavy-barreled rifles such as this are not as popular in 243 chambering as the lighter sporters.

published velocity figures in factory loadings. Now let's examine some of its proclaimed virtues with an equally analytical eye.

The 243 is renowned for its accuracy. I used to hold the opinion that the reputation was overdone. No more. I know the 243 to be accurate in the right rifle, sometimes *astoundingly so*. One of the chief reasons for its rapid rise to fame was the level of accuracy displayed by lightweight hunting rifles. Writing in the 15th Edition of *Gun Digest,* Warren Page opined that any well-bedded 243 sporter was capable of 1½-inch, five-shot groups, fired from benchrest at 100 yards with good ammunition. I believe a good lightweight 243 will stay in less than 1¼ inches, and I've done a lot of work with 243s over the years. For example, a Ruger Model 77 I once owned would average .98-inch with its favorite handload; another M77 would put string after string of various factory loads into 1½ inches with no load tuning at all. Handloading the 243 will usually cut group size by 30 percent, so I have no doubt the rifle could have grouped around an inch with little trouble. One Remington Model 788 I tested would average .95-inch with its favored load, for seven, five-shot strings! A second load with a different bullet and powder would do nearly as well. My Ruger Number 1 light sporter would aver-

age 1.10 and 1.19 inches with its two best loads.

How about varmint-shooting accuracy? Let me quote Mr. Page:

"As a class, 6mm varmint rifles, whether standard or wildcat, can be tuned and loaded to give five-shot 100-yard groups of about .75-inch, usually without much sweat . . . To squeeze any one of 'em tighter than that seems darned near impossible so long as we talk about averages or a string of test groups, not freak one-holers like the target you carry around in your wallet."

My experience roughly parallels that of Page. My most accurate varmint-weight 243 was a Model 70 Winchester; it printed into .83-inch for a nine-group average. Its runner-up load went .91. Not quite the ¾-inch group Page predicted, but close. A Browning Safari Heavy-Barrel I once owned, built on a medium-length Sako action, would group into .85-inch with a mild load, one unsuitable for varmint shooting.

Which brings me to my most recent 243, a plain-Jane Remington 788 sporter with 22-inch barrel. The gun has never been tuned or altered in any way; it came from a dealer, not hand-chosen by the factory. With its pet load, the little rifle fired an average of .70-inch for 13 five-shot strings at 100 yards! Even with the 90-grain Speer game bullet, that 788 will print a .78-inch aver-

Shooter Dale Hawks illustrates the fact that recoil of the 243 is so light, it can be fired comfortably in shirt sleeves. That's a real asset for the summertime varminter. Rifle is a Remington M700.

age. Which makes it the most accurate 243 I've ever seen, shot, heard of or read about.

Not only is a 243 inherently accurate, it is also eminently shootable. The recoil is so mild it is scarcely noticed except by the most tender of shoulder. Such impeccable manners enable the average hunter to connect on distant animals much easier than with a gun of heftier kick. This broadens his grin and convinces him he's one hell of a rifle shot. In actuality, the 243 is less potentially accurate than some other big-game cartridges, most notably the 308 Winchester and 25-06. It's just much easier to hit with and more shootable. And thereby developed its distinction as an *accurate* cartridge.

Varmint Use

The most controversial area of the 243's mystique is its hunting application. As a varmint cartridge, many swear by it, claiming it to be without peer as a long-range load, particularly on a windy day. The heavy (by varminting standards) 24-caliber bullets are said to fly unerringly to their target, seemingly impervious to vagrant gusts that would blow a high-velocity 22-caliber bullet into the next valley.

Many others swear *at* the cartridge, citing its heavy recoil (by varminting standards) and loud muzzle blast as not only unnecessary but deleterious to the accuracy requisite to varmint shooting. A true hunter, they advance, should be able to stalk within range of a more mild-mannered load. The 243, they insist, is just too much gun.

Some big-game hunters harangue a similar line, disdaining the 243 as too small and impotent for even the most under-nourished deer, let alone something bigger. Plink a black bear with this puny number, they dolefully exclaim, and you're certain to become bruin fodder.

An equally vociferous clique claims the 243 to be as effective as controlled nuclear fission. Smack a big buck

with one of those zippy 100-grain slugs and, as Jack O'Conner used to say, all you'll have left will be a red mist and a whimper.

As usual, the truth lies somewhere in between. As a varmint cartridge, the 243 is indeed near the top of the ballistic heap. If your normal varminting ranges fall short of 300 yards, one of the lesser 22 centerfires will fill the bill with little fuss and no bother. However, if you find an occasional 400-yard chuck filling your scope, you need stiffer medicine. Something like a 22-250. Maybe a 220 Swift. Or a 243.

Using the 22-250 as the example, let's compare. The better 22-250 loads utilize a 55-grain bullet at about 3700 fps from a 24-inch barrel. A 55-grain Nosler boat-tail beginning at that speed and zeroed for 200 yards, will show a 400-yard drop of 14.7 inches. An 85-grain Nosler boat-tail 24-caliber bullet exiting the muzzle at 3300 fps, with the same 200-yard zero, drops 16.8 inches at 400. That's a 2.1-inch advantage for the 22-250. I can scarcely see that increment at 400 yards; I doubt I could use it to my advantage.

Even if I could, there is yet another factor to consider—wind drift. The above-mentioned 55-grain Nosler drifts 30.8 inches at 400 yards, assuming a 20 mph crosswind and 3700 fps muzzle speed. The 85-grain, 24-caliber drifts 25.9 inches, 4.9 inches less. More significant than the drop figures? I think so. Moreover, it takes a 24- or 26-inch barrel to realize such figures in either the 22-250 or the 220 Swift. Using a comparable barrel chambered for the 243 increases its advantage.

So where's the rub? Why doesn't everyone use the 243 for varmints? Well, the high-intensity 22 centerfires have less recoil, they're cheaper to shoot, and they are generally a little more accurate. Not a great deal more precise, but nonetheless a demonstrable amount. And the 243 gets serious competition from the 6mm Remington and the 25-06, both of which offer ballistic advantages similar to those the 243 enjoys over the hotshot 22s.

The upshot is that the 243 is a fine varmint cartridge, but a middle-of-the-roader, not as potent as the 25-06, nor as pleasant and cheap to shoot as the 22-250 or 220 Swift. And there you have the reason for the scarcity of 243 *varmint-weight* rifles: it's a compromise varmint load.

Big Game Use

As a deer cartridge, the 243 comes into its own in popularity, although its suitability remains suspect. *Fact:* The light-recoil of a 243 enables knowledgeable and skillful riflemen to hit game animals with remarkable ease at absurd ranges. *Fact:* With good, maximum handloads, the 243 retains enough kinetic energy at 400 yards to kill cleanly a normal-sized deer if the correct bullet is chosen and the shot is placed in the right spot. *Fact:* Not many hunters can always place their slug in the right spot, particularly at long range, and some don't even know where the right spot is. *Fact:* The level of energy provided by the 243 is such that there is no surplus of power to help make up for a hit that is just slightly off the mark.

Stories abound of the 243's failure to drop a deer neatly in its tracks. Linda Jamison smacked a fat nine-point mule deer in the brisket from about 75 yards. The buck spun around and ran off, seemingly unhurt. She searched the area but found no blood, no hair, no nothing. Undaunted, she circled until she found her buck, dead, 50 yards from where he'd been hit.

This is the jacket of Linda Jamison's 100-grain Nosler Solid Base bullet after it traversed a buck's chest cavity on into the intestines. The core separated and was not found. The deer was shot from about 75 yards. Rifle: Remington Model 600 Mohawk. Load: 34.5 grains of IMR 4064.

Her 100-grain Nosler Solid Base had removed part of the deer's heart, going on to lodge in the intestines. The bullet's core had been shed, yet expansion had been excellent. No problem there. The snag was that there had been no blood trail, primarily because there had been no exit wound. This is often the case with the 6mm class of cartridges. If Linda hadn't been dead sure of her aim, she might have assumed a miss and left a fine buck to feed scavengers.

Rick Jamison was nearly run over by a huge whitetail buck in Pennsylvania a few seasons back. Rick tagged him with a 100-grain Hornady as the deer plowed by. Knocked the buck for a loop. Unfortunately, the animal regained its feet and scampered off. Rick fired again, the buck staggered but kept going. A few minutes later, as he trailed the deer, Rick heard a fusillade of shots. Presently, he found his deer . . . surrounded by other hunters, all of whom claimed the carcass. Since the hapless buck was shot to pieces, Rick swallowed his objections and left the fussing to others.

So the 243 won't down a deer, right? Wrong, if you ask Dave Coffee. Last year he watched a spike buck for 45 minutes before he decided it might be his best chance of the season and lowered the boom. His 100-grain Hornady Spire Point slipped between the ribs of the little buck, wrecked the lungs, and exited the off shoulder. The deer reared halfway up on its hind legs and fell over dead. Never even kicked. Dave's load of 41.0 grains of Winchester 760 yields 2750 fps at the muzzle of his Remington 788, a tad less than most factory ammo gives. Despite the mild load, the buck likely never knew what hit him. Why? Because Dave can shoot, that's why, and he has studied charts of his quarry's anatomy like a fortune teller gazing into her tea leaves. He knows where to stick a bullet.

Harry Goodwin is another 243 fan, at least when he's not using a 220 Swift. He shot a big six-point that was standing, quartering away, at 170 yards. His 80-grain Speer, propelled by a moderate charge of DuPont 3031, pierced the short-ribs and exited the frontal chest. The deer humped up, walked a few feet, stopped for a last look around, then buckled.

That seems to be the normal way of things with the 243. If a deer is calm, reasonably close, and unaware of danger, it seldom moves far if hit vitally with a good bullet. Problems arise with a peripheral hit, an excited deer, too-rapid or too-slow bullet expansion. Exacerbating the difficulty is the frequent lack of a profuse blood trail, something that requires a surplus of power or penetration. The 243 has a surfeit of neither.

Let's compare 243 ballistics with a better deer round, one of proven performance and unblemished reputation, the 270 Winchester. Kick a 100-grain Sierra boat-tail out of a 243 at 3000 fps and you get 2000 fpe at the muzzle. Using a 130-grain Sierra boat-tail in the 270 at 3100 fps gives a muzzle energy of 2775 foot-pounds. Out at 400 yards, the 243 retains 1069 foot-pounds, barely enough for a sure kill if all else is perfect. The 270 still shows 1443 foot-pounds, a considerable advantage, and carries a heavier slug to boot. It shoots a little flatter too, showing a 37.5-inch drop compared to 39.4 inches for the 243, both at 400 yards.

Distilled to its essence, the foregoing discussion indicates that the 243 is adequate for deer hunting if used by

From left to right is a lineup of some excellent 24-caliber bullets: 70-grain Sierra HPBT benchrest; 85-grain Sierra JHPBT benchrest; 95-grain Nosler Partition; the 100-grain Hornady Spire Point and the 100-grain Nosler Solid Base. The 85-grain Sierra may well be the most popular 6mm varmint bullet, with the 95-grain Nosler Partition getting the nod for big game use.

a cool-headed hunter who is an excellent shot, knows where to place his bullet, and will pass up questionable opportunities. Sound like an expert? Absolutely! The 243 is an *expert's* deer cartridge, not for the duffer, beginner, nor yet Mr. Average.

Which brings us to this point: Don't choose the 243 for a budding teenager wanting his first deer rifle. Don't select one for your hunting wife or daughter because of the low recoil level. It just isn't necessary; anyone of normal stature can learn to handle a 7mm-08 or a 270, either of which is a much better selection for deer-sized animals.

For game larger than the deer-and-black-bear class, forget the 243 and buy a rifle chambered for a more powerful load. Period.

Handloading the 243

When it comes to handloading the 243, no problems arise. Cases are long-lived and require trimming no more often than most other high-intensity cartridges, despite what you may have heard. I trim every fourth or fifth firing, depending on the rifle and pressure level of the load.

The best powders are those of a relatively slow burning rate. Although such propellants as IMR 4064 and IMR 3031 offer fine accuracy, the muzzle speeds aren't usually up to adequate hunting standards. My favorites are Olin's 785 with bullets of 90 grains and under, and Norma MRP with the heavies. IMR 4831 and IMR 4350

are also good choices, the latter with all bullet weights.

Incidentally, the 243 Winchester is ideally suited to the use of 785, in my experience. It offers superb accuracy potential, excellent shot-to-shot velocity uniformity, and fine muzzle speeds with varmint-class bullets. For some reason, 785 often performs erratically in other cartridges; I'm not sure why. I've been told that 785 was designed around the 243. I believe it. I would also suggest you get a copy of the Lyman Reloading Handbook, 46th Ed., and explore their recommended Olin 785 loads for the 243. You will find a winner, I'm sure.

For bigger game I like the 100-grain Nosler Solid Base and 46.0 grains of MRP ignited by a hot Federal 215 cap. It'll come close to 3000 fps in most rifles, though it gives only 2917 fps in my long-throated Ruger. If I ran out of MRP, I'd load 42.0 grains of IMR 4350 under a good 100-grain hunting bullet and get about the same speed and accuracy at perhaps a tad higher pressure.

That's the pick of the litter. See the Handload Data chart for other loads; you might prefer one of them. Or your rifle might decide for you.

The 243 Winchester is undoubtedly a fine cartridge. Adequate for deer, while not actually ample; near the top of the heap for varmints, while not quite the best. In the top three as a combination deer/varmint load, the 243 will be with us for years to come, holding its popularity if not actually gaining. It's controversial but it's worth it.

243 Winchester

HANDLOAD DATA

Bullet Wt. Grs. Type	Powder Wt. Grs. Type	Primer	Case	MV (fps)	ME (fpe)	Rifle/ Bbl. (in.)	Remarks
75 Speer SP	**39.0** IMR 4895	Rem. 9½	Rem.	**3407**	**1934**	Univ. Rec./26	Lym. Hndbk., 46th Ed., (Acc. Ld.)
80 Speer SP	**49.0** H450	Rem. 9½	Rem.	**3455**	**2121**	Univ. Rec./26	Lym. Hndbk., 46th Ed., (Acc. Ld.)
85 Sierra JHPBT	**44.0** IMR 4350	Rem. 9½	Rem.	**3283**	**2034**	Univ. Rec./26	Lym. Hndbk., 46th Ed., (Acc. Ld.)
85 Sierra JHPBT	43.0 H205*	8½-120	Fed.	3150	1869	Sav. 111/22	Grp. av. 1.14(3)
85 Sierra JHPBT	38.0 IMR 4350	RWS	Rem.	2783	1462	Browning Varm./23	Most acc. ld. this rifle; grp. av. .85(11)
85 Sierra SP	**44.5** IMR 4350	8½-120	Fed.	**3263**	**2010**	Win. 70-V/24	Very accurate; grp. av. 1.00(4)
85 Sierra SP	**46.5** IMR 4831	8½-120	Fed.	**3308**	**2066**	Rem. 788/22	Grp. av. 1.45(2)
85 Sierra SP	49.4 MRP	8½-120	Fed.	3313	2068	Rem. 788/22	Grp. av. 1.10(8)
90 Speer SP	**43.5** IMR 4350	Rem. 9½	Rem.	**3161**	**1997**	Univ. Rec./26	Lym. Hndbk., 46th Ed., (Acc. Ld.)
100 Hrndy. SPBT	**36.0** IMR 4320	Rem. 9½	Rem.	**2853**	**1807**	Univ. Rec./26	Lym. Hndbk., 46th Ed., (Acc. Ld.)
100 Hornady SP	43.5 IMR 4831	CCI 250	Fed.	3009	2011	Rem. 788/22	Accurate; grp. av. 1.25(4)
100 Nosler SB	**46. 0** MRP	Fed. 215	Fed.	**3025**	**2032**	Rem. 788/22	Grp. av. 1.25(12)
105 Speer RN	43.0 IMR 4831	8½-120	Fed.	2987	2081	Win. 70-V/24	Very accurate; grp. av. 1.33(4)
105 Speer SP	45.1 IMR 4831	8½-120	Win.	3100	2235	Rug No. 1-S/22	Grp. av. 1.97(4)
105 Speer SP	46.6 MRP	8½-120	Fed.	2950	2029	Rem. 788/22	Grp. av. 1.25(4)

*Discontinued powder

SP—Soft Point; JHPBT—Jacketed Hollow Point Boat-Tail; SPBT—Soft Point Boat-Tail; RN—Round Nose.
The number in parentheses after the group size indicates the number of five-shot groups fired for that average from 100 yards benchrest.

FACTORY LOAD DATA

Bullet Wt. Grs. Type	Savage 111 MV (fps)	ME (fpe)	Grp. Avg.	Remington 788 MV (fps)	ME (fpe)	Grp. Avg.	Remarks
75 Hrndy. JHP Front.	3050	1550	1.28	3056	1555	1.93	Mild load
80 Fed. SP	3183	1797	1.23	3185	1798	1.60	Fine varmint load
80 Rem. SP	3157	1766	2.17	NT*	NT*	NT*	
80 Win. SP	3346	1985	1.44	3352	1992	1.32	Very fast and acc.
85 Fed. Prem. JHPBT	3121	1835	2.72	3149	1868	1.43	————
100 Fed. SP	2894	1860	1.69	2853	1808	2.33	
100 Fed. Prem. SPBT	2789	1727	4.02	2756	1685	1.44	Slow; erratic acc.
100 Hrndy. SP Front.	2948	1930	1.93	3102	2132	2.15	Two different lots
100 Norma SP	3096	2123	5.10	3097	2125	2.98	High vel.; inacc.
100 Norma FMJ	3087	2114	1.35	NT*	NT*	NT*	Fast and accurate
100 Rem. SP	2853	1808	2.43	NT*	NT*	NT*	
100 Rem. SP	2839	1790	5.29	2874	1835	2.41	Inacc. in test rifles

*NT—Not Tested.
JHP—Jacketed Hollow Point; SP—Soft Point; JHPBT—Jacketed Hollow Point Boat-Tail; SPBT—Soft Point Boat-Tail; FMJ—Full Metal Jacket.

Test rifles had 22-inch barrels. The group average is for several five-shot strings fired from benchrest at 100 yards and is given in inches.

CAUTION:

Loads recommended and suggested herein have been carefully listed, but are intended solely as a guide to readers and neither the publisher nor author accept any responsibility for results of their use.
Maximum loads, listed in bold, should be reduced by 10 percent and worked up to cautiously.

243 COMPARISON DATA

Varmint Load				Deer/Antelope Load			
243 Winchester **Bullet:** 85-gr. Nosler SB **MV:** 3300 fps **Zero:** 200-yard	**22-250 Remington** **Bullet:** 55-gr. Nosler SB **MV:** 3700 **Zero:** 200-yard			**243 Winchester** **Bullet:** 100-gr. Sierra SPBT **MV:** 3000 fps **Zero:** 200-yard	**270 Winchester** **Bullet:** 130-gr. Sierra SPBT **MV:** 3100 **Zero:** 200-yard		

Drop

	200 yds.	300 yds.	400 yds.	500 yds.		200 yds.	300 yds.	400 yds.	500 yds.
243	—	−5.7″	−16.8″	−34.6″	243	—	−6.7″	−19.4″	−39.4″
22-250	—	−4.8″	−14.7″	−31.2″	270	—	−6.3″	−18.4″	−37.5″
Difference	—	.9″	2.1″	− 3.4″	**Difference**	—	.4″	1.0″	− 1.9″

Deflection (20 mph Crosswind) / Retained Energy

	200 yds.	300 yds.	400 yds.	500 yds.		200 yds.	300 yds.	400 yds.	500 yds.
243	—	13.9″	25.9″	42.5″	243	—	1263	1069	898
22-250	—	16.3″	30.8″	51.3″	270	—	1718	1443	1203
Difference	—	2.4″	4.9″	8.8″	**Difference**	—	455	374	305

SPECIFICATIONS

Shell Holders
RCBS: 3
Bonanza: 1
Lyman: 2
Pacific: 1

Bullet Diameter
Jacketed: .243″

Lengths
Trim: 2.035″
Maximum Case: 2.045″
Maximum Overall: 2.710″

The fast, Norma 100-grain semi-pointed factory soft point is shown here, together and broken down. The charge is 46.0 grains of a powder resembling Norma MRP. Note cannelured bullet.

6mm Remington

"When Remington reintroduced the 244 in 1963 as the 6mm Remington . . . The red ink disappeared and the 6mm came into its own."

[Diagram of cartridge with dimensions: 2.233", 26°, .472", .470", .429", .276", 1.724", 1.881"]

WHEN Winchester brought out their 243 in early 1955 and Remington the 244 shortly thereafter, quite a stir was created in the shooting world. The 243 fared nicely in popularity while the 244 didn't do so well, but the two of them together virtually buried the 257 Roberts overnight. For 10 years, the shooting press sang the praises of the six-millimeters, some articles suggesting their use on game up to elk and caribou in size. One story I read in the early '60s recounted the taking of a polar bear with the 243! Not me!

Today, cooler heads prevail and the pendulum is swinging a tad too far in the opposite direction with some writers berating the use of either of the sixes on deer-sized fauna. Horse apples. But before we delve deeper into the practical aspects of 6mm killing power, let's examine the history of the two popular 24-calibers.

Several reasons have been advanced for the 243 Winchester's rapid rise to fame while the equally good, if not a little better, 244 Remington foundered in seas of red ink. The 243 was initially offered in two high-quality rifles, the Model 70 bolt-action and the Model 88 lever-gun. Remington at first chambered only the Model 722 turnbolt for their 244, although the Model 760 slide-action followed shortly. (The 742 semi-auto was chambered for the 244 for a brief period, but the 243 was already off and running by that time.) Savage helped out the Olin contingent by reaming their famous Model 99

lever-action and the Model 110 bolt gun for the Winchester load, eschewing the Ilion offering. A whole bevy of imports crossed the ocean, chambered in 243 but not 244. This availability of such a vast array of rifles in caliber 243, plus the undeniable fact that the Remington 722 wouldn't win many beauty contests, enabled the Winchester cartridge to outdistance Remington's load in retail sales.

Some writers have advanced the theory that the 1-in-10 inch rifling twist of the 243 (as opposed to Remington's 1-in-12), which enabled it to stabilize the heavier 6mm slugs of 100 to 105 grains, hammered home most of the nails in the 244's coffin. It's possible, but I'm unconvinced. I suspect that most astute hunters realized that a well-constructed 90-grain bullet would kill deer-sized game as well as a 100-grain slug of equally stout construction. Rather than considering the twist rate and its effects on accuracy, I suspect that most nimrods simply chose the cartridge that provided the heavier bullet in factory-loaded form. That was the 243. Thus, Remington's marketing error may have been in presenting the 244 as a long-range varmint buster, instead of bally-hooing it as a *combination* cartridge suited for varmints and deer.

When Remington reintroduced the 244 in 1963 as the 6mm Remington, complete with a brand new head-stamp, barrels were rifled with a 1-in-9 twist, perhaps with a touch of malice. (The twist change had been

6mm Remington: Varmint/Deer

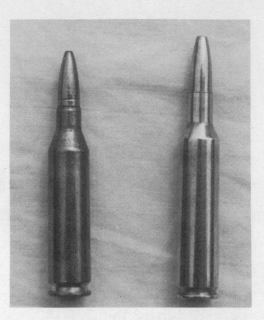

(Right) The 243 (left) and 6mm have long been rivals, with the 243 being the more popular for years. They are ballistically twins, both having been inspired by gunwriter Warren Page.

(Left) Two of the finest varmint cartridges ever developed are the 222 (left) and the 6mm Remington (right). The 222 was a runaway best seller when introduced and is good for ranges up to about 250 yards. The 6mm, however, covers ranges on out as far as the bullets will expand, about 400 yards or so.

done earlier, but was not widely known.) Remington also redesigned the 721-722 series into the handsome new Model 700. In the late '60s, Sturm, Ruger introduced the Model 77 and one of its chamberings was the 6mm Remington. Ruger also made up some Number 1 single shots in 6mm; Browning listed it for their Model 78 single shot; Remington stuck it in their budget-priced but super-accurate 788; and several imported brands picked it up. The red ink disappeared and the 6mm came into its own.

Today you can buy domestic 6mm ammunition not only from Remington but from Federal and Winchester as well. Of the major producers, only Frontier fails to offer the 6mm Remington.

The 6mm Remington cartridge is .19-inch longer than the 243, has a longer neck, a sharper shoulder. Handloaders cite these as distinct advantages over the 243. Maybe. A sharp shoulder I can take or leave, but I like the 6mm's slightly greater capacity, which is a by-product of the longer case. The advantages of a long neck are theoretical at best. A long neck merely means that a reloader might not have to load his ammo with the powder level quite so near the case mouth as might be the case with a short-necked cartridge such as the 243. Conversely, if the case body is lengthened to the point where it shortens the neck, case capacity is increased if all else is equal. In one instance, the base of the bullet does not extend very far into the powder chamber; in the other you have more capacity to work with.

Additionally, the longer a case neck is, the more stress it puts on a seated bullet. If neck thickness or tension on the seated slug is uneven, there is greater chance of a "cocked" bullet, which does nothing good for accuracy. Some handloaders advance the idea that the longer neck contributes to bullet-bore alignment.

I don't buy that. If that were the case, why do so many handloaders resize just a portion of the case neck, usually just to the base of the seated bullet? They would certainly be cheating themselves out of the virtues of a long neck if they didn't use it to the fullest, right? The fact that many handloaders do not says volumes, in my opinion.

The potential accuracy demonstrated by such cartridges as the 300 Winchester Magnum and the 7mm Remington Magnum, both short-necked wonders, in long-range target competition gives the lie to the "long-necks-are-always-better" advocates. Before leaving this business of long-necked cartridges versus short, one last word. If you own or intend to purchase (or have built) a benchrest-quality rifle, one capable of sub-¼-inch accuracy at 100 yards, you might give neck length a thought when you are considering your cartridge. For all the rest of you, forget neck length and go on to something of more significance like what type of recoil pad to buy or what color to paint your fiberglass stock.

The 243 is adduced to be a real case-stretcher because of its gentle 20-degree shoulder slope. Having a sharper 26-degree shoulder, the Remington case does resist stretching somewhat better, but the difference is negligible. High pressure loads or rear-locking actions are more often causes for atypical case lengthening than esoteric shoulder angles. Quite a number of popular rifle cartridges sport shoulder angles similar to the 243, among them the 257 Roberts, 25-06 Remington, 270 Winchester, and the 30-06. Only the 270 is known as a case stetcher—it's routinely loaded to high pressures, just like the 243.

One clear point of superiority the 6mm can claim is a greater case capacity. Most brands of 243 brass average around 50.6 grains of water; the 6mm case holds around

51.5 to 52.0, depending on headstamp. That's about a 2 percent advantage, and it enables the 6mm to outdistance handily its smaller cousin in the velocity sweepstakes.

As an example, I recently worked with two Remington Model 7 rifles, both with 18½-inch barrels. One was a 243, the other a 6mm. The 243 gave the following muzzle speeds with factory ammunition: 80-grain Remington soft point, 3017 fps; 100-grain Remington SP, 2674; 100-grain Frontier SPBT, 2623 fps. My identical 6mm Model 7 showed the following: 80-grain Remington SP, 3320; 80-grain Winchester SP, 3340; 100-grain Federal SP, 2900; 100-grain Winchester SP, 2950. The average velocity advantage in favor of the 6mm was a whopping 356 fps!

Before you express incredulity that such an insignificant advantage in case capacity can give such a whopping superiority in achieved ballistics, let me hasten to say that the above-mentioned 356 foot-second advantage in favor of the 6mm is not due to case capacity alone. It is as much due to sub-maximal factory-load pressure levels as to volumetric considerations.

For some years now, the 243 has been developing a reputation for blowing rifles apart at the seams. In fact, the 243 rivals the disreputable 220 Swift in that regard. The reasons for these blowups are complex and discussed in detail in the chapter devoted to the 243, so I shan't detail them here. The salient point is that the 6mm, for whatever reasons, is not known as a gun-destroyer; however, pressures for it are as fulsome as ever. Not so with the 243. For several years now, manufacturers of 243 ammunition have throttled back on the juice with the heavy 100-grain bullets, to preclude disintegrated rifles, or the tendency for same. When you lower chamber pressures, you lower muzzle velocities if all else is equal. The upshot is that while the varmint-weight 243 factory loads are still up to snuff, the deer-killing loads are but a flaccid shadow of their former selves.

Some years ago, I averaged the muzzle speeds of top-listed loads shown in various handloading manuals in the sections devoted to the 243 and the 6mm Remington. The results: the 243 was .2 percent faster with 75-grain bullets, .5 percent faster with 80-grain bullets, and .2 percent ahead with the 100-grain projectiles. The 6mm was quicker with the 85- and 87-grain slugs by 2.2 percent, with the 90-grain bullets up by .4 percent, and was ahead 1.7 percent with the 105-grain Speer. On the whole, the 243 ran 1.1 percent behind in average velocity with all weights tested. That means that with a given load at a certain velocity level, for example 3000 fps muzzle velocity in the 6mm, a comparable load in the 243 would clock about 2967 fps.

My own tests verify this. I have owned several 243s that would reach (in safety) about 3025 fps, assuming at least 22 inches of barrel. While I haven't matched that speed with a 6mm, I have come close. In addition, I have chronographed 100-grain Remington factory ammunition in a 24-inch 6mm at an *amazing* 3207 fps! No 243 load I've shot would come close to that, not even the ultra-fast 100-grain Norma factory load. Not belaboring the issue, let's just say that the 6mm will usually outrun a similar 243 by roughly 100 fps and leave it at that.

In case you're not aware of it, Warren Page is the father of both the 243 and the 6mm Remington. Page and a fellow by the name of Al Marciante dreamed up the 243, according to an account in Page's *The Accurate Rifle,* basing their wildcat on a sample of 7.62 NATO brass in their possession. Offering his idea to Winchester, Page met with a cold shoulder, at least on the surface. Some time later, he discovered by accident some activity in East Alton focusing on a modified version of his 240 Page Souper Pooper. The Olin experimental cartridge had a more slope-shouldered profile than the 240, being simply the 7.62 NATO (308 Winchester by that time) necked down. Initially, the new Winchester load was dubbed the 6mm Winchester. When introduced to the public in the Model 70 Featherweight, the 243 quickly acquired a reputation for accuracy, particularly for a lightweight sporting rifle.

In the meantime, Page, a tad miffed at the Winchester rebuff, offered the 6mm idea to Remington in the form of the 243 Rockchucker, a Fred Huntington-inspired wildcat. Page and Huntington had shot several rifles so chambered, some varmint models and one nifty little sporter stocked by Monte Kennedy. The wildcat ballistics attained in such arms were about 3400 to 3500 fps with 85-grain varmint slugs and about 3100 fps with the 100-grain bullet. The Bridgeport firm liked the idea and the cartridge, but stumped for varmint-deer stress rather than the other way around. Consequent to that decision, Remington opted for the now-infamous 1-in-12 twist and housed their new load in the ungainly Model 722 semi-sporter. Winchester ate their lunch.

Page wrote that any difference in intrinsic accuracy between the two rounds was insignificant. I'm not so sure. I've read that the 6mm is quite finicky and a bit difficult to load for when it comes to accuracy. My hunting chrony Lewis Dawkins, alias "Hawkeye," disagrees. Lewis shoots a Ruger M77, which left the Southport plant as a 243 sporter. Not happy with the barrel that graced the rifle when he bought it, Hawkeye had ace gunsmith Raymond Cain of Asheboro, NC, screw in a medium-heavy stainless Hart tube, lop it off at 25 inches, and chamber it for the 6mm Remington.

Dawkins is an inveterate tinkerer, load experimenter and amateur ballistician. He likes developing handloads and shooting them for group even better than dipping snuff. Right now, Hawkeye is vacillating between

6mm Remington: Varmint/Deer

loads. One is the 75-grain Hornady hollow point and 44.0 grains of Hodgdon H380, sparked by a Federal 215 magnum cap. The other is from 40.5 to 41.0 grains of Du Pont IMR 4895 under the 75-grain Sierra hollow point.

Not long ago, Lewis was placidly glassing a huge meadow, polluting the air with his foul-smelling pipe, enjoying the mild summer weather. A band of crows alighted in the corner of a cornfield and proceeded to decimate the crop. As is the norm for the black bandits, a sentry was posted high in a tree bordering the field. Hawkeye watched that sentry bird for a spell. He dug out his range finder and zeroed in; it read off 385 yards. Setting up his home-made "buffalo sticks," Dawkins adjusted the bullet-drop compensation feature of his scope to 400 yards and centered the crosswires on the bird's chest. I was on another mountain, hoofing it after woodchucks, so I didn't see the shot. If I *had* seen Lewis drawing a bead on a crow nearly four football fields away, I'd have given him the horselaugh. I would have choked on my chuckle. Hawkeye dropped the bird with one shot; the 75-grain Hornady hollow point entering the crow's skull just aft of the right eye. It was the best field shot I've ever "almost witnessed." Incidentally, I saw Dawkins pick up his crow, and I knew where he had been sitting when he fired. There was no question about the validity of the shot. (I wish there had been. Hawkeye has been insufferable ever since.)

Obviously, Lewis Dawkins has no trouble with accuracy in his Hart-barreled 6mm Ruger. I've seen him shoot many ¾-inch five-shot clusters, and I fired one that measured .63-inch while chronographing a load for him. My own experience with three different 6mm rifles supports Dawkins' findings; none of my 6mm's has been unusually persnickety.

The most accurate was a Remington Model 700-V. That gun would print nearly any handload into well under an inch, and it went .64-inch for a five-shot average with 47.0 grains of Norma MRP and the excellent 85-grain Sierra JHPBT. A couple other loads shot under ¾-inch.

Less accurate but still laudable considering its action type and purpose in life is my Remington Model 6 pump. With 80-grain Remington Power-Lokt factory loads, the M6 grouped four, five-shot strings into 1.62 inches. Its favorite handload, the 75-grain Speer hollow point over 43.0 grains of H380, groups 1.72 inches. So far, three different bullet weights have gone under 2 inches, and one more just over. Not bad for a quick-firing trombone action.

(Right) This is the Remington 700 varmint the author tested so many loads in. It is also the most accurate 6mm the author has ever shot; with the best load, 100-yard, five-shot groups average .64-inch.

From the bench, this 6mm Remington Model 6 pump is good for 1⅝-inch, 5-shot groups at 100 yards. Excellent accuracy from a trombone repeater. Scope is a Redfield Lo-Profile in 4x.

Topped with a Bushnell 3-9x Sportview, this Remington Model 7, in 6mm, will average just over 1½-inch groups at 100 yards, with a good load.

My favorite 6mm is a Remington Model 7, a trim little 6½-pound sporter that carries like a dream and groups its best handload to date into 1.55 inches. Several additional loads will stay under 1¾ inches, and quite a few will group below the 2-inch mark.

To recap, my three 6mm rifles have shot into about ⅝-inch, 1½ inches, and 1⅝ inches. While my most accurate 243 won't quite shade the average turned in by the heavy-barreled 700-V, it would average .70-inch which isn't far away. The clincher is that the 243 was a *sporter,* not a varmint-weight rifle. Further, I've owned two more 243 sporting rifles that would average under 1 inch from the bench at 100 yards with their pet loads. Nearly every 243 I ever fired would group under 1½ inches.

The big advantage the 243 enjoys over the 6mm is an availability of a somewhat broader range of factory loads. In domestic brands alone, the 243 user had his pick of 12 different loads using bullets in 75-, 80-, 85- and 100-grain weights and in hollow point, hollow-point boat-tail, soft point, full metal jacket, and soft-point boat-tail configuration. The odds of not finding an accurate combination in a properly tuned, scope-sighted 243 are virtually nonexistent.

To be sure, there are several good 6mm Remington factory loads available, most notably the 80 Remington Power Lokt and the fine 80-grain Federal factory soft point, but the array of choices is sparse compared to the 243. Perhaps that's because the average 6mm shooter is more apt to be a handloader than his counterpart with a 243. Of all the gunners I've known who owned a 6mm, only one was not a handloader. Conversely, I've met many 243 users who made do with store-bought ammo exclusively.

What does this prove? I'm not sure. I suspect it indicates that the 243 Winchester just might outshoot the 6mm Remington in comparable guns with good ammunition, but it doesn't *prove* that it will. The 243s I've shot have shown less load-to-load group variations than my three 6mm Remington rifles, but I've used several times as many 243-caliber guns as 6mm. Let's say the jury is still out and go on to other things.

The 6mm and Big Game

Many heated arguments have taken place within the pages of gun magazines as to whether the 6mm family of cartridges will take deer-sized game cleanly. The answer is yes, they will if: A) the shot is placed in the chest area, or the brain or spine; B) the bullet used offers sufficient penetration to breach the chest wall even if bone is struck; C) the bullet expands acceptably but does not blow up; D) the range is reasonable, say 250 or 300 yards as a maximum.

Friend Fred Ritter uses a Remington Model 7 6mm on North Carolina deer. Using the 80-grain Remington pointed soft point factory load, Fred bagged his first

Only in recent years has the shooting public had such a wide choice of 6mm Remington ammo. From top to bottom: Federal 100-grain Soft Point; Winchester 100-grain Pointed Soft Point; Federal 80-grain Soft Point and Remington 80-grain Soft Point. During testing, this factory ammo proved among the best 6mm factory fodder available.

one from about 120 yards. The buck, a mature six-point, took the little bullet just aft of the right shoulder. Breaking two ribs on entrance, the slug coursed on through the chest cavity to wreck the lungs and heart, lodging just beneath the skin on the off side. Fred said expansion was just fine and the bullet held together well. The buck dropped at the shot.

Fred's next deer was a fat spike that eased up behind to catch him daydreaming in his tree stand. Fred tagged him as he quartered away, heading back into a thick swamp. The bullet made its entrance just behind the last rib on the right side and exited behind the left shoulder—20 yards was as far as the buck could go.

The final deer was a little tougher. Fred had been up his tree for about 2 hours, overlooking a stand of small oak trees and scattered pines. The area was profuse with sign; the deer were definitely there. Just before dark, a nice buck approached from the right, roughly 150 yards out. It was feeding along, nibbling mushrooms and acorns. No hurry. Abruptly, it changed directions and began to feed away from Fred's stand. Stopping in a coppice of pine trees, the deer tested the wind. Fred could make out the shoulder and part of the neck and head, but too many small limbs and pine needles blocked the path to the chest area. Concerned about the brush, but aware that this was likely to be his best opportunity, Fred painted the crosswires on the junction of neck and shoulder and cut loose. The buck disappeared!

6mm Remington: Varmint/Deer

Fred climbed down and checked on his deer. It hadn't moved. The bullet had struck the base of the neck and stopped under the skin just above the right shoulder, perfectly expanded. The spine was not hit.

Before you decide that the 80-grain load is the only way to go, let me hasten to explain that such may not be the case. Fred is a careful hunter, an excellent shot, and knows where to put his bullet. More importantly, he knows *when* to shoot and when *not to shoot*. He would be first to admit that light, varmint-weight slugs are not the perfect buck medicine. He chose it because he wanted to salvage as much muzzle velocity from the short Remington barrel as possible.

Larry Bishop is another 6mm fan. Larry has taken eight deer in 12 years with an old Herters J9 bolt-action rifle made up on a Mauser action into which is screwed a 23½-inch 6mm barrel. Larry retains a hoard of 100-grain Remington Pointed Core Lokt bullets. He loads them ahead of 43.5 grains of IMR 4350.

Recently, Larry was using a tree to hold his back up while watching the far side of a valley. The timber on yonder ridge was cut halfway up; visibility was pretty good, except for some morning fog. He spotted a fine eight-point buck negotiating a patch of loose shale across the way. Figuring the deer for 275 yards, he held a little below the backbone and touched one off. The deer vanished. Larry couldn't believe his scope! He searched the ridge frantically, saw no downed buck nor one scampering off. After a moment or two of apprehension and confusion, he spied a patch of white directly down the mountain from the spot his buck had last been seen. What he saw was light-colored throat hair; his buck had dropped instantly and slid down the slope. It kicked a short while, then lay still.

Fred Ritter hunts from a tree stand with a Remington Model 7 in 6mm. Fred has slain three deer with that rifle this season alone. None moved very far.

From the bench at 100 yards, this Remington Model 7 in, 6mm turned in its best groups with 46 grains of 760 and 75-grain Hornady hollow points.

The recovered slug weighed a tad more than 80 grains. It had struck right where Larry had held and traversed the chest from side-to-side. He checked the distance some time later with a rangefinder and came up with 230 yards.

Seven of the eight deer Larry slew with his old Herters' J9 fell on the spot. One deer, a little spike that was following three does, nose to the ground, didn't realize he was dead and covered about 40 yards before collapsing.

Counting the deer taken with the 243 and 6mm by just these two men, we arrive at a tally of close to 25 deer. Many other hunters of my acquaintance use 6mm-class rifles and have no complaints. I will, however, say that all of the hunters I know are experienced hunters and shooters. In short, they know when, where and how to place a 6mm slug.

The best shot I ever heard about that was made with a 6mm Remington, excepting possibly Lewis Dawkins' unlucky crow, was one made by a gentleman I hunted with nearly 15 years ago. His name was Troy Pickett, and he decked a buck with such finality at 400 yards that the animal's antlers dug into the turf and turned the hapless buck a somersault.

Troy had surprised the buck in the middle of a very large soybean field. The deer was far out and running broadside. Troy pumped shot after shot at him, kicking up sod but drawing no blood. Finally, his fourth shot geysered in front of the flying hooves and turned the deer so that it sped directly away. Troy held at the top of the wide rack and squeezed. The result was instantaneous. Upon such events are we made believers.

For deer-sized game, I'd use the 100 Remington Core Lokt factory load in my Model 6 simply because none of my handloads will equal it for accuracy. The same goes for the 100-grain Winchester factory soft point in my Model 7. I wouldn't use any load for deer with my 700-V; I couldn't bear to lug it around.

For varmints, I like the 75-grain Hornady JHP over 46.0 grains of Winchester 760, which shoots into 1.55 inches in my Model 7 while chronographing 3200 fps out of the stubby 18½-inch barrel.

As a varmint cartridge, the 6mm Remington is tough to beat. This varmint hunter is using a Ruger 77 with a 6mm Hart barrel.

I once penned an article comparing the two popular 24-bore cartridges. My closing paragraph went as follows:

So which to choose? If an individual is *not* a handloader, I'd lean toward the 243 every time. For a handloader thinking about buying a new rifle that is chambered for both calibers, I'd suggest he look at one example of each and decide on the individual rifle that he prefers, not basing his choice on caliber but on subtleties of fit, finish, or wood quality. If the rifle brand he was considering was offered only in 243 caliber, I would admonish him not to buy a different brand just to avail himself of a 6mm Remington. Finally, if a handloader is having a custom rifle built to his specifications, I'd pump for the 6mm.

I stand by that opinion.

6mm Remington

HANDLOAD DATA

Bullet Wt. Grs. Type	Powder Wt. Grs. Type	Primer	Case	MV (fps)	ME (fpe)	Rifle/ Bbl. (in.)	Remarks
75 Speer JHP	44.0 H380	Fed. 215	Win.	3350	1869	Rem. M6/22	Most acc. ld. this rifle
75 Hrndy. JHP	46.0 Win. 760	Rem. 9½	Fed.	3200	1706	Rem. M7/18½	Most acc. ld. this rifle
80 Speer SP	36.0 IMR 3031	Fed. 210	Fed.	2880	1474	Rem. M7/18½	Very accurate
85 Sierra JHPBT	43.0 H205*	Fed. 210	Rem.	3220	1952	Rem. M700-V/24	Very fast and acc.
85 Sierra JHPBT	45.0 IMR 4350	CCI 200	Win.	3042	1747	Rem. M6/22	Accurate
85 Speer SPBT	45.0 IMR 4350	CCI 200	Win.	3055	1762	Rem. M6/22	Very accurate
85 Sierra JHPBT	47.0 MRP	Fed. 215	Rem.	3218	1955	Rem. M700-V/24	Most acc. ld. this rifle
85 Sierra JHPBT	47.0 Win. 785	Fed. 215	Rem.	3157	1882	Rem. M700-V/24	Accurate
100 Nosler SB	47.0 H4831	Rem. 9½ M	Win.	2972	1962	Rem. M6/22	Good velocity
105 Speer SP	44.0 MRP	Fed. 215	Rem.	2922	1991	Rem. M700-V/24	Highest vel./this bullet

*Discontinued powder.

JHP—Jacketed Hollow Point; SP—Soft Point; JHPBT—Jacketed Hollow Point Boat-Tail; SPBT—Soft Point Boat-Tail; SB—Solid Base.

FACTORY LOAD DATA

Bullet Wt. Grs. Type	MV (fps)	ME (fpe)	Rifle/ Bbl. (in.)	Remarks
80 Rem. PLHP	3346	1985	Rem. M700-V/24	Accurate
80 Rem. PLHP	3220	1838	Rem. M6/22	Most acc. ld. in this rifle
80 Rem. PSP	3320	1954	Rem. M7/18½	Very acc. and fast
80 Fed. SP	3372	2016	Rem. M6/22	Very fast
80 Fed. SP	3213	1830	Rem. M7/18½	Extremely accurate
80 Win. SP	3340	1978	Rem. M7/18½	Very high velocity
90 Rem. PSP	3189	2029	Rem. M700-V/24	Most acc. fact. ld. in this gun
100 Rem. PSPCL	3207	2280	Rem. M700-V/24	Excellent energy levels
100 Rem. PSPCL	2943	1923	Rem. M6/22	Superb acc.; good velocity
100 Fed. SP	2934	1911	Rem. M6/22	————
100 Fed. SP	2900	1867	Rem. M7/18½	
100 Win. SP	2950	1932	Rem. M7/18½	Excellent vel. in this barrel length

PLHP—Power Lokt Hollow Point; PSP—Pointed Soft Point; SP—Soft Point; PSPCL—Pointed Soft Point Core Lokt.

SPECIFICATIONS

Shell Holders
RCBS: 3
Bonanza: 1
Lyman: 2
Pacific: 1

Bullet Diameter
Jacketed: .243″

Lengths
Trim: 2.223″
Maximum Case: 2.233″
Maximum Overall: 2.825″

CAUTION:

Loads recommended and suggested herein have been carefully listed, but are intended solely as a guide to readers and neither the publisher nor author accept any responsibility for results of their use. **Maximum loads, listed in bold, should be reduced by 10 percent and worked up to cautiously.**

240 Weatherby Magnum

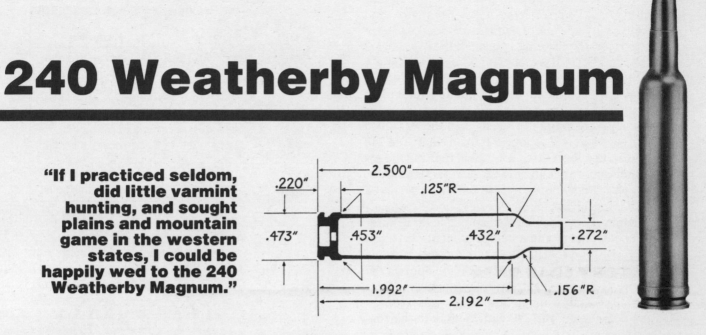

"If I practiced seldom, did little varmint hunting, and sought plains and mountain game in the western states, I could be happily wed to the 240 Weatherby Magnum."

THE 240 Weatherby Magnum, spawned in 1968, is another example of Weatherby one-upmanship. As with most of the Weatherby line of belted magnums, the 240 is the most potent commonly-available cartridge of the respective bore size, which is 6mm (.243-inch), not .240-inch. The two rounds which do not exceed their competitors in ballistics are the 224 and 7mm Weatherby Magnums, although the 7mm does *slightly* outdo the 7mm Remington and Sharpe & Hart belted loads.

The 240, on the other hand, quite handily outraces its smaller brethren, the 243 Winchester and the 6mm Remington. In factory persuasion, the 243 shows an 80-grain spitzer at a listed 3350 fps for 1994 fpe, and a 100-grain soft point at 2960 fps for 1945 fpe. The 6mm, again according to factory data, carries the 80-grain payload to 3470 fps for 2139 fpe, and bumps the 100-grain soft point up to 3100 fps and 2134 fpe. In real life, the 243 will most often fail to reach its advertised ballistics, particularly in 22-inch tubes and with the heavyweight slug. The 6mm comes closer, and in some lots will actually beat the published numbers slightly if fired in at least 24 inches of barrel.

Consulting *The Weatherby Guide,* I came up with these figures for the 240: 70-grain bullet (now discontinued) at 3850 fps with 2305 fpe; 87-grain bullet at 3500 fps for 2367 fpe; 100-grain bullet at 3395 fps for 2560

From the bench, at 100 yards, the 240 Weatherby usually provides fine accuracy. Groups of 1 inch, or better, are not unusual.

fpe. If the cartridge actually reaches such numbers, that is quite a difference. Is it important? Depends.

If I hunted only deer and antelope at long range, and did not handload, and liked the Weatherby Mark V, and could afford one, and always wore ear protection when I hunted, I can think of no better cartridge for such enterprise. The 257 Weatherby is equally good ballistically, but kicks more and is *really* loud. On such animals as deer, the increased punch of the 25-caliber is not needed. The 264 Winchester Magnum is simply more of the same.

The way I see it, the only real competitor for the 240 Weatherby is the 25-06. Either will outpunch the lesser 6mms by a goodly margin. The 243 is in the 1900-2000 fpe class; the 6mm adds about 200 fpe to that. The 240 jumps the energy level up to 2300-2500 fpe, and the 25-06 is in the same range in comparable barrel lengths. That's a solid 400-500 fpe increase over the 243, and a tidy 200-300 fpe advantage (between 15 and 20 percent) over the 6mm. I consider the 240 and 25-06 to be surer killers on deer, sheep, and antelope at all normal hunting ranges. Despite that, I don't think either cartridge becomes an elk load by virtue of a 300 fpe edge on the 6mm. More room for slight errors in holding on deer-class animals, yes; moving up into the elk class, no.

On the deficit side, the 240 and 25-06 both show increased barrel wear compared to the small-cased 6mms. If you shoot a lot, that could make a difference. Also, for varmint hunting on a regular basis, the 240 (and 25-06) offer a bit more recoil than is ideal for making those pinpoint long shots with a normal-weight rifle. Combining the bore-wear problem with the heavier recoil, I would consider the 240 inferior to either the 243 or 6mm as a steady-diet varmint cartridge.

Accuracy is not a problem inherent to the 240 Weatherby. In the 1969 *Gun Digest,* John Lachuk wrote of his extensive experiments with three 240 rifles. One was a 30-pound target-type rifle. Groups ran from ⅜-inch to ¾-inch with one exception, and that was with a too-warm load. One of the most accurate loads was 55.0 grains of Hodgdon's H4831 under an 85-grain Sierra Spitzer, for ⅜-inch clusters and 3500 fps.

The other two rifles were standard Mark V Weatherbys, although each had a different barrel contour. Lachuk wrote that both of his Mark Vs would easily exceed the manufacturer's accuracy guarantee of three shots in 1½ inches. In fact, both guns would better that by a third when firing *five-shot* strings. I quote:

> The first rifle grouped tightest with bullets from Speer and Hornady, with ¾- to 1-inch groups the rule. The southpaw Weatherby shot best with Sierra bullets. 5-shot, 100-yard groups averaged 1 inch with every bullet weight bearing the tall mountain trademark. Remington 80-gr. "Power-Lokt" bullets punched in equally tight. Occasional groups with both makes ran as tight as ½ to ⅝-inch.

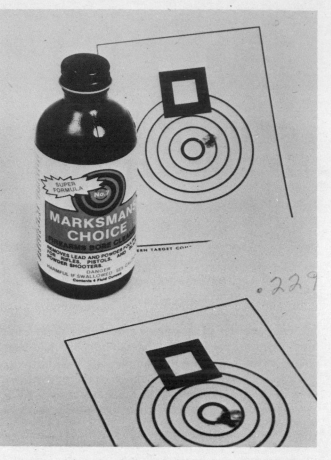

All small-bore, large-capacity cases foul their bores badly. A good cleaning with bore solvent is a must after every few rounds to sustain good bench accuracy.

Since the 240 Weatherby Magnum has the same case head size as the 30-06, it can be chambered in standard, long-action rifles without having to go through all the fuss of opening up the bolt face.

(Opposite page) Unlike most magnums, the 240 Weatherby does not have a typical-size cartridge head. The 338 Magnum shown at right illustrates the normal magnum head size. The 240 has the same size case head as the 30-06, shown at left.

Mr. Lachuk pointed out another item of interest to the hunting owner of a 240 Mark V: "Both rifles possessed the one essential attribute for a successful hunting rifle. They put the first shot from a cold, *fouled* barrel well inside of the final group."

This latter remark puzzles me. Nearly all of my rifles, and most that I have tested, will put the first shot from a cold, fouled barrel into the group. No sweat. Having the *first* shot wind up in a group from a cold, *clean* bore is something else again. Many, many rifles will not. If the Weatherbys in question would do *that,* then I'd certainly join Mr. Lachuk in rejoicing. If not, then I feel that the test rifles merely performed as should be expected.

Regardless, the 240 Magnum is obviously an accurate cartridge. It would seem to offer about as much potential as either of the other two popular 6mms.

Incidentally, the 240 is the only Weatherby magnum cartridge besides the 224 that has a non-magnum head size. The 240 is sort of like a 30-06 case that has had a belt swaged on it. In fact, Jim Carmichel wrote of doing just that in his book, *The Modern Rifle.* Jim had been having trouble getting his sample 240 Weatherby to shoot well. Assuming the fault lay with the rifle, he suspended his testing. Here's Jim:

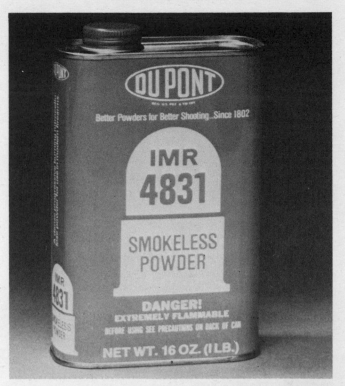

Du Pont's IMR 4831 is an excellent choice for the 240 Weatherby. The *Hornady Handbook,* 3rd Edition, shows IMR 4831 to be the *only* propellant capable of launching a 100-grain bullet to a muzzle velocity of 3400 fps.

Currently, the Weatherby Mark V is the only commercial rifle available in 240 Weatherby Magnum.

H380 often provides excellent accuracy in the 240 Weatherby when used with magnum, large rifle primers. Winchester's 760 is also a good choice for the 240.

Later, just to see how hard it was to swage a belt on a 30/06, I ran a few surplus G.I. cases into the 240 sizing die. The operation was easy enough and resulted in a few cases with a belt neatly squeezed in place. So, with these cases on hand and nothing else to do, I loaded them up and gave the rifle another benchtest. Groups for three, five-shot strings were under an inch, by far the best accuracy so far. The experiment was repeated and again groups were small.

And now you know how to obtain brass if 240 factory cases are hard to come by. In case you're worried about that double-radius shoulder, don't. Remember that the belted cartridges are designed to headspace on the belt. Besides, after fire-forming, the 30-06 brass will have a neat double-radius shoulder. Like magic.

For real long-range performance on deer and suchlike, zero your 240 at 300 yards. Assuming for the sake of this confabulation that the published ballistics are correct, your 100-grain bullet would then strike only 8.8 inches low at 400 yards, a mere 3½ inches high at 200. If you are a dead shot, firing from a steady position at a standing, broadside animal, you can hold on the center of its chest and never trouble yourself with such esoteric items as the exact range. Handy.

The Weatherby Guide goes only out to 300 yards when giving retained energy, so I repaired to the *Hornady Handbook* to see what the 100-grain Hornady spire point has left over, way out at 400: nearly 1200 fpe. Handload the streamlined Hornady boat-tail spire point and you have a residual energy of over 1300 fpe. The 243 shows 882 fpe at the same distance with factory-equivalent ammo; to that the 6mm adds another 100 fpe. The 240 beats them by more than 20 percent out where it counts, and for the type of hunting best suited

Slow burning propellants like Norma MRP provide a good bullet weight/velocity ratio in big-case, small-bore cartridges such as the 240 Weatherby.

to the 240/Mark V combination.

I would not prefer the 240 to the 25-06 for most types of hunting, but I wouldn't walk far for a 25-06 if I had a Weatherby at my disposal. Since I view the 6mm class of cartridges as combination varmint/deer loads, I personally would choose the 243, 6mm, or 250-3000 over the 240 Weatherby. But that is more a function of the pleasant qualities innate to the smaller-cased loads—relative to blast and recoil and barrel wear—than it is to ballistic merit. If I practiced seldom, did little varmint hunting, and sought plains and mountain game in the western states, I could be happily wed to the 240 Weatherby Magnum.

The 240 chambering can also be had in one of Weatherby's more fancy Mark Vs, the Lazermark. Note the laser-cut patterns at the toe, wrist and forearm of the stock. Scope is a 3x9 Weatherby Premier.

240 Weatherby Magnum

HANDLOAD DATA

Bullet Wt. Grs.	Type	Powder Wt. Grs.	Type	Primer	Case	MV (fps)	ME (fpe)	Rifle/ Bbl. (in.)	Remarks
70	Hrndy. SP	54.0	IMR 4350	Fed. 215	Wby.	3700	2128	Wby. Mk. V/26	Lym. Hndbk., 46th Ed. (Acc. Ld.)
80	Rem. PL	52.5	H450	Fed. 215	Wby.	3301	1936	Wby. Mk. V/26	Lym. Hndbk., 46th Ed. (Acc. Ld.)
85	Sierra SP	**54.5**	H4831	Fed. 215	Wby.	**3426**	**2216**	Wby. Mk. V/26	Lym. Hndbk., 46th Ed.
100	Hrndy. SP	**53.0**	H4831	Fed. 215	Wby.	**3210**	**2288**	Wby. Mk. V/26	Lym. Hndbk., 46th Ed.

SP—Soft Point; PL—Power-Lokt.

FACTORY LOAD DATA

Bullet Wt. Grs.	Type	MV (fps)	ME (fpe)	Rifle/ Bbl. (in.)	Remarks
87	Wby. SP	3500	2367	Wby. Mk. V/26	The Wby. Guide
100	Wby. NP	3395	2560	Wby. Mk. V/26	The Wby. Guide
100	Wby. SP	3395	2560	Wby. Mk. V/26	The Wby. Guide

SP—Soft Point; NP—Nosler Partition.

SPECIFICATIONS

Shell Holders
RCBS: 3
Bonanza: 1
Lyman: 2
Pacific: 1

Bullet Diameter
Jacketed: .243"

Lengths
Trim: 2.490"
Maximum Case: 2.500"
Maximum Overall: 3.00"

The 240 Weatherby Magnum (center) is flanked by the 243 Winchester (left) and the 6mm Remington (right). Note the obvious difference in over-all cartridge length and case capacity.

CAUTION:
Loads recommended and suggested herein have been carefully listed, but are intended solely as a guide to readers and neither the publisher nor author accept any responsibility for results of their use.
Maximum loads, listed in bold, should be reduced by 10 percent and worked up to cautiously.

250-3000 Savage

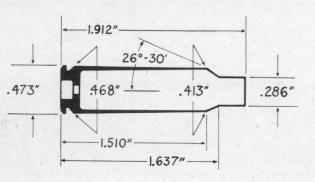

1.912"

26°-30'

.473" .468" .413" .286"

1.510"

1.637"

"It is the single most accurate big game cartridge I've ever seen, on a gun-by-gun basis. Taking all factors into account, I can think of nothing better for use on game up to 250 pounds in weight. Nothing."

THE little 250-3000 Savage is of no account. Everyone knows that. It came into being during the reign of celluloid collars, even before public radio; anything that old can't be much good today. Sure. The only thing it's good for is killing game up through deer in size like a bolt of triple-forked lightning, shooting flat as a taut wire at all reasonable varmint hunting ranges, grouping all its shots into uncannily small clusters from most any type or brand of rifle, and doing the foregoing with such a minimum of fuss and bother that an arthritic leprechaun can handle it with ease.

Before you read on, let me disencumber my conscience: I am bewitched by the 250 Savage cartridge. Although my objectivity is carefully guarded, I must warn you in advance that the 250 is so replete with virtue I may lose sight of my control during this exercise. Let's begin at the beginning.

For many years, Charles Newton has been given credit for fathering the 250-3000. The credit is misplaced. The cartridge that Mr. Newton touted to the Savage firm way back in 1912 or so was a 25-caliber based on the 30-40 Krag cartridge. He had cut the case back to approximately 30-30 length, then reduced the taper and necked it down to 25. The Savage officials turned up their corporate "beezers" at Newton's proposal. It seems that the 30-40 case had a rim of such girth the Savage Model 99 action wouldn't accept it.

Of course, friend Charles was undaunted. He suggested that Savage revamp their rifle to fit his cartridge. The boys at Utica nixed that idea, too expensive. Miffed, Newton betook himself to Winchester with his brainstorm, where he was promptly disposed of. The New Haven firm already had a 25-caliber entry, the 25-35 Winchester.

About this time, enter one Harvey Donaldson of Rome, New York, which is just a few miles up the road from Utica, home of Savage Arms at that time. Harvey was acquainted with John Pierce, ballistic engineer for Savage, and often had him run chronograph tests of whatever cartridge design Harv was playing with at the moment. On one of these trips, Harvey asked Pierce what had become of Newton's bastard 25-caliber. Pierce replied that nothing had or would become of it, at least from the Savage viewpoint. He spilled his tale of woe on Harvey, recounting the problem stemming from the fat rim. Harvey mused a spell, said, "Why not use a case with a smaller rim?"

Pierce replied, "Just what case would you suggest?"

Harvey suggested that Pierce take the 30-06 Springfield case, cut it off to whatever length necessary to function in the Model 99 action, and neck it to 25-caliber. He further suggested that it be given a gradual taper, a 30-degree shoulder, and be capped with a 75-grain bullet for chuck shooting.

Pierce hemmed and hawed and allowed as how Savage had never made up a Model 99 chambered to a rim-

The little 250 is shown here with its bigger brethren. The 250-3000 is at left, the 257 Roberts is in the center, and the 25-06 is on the right.

Although this rifle is not circa 1915, the Savage M99 is the one that started it all as far as the 250-3000 is concerned. This 99 is reliable, accurate, and reasonably handy.

less design. Harvey asked why not. All that would be required was a change in the extractor and method of headspacing. No problem.

And indeed it wasn't. Newton must have gotten wind of the development; I have it on pretty reliable authority that he made it known to Savage that they would be remiss if they didn't load a 100-grain hunting bullet in the nascent cartridge. Since that was the bullet weight he had stumped for with his original 25 Krag idea, it came as a surprise to no one. Savage, however, was foaming at the muzzle for a load giving 3000 fps. What a sales tool! After careful experimentation, it was determined that if the 3000 fps muzzle speed was to be realized, bullet weight could not exceed 87 grains if you wanted to keep your face free of gas and debris. And it came to pass that Savage produced its new cartridge, with Newton somehow finagling the credit for it.

The 250 took off like gangbusters. At first, old-timers took one look at that little cartridge, peered one-eyed into the rifle muzzle, then announced that anyone caught in the woods with one was a milquedtoast and should likely get "et" by bears. Soon, word filtered down that all manner of game was being slain by the 250, with few hunters winding up as bruin fodder. Of course big, mean bears are not exactly the province of the little 250-3000 although many have met their demise at its behest.

Deer and antelope are more like it. Even today, I

doubt that a better deer cartridge exists for ranges up to 250 or 300 yards if the hunter is not enamored of recoil and muzzle roar. Henry Stebbins once wrote: "In killing power on deer [the 250] is generally a little ahead of the 30-30, though it's vastly different in its effects. . . ."

The great Larry Koller was an early user of the 250-3000. In his book *Shots at Whitetails,* he had this to say: " . . . I killed the first three bucks shot at with this rifle. One buck was struck in the neck, the others through the chest cavity; all three dropped as though struck by lightning."

Larry sold his 250 Savage Model 99 to a fellow hunter. Four years later, the rifle had taken four bucks with six cartridges. "Missed one," the hunter explained, "and had to finish another one off with a second shot. But man, I never saw a deer killed any quicker than that little 250 does the job."

Larry summed the 250 this way: "Of all the calibers suited to deer hunting the 250 Savage is without doubt one of the most pleasant to shoot. It is highly accurate, even in lever-actions; has a very flat trajectory, light report and little recoil effect — altogether a highly versatile cartridge for deer."

The mention of accuracy in the above quote makes a fine lead in. Let me quote Jack O'Conner: "I have had three Model 99 Savage rifles for the cartridge, an FN Mauser, and one of the rare Savage Model 1920 bolt-actions. I have never seen a 250-3000 that did not shoot well. One of the first rifles I ever saw that would consistently group into less than a minute-of-angle was a 250-3000 Model 70 Winchester."

In *Mister Rifleman,* Townsend Whelen wrote:

> This rifle [a Savage Model 99] was given to me, probably about 1915, by Pascal De Angeles, then the sales manager of Savage . . . I experimented with it with a number of loads, and it was the first rifle that I ever shot with which I got quite a number of minute [of] angle groups. I mean 10-shot groups, for that was the only kind of groups we shot in those days.

Henry Stebbins said this of the 250's accuracy: "The length, body taper, and shoulder of the 250 resulted in an accurate cartridge that did well with the old powders and with the new ones, in spite of their deterrant coating."

Allow me to make a quorum. I have done pretty extensive bench testing with six different 250-3000 rifles over the past 7 or 8 years, and have recently acquired a new one. The least accurate of the six mentioned were a pair of Model 99 Savage rifles, one a 99-A and the other a 99-E. The two fired exactly the same group average — 1.32 inches. That is for several *five-shot* groups, not three-shotters as are often seen. The most precise of the half-dozen was a Savage Model 111 prototype; it grouped into .99-inch for nine, five-shot strings. The other three rifles were Rugers, a pair of the standard-weight Model 77-R turnbolts and a Mannlicher-stocked M77 International with a light 18½-inch barrel. One of the M77-R's printed 1.15 inches with its pet handload, the other 1.24. The International grouped 1.22 inches with its favorite recipe. Averaging the top loads for all six rifles, we get 1.21 inches! Bear in mind that none of these guns had a heavy barrel, or even a medium-heavy sporter contour. *All* were standard or lightweight sporters.

Incidentally, the seventh gun mentioned is a new Ruger Ultra Light turnbolt. I sighted it in just this weekend, using the only 250 ammo I had on hand — the 100-grain Winchester Silvertip factory load. After expending five rounds zeroing, I fired three, five-shot strings; the average was 1.68 inches, and with factory stuff at that.

Now let me sink the hook. Like Jack O'Conner, I have never fired a 250-3000 that failed to shoot well. The Savage 111 is one of only seven sporters I have ever tested that averaged under 1 inch. The pair of Model 99s are the only leverguns I've fired that would group under 1½ inches for an average. The Ruger International is the most accurate lightweight carbine (6¼

Scoped with a 3x9 Bushnell, this Savage Model 99-E grouped into a 1.32-inch average of four, five-shot strings. A sister M99-A showed the exact same aggregate. The Model 99 will shoot!

The author's Savage Model 111 is the most accurate 250-3000 he's ever owned. It averaged .99-inch for nine, five-shot groups. It's accuracy like this that makes the 250-3000 so popular with experienced hunters.

This is the Ruger International. The author's sample grouped a 1.215 inches average for four, five-shot strings with 41.8 grains of H380 under the 75-grain Sierra JHP. Accurate?

pounds or less, unscoped and unloaded) I have shot in a caliber suitable for deer. Thinking back on all the calibers I've test-fired in the line of duty, and including only those loads with which I have handled four or more samples, none of them has been as consistent as the 250.

The 243 comes close. I've forgotten how many 243 rifles there have been, but it must approach 10 or more. One of them wouldn't stay under 2 inches, although I suspect the gun was at fault in a serious way. A recent bolt-action of popular brand would not do better than 1.34 inches, and it took some doing to get it down there.

The 308 Winchester is another contender. A Colt-Sauer I had would beat ⅞-inch if carefully attended to. But a couple of lever-actions would group over 2 inches, which kills the overall picture. Most of my 270s have

been precise, except for one . . . And I have had uncommon good fortune with the 7mm Remington Magnum . . . and the 30-06, except for a pre-War Model 70. . . . Nope, nothing, equals the 250.

To be fair, the 6mm Remington has been tested in only three guns. Thus far, none has been a stinker. Included were a Remington M700-V — which naturally should have done well with its heavy barrel, a Remington Model 6 pump which surprised me with its accuracy, and a Remington Model 7. But then, only one of this trio would group under 1½ inches, whereas *not one* of the 250-3000s grouped *as poor* as 1½ inches with its best load.

Maybe the 223 Remington? There have been a Savage Model 112-V that was a bell-ringer, and a pair of super-accurate Remington Model 788s. Oops, there was

The author's shooting companion, Mike Holloway, owns this particular Ruger 77 in 250-3000. It consistently groups 1.15 inches with pet loads.

250-3000 Savage: Varmint/Deer

(Right) Varmint hunter Lewis Dawkins has used his Ruger 77 Ultra Light 250-3000 to take woodchucks out to 300 yards or so. Lightweight 250-3000s, like the Ruger, are not only easy to carry into the field, they are capable of bringing home the bacon.

The 250-3000 is right at home in this type of deer cover, despite its speedy little bullets. It made its reputation in wooded terrain back East, although it also became popular in the West.

also the Ruger Mini-14, which grouped well up in the 3-inch class.

Try as I might, I can't conjure another load that has averaged even close to 1.21 inches in *six different untuned* rifles, regardless of weight and barrel configuration. And the Ultra Light might prove to be the most accurate yet.

Ballistically, the 250 is sound as a dollar, or at least as sound as a dollar used to be. Its competitors are the 243 and the 6mm Remington. If you want to include the 257 Roberts, okay by me, although the Roberts is at its best in a long-action rifle. The others fit just fine in the shorties. With 22 inches of barrel, the 250 will drive 75-grain varmint slugs to about 3350 fps with no pressure pains; 87-grain bullets with the right powder, can manage better than 3100 fps, no problem; 100-grain bullets are easily started at 3000 fps with some guns showing better than 3050 fps with no signs of strain.

The 243 in comparable barrels will do this: with 75-grain bullets, roughly 3450 fps; 85-grain, about 3250 fps; 100-grain, around 3050 fps using top handloads at high but acceptable pressures. Thus, the 243 shades the 250-3000 by around 100 fps with the lighter slugs, 140-150 fps with the intermediate 85- to 87-grain class, and virtually equals it with the 100-grain bullets, although I'll grant it 50 extra fps to keep it clean. Since neither cartridge is really a load for game larger than deer —

except for the coolest, most expert hunter — I doubt that the added 50 fps is of any consequence with the deer-weight bullets. Certainly no whitetail could ever tell the difference, nor would the most careful autopsy reveal which cartridge did the damage.

Energy levels are comparably close. Most of the better 250-3000 loads yield muzzle whoosh in the 1800-2000 fpe neighborhood, with an occasional one showing about 2100. The 243 will get about the same, with the rare one achieving 2200 foot-pounds. Not much difference here.

With the varmint-weight bullets, the 243 is surely superior in the trajectory department to the pipsqueak 250, right? Let's see. With a 75-grain Sierra starting out at 3350 fps, the 250 would show this trajectory zeroed in for 200 yards: 100-yard rise, 1.3 inches; 200-yards, zero; 300-yard drop, 6.8 inches; 400-yard drop, 21.4 inches. With the same weight and brand of bullet but of .24-inch diameter and starting at 3450 fps, the 243 produces this path zeroed for 200 yards: 100 yards, up 1.1 inches; zero at 200 yards; 300-yard drop, 6.0 inches; drop at 400 yards, 18.4 inches. As you can see, the 243 shows only .8 inch less dip at a full 300 yards than the elderly 250-3000, and even at 400 has only a 3-inch advantage in trajectory.

Naturally the 6mm Remington will improve on the 243's performance a little, and thus widen the gap be-

H380 is the powder for accurate vermin loads in the author's 250s, especially with the 75-grain Sierra JHP. Winchester 760 is the stuff for fast-steppin' deer loads now that H205 is no longer with us.

tween it and the 250. How about the 257 Roberts? Well, the fastest 75-grain handload I've ever tried in my *26*-inch barreled Ruger Number 1 gave only 3475 fps. With that much barrel to play with, I suspect the 250 Savage could push 3425 fps, or a little better given the same bullet weight. My swiftest 100-grain reload clocked 3090 fps in the Ruger 257, just 8 fps quicker than the top load in my Savage M111 250-3000, despite its disadvantage of 4 inches less barrel. I have yet to beat 3000 fps in any *22*-inch barreled Roberts; I have passed that figure in three of my six 250-3000's with no excessive-pressure symptoms. I realize that the 257 Roberts has a greater case capacity, but so far that fact has not stood it in noticeably better stead, at least in my guns.

The 243 and 250 perform about the same on deer, as their respective ballistics would indicate. In fact, Henry Stebbins commented: "Many of . . . [the 6mm's] publicized 'advantages' over pretty competent 25s, even, to say nothing of larger calibers, can be put down to natural enthusiasm over a new product."

In *The Rifle Book*, Jack O'Conner penned this wise assessment: "In my opinion, the 243 has been greatly over-praised. I consider it inferior . . . to the 250-3000 Savage cartridge which it drove from the Savage line. . . ."

Allyn Tedmon referred to the 250-3000 as, " . . . the most nearly perfect of any commercial cartridge case."

He called the Savage Model 99 250-3000 combination the "Miracle Rifle of 1915."

In the 1952 edition of O'Conner's *The Big-Game Rifle,* we find:

> The 250-3000 cartridge was and is a most excellent one. It was the first of the sharp-shouldered cartridges. Its shoulder with a 26 degrees-30 minutes angle has been shown to be exceedingly efficient for burning modern smokeless powder. The relationship of case capacity to bore diameter is very good and the 250-3000 has always given top accuracy even in fairly light rifles.

Handloading

Obviously everyone agrees that the 250 case is efficient, that the sharp shoulder enables it to burn a good deal of its propellant in the combustion chamber rather than in the barrel. (Or what's worse, out in front of the barrel.) So which powders work best? I've had the best luck with such medium-slow burners as H380, IMR 4350, and lately Winchester's 760 ball. Winchester 785 performed like a champ in some of my 250s, but it too seems to have gone by the board, and I am unfortunately void of any remaining stock. I've found H380 a more than suitable replacement. Du Pont IMR 4320 has been recommended for use in the 250, but the one load I finalized on that featured the stuff wasn't particularly noteworthy in any aspect.

Harvey Donaldson liked IMR 3031 for his 250. In *Yours Truly, Harvey Donaldson,* I discovered: "With my own swaged 25-caliber bullets in the 250-3000 I have had the best accuracy with those of from 83 to 85 grains with 34 to 35 grains of No. 3031. . . . I have never found any load in the 257 Roberts to equal it." (It is comforting to know that not everyone dotes on the 257 Roberts.)

I haven't gotten around to trying Harvey's load, but I intend to. So far, the most accurate load in two of my rifles is built around 41.8 grains of Hodgdon H380 and the 75-grain Sierra hollow point. My Savage 99-E grouped four strings into 1.32 inches and chronographed 3338 fps while doing so. I was so surprised by the extremely high muzzle speed that I ran the test again the following day; the average was 3350 fps. The temperature was a few degrees warmer on the second day, accounting for the slight increase in velocity.

I immediately tried the load in my Ruger International which at its best had previously averaged 1.55 inches. Four strings with the H380/75-grain Sierra duo averaged 1.22 inches, a 21 percent improvement. Excellent accuracy.

That brings up a couple of points about H380 powder. In my experience, it works best at near-maximum charge levels. Other cartridges in which I've used it reinforce that conclusion. Secondly, I recommend the hottest primers you can find; H380 is unusually difficult to ignite. Despite these caveats, I think the powder is worth the extra attention to details. While H380 doesn't always provide the highest muzzle velocities (the 250 is an exception to the rule), it frequently exhibits excellent accuracy. My buddy Lewis Dawkins burned it in a 6mm to win seventh place in a Hunter benchrest match recently.

I've spent little time on the original bullet weight of 87 grains. Like Harvey Donaldson, I have long felt the 75-grain slug to be first choice as a varmint bullet. Considering the 100-grain bullet to be apropos for deer-sized animals, I have nearly ignored the medium weight bullets.

When we get to the 100-grain bullets, two powders stand out from the pack. Du Pont 4350, and Winchester 760. Both are excellent; both kick the heavy bullets out at comparable speeds.

I have scant use for the heavier 25-caliber bullets in the little Savage case; I don't plan to hunt a moose. If I did, I'd likely stick with 100-grain Noslers and poke the bullet in the right spot. For you fellows who stoutly maintain that the heavier the better, I have included one load utilizing the 115-grain Nosler Partition: 39.5 grains of Norma MRP drives it to 2600 fps at the nozzle,

almost reaching factory specs.

The Norma 100-grain loading was the star of the show. In my Savage 99-A it clocked a rousing 2875 fps and grouped just over 1½ inches for three strings. Good load.

Let's close with a hunting tale or two, beginning with Jack O'Conner from *The Big-Game Rifle:*

> . . . The 87-grains bullet, particularly for open country shooting, was adequate for animals the size of deer, antelope, and sheep and that little bullet in the 250/3000 was even advertised as being deadly on grizzly, moose, etc. The late Gene Jacquot, sourdough who outfitted hunting parties for many years in the Yukon, used a 250/3000 and killed many grizzlies with it.
>
> To inject a personal note into this, I have used a 250/3000 off and on since 1917. I have never killed anything larger than a deer with the 250/3000, but I can testify that it is a grand cartridge. I killed a lot of whitetails with the old 87-grain soft-point bullet, and when I hit them in the chest they were almost always killed instantly in their tracks.

In the September, 1971, issue of *Shooting Times,* John Wootters recounted the saga of Uncle Dick Fon-

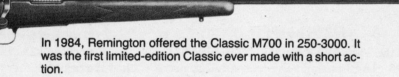

In 1984, Remington offered the Classic M700 in 250-3000. It was the first limited-edition Classic ever made with a short action.

as good a heavy load as I've found.

Factory loads are generally pretty good in the 250-3000, at least in the heavier (117-120 gr.) weights. Although I've tried several lots of the 87-grain Winchester and Norma factory stuff in different rifles, none has grouped tightly. The Norma ammo is very fast, showing 3021 fps from my 99-A and 3081 fps in the Savage M111. The Winchester loads run from 2830 to 2939 fps, depending on gun and ammo lot.

Switch to the 100-grain loads and things perk up. One lot of 100-grain Winchester Silvertips chronographed 2788 fps and grouped very well indeed in my Savage M111. Another batch clocked only 2645 fps in my Ruger Ultra Light, although accuracy was fine at 1.68 inches for three strings. Two of the four lots of 100-grain Remington soft points I've tested have performed beautifully. In my International the average was 1.55 inches; only one handload would outgroup it. The Savage 99-A liked the load nearly as well. A third lot was shot in the Ruger International and fared poorly, both in accuracy and velocity. The fourth batch shot lousy groups in the Savage M111, but velocity was very good,

ville. This is the way the story went:

> When I was a boy, growing up in a roughhewn deer camp on the frying pan-flat, oak-studded coastal prairies of Texas, the grand old man of the camp carried a neat little Savage Model 99A chambered for the 250-3000 Savage cartridge. Aside from the fact that, in my young eyes, this man knew everything in the world about guns and cartridges, the results he got impressed me.
>
> They still do.
>
> When the rest of us hunters heard the spiteful crack of that rifle, we knew that nobody needed to shoot camp meat; Uncle Dick Fonville had a deer. And, during the 13 years I was privileged to hunt with this fine old sportsman, I don't recall hearing the 250 bark more than one time per deer very often.

The only critters I have hunted with any of my 250s have been woodchucks. Actually, I should say hunted *successfully;* I have sought whitetails while carrying a 250, but the deer refused to cooperate. The last chuck I slew with a 250-3000 was not much more than 100 yards away. He had propped himself in the sun and was partially obscured by high grass as he munched his afternoon snack. I was sitting on a mound of dirt, watching a hole wherein resided a gorgeous red-coated chuck that had been making a monkey out of me. The slight movement of the second chuck caught my eye. Shifting my position to starboard, I upped the International and put the crosswires on his shoulder. At the shot, he disappeared. Peering through the scope, I detected a blur of movement at the mouth of the chuck's den. A twitching hind leg. I walked over and examined the result. Never knew what hit him.

My pal Mike Holloway has hunted with a 250 Savage for years. He owns no other centerfire rifle. The last day of deer season, Mike was freezing in a treetop, contemplating the mysteries of the universe and trying not to fall out of the tree. That season had seen Mike with no buck hanging in front of his wickiup; if he didn't snare one today, he'd be reduced to eating TV dinners and kicking the dog. As the last rays of the sun melted away, a band of does scooted out into the cornfield and dug in. Supper.

One old crone hung back. She stood in a sort of fold in the field and eyed Mike suspiciously. Mike commiserated with the doe; folks often eye him suspiciously.

But this was an unfortuitous time and place. Mike scanned the treeline, searching for something with which to stuff his freezer. The doe did not relent. She stood her ground. Nerves were on edge in that field.

A smallish buck sashayed into the open and joined the does for dinner. Mike thought, "There's the beef," and shouldered his Ruger. His shot sent the buck dashing for the woods, whereupon it crashed into a tree, staggered drunkenly a few yards and dropped. Mike descended from his perch, trailed the deer. A postmortem revealed that the 100-grain Nosler Solid Base had wrecked the lungs and exited in front of the shoulder. A very dead deer.

As I said at the beginning, the 250-3000 ain't much count. It has merely been used successfully to take Bengal tigers, Yukon grizzlies, bull elk, and other assorted fauna from here to Tangiers. It shoots nigh as flat as the 243, and that, friends, is *flat*. Recoil and muzzle rip are pleasant enough for geriatric users. It is the single most accurate big game cartridge I've ever seen, on a gun-by-gun basis. Taking all factors into account, I can think of nothing better for use on game up to 250 pounds in weight. Nothing.

Jimmy Michael illustrates the advantage of such lightweights as this 250-3000 Ruger International. The slung rifle offers scant impediment to Jimmy's chuck search.

250-3000 Savage

HANDLOAD DATA

Bullet Wt. Grs.	Type	Powder Wt. Grs.	Type	Primer	Case	MV (fps)	ME (fpe)	Rifle/ Bbl. (in.)	Remarks
75	Sierra JHP	41.8	H380	Fed. 215	Win.	3338	1856	Sav. M99-E/22	Most acc. in this gun
75	Sierra JHP	41.8	H380	Fed. 215	Win.	NC*	NC*	Rug. M77 Int'l./18½	Most acc. in this gun
87	Speer SP	34.5	IMR 3031	CCI 200	Win.	2812	1528	Rug. M77 Int'l./18½	Fair accuracy
87	Sierra SP	**41.0**	Win. 760	Fed. 210	Win.	**2852**	**1572**	Rug. M77 Int'l./18½	_____
90	Sierra JHPBT	**40.5**	IMR 4350	Fed. 210	Win.	**2830**	**1601**	Rug. M77 Int'l./18½	Fair accuracy
100	Hrndy. SP	36.0	IMR 4320	CCI 200	Win.	2890	1855	Sav. M99-E/22	Fair accuracy
100	Sierra SP	40.0	Win. 760	Fed. 215	Win.	2914	1886	Sav. M99-E/22	2nd most acc. ld.
100	Sierra SP	40.0	Win. 760	Fed. 215	Rem.	3022	2028	Sav. M111/22	Very acc. and fast
100	Speer SPBT	40.0	Win. 760	Fed. 210	Win.	2875	1835	Rug. M77 Int'l./18½	Fastest heavy-bullet ld.
115	Nosler Part.	39.5	MRP	8½-120	Nor.	2600	1726	Sav. M99-A/22	Fair accuracy

*NC—Not Chronographed.

JHP—Jacketed Hollow Point; SP—Soft Point; JHPBT—Jacketed Hollow Point Boat-Tail; SPBT—Soft Point Boat-Tail.

FACTORY LOAD DATA

Bullet Wt. Grs.	Type	MV (fps)	ME (fpe)	Rifle/ Bbl. (in.)	Remarks
87	Win. SP	2939	1669	Sav. M111/22	Mediocre accuracy
87	Win. SP	2830	1547	Rug. M77/22	_____
87	Norma SP	3081	1834	Sav. M111/22	Mediocre accuracy; fast
87	Norma SP	3021	1763	Sav. M99-A/22	Poor accuracy
100	Win. ST	2788	1726	Sav. M111/22	_____
100	Win. ST	2645	1554	Ruger M77 U.L./20	Accurate
100	Rem. SP	2811	1755	Sav. M111/22	Poor accuracy
100	Rem. SP	2769	1703	Sav. M99-A/22	Accurate
100	Rem. SP	2590	1490	Rug. M77 Int'l./18½	Very accurate
100	Norma SP	2875	1836	Sav. M99-A/22	Extremely accurate

SP—Soft Point; ST—Silver Tip.

SPECIFICATIONS

Shell Holders
RCBS: 3
Bonanza: 1
Lyman: 2
Pacific: 1

Bullet Diameter
Jacketed: .257"

Lengths
Trim: 1.902"
Maximum Case: 1.912"
Maximum Overall: 2.515"

CAUTION:
Loads recommended and suggested herein have been carefully listed, but are intended solely as a guide to readers and neither the publisher nor author accept any responsibility for results of their use. **Maximum loads, listed in bold, should be reduced by 10 percent and worked up to cautiously.**

257 Roberts

"The Roberts is plenty precise for big game hunting under virtually all conditions. No rifle cartridge capable of grouping consistently into from 1.40 inches to 1.60 inches can be dubbed a dud. No sir."

I HAVE tried to like the 257 Roberts. Growing up reading Jack O'Conner and Townsend Whelen, I was exposed to the cartridge early, at least vicariously. Both O'Conner and Whelen were unabashed admirers of the 257. I read about Eleanor O'Conner's successes with the little 25-caliber, about both of Jack's sons using it on southwestern deer, about Whelen's experiences with it on big game and varmints. The more I read, the more I faunched for one.

The happy day arrived in 1974. I became the proud and expectant owner of one of a special run of Ruger 77 turnbolts, complete with a 24-inch medium-heavy sporter barrel and iron sights. After an affair with that rifle, my ardor tended to bank a mite.

There was nothing really wrong with the gun. At its best, it grouped 1½ inches from the bench at 100 yards. Not shabby, but nothing to put up in lights either. And muzzle velocities ran a little less than I'd been led to expect from the articles circulating at that time. (*Not* ones authored by O'Conner or Whelen.) After a brief period of indecision, I swapped that 257 off, thinking it had a barrel not quite up to snuff.

A few years later, I met a local doctor who was an accuracy buff of the first magnitude. An inveterate gun buyer (I don't think he ever *traded* one away) and experimenter, he owned a 257 Roberts identical to the one I'd had. His was a mediocre shooter as well.

Now I became convinced that Ruger had indeed latched unknowingly upon some sub-standard 25-caliber barrels. A few years later, I acquired, tinkered with, and generally got to know well a pair of Ruger 77s in 250-3000. Nothing wrong with those rifles! Both grouped under 1¼ inches with good ammunition, and it didn't take much experimenting to find such loads.

I continued to read articles and books by O'Conner and Whelen, occasionally found a good word about the 257 in works by Harvey Donaldson. Ken Waters, a writer I respect and admire immensely, had penned a piece in an issue of *Handloader* magazine about the Roberts. I reread it countless times. When Winchester announced the return of the Model 70 Featherweight, and subsequently that the 257 was to be one of the chamberings, I began to feel another 257 deep in my bones.

Before finding a Winchester Featherweight for sale, I happened to mention in conversation with Mike Bussard (then of Sierra Bullets) that I was itching all over for a 257 Roberts. Mike informed me that there was a spanking new Ruger Number 1-B sitting in Sierra's vault; I could buy it at a good price if I couldn't live without it. A week later it was sitting in a corner of my gun room. Again I was expectant, though not quite as proud; perhaps the years had jaded me.

After the smoke cleared, I was convinced that Ruger's earlier barrels had not been to blame. The Roberts cartridge was. That Number 1 shot pretty fair, as most Number 1s do, but try as I might, I couldn't get

While Winchester's Model 70 Featherweight is a fine hunting rifle, the author found himself disappointed with its accuracy. Groups of 1.94 inches, at 100 yards, was the best it could do.

it to average under 1½ inches for five-shot groups. I came close, getting 1.57 inches with the best load. I began to wonder about the good ol' Roberts.

I dug out my books and magazines and dug in. In his masterpiece *Mister Rifleman,* Townsend Whelen wrote:

> My records show that I have to date made 72 separate accuracy and trajectory tests of this 257 Roberts Model 70 rifle with many different loads. During the past few years I have been testing it with modern bullets and powders, and here is the dope on *the most successful loads.* [Italics mine].
>
> The 100-grain Sierra spitzer bullet with 46 grains Du-Pont No. 4350 powder. Winchester cases. Winchester No. 120 primers. Bullets seated to an overall cartridge length of 2.90 inches or almost to touch the lands in your rifle. Muzzle velocity 3,034 fps. Benchrest accuracy at 100 yards with 2½X scope, five-shot groups—smallest 1.00 inch, largest 2.10 inches, average for seven groups 1.39 inches.
>
> The 117-grain Sierra spitzer boat-tail bullet with 45 grains of Du Pont No. 4350 powder. Winchester cases. Winchester No. 120 primer. Overall length 2.90 inches. M.V. 2,975 fps. Five-shot groups at 100 yards were: smallest 1.30 inches, largest 1.85 inches, average for seven groups 1.60 inches. (Note: In the Niedner rifle this load gave three groups: 1.45 inches, 1.60 inches, and 1.25 inches.) [That last parenthetical is Whelen's and please note that the average for the Niedner rifle mentioned was 1.43 inches.]

Now here we have evidence that the 257 is not quite as accurate as folks let on, at least in my opinion. While Whelen's rifles did outgroup both of mine, it was only

after 72 range sessions with one and goodness knows how many with the Niedner. Also, the Niedner outgrouped my Ruger Number 1 by only .14-inch and my M77 by half that. The Model 70 was the most accurate of the four guns we're discussing, by from about ⅛-inch in one instance to .18 in the other. And Whelen's second-place handload in the Model 70 was less accurate than either of my rifles. The relative accuracy, however, is not the point. Note that *all four rifles* grouped in the 1½-inch neighborhood, or 1⅜ for the Model 70 if you want to be picky.

If I tested a standard-weight sporter chambered in 243 Winchester, 6mm Remington, 250-3000 Savage, or 25-06 Remington that grouped as poorly as 1½ inches with its favored ammunition, I'd consider it to be a mediocre performer indeed. All these cartridges are direct competitors of the 257 Roberts; the two 24-calibers nearly drove the Roberts to extinction.

Okay, so four guns do not make a consensus, right? Right. Let's see what other writers have had to say. In his tome, *The Deer Rifle,* copyrighted 1978, the respected Bob Wallack wrote:

> Accuracy is something that's a little hard to define and pinpoint. A rifle that delivers its shots into a minute of angle is usually considered to be a very accurate rifle . . . A minute of angle is defined as 1 inch for every 100 yards of range—an inch at 100 yards, 2 inches at 200, and so on. Just how accurate you need your rifle to be depends on many things, not the least of which are your ability, your sighting equipment, and the range over which you will shoot.

Browning's BBR (short action) is currently offered in 257 Roberts. While the light, 22-inch barreled version is seen here, a 24-inch heavy barrel option is available at no extra cost.

Although they're a little hard to find, the Ruger 77 is offered in 257 Roberts. The author's 77 Roberts came with a factory, 24-inch, medium-heavy barrel. It proved to be his most accurate 257, grouping into 1½ inches at 100 yards.

For reasons that are hard to determine, rifles in 250 Savage caliber have always shot better than rifles chambered for the 257 Roberts. This is a hard one to figure, because the shape or size of a cartridge case really has nothing to do with accuracy, within reasonable limits. This is one of the things many 250 Savage owners like about their rifles. They can be depended upon to put a bullet right where the sights are, and you can't say that about every rifle.

I have shot a good many 257 rifles, and *I have never had one that would hold a candle to the 250 Savage, nor any of the 6mms.* [Italics mine.]

In a letter to Neal Knox, printed in the book, *Yours Truly, Harvey Donaldson,* Harvey had this to say: "With my own swaged 25-caliber bullets in the 250-3000 I have had the best accuracy with those from 83 to 85 grains with 34 to 35 grains of [IMR] 3031 . . . I have never found any load in the 257 Roberts to equal it." However, since there is no mention of group size, we can't really judge how accurate Harvey's 257 rifles were.

In an article published in an outdoor magazine a couple of years ago, a well-known writer waxed ecstatic about the 25-caliber cartridges in general and the Roberts in particular. An interesting photograph was included with the piece, showing the author standing in front of a target frame, holding his rifle and pointing proudly at a series of groups obviously fired only moments before. The photo caption read: "All of the quarter-bore cartridges are extremely accurate, as is the author's 722 Remington chambered for 257 Rob."

As I type these lines, I have the magazine open beside me. There are three five-shot groups clearly visible on the target (which has eight aiming points stamped on it), and three more that are not so easily made out, at least in their entirety. Near as I can tell, the aiming points are about 1½ inches square. If that assumption is correct, then the tightest group shown measures around 1⅜ inches. A couple more appear to be about the same size, but two others are quite noticeably larger, more in the 2-inch range.

So why the beef? Simply this: first, the Roberts' competitors—as listed above—are capable of much better accuracy than this. Second, the 257 Roberts was not conceived as a big game cartridge in its *primary* role, and with a varmint cartridge, groups of 1½ inches cut no ice.

In talking to Steve Hornady recently, he warned me that if I disparaged the 257 Roberts I'd be burned in effigy. He also told me that his company has a test barrel chambered to the Roberts load that is used to sanction test lots of bullets. Further, he admonished, such test barrels *must* be extremely accurate; he can't afford to waste money on an inaccurate barrel.

"How heavy are these test barrels?" I inquired.

"An inch and a half at the muzzle," he answered.

"No wonder they're so accurate," I replied.

"Still," he said, "some cartridges *are* more inherently accurate than others."

"Is that why they used the 257 in lieu of the 250-3000?" I queried.

257 Roberts: Varmint/Deer

"Not at all," said Steve, "the 250 is just a little slow to cover the entire 25-caliber velocity field." Oh.

So let's put it in plain English. I am convinced that some cartridges are more "accurate" than others. So was Harvey Donaldson, one of the greatest firearms experimenters we ever had. So are many, many benchrest competitors. So is Steve Hornady. A consensus.

Further, I believe that the *average* 257 Roberts will not shoot as well as the *average* 243, 6mm, 250-3000, or 25-06. (Or the 270, 284, 308, 30-06, 300 Winchester Magnum, 7mm Remington Magnum, 375 Holland & Holland, and virtually all the small-bore Weatherby Magnums, for that matter.) If chambered in a true bull-barreled-universal-receiver test "rifle," the 257 Roberts is very likely quite accurate. If not, Steve Hornady would have no truck with one. In a hunting rifle, I have never read about nor met a Roberts that would equal similar rifles chambered for one of its competitiors as listed above.

Before you light the bonfire, let's put this in perspective. The Roberts is plenty precise for big game hunting under virtually all conditions. No rifle cartridge capable of grouping consistently into from 1.40 inches to 1.60 inches can be dubbed a dud. No sir. But for a varmint rifle (*not* a big game rifle *used* on varmints; there's a big difference), such grouping is pretty sad. Why all this emphasis on the 257 as a varminter you ask?

Quoting again from Whelen's *Mister Rifleman:*

A student of rifles wrote me that he thought the 257 Roberts rifle and cartridge were on their way out. I do not think so. Probably he based his opinion on the recent volumes of factory ammunition sold. This rifle with factory ammunition, while it is good, is not in any way outstanding. Ned Roberts was a personal friend, and we were together many months on the range and in the chuck pastures when he was developing his cartridge. *He thought of it only as a cartridge for woodchucks.* [Italics mine.]

Ned Roberts, as I'm sure you realize, had a great deal to do with the development of the 25-caliber cartridge that came to bear his name. In the January, 1935, *American Rifleman,* he wrote:

As many of our readers know, the 25 Roberts case was designed by my friend F.J. Sage, and myself, with the assistance of our mutual friend, A.O. Niedner, of the Niedner Rifle Corporation. Before tooling up for this cartridge Mr. Niedner was advised by Col. Whelen, Mr. L.C. Weldin . . . of the Hercules Powder Company, and also one of the ballistic engineers of Frankford Arsenal to make the slope of the shoulder of the new cartridge case on an angle of 15 degrees . . . Thus it will be seen that the 25 Roberts cartridge was designed by . . . the ideas of our best ordnance experts and ballistics engineers.

Harvey Donaldson wrote: "I firmly believe that most of the early experimenting on this case was done by Col. Whelen. Whelen had the experience and the time for

As a deer cartridge (below), the 257 Roberts will fill the bill. As a long range, open-field varmint cartridge, the Roberts round may not be the best choice. Why? The author's groups averaged, at best, 1½ inches at 100 yards. At 200 yards those groups turn into 3-inchers. If you're content to keep the distance short, i.e., under 200 yards, the 257 will work (right) just fine.

If you feel you have to get the most out of a 257 Roberts, you might consider looking for a Remington 700 Classic. A limited run of these rifles, in 257 Roberts, was done in 1983.

Using his Ruger No. 1, the author managed to shoot 100-yard groups averaging 1.57 inches with his best load (47.3 grains of IMR 4350 and the Sierra 90-grain JHPBT). The accuracy is acceptable, but not exceptional.

this work, as well as the use of the Springfield Arsenal and its ballistic engineers."

Remington legitimized the load in 1934, changing the shoulder angle for some obscure reason to 20 degrees. The cartridge was officially christened the 257 Remington Roberts.

The 257 may not have made a big name for itself as a varmint round, but it was long considered tops as a mild-recoil load for big game. When Winchester jumped on the 257 bandwagon with the Model 70, Townsend Whelen began to get mail from all over, recounting the 257's successes on large animals, even elk and moose. Jack O'Conner once knew a very experienced elk hunter who had slain more than 30 of those animals with a Roberts, losing nary a one.

When O'Conner was still acting as Executive Editor of *Peterson's Hunting,* he wrote in that magazine: "Don't let anyone tell you that such cartridges as the 250-3000, the 257, as well as the two 6mms, aren't adequate for deer. I have seen at least 100 shot with the two 25s and I have never seen one get away wounded."

O'Conner so liked the 257 that he closed his piece this way: "To my way of thinking the best of the 25s—in versatility, accuracy, light report, and recoil—is the 257 Roberts, and it is the most moribund of the lot. Lots of things in this world don't make sense to me. The fate of the 257 is one of them!"

Famed gun writer Bob Milek has used the 257 for years, on game large and small. In the March, 1982, *Peterson's Hunting,* Bob opined: "I consider the 257 Roberts to be one of the best-balanced cartridges ever developed—a natural for medium-sized game . . . " And: ". . . shooters have come to realize that the Roberts will, when handloaded, do everything any of the 6mms will and a good many things they won't."

You may be pondering just why everyone scoffs at the factory ammo. The reason is that as put up by the factories, the 257 is a weak reed. For some inexplicable reason, the factories have always under-loaded the Roberts. In my 26-inch barreled Number 1, the new Plus-P Winchester 117-grain round nose clocked only 2610 fps, although the published figures read 2780 fps. Not much "plus" in that stuff. My newest 257, a Featherweight Model 70 with 22-inch tube, chronographed as fast as the Ruger at 2609 fps. Strange. I've never checked any of the 100-grain factory fodder, but the Speer manual shows the 100-grain Winchester loading at 2762 fps from a 24-inch barreled Ruger 77. See why the factory products draw such cutting remarks?

For comparison, the 100-grain Winchester Silvertip, 250-3000 ammunition gets 2788 fps in my 22-inch barreled Savage Model 111 and 2645 fps in a 20-inch barreled Ruger Ultra Light. Remington's 100-grain soft point loading shows 2811 fps from my Savage 111, 2769 fps in a Savage 99-A, and 2590 fps in a stubby Ruger International with 18½-inch barrel. The 100-grain Norma ammo is faster yet, at 2875 fps in a 22-inch barreled Savage 99. Thus, the 250-3000 is *more* powerful than the 257 in factory persuasion, not the other way around.

Handloading the 257

Handloading rearranges things, but not as much as you might suspect. My best load with a 75-grain bullet in the 257 runs to 3475 fps; in my Savage 99-E 250, the same slug is goosed to 3338 fps. With the 90-grain bullet, I get 3355 fps in the 257 and 3113 fps from the 87-grain bullet in my 250. The 100-grain slugs show 3090 fps in my fastest 257; it's no trick to reach 3082 fps in my Savage 111 250, and 3068 fps in a Ruger 77. If the 257 seems to have an inordinate lead in muzzle speeds, particularly with the lighter bullets, please note that the Ruger Number 1 from which these handload velocities were taken sports a 26-inch tube; the rifles chambered in 250-3000 carry 22-inchers. Makes a difference.

The upshot is that the 243 and 250-3000 both get a 100-grain deer bullet into the low-3000 fps range in most guns having at least 22 inches of barrel, with an occasional rifle shading that by a few fps. The 6mm Remington and 257 Roberts add perhaps 75 fps to that, maybe 100 if you pit a fast 257 or 6mm against a slow 250 or 243. With the lightest bullets, the 243 picks up about 100 fps on the 250, and the 257 and 6mm run a little ahead of the 243. You could use any of the quartet for years and never know which one you were shooting without looking. (Or perhaps hearing; the 250-3000 is usually a tad quieter than the others.)

My favorite 257 loads feature IMR 4350 in their makeup. That's the traditional propellant in the Roberts, and a very good one. The most accurate load in my Numer 1 is 47.3 grains of IMR 4350 and the 90-grain Sierra JHPBT; groups run 1.57 inches and velocity 3355 fps. It's a great varmint load at distances where 1½-inch accuracy is sufficient.

Second best in the Ruger single shot is 45.0 grains of IMR 4350 under the 100-grain Speer hollow point. Groups average 1.77 inches, velocity 2940 fps. In third slot is 45.0 grains of Winchester 760 and the 100-grain Sierra soft-point.

Interestingly, I tried the top three loads from the Number 1 in my new Winchester Model 70 Featherweight, along with several others. The order was the same for the first three places in both guns, with the loads tried in both. Remember that when you hear that, there is no such thing as an "accuracy" load.

My Featherweight was the least accurate 257 I've fired to date. In desperation, I tried a load from Ken Waters' "Pet Loads" article, one he had found worked well in his rifles. The load: 40.0 grains of IMR 4064 be-

neath the 75-grain Sierra hollow point. It averaged 1.94 inches in the Model 70, for four, five-shot strings, and was the only load that stayed under 2 inches. Muzzle velocity was 3052 fps, a mild load.

One other point I'd like to touch on before leaving the 257 Roberts. For years the cartridge was offered in such short-action rifles as the Remington 722. Even the lengthy Winchester Model 70 had a short throat to accommodate factory seating depth, and a shortened magazine and bolt throw to match. Every gun writer I can think of has lamented such a state of affairs, suggesting deepening the chamber throat and seating the bullets "out where they belong" in rifles having sufficient action length. In the days before the 25-06 was made into a factory round, such advice had merit. As far as I'm concerned, when the 25-06 saw the legitimate light of day, the long-throated Roberts became instantly obsolete. Why in the world should you carry a long-action rifle and stuff it with a medium-length cartridge when there is available a load of the proper length that will outdo the shorter cartridge in every way? *Every* way. Sure, the 25-06 kicks a tad more, uses a little more powder, wears out barrels a bit quicker. It also groups more tightly, shoots flatter and is available in more guns. Now, I wouldn't trade off a trusted long-throated 257 for a new-fangled 25-06. But if I were in the market for a new ¼-inch bore that would fit in long actions, I'd never cast a glance at the 257 from a purely pragmatic standpoint. Nostalgia, yes. Curiosity, sure; I'd still like to find a 257 that will *really* shoot. But from a hard-nosed ballistic standpoint? No thanks.

There *is* one 257 rifle on the market that interests me: the Browning BLR. The action is short, like it should be. The only BLR I have shot—a 358 Winchester—was very accurate. My friend, Ed White had a 22-250 that was a bell-ringer, as was the *American Rifleman's* test gun. Yep. I'd like to try one of those. I might find an accurate 257 Roberts yet.

The Winchester Model 70 Featherweight, chambered in 257 Roberts, has a long action, as can be seen here; but, the chamber doesn't have a long throat. The result is that handloaders can't take advantage of the additional performance potential a long-actioned 257 offers.

257 Roberts

HANDLOAD DATA

Bullet Wt. Grs. Type	Powder Wt. Grs. Type	Primer	Case	MV (fps)	ME (fpe)	Rifle/ Bbl. (in.)	Remarks
75 Sierra JHP	40.0 IMR 4064	8½-120	Win.	3052	1552	Win. M70 Fwt./22	Most acc. in this gun
75 Sierra JHP	**48.0** H380	Fed. 215	Win.	**3475**	**2012**	Ruger No. 1-B/26	Fastest load tested
75 Sierra JHP	**48.0** H380	CCI 250	Win.	**3360**	**1881**	Win. M70 Fwt./22	Fastest load tested
90 Sierra JHPBT	**47.3** IMR 4350	CCI 200	Win.	**3355**	**2250**	Ruger No. 1-B/26	Most acc. in this gun
90 Sierra JHPBT	**47.3** IMR 4350	CCI 200	Win.	**3040**	**1847**	Win. M70 Fwt./22	2nd most accurate
100 Sierra SP	37.0 IMR 4064	Rem. 9½	Win.	2833	1783	Ruger M77/24	Fair accuracy
100 Hrndy. SP	44.0 IMR 4350	Rem. 9½	Win.	2931	1908	Ruger M77/24	Accurate
100 Sierra SP	**45.0** Win. 760	Rem. 9½	Win.	**3090**	**2111**	Ruger No. 1-B/26	Very accurate
100 Sierra SP	**45.0** Win. 760	Rem. 9½	Win.	**2947**	**1929**	Win. M70 Fwt./22	Very accurate
100 Speer JHP	**45.0** IMR 4350	CCI 200	Win.	**2875**	**1836**	Win. M70 Fwt./22	Very accurate
100 Speer JHP	**45.0** IMR 4350	CCI 200	Win.	**2940**	**1920**	Ruger No. 1-B/26	Very accurate
120 Nosler SB	**45.0** IMR 4831	CCI 200	Win.	**2740**	**2001**	Win. M70 Fwt./22	Poor accuracy

JHP—Jacketed Hollow Point; JHPBT—Jacketed Hollow Point Boat-Tail; SP—Soft Point; SB—Solid Base.

FACTORY LOAD DATA

Bullet Wt. Grs. Type	MV (fps)	ME (fpe)	Rifle/ Bbl. (in.)	Remarks
117 Win. RN+P	2609	1768	Win. M70 Fwt./22	Fair accuracy
117 Win. RN+P	2610	1769	Ruger No. 1-B/26	Fair accuracy

RN+P—Round Nose Plus P.

SPECIFICATIONS
Shell Holders
RCBS: 11

Bonanza: 1

Lyman: 8

Pacific: 1

Bullet Diameter
Jacketed: .257"

Lengths
Trim: 2.223"

Maximum Case: 2.233"

Maximum Overall: 2.775"

CAUTION:
Loads recommended and suggested herein have been carefully listed, but are intended solely as a guide to readers and neither the publisher nor author accept any responsibility for results of their use. **Maximum loads, listed in bold, should be reduced by 10 percent and worked up to cautiously.**

25-06 Remington

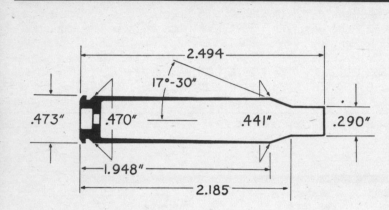

2.494

17°-30"

.473" .470" .441" .290"

1.948"

2.185

"It's an excellent limited-scope cartridge, and one of the best for really long-distance shooting of pests. Ditto for pronghorns and deer in the wide open spaces."

I'VE never been a particular fan of the 25-06 Remington. Not, at least, until recently. Some years ago I authored a piece on reloading the 25-06 with modern slow-burning propellants. Before that, I had never worked with a 25-06 at all. A year or two after writing the handloading piece, I was assigned the task of wringing out the new line of Federal "Premium" rifle ammunition, a portion of which was headstamped 25-06. I used three rifles so chambered, but handloaded for none of them. The results obtained from the long 117-grain Federal boat-tail (made for them by Sierra) were not unusually impressive.

Some time later I acquired through a complicated gun swap an Interarms Mark X Mauser. The rifle was about as "standard" as a gun can be, complete with a military-type trigger having a yard of creep and overtravel. Oddly, the gun also had a non-standard barrel twist rate of 1 in 14 inches; the normal twist is 1 in 10. That rifle would throw the long 117-grain boat-tails all over the target, due to the slow twist, but man would it group the lightweight slugs! Using a charge of Norma MRP that had proved accurate in another rifle, that Mark X printed an average of 1.02 inches with the 87-grain Hornady soft point.

I began to reappraise my position on the 25-06. Of the two rifles I had handloaded for, one would group right at one minute-of-angle, and the other—a full-fledged target rifle—would group just over ½-inch. Ob-

viously some potential here.

Recently, I secured yet another ¼-incher, this one a new Kleinguenther lightweight turnbolt. Barrel length is a little out of the ordinary for a 25-06; it measures just 22 inches from breech to crown. I'm certain many of you are shaking your heads sagely and *tsk-tsking* my misfortune. Save your effort; if I've suffered any loss by going to a 22-inch pipe, I'm having great difficulty detecting it.

I chronographed my Kleinguenther side by side with a Ruger Number 1 Varminter; the Ruger boasts a 24-inch tube. The best load to date in the Kleinguenther utilizes 52.0 grains of IMR 4831 and the 120-grain Nosler Solid Base. (This is the top-listed load in the new Nosler manual, so work up to it carefully like I did.) The Kleinguenther gave 3077 fps with this load, the Ruger 3056. I checked the muzzle speed of the accurate 90-grain Federal hollow point in both guns; the K15 showed 3220 fps, the Ruger 3375 fps. Aha, you say, that's more representative of the norm. Is it? I clocked the 120-grain Remington soft point Core Lokt; the K15 managed 2988 fps, while the Ruger made it to 3003 fps. You call that a big difference?

Averaging all loads chronographed in both rifles, the Kleinguenther K15 comes up 49.4 fps short of the longer-barreled Ruger, which amounts to 24.7 fps per inch of barrel abbreviation. Big deal. I'll take the shorter barrel, thanks very much.

The author's favorite 25-06 load uses 52 grains of IMR 4831 and the Nosler 120-grain Solid Base. IMR 4831 is an excellent choice for the 25-06.

The editor of this book once sat down behind a Ruger No. 1, 25-06 Varmint and proceeded to shoot a .75-inch, five-shot group. The load was 55.5 grains of H4831, Speer 100-grain hollow points and CCI Large Rifle Magnum primers. That load has proven to be a consistent performer in a large number of rifles chambered for the 25-06.

And now perhaps you're wondering if the super light tube gracing the K15 has caused any accuracy problems. Not so's you'd notice. The above mentioned reload of 52.0 grains of IMR 4831 and 120-grain Nosler Solid Base slugs printed an average for three, five-shot strings of .697-inch. *That's .697-inch!* From a sporter! For *five-shot* groups! If you don't think that deserves a brass band, then you've shot few sporter-weight rifles in calibers with a bore diameter larger than .224-inch.

I am now a staunch 25-06 supporter; I dote on accurate rifles. However, as a hunting cartridge, the 25-06 is not exactly what you'd call the ideal all-rounder. Let's examine it in that light.

Factory-quoted ballistics for the 25-06 run like so: Federal offers a 90-grain hollow point at a listed 3440 fps muzzle speed, and a 117-grain soft point at 2990 fps, neither of which was reached in any of my sporters; Remington shows an 87-grain Power Lokt at 3440 fps, a 100-grain soft point at 3230 fps, and a 120-grain soft point at 2990 fps, with only the 120-grain matching up with advance notice in my sporting guns; Winchester makes a 90-grain hollow point at a catalogue figure of 3440 fps, and a 120-grain hollow point at 2990 fps. Since the only rifle I've clocked these rounds in had a 27¼-inch barrel, it is not really fair to the previously-mentioned Federal and Remington ammo. But with that caveat duly noted, I'll report that both Winchester loads exceeded their published data by a good margin; the 90-grain clocked a sizzling 3660 fps, the 120-grain a fast 3132 fps. (Incidentally, an old lot of the 87-grain Remington Power-Lokt chronographed 3483 fps in my long-barreled Remington.)

Now, considering the above ballistics, you'd think that the 25-06 was a real hollerin' terror in the hunting fields. It is, kinda. It'll reach out and ruin a chuck's day to 400, maybe 450 yards, if you can hit it, and shoot flat as the 6mm Remington while doing so. That's not damning with faint praise; the 6mm is one of the flattest-shooting cartridges ever carried into a chuck pasture. So if the 25-06 shoots as flat as the 6mm, and hits at least as hard or a tad harder way out yonder, why isn't it the berries when it comes to decimating the var-

25-06 Remington: Varmint/Deer

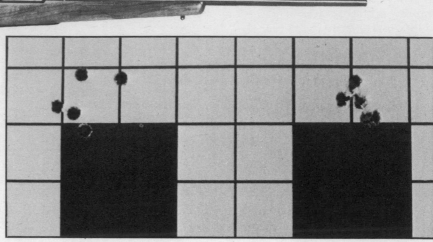

(Above) One of the most popular varmint-style 25-06 rifles available is the Ruger 77V. It has an excellent reputation for accuracy in this chambering.

(Right) Groups like these are quite common from a quality 25-06. The group on the left measures 1.22 inches, the group on the right—fired with 120-grain Noslers—measures .7-inch. Excellent performance.

mint population? It r'ars back too much for the tender of shoulder, barks a mite loudly for those who prefer to speak in normal tones, and it uses up powder and barrels in imprudent fashion. By the dedicated vermin seeker, such blemishes are not taken lightly. Remember, the serious varminter will burn up more ammo in a month than an average shooter will in a year, maybe two. Powder cost, barrel replacement, ringing ears—all are truly meaningful to the nimrod who considers a groundhog, crow, or prairie dog a target worthy of businesslike attention.

If the 25-06 is a bit too much for the smaller species, it must be ideal for the big boys, right? Well, not the *real big* boys. Actually, the 25-06 is in its bailiwick on pronghorn antelope and mule deer, and whitetails if you hunt over soybean fields or corn rows. Loaded with a sharp-pointed slug like the 100-grain Nosler Solid Base or Speer spitzer boat-tail, retained energy out at 400 yards—which is what I consider maximum range on any big game animal with any cartridge — is around 1250 fpe, assuming a 3300 fps starting speed. Zero your rifle at 200 yards and your bullet will dip only 16.1 inches at 400. That, my friend, is *flat*.

If you like a little more bullet weight, you can goose the 117-grain Sierra spitzer boat-tail to 3100 fps if you know what you're about. Retained energy at 400 yards would then be 1272 fpe, and the drop would be 18½ inches. Personally, I'd rather use the 100-grain bullet on deer and antelope taken at long range. I've seen what that wicked 100-grain Nosler Solid Base will do to a buck.

On bigger animals, say elk, moose, or grizzly bears, I think the 25-06 is borderline. I know folks who have taken such game, and humanely. I also know a guy who rode a moped from Orlando to St. Paul, but I would hesitate to recommend the practice. If I were determined to pursue an elk or moose while armed with a 25-06, I'd want it to be loaded with ammo featuring the 120-grain Nosler Partition over as much Hodgdon H4831 as my rifle would stand. Then, if I were careful to place my shot *just so,* I'd likely dine on elk steaks.

If the foregoing sounds as if I'm condemning the 25-06, such is not my intention. I genuinely like the cartridge, ranking it in the top 10 of my personal favorites. After all, when you consider that the 25-06 is as good at taking long-range varmints as the excellent 6mm Remington, while nearly equaling the 270 Winchester or 6.5 Remington Magnum as a downer of medium-sized big game, you must admit that this ¼-incher is a capable cartridge. A whole bevy of folks think the 25-06 will do nearly anything.

One of the best stories I ever read about the 25-06 appeared in the January-February, 1974, issue of *Handloader* magazine, under John Wootter's byline. John is one of the most knowledgeable and entertaining gun writers in the business, and this particular piece was one of his best efforts. In said article, John was relating how popular the wildcat 25-06 was in the Houston area during the mid-50s. He opined that RCBS sold more 25-06 dies in Texas than any other state, and that the bulk of those went to the Houston area.

Although John was aware of the ballistic virtues of the wildcat 25, he couldn't quite grasp just what in its makeup was creating such holy fervor among its disciples. One day he bearded one of the zealots and pressed him as to what virtues inherent to the 25-06 were so addictive. Let John take it from here:

He kept mumbling about some rare and wondrous perfect matching of bore diameter versus case capacity, although when pressed he admitted that the wildcat was essentially a one-powder, one-bullet cartridge. The one powder in those days was Hodgdon's 4831 and the bullet was the 117-grainer (or thereabouts). He mentioned trajectories which patently defied all natural law, and raved about killing effectiveness out of all proportion to the obvious ballistics of the cartridge. Finally, after listening for about half an hour, I observed, "In other

For some reason, Ruger No. 1s in 25-06 show up in varmint persuasion more often than not. For those who want a Ruger 25-06 single shot in a more carryable weight, the No. 1B, seen here, fills the bill nicely.

The 270 (left) and the 25-06 (right) are both offspring of the 30-06. With the right bullet, and load, the 25-06 comes close to the 270 and makes for a fine deer/antelope round.

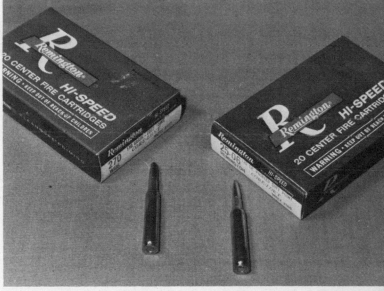

words, what you're really trying to tell me about this super cartridge is that it's *magic*."

"Right!," he yelped, "That's exactly right. It's just magic. There's no explaining it any other way!"

I've run across the claim of magic being included in the structure of a cartridge before, relative to such loads as the 257 Roberts, 7x57 Mauser, the 300 Holland & Holland Magnum, and the 375 Holland & Holland Magnum. It's incredible what a grown man will believe. But then, maybe not. For years one particular gun scribe pounded our senses with the theory that anything less than a 250-grain bullet of at least 33-caliber would bounce off the hide of an elk or moose; you'd be awed at the number of otherwise perfectly sensible people who swallowed that hypothesis! It's no real surprise, then, that such avidity should surround the 25-06.

Remington took a reading of the public pulse and in 1969 made an honest cartridge out of Mr. Niedner's famous wildcat. According to many sources, my favorite being the inimitable Warren Page, former gun-editor-in-residence of *Field & Stream,* the Niedner firm was producing rifles for the illegimate cartridge in fair quantity by 1920. The idea of necking the 30-06 down in varying increments—not only to 25-caliber—had doubtless occurred many years before that. Heck, the forerunner (in a manner of speaking) of the 250-3000 was a necked-down 30-40 Krag. The 250-3000 itself was a necked and abbreviated 30-06. It's not entirely remiss to consider the 25-06 simply a lengthened version of the little 250. That might also explain its superb accuracy, as the 250 is legendary in that regard. (Interestingly, the 257 Roberts, being fabricated from another cartridge case entirely, is not generally as close-grouping as its 25-bore siblings.)

And so for more than 50 years the 25 Niedner, as it was once known, had no home. When Remington picked up on it in 1969, there were no ¼-inch cartridges being chambered except for the proprietary 257 Weath-

erby Magnum. After the 25-06 made its official debut, Savage reinstated the superb 250-3000 via their Model 99 lever-action. Ruger revived the 257 Roberts, and tooled up the 250-3000 for good measure. Thus you could, and still can, buy a 250, 257, and 25-06 with the Ruger phoenix emblazoned in the grip cap. God bless Bill Ruger.

If you want to throw your money around, you can purchase a 25-06 from the following makers: Bighorn, Browning, Colt-Sauer, Champlin, DuBiel, Klieinguenther, M-S Safari Arms, Interarms (Mark X), Remington (700), Ruger (77 and Number 1), Sako, Smith & Wesson, Steyr-Mannlicher, Weatherby (Vanguard), and perhaps the Wichita Magnum. Actually, if you delete the semi-custom rifles from this list, you are left with a rather limited selection. Also note that with the exception of the Ruger Number 1 single shot, all the rifles mentioned are bolt-actions. While this may not surprise you, perhaps it should. You can buy the 243 Win-

25-06 Remington: Varmint/Deer

There is a pretty good selection of 25-06 rifles available that are reasonably priced. One is the S&W M1500, scoped here with a 3-9x Bausch & Lomb.

This Remington 40x is the most accurate 25-06 the author ever shot, and the third most accurate rifle he has owned. It would group in .53-inch, with pet loads, at 100 yards.

(Left) From left to right: 75-gr. Sierra JHP, 87-gr. Hornady SP, 100-gr. Nosler SB, and 115-gr. Nosler Partition. Any use you may have for a 25-06 can be covered by these four bullets.

chester in such long-action ordnance as the Remington Model 4 auto, the Browning BAR, and the Remington Model 6 pump, all of which are thought of primarily as deer rifles. Since all have actions of sufficient length to handle the 25-06, since the 25-06 is nearly as mild of recoil as the 243, and since the 25-06 is a better big game cartridge than the 243 any way you slice it, I can think of no reason why the 25-06 shouldn't be offered in the same guns. On second thought, I can think of one reason. Popularity.

Handloading

On the annually-published RCBS Top 30 die-popularity chart, the 25-06 placed 15th in 1983. The 243 made it to ninth spot. That's a pretty broad gap. Shucks, even the 300 Winchester Magnum placed ahead of the 25-06. (That's likely Rick Jamison's fault; he ballyhoos the 300 Mag. at every opportunity.)

The 25-06 might not be a one-powder cartridge like it used to be, but it definitely requires the slow-burning numbers to make it percolate. I like Norma MRP (at least I used to; trying to get some nowadays is akin to rowing a boat with a pitchfork—you expend a lot of effort but get nowhere), Du Pont IMR 4350 (with the lighter bullets) and IMR 4831, Hodgdon's H4350 and H4831, and Olin's 785 (again, if you can locate some).

My favorite loads depend on what rifle and what purpose. For tight grouping, my Remington 40X used to like 42.5 grains of now defunct H205 behind the 117-grain Sierra soft point boat-tail. With that recipe,

groups averaged .53-inch from the bench at 100 yards. (I said "used to like" because the throat burned out of that rifle in about 700 rounds. Now, it doesn't like anything.)

Next best in that Remington was 55.5 grains of Norma MRP with the fine 87-grain Hornady soft point. The group average was .56-inch and the muzzle speed was a lusty 3453 fps. Good varmint load.

Finally, the 40X did good work with 51.0 grains of Winchester 785 pushing the 117-grain Sierra boat-tail. The velocity was 3038 fps; groups ran .60-inch for the average.

I detailed the Kleinguenther's pet recipe earlier in this chapter. It's runner-up load consists of the 117-grain Hornady round nose over 51.9 grains of Hodgdon H4831, for a 1.04 inch average of four, five-shot strings.

Perhaps the best varmint and deer load in the Kleinguenther is 55.5 grains of IMR 4831 and the 100-grain Hornady spire point. The muzzle speed is noteworthy at 3307 fps, for 2429 fpe, and the groups are well under 1½ inches.

And so we wind up the 25-06 Remington. It's an excellent limited-scope cartridge, and one of the best for really long-distance shooting of pests. Ditto for pronghorns and deer in the wide open spaces. As for bigger game, Warren Page said it best, " . . . he who considers the 25-06 to be a big game cartridge surely effective on beasts over 500 pounds, say on elk, may be due for some rude shocks in the field."

I could scarcely have put it better.

25-06 Remington

HANDLOAD DATA

Bullet Wt. Grs.	Type	Powder Wt. Grs.	Type	Primer	Case	MV, (fps)	ME, (fpe)	Rifle/ Bbl. (in.)	Remarks
87	Hrndy. SP	53.0	H205*	CCI 250	Rem.	3630	2546	Rem. 40X/27¼	Very acc. and fast
87	Hrndy. SP	54.5	Win. 785	CCI 250	Win.	3356	2176	Rem. 40X/27¼	Accurate
87	Hrndy. SP	55.5	MRP	Fed. 215	Rem.	3453	2304	Rem. 40X/27¼	Extremely accurate
87	Hrndy. SP	55.5	MRP	Fed. 215	Fed.	3301	2106	Intrms. Mk. X/24	Most acc. ld. this gun
100	Hrndy. SP	55.5	IMR 4831	CCI 250	Fed.	3307	2429	Klein./22	Accurate and fast
100	Speer SP	52.0	Win. 785	Fed. 215	Win.	3234	2323	Rem. 40X/27¼	Fair accuracy
115	Nos. Part.	**46.0**	H205	Fed. 210	Win.	**3000**	**2300**	Rem. 40X/27¼	Accurate
117	Hrndy. RN	51.9	H4831	Fed. 210	Fed.	2786	2017	Klein./22	Extremely accurate
117	Sierra SPBT	42.5	H205*	8½-120	Rem.	2871	2142	Rem. 40X/27¼	Most acc. ld. this gun
117	Sierra SPBT	51.0	Win. 785	CCI 250	Win.	3038	2398	Rem. 40X/27¼	Extremely accurate
120	Nosler SB	52.0	IMR 4831	CCI 250	Fed.	3077	2523	Klein./22	Most acc. this gun; fast

*Discontinued powder.

SP—Soft Point; RN—Round Nose; SPBT—Soft Point Boat-Tail; SB—Solid Base.

FACTORY LOAD DATA

Bullet Wt. Grs.	Type	MV, (fps)	ME, (fpe)	Rifle/ Bbl. (in.)	Remarks
87	Rem. PL	3483	2340	Rem. 40X/27¼	Accurate
87	Rem. PL	3271	2067	Rug. No. 1-V/24	Accurate
90	Win. JHP	3660	2678	Rem. 40X/27¼	Extremely acc. and fast
90	Fed. JHP	3375	2276	Rug. No. 1-V/24	Most acc. in this gun
90	Fed. JHP	3220	2072	Klein. K15/22	Accurate
100	Rem. SP	3143	2193	Rug. No. 1-V/24	Erratic accuracy
100	Rem. SP	3095	2127	Klein. K15/22	Accurate
117	Fed. SP	2878	2151	Rug. No. 1-V/24	Fair accuracy
117	Fed. SP	2828	2077	Klein. K15/22	Most acc. facty. ld.
117	Fed. SP	2990	2322	Rem. 40X/27¼	Most acc. facty. ld.
117	Fed. SPBT Premium	3037	2396	Rug. M77/24	Accurate
120	Win. JHP	3132	2608	Rem. 40X/27¼	Very fast
120	Rem. SP	3003	2402	Rug. No. 1-V/24	Fast
120	Rem. SP	2988	2379	Klein. K15/22	Fast

PL—Power-Lokt; JHP—Jacketed Hollow Point; SP—Soft Point; SPBT—Soft Point Boat-Tail.

SPECIFICATIONS

Shell Holders
RCBS: 3
Bonanza: 1
Lyman: 2
Pacific: 1

Bullet Diameter
Jacketed: .257″
Lengths
Trim: 2.484″
Maximum Case: 2.494″
Maximum Overall: 3.250″

CAUTION:

Loads recommended and suggested herein have been carefully listed, but are intended solely as a guide to readers and neither the publisher nor author accept any responsibility for results of their use.
Maximum loads, listed in bold, should be reduced by 10 percent and worked up to cautiously.

257 Weatherby Magnum

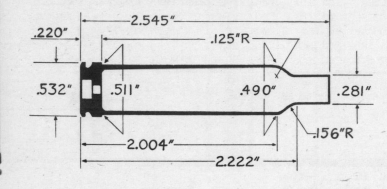

.220" 2.545" .125"R
.532" .511" .490" .281"
2.004" .156"R
2.222"

"One of the reasons the 257 is so widely liked and purchased is, you guessed it, its accuracy."

TWENTY-FIVE-caliber rifle cartridges have long been renowned for their accuracy. The 25-35 was held in awe by some users of Model 94 Winchester carbines. When the 250-3000 Savage was introduced in the Model 99, many shooters found, for the first time, a rifle/cartridge combination that would group around 1 inch at 100 yards from a solid rest. Frequently. The 25-06 Remington provokes even greater glassy-eyed devotion, its disciples brandishing tiny clusters on target paper with ardent fervor.

I haven't read all that much about the velocity king of the ¼-inch bore, the 257 Weatherby Magnum. A few writers have paid homage to it in print, but largely the big-case 257 has gone unnoticed.

The 257 Weatherby was introduced around 1944, about a year before Roy Weatherby ventured into the commercial gun business. Like many Weatherby cartridges, the 257 is based on a shortened and modified version of the 300 Holland & Holland Magnum of British ancestry. It sports the old double-radius shoulder common to other Weatherby magnums, the same belted case, the slight body taper. Commercial ammo has been available under the Weatherby name since 1948, and since 1951 has been fabricated of Norma components.

According to Barnes' *Cartridges of the World*, the 257 Weatherby was one of the first ultra-velocity, small bore rifle cartridges produced commercially that has

managed to achieve, and hang onto, a large degree of popularity. Tom Hall of Weatherby tells me that the 257 is the fourth most popular of the Weatherby line of cartridges.

One of the reasons the 257 is so widely liked and purchased is, you guessed it, its accuracy. Despite the fact that no heavy-barreled varmint rifles are chambered for it by any factory I know of, the load is used for long-range varmint sniping. Sure it shoots flat enough, and of course it hits hard enough, no question. But a long-range varmint rig has to be accurate with a capital "A." Is the average 257 Weatherby accurate enough for such hunting? Obviously a lot of folks think so.

I recently borrowed a 257 Weatherby Mark V from Tom Hall, for use in an upcoming handloading article about the whole family of modern 25s. I haven't had a chance to handload for the gun yet, but the results obtained with factory loads arched my brows a tad. The 87-grain factory soft points didn't perform any feats of legerdemain, grouping into 1.95 inches, but the heavier 117-grain round-nosed soft points did much better at 1.37 inches for three, five-shot strings. The 100-grain loads were the show ponies, averaging just over 1¼ inches for three groups. That's pretty darned good for factory loads in a full-blown magnum rifle. In fact, I have shot only one other magnum that would beat that group average, and then only with handloads.

Weatherby guarantees their Mark V rifles to shoot a

With the right handloads, the 257 Weatherby can turn in superb accuracy. This 5-shot, 100-yard group measures ¾-inch.

three-shot group of 1½ inches or less before the gun leaves the factory. Enclosed with my sample 257 was a three-shotter fired by one Y. Yamamoto using 100-grain factory stuff. It measured .67-inch.

Even more impressive, amazing actually, was a five-shot string fired by a tester named Scott. The group measured .70-inch center-to-center of the widest holes! The target has "100-gr." handwritten on it. I don't know if it was a handload or factory ammunition, but it certainly was accurate. I'll have my work cut out just trying to equal that group.

But this is only one rifle, right? Do I know of any oth-

From the bench, at 100 yards, the author gets 1¼-inch, five-shot groups from the Weatherby Mark V. Excellent accuracy is one of the keys to the 257 Weatherby's popularity.

er reliable tests that support my contention that the 257 Weatherby is extremely accurate? Yes. I do.

Writing in the September-October, 1983, issue of *Handloader* magazine, Ken Waters wrote of his 257 Weatherby Mark V:

Accuracy with factory ammo was phenomenal for a cartridge of this intensity. I was able to beat it by only modest margins with 87- and 100-grain handloads, and I am chagrined to report that I failed to even equal the minute-of-angle accuracy of 117-grain Weatherby factory loads, some of which grouped in slightly under ¾-inch!

As you should see, there is more than one very, very accurate 257 Weatherby running loose. I don't know if my Mark V will live up to the precision of Ken's rifle, but I'll give it my best shot. Regardless, Ken's Weatherby shows that it definitely isn't folly to consider seriously the big ¼-incher as a varmint round.

But the 257 Mag. kicks, doesn't it? Yep. And isn't it loud? It'll curl your toenails. Then why is it such a terrific varmint cartridge? I didn't say it was a terrific varmint cartridge; I said it was accurate enough *to serve* as a long-distance vermin slayer. I never said *I* would choose it for such work. I wouldn't, expect for an occasional experiment. But not because it recoils too much. I'll pass on the 257 Weatherby simply because it talks too loud for a day-in, day-out varmint load. For big game, it's

257 Weatherby Magnum: Varmint/Deer

Mule deer like this, taken at long range in the western plains and mountains, are the 257 Weatherby's forte. The cartridge is flat shooting, and packs a good punch.

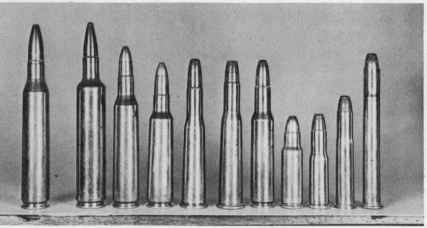

The family of 25-caliber cartridges is a large and old one. From left to right: 25-06; 257 Weatherby; 257 Roberts; 250-3000 Savage; 25-35 Winchester; 25-36 Marlin; 25 Remington; 256 Winchester; 25-20, 25-20 S.S. and the 25-21 Stevens.

vaulting-pole length constitutes less of a handicap.

You may be interested in knowing just what these nigh-legendary ballistics actually are. According to *The Weatherby Guide,* the 257 shows 3825 fps from the 87-grain factory load, for 2827 fpe; the 100-grain loading is listed at 3555 fps at the muzzle, for 2807 fpe; the 117-grain round nose gets 3300 fps and 2830 fpe. All figures are for a 26-inch barrel.

I chronographed a sampling of each weight in my 26-inch barreled Mark V. My trusty Oehler Model 33 read off 3730 fps for the 87-grain load, 3550 fps with the 100, and 3277 fps when I slid the 117-grain fodder across the screens. Respective muzzle energies are 2688, 2799, and 2791 fpe. Thus were my 87-grain loads 95 fps shy of the mark projected by the ballistics sheet, the 100-grain stuff only 5 fps short of expectations, and the 117-grain blunt-prowed loading a mere 23 fps this side of adver-

another matter.

In *Cartridges of the World,* Frank Barnes wrote:

> . . . [The 257 Weatherby] delivers sufficient velocity and energy to take on almost any North American big game . . . A superb deer, antelope, sheep, goat or black bear cartridge, it has also been used successfully on elk, moose, brown bear, lion, buffalo and zebra . . . it is not intended as a woods rifle . . . It is in its element for long-range plains or mountain hunting.

In *The Rifle Book,* Jack O'Conner wrote the following: "The 257 Weatherby has been surprisingly popular, and spectacular long-range kills have been made with it . . . this is a high-performing outfit for the plains or mountains."

And so on. The consensus is that the 257 Mag. is a real hollerin' terror as a cartridge for taking game spotted one county over. The reference to its unsuitability for use in densely-wooded terrain is cogent. It's not that the 257 is useless in the forest, just that since the rifle is so long, relatively heavy, and awkward, it is not the *ne plus ultra* of close-in deer guns. On the high plains, the

tised speeds. That's pretty fair matching up, except for the lightweight varmint bullet. (Let me remind you that the same load was far and away least accurate in my rifle. That 87-grain ammo was the klutzy ballerina for certain.)

It might be possible to equal the factory ammunition as far as velocity is concerned, but it would be tough indeed to exceed it. Ken Waters managed to beat his lot of 100-grain factory loads with one handload, but he couldn't quite reach either of the other two. (He did come close with the 117-grain handloads.)

For impressive muzzle speeds, IMR 4350 is a good powder selection for use with slugs, weighing 90 grains or less. Hodgdon H4831 would be my second choice for speed with the varmint-weight bullets, and my preference with the 100-grain projectiles. From what I read, the slow spherical numbers like Winchester 785 and Hodgdon H450 offer the best possibilities with the heavy jobs, although not all sources agree. Lyman, for example, goes with IMR 4350 when goosing the heavyweights; Speer prefers IMR 4831. Point is, stick with the slow burners in the 257 Magnum.

From the foregoing, you may be inclined to think that I am purposely dodging all the 257 Weatherby Magnum's faults. I demur. Already I have castigated the cartridge politely for its big mouth, and gently chided it for recoil that, while not in any way excessive for big game hunting, is on the pushy side for a varmint round. Only the noise-pollution aspect is of any real import of the complaints heretofore mentioned.

There *is* one justifiable gripe, and it surfaces every time the 257 Weatherby is mentioned. I'll let the late Warren Page introduce it, from the August, 1969, *Field & Stream:*

> The general feeling is that the . . . 257 Weatherby Magnum, however hot it may be for flatness of trajectory, vicious effectiveness on far-out varmints, antelope, even deer [even?], is also too rough in its erosive effects on barrels . . . clearly any big 70-grain magnum will wash into alligator skin a barrel throat quicker than will, say, a 45-50 grain cartridge such as the original 257 [Roberts].

And there you have it: dreaded barrel wear. Take your 257 Magnum on a woodchuck foray, and you had better be careful, say the savants. Fire three shots in a minute or two and the barrel will get hot enough to roast marshmallows. Should you be so unfortunte as to be offered perhaps five chances at a clutch of hapless chucks, your barrel is apt to turn scarlet from the heat. You've been warned.

I suspect there is more than a small grain of truth in the assertion that the 257 Weatherby is tough on barrel steel. I wore the throat out of a stainless-steel barrel chambered to 25-06 in about 700 rounds, believe it or not. The barrel was button rifled, so a tad on the soft side, but it happened nonetheless. Since the Weatherby Mark V tube is hammer-forged, it should last pretty well.

All this is academic, as I see it. In the first place, if you use your 257 Magnum for regular varmint hunting, and don't wear muffs, you will in a few weeks be confronted with more serious problems than barrel wear. You'll be deaf. Secondly, most shooters have little conception of just how much shooting is involved in 800 or 1000 rounds. It's a lot. With a yammering magnum, it's a *whole* lot.

If you pine for a long-range magnum, hanker for one of the handsome Weatherby Mark V rifles, are not exactly immune to recoil, are not a dedicated varmint hunter who can afford only one rifle, will spend most of your big game efforts on animals less than ¼-ton in heft, then take a long look at the 257 Weatherby Magnum. It fills your bill.

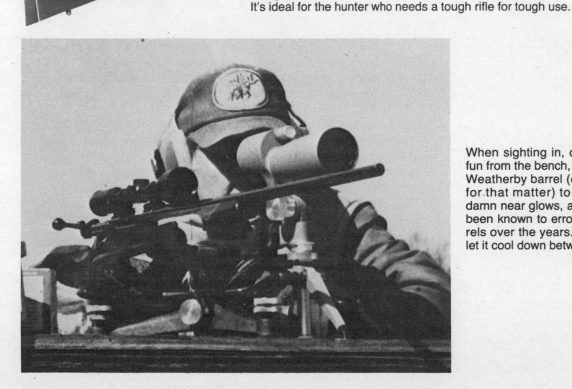

Weatherby's new Fibermark is available in 257. It features a fiberglass stock and bead-blast (non-reflective) metal finish. It's ideal for the hunter who needs a tough rifle for tough use.

When sighting in, or just plain having fun from the bench, don't heat up a 257 Weatherby barrel (or any other barrel, for that matter) to the point where it damn near glows, as this cartridge has been known to errode its share of barrels over the years. Open the bolt and let it cool down between strings.

257 Weatherby Magnum

HANDLOAD DATA

Bullet Wt. Grs.	Type	Powder Wt. Grs.	Type	Primer	Case	MV (fps)	ME (fpe)	Rifle/ Bbl. (in.)	Remarks
87	Rem. SP	**69.0**	IMR 4350	Fed. 215	Wby.	**3759**	**2730**	Wby. MK. V/26	Lyman Rld. Hndbk., 46th Ed. (Acc. Ld.)
100	Rem. SP	**66.0**	IMR 4350	Fed. 215	Wby.	**3472**	**2677**	Wby. MK. V/26	Lyman Rld. Hndbk., 46th Ed. (Acc. Ld.)
100	Rem. SP	**70.0**	H4831	Fed. 215	Wby.	**3436**	**2622**	Wby. MK. V/26	Lyman Rld. Hndbk., 46th Ed.
117	Rem. SP	**64.0**	IMR 4350	Fed. 215	Wby.	**3322**	**2868**	Wby. MK. V/26	Lyman Rld. Hndbk., 46th Ed. (Acc. Ld.)

SP—Soft Point.

FACTORY LOAD DATA

Bullet Wt. Grs.	Type	MV (fps)	ME (fpe)	Rifle/ Bbl. (in.)	Remarks
87	Wby. SP	3730	2688	Wby. MK. V/26	Fair accuracy
100	Wby. SP	3550	2794	Wby. MK. V/26	Extremely accurate
117	Wby. RN	3277	2783	Wby. MK. V/26	Accurate

SP—Soft Point; RN—Round Nose.

SPECIFICATIONS
Shell Holders
RCBS: 4
Bonanza: 2
Lyman: 13
Pacific: 5

Bullet Diameter
Jacketed: .257"

Lengths
Trim: 2.540"
Maximum Case: 2.545"
Maximum Overall: 3.250"

CAUTION:
Loads recommended and suggested herein have been carefully listed, but are intended solely as a guide to readers and neither the publisher nor author accept any responsibility for results of their use.
Maximum loads, listed in bold, should be reduced by 10 percent and worked up to cautiously.

Popular Sporting Rifle Cartridges

6.5 REMINGTON MAGNUM
270 WINCHESTER
270 WEATHERBY MAGNUM
7mm-08 REMINGTON
7x57 MAUSER
280 REMINGTON
284 WINCHESTER
7mm REMINGTON MAGNUM
7mm WEATHERBY MAGNUM
30-30 WINCHESTER
300 SAVAGE
30-40 KRAG
308 WINCHESTER
30-06 SPRINGFIELD
300 HOLLAND & HOLLAND MAGNUM
300 WINCHESTER MAGNUM
300 WEATHERBY MAGNUM
32 WINCHESTER SPECIAL

DEER/BEAR

6.5 Remington Magnum

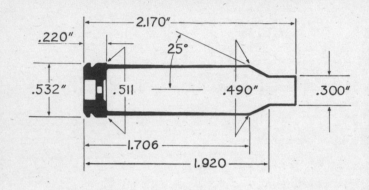

.220" .532" 2.170" 25° .511 .490" .300" 1.706 1.920

"Today, if you desire a new 6.5 Remington Magnum, you have two choices. Have a custom rifle built, or go without. It may be possible to find a nice used one, but I have seen few on the used-gun market in my area."

WHEN I was a boy, I was regaled by tales of the hunt. My father was not a big game hunter, but many of his cronies were. One of his most eccentric acquaintances was a ne'r-do-well named Clifford Prisely. Clifford was in his early 30s when I met him; I remember he was 15 years younger than my dad. He had received little formal education. As I recall, he had dropped out of school after the 6th or 7th grade. Clifford worked some for my father, who owned and operated a commercial recreational lake. In return, he was granted semi-permanent use of a log cabin my father had built on our property.

I never knew exactly what Clifford did to earn his keep, but I suspect he transported the occasional beverage on which the taxes have yet to be paid. Didn't matter to me. Clifford was a godsend. He knew more about hunting and shooting than anyone I had ever met except my shooting uncle, who lived far away.

Clifford kept journals of his hunting trips and shooting projects. He never let me read them, I suspect because he had atrocious handwriting and was embarrassed by it. Instead, he would sit for hours relating details of a recent foray after deer or sojourn to the range. (Clifford's range was set up alongside a pasture belonging to one of his "business associates.") He was a master deer hunter, a superb marksman, and an expert amateur ballistician. So far as I know, Clifford never lied about his shooting and hunting exploits. He was no

saint; he often lied about many things. But when he told you his 30-06 had fired five, five-shot strings into a 1.14-inch average, you could put it in the bank. If he said that a buck took a 45-caliber round ball through the shoulder and ran 30 yards before piling up, you didn't need to step it off or look for the wound. Clifford was just what a budding gunner needed—a friend to shine the light.

The first 6.5 Remington Magnum cartridge I ever saw lay gleaming sweatily in Clifford Prisely's palm. He handed it to me, said, "Whatcha think?"

Trying to appear erudite, I turned the cartridge over in my hand, hefted it, squinted closely at it, handed it back. "Looks like a lollapaloozer to me. Oughta transmogrify a whitetail." (I had just learned that word; a girl at school had told me that if I didn't keep my hands off her she would transmogrify my face.)

"Why?" Clifford wanted to know.

"You kiddin?" I replied, "With that fat belted case, the energy must be enormous."

"About like my 270," said Clifford.

"What!"

"Sure. Look close now. Note how short it is. It's got a magnum-sized body all right, just a tad short on length is all. That belt don't mean nothing, just cashin' in on the magnum craze."

I was dubious. I knew what "magnum" meant: Power! We walked over to the door of Clifford's/my dad's cabin, whereupon he reached just inside the door and

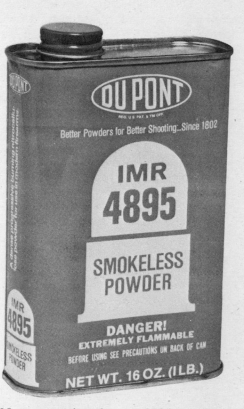

Du Pont's medium-burning IMR 4895 works well when it comes to top accuracy in the 6.5 Remington Magnum.

withdrew a rifle. I'd seen one similar to it before, but not exactly like it. This one had the familiar ventilated rib, short stubby barrel, and gnarled (not knurled) bolt handle. What wasn't familiar was the multi-hued laminated stock with its rubber butt pad.

Clifford said, "This is the Remington Model 600 Magnum. It's about the same as the standard Model 600 except for the laminated stock, recoil pad, and sling installed at the factory. From that 18½-inch barrel, the 120-grain factory load is supposed to get around 3000 fps. Factory sheet says 3030, but that's for a 20-inch barrel. Muzzle energy is a little over 2400 fpe. If I zero her in at 200 yards, she's gonna drop a mite more than 7 inches at 300. Like I said, about like my 270 with a 130-grain ball."

I was deflated. Any cartridge that wore a belt and featured the word "magnum" in its title was supposed to outdo any standard load made. I didn't give up. "What if it had a barrel as long as the one on your 270?"

"I'd likely get 3150 or 3200 feet per second. You're right, that'd be a little faster than my 270. But with a bullet 10 grains lighter. The two are pretty close."

"If this new magnum is so near like your 270, why did you buy it?" I tended to be a bit obtuse, something I've grown out of.

His gray eyes twinkled at me. "Because my 270 weighs almost 9½ pounds field-ready, and this little carbine here sticks the scale needle just under 8—scope, ammo, and all. Not to mention that my 270 is more'n 7 inches longer than this little feller."

"You becoming a pantywaist? Heck, you run around in the woods all the time. You lift all them weights. What's a pound or two here and there?"

Clifford took up his new rifle, went into the cabin, closed the door. In my face. I often seemed to affect people that way.

Ken Waters did a short write-up on the new 6.5 Mag. in the 1967 *Gun Digest*. Reflecting on the 350 Remington Magnum case, gun writers had been having a field day trying to second-guess each other as to which bore size Remington had up its corporate sleeve. When the 6.5 came out in 1966, they all said, "I told you so" to each other. Actually, it wasn't so hard to figure which bullet diameter the Bridgeport outfit would pick.

The 25-caliber cartridges were as unpopular as pimples back in the mid-'60s. Although there was some speculation that a new 25-caliber was brewing, most folks didn't take the rumor seriously. Remington already had a 7mm Magnum, with a full-sized cartridge and ballistics to go with it. On the smaller side, the excellent 6mm Remington was gaining a new lease on life under its new name; Remington obviously wouldn't heap trouble on it by adding a competitor. The 27-caliber was out; the 280 Remington had that base covered.

What was needed, it seemed, was something a little bit different. A load that would offer 270-class ballistics in short-barreled, lightweight carbines. Folks who doted on the 270, but were less than ecstatic about climbing over, under, and around rocky outcroppings with a rifle as long as a vaulting pole, would love it. In theory. Maybe folks did love it, but they didn't buy it.

After three hunting seasons, the handy little Model 600 turned into the less-handy little Model 660 by shedding its shark-fin front sight, tossing its flimsy ventilated rib, gaining 1½ inches of barrel and several ounces of *avoirdupois*. Lousy trade. By 1970, the Remington magnum carbines were no more. A pity. They were very nice rifles.

As a last-ditch effort to salvage their investment, Remington stuck the 6.5 and 350 Magnums in their Model 700 lineup. Buyers stayed away in record numbers. Ruger tried to help out by chambering a few Model 77 turnbolts for the two loads. Those who had been neglecting Remington ignored Ruger with equal fervor.

the belt. For comparison, the 308 Winchester is listed in the Lyman manual at 2.80 inches overall, with a case length of 2.015 inches. Thus the loaded cartridges are comparable in length with the 6.5 *case* being a little longer than that of the 308. The 7mm Remington Magnum mikes .532-inch at the head and .511-inch just in front of the belt, exactly the same as the 6.5 Magnum. The shoulder angle is 25 degrees on the 6.5, the same as on the 7mm Mag., 264 Winchester Magnum, and the 300 Winchester Magnum.

The propellants that work best in the 6.5 Magnum are those of relatively slow burning rate, as is the case with the 270 Winchester. Such powders as IMR 4350 and IMR 4831, Hodgdon H4350, H450, and H4831, Norma N204 and Norma MRP give both high velocities and ample accuracy. In the "Pet Loads" section of the January-February, 1972, issue of *Handloader* magazine, Ken Waters wrote:

Years ago, Ruger chambered a few 26-inch barreled single shots (left) for the 6.5 Rem. Mag. If you ever happen to run across a Ruger No.1-B with a barrel marking like this (above), snap it up. You'll have yourself a collector's item.

I know of at least one Ruger Number 1 chambered to 6.5 Mag. Layne Simpson owns it, swears by it, will bore you to death with tales of its prowess. Perhaps there are a few more out there as well.

Today, if you desire a new 6.5 Remington Magnum, you have two choices. Have a custom rifle built, or go without. It may be possible to find a nice used one, but I have seen few on the used-gun market in my area. Obviously, the guys who bought 6.5 Magnums like them. Or think they're a wise investment.

In case you haven't seen a 6.5 Remington Magnum cartridge and are having trouble visualizing it, let me describe it for you. Overall loaded length is limited to 2.79 inches in order to work through the short Model 600 action. The case itself is 2.17 inches long, has a head diameter of .532-inch, is .511-inch in girth just ahead of

Norma-204 . . . together with its American-made counterpart, [IMR] 4350, are I believe, the two most suitable powders for all-around use in the 6.5 Rem-Mag. Ideal for 120-grain bullets, either is sufficiently flexible to handle . . . bullets at opposite ends of the weight scale. I consider my load of 55 grains 4350 with 125-grain Nosler bullet to be *the* best load for this cartridge, delivering 3,050 fps from my 22-inch barrel Ruger, with 2,582 foot-pounds muzzle energy.

Ken also noted that some of the medium-rate propellants gave excellent accuracy, if not the highest muzzle speeds. His most accurate load featured the 120-grain Sierra spitzer over 45.0 grains of IMR 4064. In his load table, Ken claimed ¾-inch MOA accuracy for this recipe. A pet load indeed.

Will the 6.5 Remington Magnum slay game? You

bet. Here's what Simpson had to say in *Handloader,* Number 87:

> For hunting big game, the factory load in short-magazine rifles makes the 6.5mm Magnum the equal of 25-06 and 270 factory loads for use on deer-size game. With good handloads using the heavier bullets seated out where they should be, the 6.5mm Magnum is superior to the 25-06 and 257 Weatherby Magnum, and it will do anything the 270 Winchester will do, on any big game, and it can put just as many horns on the wall as the 7mm Express Remington and 30-06 when these two larger bores are loaded with 150-grain bullets.

And Les Bowman, in *Handloader,* Number 6:

> After seeing over 50 head of big game killed, from antelope to elk, with the new Remington 120-grain bul-

let [a semi-pointed Core Lokt], I am confident this bullet will be the answer to the success of the 6.5

Clifford Prisely found the 6.5 Remington Magnum cartridge and carbine to his liking. The first year he hunted with it, he jumped a spike buck out of its bed in a pine thicket. While the buck was hopping, Clifford was aiming. He had planted a 2x scope with long eye relief atop the *barrel* of his Remington; claimed it jumped into line quicker than a toad's tongue. It did so then. He slanted a 120-grain factory-loaded bullet through the paunch, into the rib-box and out the chest. The deer ran a few yards and slumped over. Later in the season he bagged a doe under similar conditions. For the next 6 months, I had to listen to how terrific that rifle was.

Come to think of it, it was pretty darned good.

When Remington's 600/660 series failed to fill the corporate coffers, the 6.5 Remington Magnum chambering was introduced in that outfit's popular Model 700 turnbolt. That didn't last long either.

Slower burning powders, like Hodgdon's H4831 would be the choice for the hunter wanting top velocity.

6.5 Remington Magnum

HANDLOAD DATA

Bullet Wt. Grs.	Type	Powder Wt. Grs.	Type	Primer	Case	MV (fps)	ME (fpe)	Rifle/ Bbl. (in.)	Remarks
100	Rem. SP	49.0	IMR 4320	Rem. 9½ M	Rem.	**2906**	**1875**	Rem. M600/18½	Lym. Hndbk., 46th Ed. (Acc. Ld.)
120	Sierra SP	45.0	IMR 4064	Rem. 9½ M	Rem.	**2638**	**1854**	Rem. M600/18½	Lym. Hndbk., 46th Ed. (Acc. Ld.)
120	Sierra SP	42.0	IMR 4320	Rem. 9½ M	Rem.	2481	1639	Rem. M600/18½	Lym. Hndbk., 46th Ed. (Acc. Ld.)
120	Sierra SP	53.0	IMR 4350	Rem. 9½ M	Rem.	**2808**	**2101**	Rem. M600/18½	Lym. Hndbk., 46th Ed.
129	Hrndy. RN	41.0	IMR 4320	Rem. 9½ M	Rem.	2398	1647	Rem. M600/18½	Lym. Hndbk., 46th Ed. (Acc. Ld.)

SP—Soft Point; RN—Round Nose.

FACTORY LOAD DATA

Bullet Wt. Grs.	Type	MV (fps)	ME (fpe)	Rifle/ Bbl. (in.)	Remarks
120	Rem. PSPCL	3210	2745	Test barrel/24	Remington Data
120	Rem. PSPCL	3030	2450	Test barrel/20	Remington Data
120	Rem. PSPCL	3106	2570	Rem. M700/24	Speer Data
120	Rem. PSPCL	2926	2281	Rem. M600/18½	Speer Data

PSPCL—Pointed Soft Point Core Lokt.

SPECIFICATIONS
Shell Holders
RCBS: 4

Bonanza: 2

Lyman: 13

Pacific: 5

Bullet Diameter
Jacketed: .264"

Lengths
Trim: 2.160"

Maximum Case: 2.170"

Maximum Overall: 2.800"

CAUTION:

Loads recommended and suggested herein have been carefully listed, but are intended solely as a guide to readers and neither the publisher nor author accept any responsibility for results of their use. **Maximum loads, listed in bold, should be reduced by 10 percent and worked up to cautiously.**

270 Winchester

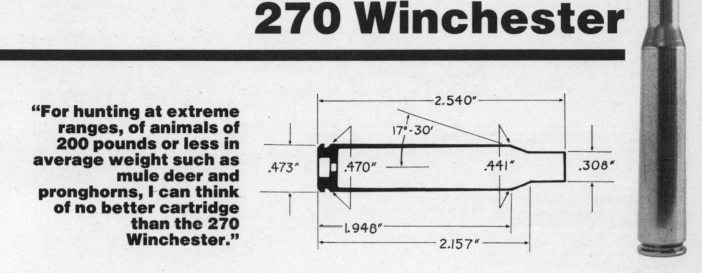

"For hunting at extreme ranges, of animals of 200 pounds or less in average weight such as mule deer and pronghorns, I can think of no better cartridge than the 270 Winchester."

2.540"
17°-30'
.473"   .470"   .441"   .308"
1.948"
2.157"

THE spike buck came out of the thicket as if he knew where he was going and was late getting there. He trotted right under the hunter's tree stand, zeroed-in on a fresh scrape 30 yards distant and made a beeline for it. Reaching the scrape, he fanned his tail like a deck of cards and "pointed" the pungent patch of ground. Fred Ritter raised his 270 and socked the little buck in the back of the neck. The deer dropped. Not fell; *dropped*. Upon examination, Fred found an exit hole he could literally stick his fist into.

Another time, another buck meandered out of a swamp, pausing periodically to peer back over its shoulder. Fred figured that a larger buck might be following, but none appeared. Deciding that the first deer was likely the only deer, he poked a 130-grain 270 bullet through its shoulder. Caught mid-stride, the buck folded up like a pastry box. Never kicked.

It was late in the day and nary a deer had been sighted when a three-pointer sashayed out of a pine thicket and began feeding in the rye field that extended in front of the hunter. Thinking it was a doe, Fred ignored it for a spell, then reconsidered and scoped it carefully. Spotting the horns, he opted for "the deer in the hand" and put the juncture of crosswires behind the right shoulder as the deer fed, slowly quartering away. The gun slapped back in recoil as the hollow *BOOM!* reverberated through the stillness. The buck did not twitch.

That's normally the way of it when you apply a well-

directed 270 Winchester to a whitetail buck. Or a mule deer. Or pronghorn, mountain goat, big-horn sheep. The rifle goes *WHAM!* and the animal goes down. Almost like alchemy.

Fred Ritter dropped the foregoing threesome in one season. Gary Wade has used his 270 for many years, tallying 20 or 25 deer with it. None ever escaped. The farthest a buck ever traveled after taking a 130-grain bullet through its chest was 250 yards or so. Most didn't go 50.

Typical is the fat eight-pointer caught munching in a soybean field one rainy day. Gary had been sitting in a downpour, rain-suited from dome to sole, wondering what in hell he was doing out on such a day. The rain lessened a tad; Gary peeked out at the bean field and spied a buck hard at lunch. Dragging his 270 from under the protective folds of his wet-weather garments, he cinched things down and popped the buck in the shoulder from about 150 yards. The deer made no further tracks. The load was the 130-grain Federal Premium boat-tail.

Another year, Gary was hunting a series of scrapes when he spooked a monster eight-point. The big buck dug in, taking long jumps, serious about putting turf behind him. Gary put his crosshairs on the deer's ribcage and touched off. A tad slow; he knew the shot was too far back. To his surprise, the buck tumbled in a heap. The post mortem revealed an entrance wound just aft of the last rib on the left side and a perfectly-expanded

Two offspring of the 30-06, the 270 (left) and the 25-06 were both designed to shoot a tad flatter than the old warhorse, recoil less, and to be used on medium-sized game. Both have taken game up to elk, and larger.

(Right) Few would argue that the 270's claim to fame is the fact that it's one of the finest big game cartridges to ever come down the pike. However, don't overlook the fact that the 270 can shine as a varmint round when light bullets are used. This fat ground hog was taken in the North Carolina mountains with a Ruger Ultra Light 77.

slug lodged in the front of the right shoulder. The bullet was a 130-grain Sierra soft-point boat-tail.

Let's go on a bit. Jack O'Connor, Townsend Whelen and Monroe Goode began using the 270 back in the mid-'20s and wrote about it in the sporting press. Although O'Connor became more closely associated with the cartridge than the other two, they all had plenty of experience with it.

Whelen used a Winchester Model 54 270 to account for a bull moose as it waded in a beaver dam. One shot, one moose. He shot another moose, some caribou, and several deer with the Model 54, all one-shot kills. One of the caribou was 325 yards away; it ran 50 paces and piled up.

O'Connor killed a dozen moose with various 270 rifles. Contrary to Whelen's experience, Jack never decked a moose with one shot. However, he wrote that his son Bradford dropped a big one from 50 feet with one slug. In addition to moose, O'Conner slew elk, black bear, grizzly, caribou, goat, pronghorn, sheep, javelina and an assortment of African game I can hardly pronounce. All with the 270.

Generally, there is little argument against using the 270 on critters of under 350-400 pounds in weight. It's when the game comes in elk-size hides that dissent rears its ugly head. Aside from the late, great Elmer Keith, who maintained that the 270 was not adequate for larger big game, the 270 has garnered few detractors.

Hosea Sarber even used a 270 on Alaskan brown bears. While I would personally draw the line somewhat short of the big bruins, many other experienced hunters have taken browns and grizzlies.

O'Connor killed an elk at 600 yards with one of his 270s. His first shot hit the bull in the mouth and exited the lower jaw. Miffed at this unpleasant intrusion on his privacy, the big boy jumped to his feet searching for the source of his discomfiture. Jack busted him again, this time in the ribcage. The bull wobbled around on rubber legs for a moment, then toppled.

Hunting with Les Bowman in Wyoming, O'Conner spotted a big bull some 250 yards distant, quartering away. He slipped a 150-grain bullet into its ribcage high on the left side. The slug angled on through the lungs, broke the off shoulder, and put the bull on the mat before Jack could rechamber a round. On surveying the damage, Les remarked, "If anyone ever tells me the 270 isn't an elk cartridge, I'll tell him he's nuts."

The level of popularity the 270 has achieved is remarkable. Consider this: The 270 was not a military cartridge like the 308 and 30-06; it was not a ground-breaking cartridge like the 30-30, which bridged the gap between blackpowder and smokeless and came in handy little carbines to boot; it was not loudly ballyhooed in the shooting press by countless erudite gun writers, indeed for several years was largely ignored; it was not a light-kicking varmint/deer load that could be

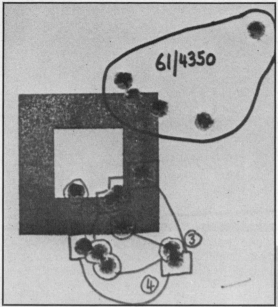

These three groups were fired in the author's Remington 270, 700 Classic. The mixed pair of 5-shot groups on the bottom were the result of 55.0 grs. of IMR 4350 and the 90-gr. Sierra JHP. The upper group: 61.0 grs. of 4350 and the same bullet. The lower groups measure around 1.2 inches, the upper running a little over 2 inches.

From the bench, the author's wife was able to put five rounds into just under 1½ inches consistently at 100 yards using a Savage Model 111 270.

H4895 and Du Pont's version of the same number should work okay with the lighter bullets, but I like slower powders. Starting with H380, I have used and liked IMR 4320 and IMR 4350, Olin's 760 ball, and Hodgdon's H4831. This last powder is traditional when it comes to the 270; O'Conner wrote of its use in more articles than I can count. He employed up to 62.0 grains with a 130-grain bullet in Winchester brass, a grain or two less in the heavier Remington cases. That, however, was with the old war-surplus lots of H4831. The newer made-in-Scotland batches should be loaded at lesser levels. Hodgdon's new Manual Number 24 lists

shot in shirtsleeves by an 80-pound grandmother. Its inclusion in the top six best-selling current rifle cartridges seems miraculous.

Handloads

The load that made the 270's reputation was, and is, the 130-grain spitzer. Fred Ritter used the Remington factory Pointed Core Lokt in that weight for all his hunting with the 270. Gary Wade likes the 130-grain Federal Premium boat-tail or his own handloads using IMR 4831 and the 130-grain Sierra soft point boat-tail. I do more varmint shooting with the 270 than deer hunting; I prefer a shorter, lighter, handier gun than the average 270 for my whitetail sojourns. Consequently, my leanings are toward the 90-grain Sierra hollow point and IMR 4350, or the 110-grain Hornady hollow point and IMR 4064.

Many propellants are well suited to 270 use. On the faster side, IMR 4064 works just fine. Jack O'Conner once wrote that if a 270 doesn't perk with a load of 49.0 grains of 4064 and a good 130-grain bullet, it is either worn out, poorly bedded, or just plain stupid. (That's not a direct quote, but it gives the gist.) Hodgdon's

60.0 grains as tops with 130-grain bullets.

My favorite bullets from an accuracy standpoint are the 90-grain Sierra hollow point and the 130-grain Sierra soft point. Handloading writer Ed Matunas likes the 90-grain Sierra and the 150-grain Speer spitzer for precise shooting. Gary Wade sticks with the 130-grain Sierra soft point boat-tail for both hunting and group shooting, being well satisfied with the bullet for both purposes.

Matunas and I both recommend 55.0 grains of IMR 4350 with the little 90-grain Sierra hollow point. My Remington 700 Classic groups 1.33 inches with that load, for an average of several five-shot strings. Muzzle speeds run just under 3000 fps in 22-inch barrels. For more sizzle at the spout, I load the 90-grain Sierra hollow point and 61.0 grains of 4350 for 3450 fps in my Remington Classic, although groups run a good deal larger than with the lighter load.

If I were planning a deer hunt for tomorrow, and planned to carry either my Model 700 Classic, my Model 70 Featherweight, or my Ruger Number 1 International, I'd load a box of 130-grain Sierra soft points or 130-grain Nosler solid base bullets over 54.7 grains of

Remington's Model 7600 (shown) and Model 6 pump actions are both chambered for the 270 Winchester. These fast repeaters have a good reputation for accuracy and reliability.

Southpaw 270 fans can get the Savage 110 bolt-action in left-hand persuasion. The 110-CL seen here is clip fed, and accurate.

Du Pont 4350. Groups run 1¾ inches in my Model 700, close to 1½ inches in the Featherweight. Muzzle velocity is around 2940 fps in both rifles, which is about the same as with most factory loads.

For elk or similar game, I'd opt for the 150-grain Nosler Partition or the 150-grain Speer soft point, and likely couple either one with IMR 4831 or the Hodgdon equivalent. So much for specific hunting choices.

Accuracy

A word about accuracy, for which the 270 is noted. O'Conner said that in his experience the 270 was a bit more accurate than a comparable 30-06, both using factory ammo. My experience supports his. My Remington Classic 270 groups 1.52 inches with 100-grain Winchester soft points, 1.55 inches with 130-grain Winchester Power-Points, 1.62 inches with the 150-grain Federal Premium boat-tails, all for four or five, five-shot strings, 100 yards, at the bench. The Featherweight goes into 1.27 inches with the 150-grain Federal Premium load, which is the single most accurate load in that rifle, handloads included. Few 30-06s I've tested would print under 1½ inches with any factory load, al-

This Winchester Model 70 Featherweight in 270 is quite accurate, grouping into 1¼ inches with its pet load. Many 270s will do as well or better. Scope is a 2-7x Redfield Lo-Profile.

though most would do around 1.20 inches or better with handloads, something only one 270 I've owned would equal.

From my experience, a good 270 can be counted on to cluster five shots, on the average, into less than 1½ inches with select handloads or factory ammo that the rifle likes. A really fine 270 ought to group in 1¼ inches or better. The most accurate 270 I've used was a Ruger Number 1 that would average around 1 inch for five shots. Unfortunately, I've lost the target files on that rifle and can't give specific details. I traded that Ruger off more than 10 years ago, for some obscure reason. Wish I hadn't.

Rifles for the 270

A list of rifles chambered for the 270 would include such luminaries as Mauser, Griffin and Howe, Mannlicher-Schoenauer, B.S.A., Holland and Holland, Husqvarna. Today you can buy one from Winchester (U.S. Repeating Arms), Ruger, Remington, Steyr, Browning, Savage, Kleinguenther, Bishop, Smith & Wesson, Weatherby, Sako, Tradewinds, Interarms, Harrington & Richardson, Krico, Mauser, Bighorn, Colt, DuBiel, Heym, Champlin, Alpine, and undoubtedly some I missed. You can get a trim, accurate turn-bolt, a quick-firing pump, an elegant single shot, a reliable semi-automatic, all chambered for the 270. Barrel lengths range from 20 inches on such models as the Harrington & Richardson 301, the Sako Mannlicher-stocked carbine, the Ruger Number 1 International and Ultra-Light, to 24 inches on such rifles as the Kleinguenther K-15, the Weatherby Vanguard, the Mauser Mark X and others. Most common length is 22 inches as found on the Winchester Featherweight and Remington Model 700.

The author's old (now discontinued) Savage Model 111 270 shoots well and functions reliably. Having been around for over a half-century, you'll find the 270 chambered in a number of well made, out-of-print rifles. In short, don't overlook the second-hand market when it comes buying your own 270.

(Top) Ruger 77 Round Top; (bottom) Browning BBR. Both of these fine bolt-actions are chambered for the 270 and both have a good reputation with shooters.

The Flat-Shooting 270 and Game

Despite the availability of autos and pumps, the classic 270 is a sleek bolt-action, preferably with a classic-style stock. The cartridge made its place in shooting history by way of its ability to reach way out yonder and smack game, with little fuss at the butt end and scant allowance for holdover. Just how flat is the 270 compared to other popular cartridges? Well, the respected 7mm Mauser, in use for nearly 100 years on all types of animals in every country in the world, drops 10 inches at 250 yards and 19.1 inches at 300 when zeroed at 150 yards with the standard 175-grain soft point. The flatter-shooting 308 Winchester, zeroed at 200 yards with a 150-grain spitzer, drops 3.6 inches at 250, 9.1 at 300 yards. The 30-06 is flatter yet, showing a mere 3.3-inch drop at 250 yards, 8.5 at 300, both with 150-grain bullet and 200-yard zero. The 270, using its most popular load, the 130-grain spitzer, drops only 2.8 and 7.1 inches at the above ranges from a 200-yard zero. That, my friends, is *flat*.

Retained energies at 300 yards are: 998 foot-pounds for the 175-grain 7mm Mauser; 1344 foot pounds for the 150-grain 308; 1445 foot pounds for the 30-06 150-grain; and 1565 foot pounds for the 270 with a 130-grain spitzer at 3060 fps muzzle speed. I realize, of course,

that I could choose different bullet weights to show different figures, but the comparison will remain about the same. The 30-06 will show higher retained energies at long ranges than any 270 factory load if the 180-grain spitzer is chosen. The same could be said of the fine 30-06 200-grain Federal soft point boat-tail, but the 270 still shoots flatter with comparable loads, kicks less, and hits nearly as hard. If I were going after game up to caribou in weight, I'd opt for the 270 over all others if striking energy and flat trajectory were the prime considerations. For elk, moose, or the larger bruins, I'd rather have a 30-06. Or a 338 Winchester Magnum.

For hunting at extreme ranges, of animals of 200 pounds or less in average weight such as mule deer and pronghorns, I can think of no better cartridge than the 270 Winchester. The 284 Winchester is its near equal (but not quite); the 280 Remington is full equal (though it kicks a tad more); the 25-06 shoots a little flatter (and hits with less authority); the 257 Roberts, 7mm Mauser, 7mm-08 Remington, and the 308 are definitely inferior ballistically.

Windy-country varmint shooting is not the 270's speciality, but only two other cartridges compete with it in popularity when the strong breezes flow— the 6mm Remington and the 25-06. All three shoot fast and flat with bullets of high ballistic coefficients, bucking the wind with the tenacity of a determined dowager intent on walking her poodle. All three hit with enough punch at 400 yards to expand their bullets for a clean kill. All three have a good bit of recoil — the 270 most of all — for shirtsleeve varminting.

And thus we cover the 270's bailiwick. It is a fine but hard-kicking varmint round, a nigh-perfect long-range cartridge for deer-sized beasts, an acceptable load for forest game approaching 400 pounds, (handicapped only by an overall length that necessitates the use of a long-action rifle), and it is adequate under most conditions for elk and moose. It's been around exactly as long as public radio, and it seems to be almost as popular. Like its long-time mentor, Jack O'Conner, it is competent at its job, respected by those familiar with it, and has traveled to many lonely isolated, romantic locales. Long may it live.

Until recently discontinued, the 100-grain factory Remington ammo was often used on vermin. Winchester made a similar 100-grain load for years, but it, too, bit the dust.

270 Winchester

HANDLOAD DATA

Bullet Wt. Grs.	Type	Powder Wt. Grs.	Type	Primer	Case	MV (fps)	ME (fpe)	Rifle/ Bbl. (in.)	Remarks
90	Sierra JHP	55.0	IMR 4350	Fed. 210	Win.	2965	1757	Rem. M700/22	Most acc. ld. this gun
90	Sierra JHP	55.0	IMR 4350	Rem. 9½	Fed.	2857	1632	Ruger No. 1 RSI/20	Very accurate
90	Sierra JHP	55.4	H380	Rem. 9½ M	Fed.	3307	2186	Rem. M700/22	Accurate
90	Sierra JHP	**61.0**	IMR 4350	Fed. 210	Fed.	**3450**	**2379**	Rem. M700/22	Accurate and fast
100	Speer JHP	**59.9**	IMR 4350	Rem. 9½ M	Win.	**3268**	**2372**	Win. M70/22	Very accurate
110	Hrndy. JHP	51.0	IMR 4064	CCI 200	Fed.	3130	2394	Rem. M700/22	Accurate
130	Sierra SP	**49.0**	IMR 4064	8½-120	Fed.	**2895**	**2420**	Ruger No. 1 RSI/20	Most acc. ld. this gun
130	Sierra SP	54.7	IMR 4350	Rem. 9½ M	Win.	2943	2450	Win. M70/22	Accurate
130	Nosler SB	**55.0**	IMR 4350	Rem. 9½	Fed.	**2884**	**2401**	Ruger No. 1 RSI/20	————
150	Sierra SPBT	51.6	H4350	8½-120	Fed.	2625	2295	Ruger No. 1 RSI/20	Very accurate

JHP—Jacketed Hollow Point; SP—Soft Point; SPBT—Soft Point Boat-Tail; SB—Solid Base.

CAUTION:
Loads recommended and suggested herein have been carefully listed, but are intended solely as a guide to readers and neither the publisher nor author accept any responsibility for results of their use.
Maximum loads, listed in bold, should be reduced by 10 percent and worked up to cautiously.

FACTORY LOAD DATA

Bullet Wt. Grs.	Type	MV (fps)	ME (fpe)	Rifle/ Bbl. (in.)	Remarks
100	Rem. PSP	3055	2073	Rem. M700/22	Fair accuracy
100	Fron. JHP	2990	2184	Ruger No. 1 RSI/20	Accurate
100	Win. PSP	3370	2769	Rem. M700/22	2nd most acc. ld. this rifle
100	Win. PSP	3277	2617	Win. M70/22	Very accurate
130	Fron. SP	2716	2129	Ruger No. 1 RSI/20	————
130	Win. SP	2964	2535	Win. M70/22	Poor accuracy
130	Win. SP	2919	2459	Rem. M700/22	Very accurate
130	Fed. Prem. SPBT	2918	2457	Ruger M77/22	Fair accuracy
130	Fed. Prem. SPBT	2954	2518	Win. M70/22	Very accurate
140	Fron. SPBT	2633	2156	Ruger No. 1 RSI/20	Fair accuracy
150	Fron. SP	2588	2229	Ruger No. 1 RSI/20	Fair accuracy
150	Fed. Prem. NP	2742	2505	Ruger No. 1 RSI/20	Fair accuracy
150	Fed. Prem. SPBT	2766	2547	Ruger M77/22	————
150	Fed. Prem. SPBT	2813	2637	Win. M70/22	Most acc. ld. this rifle
150	Fed. Prem. SPBT	2814	2639	Rem. M700-C/24	Very accurate
150	Fed. Prem. SPBT	2848	2703	Sako M74/24½	Good accuracy

PSP—Pointed Soft Point; JHP—Jacketed Hollow Point; SP—Soft Point; SPBT—Soft Point Boat-Tail; NP—Nosler Partition.

SPECIFICATIONS

Shell Holders
  RCBS: 3
  Bonanza: 1
  Lyman: 2
  Pacific: 1

Bullet Diameter
  Jacketed: .227"

Lengths
  Trim: 2.530"
  Maximum Case: 2.540"
  Maximum Overall: 3.340"

The 270 Winchester was famed gun writer Jack O'Conner's favorite elk cartridge. In the eyes of many, the 270 is the finest deer-class cartridge to ever see the light of day.

CAUTION:
Loads recommended and suggested herein have been carefully listed, but are intended solely as a guide to readers and neither the publisher nor author accept any responsibility for results of their use. **Maximum loads, listed in bold, should be reduced by 10 percent and worked up to cautiously.**

270 Weatherby Magnum

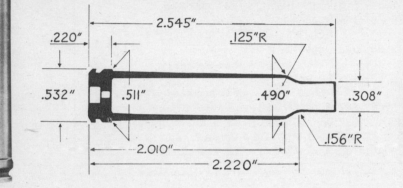

"For long-range shooting of mule deer, caribou, or pronghorn, I'd take the 270 Weatherby over any larger caliber having a belted case."

ASIDE from the 270 Winchester, the only other cartridge available in this country taking bullets of .277-inch diameter is the 270 Weatherby Magnum. The Weatherby cartridge is not a great deal younger than the 270 Winchester itself, something less than 2 decades. Sometime during WWII, Roy Weatherby began experiments with a shortened, necked-down 300 Holland & Holland case, choosing the 270-caliber as his testbed. Results were encouraging. The 270 Weatherby was actually introduced before the famous 300 Weatherby Magnum, not the other way around as is commonly thought.

Also erroneous is the notion that the 270 and 300 Weatherby Magnums share the same case. Not so. The 270 shares its brass with the 257 and 7mm Weatherby cartridges, and has a length of 2.545 inches compared to the 2.820-inch length of the 300 and 340 Weatherby Magnums. The 270 Weatherby has a capacity similar to that of the 264 Winchester Magnum and the 7mm Remington Magnum. The Weatherby cartridge accepts larger doses of propellant because of the long throating common to Weatherby rifles. (This long throat used to be termed "free bore," although the newer Weatherby rifles show much less of it than they used to.)

Is the 270 Weatherby popular? Not if compared to the 270 Winchester, but it is as far as Weatherby cartridges go, ranking second in the Weatherby line. That kind of surprised me a little; I figured the 7mm for number-two slot. Tom Hall of Weatherby tells me different.

Let's glance at the factory-quoted ballistics for the 270 Weatherby, as taken in a 26-inch barrel.

The 100-grain pointed expanding:
Muzzle velocity, 3760 fps; 100 yards, 3341 fps; 200-yards, 2949 fps; 300-yards, 2585 fps. Muzzle energy, 3140 fpe; 100-yards, 2479 fpe; 200-yards, 1932 fpe; 300-yards, 1484 fpe.

The 130-grain pointed expanding:
Muzzle velocity, 3375 fps; 100-yards, 3110 fps; 200-yards, 2856 fps; 300-yards, 2615 fps. Muzzle energy, 3289 fpe; 100-yards, 2793 fpe; 200-yards, 2355 fpe; 300-yards, 1974 fpe.

The 150-grain pointed expanding:
Muzzle velocity, 3245 fps; 100-yards, 3012 fps; 200-yards, 2789 fps; 300-yards, 2575 fps. Muzzle energy, 3508 fpe; 100-yards, 3022 fpe; 200-yards, 2592 fpe; 300-yards, 2209 fpe.

To see how closely those figures jibed with normal ammo in a hunting rifle, I clocked each weight in a 26-inch barreled Weatherby Mark V. The 100-grain pointed expanding chronographed 3670 fps for 2991 fpe. The 130-grain pointed expanding showed a 3307 fps average and 3158 fpe. The 150-grain pointed expanding read off 3183 fps, 3375 fpe. (I use the antiquated term "pointed

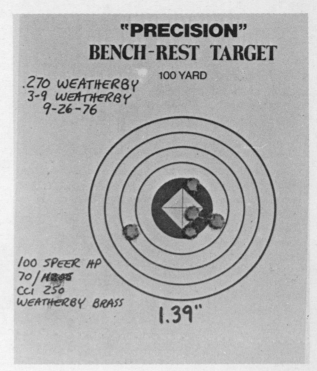

"PRECISION"
BENCH-REST TARGET
100 YARD

.270 WEATHERBY
3-9 WEATHERBY
9-26-76

100 SPEER HP
70/H205
CCI 250
WEATHERBY BRASS

1.39"

This particular five-shot group is representative of the 270 Weatherby's accuracy potential. The group was fired from 100 yards and measures 1.39 inches.

expanding" because Weatherby does, to distinguish that projectile from the Nosler which is also loaded in Weatherby cartridges.) That is 90 fps short with the 100-grain slug, 68 fps down with the 130-grain bullet, and 62 fps shy with the 150-grain bullet. The average for all weights was 73 fps on the deficit side.

In *Handloader* magazine's March-April, 1983, issue, Ken Waters listed his chronograph testing of a 24-inch barreled German-built Mark V. Ken achieved the following: 100-grain bullet, 3615 fps; 130-grain bullet, 3370 fps; 150-grain bullet, 3206 fps. Ken's ammo averaged 47 fps faster than did mine, across the weight range. This is normal; I've clocked various lots of many cartridges that showed a much broader disparity than that.

In fact, in the May-June, 1976, *Handloader,* Bob Hagel showed the 130-grain factory load as giving 3230 fps in his sample 24-inch barreled Mark V. That's much slower than either mine or Ken's. The Speer Number Nine loading manual shows the 150-grain load at 3425 fps in a 26½-inch barreled custom 270 Weatherby Magnum, considerably swifter than any of our rifles. And so forth. Guns vary, ammo varies, conditions change, temperatures, chronographs, *ad infinitum.*

Regardless of which figures you go by, the Weatherby cartridge stomps the 270 Winchester pretty thoroughly. The fastest 270 loads I've ever checked read like this: 100-grain bullet, 3370 fps in factory persuasion, 3455 fps for handloads; 130-grain bullet, 2964 fps in factory form, 2943 fps for handloads; 150-grain bul-

The 270 Weatherby Magnum (right) possesses a slightly longer case (and a radiused shoulder) when compared to the Remington 7mm Magnum (left).

270 Weatherby Magnum: Deer/Bear

From left to right: 100-grain Speer JHP; 130-grain Hornady SP; 150-grain Sierra SPBT. All three of these .277-inch diameter slugs have proven to be accurate, reliable performers in the author's Mark V 270 Weatherby.

The author's test Weatherby Mk. V in 270 Weatherby Magnum is the most accurate "magnum" rifle the author ever fired. Groups of 1¼ inches, at 100 yards, are not uncommon.

The 270 Weatherby will handle bullets from 100 to 130 grs. while the newer 1-in-10 twist Mark Vs will do well with the heavier slugs.

let, 2848 fps for the factory stuff.

I realize that these figures are slower than you may be used to seeing, but my 270s obviously aren't as fast as everyone else's. Except perhaps, for the 100-grain slugs. The current Speer manual shows only 3362 fps with the same weight, and the Lyman No. 44 only 3436 fps in a 26-inch test barrel. (Both figures are for the fastest loads listed.)

How does the 270 Weatherby stack up against another close competitor, the 264 Winchester Magnum? The Speer Number Nine manual gives this data, derived from a 26-inch barreled Model 70 Winchester: 140-grain Winchester soft point, 3139 fps; 140-grain Remington SP, 3025 fps. In a 24-inch barreled Model 700 Remington, these are the numbers: 100-grain Winchester soft point, 3390 fps; 140-grain Winchester SP, 3077; 140-grain Remington SP, 3039. As might be construed, the 264 Magnum seems a mite watered-down. It runs a short second to the 270 Weatherby, at least with the lots mentioned.

The 7mm Remington Magnum comes closer. In my 24-inch barreled Interarms Whitworth, I got this: 125-grain Winchester soft point, 3293 fps; 150-grain Winchester SP, 3089 fps; 150-grain Norma SPBT, 3155 fps; 175-grain Remington PCL, 2825 fps. Thus, in the 7mm Rem.-Mag., the 125-grain load was only 14 fps abaft of the 130-grain 270 Weatherby, and in a shorter barrel at

that. The 150-grain Norma 7mm factory load was hot on the heels of the 270 Weatherby, 3155 to 3183 fps. The extra 2 inches of pipe definitely made the difference. Let's say that the 270 Weatherby and the 7mm Remington Magnum are in a dead heat.

The 7mm Weatherby is another story. I clocked the 139-grain factory load at 3227, the 154-grain at 3132, and the 175-grain at a sizzling 2985 fps, all from a 24-inch barreled Mark V. Since none of the bullet weights match, let's look at muzzle energy for the story on delivered power. With its lightest bullet, the 270 Weatherby managed 2991 fpe; with its lightest slug, the 7mm Weatherby showed 3208 fpe. Big difference. Turning to mid-weight loads, the 270 carried 3151 fpe with its 130-grain soft point; the 154-grain bullet in the 7mm Weatherby Magnum got 3348 fpe. The 270 is still in arrears. Comparing the 150-grain 270 slug to the 154-grain 7mm Weatherby Magnum slug leaves the 270 on the winning side, 3373 fpe to the 7mm's 3348 fpe. But switch to the heaviest 7mm load with its 175-grain slug, and the 28-caliber is back on top at a thundering 3462 fpe.

And that about tells the story of the 7mm Magnums versus the smaller 270 Weatherby. Until the weight climbs past 160 grains or so, the 270 Weatherby stays in there kicking. But load up with the big 175-grain bullet and it's all over but the crying. That is exactly what the late Warren Page claimed for years: It's the heavy bullet

Reloading the big 270 Weatherby is not a difficult task. Just be sure to use a press that has sufficient leverage to handle the big case. The Bonanza Co-Ax seen here is ideal for sizing large, belted cases.

(Left) In the wide-open spaces of the West, the 270 Weatherby is a winner on mule deer. The cartridge really shines when the shooting distance stretches out to three or four football fields.

that makes the big seven the *Big Seven*.

Incidentally, my one and only 270 Weatherby leads me to believe the cartridge is nearly as accurate as its brother, the 270 Winchester. My Mark V grouped 1.22 inches for an average with the 130-grain factory load, and 1.37 inches with the varmint-weight permutation. My top handload printed 1.10 inches, the runner-up 1.24 inches, and the third-place finisher still grouped into 1.27 inches for several five-shot strings. That is *accurate,* folks. Remember that the Mark V has a relatively skinny barrel, and remember also that the 270 Weatherby Mag. uses nigh a cupful of propellant at every discharge. That slender barrel gets hot damn quick.

Want verification? In the aforementioned *Handloader* article by Ken Waters, I found this:

The accuracy produced by the slim barrel of this rifle despite the intense heat generated in firing five-shot groups was a continual source of wonder to me. Minute-and-a-half [1½-inch] groups were commonplace, and spreads as small as one to one and quarter minutes [an inch to 1¼ inches] . . . were frequent.

In the *Handloader* piece by Hagel:

. . . the new style 160-grain semi-pointed Nosler, which is slightly longer than the 170-grain Speer round nose, gave beautiful groups that ran an average of just over 1-inch. [I believe these were three-shot groups.]

The ultra-slow powders work best in the 270 Weatherby, which should come as no shock. Such numbers as IMR 4350, Winchester 760, Hodgdon H450 and H4350 work well with the lighter bullets, say up to 110 grains, although H450 handles the heavier weights as well. IMR 4831, Norma MRP, Winchester 785, and Hodgdon H4831 and H870 perform best in the heavyweights, with H870 at its peak with those slugs of 160 grains and up. (Incidentally, some older 270 Weatherby rifles have a 1-in-12 twist and will not stabilize bullets heavier than 150 grains. The guns built since 1973, I understand, have 1-in-10 barrels.)

One of my best, most accurate handloads, was 76.0 grains of the great Norma MRP pushing the 100-grain Speer hollow point. Groups were tight and the muzzle speed was a spectacular 3656 fps, nearly as quick as the factory stuff of the same weight.

The best all-around handload consisted of 72.0 grains of MRP and the 130-grain Hornady spire point, yielding groups around 1¼ inches and speeds of 3353 fps, for 3246 fpe. Amazingly, that handload was faster than the 130-grain factory load, something not easy to achieve in the Weatherby magnum cartridge in my experience.

It should also be said that the *worst* groups that rifle shot averaged just over 1⅝ inches. That is truly amazing, and the best performance I have ever received from a magnum rifle regardless of brand or caliber. (Discounting the 222 Remington Magnum, of course, which is no more a magnum than my grandmother was Cleveland Amory.) My two other Mark Vs, a 7mm and a 257 Weatherby Mag., shoot about as well as the 270; the 7mm goes 1.27 inches with its pet handload, and the 257 exactly the same with the 100-grain factory load. (Why do Mark V rifles tend to shoot so well?)

I don't see much in the current sporting press about the 270 Weatherby Magnum. Did the old-timers write about it? In *The Rifle* Book, Jack O'Conner had this to say:

> The 270 Weatherby Magnum is more popular than the 7mm [Weatherby] Magnum, but probably a bit less efficient, as that hole in the barrel is a bit small for the powder capacity. However, it is an excellent long-range cartridge. Most widely used load [two decades ago] is 65 grains of [IMR] 4350 with the 130-grain bullet for 3,300.

One writer who isn't exactly an old-timer, although he knows whereof he speaks in the hunting and shooting field, is Bob Hagel. In his book *Game Loads and Practical Ballistics for the American Hunter*, he wrote of the 270 Weatherby Magnum:

> For long shots at heavy game the 270 Weatherby is a better choice than either the 270 Winchester or the 264 [Winchester Magnum]. The 270 Weatherby Magnum will start a 150-gr. bullet just as fast as the 270 Winchester starts the 130-gr. if you use the right powder in both. In fact, there are several of the slower powders that will give the 150-gr. over 3150 fps from a 24″ barrel and the very slow H-870 spherical powder will send it along at 3200 fps without excessive pressures . . . In fact, due to the high velocity attained with the 270 Weatherby with all bullet weights, anything except bullets with full ex-

pansion control like Nosler should not be used for shooting heavy game at any range, because of the liklihood of bullet breakup.

As for me, if I were planning to carry a rifle as big and heavy as the Mark V after game the size of elk, I'd about as soon have the 270 Weatherby as anything else. Offered my druthers, I'd choose either of the popular 7mm magnums stoked with the 175-grain Nosler Partition. Relieved of that choice, I'd toss a coin between any of the above three cartridges, stick a 150- or 160-grain Nosler Partition in the case, and care not what legend was stamped on the barrel. As Jack O'Connor was wont to say, any real difference between the three would reside in the imagination.

For long-range shooting of mule deer, caribou, or pronghorn, I'd take the 270 Weatherby over any larger caliber having a belted case. Ditto if hunting whitetails from a tree stand overlooking considerable acreage.

Although accuracy is sufficient, and the recoil not unbearable even in shirt-sleeves, I'd eschew the 270 Magnum if in pursuit of vermin unless I had only the one rifle and was bound for only an occasional hunt. Too loud. Too long and heavy to tote far on foot. Barrel heats up too rapidly. The 270 Weatherby is a big-game load, not a prairie dog demolisher.

As magnum cartridges go, the 270 Weatherby Magnum is pretty versatile. I find the impressive accuracy its most endearing feature. But I'm lazy; I don't like to carry more cargo than I absolutely must. However, for the nimrod who drives to within a couple hundred yards of his stand, and is likely to be offered shots at game three or four football fields distant, the 270 Weatherby is hard to beat.

270 Weatherby Magnum

HANDLOAD DATA

Bullet		Powder				MV	ME	Rifle/	
Wt. Grs.	Type	Wt. Grs.	Type	Primer	Case	(fps)	(fpe)	Bbl. (in.)	Remarks
100	Speer JHP	76.0	MRP	Fed. 215	Wby.	3656	2969	Wby. Mk. V/26	Fastest load tested
130	Hrndy. SP	72.0	MRP	Fed. 215	Wby.	3353	3246	Wby. Mk. V/26	Extremely accurate
150	Sierra SPBT	67.0	Win. 785	Fed. 215	Wby.	2957	2912	Wby. Mk. V/26	Consistent velocity
150	Sierra SPBT	69.0	MRP	Fed. 215	Wby.	3165	3337	Wby. Mk.V/26	Highest energy any load

JHP—Jacketed Hollow Point; SP—Soft Point; SPBT—Soft Point Boat-Tail.

FACTORY LOAD DATA

Bullet		MV	ME	Rifle/	
Wt. Grs.	Type	(fps)	(fpe)	Bbl. (in.)	Remarks
100	Wby. SP	3670	2991	Wby. Mk. V/26	Very accurate
100	Wby. SP	3307	3151	Wby. Mk. V/26	Most accurate
150	Wby. SP	3183	3373	Wby. Mk. V/26	Accurate

SP—Soft Point.

SPECIFICATIONS

Shell Holders
RCBS: 4
Bonanza: 2
Lyman: 13
Pacific: 5

Bullet Diameter
Jacketed: .277"

Lengths
Trim: 2.540"
Maximum Case: 2.545"
Maximum Overall: 3.250"

In searching for load data for the 270 Weatherby Magnum, or any other cartridge, the handloader should build a library of loading manuals. Lyman gives the shooter "Accuracy" and "Factory Duplication" loads.

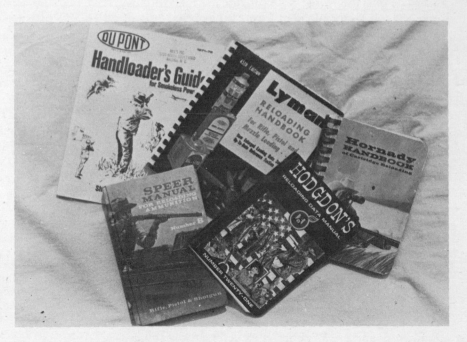

CAUTION:
Loads recommended and suggested herein have been carefully listed, but are intended solely as a guide to readers and neither the publisher nor author accept any responsibility for results of their use.
Maximum loads, listed in bold, should be reduced by 10 percent and worked up to cautiously.

7mm-08 Remington

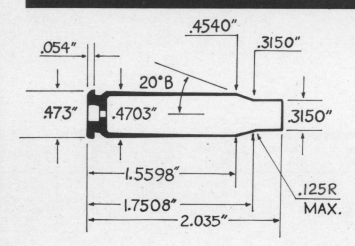

.4540"
.054"
.3150"
20°B
.473"   .4703"
.3150"
1.5598"
.125R
MAX.
1.7508"
2.035"

> **"The 7mm-08 has attained a fair amount of popularity during its brief life as a factory round, but it hasn't received the attention or the positive press it deserves."**

AS I write this, the 7mm-08 Remington has been with us for 4 years in factory-loaded form. It has been around for quite some time in wildcat guise and was used extensively by metallic silhouette competitors as such. Remington pretty well had the 7mm bore size to itself with the 280 Remington (7mm Express Remington) and the immensely popular 7mm Remington Magnum, so another horse in the stable was a logical move. Of course there are 28-caliber cartridges that bear not the Bridgeport name, such as the ubiquitous 7x57 Mauser, the dying but excellent 284 Winchester, and the reasonably popular but proprietary 7mm Weatherby Magnum, but the Remington offerings cover the ground pretty well.

The 7mm-08 has attained a fair amount of popularity during its brief life as a factory round, but it hasn't received the attention or the positive press it deserves. Of course, all the stuff printed about the 7mm-08 hasn't been negative. In the 1981 *Gun Digest,* Layne Simpson had this to say: "Some will surely say that the 7mm-08 should have a longer barrel [than 18½ inches] but I disagree. With cartridges such as the 7mm Express [280 Remington] and 270 Winchester available in longer barrels, I see no need for it, but I do see a need for a quick handling, accurate and compact bolt-action carbine, chambered for a flat-shooting cartridge." Amen.

Layne went on to compare the performance of the 7mm-08 to a wildcat 7mm cartridge he designed, based on the 308 Winchester (as is the 7mm-08). He wrote: "I

have two rifles chambered for this wildcat . . . Thus far, these two rifles have accounted for 16 big game animals such as moose, deer, pronghorn and greater kudu, with the expenditure of 19 cartridges. I'm saying all this to say that I know what a short 7mm cartridge will do on big game and am no stranger to handloading the efficient little rascal."

Further on, this from Layne: "For heavier or tougher game, such as black bear, the 139-grain Hornady, 140-grain Sierra, and the 145-grain Speer . . . will perform out to a *good 400 yards* when started at 2800 fps from the shorty carbine(s)." (Italics mine.)

With his usual insightful approach, Layne concludes:

> There will be wild claims about the amazing performance of the 7mm-08 and others that label it just short of useless for big game shooting. Somewhere between these two extremes sits the mild-mannered 7mm-08.
> Perhaps the 7mm-08 Remington can be called a modern, souped-up version of the 7x57 Mauser as it certainly lives up to that name in performance. That's not a bad pedigree to hang on the runt of Remington's litter.

Well said.

Want more? Okay. In the November-December, 1980, issue of *Handloader* magazine, Ken Waters began an article this way:

> At the risk of inviting the oft-heard criticism of writers who praise new products, I'm going to say flat-out

From left to right: the 7mm-08; the 7x57 Mauser (ballistically close to the 7mm-08); the 284 Winchester (the only other factory 7mm cartridge that will work in short actions); the 280 Remington and the 7mm Remington Magnum.

that Remington's 7mm-08 is one of the finest, most practical, and useful cartridges for the average hunter that it has been my good fortune to work with . . .

There's been much shooting from the hip in recent stories about this cartridge. It's new, and the lack of tested load data, I suppose, induced some early reviewers to make assumptions based upon logic rather than upon thorough trials. This has led to a number of erroneous conclusions.

Using two 7x57mm rifles—a Model 1909 Venezuelan Mauser and a Savage Model 111 sporter—I was unable to equal 7mm-08 velocities with the military rifle, probably because of the freebore effect of the long military chamber throat, and with heavy loads in the Savage was able to beat the fastest load with the 160-grain bullet in the 7mm-08 by just 7 fps . . . Most loads I tried in the 7x57mm Mauser produced *lower* velocities despite the use of heavier charges.

So let's set the record straight before going on to other matters. The 7x57 Mauser, if loaded to maximum pressure levels (by modern standards, not SAAMI specs) in strong, current rifles, can shade the similarly-loaded 7mm-08 by from 50 to 100 fps at most. As we've seen, in some rifles the ancient Mauser creation won't equal the 7mm-08 regardless of pressure. And domestic factory-loaded 7x57 ammo, because of its lower pressure limits, won't come close to equaling the 7mm-08 factory stuff.

Performance

So just what will the seven-oh-eight do? Currently, the only factory load available is the Remington 140-grain pointed soft point. In my 18½-inch-barreled Remington Model 7, this factory load churned up 2741 fps for 2335 fpe. A Savage Model 110-S silhouette rifle with 22-inch tube got 2801 fps for 2440 fpe, and a similar-length Browning BBR clocked 2807 fps for 2449 fpe. In a 24-inch barreled Remington Model 700 Varmint, the same lot of ammo chronographed 2895 fps for 2605 fpe, while a different lot produced 2937 fps and 2681 fpe.

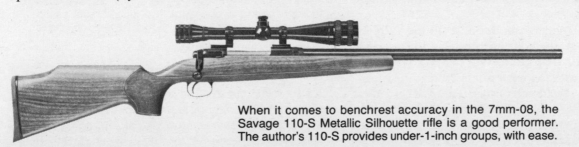

When it comes to benchrest accuracy in the 7mm-08, the Savage 110-S Metallic Silhouette rifle is a good performer. The author's 110-S provides under-1-inch groups, with ease.

7mm-08 Remington: Deer/Bear

The author's Model Seven Remington 7mm-08 is very accurate, grouping into less than 1¾ inches with several loads, from the bench at 100 yards.

Bear in mind that factory-quoted ballistics are 2860 fps from a 24-inch barrel.

My 7x57 Model 70 Featherweight gave the following factory-ammo figures from its 22-inch barrel: 140-grain Federal PSP, 2613 fps for 2123 fpe; 140-grain Remington PSP, 2613 fps for 2123 fpe; 150-grain Norma SP, 2720 fps for 2464 fpe; 175-grain Federal RN, 2390 fps for 2219 fpe. Note that only with the hot Norma loading did the 7mm Mauser keep pace with the 7mm-08 loading in barrels of the same length.

I've even clocked 280 Remington factory ammunition that didn't exactly embarrass the 7mm-08. In a 22-inch barrel Remington Model 7400, the 150-grain factory Remington load gave 2673 fps for 2379 fpe; the 165-grain Remington RN load gave 2631 fps for 2536 fpe. That makes the little 7mm-08 look pretty potent after all.

With handloads, the following 7mm-08 velocities are easily achieved: from 115-grain bullets, 3200 fps-plus; with 120-grain slugs, 2960 fps or better; the 130-grain class will reach nearly 2900 fps; the 139-140 groups will show over 2800 fps with ease; the long 160-grain boat-tails will crowd 2800 fps with the 170-grain bullets surpassing 2450. All the foregoing data assume barrels of 22 inches or longer except for the 130-grain example, which was clocked in my 18½-inch barreled Model 7. I'd suspect that 3000 fps would be handily within reach in a 22-inch tube, using the 130-grain load listed in the accompanying chart.

My 22-inch Winchester 7x57 has managed the following speeds: 139-140-grain class, 2920 fps; the 150-grain about 2680 fps; the 160-grain boat-tails will reach a little over 2600.

Energy levels range from about 2340 fpe with the lighter (130-139-grain) bullets in the 7mm-08, to 2735 fpe with the heavy 160-grain slugs. The 7x57 exhibits around 2630 fpe with the lighter deer bullets and roughly 2425 fpe with the heavier ones. The two cartridges are obviously dancing at the same church social when it comes to velocity and energy levels.

How about trajectory? As you might expect, the two are neck and neck in the stretched-string sweepstakes. Using the 140 Nosler Solid Base for comparitive purposes, with the 7mm-08 kicking it along at 2800 fps and the 7x57 managing 2900, we find that the faster load shoots .2-inch flatter getting to 200 yards, drops .6-inch less out at 300, and is down 1.7 inches less at 400 yards than the more leisurely load, all assuming a 200-yard zero and scope sight. Really pronounced difference, right? Right.

Things reverse when we switch to the 160-grain Sierra spitzer boat-tail at 2600 fps in the 7x57 Mauser and an easy 2700 fps in the 7mm-08. The swifter load shows .2-inch less rise making it to 200 yards, drops .7-inch less at 300 yards, and plunges 2.1 fewer inches at four football fields away.

The only real difference you'll detect between the 7x57 and the 7mm-08 is how much handier the rifles are when chambered to the shorter round. And how much lighter. And how much easier they squeeze through brushy terrain. And with what snap and vigor they jump to your shoulder.

Enough dry ballistics, a surfeit of comparisons. The 7mm-08 doesn't need to be compared to other loads; it can stand well enough on its own. You will look hard to find a better deer cartridge, all things considered, than the 7mm-08. It is mild of bark at the front end and push at the rear, while delivering more energy than you need for the largest deer, black bear, or bighorn sheep that ever walked. As a reloader's cartridge, it is efficient, tolerant of varying propellants and bullet weights, and pleasant enough for use on off-season varmints. For elk at reasonable distances, it has punch to spare if the proper bullets are chosen and rear-end shots are avoided. Quite a resumé.

Accuracy

As a target cartridge, the 7mm-08 has well entrenched itself among the iron-chicken shooters. There is a plenitude of reasons. The load offers an abundance of knockdown punch for the heavy steel plates, even

(Above) One of the most beautiful 7mm-08 factory rifles you can buy is Remington's Model 700 Custom bolt-action. The fit, finish and execution is superb, the accuracy top notch.

(Right) Who says light sporters can't shoot? This five-shot group was fired *offhand* from 100 yards and measures 5¼ inches. The rifle used was a Remington Model Seven in 7mm-08.

way out at 500 meters. When a 168-grain Sierra Matchking is kicked along at about 2600 fps, for example, retained energy at 500 yards is just shy of 1400 fpe. For reference, that's superior to *anything* Remington factory-loads in the 30-06, including the streamlined 180-grain Bronze Point, by more than 200 fpe. You thought the seven-oh-eight wouldn't shoot flat?

On the other hand, Remington's littlest Seven doesn't drill holes through target plates like one of the big magnums. Such anti-social behavior will get you invited away from a range in short order. Being bereft of a magnum cartridge's hitting power at the front end, naturally the 7mm-08 has a concomitantly pleasant shove at the back end. It neither loosens your bridgework nor puckers your rhomboid muscles.

As might be expected, intrinsic accuracy is present in prodigious quantities. Metallic silhouette shooters wouldn't have taken to the cartridge so readily if it were not precise indeed. I have two heavy-barreled 7mm-08s, a Savage Model 110-S and a Remington Model 700-V. I've not had them long, so tests are still proceeding. To date, the Savage has grouped as tight as .75-inch with 43.5 grains of Hodgdon's H380 under the 145-grain Speer Gold Match boat-tail and will average .96-inch. The Remington Varmint Special has printed down to .86-inch so far, but won't quite hold it for an average. As I said, work proceeds apace.

My Browning BBR Lightning Bolt prints 1⅝ inches with its favored recipe, 46.0 grains of IMR 4064 and the 115-grain Speer hollow point, designed for vermin hunting. The same load manages 1.69 inches in my Remington Model 7 lightweight; it's also the most accurate load, to date, in that rifle.

I must admit the accuracy of my four 7mm-08 rifles has not equaled the average levels usually provided by its parent case, the 308 Winchester. At least not yet. My Remington 700-V averages .74-inch in the 30-caliber; a Winchester Model 70-T 308 prints about the same; my 40-XB stays under .40-inch if I'm up to it; my Savage 110-S 308 will shoot into .89-inch on average; one of my

Du Pont's IMR 4895 is a superb powder for most 7mm-08 uses. Gunwriter Layne Simpson used this propellant to take a "First" in a "Hunter Class" benchrest match. The rifle was an *out-of-the-box* Remington Model 788 in 7mm-08!

7mm-08 Remington: Deer/Bear

All of the propellants seen here are suitable for the 7mm-08. Hodgdon's H380 provides the best accuracy in the author's Savage 110-S, with IMR 4064 proving best in his Remington Model Seven and 700-V.

Bullets such as these are excellent choices for the 7mm-08. The 140-gr. Nosler Partition, and 130-gr. Speer soft point are suitable for medium-size game; the Speer 160-gr. Grand Slam for larger game.

Ruger Model 77-Varmint guns clusters into .93-inch for the mean. Even my light-barreled Colt-Sauer 308 has averaged .86-inch for eight, five-shot strings. No, none of my seven-oh-eights has eclipsed such performances yet, but I have great expectations.

The best propellants for the 7mm-08 start with IMR 4064 on the fast side and go to Winchester 760, Hodgdon H205 and H380, and IMR 4350 on the slow-burning end. For accuracy, H380 and IMR 4064 are tough to beat. For speed I like 4064 and Winchester 760. For high velocity coupled with adequate accuracy, I'd choose Winchester 760 and never look back. Of course there are many other powders that are far from worthless in this little case, but these are my favorites.

When selecting bullets, we must first settle on our primary purpose. For varmint gunning, the 115-grain Speer hollow point is my first choice. It's accurate and expands well, even on relatively light resistance. Started at about 3200 fps, or a tad more, 300-yard drop is only 7.2 inches from a 200-yard zero, about like 130-grain factory loads in the 270 Winchester and considerably flatter than the 222 Remington factory stuff.

The 120-grain Nosler Solid Base would be my backup choice on varmints. My Browning handles it well and moves it out the muzzle not much shy of 2900 fps.

For deer-sized game at ranges long and short, I'd be happy with whatever slug shot well in my rifle and weighed between 139 and 150 grains. The 140-grain Nosler Solid Base and 145-grain Speer soft point boattail are particular favorites of mine. On animals just a little tougher than deer, but in the same class—like black bear and caribou—I'd load my ammo with either the 140-grain Nosler Partition or the 154-grain Hornady soft point. For deer and black bear in heavy cover, I'd consider the 170-grain Sierra round-nose soft point kicked along at 2330 fps-plus.

If I were after elk or moose, I'd load the 160-grain Speer Grand Slam if ranges were expected to be under 250 yards or so, and opt for the 160-grain Nosler Partition if I anticipated an occasional long-range opportunity. Although I might not turn tail and run from a grizzly if armed with one of my 7mm-08 rifles, I sure wouldn't seek one out. In fact, if I were after elk or moose specifically, I'd prefer something a little bigger than a 7mm-08 as my first choice.

The 7mm-08 wasn't designed as an elk cartridge, although it will do a good job on one if a good bullet is stuck in the proper place. Just as the 270 will. The "Little Seven" wasn't intended to be the last word as a silhouette load, but it will certainly slap a ram down with authority. Just like a 308. For plains game such as pronghorn antelope, the 7mm-08 isn't the *ne plus ultra,* but it will reach out 400 yards across a sage flat and deal a decisive blow to a buck's vitals, while dropping only about 21 inches from a normal zero. Just like a 25-06 Remington factory big game load. And it will start a 175-grain Nosler Partition at around 2500 fps, drive it deep into a bear's shoulder, smashing and tearing along the way. Just like a 7mm Mauser. All without using a cupful of powder, without rendering your eardrums useless tissue, without pulping your shoulder. All from a cartridge case that is *sans* a belt, isn't as lengthy as a cane pole, doesn't wear a fancy title like Swift or Magnum or Bone-Crusher. A modest little number. And a very good one.

7mm-08 Remington

HANDLOAD DATA

Bullet Wt. Grs.	Type	Powder Wt. Grs.	Type	Primer	Case	MV (fps)	ME (fpe)	Rifle/ Bbl. (in.)	Remarks
115	Speer JHP	46.0	IMR 4064	CCI 200	Rem.	3100	2455	Brown. BBR/22	Most acc. ld. this gun*
115	Speer JHP	46.0	IMR 4064	CCI 200	Rem.	3212	2635	Rem. 700-V/24	Most acc. ld. this gun*
120	Nosler SB	46.2	H380	Rem. 9½M	Rem.	2820	2119	Brown. BBR/22	Accurate
130	Speer SPBT	45.0	IMR 4064	CCI 200	Rem.	2883	2399	Rem. M7/18½	Potent but inacc.
140	Sierra SPBT	42.0	IMR 4064	CCI 200	Rem.	2739	2333	Brown. BBR/22	————
140	Nosler Part.	43.3	H380	Rem. 9½M	Rem.	2580	2069	Brown. BBR/22	2nd most acc. ld. this gun
140	Nosler Part.	42.0	IMR 4064	CCI 200	Rem.	2735	2325	Brown. BBR/22	Accurate
140	Nosler Part.	47.0	Win. 760	Fed. 215	Rem.	2783	2408	Brown. BBR/22	LOA 2.80″; very acc.
140	Nosler Part.	47.0	Win. 760	Fed. 215	Rem.	2809	2454	Brown. BBR/22	LOA 2.75″; doubled grp. size and Std. Dev.
145	Speer JHPBT(M)	43.5	H380	Fed. 215	Rem.	2630	2227	Sav. 110-S/22	Accurate
145	Speer JHPBT(M)	46.0	Win. 760	Fed. 210	Rem.	2782	2493	Rem. 700-V/24	Very accurate
170	Sierra RNSP	42.0	IMR 4350	CCI 200	Rem.	2335	2058	Brown. BBR/22	————

*Load data verified by Omark/CCI.

JHP—Jacketed Hollow Point; SB—Solid Base; SPBT—Soft Point Boat-Tail, JHPBT(M)—Jacketed Hollow Point Boat-Tail (Match); RNSP—Round Nose Soft Point.

FACTORY LOAD DATA

Bullet Wt. Grs.	Type	MV (fps)	ME (fpe)	Rifle/ Bbl. (in.)	Remarks
140	Rem. PSP	2741	2335	Rem. M7/18½	Fair accuracy
140	Rem. PSP	2801	2440	Sav. 110-S/22	Very poor accuracy
140	Rem. PSP	2807	2449	Brown. BBR/22	Poor accuracy
140	Rem. PSP	2895	2605	Rem. M700-V/24	Lot 1; Fair accuracy
140	Rem. PSP	2937	2681	Rem. M700-V/24	Lot 2; Poor accuracy

PSP—Pointed Soft Point.

SPECIFICATIONS

Shell Holders
RCBS: 3
Bonanza: 1
Lyman: 2
Pacific: 1

Bullet Diameter
Jacketed: .284″

Lengths
Trim: 2.025″
Maximum Case: 2.035″
Maximum Overall: 2.800″

CAUTION:
Loads recommended and suggested herein have been carefully listed, but are intended solely as a guide to readers and neither the publisher nor author accept any responsibility for results of their use. **Maximum loads, listed in bold, should be reduced by 10 percent and worked up to cautiously.**

7x57 Mauser

Diagram dimensions: 2.235 — 20°-45' — .473" — .470" — .431" — .321" — 1.730" — 1.895"

"The cartridge is a deadly big game load, moderate of recoil, not strident of voice, eminently shootable. A 7mm Mauser user is doubtless well-gunned."

I'M NOT sure how many of my readers are familiar with the name Harvey Donaldson. Mr. Donaldson was a wildcatter, machinist, sports-car driver, competitive benchrest shooter, ballistician, varmint hunter, and gun writer who died in November, 1972, at the age of 89. He was still active in shooting at the time of his demise, indeed was working on yet another wildcat cartridge. He was best known for his 219 Donaldson Wasp.

The reason I mention Harvey Donaldson is that he was an unabashed admirer of the cartridge featured in this chapter, the 7x57 Mauser. In a column he authored for *Handloader* magazine, he wrote: "My own favorite [hunting] caliber happens to be . . . 7x57mm . . . Having used several rifles in this caliber from 1898 to the present time, I have never found an occasion to change."

And this:

Down through the years I have used many good rifles, two of them being in 270 [Winchester] caliber—which I still have in my gun rack. These have shown wonderful accuracy, and for years I had the idea no rifle could beat a 270 for accuracy in the hunting field. But, when I started trying out the fine Hornady bullets in 7mm caliber, I soon found that my 7x57 rifles would give equal accuracy with any of my 270 Winchesters.

So, I still use my 7x57 rifle, and the 270s stand in the gun rack. Everyone to his choice, as the old lady said when she kissed the cow, but I still maintain that if any of the younger shooters are looking for an all-around hunting rifle, they might do worse than to select a rifle in 7x57 caliber.

Further testimonials are not hard to come by. In *The Rifle Book,* Jack O'Conner had this to say:

About the lightest cartridge that I would classify as being perfectly satisfactory for all-around use is the one known in Europe as the 7x57, and in this country as the 7mm Mauser or the 7mm Spanish Mauser.

The 7mm is a fine little cartridge. It will do just about anything the 30-06 will do, and the recoil is much less. The late Captain Paul Curtis and Colonel Townsend Whelen both praised the caliber in their writings and were responsible largely for the run of popularity it had.

On killing power:

I got a fine custom-made lightweight 7mm with a Sukalle barrel and a beautiful stock by Adolph Minar in 1934. I used it to shoot ten head of big game, and the experience left me with a lot of respect for the . . . 139-grain Western Cartridge Company load.

Jack went on to list the 10 animals and the results of the shots. Only one, a mule deer hit in the rump, required a finisher. He closed with this: "All of these shots were not farther than 200 yards, and most of them were under. They show that the 7mm kills well."

Such accolades have surrounded the 7x57 for many years, and under its many names. In the United States,

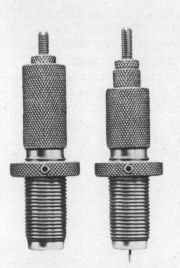

IMR 4320 is a good bet in the 7x57. In the author's M70, 45.0 grains of that propellant kicks the 139-grain Hornady SPBT out at 2920 fps.

Those who have not handloaded the 7x57 will be surprised to learn that RCBS shows the die sales for this cartridge to be nicely ahead of the 45-70 for 1981, '82 and '83. In short, the 7x57 is indeed a winner with experienced riflemen.

we have long referred to it as the 7mm Mauser or 7mm Spanish Mauser. The British call it the 275 Rigby; I've also seen it written up as the 276. Today everyone has pretty well standardized on the sobriquet "seven-by-fifty-seven." That's as good as any.

Some minor confusion engulfs its birth date. In the respected tome, *The Book of Rifles,* by Smith & Smith, the cartridge is listed under the heading, "Spanish 7mm Mauser M1893," which to me implies that the load was birthed in 1893. However, just four pages away from the above heading we find this: "The next Mauser rifle and carbine to be purchased in quantity by Spain was the 7mm Model 1892: this weapon introduced the 7mm cartridge and used an 'in line' magazine similar to the M1891."

Oh well, such discrepancies spice an historical researcher's dreary task. Since Barnes' *Cartridges of the World* supports the earlier date, let's go ahead and settle on that one.

One simply cannot write about the 7x57 without mentioning its most celebrated user, W.D.M. "Karamojo" Bell. Bell was an ivory hunter in Africa for many years. The story goes that he slew nearly 1,000 pachyderms, a good many with his little 7-pound 275 Rigby. Bell was an ardent practitioner of the brain shot. He wrote in the 1923 work, *Wanderings of an Elephant Hunter,* this:

Speaking personally, my greatest successes have been obtained with the 7mm Rigby-Mauser or 276, with the old round-nose solid . . . It seemed to show a remarkable aptitude for finding the brain of an elephant. This holding of a true course I think is due to the moderate velocity, 2,300 ft., and the fact that the proportion of diameter to length of bullet seems to be the ideal combination.

Incidentally, don't let Bell's referring to the 7x57 as the "276" throw you. In the very next sentence he called it the "275." A cartridge of many names.

The great Henry Stebbins once wrote of the 7x57: "Handloads or imported ammunition make this durable old cartridge almost equal the 270 for long-range shooting." He went on to praise the defunct 150-grain Winchester load and the 160-grain U.S. Cartridge Company's boat-tail hollow point. Of the latter he said: " . . . a splendid design, with the old Ross-type capped hollow point, very sharp but pretty rugged in magazine handling, compared to a plain soft point." (Could this

7x57 Mauser: Deer/Bear

(Above) The 7x57 is currently being chambered in Ruger's No. 1 International, an excellent choice for the deep-woods hunter who has a taste for things "Mannlicher."

(Right) Since its introduction, the Remington 700 Classic has been offered in a few "limited-run" chamberings. Fortunately, the 7x57 was part of those "limited-runs" and is considered a prize by those who love the cartridge.

spitzer had sailed through the doe to ax the buck.

Jim Corbett, famous hunter of the earlier part of this century, slew many man-eating tigers and leopards with his 7x57. It was his "second" rifle, his primary armament being variously a 450-400 Jeffery double and a 500 Express. Obviously, Corbett reckoned the 7mm to be big enough for large cats. Far as I know, he wasn't "et" by one. He lived out his later years in Kenya.

The 7mm Mauser is one of the oldest military cartridges still in relatively common sporting usage. Not the eldest; the 45-70 predated it by nearly two decades and is still fairly popular. In fact, the die-popularity sheet published annually by RCBS shows the 7x57 at 22nd place in 1981, and 21st in both 1982 and 1983. The 45-70 ranked 23rd, 24th, and 28th respectively. The 8x57 Mauser placed 27th, 28th, and 29th during the

latter bullet have been the progenitor of the popular Remington Bronze-Point design, and even more recently the Nosler Ballistic Tip?)

We seem to have general agreement here as to the ballistic and hunting merits of the ancient 7x57. For nigh onto a century, hunters from Townsend Whelen and "Karamojo" Bell, through the O'Conners—both Jack and Eleanor—up to Jim Carmichel, have used and liked and trusted the little 28-bore.

Eleanor O'Conner used it on elk, black bear, mountain sheep, mule deer, Rocky Mountain goat, greater kudu, sable, waterbuck, roan antelope, zebra, and similar-sized critters. On one African safari, she was nicknamed "One-shot Eleanor" because she took 17 head of big game with only 19 shots.

Her husband, Jack, added javelina and whitetails to the list. Once he was hunting on the Snake River with Vernon Speer, the bulletmaker. Jack popped a fat, dry doe for camp meat. The doe tumbled down the mountain, along with a spike buck that had been feeding unseen on the far side of the doe. The 145-grain Speer

same periods; it is 4 years older than the 7x57. The 30-40 Krag, of identical vintage to the 7x57, is dead as spats. Hasn't made the Top-30 RCBS chart since I've been keeping track, nearly 10 years.

In addition to Spain, Mexico, Serbia, Brazil, Colombia, Chile, Honduras, and Uruguay utilized the little 7mm Mauser as their battle cartridge. Note that I haven't stated that those are the *only* countries to have nationalized the round. If I said that, someone would send me proof that Patagonia or Sri Lanka used the load in their skirmishes with the Hottentots, sure as lumps in mashed potatoes.

Since many of the surplus military arms chambered to 7x57 were 1893 and 1895 Mausers, not to mention the one-lug M1892, the ammo manufacturers in this country have kept the lid on breech pressures. The above rifles boast no auxilliary locking lug like the Mauser '98 and are reputedly of relatively soft steel. Nothing to fret over, just something to bear in mind when settling on powder charges. As Henry Stebbins mentioned, some of the foreign ammunition is loaded a bit stiff. I clocked a batch of Norma 150-grain factory stuff recently; it showed a 2720 foot-second muzzle speed from a 22-inch Model 70 Featherweight. Whew! That's more than 100 fps faster than the swiftest *140-grain* domestic brand, the Federal pointed soft point. If that lot of Norma ammo was loaded to 45,000 CUP, Mean Joe Green wears panty hose.

One of the most common 7mm permutations was the little Mexican carbine. Sporting a barrel in the neighborhood of 18½ inches long, and wearing the Mexican coat of arms on the receiver ring, these little guns often turned up in pawnshops all along the Mexican border during the '20s, and could be had for as little as 5 bucks. They made dandy deer rifles.

Sometime between 1908 and 1912, the prestigious Mauser Werke at Oberndorf introduced a turnbolt designed around the 7x57. It was a bit shorter than the Mauser '98 and is sometimes seen with a square bridge. This iteration was intended strictly for sporting rifles, and many British-built 275 Rigby sporters used the action.

Such imports as Whitworth, Mauser Mark X, BSA, Heym, Krico, and Steyr-Mannlicher are available reamed for the 7mm Mauser. Most of these latter rifles are expensive, with the exception of the Mark X. They are all fine rifles. If you long for a 7x57, there is a plenitude of firms waiting to take your money.

Accuracy

No one but Harvey Donaldson seemed interested in making much of the 7x57's accuracy. Certainly it is more than sufficiently precise for any kind of big-game hunting, but there is where the discussion of accuracy usually begins and ends. I can find no group size quoted in Mr. Donaldson's writings, only that he felt his 7x57 would out-group either of his 270s. There is a qualifier here that does not surface without careful examination. Harvey's 7x57 rifle had a 1-in-12-inch twist, not the 1-in-8.6 or 1-in-9-inch common to most 7mm Mauser rifles.

My own two 7x57s shoot well, but not uncommonly so for light sporters. The Ruger M77 groups around 1½ inches with its favored fodder. My Model 70 Feather-

Interarms' Whitworth Express is also available in 7x57; it's an excellent example of a classic gun/cartridge combination.

Current Rifle Availability

For quite a number of years new 7x57 rifles were hard to come by. From a period in the mid-'50s when Winchester built their last 7x57 pre-'64 Model 70 for the late Jack O'Conner, until Ruger made a special run of Model 77 bolt-actions for the cartridge nearly two decades later, there were no domestic 7x57s produced (discounting custom and small-time operations, of course). Some years after the trial run, Ruger added the load to their list of standard chamberings for the M77 as well as the Number 1 single shot rifle. Savage and Remington followed Ruger in offering a limited run of 7mm turnbolts; both sold out their production, but neither has retained it in their line. Winchester returned the 7x57 to their queue when they reintroduced the Model 70 Featherweight a few years ago. It is still catalogued. Kleinguenther makes it in the K-15 Insta-Fire and guarantees ½-inch accuracy for three-shot groups, assuming proper loads.

weight is more accurate, going into 1.38 inches with its pet provender. Now, that is certainly naught to complain about in a light sporter, but it isn't really bragworthy. And it certainly doesn't shame any 270 I can remember. In fact, most of the 270s I have fired would group around 1¼ inches or better with one load or another. A few would better that considerably. Point is, I doubt seriously if a standard-twist 7x57 will outgroup a similar 270. More likely the other way around. Sorry, Mr. Donaldson.

I know of no one who has used the 7x57 to win matches in this country, although I have read that it is a popular competition load in Europe. (If anyone *has* used the 7x57 in serious competition in the United States, I haven't heard of him inundating his opponents.) Although I'm sure that some hapless chuck or prairie dog has met its demise at the hands of a well-pointed 7x57, I have no doubt that the vermin population would show a healthy increase if we all were limited to its use. If benchrest matches were restricted henceforth to 7x57

(Above) Shooter Jimmy Michael is firing this Winchester Model 70 Featherweight in 7x57. This particular rifle provides 5-shot groups that average well under 1½ inches at 100 yards; the most accurate load being 51.0 grains of H4831 and the 160-grain Sierra boat-tail soft point.

(Right) From the bench, at 100 yards the author's out-of-print Savage 111 in 7x57 turns in 5-shot groups averaging 1½ to 1¾ inches with handloads.

H4831. Muzzle speed is just over 2600 fps in my Model 70, which is good for better than 2400 foot-pounds.

While I have had my best results with extruded propellants in my 7x57 rifles, such ball powders as Hodgdon's H414 and Winchester 760 work well in some guns. The only ball-powder loading my Winchester accepts at all is a near-maximum load of H414 and the 145-grain Speer Gold Match boat-tail. Groups run in the 3-inch range, which limits its versatility considerably, but the velocity is fine at nearly 2800 fps. In a gun that grouped it well, that load would have promise.

The traditional 175-grain round nose does yeoman

rifles, the current world records would themselves set records for perpetuity.

The foregoing is no diatribe against the 7x57, merely a frank and honest appraisal of its strengths and weaknesses. The cartridge is a deadly big game load, moderate of recoil, not strident of voice, eminently shootable. A 7mm Mauser user is doubtless well-gunned. But let's not give it attributes it doesn't possess.

Handloading the 7x57

Reloading the 7x57 is pretty straightforward. In fast-twist rifles such as my Model 70, accuracy is sketchy, indeed, with handloads until bullet weight approaches at least 160 grains. For some inexplicable reason my Winchester handles the 140-grain factory loads with alacrity, grouping around 1⅝ inches. But no handloaded bullet lighter than the 160-grain Sierra soft point boat-tail will print under 2 inches.

Despite its mediocre performance on target paper, if I were to take my 7x57 after a whitetail buck tomorrow, I'd stoke it with loads featuring the 139-grain Hornady soft point boat-tail over 45.0 grains of IMR 4320. The muzzle speed is 2920 fps, hard onto factory-brewed 270 Winchester 130-grain loads. Shoots as flat, hits as hard.

For elk or moose exclusively, I'd want a 160-grain Sierra or Nosler spitzer riding 51.0 grains of Hodgdon's

work in the 7x57 if all your shots will be limited to 200 yards or less. For elk, moose, and what-have-you at such distances, the semi-pointed Nosler Partition would be as good as you could get. Pushed to perhaps 2500 fps in a strong rifle, 200-yard energy is nearly 1800 foot-pounds. (If Nosler would redesign that slug to spitzer form, it would extend its usefulness to a full 300 yards in this cartridge.)

The 7x57 Mauser is a fine old cartridge. While it makes sense as a light-recoiling rifle for big game, I can't help but feel that its popularity stems mainly from nostalgia. It is not as versatile as the 270, although a near equal as a big game round. While the 7x57 exhibits somewhat milder blast and comeback, the 270 is much better at the dual role of varmint/deer cartridge. Action lengths are identical for each as currently manufactured, so the shorter 7x57 can show no advantage in bolt throw or brevity of firearm.

The newer 7mm-08 Remington enjoys the advantages of a shorter action (enabling its use in lever-action rifles and turnbolts of truly elfine proportions) and greater variety of domestic factory rifles. Anything the 7x57 will do ballistically, the 7mm-08 will duplicate. The newer round is undeniably more accurate and thus makes a better competition and varmint cartridge as the silhouette shooters have discovered. The 7x57 in turn provides a greater selection of factory ammo.

For the largest game, the 284 Winchester and 280 Remington both offer energy levels demonstrably superior to the 7x57, albeit with attendant increased recoil and muzzle noise. Naturally, the 7mm Magnums outclass them all ballistically.

Despite the above, the 7x57 has much going for it. It is mild-mannered and shootable. It offers enough power for most any hunting task asked of it, if directed pru-

dently and loaded with good bullets. Factory ammunition is available in several weights and isn't hard to come by. Rifles chambered for it are plenty accurate for big game shooting at any reasonable distance if some degree of load selection is undertaken. For 90 percent of the big game hunting done in the continental United States, the 7x57 is enough but not too much. And contrary to what some will tell you, you *can* have too much. The 7x57 is just right.

7x57 Mauser

HANDLOAD DATA

Bullet Wt. Grs. Type	Powder Wt. Grs. Type	Primer	Case	MV (fps)	ME (fpe)	Rifle/ Bbl. (in.)	Remarks
139 Hrndy. SPBT	45.0 IMR 4320	Rem. 9½	Rem.	2920	2631	Win. M70 Fwt./22	Fine deer/antelope ld.
150 Sierra JHPBT(M)	46.0 IMR 4350	Fed. 210	Rem.	2595	2243	Win. M70 Fwt./22	————
150 Nosler Part.	**52.3** H4831	Rem. 9½	Rem.	**2677**	**2388**	Win. M70 Fwt./22	Good velocity
160 Sierra SPBT	**51.0** H4831	CCI 200	Win.	**2608**	**2417**	Win. M70 Fwt./22	Most acc. ld. tested
162 Nosler SB	**51.0** H4831	CCI 200	Win.	**2510**	**2267**	Win. M70 Fwt./22	Accurate

BTSP—Soft Point Boat-Tail; JHPBT(M)—Jacketed Hollow Point Boat-Tail (Match); SB—Solid Base.

FACTORY LOAD DATA

Bullet Wt. Grs. Type	MV (fps)	ME (fpe)	Rifle/ Bbl. (in.)	Remarks
140 Rem. PSP	2595	2093	Win. M70 Fwt./22	Very accurate
140 Fed. PSP	2613	2122	Win. M70 Fwt./22	Most acc. fact. ld.
150 Norma SPBT	2720	2464	Win. M70 Fwt./22	Warm
175 Fed. RN	2390	2219	Win. M70 Fwt./22	Good energy

PSP—Pointed Soft Point; SPBT—Soft Point Boat-Tail; RN—Round Nose.

SPECIFICATIONS

Shell Holders
RCBS: 11 or 3
Bonanza: 1
Lyman: 2
Pacific: 1

Bullet Diameter
Jacketed: .284"

Lengths
Trim: 2.225"
Maximum Case: 2.235"
Maximum Overall: 3.065"

CAUTION:
Loads recommended and suggested herein have been carefully listed, but are intended solely as a guide to readers and neither the publisher nor author accept any responsibility for results of their use.
Maximum loads, listed in bold, should be reduced by 10 percent and worked up to cautiously.

280 Remington
(7mm Express Remington)

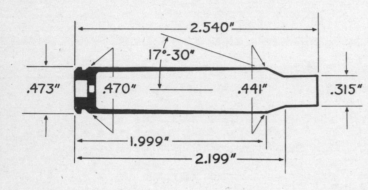

2.540"

17°-30'

.473" .470" .441" .315"

1.999"

2.199"

"The 280 is languishing, for no good reason. As an all-purpose cartridge, it is as good as anything we have ballistically."

THE fortunes of the 280 Remington/7mm Express Remington cartridge have been fraught with as many ups and downs as a Swiss chamois. When introduced in 1957 by way of the Remington Model 740 autoloader, it seemed likely that the load would gain a heavy following. It didn't. It has managed to achieve some popularity among the dedicated gun-buff crowd, the guys who read all the magazines and roll their own ammunition. The 280 was aimed at a very broad niche in the shooting scheme of things, that of the talented all-rounder. Since its inception, it has been touted as a do-anything cartridge, a role it fits quite admirably. Why, then, has it failed to separate shooters from their savings in unprecedented numbers?

First, it will do absolutely nothing in practical terms that the much older and better established 270 Winchester can't equal. Secondly, Remington slipped a joker in its own deck 5 years after the birth of the 280 via the 7mm Remington Magnum, a cartridge that has gone on to fame and corporate fortune. The only real advantage the 280 enjoys over the 7mm Magnum is its adaptability to the Remington line of pump and semi-automatic rifles. In a bolt-action, the 280 demands the same action length as the belted case 7mm Magnum. It thus offers no practical enhancement except a slight decrease in muzzle blast and recoil at the expense of slightly reduced punch.

In the book, *Mr. Rifleman*, by Colonel Townsend Whelen, we find this:

. . . I recently had a new hunting rifle built which I thought would be just a little superior to the .270 or the .30-06. It has a Douglas 7mm, 26-inch barrel with a groove diameter of .284-inch and a twist of 10 inches. Just as I was about to order this barrel the .280 Remington cartridge was announced, so I had it chambered for that case to avoid the trouble of necking down .30-06 cases, and because the .280 case holds about two grains more powder than does the .30-06. I had it fitted to a Winchester Model 70 action I had.

I had this rifle made with a 26-inch barrel . . . You might say this rifle is nothing but a glorified .280 Remington, except that its 26-inch barrel can be expected to give about 160 fps more velocity with loads containing slow-burning powders than will the 22-inch barrel of the Remington rifle.

So after . . . testing and dickering around I settled down to charges of 52 grains of [IMR] 4350 or 55.5 grains of [Hodgdon] 4831 powder with the 160 Sierra [boat-tail] bullet, and 52 grains of [IMR] 4350 or 54 grains of [Hodgdon] 4831 powder for the 175-grain bullets. [Nosler Partition and Hornady spire point.]

On accuracy, he wrote this about his new rifle:

When I fired 10 five-shot groups with each of these last loads, there was no apparent difference in accuracy with any of them. Groups with all six loads have run from one inch to 1.7 inches for five-shot groups at 100 yards. Occasionally one group has been spoiled by one shot half an inch or so off, a matter that always occurs

Confusing? Even though the headstamps are different, it's all the same round. The current factory designation is 280 Remington, *not* 7mm Express Remington.

with factory bullets produced in quantity. [This last comment is not true today.]

On recoil and killing power:

The recoil, so far as I can determine, is just about the same as from my .30-06 Springfield rifle of similar weight with a load shooting the 180-grain bullet at 2725 fps. In other words, I seem to have a rifle and loads which are just a little better than that of the .30-06 rifle at its best; better in killing power, trajectory, and in resisting wind deflection.

I do not believe it would pay the hunter who had a first class .270 or .30-06 rifle to discard it, and get one of these, but if he is starting from scratch I do think it would . . . it seems to be just a little better outfit.

Of course Mr. Whelen was not the only user of the new 280. Jack O'Conner gave it a thorough trial, pronounced it the equal of his beloved 270. But no better. In his tome, *The Hunting Rifle,* Jack wrote the following: "The .284 Winchester and the .280 Remington are so much like the .270 ballistically that if similar bullets are used any difference between the three cartridges would be a matter of imagination." Take note of that; you'll never read a truer sentence. To my notion, Jack could have included the 7x57, 7mm-08 Remington, 308 Winchester, 30-06, and 8mm Mauser and remained equally correct.

Jack had killed enough game with the 270 to know what to expect from the 280 Remington. In the same

work, he also wrote the following about a 150-grain 280 bullet backed by a stiff charge of H4831:

"I have yet to see a game animal that didn't join his ancestors with commendable rapidity after being socked in the ribs with such [150-grain] bullets, and that goes for anything from 40-pound javelinas to 1,400-pound moose, 900-pound elk, 600-pound grizzlies, 450-pound African lions, 750-pound zebras, or 800-pound bull elk."

Available Rifles

Under the name "280 Remington," the cartridge has been offered in a reasonably broad array of hardware. Remington chambered it in their Model 740 auto, Models 721 and 725 turnbolts, and Model 760 pump. Ruger makes up a few Model 77 bolt-actions and an occasional Number 1 turns up. Several European manufacturers have also added it to their lines, which strikes me as a little odd. The much older 7x64 Brenneke is virtually identical to the 280, in appearance as well as performance; I fail to perceive much advantage from the European viewpoint in abandoning the entrenched 7x64 for the American 280. Interestingly, the new rank of bolt-action rifles from Beretta includes the 7x64 as a standard chambering, but not the 280.

In 1979, Remington was seemingly about to give up on the 280. Sales figures for both rifles and ammunition were less than buoyant with health. Since they had once

The author's Remington 700 BDL in 280 was very accurate at 100 yards. Five-shot groups ran 1½ inches with the best loads. Complete with Redfield Lo-Profile 4x scope, this combo wouldn't make a bad deer/antelope rig.

been successful in yanking a cartridge back from the grave merely by changing its *nom de guerre,* they decided a similar ploy might work again. As had been done earlier with the 244, Remington tagged the 280 with a metric designation to give it European flavor, then sat back to roll in the dividends. Lazarus failed to come forth.

For the record, the original intent of the Bridgeport firm was to bedub the cartridge the 7mm-06, since its parent case is obvious and the 7mm-06 had been a reasonably popular wildcat cartridge for years. An eleventh-hour panic scotched such plans. There were concerns that since the 280 was not *exactly* a 7mm-06 (it is longer in the critical head-to-shoulder dimension than an unmodified 30-06 case), it shouldn't be so labeled. A frenzied last-minute change was instituted and no rifles marked 7mm-06 were thought to have left the plant. Wrong. I've seen one, and know of others, although specimens are scarce and today are bringing a premium on the collector's market.

Remington marketed their Model 700 boltgun and their Models Four and 7400 semi-autos for the 7mm Express Remington, as it had officially been entitled. Buyers with fistfuls of greenbacks were notable by their absence. The old name game hadn't worked its magic a second time. In 1983, Remington quietly switched back to 280 nomenclature. The load was dropped from the 700 series and is now available from Remington only in the self-loaders.

Strange. I can't imagine why anyone would want a self-shucker chambered to 280 Remington. A turnbolt, certainly, but an auto? Word has come down that the reason Remington brought the 280 out in the first place was to have a 270-class cartridge that was loaded to slightly lesser pressures, thus mollycoddling the 740 automatic. True? I doubt it, but what do I know?

In the first place, if you take a case of similar bore size and powder capacity and slow up some on breech pressure, you slow up some on velocity as well. No way around it. Secondly, if the poor ol' 740 was such a fragile creature, then how did it manage to hold up under the 270 Winchester and its attendant pressures of 54,000 CUP? Or the 52,000 provided by the 308 Winchester and 243? How many 270-chambered Remington semi-automatics have you seen that were blown apart or battered into a useless pile of weakened metal? I thought so. Of course, it's possible that *at the time* Remington didn't feel the 740 could handle such loads as the 270 Winchester.

My opinion, for what it's worth, is that Remington merely wanted a 270-class cartridge with their own name on it for their popular hunting auto. After all, in 1957 the only Remington load chambered in the 740 was the 244, and it was about as well-received as Jane Fonda at a John Birch Society picnic. It is only natural that the Bridgeport house would seek to rectify that situation. The 280 was to be the vehicle. It didn't work.

And so the 280 Remington, aka the 7mm Express Remington (not *Remington Express* as is often seen), aka the 7mm-06 Remington (against Remington's will), has become what it is today, a gun enthusiast's load.

Handloading the 280

As the proverbial all-rounder, the 280 is as good as any other cartridge if you are willing to tote a rifle a little longer and heavier than necessary. If standard length strikes you as about right, then competitors for the 280's crown would be the 270 Winchester, the 7x57, the 7mm Magnums, and the 30-06. (The 8mm Mauser is about dead, commercially.)

We can dispose of the 7x57 right off. Anything the 7x57 can do, the 280 can do better. Period. You gain a useful advantage in terminal ballistics, a demonstrably flatter trajectory, and a barrel of a more reasonable

Even though the 280's recoil is not exactly "light," it's easily handled by experienced shooters.

twist rate without having to go the custom-barrel route. The only drawback is slightly increased recoil and blast, which is of little import in this instance; if you can't handle a 280, then it is unlikely you can manage a 7x57. If the 7x57 would fit in a shorter action than the 280, then I'd gaze more kindly on it. Since you're stuck with the same action length, you might as well make the most of it.

The 270 is harder to dispose of. Recoil and muzzle blast are so nearly identical, only a guru of heightened awareness could discern any difference. Both are very accurate, although the 270 *might* win on points. Then again, the 280 has several match-grade bullets available in its bore size; the 270 does not. But the 270 may not

As a woods rifle, the Remington Model 7400 autoloader in 280 may be a good bet. It's reasonably accurate, flat shooting and provides the deer hunter with fingertip follow-up shots. It is not, however, a Remington 700 bolt-action—a much better choice when it comes to squeezing out top accuracy and energy.

need them, shooting as well as it often does with hunting projectiles. The only real advantage for the 28-bore, from where I sit, is the availability of the superb 175-grain Nosler Partition 7mm slug. Of course, you can purchase the excellent 160-grain Nosler Partition in 277 caliber, but it just doesn't enjoy the reputation for awesome penetration that the 175-grain 7mm does. You can't hedge by saying that you don't plan to shoot game requiring such deep penetration; we're discussing these loads with an eye toward all-around use, which includes really big game like elk and moose. I'll have to go with the 280.

The 30-06 has its adherents, and rightly so. Less than 3 months ago, as I write this, I asked Rick Jamison and Layne Simpson which cartridge they considered the best for all-purpose use in the United States. They unhesitatingly chose the 30-06. Over supper, they backed up their selection with a good case. As far as I'm concerned, it's a tossup. I'm not especially enamored of "large caliber" as an important element in killing power, particularly if the difference in diameter amounts only to .024-inch. Since both cartridges produce energy levels on the same plane, and since the 175-grain Nosler Partition will penetrate as well as any bullet you can stuff in a 30-caliber case, I feel there is no difference in effective killing power between the two. Therefore, I'll go with the cartridge having lesser recoil and be done with it.

The Seven Mags are another story. Either the 7mm Weatherby or Remington Magnum will drive a similar-weight bullet from 200 to 250 fps faster than will the 280 Remington, assuming barrels of standard length for the cartridges in question and pressures approximating SAAMI specs. Equalize the barrel length and up the 280's operating pressures to that of the magnums, and the difference drops to a less significant level. But it is still there.

Du Pont's IMR 4350 is one of the top powders for use in the 280 Remington. (The author has used IMR 4350 in more 280 handloads than any other powder.)

My fastest 280 Remington handload velocities are as follows: 150-grain bullets, 2943 fps for 2886 fpe; 160-grain bullets, 2760 fps for 2706 fpe; 175-grain bullets, 2680 fps for 2791 fpe. The fastest factory load I've clocked was the 150-grain Norma soft point at 2985 fps and 2968 fpe. The most potent domestic stuff was a lot of 165-grain Remington ammo headstamped "280 Remington," which managed 2715 fps and 2701 fpe. All loads were fired in a Remington Model 700 with 22-inch barrel; all loads were chronographed.

Bearing in mind that my 7mm Remington Magnums have been graced with 24-inch barrels, here are the numbers for reloads: 150-grain bullets, 3104 fps for 3210 fpe; 160-grain bullets, 2980 fps for 3156 fpe; 175-grain bullets, 3008 fps for 3517 fpe. Averages for all factory 7mm Magnum loads ran thus: 150-grain bullets, 3089 fps and 3172 fpe; 175-grain bullets at 2824 fps and 3100 fpe.

From these representative samplings, we can see that the 150-grain 280 loads run 161 fps shy of the 7mm Remington Mag; the 160-grain 280's show a 220 foot-second deficit; and the 175-grain 280 loads run 328 fps aft of the Big Seven. When timed on my Oehler chronograph, the 150-grain domestic 280 fodder shows a 254 fps disadvantage compared to the 7mm Magnum. The hot 150-grain Norma soft point 280 Remington load is 202 fps behind the same brand in 7mm Remington Magnum. Allowing about 60 fps for the shorter barrel of the 280, it is still in arrears 150 fps on the average for handloads and factory.

Is that figure significant? Probably not. Even on large animals, I doubt that the difference in killing power can be detected. Let me note that since I'm not uncommonly sensitive to recoil, I doubt I'd buy a 280 rifle instead of a 7mm Magnum. However, if I owned both a 280 and a Big Seven and liked them equally, the only time I'd choose the 7mm Magnum over the 280 would be for use on game large enough and tough enough to warrant the 175-grain Nosler Partition. Animals like elk or moose.

I have neglected the 7mm Weatherby Magnum simply because it is even farther ahead of the 280 than the 7mm Remington Magnum. Choosing between the 7mm Weatherby and the 280, I'd opt for the Weatherby. A recoil-sensitive shooter would have other considerations, of course.

The 280 is languishing, for no good reason. As an all-purpose cartridge, it is as good as anything we have ballistically. It has never achieved much public approbation and likely never will. It is an unusually useful number surrounded in the picket fence of rifle cartridges by many that will perform the same functions at least as well. Its competitors have such advantages as military subsidy, a head start in years, more charisma, a better reputation for accuracy, or a combination of the above. Despite this, there is nothing wrong with the 280 Remington, and it is significantly overshadowed by no other cartridge. But then it overshadows none, either.

280 Remington

HANDLOAD DATA

Bullet Wt. Grs.	Bullet Type	Powder Wt. Grs.	Powder Type	Primer	Case	MV (fps)	ME (fpe)	Rifle/ Bbl. (in.)	Remarks
139	Hrndy. SPBT	54.0	IMR 4350	Rem. 9½	Rem.	2765	2359	Rem. M7400/22	Sub-max in autos
150	Nosler Part.	55.5	IMR 4350	8½-120	Nor.	**2943**	**2888**	Rem. M700/22	_____
162	Nosler SB	51.5	IMR 4350	Rem. 9½	Rem.	2576	2387	Rem. M7400/22	Most acc. ld. this gun
175	Hrndy. SP	53.0	IMR 4831	8½-120	Nor.	2680	2791	Rem. M700/22	Very accurate

SPBT—Soft Point Boat-Tail; SP—Soft Point; SB—Solid Base.

FACTORY LOAD DATA

Bullet Wt. Grs.	Bullet Type	MV (fps)	ME (fpe)	Rifle/ Bbl. (in.)	Remarks
150	Rem. PSPCL	2673	2379	Rem. M7400/22	Headstamped "7mm Express"
150	Rem. PSPCL	2835	2678	Rem. M700/22	Headstamped "7mm Express"
150	Rem. PSPCL	2768	2552	Rem. M700/22	Headstamped "280 Remington"
150	Norma SP	2985	2968	Rem. M700/22	Headstamped "280 Romington"
165	Rem. RNCL	2631	2536	Rem. M7400/22	Headstamped "280 Remington"
165	Rem. RNCL	2715	2701	Rem. M700/22	Headstamped "280 Remington"

PSPCL—Pointed Soft Point Core Lokt; SP—Soft Point; RNCL—Round Nose Core Lokt.

SPECIFICATIONS

Shell Holders
RCBS: 3
Bonanza: 1
Lyman: 2
Pacific: 1

Bullet Diameter
Jacketed: .284"

Lengths
Trim: 2.530"
Maximum Case: 2.540"
Maximum Overall: 3.330"

Lewis Dawkins fires the M7400 Remington 280 from a benchrest.

284 Winchester

> "The 284's *raison d'être* is its magnificent application to lightweight, short-action hunting rifles. For that purpose it has no peer."

MY FIRST 284 Winchester rifle was a Ruger Model 77 I purchased from a drug store, of all places. That particular apothecary had one helluva gun department, and the guy responsible for that part of the store's business really knew his. I had lusted after that particular Ruger for many months before I finally accumulated enough jack to bail it out.

The first trip to the range let the wind out of my sails a tad. The gun wouldn't group on a tobacco tin at 100 yards. Wow! I'd had some recalcitrant turnbolts before but nothing like this. Neither the 125-nor the 150-grain Winchester factory soft point fodder would shoot. No one else made ammo, so I retired to my loading bench.

I'd been into handloading all of a couple of years, but I knew enough to begin my search for an accurate load by reading. Couldn't find a thing on the 284. Chagrined, I consorted with my Speer handbook, then charged my empties with 54.0 grains of IMR 4350, the 130-grain Speer spitzer, and CCI 250 primers. My next four groups averaged 1.19 inches! With confidence thus reinstated, and respect for the 284 cartridge and the Ruger 77 rifle imbued, I went happily on my way.

I've owned two more 284s since then, another Ruger 77 and a Shilen DGA sporter. I wish I had one now. The unsung 284 Winchester just might have been the best all-around cartridge produced in this country. Big talk? Let me state my case.

The attributes of the 284 are impressive. First, and

way ahead of most of the others, is that it is a short cartridge. It was orginally designed, back in 1963, to function in the Winchester Models 88 and 100 rifles, both of which handled cartridges of 308 Winchester length. As far as I'm concerned, the shorter a cartridge the better, within reasonable limits. A short cartridge enables a short action, which in turn creates a handier rifle without having to abbreviate the barrel. A short action is a stiffer action, all else equal, and generally gives better accuracy. (If you doubt the accuracy advantage, let me note here that I've owned only one sporter-weight bolt-gun that would average an inch or less that was chambered for *any* cartridge longer than the 308.)

Secondly, the 284 has a sharp shoulder which enhances powder combustion and reduces case stretching, providing pressures are held within normal limits. Sharp-shouldered brass is reputed to be difficult to resize, but I've noted no such tendency in my 284 rifles.

Third, the 284 has a greater case capacity than any non-belted cartridge of its length, due to a body diameter of near-magnum proportions and a 35-degree shoulder. The case head is of .473-inch diameter, thus is smaller than the body. This type of cartridge configuration is known as a *rebated rim;* it enables the use of a standard-size boltface.

In toto, what we have is a beautifully engineered 28-caliber combustion capsule that works through medium-action guns, stretches itself little upon firing, and

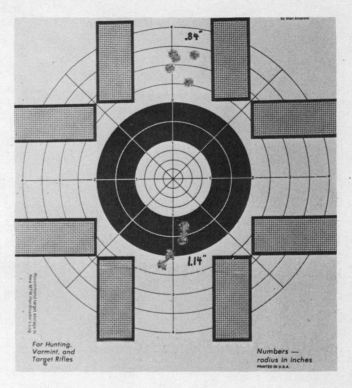

This pair of 5-shot 284 groups averaged .99-inch—you can't ask for much better. They were fired from the author's Shilen DGA.

has a voluminous capacity. There are reportedly two strikes against it. Let's examine them.

The rebated rim is said to create feeding problems in standard-rail bolt-actions. None of the three rifles I owned exhibited any such difficulty. I suspect that custom bolt-actions of 30-06 length were built for the round and that gunsmiths didn't alter the feed rails correctly to handle the fat-bodied 284. I have never read or heard of a Savage M99, Winchester 100 semi-auto, or Winchester 88 lever-action that gave a problem. My opinion is that the reported feeding miscues were *gun* failures, not cartridge failures.

The most common complaint is that the 284, being of such short stature, requires deep seating of its bullets. Golly. How terrible. Such a complaint gives me acute indigestion. *Of course the bullets have to be seated deeply, so what.* You think a 200-grain boat-tail 30-06 bullet, chambered in a standard-throat rifle, doesn't poke its base down below the case neck? You don't believe a 180-grain slug stuffed in a 308 Winchester case doesn't protrude well into the basement? Again, so what? You lose a little powder capacity. No great loss; there is capacity aplenty. Besides, that is one of the trade-offs for a short action. You don't get something for naught.

This whole business reminds me of the problems created by the gasoline shortage. When grizzled and gruff old-timers—weaned on gargantuan automobiles that rode like a cloud, handled like a tricycle, braked like a mule on ice—were forced by economic necessity to consider alternative modes of travel, they chose down-sized imported cars. After living with them for a while, they would brag long and loud about the terrific gas mileage, then turn around and complain interminably about the lack of room or the choppy ride. Two morals here: everything is a compromise in one way or another, and some people will grouse about *anything.*

As far as I'm concerned, the 284 has no flies on it and every gun company should have it in their line, preferably in several models. Is this likely to happen? Not so's you'd notice. Why, you ask? Pull up a chair.

The 284 never really got off the ground except as a vehicle for wildcatters to neck up and down, willy-nilly. The Winchester Models 100 and 88 are defunct. Neither Browning, Savage, nor Ruger continues to offer 284-chambered rifles. Perhaps one of the semi-custom outfits such as Kleinguenther, DuBiel, or Shilen would make you up a gun if you can swallow the price tag. There's the first problem: guns are hard to find.

The second obstacle is that the 284 competed head-on with the 280 Remington, which is barely kicking, and the 270 Winchester, which is very much alive and well, thank you. Casual gunners peruse the ballistics charts and note that the three cartridges are as alike as three crows on a cornstalk, so why buy something they never heard of? The 270 is well entrenched; everybody knows

284 Winchester: Deer/Bear

At one time you could get a good quality bolt action 284 from a number of manufacturers. For those who have a well-deserved affection for things 284, the Ruger 77 seen here is a prize catch in the used-gun market.

From left to right: IMR 4320; IMR 4064; H-380; Winchester 760; IMR 4350. All of these propellants are suitable for use in the 284.

Du Pont's IMR 4350 is well suited for use in the 284. Using 54.0 grains of IMR 4350 and Speer's 130-grain soft points, the author got superb accuracy from his Ruger 77—his average for four, 5-shot groups ran 1.19 inches.

someone who owns one and swears by it. The non-handloading hunter has no interest in such an esoteric cartridge.

Handloaders, on the other hand, are frequently voracious readers. If the 284 Winchester ever had any good press, I must have missed it. The reader is admonished of the terrible feeding problems he can expect with his 284. Then he is beat over the head with the old "bullet-base-intruding-down-the-stairwell" syndrome until he envisions himself and his dandy new rifle being scattered over 3 acres of farmland. Why, he asks himself, should he purchase a play toy that is so fraught with engineering *faux pas* when he can settle on the much-ballyhooed 280 Remington and live blissfully ever after? Why, indeed.

Handloading

The 284's *raison d'être* is its magnificent application to lightweight, short-action hunting rifles. For that purpose it has no peer. None. Lest you accuse me of favoritism, let me hasten to note that I cherish the 308 Win-

chester, dote on the 243, respect the 6mm Remington. However, none of these is quite so adept at its life's work as the 284.

You could have a 22-inch-barreled 284 (if one were made) that weighed no more than 6¼ pounds and would zip a 130-grain Speer spitzer along at 3111 fps with a maximum load of 64.0 grains of Norma MRP, or get 3039 fps from a maximum load of 59.0 grains of IMR 4831, according to the current Speer manual. If you were going after elk, you could ladle a maximum of 54.0 grains of IMR 4350 behind the 160-grain Speer Grand Slam and reach 2800 fps or a little better. You might be able to equal those figures with a 270 or 280 (I've never been able to), but the rifle would run about 1-inch longer and likely ½-pound or more heavier.

Should you worry that the Speer test rifle was an unusual specimen, with a throat ½-inch long and a grossly oversized chamber, fear not. Velocities from my Shilen DGA should be pretty representative, if not conservative, and they support the Speer data. Despite the fact that it had a 24-inch barrel, my Shilen also boasted a

Groups of around 1 inch or better are not uncommon with the 284. This shooter managed to get that sort of performance from a Remington 788 rebarreled to 284 Winchester.

The author's Shilen DGA in 284 Winchester proved to be a superbly accurate rifle. If you want a bolt action 284, you're going to have to hit the used-gun trail or turn to custom outfits like Shilen.

very short throat. So short that 125-grain Winchester factory ammunition would not chamber as they came from the box. (I had to seat them deeper in order to test them.)

Here are the top velocities achieved in my 284 Shilen; 120-grain bullet, 3225 fps; 130-grain, 3150; 139-grain, 2990; 150-grain, 2907; 168-grain, 2788. Winchester factory stuff went as follows: 125-grain, 3290 fps(!); 150-grain, 2984.

To provide some perspective on those factory-load velocities, permit me to make a couple of comparisons. I once tested a batch of 125-grain 7mm Remington Magnum factory loads in a Winchester Model 70 with 24-inch barrel. Muzzle speed was 3198 fps, almost 100 fps *slower* than the same bullet weight in my Shilen 284. The fastest domestic 7mm Remington Mag. 150-grain ammo I've clocked gave 3089 fps; my 284 showed only 105 fps less.

The top muzzle speeds I've achieved from any handloaded 270 Winchester were as follows: 3130 fps with 110-grain bullets, 2943 fps with 130-grain slugs. Fastest

factory loads were 3370 fps with 100-grain Winchester soft points, 2964 fps with 130-grain Winchester soft points, and 2814 fps with 150-grain Federal Premium boat-tail, all in 22-inch barrels. (One batch of 150-grain Federal Premiums clocked 2848 fps in a 24½-inch Sako.)

The 280 Remington went as follows: 150-grain Remington factory ammo (headstamped 7mm Express Remington), 2835 fps; 150-grain Norma, 2985 fps; 165-grain Remington RNCL, 2715 fps. Top 280 handloads: 150-grain, 2943 fps, 160-grain, 2760 fps.

Compare the foregoing with the data from the Shilen 284. I think you'll agree that 284 will hold its own quite well, despite the dreaded deep-seated bullets. It was not any lack of merit that killed the 284. Instead, it was poor press, public apathy, and ignorance of the cartridge's actual capabilities that did it in.

It might be apropos to mention that a few of my colleagues have penned articles recommending that such long-actioned rifles as the Winchester Model 70 be chambered to 284, enabling long-throating and consequent shallow seating of bullets. This procedure would achieve increased case capacity and thus velocity. If we apply such logic to other cartridges, we can envision a 22 Hornet built on a medium-length Sako Forester action, doing away with such trivialities as the short bolt throw and elf-like handling qualities of the tiny Vixen. Perhaps we could stuff the 308 Winchester into a long FN Mauser action and seat the bullets *way* out, ignoring the handiness of such abbreviated ordnance as the Remington Model 7, one of the rifles *designed* around medium-length cartridges. Better yet, we could dig up a Brevex Mauser of true magnum proportions and chamber it for the 30-06. We'd get another 100 fps or so at the expense of unburdensome heft, balance, and aesthetic appeal—whimsical attributes at best.

Folks tend to overlook common sense when discussing rifles and their cartridges. If I'm willing to tote a standard-length rifle, I'll buy one chambered for a standard-length cartridge. Short actions have their places, just as do the magnum lengths. Velocity and case capacity aren't everything.

Original factory-quoted ballistics tables listed the 125-grain load at 3200 fps, the 150-grain at 2900 fps. Current data shows 3140 and 2860 fps respectively. As mentioned, the lots of ammo I've tested handily outstripped factory-quoted figures, which is most unusual. Early lots left a tenacious residue in rifle bores and accuracy was pretty sour. More recent batches have shown no tendency to foul, but accuracy is still naught to write home about.

The only problem I've run into with any of my 284's was a moderate difficulty in cramming cartridges into my Shilen's magazine. The procedure was akin to stuffing size 13 feet into size 10 shoes; it was a dang sight easier gettin' them out than in! With my Rugers, I experienced no such difficulties.

Favorite powders for the 284 are such medium-slow burners as IMR 4350 and Winchester 760 and Hodgdon H205. Alas, the Hodgdon propellant has bit the dust. Fifty-two grains of it kicked the 140-grain Nosler Solid Base along at 2917 fps and grouped just over 1¼ inches for three five-shot strings. That makes for a dandy deer and pronghorn load.

If I planned to compete in metallic silhouette competition, I'd load my 284 with 50.0 grains of H205 under the 162-grain Hornady JHPBT Match, or 49.0 grains behind the 168-grain Sierra Matchking. Either load would group around 1⅛ inches in the Shilen. If my supply of H205 was exhausted, I'd opt for 50.0 grains of Winchester 760 and the 162-grain Hornady for a muzzle velocity of 2752 fps. Velocities are a bit slower with 760, but accuracy is even better.

For big game, I like 55.0 grains of Norma MRP and a good 160-grain premium bullet such as the Speer Grand Slam. Velocities ran around 2800 fps in my Shilen DGA, with 2774 fpe to do the work. For hunting in timber, I'd consider a 175-grain round nose and a maximum load of 49.0 grains of 760 for about 2560 fps, and 2550 fpe.

I'd love to relate a hunting yarn or two, but I know of no one who hunts with a 284. Heck, I don't know anyone who *owns* a 284. I've hunted a little with mine, but never ran across any game while carrying one.

The 284 Winchester is not popular. It never was. I included it in this book because it is a good cartridge, very useful, quite unappreciated, and it fathered a veritable basketful of wildcats. (I suspect that the 25-284 is more widely known than its parent cartridge). If I were restricted to one rifle and cartridge for all hunting on this continent, I'd choose the 284 with scant hesitation. I never fired one that was not exceptionally accurate or that failed to reach ballistic levels concomitant with its case capacity. It is one cartridge that lives up to its potential. That's saying a lot.

284 Winchester

HANDLOAD DATA

Bullet Wt. Grs. Type	Powder Wt. Grs. Type	Primer	Case	MV (fps)	ME (fpe)	Rifle/ Bbl. (in.)	Remarks
120 Nosler SB	56.0 IMR 4350	CCI 250	Win.	3225	2640	Shil. DGA/24	Fastest handload tested
130 Speer SP	54.0 IMR 4350	CCI 250	Win.	NC**	NC**	Ruger M77/22	Superbly accurate
130 Speer SP	**56.0** Win. 760	Fed. 215	Win.	**3150**	**2859**	Shil. DGA/24	Gd. open-cntry. deer ld.
139 Hrndy. SP	60.0 MRP	Fed. 215	Win.	2990	2759	Shil. DGA/24	Mediocre accuracy
140 Nosler SB	52.0 H205*	Fed. 215	Win.	2917	2645	Shil. DGA/24	Extremely accurate
150 Nosler SB	58.0 MRP	CCI 250	Win.	2907	2813	Shil. DGA/24	Accurate
160 Speer GS	55.0 MRP	Fed. 215	Win.	2794	2774	Shil. DGA/24	For heavier game
162 Hrndy. JHPBT	50.0 Win. 760	Fed. 215	Win.	2752	2724	Shil. DGA/24	2nd most acc. ld.
168 Sierra JHPBT	49.0 H205*	Fed. 215	Win.	2788	2900	Shil. DGA/24	Most accurate ld.
175 Win. RN	**49.0** Win. 760	Fed. 215	Win.	**2562**	**2552**	Shil. DGA/24	For brush country

*Propellant discontinued; **NC—Not chronographed.
SB—Solid Base; SP—Soft Point; GS—Grand Slam; JHPBT—Jacketed Hollow Point Boat-Tail; RN—Round Nose.

FACTORY LOAD DATA

Bullet Wt. Grs. Type	MV (fps)	ME (fpe)	Rifle/ Bbl. (in.)	Remarks
125 Win. SP	3290	3000	Shil. DGA/24	Poor acc. in this rifle
150 Win. SP	2984	2966	Shil. DGA/24	Poor acc. in this rifle

SP—Soft Point.

SPECIFICATIONS

Shell Holders
RCBS: 3
Bonanza: 1
Lyman: 2
Pacific: 1

Bullet Diameter
Jacketed: .284"

Lengths
Trim: 2.160"
Maximum Case: 2.170"
Maximum Overall: 2.800"

The author's 284 Shilen DGA produced these excellent five-shot groups which average .97-inch.

CAUTION:
Loads recommended and suggested herein have been carefully listed, but are intended solely as a guide to readers and neither the publisher nor author accept any responsibility for results of their use. **Maximum loads, listed in bold, should be reduced by 10 percent and worked up to cautiously.**

7mm Remington Magnum

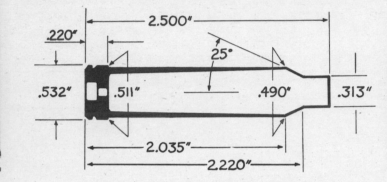

"It will group under 1½ inches in most any turnbolt sporter without 6 months worth of tuning, and it's not so heavy you can't carry it all by yourself. Good cartridge, this 7mm Remington Magnum.

BIG-CASED 7mm cartridges are nothing new. The 280 Ross came out in 1906 chambered in the Canadian straight-pull Ross rifles. Although referred to as a rimless case, it actually had a semi-rim like the 220 Swift. I have read that the ballistics of the Ross were: a 145-grain game bullet at 3050 fps, and a 180-grain match load at a quoted 2900 fps. I suspect it took a barrel 28 or 30 inches in length and a very friendly chronograph to reach such lofty numbers in 1906!

The Ross was originally intended as a military load, but it made its reputation in the game fields. A contingent of Canadian sharpshooters made hay with it prior to World War I in British long-range rifle matches, which did its popularity no harm. The well-heeled sportsmen of that distant time betook the 280 Ross all over the world and shot all manner of game. Unfortunately, a few got et up or trampled in the process; the Ross fell into disfavor. Although loaded at one time by both Remington and Winchester, the 280 Ross is a dead bird today and was pretty much by the start of World War II.

For some years an emasculated version was loaded in England, featuring a 140-grain slug at 2900 fps and a 180-grainer at 2550 fps. But a shadow of its former self, the sickly iteration was dubbed the 280 Rimless Nitro Express. Hunters did not engage in fistfights to acquire one.

We got World War I out of the way, then went back

to the business of developing a serious 7mm cartridge. The Germans tried a sneaky by reviving the 280 Ross, renaming it the 280 Halger (for the firm of *Hal*be & *Ger*lich, get it?), and quoting all manner of hot ballistics.

Along the way the British brought forth the 275 Holland & Holland (also called the 275 Belted Rimless), which like the Ross used .288-inch bullets instead of the .284-inch slugs used in such as the 7x57 Mauser. The 280 Rimless Jeffery, or 280 Jeffery Nitro Express, was a necked-down 333 Jeffery; a 140-grain bullet was said to reach 3000 fps from this cartridge. The 275 H&H was loaded to 2650 fps with the 140-grain bullet in Britain but the Western Cartridge Company here in America kicked a 175-grain slug along even faster.

When the Winchester outfit began work on a necked-down 338 cartridge, they concentrated on the 6.5mm (which became the 264 Winchester Magnum) instead of the 7mm because of the poor sales of the 275 Holland & Holland. Considering that the 7mm Remington Magnum is simply the 338 Magnum case necked down, and that the 264 has not been exactly a banner success, I suppose there is much gnashing of teeth at Olin.

Sometime in the late '40s Roy Weatherby began work on his 7mm Weatherby Magnum, a shortened, modified 300 Holland & Holland Magnum. Also at work were such luminaries as John Dubiel, formerly of the Hoffman Arms Company, who devised the 276 Du-

The author's favorite 7mm Magnum load is built around Norma MRP, the 150-grain Nosler Partition or Solid Base, and Federal 215 primers.

biel, a reshaped 275 H&H. Dubiel similarly changed and necked-down the 300 H&H and came up with the 280 Dubiel. Parker Ackley designed a short magnum 7mm in the '30s.

Just before the start of World War II, Remington was at work with two 7mm cartridges. One was similar to today's 280 Remington, being based on the 30-06 case, and the other was merely the 300 H&H necked to 284. The belted number appeared similar to the 280 Dubiel and also to the German 7x73 Von Hofe Belted. The War put the kibosh on further work, and it was many years before Remington finally brought out their 7mm magnum.

Subsequent to the second World War, renewed interest in the hot sevens brought forth such items as the one dreamed up by Santa Barbara gunsmith Roy Gradle. This number was made from the 348 Winchester case with the rim turned off, an extractor groove cut in the case, and the body blown out by fire-forming. The Mashburn Arms Company fabricated two versions, one on a short belted case and the other on a longer one. Gun writer Phil Sharpe came up with the 7x61 Sharpe and Hart, had ammo imported from Sweden and rifles from Denmark. The 7x61 S&H attained a small following, but since it didn't have the case capacity or ballistics of the older 7mm Weatherby Magnum, it didn't have much staying power. I have never seen a rifle chambered for the 7x61.

In the '50s Winchester started playing around with various offspring of the 458 Winchester Magnum. The 338 was the second Olin offering based on the short belted-case format, with the 264 following closely after. Les Bowman, at the time a rancher, outfitter, and gun bug, had "inherited" from Jack O'Conner an old 275 H&H Magnum. Les had Fred Huntington of RCBS re-barrel the gun for the 338 Magnum necked down to 7mm. I understand the barrel was stamped ".280 Remington Magnum."

Bowman took a few head of game with that gun, lent it to other hunters who did likewise, got Mike Walker of Remington interested in the load. Much of the initial experimenting and chronographing for the nascent 7mm Remington Magnum was done at the Bowman ranch near Cody, Wyoming. When Remington announced the new Model 700 Remington, one of the rounds chambered in it was the 7mm Remington Mag.

Remington's new baby was akin to many of the short magnums that had preceded it. It had a loaded overall length of 3.29 inches, just a bit short of the 30-06 at 3.34 inches. Case length of the magnum seven was 2.50 inches versus 2.494 for the ought-six. As you can see, any action long enough to house the 270 Winchester or 30-06 was ample for the 7mm Magnum. Of course the magnum cartridge had a belt, a fat case, a shoulder angle of 25 degrees, and a large head diameter of .532-inch. (The '06 clan sports a .473-inch head size.)

7mm Remington Magnum: Deer/Bear

South Carolina gun writer and big game hunter Layne Simpson took this mule deer buck out West using a Remington M700 7mm Magnum in a Six fiberglass stock. Under such snowy conditions, a "glass" stock is great! (Photo courtesy of Layne Simpson.)

When the new Remington load hit the market, its advertised ballistics were: 3260 fps from a 150-grain pointed Core Lokt, and 3020 fps from a 175-grain round nose Core Lokt. Muzzle energy was 3540 fpe with both. Today, things have been toned down a mite: the 150-grain bullet is now listed at 3110 fps for 3221 fpe; the 175-grain slug is shown at 2860 fps and 3179 fpe. Additionally, Winchester makes a 125-grain factory load at 3310 fps for 3042 fpe; Federal offers a 160-grain Nosler Partition at a listed 2950 fps and 3093 fpe, and a 165-grain soft point boat-tail at 2860 fps and 2998 fpe.

The Big Seven has been an unqualified success. In the two decades since its intro, it has climbed to the top half-dozen big game cartridges in ammo sales. Among reloaders, its approbation is at least as great; no non-military cartridge introduced since the mid-'50s has equaled it in reloading die sales, according to RCBS.

Why, you ask yourself? The reasons are ballistics, hunting success and ability, accuracy, availability, and manageable recoil from a truly super-potent magnum. All in all, quite a combination of attributes. Let's take a look at them individually.

Ballistics and Hunting

Going by factory-quoted figures, the 7mm Magnum retains 1930 fpe at a full 400 yards with the 150-grain Federal Premium soft point boat-tail. Know what beats that? The Federal Premium loading in the 300 Winchester Magnum, which consists of a 200-grain soft point boat-tail starting at 2830 fps and reaching 400 yards with 2240 fps remaining for 2230 fpe. The 225-grain Winchester pointed soft point in the 338 Winchester Magnum, starting at 2780 fps and arriving at the 400-yard mark with 2005 fpe of punch. Discounting proprietary cartridges, those are the *only* two loads that shade the 7mm Remington.

In return for their slight energy advantage at long range, each of the cartridges mentioned kicks a great deal more strenuously. The 300 Magnum drops 2.7 inches more at 400 yards, which is 13 percent (17.6 vs 20.3 inches). The 338 dips more yet, showing a 25.0-inch drop. Thus, the 7mm Remington Magnum hits with 300 fewer fpe than the Super Thirty out at 400 long yards, while smacking you much less forcefully at the buttpad and exhibiting a flatter trajectory than the top 300 Winchester Magnum loading. And, it yields only 75 paltry fpe to the 338 while showing a trajectory 30 percent flatter and *much* less recoil.

The hunting success stories of the 7mm Remington Magnum are legion. When the cartridge first came out, Bob Hagel took one along with him in Idaho, slaying a fine bighorn ram, a big elk, a mule deer, and a Rocky Mountain goat. Only the goat required a second hit; the shot angle was tricky and the first slug didn't get inside the animal.

In the 1964 *Gun Digest* a fellow by the name of Sam B. Saxton related his African experiences with the new 7mm Remington. Saxton slew gerenuk, oryx, Thomson's gazelle, eland, Grant's gazelle, wildebeeste, impala, Grevy zebra and common zebra, waterbuck, greater kudu, bushbuck, duiker, jackal, hyena, and leopard. In all, he took more than 40 head while on a 50-day safari. He concluded his article:

. . . the new 7mm Remington [was] a pleasure to shoot and extremely capable in all capacities when we used the correct loads under the conditions for which they were designed. Remington's efforts represent a major breakthrough on the part of one of our oldest gun companies, not only in the design of the new rifle, but in bringing to fruition the potential of the time-proven 7mm caliber.

John Wootters is another fan of the 7mm Remington Mag. In the October, 1980, issue of *Guns & Ammo* he had this to say:

In looking over my notes, I find that I've collected more than 35 different species of game animals around the world with the 7mm [magnum]. The largest was a Cape buffalo, but that was a stunt, and I do not mean to sound as though I'm touting the 7mm Magnum for such brutes. American elk and big African greater kudu—almost as large as most trophy elk—have been the largest animals I've taken with the cartridge which I consider reasonable game . . . On this continent, I've used the 7mm Remington for such game as Stone rams, mountain goat, pronghorn, whitetails and mulies.

All things considered, the 7mm Remington Magnum has handled all the above listed animals for me, plus scores more in Africa, America, and Canada, with a certain comforting certainty that no other round has ever quite equalled in my own experience. Obviously, it has done the same for thousands of other hunters, judging from the fact that it has always been and remains today one of the hottest-selling big-game rounds on the list, almost from its introduction in 1962.

My elk hunting partner, Dave Jacobson, dropped a big Idaho bull in the Bitterroots back in 1978. Dave and his guide had topped a rise in an area thick with spruce when a bull bugled at them. They stalked a while, then sat down to wait. When it seemed that the bull was coming no closer, they moved again. Spotting the elk at about 70 yards, Dave slipped a 175-grain Nosler into its ribs. The bull stepped into an opening, stopped, looked back dolefully over its shoulder. Dave shot again, breaking the bull's neck.

Jacobson uses that 7mm Remington Magnum for everything. Once he shot just over the backline of a nice pronghorn because he had misjudged the range. He told me the buck looked very small, so he assumed it was way out yonder. He tossed a shot, aiming high at the shoulder. The buck just stood there. Dave fired again; now the buck was becoming nervous. Just as the antelope decided things were getting a bit uncomfortable, Dave tried again. Off galloped the buck. After much time and some sneaking around, Jacobson maneuvered himself within 100 yards and made his shot good. Upon dressing the animal, he discovered that his first three shots had hit right above where he'd aimed; each bullet had cut a groove through the hair on the buck's back! Dave guesses that the antelope was about 150 yards away when he first fired at it.

Bill Haworth, of High Point, North Carolina, took a Big Seven after mule deer in the Powder River Breaks of Montana. He was hunting high atop a ridge when he spotted a big buck down in a draw. The deer took off before Bill could get settled, but it reappeared on the opposite slope where it stopped running, turned broadside, and ambled along. Placing the vertical crosswire on the chest and the horizontal wire on the backline, Haworth let drive. The buck tumbled. Bill figured the range for around 400 yards. He was using the fine 162-grain Hornady soft point boat-tail in a Remington Model 700. Another time he used the same load on another buck with the same results. Bill is partial to his Seven Mag.

About recoil. I have always found the 7mm Magnums easy to handle. Not so the 300 Mags and up. To my educated shoulder, the Big Seven feels a lot like a 30-06, and it's about the same with everyone I know. In the previously-mentioned article, John Wootters wrote: "Most shooters maintain that they cannot detect any difference in recoil between a 7mm Magnum and a 30-06, and I agree." So do I.

Of course, in actual foot-pounds of recoil, there is a

As you can see, this Six-stocked Remington M700 7mm Mag comes in at a feathery 7½ pounds scoped, which is very light for a magnum.

7mm Remington Magnum: Deer/Bear

Weatherby makes the Vanguard VGX in 7mm Remington Magnum. It's accurate.

Doctor Bill Barry uses and dotes on this "Super Seven" as he calls it. It's a Weatherby Vanguard 7mm Remington Magnum.

difference; the Big Seven kicks up about half-again as much ruckus. But I can't *feel* it. It seems that most folks can't. So much for the 7mm Mag's recoil; if you can handle a 30-06, you can likely conquer a Big Seven without a hitch.

When it comes to availability, the 7mm Remington Magnum is in its element. Ruger makes his Number 1 single shooter for the round, and Browning tools up their BAR semi-auto. Aside from those two notables, the Seven Mag is a bolt-action proposition. According to the current *Gun Digest*, you can have your pick of Alpine, BSA, Bighorn, Browning, Colt-Sauer, DuBiel, Heym, Kleinguenther, Krico, M-S Safari Arms, Interarms Mark X, Remington M700, Ruger M77, Sako, Savage 110-C, Smith & Wesson M1500, Steyr-Mannlicher, Weatherby Vanguard, Whitworth Express, Wichita Magnum, Winchester M70. There oughta be something in that list to suit your fancy.

Accuracy

I recently prepared an article for *Shooting Times* magazine in which I detailed the results of accuracy testing more than 100 rifles of many types, brands, and calibers. While preparing that piece, it surprised me just how precise my Big Sevens have been. I've tested eight in all, seven of them extensively. They are: Remington M700 Classic, Interarms, Cavalier, Colt-Sauer, Ruger M77, Ruger Number 1, Winchester M70, Golden Eagle M7000, and the Whitworth Express.

The two most accurate were the Interarms Cavalier and the Colt-Sauer, both of which averaged 1.30 inches for several five-shot groups from the bench at 100 yards. The Cavalier liked a handload consisting of 52.0 grains

of H205 under the 175-grain Speer Mag-Tip; the Colt preferred the excellent 175-grain Hornady soft point factory load to any of my handloads.

If we took an average for the top two loads, the Cavalier would come out on top by the tiniest of margins. With the 150-grain Nosler Partition ahead of a top charge of H205, groups ran 1.31 inches. The Colt summoned a 1.34-inch aggregate with its runner-up recipe, 66.0 grains of Norma MRP and the 150-grain Nosler Solid Base.

Next in the accuracy sweepstakes was my beautiful and portable Ruger Number 1. Its favored load was 78.0 grains of Hodgdon H870 pushing the 175-grain Nosler Partition, with eight groups averaging 1.33 inches. The muzzle speed was an impressive 3008 fps for a whopping 3517 fpe! Great load; great rifle. Another good load in the Ruger features a maximum load of Norma MRP and the 140-grain Nosler Solid Base; the average was 1⅞ inches.

My Whitworth Express and Model 70 Winchester tied for the next position, both grouping 1.40 inches for the average. The Model 70 did its best with the 154-grain Hornady soft point factory stuff, while the Whitworth liked 66.0 grains of MRP and the 150-grain Nosler Solid Base (as several of my guns have). Second spot in the Whitworth Express went to the hot 150-grain Norma factory ammo. The Model 70 liked the old 175-grain Federal Premium soft point boat-tail factory load as bride's maid.

The Golden Eagle averaged 1.43 inches with the same Norma MRP/150-grain Nosler handload the above rifles liked. Just off the pace was 60.0 grains of Winchester 785 under the 175-grain Speer Grand Slam for a 1.64-inch mean. Staying right with the latter hand-load was the Hornady 175-grain factory load, and it was quite a bit faster in that rifle to boot.

My Remington Model 700 Classic turned in its best performance with the 175-grain Hornady soft point factory ammo (that stuff sure shoots well in a *lot* of guns), printing 1½ inches on the nose. The 165-grain Federal Premium was in the hunt at 1.65 inches.

Least accurate but also the least fired was the Ruger 77. The 150-grain Federal soft point load showed a 1.82-inch spread for three, five-shot groups.

Averaging the best load in all eight guns gives us a

1.435-inch aggregate. That is pretty danged good in my opinion for untuned magnum rifles, none of which had a great deal of load development except the Cavalier.

I'm sure you've noticed that my favored propellants for the Big Seven are all on the slow side. Even with the relatively lightweight slugs like the 140-grain Nosler, I like nothing faster than IMR or Hodgdon 4350. In rifles with fairly long throats, like my Number 1, I'll pick the ultra-slow H870 if my gun will group it at all.

Hornady makes a neat 100-grain hollow point, Speer offers a dandy 115-grain hollow point, Nosler, Sierra and Hornady all catalogue 120-grain spitzers in 7mm

Fine 7mm bullets include (left to right) 139-grain Hornady SP, 150-grain Nosler Partition, 160-grain Sierra SPBT, and the 175-grain Speer Mag-Tip.

Across a broad range of guns, the most accurate 7mm Magnum factory load the author has used is this 175-grain Hornady soft point. In some guns, handloads wouldn't equal it.

(Left) Perhaps the author's favorite 7mm Remington Magnum was this Interarms Cavalier. From coyotes to elk, it would do the job.

This Colt-Sauer was tied with the Cavalier as the most accurate Big Sevens the author has fired, although all 7mm Magnums group well. The big Colt averaged 1.3 inches at 100 yards.

The Savage 110-C is made up in 7mm Remington Magnum. It features a handy detachable clip, something of value to hunters.

caliber. If I planned to use a Big Seven for varminting, I suppose I'd try one or more of those. But I don't plan to. Despite the fact that the recoil is not decapitating, it isn't really fun in shirtsleeve weather. Nor is the muzzle blast. I'll ignore the 7mm Magnum for vermin, thanks just the same.

But for most anything else in this country short of the big bears, the 7mm Remington Magnum will do quite nicely. As a deer-only rifle, you can do much better. For pronghorns specifically, the 7mm Remington Magnum is good but a bit too much. If shots at elk both in the timber and at very long range were my prime con-

cern, there are a couple or three other cartridges I'd choose if I could have my druthers. But for all the above, there is no better load than the 7mm Magnum. It shoots flatter than the 25-06, thumps harder at really long range than the 8mm Remington Magnum, will penetrate with the best heavy-game loads if stoked with the 175-grain Nosler Partition, and do it all with a backward shove that feels about like a 30-06. It will group under 1½ inches in most any turnbolt sporter without 6 months worth of tuning, and it's not so heavy you can't carry it all by yourself. Good cartridge, this 7mm Remington Magnum.

7mm Remington Magnum

HANDLOAD DATA

Bullet Wt. Grs.	Type	Powder Wt. Grs.	Type	Primer	Case	MV, (fps)	ME, (fpe)	Rifle/ Bbl. (in.)	Remarks
139	Hrndy. SP	58.0	H205*	CCI 250	Win.	2969	2721	Cavalier/24	Consistent velocity
139	Hrndy. SP	66.0	Win. 785	Fed. 215	Win.	3033	2840	Cavalier/24	Poor accuracy
140	Nos. SB	**68.0**	MRP	Fed. 215	Fed.	**3164**	**3113**	Rug. No. 1/26	Accurate
150	Nos. SB	**66.0**	MRP	Fed. 215	Win.	**3104**	**3210**	Cavalier/24	Fair accuracy
150	Nos. SB	**66.0**	MRP	Fed. 215	Win.	**2902**	**2806**	Gold. Eagle/24	Most acc. in this gun
150	Nos. SB	**66.0**	MRP	Fed. 215	Win	**3016**	**3030**	Whit. Expr./24	Most acc. in this gun
150	Nos. Part.	53.0	H205*	CCI 250	Win.	2853	2712	Cavalier/24	Most acc. in this gun
150	Nos. Part.	63.0	Win. 785	Fed. 215	Win.	2941	2882	Cavalier/24	Fair accuracy
160	Sierra SPBT	**64.0**	Win. 785	Fed. 215	Win.	**2889**	**2966**	Cavalier/24	Fair accuracy
160	Sierra SPBT	**65.0**	MRP	Fed. 215	Win.	**2985**	**3167**	Cavalier/24	Good velocity
175	Speer MT	52.0	H205*	Fed.215	Win.	2647	2723	Cavalier/24	Extremely accurate
175	Speer MT	60.0	Win. 785	Fed. 215	Win.	2674	2779	Cavalier/24	2nd most acc. this gun
175	Speer GS	60.0	Win. 785	Fed. 215	Win.	2690	2812	Whit. Exp./24	Accurate
175	Speer MT	62.0	MRP	Fed. 215	Win.	2860	3179	Cavalier/24	Good energy level
175	Nos. Part.	**78.0**	H870	Fed. 215	Fed.	**3008**	**3517**	Rug. No. 1/26	Most acc. this gun; fast

*Propellant discontinued.

SP—Soft Point; SB—Solid Base; SPBT—Soft Point Boat-Tail; MT—Mag-Tip; GS—Grand Slam.

CAUTION:
Loads recommended and suggested herein have been carefully listed, but are intended solely as a guide to readers and neither the publisher nor author accept any responsibility for results of their use.
Maximum loads, listed in bold, should be reduced by 10 percent and worked up to cautiously.

FACTORY LOAD DATA

Bullet Wt. Grs.	Type	MV, (fps)	ME, (fpe)	Rifle/ Bbl. (in.)	Remarks
125 Win.	SP	3224	2886	Colt-Sauer/24	Fair accuracy
125 Win.	SP	3293	3011	Whit. Expr./24	Very high velocity
125 Win.	SP	3362	3138	Rug. No. 1/26	Extremely high vel.
150 Fed. Premium	SPBT	2932	2864	Rug. No. 1/26	Extremely accurate
150 Fed. Premium	SPBT	2855	2715	Colt-Sauer/24	Fair accuracy
150 Win.	SP	3048	3095	Cavalier/24	Good accuracy
150 Rem.	SP	3047	3093	Gold. Eagle/24	Good velocity
150 Rem.	SP	3073	3146	Whit. Expr./24	Fair accuracy; fast
150 Norma	SPBT	3187	3384	Gold. Eagle/24	Most potent load tested
150 Norma	SPBT	3155	3316	Whit. Expr./24	Very accurate
154 Hrndy.	SP	2950	2977	Win. M70/24	Fair accuracy
154 Hrndy.	SP	2952	2981	Rug. M77/24	Fair accuracy
165 Fed. Premium	SPBT	2881	3042	Rug. No. 1/26	Poor accuracy
175 Fed.	SP	2824	3100	Rug. No.1/26	Very accurate
175 Fed.	SP	2849	3155	Ruger M77/24	Accurate
175 Fed.	SP	2771	2985	Cavalier/24	Most acc. in this gun
175 Fed. Premium	SPBT	2711	2857	Colt-Sauer/24	Very accurate
175 Rem.	SP	2825	3102	Whit. Expr./24	Good velocity
175 Hrndy.	SP	2654	2738	Colt-Sauer/24	Most acc. in this gun
175 Hrndy.	SP	2680	2792	Gold. Eagle/24	Extremely accurate

SP—Soft Point; SPBT—Soft Point Boat-Tail.

SPECIFICATIONS

Shell Holders
RCBS: 4 or 26
Bonanza: 2
Lyman: 13
Pacific: 5

Bullet Diameter
Jacketed: .284"
Cast: None

Lengths
Trim: 2.490"
Maximum Case: 2.500"
Maximum Overall: 3.290"

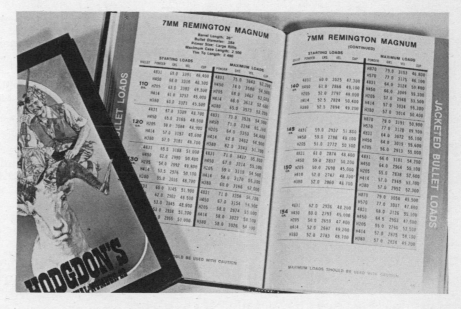

Good handload data for the 7mm Magnum, like that found in the Hodgdon Manual, is a must for the reloader.

CAUTION:

Loads recommended and suggested herein have been carefully listed, but are intended solely as a guide to readers and neither the publisher nor author accept any responsibility for results of their use. **Maximum loads, listed in bold, should be reduced by 10 percent and worked up to cautiously.**

7mm Weatherby Magnum

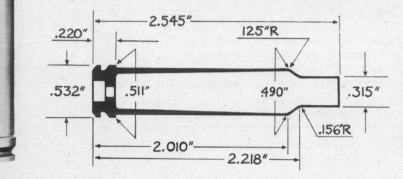

2.545" *125"R* *.220"*

.532" *.511"* *.490"* *.315"*

.156"R

2.010" *2.218"*

". . . The Weatherby 7mm Magnum offers muzzle energies well in excess of the 30-06 class, coupled with a stretched-garter trajectory and manageable recoil."

ACCORDING to some sources, the 7mm Weatherby Magnum was introduced by Roy Weatherby in 1944, concurrent with the 300 Weatherby Magnum. While my collection of *Gun Digest* is not complete—missing the years between the Second Edition, copyrighted 1946, and the Fifth Edition, labeled 1951—the Second Edition carries no mention of Weatherby rifles at all. My Fifth Edition does show the "Weatherby Bolt-Action Magnum Rifles" as available in 220 Weatherby Rocket (a Swift variant), 257 Weatherby Magnum, 270 Weatherby Magnum, and 300 Weatherby Magnum (also referred to as the "Improved 300 H&H Magnum"). Retail prices were $165 for the standard permutations, up to $350 for custom versions built on military Mauser, commercial Mauser or Winchester Model 70 actions.

Why no mention of the 7mm Weatherby? My theory is that specs for the cartridge had not been settled on at that time. I've searched meticulously, to very little avail, to dig up an authority who satisfies me as *knowing* when the 7mm Weatherby was first proffered to the shooting public. The best I could do was the following, quoted from *The Big-Game Rifle,* copyright 1952, by Jack O'Conner:

> Latest Weatherby Magnum cartridge is also a 7mm, and in the present state of technical development in this sinful world I think it is about as good a long-range mountain cartridge as one can get . . . .
> Weatherby's first version of his [7mm] Magnum came

about because G.I.'s returning from the European theater brought in dozens of 7x64 rifles for which no American ammunition was available. Others brought in standard 7x57s and wanted some goat glands put in them. Weatherby made up reamers to rechamber these rifles for the shortened Magnum case with a conventional 30-degree shoulder and did some loading and chronographing so he could furnish some dope.

> Results were encouraging, so the next step was to make up a set of reamers using the radius shoulder which is a trademark of the Weatherby cases . . . .

> The 7mm Weatherby Magnum cartridge *is still not so completely developed* [italics mine] but that the curious experimenter could add to the knowledge about it. For example, so far as I know, chronograph tests have not been made with cases with the new shoulder and 175-grain and 180-grain bullets.

Based on the foregoing, and considering what I've gleaned elsewhere, my opinion for what it's worth is that the 7mm Weatherby Magnum was not offered as a factory-standard cartridge until sometime subsequent to 1952.

Unlike the larger-cased 300 Weatherby, the 7mm shares its brass with the 257 and 270 Weatherby Magnums. All are relatively straight-sided cartridges with a double-radius shoulder, belted case, and an overall case length of 2.549 inches. As with all Weatherby cartridges except the 224 Magnum, there is more power on tap than with similar-caliber American offerings.

Although such Weatherby numbers as the 257, 270,

The author's favorite 7mm Weatherby Magnum propellant is IMR 4831. Using 63.0 grains of that powder and the 175-grain Hornady soft point, the author got consistent, five-shot groups that hovered around 1¼ inches.

Both Remington and Weatherby 7mm Magnums have differing throat lengths. The Mark V has a virtual free bore, illustrated by the 7mm Weatherby Magnum cartridge at the far right with the bullet seated backward.

300, 375, and 460 Magnums have been chambered in rifles other than those of the South Gate firm, I can find no evidence that the same holds true for the 7mm Weatherby Magnum, at least in production guns. (Of course, while outfits such as DuBiel and Champlin advertise that they will build nearly anything you want, they don't qualify under my definition of "production guns.") In fact, the 7mm Weatherby seems to have been singularly ignored.

For example, the Kleinguenther K-15 bolt-action is available in 257, 270, and 300 Weatherby Magnums—plus the 308 Norma of all things—but is not obtainable in 7mm Weatherby, according to current Kleinguenther literature. You can purchase a Colt-Sauer chambered to 300 Weatherby but not the 7mm. Mauser will sell you a Model 66S Magnum rifle with 300 Weatherby

stamped on the barrel; not so if you long for a 7mm. And so on.

I find this state of affairs passing strange. The 7mm Remington Magnum took off like designer jeans when it was birthed in 1962, despite the fact that no 7mm cartridge, magnum or otherwise, had done more than passably well in this country, ever. The 7x61 Sharpe & Hart was an early factory-loaded belted magnum, gestated about the same time as the 7mm Weatherby. Like the Weatherby Big Seven, the 7x61 lined no coffers with gold. Earlier yet were such antecedents as the 7mm Mashburn Magnum, the 7mm Barnes Magnum, and the 275 Holland & Holland Magnum. All dead. In fact, if it hadn't been for the late Warren Page, shooting editor of *Field & Stream,* who toted his 7mm Mashburn, Ole Betsy, from Montana to Tanzania, the Big Sevens would

7mm Weatherby Magnum: Deer/Bear

Weatherby's Mark V is available in a number of styles and grades. Seen here is the "Crown Custom," available in 7mm Weatherby Magnum.

The author and others feel the Weatherby 7mm Magnum is ballistic poison on large game such as elk and moose. If you're planning a pack hunt for elk in the Rockies, consider taking a Mark V chambered for the Big Seven—it won't let you down.

have remained obscure until Remington entered the fray.

Remington's 7mm Magnum pretty well mopped up the competition. Weatherby, maintaining as it does a sort of captive audience of "Weatherbyphiles," hung on to such popularity as the 7mm Weatherby exhibited. Meanwhile, other 28-caliber factory cartridges hoed a tough row. The 7x61 hung on a few years, then expired. Remington's own 280, introduced only a few years prior to the Seven Mag and aimed at the 270 Winchester, suffered at the hands of the new, belted cartridge. It is still around, catered to by died-in-the-wool rifle buffs who consider it nearly an ideal cartridge in several aspects, but it heads no pop charts. The 284 Winchester was a flash in the pan; today it's as dead as the Brooklyn Dodgers. Still doddering on is the ancient 7x57 Mauser, kept afloat by legions of surplus weaponry and a fervently reverent press. The upstart 7mm-08 is not in direct competition with the 7mm Remington Magnum; it has garnered its own glassy following.

Why then, if the 7mm Remington is so terrific, should anyone want a 7mm Weatherby. Well, perhaps because said person is enamored of the Weatherby Mark V rifle, an understandable position since it's an excellent gun, and you can't buy one chambered for the belted Remington 28-bore. The Weatherby wins by default. Maybe our prospective buyer is a southpaw; no one but Weatherby offers a 7mm Magnum for the sinistral shooter. Perchance our budding hunter is after the Mag Seven that delivers the most zip for his "moolah," in factory form. The Weatherby wins hands-down.

Ballistics

Weatherby quotes the following for its 7mm factory ammo: 139-grain soft point, 3300 fps for 3362 fpe; 154-grain soft point, 3160 fps, and 3415 fpe; 175-grain soft point, 3070 fps for 3663 fpe. All are from a 26-inch barrel. How realistic are those figures?

Chronographing a 24-inch Weatherby Mark V, I received the following data: 139-grain, 3227 fps and 3215 fpe; 154-grain, 3132 fps and 3355 fpe; 175-grain, 2985 fps and 3463 fpe. Recently, I clocked a different batch in a 24-inch barreled Weatherby Fibermark. The results: 154-grain, 3186 fps and 3472 fpe; 175-grain, 2980 fps for 3451 fpe. Two different guns, two different lots of ammo. Both pretty damn good.

The fastest 175-grain factory load I've chronographed in any 24-inch barreled 7mm Remington Magnum was one lot of 175-grain Remington Pointed Core Lokt that managed 2825 fps in an Interarms Whitworth Express, for 3102 fpe of punch. Several rifles have sent the 150-grain Norma factory load sizzling across the screens in excess of 3140 fps, the fastest giving 3187 fps for 3384 fpe. Top 125-grain load was the Winchester Pointed Soft Point at 3293 fps in the Whitworth. That's good for 3011 fpe.

Thus, we find that the best factory fodder yields around 3000 fpe with 125-grain loads, 3380 fpe from the 150-grain Norma (nothing else will approach the Norma loading), and about 3100 fpe with the 175-grain load in the Remington cartridge. The Weatherby rendering gets about 3230 fpe with the light 139-grain load, 3470 fpe from the 154-grain, and 3460 fpe with the 175-grain soft point. Decide for yourself which is more potent. (Remember that all loads were chronographed by me in standard rifles of identical barrel lengths, and that the results shown for the Remington cartridge are for the *best* loads I've tried, not the norm.)

Handloading

When it comes to handloads, my experience has been that the 7mm Weatherby Magnum maintains a slight lead over the Remington offering. I've safely reached just under 3000 fps with a 160-grain Sierra soft point boat-tail and 66.0 grains of IMR 4831 in my Weatherby. The fastest 160-grain load I've clocked in a 7mm Remington Mag was 2985 fps.

The best powders happen to be the same for each cartridge. I like such slow numbers as Norma MRP, Hodgdon H870, and DuPont IMR 4831. Top handload in my Mark V was the 175-grain Hornady Spire Point over 63.0 grains of IMR 4831. Groups ran just a hair over 1¼ inches for five shots at 100 yards. Only one magnum rifle I've tested would beat that accuracy performance, and that was another Weatherby. Muzzle speed with that load is nothing to glue on a billboard, but it is adequate for most hunting situations at 2817 fps for 3084 fpe.

Which brings up the hunting angle. In the aforementioned book, *The Big-Game Rifle,* Jack O'Conner said of the Big Seven Weatherby:

> For the man who wants great power and long-range

(Right) This Weatherby Mark V 7mm Weatherby Magnum shot well, grouping just over 1¼ inches for five-shot groups at 100 yards. (The scope is a 3×9 Weatherby Premier.)

For those who like to load large-capacity, belted cases, be sure to select a press that affords you lots of leverage—it will only make the job easier. The RCBS Big Max shown here is the largest press that firm offers. It will suffice to say that loading up a batch of 7mm Weatherby brass, on this press, is as strain-free as you could ask for.

> accuracy, yet with recoil and muzzle blast that won't knock a man out from under his hat, this [cartridge] looks like our baby.
>
> With the 160-grain bullet, which is probably the best bet for long-range big-game shooting, the 7mm. Magnum should be poison on elk, moose, and grizzly, and probably very bad medicine on the Alaska brownies, which I have never hunted.

(Remember, this was written prior to 1952.) Further on, he adds this:

> For big-game shooting the 160-grain bullet [has] high velocity [that] is well retained because of the good sectional density, and killing power out where the game is should be spectacular. Here is a cartridge with more power and a flatter trajectory than the 300 [Holland & Holland] Magnum, yet with a light enough recoil so that it can be shot accurately. No one will think he is touching off a 22 rim-fire when he lets go with the 7mm Magnum, but the recoil is not too bad.

That about sums it up. The Big Seven Weatherby is at its best when used on large animals at long range. Al-

The author's choice for large game (above 400 pounds in weight) is the Weatherby Fibermark 7mm Magnum. With its "dust" finish and durable fiberglass stock, the Fibermark is one of the finest hunting rifles available commercially.

From left to right: 150-grain Nosler Solid Base; 175-grain Speer Grand Slam; 160 grain Sierra soft point boattail; 160-grain Speer Grand Slam and the 175-grain Hornady soft point. All of these 7mm bullets are potentially superb performers in the 7mm Weatherby Magnum.

though there is nothing wrong with shooting big critters at close range, that is not the forte of the belted 7mm calibers. In the shooting scheme of things, the 7mm Weatherby (and the 7mm Remington Magnum) is as close to the mythical all-around big game cartridge as we're likely to get. (Note that I stipulate all-around *big game* cartridge; there is *no* cartridge that is ideal on all game from marmots to musk oxen, regardless of prodigious arguments mounted to the contrary.) As O'Conner pointed out, the Weatherby 7mm Magnum offers muzzle energies well in excess of the 30-06 class, coupled with a stretched-garter trajectory and manageable recoil. In fact, if I lived out West or planned to spend a lot of time hunting there, or farther north where game grows big and carnivores wax heavy, I would select just such a combination. In fact, just this year I did exactly that.

A rifle I've recently received for testing, the new Weatherby Fibermark, would fill the bill nigh perfectly.

It boasts a fiberglass stock that won't warp under extremes of heat, cold, or humidity. The metalwork is finished in a subdued luster, so as not to flash sunbeams and spook unwary fauna. The fiberglass stock enables a relatively light rifle, which assists in keeping my pulse under control as I wheeze my way up a mountain. Additionally, the glass stock will give under recoil. Not much; just enough to take the sting off. The gun has back-up iron sights in case my scope fogs or gets knocked out of whack.

The rifle is chambered for the 7mm Weatherby Magnum. Not coincidentally; I ordered it that way. Perhaps a 7mm Remington Magnum or 300 Winchester would serve as well. Then again, perhaps not. The Remington Magnum doesn't come out of the box dressed in glass. Neither does the 300 Winchester Magnum, and it kicks the stuffing out of you to boot. No, I'll stick with my Weatherby Fibermark Seven Mag. Its beauty is more than skin-deep.

7mm Weatherby Magnum

HANDLOAD DATA

Bullet Wt. Grs.	Type	Powder Wt. Grs.	Type	Primer	Case	MV, (fps)	ME, (fpe)	Rifle/ Bbl. (in.)	Remarks
160	Sierra SPBT	66.0	IMR 4831	Fed. 215	Wby.	2990	3176	Wby. Mk.V/24	Good velocity
160	Speer GS	80.0	H870	Fed. 215	Wby.	2882	2950	Wby. Mk.V/24	Poor accuracy
175	Hrndy. SP	63.0	IMR 4831	Fed. 215	Wby.	2817	3084	Wby. Mk. V/24	Extremely accurate

SPBT—Soft Point Boat-Tail; SP—Soft Point.

FACTORY LOAD DATA

Bullet Wt. Grs.	Type	MV, (fps)	ME, (fpe)	Rifle/ Bbl. (in.)	Remarks
139	Wby. SP	3227	3215	Wby. Mk. V/24	Fastest load tested
154	Wby. SP	3132	3355	Wby. Mk. V/24	Accurate
154	Wby. SP	3186	3472	Wby. Fmark./24	Accurate
175	Wby. SP	2985	3463	Wby. Mk. V/24	Most acc. in this gun
175	Wby. SP	2980	3451	Wby. Fmark./24	Fair accuracy

SP—Soft Point.

SPECIFICATIONS

Shell Holders
RCBS: 4
Bonanza: 2
Lyman: 13
Pacific: 5

Bullet Diameter
Jacketed: .284″

Lengths
Trim: 2.540″
Maximum Case: 2.550″
Maximum Overall: 3.260″

The flat-shooting 7mm Weatherby Magnum has a reputation for both accuracy and stopping power. Out West it is considered to be a superb elk cartridge.

CAUTION:
Loads recommended and suggested herein have been carefully listed, but are intended solely as a guide to readers and neither the publisher nor author accept any responsibility for results of their use. **Maximum loads, listed in bold, should be reduced by 10 percent and worked up to cautiously.**

30-30 Winchester

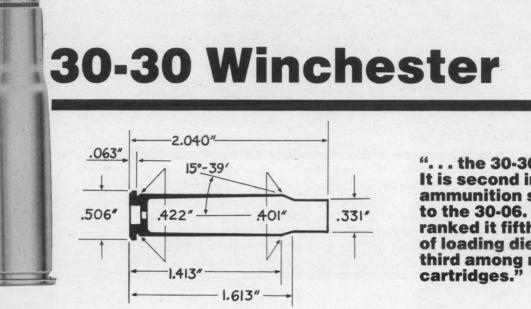

2.040"
.063"
15°-39'
.506"
.422"
.401"
.331"
1.413"
1.613"

". . . the 30-30 lives on. It is second in rifle ammunition sales only to the 30-06. RCBS ranked it fifth in sales of loading dies in 1982, third among rifle cartridges."

AFTER years of disparaging press, through two world wars and two "police actions," despite the advent of faster, more exciting, more powerful cartridges, the 30-30 Winchester lives on. It is second in rifle ammunition sales only to the 30-06. RCBS ranked it fifth in sales of loading dies in 1982, third among rifle cartridges. Winchester (now U.S. Repeating Arms) has built more than 5,000,000 Model 94 rifles and carbines; Marlin peddles thousands of lever-action 30-30's each year; Savage fabricates a bevy of inexpensive Model 340 bolt-guns per annum; Harrington & Richardson sells more than a few Topper single shots. Legions of orange-clad hunters take to the deer woods each fall, clutching light, handy 30-30 rifles in their mittened hands.

All this from a cartridge that is scarcely as long as your index finger, wears no belt, has no "magnum" appendage attached to its sobriquet, fails to shoot as flat as a taut wire, carries not a ton of energy within its limited confines. It is older than my maiden Aunt Mildred; carbines and rifles chambered to it are doing quite well if they keep all their shots within a 3-inch circle at 100 yards; and its trajectory is as curved as a bald man's pate. Despite the foregoing, the 30-30 is as popular as a wet T-shirt contest. Why?

To cast some light on the caprice of public whim, let's shift the scene to the mid-1890s. John Browning has just designed a strong, light, handsome lever-action rifle, and Winchester plans to tool up for it. The new gun en-

ters the commercial fray in 1894, chambered for the black powder 32-40 and 38-55 cartridges, and causes only a faint stir. Ah, but waiting in the wings . . .

Smokeless powder and jacketed bullets are not unknown in 1894, just very new. The French army had started the trend in 1888 with the 8mm Lebel, and nearly every other military organization in the world has seen the advantages and followed suit. The United States adopts the 30-40 Krag in 1892, loads it with jacketed slugs and smokeless powder. Winchester builds a few Model 1885 single shots, barreled for the 30-40 Krag, and sells them prior to 1894. And thus the stage is set to perpetrate some of the most prolific factual errors ever to be repeated and distorted by the firearms press.

The 30 Winchester Center Fire, or 30 WCF as the 30-30 was dubbed upon its debut in 1895, was first loaded with a 160-grain jacketed bullet at a nominal muzzle speed of 1960 fps. The Model 94 lever-action in which it appeared was the first American sporting rifle to be offered with a nickel-steel barrel as standard. The cartridge was loaded with 30 grains of smokeless propellant. Those are the facts ma'am. Let's examine some popular misconceptions.

Error number one: the 30-30 was introduced in 1894 along with the Model 94 Winchester. Wrong. As mentioned above, the 30-30 was introduced in 1895, although it *was* through the Model 1894 Winchester. Error number two: the 30-30 was the first smokeless-

Many years ago, Winchester chambered their Model 54 bolt-action (and then the Model 70) for the 30 WCF. Today, the only bolt-action chambered for this venerable cartridge is Savage's 340, accuracy from which can oftentimes be excellent. (Photo courtesy of Layne Simpson.)

powder cartridge produced in the United States. Nope. The 30-40 Krag was. Error number three: the Model 94 30-30 was the first sporting rifle chambered for a smokeless-powder cartridge. Close, but no cigar. The 1885 Winchester in 30-40 Krag gets the prize. Before we get to the final error, let me admit to being one of those who has made it. In print. In the October, 1983 edition of *Shooting Times* magazine I wrote: ". . . the 30-30 was the first *sporting* rifle cartridge designed in this country expressly for smokeless powder. . . ." How embarrassing. I can only offer the weak excuse that nearly every knowledgeable gun writer in the country harbors the same erroneous notion. (The less erudite gun writers most often subscribe to error number two.)

Let's set the record straight once and for all regarding the 30-30 and the origin of sporting-rifle usage of smokeless powder. The 30-30 was *not* the first sporting cartridge to utilize smokeless powder in its makeup , or if it was, it would be impossible to prove. The 30-30 was *tied* for first. It was first listed and offered for sale in August, 1895 *along with the 25-35 Winchester*. Simultaneously. Now you know the truth. Tell everyone you read it here.

On to less weighty matters. Splashing into the world amid the Gay Nineties, the 30-30's rise to fame was meteoric. Most blackpowder numbers of the period showed a mid-range rise of from 11 to 18 inches at 100 yards when zeroed at 200. The upstart 30 WCF carried a mere 5¾-inch maximum ordinate! That made hitting at long ranges ludicrously easy compared to what had gone before. In addition, striking energies were similar because of the sizzling muzzle speed generated by the hot new cartridge. Deer and similar-sized game fell as readily to the 30-30 as they did to the big-bore blackpowder loads. The combined attributes of light weight, mild recoil, flat trajectory, and adequate hitting power virtually inundated the entire class of blackpowder cartridges in less than 20 years. The old blackpowder cartridges that did manage a stay of execution did so by converting their fabrication to the use of smokeless powder and jacketed bullets.

The 30-30 created a storm of controversy among the hot-stove league. Wrinkled old-timers took one look at the puny little copper-clad slug and predicted that it would bounce off a deer's hide to go singing off through the forest. No way, they stated, could such a miniscule missile handle anything larger than a opossum. A few intrepid hunters tried the little cartridge in the face of public disapprobation. Eskimos slew Barren Ground grizzlies and polar bears with it; Mexicans used it on the great bears of Sonora and Chihuahua; stockmen in Arizona at the turn of the century considered themselves well-armed when tackling *ursus horribilis*. Frank Golata, Stone sheep guide and outfitter, used his 30-30 on grizzlies for years, owning no other rifle until 1946 when he acquired a 30-06. Word got out. When you shot an

From top to bottom: Marlin 336C; Savage 340; Winchester Model 94. All three of these rifles, and their variants, are chambered for the 30-30 Winchester. In the minds of many, the Model 94 has accounted for more whitetail deer than any other modern-day firearm.

animal, even a big one, through the heart, lungs, or shoulder with a 30-30 it generally fell over dead. More hunters tried it.

In 1901, Townsend Whelen resigned his commission in the National Guard and headed off to British Columbia in search of adventure. He traveled deep into the northern portion of the province, jumping off with his pack outfit from Ashcroft, near the Fraser River. He carried a pair of long guns, a 40-72 Model 95 Winchester and a Model 94 30-30. He shot a lot of game with both. Using the 30-30, he killed three mule deer with seven shots at very long range. Pacing it off, he found it just short of 300 yards.

After a good bit of experience and much deliberation, Whelen decided that 200 yards was the maximum range he could be certain of a killing hit on deer and reserved his shots to that distance or less from then on. (That was still 50 yards farther than he could rely on his 40-72.) Before swapping his 30-30 in 1906, Whelen killed many deer with it, all with lung shots. The bullets punched on through the deer, leaving exit wounds 2 inches in diameter.

The 30-30's rapid acceptance flushed many similar cartridges out of the swamp. Winchester introduced the 32 Special in 1902, giving it a bullet of slightly larger caliber and about 50 fps more velocity. The 32 Special was rifled with a 1-in-16 inch twist, theoretically to enable the handloader to use black powder for reloading. The slower twist, while indeed more amenable to black-powder usage, is reputed to have caused accuracy problems when the barrels became worn or rusted.

During the early years of this century, the firearms press crackled with controversy over the merits of the 30-30 versus the 32 Special. Writers with opposing viewpoints squared off in print and waged heated verbal warfare, each side offering lengthy and tedious support for their stance. Much ado over nothing. There was no demonstrable difference. Never has been, never will.

The 303 Savage, unleashed in the excellent Model 99 lever-action, gained some ground on the 30-30. Loaded with a 190-grain bullet of approximately the same diameter at roughly 100 fps less velocity, the 303 gained wide repute as being fine grizzly and moose medicine. I must admit, if forced to choose one or the other, I'd have opted for the 190-grain bullet in the 303 over the 170-grain slug in the 30-30. I'd likely have preferred climbing a tree to using either.

Remington spawned the 30 Remington Rimless, along with a bevy of similar loads designed to lure customers from the folds of Winchester. The 30 Remington was a dead ringer ballistically to the 30-30, but since it was offered in such popular and well-made arms as the Remington Model 14 pump and Model 8 semi-auto, it hung around for a long time. Full-metal-case bullets were produced by the factory, ostensibly for police use, which didn't hurt its popularity any.

Today the 303 Savage and 30 Remington are dead as the dirigible, and even less likely to be resurrected. The 32 Special is moribund, although Winchester revived it in 1983 in a special version of the Model 94. Sales of 30-30 rifles and ammunition on the other hand are healthy indeed, as we have seen.

Ballistics and Accuracy

Current 30-30 ballistics surpass anything available during Townsend Whelen's time, when the cartridge was gaining its reputation. The factories load a 170-grain bullet to 2200 fps, and a 150-grain at 2390. Federal offers a 125-grain varmint load, listed at 2570 fps. Remington sells their "Accelerator," which kicks a sabot-encased 22-caliber bullet weighing 55 grains out of the muzzle at a listed 3400 fps. This last load makes the 30-30 a respectable varmint slayer at reasonable distances in a rifle that handles it well, and roughly duplicates the 223 Remington ballistically.

When chronographed in 20-inch-barreled carbines, the 30-30 falls a bit short of the above numbers. Muzzle speeds run around 2050 fps with most brands, with an occasional lot achieving 2100 fps. In my 24-inch Marlin Model 336-A, the 170-grain Winchester Power Points clocked 2213 and the 170-grain Remington Round Nose Core-Lokt managed 2295 fps. I suspect that a 22-inch Savage Model 340 or Remington 788 would give just about factory-quoted ballistics.

Handloads for the 30-30 approximate the factory stuff; it is very difficult to better the quoted figures within acceptable pressure limits. After all, the ammunition companies have had 90 years to work out every conceivable combination. Common sense indicates that they'd have it right by now.

My best results loading for a pair of 30-30's has come with Winchester 748, although such medium-burning propellants as IMR 3031, IMR 4895, IMR 4064, and IMR 4320 are useful to varying degrees. Hodgdon's BL-C(2), H335, and H4895 as well as Hercules Re-Loder 7 have promise. Indeed, one of the most accurate

Federal and Nosler recently teamed up to provide factory 30-30 ammo loaded with 170-grain flat nose Partition bullets. Unfortunately, these bullets are not available to handloaders.

Du Pont's IMR 3031, in some 30-30s, will prove to be an excellent choice for the handloader.

Hodgdon's H4895 provided excellent accuracy with the 170-grain Hornady Flat Nose bullet in the author's Model 94. (See Handloading Data for load.)

Your old 30-30 can be turned into a passable varmint buster with the Remington Accelerator cartridge. It kicks a 55-grain, 22-caliber bullet out of the muzzle at about 3400 fps.

loads in my Model 94 consists of the 170-grain Hornady Flat Nose and 31.5 grains of H4895. Muzzle velocity is 2036 fps and groups run a little over 3 inches at 100 yards.

The single best handload for my Model 94 is a maximum charge of 35.0 grains of 748 under the 170-grain Hornady, ignited by a CCI 200 primer. Groups are a tenth of an inch tighter than the H4895 load while velocities run nearly 100 fps higher.

Decanting 30.5 grains of IMR 3031 behind the 170-grain Hornady FN yields 2118 fps in my Model 94, probably 2200 or so in the Marlin. Coupling the 150-grain Speer Flat Nose with 36.5 grains of 748 yields 2245 fps with acceptable accuracy in the Model 94.

For years, the 30-30 cartridge and the rifles that house it have been castigated in the shooting press for being inaccurate. I've read that the "average" Model 94 Winchester would do well to group all its shots in 4 or 5 inches from benchrest at 100 yards, with the typical Marlin or Savage 99 doing only marginally better. That's a heap of compost, partner. My personal Model 94 Winchester, which I purchased over the counter at Montgomery Ward, groups 2.40 inches with its pet load, the 170-grain Remington Core-Lokt. That is for several five-shot strings, from the bench at 100 yards, with a Lyman receiver sight. The Winchester 170-grain Power Point will do almost as well. My Marlin 336-A will print 2.96 inches with its favorite handload and 3 inches on the button with the 170-grain Remington factory load. Other 30-30s I've tested over the years will do as well. Anyone who suggests that such accuracy is insufficient for deer hunting, at the ranges within which the 30-30 is ballistically suited, is full of chicken-noodle soup.

The 30-30 for Deer

The same individuals who claim insufficient accuracy may tell you that the 30-30 is not even adequate for deer hunting. Should someone do so, merely excuse yourself politely and make good your escape; your conversant is obviously suffering delusions. The 30-30 has killed many millions of deer; not all of them ran off to become buzzard fodder. If such were the case, the cartridge would have been buried years ago. No, in the hands of a careful shot who knows a deer's anatomy and does not take risky shots at extended ranges (past 175 yards or so), the 30-30 will drop a whitetail quite neatly. Bear in mind that the bullets loaded in it were designed expressly for it and will expand properly at normal hunting ranges while penetrating adequately.

My old college crony, Fred Ritter, killed his first buck with a Model 94 30-30 carbine. Fred jumped the buck at 50 yards or so; by the time he had gathered his wits and upped his rifle, the deer was 70 yards out. A 170-grain load between the hams decked the buck on the spot.

Fred used the 30-30 on seven or eight more deer. He recently told me that within a 100 yards the 30-30 will drop a buck as decisively as any cartridge he's used. In fact, he opined that the 30-30 slug expands better on lung shots than the 35 Remington 200-grain, a load he also used for a while. He says he would not hesitate to use his 30-30 on deer any time. The reason he abandoned it was purely esoteric, having nothing whatever to do with any inadequacy of the load. Being the manager of a sporting goods store, he feels compelled to use a variety of cartridges, thus enabling him to advise his customers through his own experience, not theory. Of the 40 to 50 deer he has taken, Fred has used such diverse cartridges as the 223 Remington (legal in his state), 243, 6mm Remington, the 308 Winchester (which is his favorite), the 270, 30-30 and 35 Remington. Considering that Fred has been hunting deer for only 20 years, his record is exemplary.

Another friend, Bernard Price, hunts with a 30-30. His gun is a Winchester 94 Canadian Centennial, circa 1967, with the long 26-inch octagonal barrel. A decade ago, Bernard was shivering in a tree stand a few minutes before shooting light of opening day. A heavy frost tinged the landscape with crystal. Having hung his rucksack on one of the steps leading up to his stand, the frozen hunter busied himself with the task of retrieving from the sack his thermos of scalding coffee. Using fingers numbed with cold, Bernard extracted the thermos and promptly dropped it to the ground many feet below, where it broke. Alternating between cussing and shaking, Price watched the eastern sky brighten. Birds abandoned their roosts; a hawk eddied on chill currents of air.

A fat, five-point buck approached from upwind, paralelling a dry creekbed. The buck walked under a tree trunk, long-since toppled over from heavy wind, and kept meandering purposefully—until a 170-grain bullet socked into its brisket. Hit low in the chest, the buck leaped into a run and disappeared behind some honeysuckle. Bernard could hear the deer thrashing around but couldn't see it. He waited 45 minutes, climbed down, sought his buck. Having been hit through the lungs, the five-pointer had run less than 20 yards.

On another occasion, Bernard shot at a spike that simply turned and ran off, exhibiting no signs of a hit. Figuring he'd missed, Bernard stayed in his stand for about 2 hours. The more he cogitated, the less he believed he had missed the deer. Finally, flushed with curiosity he descended the tree and went to the white oak beside which the buck had been standing at the shot. Chunks of venison were all over the place with white chest-hair littering the ground. The blood trail was easy to follow: Bernard found his buck within 40 yards, stone dead.

One salient point: Bernard owns a half-dozen centerfire rifles, among them a 375 Winchester, a 444 Marlin, and a couple of 30-06s. Despite his ample battery, he has never killed a deer with any other rifle cartridge than the 30-30, indeed never hunts with anything else. His 30-30 works just fine, thank you.

And so, the old 30-30 plugs on. It has been a movie star for 50 years, has slain moose, caribou, polar bear and grizzlies. It served Pancho Villa's troops well in various Mexican donnybrooks, rode in a scabbard on many a cowhorse. It has become the definitive deer cartridge, by which most others are judged. In modern loadings, it is better than ever. In these days of deer hunting with handgun calibers approximating the power of the ancient 44-40 rifle cartridge, a load the 30-30 made obsolete virtually overnight, the grizzled old-timer is decried as underpowered, inadequate. Don't believe it.

30-30 Winchester

HANDLOAD DATA

Bullet Wt. Grs.	Type	Powder Wt. Grs.	Type	Primer	Case	MV (fps)	ME (fpe)	Rifle/ Bbl. (in.)	Remarks
150	Speer FN	36.5	Win. 748	CCI 200	Win.	2245	1679	Win. M94/20	Fastest tested
170	Hrndy. FN	30.5	IMR 3031	CCI 200	Win.	2118	1694	Win. M94/20	Not very acc. in Win. 94
170	Hrndy. FN	31.5	H4895	CCI 200	Win.	2036	1565	Win. M94/20	Accurate
170	Speer FN	34.5	Win. 748	CCI 200	Win.	2100	1665	Win. M94/20	Approx. fact. ball.
170	Hrndy. FN	**35.0**	Win. 748	CCI 200	Win.	**2130**	**1713**	Win. M94/20	Most acc. ld. in Win. 94

FN—Flat Nose.

FACTORY LOAD DATA

Bullet Wt. Grs.	Type	MV (fps)	ME (fpe)	Rifle/ Bbl. (in.)	Remarks
170	Fed. FN	2030	1556	Win. M94/20	Not very acc. in Win.
170	Fron. FN	2070	1618	Win. M94/20	Good deer load
170	Rem. RNCL	2110	1681	Win. M94/20	Most acc. ld. in Win.
170	Rem. RNCL	2295	1989	Mar. 336-A/24	Fastest load tested
170	Win. RNPP	2057	1598	Win. M94/20	Very accurate
170	Win. RNPP	2213	1849	Mar. 336-A/24	High velocity

FN—Flat Nose; RNCL—Round Nose Core Lokt; RNPP—Round Nose Power Point.

SPECIFICATIONS

Shell Holders
RCBS: 2
Bonanza: 4
Lyman: 6
Pacific: 2

Bullet Diameter
Jacketed: .308"

Lengths
Trim: 2.029"
Maximum Case: 2.040"
Maximum Overall: 2.550"

CAUTION:
Loads recommended and suggested herein have been carefully listed, but are intended solely as a guide to readers and neither the publisher nor author accept any responsibility for results of their use.
Maximum loads, listed in bold, should be reduced by 10 percent and worked up to cautiously.

300 Savage

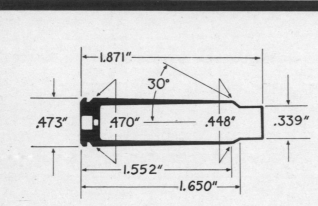

1.871"

30°

.473" .470" .448" .339"

1.552"

1.650"

"... the 300 Savage has all it takes and then some to hang venison from the meatpole."

SAVAGE Arms Company introduced the 300 Savage in either 1920 or 1921, depending on your source, in the Model 99 lever-action. (Ken Waters says September, 1921, so that's good enough for me.) Subsequently, Savage added it to their turnbolt Models 20, 40 and 45; Winchester offered it in their Models 54 and 70; and Remington produced a few bolt-action, slide and semi-automatic rifles for the cartridge. Today, only Savage continues to make it, and only in their economy-grade Model 99-E. So why did we need the cartridge in the first place?

The 300 was intended to offer ballistics in the 30-06 class, but in a cartridge short enough to function in Savage's bread-and-butter levergun. At the time of the 300's introduction, 30-06 ballistics consisted of a 150-grain bullet at 2700 fps. The new Savage round was so advertised. It didn't reach it, but it did exceed 2600 fps in 24-inch barrels. The little load took off.

Combining to insure the cartridge's popularity were the excellent ballistics (for that time), and its availability in a lever-action rifle. Remember, the American hunter of the 1920s was only beginning to be weaned from the levergun; that action type would continue to reign supreme for many years to come. Any cartridge that offered advanced ballistics in such a popular firearm type would certainly cause folks to sit up and take notice.

According to Jack O'Conner, still a young man when

the 300 Savage belched its first, the cartridge became successful virtually overnight. Western nimrods in particular took the 300 to their collective bosoms. In *The Rifle Book,* Jack had this to say:

> The 300 has been especially popular in the Western states, where so many of even the most conservative hunters want higher velocity and flatter trajectory than can be got with rifles of the 30/30 class. Throughout the West the Model 99 Savage in the 300 has been a best seller for a good many years. Back about 1941 more 300 Savage rifles were used on an Arizona antelope hunt than rifles of any other caliber . . . the 30/30 . . . for so many years . . . the favorite Western caliber, came out in third place.

Jack went on to tell of an old-time outfitter he knew who had slain a quartet of bucks as they ran along a canyon wall, using only four cartridges. Simply *blam, blam, blam, blam,* one right after another. All lung-shots. All very quickly dead.

Despite such stellar performance, O'Conner didn't think much of the 300's accuracy. He wrote:

> The 300 is not the most accurate of cartridges, and I wouldn't select one for use at the longest ranges. With a 150-grain bullet it becomes, however, a good 250-yard rifle. With a scope sight most 300s will group into around 3 inches at 100 yards and will stay in a 10-inch circle at 250.

The 300 Savage (left) was introduced about 1921, the load roughly duplicating the ballistics of the 30-06 (center). The 308 Winchester (right) has virtually eliminated the 300 Savage from the short case, 30-caliber popularity charts.

There are still plenty of 300 Savage 99As to be had. Unfortunately, you'll have to hit the used-gun market to find

My limited experience with one 300 Savage, a relatively recent Savage 99-E, supports Jack's opinion. With factory ammo, my sample 300 is no better than a 3-inch grouper at best. But, considering the range limitations of normal 300 Savage loads, such accuracy is sufficient.

John Hayden, policeman from Greensboro, North Carolina, worries not at all about his 300's accuracy. The little Model 99 Featherweight has been bringing home John's venison for more than 20 years. He's not certain how many deer that rifle has dropped, but he figures it's between 20 and 25. Hayden uses the Remington Core-Lokt factory loads exclusively, divided about equally between the 150- and 180-grain round nose versions.

Some years back, John was hunting from a South Carolina tree stand when he spied a fat five-point buck out around 70 yards and coming closer. The buck walked right up to John's tree, stopped, turned its head away. The Core-Lokt slug ripped into its chest, destroying the heart. Then, John told me, that buck did a crazy

Currently, the only rifle chambered for the 300 Savage is the lever-action Savage 99E.

Never underestimate the 300 Savage. Out West, that cartridge won the hearts and minds of a lot of open-terrain deer hunters. Mule deer like these can be handily taken out to 250 yards with the 300 Savage.

thing. It cut a backflip, spraying blood in a rainbow-shaped geyser out the exit wound, and landed square on its horns. It then, quite discourteously according to John's view, rolled all the way to the bottom of a ridge. He had to fetch it back up the slope.

Once, hunting on Mount Mitchell in 6 inches of snow, John spotted a plump whitetail romping around, having a grand ol' time. It was 5 degrees above 0. John was freezing his kazoo. He shot that deer in the heart from virtually point-blank. It fell right over.

John's best whitetail was another South Carolina buck. He and some compadres were hiking into a thick-ly-wooded area slashed with steep ridges. John lagged behind, reasoning that when his partners topped out on the other side of the ridge, they'd likely run all the deer from that side over to this side. He sat down for a spell.

Directly, he saw a big eight-pointer sauntering his way, accompanied by a doe. The pair stopped short of a partial clearing dotted with pine second-growth. As dictated by whitetail SOP, the doe went into the clearing on recon while the buck hung back. John had his Savage at his shoulder, was squinting down the irons, as the sassy doe pranced right up to him. He was running out of breath, patience, and will power. Finally the buck moved just enough to offer a clear shot. The doe had stopped about 2 yards away from our intrepid hero, sniffing him out. John dropped hammer on the eight-point. Bad shot. Gut. The deer ran off.

As usual with a gut-shot deer, the blood trail was no-table in its absence. John walked nearbout to Mississip-pi, the way he tells it. He enlisted a fellow hunter to help find the buck. Naturally, the draftee found the deer, hung up in a honeysuckle thicket not 60 yards from where John had shot it. John broke its neck with a shot from the little Savage.

John Hayden has also used that same Savage 99 to kill enough squirrels to feed Kansas City for a week. He handloads a 90-grain cast spire point for the job. His longest shot on squirrels was about 50 yards. His longest shot on deer? The eight-pointer. Fifty steps, maybe 40 yards. John doesn't believe it's necessary to take long shots at deer.

The story John Hayden likes to tell the most is about his "wild cat." (In many parts of the South, a bobcat is always referred to as a wild cat.) One pleasant day John sat musing on one end of a rotting 20-foot log. He was sitting right still, so he says, moving only his lungs and his eyeballs. On one of his right-to-left swings, the left orb picked up a blur of movement directly to port. And close. Very, *very* close.

John swung both his face and his rifle barrel simulta-neously, discovering to his discomfiture that he was sharing the log with a "wild cat" bigger than a Packard. (Things with teeth and claws do indeed look quite large viewed unexpectedly from up close.) By the time he swallowed his ticker back into place, John had sent a 180-grain package Special Delivery. When that big kitty received her mail, she elevated herself with such alacri-ty and suddenness that John tried to shoot her again without pumping the lever. Meantime, the bobcat fell off the log, began thrashing around amid the leaves, chewing on her end of the log with vehemence sufficient to raise goosebumps on a mummy. John is no mummy. His gooseflesh had goosebumps.

Directly the cat expired. After several hours, John, feeling reasonably certain of her demise, took a look-see. She was dead, as expected. The bullet had removed a lung, traversed the abdominal cavity, come to rest in a hind leg.

Ask John Hayden if he needs anything bigger than the antiquated 300 Savage for deer and he'll probably arrest you for loitering. He won't abide stupid questions.

Handloading

John Hayden handloads only small-game ammunition in his 300. Not big game loads. The cartridge has acquired a reputation over the years as being eminently unreloadable. Reasons cited are its short neck—which at .22-inch is *really* short—and its slight body taper. Coupled with a very sharp 30-degree shoulder angle, full-length resizing is said to be quite difficult. I can neither verify nor refute; I have never reloaded a 300 Savage case in my life.

Another area of disputation regarding the little Savage cartridge is its normal operating pressure. Everything from 40,000 to 49,000 p.s.i. has been quoted somewhere or other, although Ken Waters has written that the SAAMI maximum-working pressure is 46,000 CUP (copper units of pressure). I'll happily take Ken's word.

The overall loaded length of 300 Savage ammo is 2.60 inches, some .2-inch shorter than the 308 Winchester, which has come to replace it as the popular deer load in the Model 99. Even so, the elderly cartridge can keep within spittin' distance of its replacement in the velocity and energy game if both are loaded to comparable pressures. According to the Du Pont Handloader's Guide, the 300 Savage reaches its top velocity with 150-grain bullets via 38.5 grains of IMR 3031, for 2575 fps. The 180-grain gets 2395 with 38.5 grains of IMR 4064, although three propellants peak at 2390 fps. Obviously, the 300 Savage is no one-powder cartridge. The velocities listed were taken from a 24-inch barrel.

The 308 Winchester shows 2830 fps with the 150-grain bullet, and 2580 from a 180-grain, but at higher pressure levels than the 300. The data for the 308 was taken in a 23-inch barrel, which hurts it a little. Nonetheless, you can see that the advantage is the 308's by more than 220 fps on the average.

However, loaded to comparable pressure in strong bolt-action rifles, the 300 closes the gap. My pal Rick Jamison ran some tests with a 24-inch barreled Remington Model 722 chambered to 300 Savage, pitting it against a 22-inch Savage Model 110-S 308. Rick tried to load the two cartridges to similar pressures, at least as far as he could determine with normal handloader's techniques. He did not have access to a pressure barrel in either caliber.

Rick safely achieved 3014 fps with 130-grain bullets in the Model 722, 3197 fps, in the 308. With the 300, he got 2839 fps with the 150-grain Nosler Solid Base, 2919 fps in the Savage 110-S. Using the 180-grain Hornady spire point, he managed 2512 fps in the 300 Savage, and 2584 fps in the 308. The average difference was 112 fps across the board, with the heavier bullets coming closer to the 308 than the lighter ones. That surprised me.

Thus, it seems that the 300 Savage comes as close to equaling the 308 Winchester as the 308 in turn comes to the 30-06. As close as the 7x57 Mauser gets to the 280

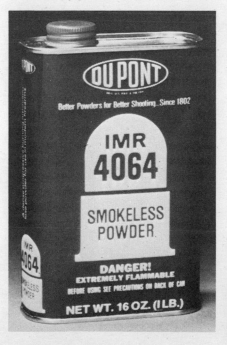

Du Pont's IMR 4064 is one of the most useful powders in the 300 Savage. The *DuPont Handloader's Guide* shows 38.5 grains of IMR 4064 providing 2395 fps with a 180-grain bullet. Good velocity, good energy.

One of the rarities: It's a Savage Model 1920 in 300 Savage. It's a very nice little rifle, and one of the first "true" short-action turnbolts. The chambering of the 300 Savage in any bolt-action rifle could be considered a rarity as the Savage 99 lever-action was considered *the* gun when it came to that cartridge.

Remington. As close as the 243 is to the 6mm Remington. In other words, *pretty close.*

Most-useful powders for the 300 Savage would include IMR 3031, IMR 4895, IMR 4064, IMR 4320, Winchester 748 and 760, Norma 202, and Hodgdon's BL-C(2), H335, and H4895. In Ken Waters' "Pet Loads" column in *Handloader* Number 64, he listed as his most accurate load 40.0 grains of IMR 4895 and the 150-grain Sierra spitzer. Ken showed several loads in his M99 as giving 2-inch groups or better, from the bench at 100 yards. Maybe the old 300 isn't as imprecise as Jack O'Conner thought it to be. Or maybe it takes good reloads to make the cartridge work.

Although factory listed at 2630 fps for 150-grain loads, and 2350 fps for the 180s, I decided to check it for myself. I clocked two batches of 150-grain Remington Core-Lokt ammunition, one an aging lot of the round nose permutation, the other from a fresh new box of the pointed variety. The two loads chronographed within 4 fps of each other: 2581 fps for the newer stuff, 2585 for the old. Since my 99-E sports a 22-inch tube, I figured those speeds to be pretty good.

A sample of the 180-grain round nose Core-Lokt was secured from John Hayden, vintage about the same as the round-nosed 150-grain ammo. The average came out 2343 fps with a mere 12 fps velocity variation. Very consistent, very fast.

As John Hayden and thousands of hunters have proved for nearly 65 years, the 300 Savage has all it takes and then some to hang venison from the meatpole. Ditto antelope, sheep and black bear. Even mean old "wild cats."

300 Savage

HANDLOAD DATA

Bullet Wt. Grs.	Type	Powder Wt. Grs.	Type	Primer	Case	MV, (fps)	ME, (fpe)	Rifle/ Bbl. (in.)	Remarks
130	Hrndy. SP	41.0 IMR 3031		Rem. 9½	Rem.	2808	2276	Sav. M99/22	Lym. Hndbk., 46th Ed. (Acc. Ld.)
150	Hrndy. SP	40.0 IMR 3031		Rem. 9½	Rem.	2695	2419	Sav. M99/22	Lym. Hndbk., 46th Ed.
150	Hrndy. SP	43.5 IMR 4320		Rem. 9½	Rem.	2672	2378	Sav. M99/22	Lym. Hndbk., 46th Ed. (Acc. Ld.)
180	Hrndy. SP	40.0 IMR 4895		Fed. 210	Fed.	2494	2486	Sav. M99E/22	R. Jamison data

SP—Soft Point.

FACTORY LOAD DATA

Bullet Wt. Grs.	Type	MV, (fps)	ME, (fpe)	Rifle/ Bbl. (in.)	Remarks
150	Rem. PSPCL	2581	2218	Sav. M99-E/22	Old lot of ammo
150	Rem. RNCL	2585	2225	Sav. M99-E/22	Consistent
180	Rem. RNCL	2343	2194	Sav. M99-E/22	Very consistent

PSPCL—Pointed Soft Point Core Lokt; RNCL—Round Nose Core Lokt.

SPECIFICATIONS

Shell Holders
RCBS: 3
Bonanza: 1
Lyman: 2
Pacific: 1

Bullet Diameter
Jacketed: .308″
Lengths
Trim: 1.861″
Maximum Case: 1.871″
Maximum Overall: 2.600″

CAUTION:
Loads recommended and suggested herein have been carefully listed, but are intended solely as a guide to readers and neither the publisher nor author accept any responsibility for results of their use.
Maximum loads, listed in bold, should be reduced by 10 percent and worked up to cautiously.

30-40 Krag

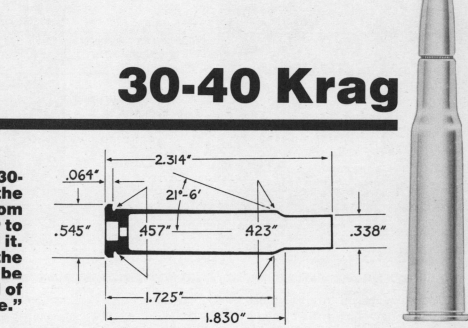

"Take note that the 30-40 did not "survive" the change from blackpowder to smokeless. It started it. For that fact alone, the cartridge should be admitted to the hall of fame."

Diagram dimensions: 2.314", .064", 21°-6', .545", .457", .423", .338", 1.725", 1.830"

IN 1892, the United States Army cashiered the roly-poly 45-70 Government in favor of the 30 U.S. Army, more commonly called the 30-40 Krag. It was a wise move. In Europe, the Kaiser had provided his troops with the 8mm Mauser, the first of the small-bore military rounds, and the Spaniards were experimenting with their new 7mm cartridge. Not to be outdone, Uncle Sam trotted out his new 30-bore.

The new military rifle built around the 30-caliber cartridge was an American-modified version of the Norwegian-invented Krag-Jorgensen bolt-action rifle, from which the Krag nomenclature for the cartridge originated. Directly, such civilian ordnance as the Remington-Lee, Remington rolling block, Winchester Model 1895 lever-action, and Winchester high-wall single shot were chambered for the new load. The high-wall was the first sporting rifle to be chambered in this country for a small-bore, smokeless-powder cartridge. A few modern rifles have been chambered to 30-40 Krag, most notably the Ruger Number 3, but today the cartridge is as passé as high-button shoes.

Still, if you have a serviceable rifle, the 30-40 will

Bullets such as these can be used in the ancient Krag because of its box magazine. Round nose bullets are not a requirement.

IMR 3031 is a fine propellant for the lighter (130 to 150 grains) Krag bullets.

When it comes to using 200- or 220-grain slugs in the Krag, IMR 4350 is a good performer.

bring home the bacon. It's been doing so for more than 90 years. Today's factory ballistics read thus: 180-grain soft point at 2430 fps for 2360 fpe at the muzzle. There was for some time a fine 220-grain round-nose soft point, but it is no longer loaded. Velocity was reported to be 2200 fps, but I've read that it gave only about 2000 fps in normal barrel lengths. The 45th Lyman reloading manual shows 2061 fps from the batch of factory ammo tried in their test rifle. The 180-grain load is shown as giving 2288 fps. Obviously the factories stoke their ammo with more restraint than enthusiasm. It's just as well; the old Krag had but one locking lug.

There is very little reason to purchase a 30-40 Krag except as an artifact. It was obsolete the day it was introduced. The 30-03 (soon to become the 30-06) made it *totally* obsolete. Even in bygone years, the 30-40 was not a real sought-after big game cartridge after the 30-06 became commonly available in sporting rifles. The guys who wanted a light 30-caliber bought the 30-30. Hunters after elk and moose who wanted more power than the 30-30 offered went to the 30-06 or something even bigger. The 30-40 didn't have much to recommend it. Nor does it today.

The Krag rifle is interesting because of its history and the velvety smoothness of its bolt operation. Its magazine design is also of interest to students of military arms. If it were chambered for the 35 Newton it would still be noteworthy; its cartridge has little to do with the fondness with which the rifle is held.

At one time, the 30-40 was quite a target cartridge. The reason is that it was the military load of the day,

and most rifle matches originated with the military. The 45-70 was also considered to be a fine competitive load, just as the 5.56mm is today used in military-rifle competition. Again, if the military cartridge had been the 35 Newton or the 219 Zipper, the load would have shown up in many matches. Merely being a military cartridge insures a place in the competitive scheme of things, regardless of its merit in that arena.

In *Mr. Rifleman*, Townsend Whelen wrote of the early days of the Krag:

My old rifle coach, Bill Foulke, was at the range almost weekly. One day he brought down a Krag rifle. This had been adopted as the standard rifle of our Regular Army in 1894 [*note this descrepancy from most sources*], supplanting the old 45-70 Springfield Single Shot.

It was a bolt-action rifle, with magazine holding five rounds. It had the foreign Krag-Jorgensen type of action, with a magazine gate on the right side of the action. It was made at Springfield Armory, the first models being produced in 1894 [*again the disagreement from "established" sources. Perhaps Col. Whelen was right. Incidentally, the Sierra Manual says 1893; take your pick . . .*] and slightly improved in 1898. It shot a 30-caliber rimmed cartridge loaded with a 220-grain round-nose bullet. The muzzle velocity was 2000 feet per second. The first bullets were jacketed with mild steel, but after about 1898 jackets were of cupro-nickel.

When Bill and I started to shoot this rifle, the first thing we noted was the peculiar whine of the bullet as it traveled down to the target as compared to that of the .45 caliber Springfield. We next became pleasantly aware of the very moderate recoil. The accuracy was also excellent.

Left to right: 25-35 Winchester, 250 Savage, 257 Roberts, 30-40 Krag and the 348. While all but the 250 Savage and the 257 Roberts are now obsolete, the 30-40 still has fans.

(Right) In years gone by, the 30-40 Krag had quite a following among deer hunters. In some areas of the U.S. the 30-40 Krag still hangs on to some of that popularity.

Before you get too excited about the accuracy he refers to, remember that he was comparing it to that obtained from the 45-70 Springfield, not exactly a benchrest rifle, although it has certainly won its share of competitions over the years.

Note Whelen's reference to the 30-40's rim. That rim was a necessity if the round was to be used in the Krag-Jorgensen rifle, but the rim is one of the design attributes of the cartridge that rendered it outmoded in a very short time. The coming thing was the Mauser-type rifle, the feeding system of which is not partial to rimmed cartridges. And thus was born the "30-03" when the Army switched to the superior 1903 Springfield rifle, virtually a Mauser clone.

Ballistically, the 30-40 remained current for many years. It was more powerful than cartridges of the 30-30 class, more like the 300 Savage. That big, long, 220-grain round-nose slug with its ½-acre of exposed lead would plow through a lot of meat, expanding itself all the while. Anything plinked through the lungs with that chunk of lead merely had to find a place to lie down. The Grim Reaper had swung his scythe.

Take note that the 30-40 did not "survive" the change from blackpowder to smokeless. It *started* it. For that fact alone, the cartridge should be admitted to the hall of fame.

If I were loading a 30-40 Krag today, I'd choose from the fast-to-medium propellants such as IMR 3031, 4895, and 4064; Hodgdon's H4895 and H414; or Olin's slower 760, for use with the 150- to 180-grain bullets. Such slower numbers as IMR 4350 and Hodgdon H4831 might work better with the heavy 220-grain slug. The 30-40 has a case capacity of roughly 47.5 grains of water, which is a tad less than the 308 Winchester and a bit more than the 300 Savage. The pressure ceiling is relatively low due to the strength limitations of the Krag rifle. Maximum average-chamber pressures should not exceed 40,000 CUP. The strong Ruger Number 3 can handle more, but in that light rifle the recoil could quickly become pretty grim. If I had one, I'd treat it like an unusually burly Krag and load for accuracy, not power.

Treat the 30-40 Krag gently—both rifle and cartridge—and you should be able to enjoy using it for many years. Just consider its age; you wouldn't ask your grandfather to run the high hurdles. Baby the old veteran. He's earned his keep.

30-40 Krag

HANDLOAD DATA

Bullet		Powder				MV	ME	Rifle/	
Wt. Grs.	Type	Wt. Grs.	Type	Primer	Case	(fps)	(fpe)	Bbl. (in.)	Remarks
130 Hrndy. SP		54.0	IMR 4350	Rem. 9½	Rem.	2617	1977	Krag/22	Lym. Hndbk., 46th Ed. (Acc. Ld.)
180 Rem. SPCL		49.0	IMR 4350	Rem. 9½	Rem.	2386	2276	Krag/22	Lym. Hndbk., 46th Ed. (Acc. Ld.)
180 Rem. SPCL		54.0	H4831	Rem. 9½	Rem.	2347	2202	Krag/22	Lym. Hndbk., 46th Ed.
220 Rem. SPCL		45.0	IMR 4350	Rem. 9½	Rem.	2127	2211	Krag/22	Lym. Hndbk., 46th Ed. (Acc. Ld.)

SP—Soft Point; SPCL—Soft Point Core Lokt.

FACTORY LOAD DATA

Bullet		MV	ME	Rifle/	
Wt. Grs.	Type	(fps)	(fpe)	Bbl. (in.)	Remarks
180 Rem. SP		2248	2019	Krag/30	Speer Manual No. Nine
180 Rem. SP		2288	2092	Test barrel/22	Lyman Handbook, 46th Ed.
220 Rem. SP		2061	2075	Test barrel/22	Lyman Handbook, 46th Ed.

SP—Soft Point.

SPECIFICATIONS

Shell Holders
RCBS: 7
Bonanza: 11
Lyman: 7
Pacific: 11

Bullet Diameter
Jacketed: .308″

Lengths
Trim: 2.304″
Maximum Case: 2.314″
Maximum Overall: 3.089″

Hodgdon's H4895 is a propellant that's suitable for use in handloading the 30-40 Krag.

CAUTION:
Loads recommended and suggested herein have been carefully listed, but are intended solely as a guide to readers and neither the publisher nor author accept any responsibility for results of their use. **Maximum loads, listed in bold, should be reduced by 10 percent and worked up to cautiously.**

308 Winchester

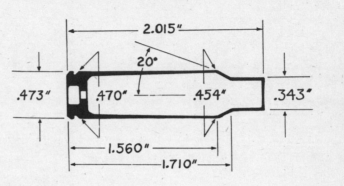

> **"The 308 deserves its public approbation. It is a pleasant load, mild of voice and kick for the energy levels it delivers, available in the broadest selection of rifle types, purposes, and actions of any centerfire cartridge."**

I FELT like I'd been riding for days. Actually, I had, but not without a rest. The sun was out, somewhere up there through the trees; I got only occasional glimpses of it. My wool breeches were soaked through with water from the dense foliage. My horse had stuck a small limb into my knee. Deep into my knee. I still carry the scar. No matter; the bleeding had stopped after 10 or 15 minutes. The crisp Idaho air stung my lungs as I sucked in a deep draught. My back hurt; my knee throbbed; my legs felt like rubber. I was having a great time.

Only moments before, I had assisted one of my hunting partners in shooting a smallish five-point elk. He had done most of the shooting; I'd been backup. The bull had been hard-hit, but he hadn't dropped. A guide and the two wranglers had escorted my partner in pursuit of the wounded animal.

The other guide, Jack Lykins, decided that we'd see what was on the other side of the mountain. I thought this side looked all right, but went along so he wouldn't get lost. We had covered perhaps ¼-mile when we broke onto a grassy park radiant with sunshine. I was intent on enjoying the view when Jack yelled, "There's one! Up the mountain! Got cows with him! Hurry up! He's movin' 'em out!"

Simultaneously, I looked up the mountain, spotted a strung-out herd of elk *way* up there, tried to jerk my rifle from its scabbard, attempted to unhorse without falling off, hurried, tried to swallow, watched the elk disappearing one by one into a draw, hurried faster, had the rifle, gained the ground, almost tripping.

Vaguely, I was aware that Jack was still yelling for me to hurry up, which I viewed uncharitably. I was nervous enough as it was. I yelled back, "How far?"

"Four hundred yards! He's bringin' up the rear! Hurry!"

I was thoroughly discombobulated. Glancing around, I could find nothing to rest my rifle on, nothing to drape my carcass across to assist a steady hold. The grass was too high to attempt a shot from the sitting position. It would be offhand or not at all. I snapped the gun to my shoulder and tossed off a shot. Literally. To this day, I have no earthly idea where the crosshairs were when I yanked the trigger. The bull disappeared behind a boulder the size of a school bus.

Jack was hollering, "Shoot again!"

Listen, stupid, I said to myself, *forget the guide, forget you have to hurry, just pretend you're on the range practicing with all the time in the world.*

It worked. It was amazing how calm I became. I tuned the guide out, ignored my unsteady nerves. There was a small open area between the rock that hid the bull and the last of his vanishing girl friends. He had to cross that open space to make good his escape. I was ready for him.

Abruptly he was in my scope. My mental machinery computed the distance he had to cover, the drop I had

This 180-grain Nosler Solid Base was recovered from the lungs of the author's bull elk; the slug now weighs 98.3 grains. Penetration was almost complete.

This is the author and his elk rack and 308 Colt rifle. The bull was taken at close to 400 yards.

(Right) Bill Barry illustrates the firing technique he uses when loosing a rapidfire string with a 308 assault rifle. The 308, or 7.62 NATO, is the most popular cartridge for use in such guns, worldwide.

to allow for, the lead necessary. Meanwhile, I was having my first real look at him; all I could see was horns. He was running with his head held high, nose in the air. It appeared that the tips of his horns were nearly even with his rump.

He was halfway across the clear space. I drew in a breath, held it, put the junction of my crosswires right above the rear of his skull, touched off. I worked my bolt so fast I wasn't aware of doing it. Through the scope I saw him drop as if he'd been switched off. Unfortunately, he bounced up immediately and ran into a clump of alders.

Jack hollered, "You busted him good! He won't go far."

I watched the alders shake, marking his slow progress down the mountain. Catching a glimpse of him through the trees, I fired again. If I hit anything, I couldn't tell it. Then a better view of him. He was negotiating a steep decline, perhaps a 6- or 8-foot vertical drop, and appeared to be standing on his head. I swear. I put the aiming point between his shoulders and let fly. He dumped like a sack of ragweed.

"Well, that's it," Jack opined. "He ain't goin' no-

where. Damn good shot. Get in the saddle and we'll go fetch 'im."

He was the biggest elk I've seen, before or since. I sat looking at him, at his massive six-point antlers, perfectly symmetrical, with long beams, heavy beading, bases much bigger than my wrists. Jack estimated his live weight at near 1000 pounds. John Rose, owner of the Bar 44 Outfitters, my hosts for the hunt, later guessed the bull's on-the-hoof heft at from 875 to 925 pounds.

At least a half-dozen people looked over the mountainside where I shot that bull. Range estimates ran from 350 to 450 yards, which corroborated Jack's original hasty guesstimate. I'm not sure that it was quite 400 yards out, but certainly farther than 350. Let's settle on 375 and leave it at that.

The rifle I used on that hunt was a Colt-Sauer. The caliber was 308 Winchester. I took quite a bit of good-natured kidding about my little gun. After I busted the elk, the joking stopped. John said he couldn't believe the damage done by the load I was using. My first bullet took the bull through the lungs and was found balled up under the skin on the off side. Expansion was perfect. The front quarters were pretty blood-shot.

Ballistics

The reason I went into so much detail concerning my elk hunt is that the 308 is often maligned for not being potent enough for really big game. When the hunt was still in the planning stage, a good friend in the bullet-making industry called me on the phone. He was planning a hunt with the same outfitter. He was to go in as I was coming out and was interested in what rifle I'd be shooting. When I told him, he was incredulous.

"You may have to take a really long shot. You oughta carry something that can handle an elk way out there."

"What are you taking?" I asked.

"My 280."

What he, and lots of others, hadn't stopped to consider is that the 308 is very close ballistically to such longer cartridges as the 280 Remington. With top loads using 150-grain Nosler Solid Base bullets, the 280 retains between 1550 and 1600 fpe of energy out at 400 yards. With the load I used in my 308 Colt, 51.0 grains of Winchester 760 under the 180-grain Nosler Solid Base for 2650 fps at the muzzle, retained energy at 400 yards was

shows a 22.9-inch drop at 400 yards, assuming a 200-yard zero. The same bullet fired from a 308 plunges only 24.3 inches. Thus the 30-06 shows an unimpressive 1.4-inch advantage. Big deal. The difference in energy at that extended range is 130 fpe in favor of the 30-06; less than 6 percent.

I could go on and on making ballistic comparisons between the 308 and a half-dozen competitive loads. The fact is that on North American game up to 400 pounds or so in weight—which includes all the deer species, most caribou, all the sheep family, Rocky Mountain goat, cougar, javelina, pronghorn antelope, black bear, wild boar, wolf, and most cow elk and not a few bulls—*any* cartridge in this class has all it takes for clean kills. On game the size of moose and big bull elk, all cartridges in the 270/30-06 class become moot. I personally feel that they are adequate for such animals under all but the most extraordinary circumstances, as did Jack O'Conner, Captain Paul Curtis, Townsend Whelen, and approximately 6 trillion successful hunters. I must admit that some writers have advocated bigger cartridges, most notably Warren Page and Elmer Keith. If someone wants to argue all day that the 30-06 or 7mm

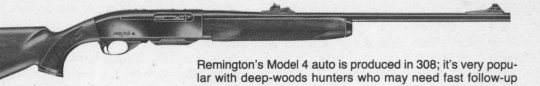

Remington's Model 4 auto is produced in 308; it's very popular with deep-woods hunters who may need fast follow-up shots.

about 1559 fpe. And that from a bullet 30 grains heavier, of larger caliber and slightly superior sectional density. Even with the 160-grain Nosler Partition at 2800 fps, 400-yard energy in the 280 would have been only 1579 foot-pounds. And he thought *I* was handicapping myself?

How about trajectory? A 150-grain Nosler Solid Base started from a 280 at 2850 fps will drop 20.7 inches at 400 yards from a 200-yard zero. In my 308, a 180-grain Solid Base, kicked out at 2650 fps, would show about a 23-inch dip at 400 yards. So the better 280 loads shade the 308 by about 3 inches at 400 yards. Significant? I think not. Even on such game as woodchucks, I doubt that such a small difference would be much of a handicap. On game the size of deer, let alone elk and caribou, 3 inches at 400 yards is practically nothing.

Similar cartridges are similarly close to these two. The 7x57, 284 Winchester, 7mm-08, 270 Winchester, 30-06, and maybe one or two others are so akin ballistically that any difference between them is merely food for disputation. No animal would know the difference.

Take the 30-06 for example. Using the excellent 165-grain Federal Premium boat-tail factory ammo, the '06

Magnum or 338 Winchester Magnum is more suitable for big bull elk or moose than a 308 or 270, that's fine with me. I have better things to do. Besides, how many hunters will have a shot this year at a *big* bull elk or a moose?

If some savant pronounces that one of the aforementioned standard cartridges is not up to taking animals *of 400 pounds or under,* or that one of them is demonstrably superior to another, then so be it. That savant is full of prunes.

Hunting

Back to the 308. The last time I spoke with Dave Sappington, he had slain a half-dozen West Virginia whitetails with his Winchester Model 88 in 308. His son had dropped two more. Dave's load at the time was built around the 180-grain Hornady round nose and 41.0 grains of IMR 4895. Although the muzzle speed likely failed to exceed 2400 fps by much, it was poison on deer.

One of Dave's bucks was caught running broadside in heavy-timbered country. His first shot slammed through a 2-inch sapling, then on through the fat six-

Remington's Accelerator is an innovative way to turn the 308 into a high-speed varmint cartridge. It works..

A rimfire conversion unit, shown installed here, is available for the H&K M770, 308. With the unit in place, practice is cheap and accuracy surprisingly good.

pointer. Just spurred the deer on. Dave fired again. This time his bullet plowed through a 6-inch pine tree, yawed another 35 yards or so, and struck the buck in the ribcage, exiting the neck. Dead buck. Although Dave claims not that such lumber-busting performance is the norm for that load, he doesn't deny it either. As far as performance on game—not trees—is concerned, Dave says that a buck absorbing that bullet usually runs 50 or 60 yards and piles up. The slug almost always exits the deer, leaving a profuse blood spoor for following up.

Fred Ritter is another staunch 308 supporter. Fred lives in North Carolina; each year he kills more deer than I *see* in 3 years. Back in 1970, Fred acquired a Browning semi-automatic chambered to the round. Since then, he has used that rifle and others of the same caliber to account for more than 30 deer. The only load he has ever used is the Remington 150-grain pointed soft point Core-Lokt.

Fred's first buck with that Browning walked out into a rye field and began nibbling the greenery. The distance was around 130 yards. Fred put the crosswires on the buck's shoulder and touched off. The deer never took a step. Fred is a firm believer in the shoulder shot if you don't want a deer making tracks after you shoot it. Of course, slivers of bone can cause excessive meat damage, but at least the animal doesn't run off, taking its excessive meat damage with it.

Some years later, Fred was presiding over three scrapes when a five-pointer came hustling out of the woods as if something were prodding it. The buck ran right under Fred's tree stand, stopped, sniffed the air, looked around haughtily, then fanned his tail and walked stiff-legged toward the closest scrape.

Let Fred tell it: "I centered the crosshairs on the top of his neck just behind the head and pulled the trigger.

He was dead before he hit the ground. The bullet exited the white throat patch leaving a hole large enough to put your fist in. Not a good shot if you plan on mounting your trophy but a sure kill with little loss of meat."

Fred told me he has shot a whole slew of deer just behind the shoulder as they trotted along. Most of them ran a short distance in the direction they were traveling, then keeled over. "This is where the 150-grain bullet has the edge over the heavier 180- or 200-grain bullets. The 150-grain is constructed so as to open up more quickly on thin-skinned game such as deer when a large bone is not hit," says Fred. He's absolutely right.

More on bullet weight and deer. Fred recounted this tale: "Some years ago I convinced a friend of mine who also used a 308 to change from the 180-grain round nose to the 150-grain Core-Lokt. He had complained of shooting several deer and not getting the performance and expansion from his bullets he felt he should be getting. We went to the range and re-zeroed his Winchester Model 100 for the 150-grain load. That afternoon, we hit the woods. Around 5:00 P.M. I heard him shoot one time and then all was quiet.

"Later that night, as he was retelling the story for the fourth time, he admitted that the 150-grain bullet had put that deer down quicker than any of his previous kills."

An astute reader may note the seemingly contradicting experiences of Fred Ritter and Dave Sappington. Bear in mind that Dave shoots a bullet designed for good expansion on deer-sized game (the 180-grain Hornady round nose soft point), and that he uses it on mountain-grown whitetails, which run larger than the scrub-oak bucks Fred hunts in eastern North Carolina. Also bear in mind that the deer Dave shoots seem to travel a bit farther than those Fred takes. Both hunters have applied considerable thought to load selection, and both are successful.

Grady Shields goes with the lightweight slugs. Grady is one of my hunting partners. The last deer he shot came out of the woods at a run, and crossed a corn field in high gear. Grady smacked it in front of the right shoulder as it quartered toward him about 125 yards out. At the hit, the deer turned to its left, ran 25 or 30 yards and tried to jump a barbed-wire fence. Didn't make it.

Grady uses handloads featuring the 150-grain Hornady spire point and a generous dollop of Winchester 748 powder in his Remington Model 788 bolt-action. Shoots it well, too.

Fred Ritter smacked a wild boar with his 308 a couple years back. The pig was running broadside to him at close range when Fred let it have one through the boiler room. The hog ran off as if unhit. Fred was about to pop it again when the pig stopped beside a tree and leaned against it for support. As Fred watched through his scope, the old boy slid to the ground. The hog's chest cavity would have qualified for federal disaster aid, said Fred.

Advantages of the 308

Stories of the 308's hunting prowess could go on and on, but I'm sure you get the picture. There is little point in disparaging the 308 as a big game load. Although it doesn't shoot *quite* as flat as the 270, 7mm-08, or 284, or hit *quite* as hard as the 30-06, the difference is negligible. In fact, undemonstrable in the field. And the 308 has distinct advantages of its own that for some of us overshadow its minor ballistic deficiencies. Let's examine some of those.

First in importance to many shooters, is the easy availability of inexpensive military brass. That is an undeniable advantage, although gunners who do little handloading play it down. Military ammunition is likewise around in quantity and often can be found pretty cheap. None of this means much to the guy who shoots less than 100 rounds a year, but to the serious shooter it is money in his pocket.

Secondly, the 308 is an easy cartridge to work with. It handles most any bullet weight well, is useful with an unusually large cross section of propellants, exhibits none of the capriciousness regarding pressures or wild groups that some cartridges are notorious for. Load data is easy to find, from many sources, and with a wide variety of components. Additionally, target loads are widely published and reliable. (Try to find target-load data on such loads as the 223 Remington, 7mm-08 Remington, 7mm Remington Magnum, or 300 Winchester Magnum, all of which are commonly used in competition and have a variety of match-grade bullets available for them.)

A third advantage is the availability of new military rifles in this caliber. Modern survivalists are deadly serious about their hardware, and many of them feel the 223 is too small for an all-purpose combat/defense load. The only real alternative is the 308. (The 30-06 is available in few combat rifles, and virtually none of the truly modern ones, unless you consider the Garand a modern battle weapon. Some do.) Thus, if you are interested in a survival rifle with up-to-date combat capabilities, the 308 is about the only game in town.

The 308 is popular. Very popular, both with big game hunters, metallic silhouette competitors, over-the-course target panners, military rifle teams, survivalists, and it was at one time big among the benchrest clan, as hard-nosed a group as ever pulled a trigger. On the RCBS dic-popularity chart, the 308 ranked third for rifle cartridges in 1983. Only the 30-06 and 223 beat it. Such popularity contributes to some of the attributes mentioned above, such as the wide array of handload information. It also insures that a broad array of factory-loaded ammo can be found on the shelf, in a meaningful range of bullet weights and constructions. This helps insure that your rifle will be full on opening day, and is also comforting if you run out of ammunition miles from a well-stocked gun shop.

Accuracy and Cartridge Length

I've saved my two favorite points til last: accuracy and cartridge length. First, accuracy. The 308 is *A-C-C-U-R-A-T-E*. No other big game cartridge will equal it,

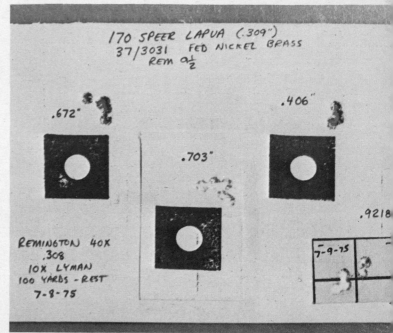

A good 308 target rifle, like the Remington 40-XB, will consistently shoot groups like this.

Good 308 match bullets, left to right: 150-grain Nosler HPBT, 168-grain Nosler HPBT, 168-grain Sierra HPBT, 168-grain Winchester HP, 168-grain Hornady HPBT, and the 170-grain Speer/Lapua BT.

Remington's ace "over-the-course" rifle is the 40-XC 308 magazine rifle. It's *ACCURATE*.

The author had a 40-XB, like this, in 308. With good loads, it averaged under .4 inch!

let alone beat it. None. Zero. The 270 Winchester? Forget it. The 243? No way. The 300 Winchester Magnum? Close, but no cigar. The 30-06? It is to laugh. Let's put it this way: how many big game loads can you think of that have set world records in benchrest competition at normal ranges? (We will not include 1000-yard shooting; that game is a function not only of accuracy, but of high velocity, which yields an attendant diminunizing of the effects of wind. No standard cartridge can win against the belted magnums under such conditions, just as no belted magnum can win against a 20mm cannon.)

If you exclude such limited-purpose loads as the 22 PPC, 6mm PPC, 6x47, and other loads dreamed up by the stool shooters (all of which are wildcats anyway), only the 222 Remington is in the 308's class for benchrest records, and the 222 is no big game round.

Eight years ago, such news items as the following were commonplace. From the July-August, 1976, edition of *NBRSA* (National Bench Rest Shooters Association) *News,* edited by Rick Jamison:

Anthony Greenwood of Fullerton, California, won the Southwest Regional Unlimited Championship held by the Northern California Bench Rest Shooters Association at the Eagle Rock Gun Club . . . April 11.

Greenwood took the 200-yard as well as the Grand [Aggregate] . . .

Greenwood shouldered a Hart-barreled Remington 308 topped with a Unertl 24. He loaded with 39.5/3031 and his own bullet.

Chet Brown of San Jose, California, captured the Heavy Varmint match . . . Brown used a Hart-barreled 308 Winchester under a Unertl 25 loaded with 39 grains of 4895 behind a Sierra bullet.

Incidentally, Mr. Brown's winning aggregate was .6534-inch MOA. That includes both 100- and 200-yard stages, and reflects the average of 10, five-shot strings. Mr. Greenwood's aggregate, which is for 10, *10-shot* groups, was .6642-inch.

Let's forget competition accuracy from benchrest guns—built by custom 'smiths with modified actions, expensive barrels, glued-on fiberglass stocks—and discuss normal guns bought over the counter. My most accurate 308 was a 40-XB Remington single shot turnbolt. That 40-X fired a four-group average of .383-inch with 42.8 grains of IMR 4895 pushing the 150-grain Nosler Match hollow point boat-tail. With 48.5 grains of H414 under the 168-grain Nosler Match MPBT, it managed a .486-inch aggregate. Accurate? Only one rifle I ever fired would shade that Remington, and it was a factory-built Remington 222 designed to be ready for benchrest competition *over the counter*. Next best was another 40-XB in 25-06 that would stay inside .53-inch if I were perking.

No 7mm-08 to date has come close to my better 308s. Even my Remington Model 700-V, which is no match for the 40-X, will outdo my best 7mm-08s. The hottest 243 I ever owned averaged .70-inch, and my varmint-weight 243s were in the ¾-inch class. Not good enough. Top 6mm Remington was a 700-V that managed .64-inch with its pet recipe; a good Swift stayed in ⅝-inch; one of my 22-250s was capable of .57-inch or so. None good enough.

The 30-06? Well, I once owned a very accurate Winchester Model 70 Target. With its favored fodder, that Model 70 would shoot a .60-inch average. That is very good indeed. But not 308 country.

Okay, so the 308 is intrinsically a more accurate load than the others. But only in super-accurate benchrest guns. What about the average sporter-weight rifle? If we compare the 308 to cartridges of its power level, say those of muzzle energy in the 2600/2900 foot-pound class, will it hold its own? Let's see.

The most precise sporters I've owned have been a 223 (.63-inch average), three 243s (.70-, .95-, and .98-inch averages), a 250-3000 (.99-inch), 25-06 (.697-inch), and a Colt-Sauer 308 that printed .86-inch for eight, five-shot strings. The 308 offers substantially higher energy levels than the other calibers listed. More goes on inside the gun than when touching off a lesser cartridge; the more turbulence, the more vehemently the barrel vibrates. The more strenuously the barrel oscillates, the more likely an erratic node will send a bullet awry. Point is that it's tougher to get supreme accuracy out of a gun as recoil and powder charge levels increase.

The most accurate 30-06 I've shot grouped into 1.10 inches, which I was most pleased with. A couple of others ran about 1.20 inches. I don't mean to downgrade the '06; I'm sure there are *beaucoup* rifles so-cham-

Gunner Mike Holloway tries his hand with the Colt-Sauer 308. This is the most accurate sporter in a caliber larger than 25 that the author has seen. With a 6X Redfield, that Colt 308 averages .86-inch for several five-shot strings.

Although this Winchester M70 Featherweight has a long action, the current (1984) Featherweight 308s carry a new short action.

Mike Holloway shooting the German-built Heckler & Koch 770, a 308: this gun is by far the most accurate semi-auto the author has tested, averaging under 1½ inches for five-shot groups.

The super-accurate Remington M788 was built in 308. Most of them have 22-inch barrels as shown here. The last few years of production showed a reduction in barrel length to 18½ inches in the "deer" calibers. The author's 788 308 groups 1¼ inches with very little load development.

(Right) Ruger makes an M77 Varmint chambered to 308. Often used by police sniper units, these guns are usually quite accurate.

30-06 or 8mm Mauser, the difference is of no practical consequence in the field. None. (Unless of course it increases your confidence.)

There are a lot of shooters out there who hunt only occasionally, spending the rest of their year trying to "load tune" their sporters into producing extra-tight clusters in target paper. The 308 is particularly amenable to such enterprise, and in *my experience* is more apt to reward you with sub-1-inch accuracy than any other cartridge within the energy range aforementioned. And here I'm speaking of an average for at least five, *five-shot* strings, discounting no groups or fliers due to wind conditions, a "pulled" shot, or the color of your socks.

And so we have come to the final advantage the 308

bered that will hit a newt's derriere at a hundred paces. I just haven't run across one. Steve Hornady once told me he had a Ruger 77 that would stay in ¾-inch. Layne Simpson says that he has had uncommonly good luck with the 30-06; believes he can get most any 30-06 turnbolt model to group in an inch, at least for three shots. Perhaps. So far I haven't been able to coax an 'ought-six below MOA for five-shot strings, but not from lack of trying.

How about the good ol' 270? I've had one or two that would group on the threshold—including a Sako Finnbear and a particularly accurate Ruger Number 1—but none that would quite squeeze under an inch.

The 7mm-08 has made the sub-MOA grade, but only in heavy-barreled varminters to date. My 284 Shilen DGA has come close. I've owned several 7mm Magnums that would shoot around 1.25 inches. My 270 Weatherby Magnum stays in 1.10 inches with good ammo. And so forth. None has equaled the 308 so far.

Don't be misled. You can choose any 30-06 class cartridge you want and achieve accuracy commensurate with whatever big game challenge you're likely to be offered. I wouldn't choose a 308 over any other big game load based on its accuracy level *alone*. Even if the average 308 groups 20 percent better than an average 270 or

enjoys over many of its competitors: it is comfortably short. Short enough to work in such rifles as the Savage Model 99, Winchester Models 88 and 100, Heckler & Koch Model 770, Harrington & Richardson Ultra-Auto, Browning BLR, Sako Forester and Finnwolf, Remington Models 600, 660, 722, and Seven, Ruger International, Weatherby VGL, and the short-action versions of such turnbolt models as the Browning Safari and BBR, Savage 110 and 111 Chieftain, Remington 700 and 40-X, Ruger 77, Weatherby Vanguard, Smith & Wesson 1500 and 1700LS, Ithaca LSA, Colt-Sauer, Steyr-Mannlicher, Winchester Model 70, and probably a few I've missed. Sure, some of these guns are no longer available, and many weren't popular when they were, and lots of them come in 30-06-length permutations. Despite that, the models mentioned should be handled and hefted and shouldered before you decide that their "slight" advantage in weight and length and balance and feel is really so slight after all.

Handloads

Now that we've covered all the esoterica, let's look at some handloads that really make the 308 perk. I have used powders as fast-burning as Du Pont IMR 3031, as slow as IMR 4831. In between there have been IMR

4064, 4895, and 4350, Hodgdon BL-C(2), H414, H4895, H380 and H205 (now unhappily deceased), Winchester 748 and 760, and Norma N202. All of them have provided accurate loads in one rifle or another.

My favorite varmint load, and one of the most consistently accurate concoctions I've tried in many of my 308s, weds 51.6 grains of Winchester 748 and the excellent 125-grain Sierra soft point spitzer. Velocities run from 3032 fps in a Heckler & Koch with 19½-inch barrel to 3142 fps from my Ruger 77-Varmint with its 24-inch pipe. Retained energy at 400 yards, assuming a starting speed of 3100 fps, is 1146 fpe. That's enough for any kind of varminting and would also do a good job on the smaller species of big game. Drop from a 200-yard zero is just over 20 inches. Pretty flat.

Accuracy in my guns is generally exceptional. Of the half-dozen I've tested it in, only the Heckler & Koch displays no taste for it. My Colt-Sauer groups it into a 1.17-inch average at 100 yards. In my Remington 700-V, it clusters into .95-inch. A Savage 99-CD liked it third best of the 11 loads shot in it.

A fine long-range pronghorn or deer load is 56.0 grains of Winchester 760 under a 150-grain Nosler. I neck-size my brass, to gain a little extra capacity, and seat my bullets out as far as practicable. The Remington

700-V will do its best at the 56.0-grain level, averaging .82-inch while sending the bullets out its muzzle at 2924 fps. The short-barreled Heckler & Koch gets 2755 fps from 56.0 grains of 760 behind the 150-grain Nosler Solid Base.

My Savage 99-CD likes 48.5 grains of Winchester 748 and the 150-grain Sierra spitzer. Muzzle speed is 2888 fps for 2779 fpe. More accurate is 50.5 grains of H380 with the same bullet, but the velocity is more than 100 foot-seconds slower. My Harrington & Richardson Model 301 prefers 46.0 grains of IMR 4064 pushing the 150-grain Sierra to 2783 fps while grouping just over 1½ inches. Not bad for a Mannlicher-stocked lightweight.

When started out at 2800 to 2900 fps, a good 150-

A careful micrometer reading of case expansion keeps the reloader within bounds. Brass life is usually good with the 308.

The handsome, new, oil-finished Weatherby Vanguard VGL comes in a short-action 308 version. To the eyes of many, the VGL is one of the most handsome 308s available.

Remington's deluxe pump-action, the M6, is made up in 308. It's one of the most popular 308s in Remington's line-up.

Savage's fine deer rifle, the M99-CD, can be had in 308 Win. The author's sample groups 2¼ inches at the 100-yard mark.

The excellent Savage 110-S silhouette gun is available in 308; the author's 110-S averages well under 1 inch for five-shots.

(Right) These components shot well in several of the author's 308s, especially the Savage M111.

grain spitzer, like the Sierra, retains from 1253 to 1366 fpe at a full 400 yards. For deer, sheep, and such, that's aplenty.

The most accurate load in any of my 308's featured the 150-grain Nosler JHPBT match slug over 42.8 grains of IMR 4895. In my 40-XB, groups ran .383-inch as earlier mentioned, and muzzle speed was good at 2843 fps. Another fine target load in the 40-X was 45.0 grains of Hodgdon's BL-C(2) with the same bullet, for 2916 fps and .61-inch grouping.

If I were going after both deer and elk on the same hunt, I'd consider a good 165-grain bullet. I think the 180-grain bullet is a tad stout for deer, and the 150-grain light for elk. The 165-grain slugs offer a viable compromise. Decanting 48.5 grains of H414 beneath the 165-grain Sierra SPBT gets nearly 2600 fps in my Savage 99-CD, and groups 2¼ inches, the best that gun will do. In the Harrington & Richardson, I'd opt for 45.2 grains of BL-C(2) and the 165-grain Nosler Partition. With a muzzle velocity of 2634 fps from the short barrel, that's as good a medium-weight load as I've tried in that gun. The same bullet gets 2712 fps and 2696 fpe when loaded atop 46.0 grains of 748 in my Colt-Sauer.

For target shooting or metallic silhouette busting, the 168-grain Nosler JHPBT match bullet does pretty fair in my heavy-barreled rifles when paired with 48.5 grains of H414. The Remington 700-V groups into an inch on the button; the Ruger 77-V clocks 2713 fps.

My all-time favorite heavy-bullet loading is a maximum charge of 51.0 grains of Winchester 760 behind a good 180-grain bullet such as the Nosler Solid Base. I killed that first elk with this heavy charge. Not only is it very fast at 2650 fps, it is quite accurate and yields more than 2800 fpe at the muzzle. My 788 Remington also likes 51.0 grains of 760 and the 180-grain Speer, for

2585 fps and 2671 foot-pounds. More accurate in that rifle is the same charge under the 180-grain Sierra round nose soft point; groups measure right at 1¼ inches. My Savage Model 111 clusters into 1.76 inches with 51.0 grains of 760 and the 180-grain Hornady spire point, and clocks 2653 fps.

Using the 190-grain Hornady match boat-tail and 40.5 grains of IMR 4895, the 700-V shows a .78-inch average; the Colt does poorly at 1.84 inches; the Ruger 77-V manages a fair (for that rifle) 1.57 inches. Velocity was quite high for such a heavy slug; 2536 fps in the Remington, 2465 in the Colt.

A lightweight Ruger International pushed the 190-grain Hornady spire point boat-tail to 2414 fps with 48.7 grains of 760. The same slug clocked 2379 fps when riding 47.4 grains of IMR 4350. Those are pretty high muzzle speeds for an 18½-inch barreled carbine.

An exceptionally accurate and potent load in three of my 308s is 46.0 grains of the discontinued H205 and the 200-grain Sierra Matchking or soft point boat-tail. The Heckler & Koch grouped its best with the soft point, averaging well under 2 inches which is certainly not bad for a semi-automatic. The Ruger 77-V also grouped this load the best of its entire repertoire, averaging 1.29 inches and clocking 2523 fps with the Matchking bullet. That, folks, is pretty danged fast. The most accurate load in my 700-V, using H205, showed a .74-inch average and 2500 fps. (It's really sad H205 is no more. It was a helluva good propellant for moderate-capacity cartridges like the 308 and the 250 Savage.)

One of the most noteworthy factory loads was the 165-grain Federal Premium soft point boat-tail. The 700-V grouped it in 1.07 inches and chronographed 2660 fps. My Savage 110-S kept five-shot groups in 1.60 inches while getting 2646 fps. The Heckler & Koch managed a tight 1.89 inches and 2579 fps muzzle speed. That's a pretty consistent load.

Most accurate factory fodder in the Heckler & Koch M770 was the 180-grain Norma "Plastic-Point"; it averaged an amazing 1.49 inches and showed 2529 fps on the chronograph. Next best was the 180-grain CIL "Kling-Kor" at 1.59 inches. (That incredible H&K was the most accurate self-loader I ever shot, by far.)

Another laudable factory-brewed product was the Federal 168-grain match hollow point boat-tail. In the 40-XB, it clustered four groups into a tight .61-inch aggregate, the best I've ever seen from factory stuff. In my Savage 110-S silhouette rifle, several strings averaged .89-inch and clocked 2562 fps. Very good ammunition.

Please note that I had one target-grade 308 turnbolt that grouped under .5-inch with two loads, a varmint-weight rifle that stayed inside ¾-inch, a sporter that printed under ⅞-inch, another sporter that hovered around 1¼ inches, a Mannlicher-stocked light-weight that went into 1.32 inches, a semi-automatic that averaged better than 1½ inches, and a lever-action that would stay in 2¼ inches. There were many others that were somewhere in between. I seriously doubt you could equal that record with *any* other caliber available in such a wide array of action types.

The 308 deserves its public approbation. It is a pleasant load, mild of voice and kick for the energy levels it delivers, available in the broadest selection of rifle types, purposes, and actions of any centerfire cartridge. Ammunition is state-of-the-art, and in factory persuasion runs the gamut from 55 (don't forget Remington's Accelerator) to 200 grains. Suitable component bullets are made in weights from 100 to 220 grains, 250 grains if you consider the custom bullet makers like Barnes. No better cartridge is available for game up through caribou, and it is the equal for all practical purposes to any other all-rounder for use on game from lemming to elk. There is no better military rifle cartridge in existence. In silhouette shooting, the 308 is still the one to beat. It has set world records in benchrest competition, won many a big-bore rifle match. Rifles available for it are both compact and lightweight. It has charisma, is controversial, maligned, resented, disparaged. And sold in ever-increasing numbers. It is truly a great cartridge.

308 Winchester

HANDLOAD DATA

Bullet Wt. Grs.	Type	Powder Wt. Grs.	Type	Primer	Case	MV, (fps)	ME, (fpe)	Rifle/ Bbl. (in.)	Remarks
125 Sierra	SP	51.6	Win. 748	CCI 250	Fed.	3032	2552	H&K M770/19½	Poor accuracy
125 Sierra	SP	51.6	Win. 748	CCI 250	Rem.	3052	2586	H&R M301/20	Accurate
125 Sierra	SP	51.6	Win. 748	CCI 250	Win.	3092	2654	Sav. M99/22	Very accurate
125 Sierra	SP	51.6	Win. 748	CCI 250	Win.	3112	2689	Colt-Sauer/24	Extremely accurate
125 Sierra	SP	51.6	Win. 748	CCI 250	Win.	3128	2716	Rem. M700-V/24	Accurate
125 Sierra	SP	51.6	Win. 748	CCI 250	Win.	3142	2741	Rug. M77-V/24	Very accurate
150 Nos.	SB	55.0	Win. 760	Fed. 210	Fed.	2691	2412	Sav. M111/22	Slow; mediocre acc.
150 Nos.	SB	56.0	Win. 760	8½-120	Fed.	2755	2528	H&K M770/18½	Mediocre accuracy
150 Sierra	SP	46.0	IMR 4064	CCI 200	Rem.	2783	2580	H&R M301/20	Very accurate
150 Sierra	SP	46.0	IMR 4064	CCI 200	Win.	2825	2658	Sav. M99/22	Accurate
150 Sierra	SP	48.5	Win. 748	CCI 250	Win.	2888	2779	Sav. M99/22	Accurate
150 Sierra	SP	50.5	H380	CCI 250	Win.	2774	2564	Sav. M99/22	2nd most accurate this gun
150 Win.	FP	46.0	IMR 4064	CCI 200	Rem.	2797	2607	H&R M301/20	Extremely accurate
150 Sierra	SP	48.5	Win. 748	CCI 250	Rem.	2794	2601	H&R M301/20	Very accurate
150 Sierra	SP	50.5	H380	CCI 250	Rem.	2653	2345	H&R M301/20	Very accurate
150 Nos. Part.		51.0	Win. 760	CCI 250	Rem.	2673	2381	H&R M301/20	Accurate
150 Nos. Part.		51.0	Win. 760	CCI 250	Win.	2759	2536	Sav. M99/22	Poor accuracy
150 Nos.	JHPBT(M)	54.0	Win. 760	CCI 250	Win.	2892	2787	Colt-Sauer/24	Sub-MOA; most acc. this gun
150 Nos.	JHPBT(M)	56.0	Win. 760	CCI 250	Win.	2915	2830	Colt-Sauer/24	Fair accuracy
150 Nos.	JHPBT(M)	54.0	Win. 760	CCI 250	Win.	2901	2804	Rem. M700-V/24	Accurate
150 Nos.	JHPBT(M)	56.0	Win. 760	CCI 250	Win.	2924	2848	Rem. M700-V/24	Very accurate
150 Nos.	JHPBT(M)	56.0	Win. 760	CCI 250	Win.	NC	NC	Rug. M77-V/24	Extremely accurate

(Continued page 182)

308 Winchester

HANDLOAD DATA (con't.)

Bullet Wt. Grs. Type	Powder Wt. Grs. Type	Primer	Case	MV, (fps)	ME, (fpe)	Rifle/ Bbl. (in.)	Remarks
150 Sierra SP	**48.5** Win. 748	8½-120	Fron.	**2795**	**2601**	Rug. M77 Int'l./18½	Most acc. this rifle
150 Sierra SP	53.0 Win. 760	Rem. 9½-M	Fron.	2638	2318	Rug. M77 Int'l./18½	Fair accuracy
150 Sierra SP	54.0 Win. 760	Rem. 9½	Rem.	2729	2481	Rug. M77 Int'l./18½	Note primer and brass change
165 Sierra SPBT	48.5 H414	Fed. 215	Rem.	2524	2335	H&R M301/20	Very accurate
165 Nos. Part.	45.2 BL-C(2)	CCI 250	Rem.	2634	2543	H&R M301/20	Most acc. this gun
165 Sierra SPBT	48.5 H414	Fed. 215	Win.	2596	2470	Sav. M99/22	Most acc. this gun
165 Hrndy. SP	**47.2** Win. 748	8½-120	Rem.	**2676**	**2624**	Rem. M788/22	Fair accuracy
168 Hrndy. JHPBT(M)	42.0 BL-C(2)	Rem. 9½	Win.	NC	NC	Rug. M77/22	Mediocre accuracy
168 Nos. JHPBT(M)	37.0 IMR 3031	Rem. 9½	Fed.	2498	2328	Rem. 40-XB/27¼	Accurate
168 Nos. JHPBT(M)	48.5 H414	CCI 250	Fed.	2754	2830	Rem. 40-XB/27¼	Extremely accurate
168 Nos. JHPBT(M)	48.5 H414	CCI 250	Fed.	2667	2654	Colt-Sauer/24	Mediocre accuracy
168 Nos. JHPBT(M)	48.5 H414	CCI 250	Fed.	NC	NC	Rem. M700-V/24	Mediocre accuracy
168 Nos. JHPBT(M)	48.5 H414	CCI 250	Fed.	2713	2747	Rug. M77-V/24	Mediocre accuracy
180 Speer SP	49.4 Win. 760	Fed. 215	Rem.	2561	2622	H&R M301/20	Very accurate
180 Hrndy. SP	42.0 N202	8½-120	Fed.	2455	2410	Sav. M111/22	Accurate
180 Hrndy. SP	**51.0** Win. 760	Fed. 210	Fed.	**2653**	**2814**	Sav. M111/22	Most acc. this gun
180 Sierra RN	**51.0** Win. 760	8½-120	Rem.	**2491**	**2480**	Rem. M788/22	Most acc. this gun
180 Speer GS	**51.0** Win. 760	8½-120	Rem.	**2585**	**2671**	Rem. M788/22	Extremely accurate
180 Win. SP	**51.0** Win.760	8½-120	Rem.	**2631**	**2768**	Rem. M788/22	Poor accuracy
180 Sierra SPBT	43.0 IMR 4064	8½-120	Fed.	2566	2632	Rem. M788/22	Fair accuracy
180 Nos. SB	**51.0** Win. 760	8½-120	Fed.	**2650**	**2807**	Colt-Sauer/24	Accurate
190 Hrndy. SP	47.4 IMR 4350	Rem. 9½M	Fron.	2379	2388	Rug. M77 Int'l./18½	Poor accuracy
190 Hrndy. SP	48.7 Win. 760	8½-120	Fron.	2414	2459	Rug. M77 Int'l./18½	Fast for heavy bullet
190 Hrndy. JHPBT(M)	40.5 IMR 4895	Fed. 210M	Fed.	2465	2564	Colt-Sauer/24	Mediocre accuracy
190 Hrndy. JHPBT(M)	40.5 IMR 4895	Fed. 210M	Fed.	2536	2714	Rem. M700-V/24	Extremely accurate
190 Hrndy. JHPBT(M)	40.5 IMR 4895	Fed. 210M	Fed.	NC	NC	Rug. M77-V/24	Accurate
200 Speer RN	46.0 IMR 4831	8½-120	Rem.	2304	2358	H&R M301/20	Accurate
200 Speer RN	46.0 IMR 4831	8½-120	Win.	2316	2383	Sav. M99/22	Poor accuracy
200 Sierra SPBT	46.0 H205	Fed. 210	Fed.	2306	2362	H&K M770/19½	Most acc. this gun
200 Sierra JHPBT(M)	46.0 H205	Fed. 210M	Fed.	2523	2828	Rug. M77-V/24	Most acc. this gun
200 Sierra JHPBT(M)	46.0 H205	Fed. 210M	Fed.	2500	2776	Rem. M700-V/24	Most acc. this gun

SP—Soft Point; SB—Solid Base; JHPBT(M)—Jacketed Hollow Point Boat-Tail (Match); SPBT—Soft Point Boat-Tail; RN—Round Nose; GS—Grand Slam.

FACTORY LOAD DATA

Bullet Wt. Grs. Type	MV, (fps)	ME, (fpe)	Rifle/ Bbl. (in.)	Remarks
125 Win. SP	2875	2294	H&K M770/19½	Accurate
125 Win. SP	2887	2314	H&R 301/20	Fair accuracy
125 Win. SP	2985	2473	Sav. M99-CD/22	Very accurate
150 Norm. SPBT	2750	2519	H&K M770/19½	Accurate
150 Fed. SP	2630	2304	H&K M770/19½	Fair accuracy
150 Rem. PSPCL	2693	2417	H&K M770/19½	Fair accuracy
150 Rem. PSPCL	2685	2402	H&R 301/20	Mediocre accuracy
150 Fed. SP	2758	2535	Sav. M99-CD/22	Fair accuracy
150 Fron. SP	2719	2463	Rem. M788/22	Accurate
165 Fed. SPBT Premium	2656	2584	Sav. M111/22	Fair accuracy
165 Fed. SPBT Premium	2579	2437	H&K M770/19½	Accurate
165 Fed. SPBT Premium	2660	2592	Rem. M700-V/24	Very accurate
165 Fed. SPBT Premium	2602	2480	Colt-Sauer/24	Fair accuracy
165 Fed. SPBT Premium	2715	2701	Sav. M99-A/22	Very fast
165 Fed. SPBT Premium	2646	2564	Sav. 110-S/22	Fair accuracy
165 Fron. SPBT	2489	2270	H&K M770/19½	Fair accuracy
168 Fron. JHPBT(M)	2343	2048	H&K M770/19½	Accurate
168 Fed. JHPBT(M)	2562	2449	Sav. 110-S/22	Extremely accurate
168 Fed. JHPBT(M)	2660	2640	Rem. 40-XB/27¼	Extremely accurate
180 Norma PP	2648	2803	Sav. M111/22	Fair accuracy
180 Norma PP	2529	2554	H&K M770/19½	Most acc. this gun
180 CIL KKSP	2463	2426	H&K M770/19½	Very accurate
180 Rem. PSPCL	2464	2426	Rem. M788/22	Fair accuracy
180 Fed. SP	2585	2670	Sav. M99-CD/22	Fair accuracy
200 Win. RN	2302	2350	H&R 301/20	Fair accuracy
200 Win. RN	2395	2546	Sav. M99-CD/22	Fair accuracy

SP—Soft Point; SPBT—Soft Point Boat-Tail; PSPCL—Pointed Soft Point Core Lokt; JHPBT(M)—Jacketed Hollow Point Boat-Tail (Match); PP—Plastic Point; KKSP—Kling Kor Soft Point; RN—Round Nose.

SPECIFICATIONS

Shell Holders
RCBS: 3
Bonanza: 1
Lyman: 2
Pacific: 1

Bullet Diameter
Jacketed: .308"

Lengths
Trim: 2.005"
Maximum Case: 2.015"
Maximum Overall: 2.800"

The Browning BBR short action is made in 308 Win. It's a well made turn-bolt, capable of good accuracy.

CAUTION:
Loads recommended and suggested herein have been carefully listed, but are intended solely as a guide to readers and neither the publisher nor author accept any responsibility for results of their use. **Maximum loads, listed in bold, should be reduced by 10 percent and worked up to cautiously.**

30-06 Springfield

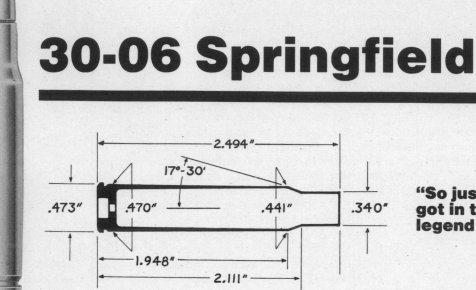

2.494"
17°-30'
.473" **.470"** **.441"** **.340"**
1.948"
2.111"

"So just what have we got in the 30-06? A legend in its own time."

TRUE OR FALSE: the 30-06 Springfield replaced the 30-40 Krag as our military rifle cartridge. False; the 30-03 replaced the Krag. The 30-06 was the first United States military rifle round to sport a pointed bullet. True; that was one of the things that distinguished it from the 30-03. The 30-06 used the same weight bullet as the Krag, 220 grains, but boosted the velocity 200 fps. False; the 30-03 used the 220-grain Krag round-nosed slug while the 30-06 went to a lighter bullet. The 30-06 can be chambered in a 30-03, but the reverse is not correct. True; the 30-06 has a shorter neck than the 30-03 so it will chamber in the earlier rifle. The 30-06 initially offered a 180-grain, full-jacketed, military loading at 2700 fps at the muzzle. False; the bullet weight was 150 grains, although the speed was indeed 2700 fps. The first rifle chambered for the 30-06 was the Springfield 1903. True; Army officers, National Guard members, and members of the NRA could purchase them from the government for private use. The first rimless 30-caliber cartridge to be chambered in the Winchester Model 1895 was the 30-06. False; it was the 30-03, since 1905. The only sporting rifle chambered to 30-06 prior to World War I was a lever-action. True; the Model '95 Winchester abovementioned. (Actually, the Newton was supposedly available in 30-06 prior to the War, but I doubt many were produced. Perhaps I should have said "regularly chambered" for the ought-six.) Last one: the first commercial 30-06 bolt-action to be brought out after World War I was produced by a major manufacturer on tooling used to build military rifles during the War. True; the Remington Model 30 turn-bolt was fabricated on machinery used to turn out the 1917 Enfield.

Wasn't that fun? Since Theodore Roosevelt took a couple of modified Springfield rifles with him on his 1908 safari, the 30-06 has been the darling of the sporting press. During the intervening years, many erroneous notions have surfaced and become imbedded in shooting folklore. We disposed of some of those in our preface.

There have been many famous users of the 30-06 over the years. Noted gun scribe Ned Crossman became a staunch fan of the rifle and round. So staunch, in fact, that in 1932 he brought forth a tidy little tome entitled *The Book of the Springfield*. In the foreword of his book he wrote;

A bit more than 25 years ago there appeared over the horizon of the American Rifleman a new arm, the new service rifle of the United States Army and called for the famous old Armory which developed it, the New Springfield.

It was shortly to become not only the most accurate military and target rifle in the world, but the most popular rifle that ever fell into the hands of the civilian rifleman. As a military rifle it established new standards of accuracy. As a sporting arm it became the rifle by which other like arms were judged.

Although the author's 30-06 S&W M1500 won't shoot like this all the time, it does so just often enough to make it interesting.

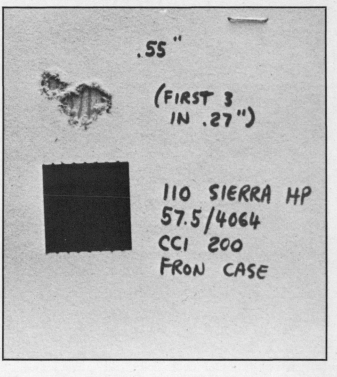

.55"

(FIRST 3 IN .27")

110 SIERRA HP
57.5/4064
CCI 200
FRON CASE

Such popular ordnance as this Remington M7400 is available in 30-06 and widely used for deer. That's Lewis Dawkins aimin'.

And so forth. Actually the "New Springfield" as Crossman called it was not as good a rifle as the Model '98 Mauser the day it was born, but that's neither here nor there. At least the 30-06 is and was a better cartridge than any of those Spanish or German rounds.

Many a gun company corralled a few shekels by remodeling, refurbishing, and generally fancying up the basic Springfield rifle. So far as I know, the first gunsmith to turn out a true Springfield sporter was Louis Wundhammer of Los Angeles. Crossman, who was in the Guard, secured a trio of Springfields and betook them to Wundhammer for modification. Fitted were gold bead front sights, Lyman 48 receiver rears, trap buttplates, and other niceties. The barreled-actions were polished and blued; new woodwork was fitted. The first sporter Springfield ever built is pictured in Crossman's book; it's a bit odd looking, with substantial

drop to the stock (okay for the iron sights that rode the deck), an odd line here and there, and the military front sight band intact. It had a schnabel forend tip, which seems to be coming back these days.

Other outfits sold customized Springfields, among them the Hoffman Arms Company, Griffin & Howe, Neidner Arms Corporation, and the firm started by August Pachmayr in Los Angeles. Such individuals as Bob Owen, Bill Sukalle, R.F. Sedgley, Ross King, and many others had a hand in more than one reworked Springfield. But all this is of only passing interest; the cartridge is what made the gun, and the cartridge is what lives today.

Ned Crossman waxed ecstatic about the 30-06 cartridge in his book, writing:

By the admission of even foreign gunmakers and foreign sportsmen our Springfield cal. 30 cartridge is the best all-round killer on the ammunition list. The high accuracy of the cartridge with practically every game type and service type bullet made; the wide range of bullet types and bullet weights, its power with the heavier bullet, proven sufficient even for the charging lion, and the comparatively light recoil of practical rifles firing this ammunition combine to make this 30 service cartridge outclass every other high-power cartridge in the world.

Wow! And this:

(Above) Colt's expensive drilling is available in 30-06 under a pair of 12-gauge barrels. While the Colt drilling is very popular in Europe, it can be had here in the U.S. As you can see, the old ought-six has been chambered in a little bit of everything.

Mike Holloway going through a rapid fire string from the sit; the ought-six doesn't kick so badly you can't shoot it in shirtsleeves.

This 30-06 cartridge in the 30 class occupies the same relative position of the 22 Long Rifle in that calibre. The keenest of target shooting competiton has compelled the ballistic engineers to lie awake nights thinking up minor details which might pinch in the angle of dispersion just a hair.

And I thought some of today's rhetoric was overdone! The 30-06 was a good cartridge then; it is today. But methinks it contains no alchemy in its makeup. When Crossman penned those immortal lines, not only had the German 8x57 Mauser been around for decades, but the 7x57 was common even in the States, not to mention the 270 Winchester or the 300 Holland & Holland Magnum. The 270 is not the target round the 30-06 is, but it was never intended to be. The 300 H&H was no slouch in the accuracy department, indeed just 3 years after Crossman's book left the presses, it took the Wimbledon Cup. The 8x57 (also called the 7.92 Mauser) was pretty close to the ought-six as the Germans stoked it up.

None of this seemed to daunt Mr. Crossman. In the chapter of his book devoted to the commercial turnbolt sporters of the day, he mentioned the new Winchester Model 54 as being the cream of the bunch. What he liked best was that it was made in 30-06. He wrote:

It is, incidentally, made for others, the list including the 7mm, the 7.65, the 9mm, the fine 270 Winchester and the triflin' .30-.30 [sic]. So these parties who can't sleep nights worrying about how to get a 7mm, since reading various magazine articles as to its merits, can now get both the rifle and a good night's rest. . .

A tad prejudiced, our E.C. Crossman. And a little xenophobic, I suspect. Let's leave him to his pithiness and search for more open minds.

Captain Paul Curtis, another writer of yon olden days, had this to say of the 30-06 in his book *Guns and Gunning,* which, as a matter of interest, was dedicated "To His Grace, The Duke of Montrose." Here's Mr. Curtis:

For heavy game the most desirable cartridges are the 270 Winchester, the 30-06, the 30-40, the 300 Savage, the 276 [7x57] and the 375. Of these the 30-06 is easily the best for many reasons. Probably more attention has been devoted to the improvement of this load than to any other the world has ever known. As a result, it is the most efficient cartridge we have today, particularly in accuracy and killing power. . .

Personally, I do not favor the 270 Winchester. I have never found it quite as accurate as the 30-06. The recoil and muzzle blast is objectionably high and I do not consider a 130-grain bullet, or even the new 150-grain bullet, heavy enough to be reliable under all conditions, nor is the load well distributed.

The 30-40 cartridge is still justifiably one of the most desirable . . . I would personally be inclined to prefer the Model No. 99 Savage for the 300 Savage.

Next to the Springfield the 7m/m [276] is probably the best. In it we have a choice of either a 175-grain bullet at 2300 feet velocity or a 139-grain bullet at 3000 feet velocity—the former developing 2110 pounds of energy and the latter 2778 pounds. With it the biggest game on the American Continent has been killed . . . For the man who is sensitive to recoil . . . it is a better load than the .06 Springfield.

Sorry I went on so long, but I had to let Mr. Curtis go

ahead and dig himself into a hole. First, he says that he objects to the 270 because of its recoil and muzzle blast! Compared to the 30-06! Now, everyone knows the 270 kicks *less* than the ought-six, and if it's any louder it would take ears more sensitive than a human's to detect it. He goes on to berate the 270 because of its lightweight bullets, then shortly after proclaims the 7x57 with 139-grain slugs adequate for all North American game! He even suggests that both the ancient and under-powered 30-40 Krag and the little 300 Savage are superior to the 270. The man was overloaded with prejudice but light on a sense of fair play.

All this was mentioned to show you how much a good press can boost a cartridge. The irony is that the 30-06 didn't need the ballyhoo; it was a fine cartridge in every respect. It is even better today.

Good old Colonel Townsend Whelen was a fan of the ought-six, but he didn't beat you over the head with it. He authored an excellent book entitled *Wilderness Hunting and Wildcraft,* which appeared in 1927. In it he listed what he considered the best choices for the larger American big game. They were the 6.5mm Mannlicher, the 270, the 7x57, and the 30-06. IIc said nice things about all of them. Of the 6.5: ". . . has been used so extensively on our big game for the past 30 years that there is no doubt as to its efficiency." The 270: "I believe that if this cartridge were modified to use a 140-grain open-point bullet . . . it would prove one of *the best cartridges* [italics his] for all American game." The 7x57: ". . . recoil is very moderate, and I think that this cartridge is most excellent for the sportsman who desires a light rifle of light recoil." The 30-06: "Two most excellent big-game loads are sold in this caliber . . . Either of these cartridges is extremely reliable on any American game, and on the thin-skinned game of other countries as well."

The above should provide an example of objective firearms journalism for all of us. Whelen used the 30-06 for many years, both in the military and on big game. He used it in competition, and on varmints. He knew what it would do. In his book *Mister Rifleman,* he assessed the 30-06 thus:

> From 1909 until 1926 I used my .30-06 Springfield rifle almost exclusively for all my wilderness hunting. From what I am reading nowadays the .30-06 seems to be beginning to be regarded as a "has been." As a matter of fact it probably never will be excelled as an all-around rifle for American game. It utilizes the capabilities of the human eye and body to the fullest extent. No other caliber does this any better. It has ample accuracy, ample power and amply flat trajectory to the distance at which any hunter can be sure of hitting right. . .
> I shot all species of American big game except Alaska bear and cougar with my old 30-06, and all but one were killed with a single shot. I fired two shots into my first moose with this rifle, but the second shot was unnecessary as it was falling when the second bullet struck . . . I certainly shot 50 head of small game for food, and many small fur-bearing animals for their trophy skins with this rifle for every head of big game. . .

Colonel Whelen was right. I doubt if any rifle cartridge will ever take the 30-06's place as an all-round varmint-to-moose cartridge.

In Dallas a few months ago, I asked Rick Jamison and Layne Simpson to buy my supper. We went anyway. While we were jawing, I queried them as to which cartridge they would choose if restricted to one. Now I figured Jamison would opt for the 300 Winchester Magnum, as it's probably his favorite cartridge, and Layne would likely take the 22 Hornet or 350 Remington Magnum or some other ridiculous load. Both chose the 30-06 without a second's hesitation. I pressed, citing advantages of various cartridges. They stuck to their guns; the 30-06 was the *only* choice.

Accuracy

Layne Simpson told me recently over the phone, while discussing the subject of inherent accuracy relative to cartridge design, that he had always had uncom-

The author's Winchester M70T would group like this consistently. It's the most precise ought-six the author has fired.

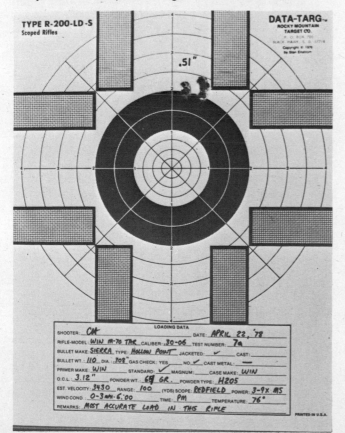

Mike Holloway shooting the author's interesting Winchester M70-Police; this gun makes a super hunting rifle, having a Parkerized finish on the metal, dull oil on the wood, but was designed for police anti-sniper work.

The author took this early-summer woodchuck with the Kleinguenther 30-06 shooting the fine 110-grain Sierra JHP. That gun will group 1.3 MOA out to 400 yards.

mon luck getting the 30-06 to shoot. He opined that he can tune most any old ought-six sporter turnbolt down into the 1-inch class, for five-shot strings. Steve Hornady backs him up, claiming that one of the Hornady test rifles—a Ruger M77—will punch out ¾-inch clusters with ease. (I suppose it requires Hornady bullets!)

While I have owned one very accurate 30-06, it was a full-fledged target rifle. That gun, a Winchester Model 70-T, will group .60-inch with its pet load. However, I've had the misfortune never to have owned a 30-06 sporter that would stay in 1 inch for five shots. My Kleinguenther K-15 will poke 'em all into a bit under 1.2 inches, as will my Smith & Wesson Model 1500. My Savage Model 111 is the most precise to date, getting 1.10 inches with its pet recipe. As you can see, these guns are hovering in the one-MOA neighborhood, but they haven't dipped beneath it on a regular basis. All of them will print sub-1-inch patterns on occasion, just often enough to keep me perking.

I have read elsewhere that 110-grain bullets won't group in the 30-06. That, folks, is a bowl of sheepdip. Every 30-06 I've shot extensively, except one, will group its *best* with the 110-grain Sierra hollow point, and that one exception has never fired a bullet under 130 grains. Even the Model 70-T does its best work with the 110-grain Sierra, that bullet being an important element of its favored load.

You might also read that even if your 30-06 does, by some quirk of fate, group the 110-grain varmint bullets in acceptable fashion at 100 yards, the poor ballistic properties of the little slug will reduce that accuracy to shambles by the time it has negotiated 300 or 400 yards of turbulence. *Wrong.* I've tried it. Out to a full 400 yards. Accuracy with my Kleinguenther was an impres-

sive 1.3 MOA. If anyone tells you the lightweight 30-caliber bullets won't group, tell him he's full of guacamole.

Hunting

What the 110-grain Sierra hollow point will do to a chuck you won't believe. I used my 30-06 on more varmints last year than any other cartridge.

Of course, the 30-06 will do for critters other than groundhogs. Last fall Rick Jamison was wild boar hunting up in New Hampshire. He had sneaked up on a bunch of the smelly porkers, could see them through the trees, but not well enough to attempt a shot. Abruptly, a big pig hove into full view. Rick let him have one, which was all it took. His rifle was one of the new Ruger Ultra Lights.

On an elk hunt a few years ago I watched my partner, Dick Sanders, deck a five-point bull elk that was alternating between feeding and bugling about 300 yards up a mountainside. Dick was using a Winchester Model 70 loaded with the 180-grain Remington Core Lokt. Took more than one hit, but that bull didn't go far.

Ron Redfield was on an elk foray with Rick Jamison once, high in the Colorado Rockies. Opening morning found Ron at 12,000 feet, watching an elk crossing through a dense fog. It was 20 degrees; Ron was cold. As if to warm his blood by suddenly increasing his heart rate, four bulls and a cow stepped into view about 400 yards away. The cow and one bull came straight toward

A good pointed 180- or 200-grain bullet like this makes the 30-06 a good long range number on caribou and elk.

him. When they had approached to within 200 yards or so, it appeared that they were about to change their compass heading. Ron let drive at the bull. First shot too far back! Another! The bull still hadn't dropped. *BOOM!* A miss! Ron fired again, then once more. Finally the bull showed signs of being hit; he stood with his head sagging. Ron slipped his last round into the spine.

Besides that last unnecessary shot in the spine, Ron had hit the wapiti with three of his six shots. Two were in the right spot; that elk was dead on its feet.

One of the finest whitetail deer I ever saw was taken on a piece of property my hunting cronies and I used to

have access to. Alas, it is now sub-divided for development. Grady Shields, one of our regulars, had invited a friend to hunt with our party during Thanksgiving week. The friend was a New Jersey resident named Hugh Brodie. Hugh had hunted deer for years but had never killed one.

Mike Holloway and I hunted the property on the first day of the season, with Mike sequestered beneath the spindly limbs of a pine tree while I stumbled around another corner of the farm. At dawn, Mike spotted a deer crossing the corn field to his front, but it was both too dark and too foggy to see the animal clearly. Mike's impression from the body size and shape was that it was a buck. We had seen tracks that a pack of cigarettes wouldn't cover, so we knew a big-footed deer frequented that field.

On the third day, Mike had to work and I had to be somewhere equally unimportant, so neither of us hunted. Grady called the night before. I told him to sit under Mike's little pine and survey the corn field for the shadowy deer. He said okay. The next day he and Hugh went hunting well before dawn.

Being a gentleman, Grady put *Hugh* on Mike's stand while he hunted the pond. Soon after first light, Hugh watched a doe cross the corn field. Directly came a second doe. Hugh saw them both disappear into the corn rows. From another direction came a lot of noise, but nothing could be seen. Hugh settled in to wait.

By 8:45 AM Grady was bored, so he headed toward Hugh at the pine. He immediately jumped two does and a fawn directly across from Hugh. Grady kneeled and scoped the does. Certain that no buck was within view, he started to stand then heard a noise and froze. Simultaneously the two men saw a heavily-antlered head appear above the corn, then flail at the stalks in mock battle. The buck was facing Grady, and was broadside to Hugh at about 100 yards. Standing not on ceremony, Hugh upped his 30-06 and fired. The buck whirled at the shot and disappeared into the brush bordering the corn.

The buck covered about 50 or 60 yards, getting up twice as the hunters followed him. There was an excellent follow-up trail, with much frothy blood indicating a lung hit. They found him in a gully where Hugh applied the finisher.

Hugh Brodie used 180-grain factory ammunition. Had he used a 150- or 165-grain load it is doubtful the buck would have covered as much ground, although 60 yards isn't really far for a deer to travel after a hit from anything.

Hugh's buck had very wide beams, long points, amazing symmetry. The beading was heavy, coloration good. A prime buck. Nice deer for the first one. Or the fiftieth.

There is little point in relating more tales. So much

(Above) The Remington M700 is made up in 30-06. This is the plain vanilla ADL version.

(Below) This is the new Browning version of the old Winchester M1895; it comes in 30-06. You have to see one of these rifles to appreciate the superb craftsmanship.

Remington's fine M700 BDL makes an accurate and reliable all-round rifle/cartridge combo in 30-06.

This fine Ruger No. 1-AB has been discontinued; it had the unusual combination of the long beavertail forend and the short 22-inch barrel. It shot like blazes.

game of all sizes has been taken with the 30-06 that its record is well known. That's why it is the most popular centerfire rifle cartridge in the United States. Even among reloaders, no centerfire rifle load is more popular. Since 1977, the 30-06 and the 357 Magnum handgun cartridge have led the RCBS die-popularity chart. In 1978 and 1979, the 30-06 actually outsold the 357!

Rifles for the ought-six come in all action types, including the lever; Browning has seen fit to bring back the Model 1895 Winchester, without the Winchester sobriquet of course. Remington makes the trombone Models 7600, Six, and the new Sportsman version. Browning and Remington offer the 30-06 in semi-automatic form, and I believe Heckler and Koch is import-

ing an elongated M770 for the round. Ruger makes up the Number 1 for the 30-06, and nearly every manufacturer of bolt-action rifles offers at least one model chambered for the old trooper. You can buy a 30-06 in any configuration, at about any price, and from nearly any country you see fit.

Factory-loaded ammunition is available in weights from 55 grains through 220, and includes the 110-, 125-, 150-, 165-, 168-, and 180-grain in between. Federal, until recently, offered a fine boat-tail 200-grain bullet as well. From the American companies alone, there are 30 different factory loads in 30-06.

Handloaders can play with slugs hefting 100, 110, 125, 130, 150, 165, 168, 170, 180, 190, 200, or 220

The reliable Savage 110-C has been made in 30-06 as long as it's been around.

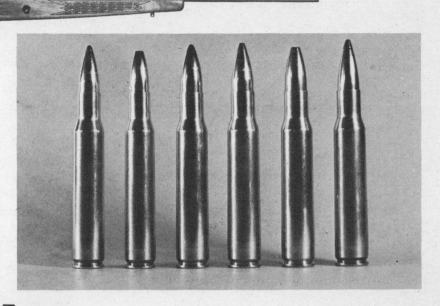

Good light-bullet 30-06 loads, left to right: 110-grain Hornady spire point, 100-grain Sierra JHP, 125-grain Sierra spitzer, 130-grain Hornady spire point, 130-grain Speer JHP, and the 150-grain Nosler Solid Base.

(Top) The new oil-finished, low-luster Weatherby Vanguard VGS can be had in 30-06. Very nice!

(Above) The new Ruger No. 1 International is made in 30-06. The styling is classic.

grains, and a few more from some of the smaller bullet makers. Nose configurations are flat, round, spitzer, spire, soft point, full-metal-jacketed, hollow point, and protected point. Can't find what you like? Just write Corbin and get tools to make up your own. Or see RCBS, Lyman, or Lee for molds and you can cast your own.

And powders. About the only powder I can see no utility for in the 30-06 is Hodgdon H870. It's just too slow. Most everything else from Bullseye to Hodgdon H4831 can be used for some type of load in the ought-six.

My favorite loads revolve around the varmint slugs because I use my 30-06s more for vermin than big game

hunting. I like 57.5 grains of IMR 4064 with the 110-grain Sierra jacketed hollow point, for fine grouping and up to 3400 fps in some rifles. Another good load for the 110-grain Sierra is 63.3 grains of Winchester 760. It's almost as accurate as the previous load, just not as fast.

My Winchester Model 70-T likes 61.5 grains of 760 behind the 125-grain Sierra soft point, another accurate and destructive varmint slug. Another good recipe in the Model 70-T is 62.0 grains of Hodgdon H205 under the Speer 130-grain jacketed hollow point. Groups run under 1 inch and the muzzle energy is close to 3000 fpe; that's a bunch from a varmint slug.

On deer-sized game I'll take the 150-grain Hornady spire point and 60.0 grains of H205. Muzzle speed with that load is just short of 3100 fps in a 22-inch barrel, for a whopping 3179 fpe. Zero that load at 200 yards and 400-yard drop is only 20.5 inches, less than a 130-grain factory-loaded 270 Winchester.

For a combination deer/elk/caribou/black bear concoction, I like the 180-grain Speer Grand Slam or Mag-Tip over 54.5 grains of H205 or 57.5 grains of MRP. Another good choice is 54.0 grains of IMR 4350 and the 180-grain Hornady spire point. I got this last load from Rick Jamison; it's the one Ron Redfield used on his elk.

Muzzle speed with all three of these loads is in the 2720 fps area, for about 2960 fpe, depending on the exact gun and load.

If you want to bump off a moose or a freight train, try either the 200-grain Nosler Partition or the 200-grain Sierra soft point boat-tail and either 52.0 grains of H205 or 56.0 grains of MRP for a little over 2600 fps and more than 3000 fpe. With the Sierra bullet, 400-yard retained energy is a lusty 1850 fpe, or about what a factory-loaded 30-30 Winchester has at the muzzle!

So just what have we got in the old 30-06? A legend in its own time. A cartridge that has won a ton of medals in competition out to 1000 yards. A load that shoots as flat as the 243 Winchester, and will do a whole bunch more

reconstruction when it gets where it's going. A cartridge that shoots with good handloads as accurately as about any other in sporting rifles, and will hold its own with most in the varmint and target models. The 30-06 is the top-selling centerfire rifle cartridge in the United States, maybe the world. A handloader's delight, with a capacious case, easy-to-get brass, and an easygoing nature.

Jack O'Conner wrote, in *The Hunting Rifle*, this homage: ". . . for all kinds of jobs in the open and in timber, on big animals and small, at long range and short, there isn't anything any more versatile than this perpetual best seller, the turn-of-the-century 30/06."

And that makes a quorum.

30-06 Springfield

HANDLOAD DATA

Bullet Wt. Grs.	Type	Powder Wt. Grs.	Type	Primer	Case	MV (fps)	ME (fpe)	Rifle/ Bbl. (in.)	Remarks
110	Sier. JHP	57.5	IMR 4350	Fed. 210	Fron.	2830	1957	Rug.No. 1-AB/22	Most acc. this gun; mild
110	Hrndy. SP	53.5	H4895	8½-120	Fed.	3375	2783	Win. M70T/26	Fast and accurate
110	Sier. JHP	57.5	IMR 4064	Fed. 210	Fed.	3406	2834	Klein./24	Most acc. this gun; fast
110	Sier. JHP	57.5	IMR 4064	CCI 200	Fron.	3265	2604	S&W M1500/22	Most acc. in this gun
110	Sier. JHP	63.3	Win. 760	CCI 250	Rem.	3235	2557	Klein./24	Second most accurate
110	Sier. JHP	64.0	H205*	CCI 250	Rem.	3341	2727	Klein./24	Good velocity
125	Sier. SP	61.5	Win. 760	Fed. 210	Win.	3245	2923	Win. M70T/26	Accurate
125	Sier. SP	61.3	Win. 760	CCI 200	Fed.	3200	2843	Klein./24	Good load
125	Sier. SP	61.2	H205*	CCI 250	Rem.	3180	2808	Klein./24	Fair accuracy
130	Speer JHP	53.4	IMR 4064	Fed. 210	Rem.	3120	2811	Klein./24	Good load
130	Hrndy. SP	53.4	IMR 4064	Fed. 210	Rem.	3062	2707	Klein./24	Fair accuracy
130	Speer JHP	62.0	H205*	Fed. 210	Win.	3207	2970	Win. M70T/26	Very acc. and fast
150	Nosl. SB	60.0	H205*	CCI 250	Fed.	3089	3179	Win. M70T/26	Very fast
150	Hrndy. SP	60.0	H205*	8½-120	Fed.	3093	3187	Sav. M111/22	Most acc. this gun; fast
165	Nosl. SB	56.5	H205*	8½-120	Fed.	2817	2908	Sav. M111/22	Fast and accurate
165	Sier. SPBT	47.0	IMR 4895	Rem. 9½	Fed.	2720	2711	Sav. M111/22	Fair accuracy
165	Nosl. SB	60.0	MRP	Fed. 215	Fed.	2850	2977	Sav. M111/22	Poor accuracy
165	Nosl. SB	61.0	Win. 785	Fed. 215	Fed.	2872	3023	Sav. M111/22	Fast and potent
180	Hrndy. SP	54.0	IMR 4350	Fed. 215	Fed.	2566	2632	Rug. No. 1-AB/22	Poor accuracy
180	Hrndy. SP	54.0	IMR 4350	CCI BR-2	Fed.	2720	2958	Sav. M111/22	Second most acc.; fast
180	Speer MT	54.5	H205*	8½-120	Fed.	2728	2975	Sav. M111/22	Fast and accurate
180	Speer MT	57.5	MRP	Fed. 215	Fed.	2716	2949	Sav. M111/22	Fast and accurate
180	Speer MT	57.5	Win. 785	Fed. 215	Fed.	2668	2846	Sav. M111/22	Accurate
200	Sier. SPBT	52.0	H205*	8½-120	Fed.	2617	3042	Sav. M111/22	Third most acc.; fast
200	Sier. SPBT	56.0	MRP	Fed. 215	Fed.	2605	3014	Sav. M111/22	Poor accuracy but fast
200	Sier. SPBT	56.5	Win. 785	Fed. 215	Fed.	2544	2875	Sav. M111/22	Mediocre accuracy

*Propellant discontinued
JHP—Jacketed Hollow Point; SP—Soft Point; SB—Solid Base; SPBT—Soft Point Boat-Tail; MT—Mag Tip.

CAUTION:
Loads recommended and suggested herein have been carefully listed, but are intended solely as a guide to readers and neither the publisher nor author accept any responsibility for results of their use.
Maximum loads, listed in bold, should be reduced by 10 percent and worked up to cautiously.

30-06 Springfield

FACTORY LOAD DATA

Bullet Wt. Grs. Type	MV, (fps)	ME, (fpe)	Rifle/ Bbl. (in.)	Remarks
55 Rem. ACL.	3988	1942	Rem. M700/22	Mediocre accuracy
55 Rem. ACL.	4016	1970	S&W M1500/22	Mediocre accuracy
55 Rem. ACL.	4040	1994	Klein. K-15/24	Excellent accuracy
55 Rem. ACL.	4119	2072	Win. M70-T/26	Lousy accuracy
125 Fed. SP	2948	2413	S&W M1500/22	Fair accuracy
125 Fed. SP	2961	2434	Klein. K-15/24	Fair accuracy
125 Fed. SP	3170	2790	Win. M70-T/26	Accurate and fast
125 Win. SP	3223	2884	Win. M70-T/26	High velocity
150 Fed. Prem. SPBT	2833	2674	Rug. No. 1-AB/22	Fair accuracy
150 Hrndy. SP	2817	2644	Rug. No. 1-AB/22	Accurate
165 Hrndy. SPBT	2670	2613	Rem. M700/22	Extremely accurate
165 Hrndy. SPBT	2685	2642	S&W M1500/22	Very accurate
165 Hrndy. SPBT	2800	2873	Klein. K-15/24	Fast and accurate
165 Fed. Prem. SPBT	2705	2681	Win. M70-P/22	Accurate
165 Fed. Prem. SPBT	2798	2869	Sav. M111/22	Good velocity
168 Hrndy. JHPBT(M)	2762	2846	Rug. No. 1-AB/22	2nd most accurate this gun
180 Fed. SP	2737	2995	Sav. M111/22	Accurate; very fast
180 Fed. SP	2729	2977	Win. M70-P/22	Very fast
180 Win. SP	2673	2857	Sav. M111/22	Fair accuracy
180 Nor. Vulc. JHP	2610	2723	Rug. No. 1-AB/22	Fair accuracy
180 Fed. Prem. Part.	2514	2527	Rug. No. 1-AB/22	Poor accuracy in this gun
180 Hrndy. SP	2410	2322	Rug. No. 1-AB/22	Poor accuracy in this gun
200 Fed. SPBT	2626	3063	Sav. M111/22	Very fast
200 Fed. Prem. SPBT	2562	2916	Win. M70-P/22	Very accurate
200 Fed. Prem. SPBT	2625	3061	Win. M70-T/26	Accurate
220 Rem. RNCL	2315	2619	Rug. No. 1-AB/22	Very accurate

ACL—Accelerator; SP—Soft Point; SPBT—Soft Point Boat-Tail; JHPBT(M)—Jacketed Hollow Point Boat-Tail (Match); JHP—Jacketed Hollow Point; RNCL—Round Nose Core Lokt.

SPECIFICATIONS

Shell Holders
RCBS: 3
Bonanza: 1
Lyman: 2
Pacific: 1

Bullet Diameter
Jacketed: .308"

Lengths
Trim: 2.484"
Maximum Case: 2.494"
Maximum Overall: 3.340"

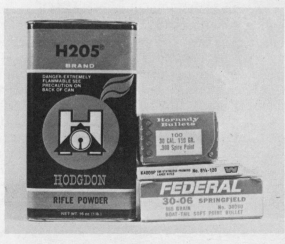

Here is an excellent choice of components for a long-range deer/ antelope load.

CAUTION:

Loads recommended and suggested herein have been carefully listed, but are intended solely as a guide to readers and neither the publisher nor author accept any responsibility for results of their use. **Maximum loads, listed in bold, should be reduced by 10 percent and worked up to cautiously.**

300 H&H Magnum

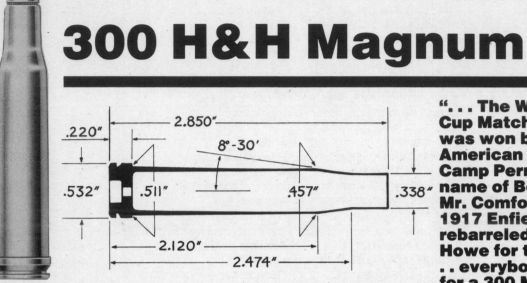

.220" 2.850"

8°-30'

.532" .511" .457" .338"

2.120"

2.474"

"... The Wimbledon Cup Match of 1935 ... was won by an American veteran of Camp Perry by the name of Ben Comfort. Mr. Comfort used a 1917 Enfield ... rebarreled by Griffin & Howe for the 300 H&H. . . . everybody hankered for a 300 Magnum."

THE FIRST belted case, so far as I know, was the British 375 Holland & Holland Magnum which debuted in 1912. In 8 years, it established a reputation for being a terror on big game of all descriptions. World War I had just ended, and the high-velocity era was gaining a firm toehold. The Brits decided that a small-bore belted cartridge based on the big 375 case would be just the thing for long-range gunning. And thus in 1920 did the 300 Holland & Holland Magnum come among us.

The 300 H&H generally gets the credit for indoctrinating Americans to the term "magnum." Since the long British cartridge was designed to use Cordite powder, which is inserted into the cartridge case before the necking-down process in a form sort of like spaghetti, the 300 has a slight 8-degree 30-minute shoulder and about as much body taper as a powder funnel. When loaded with Cordite, ballistics of the 300 H&H barely exceeded those of the 30-06. American ammo makers, using proper propellants of course, improved the ballistics a bit. The H&H also developed the reputation of being tough on barrels due to its slight shoulder angle, which caused too much powder to burn in the barrel instead of within the case, and a case stretcher because of its considerable body taper. Yes, I suppose it could be said there are some shooters who don't lament the passing of the 300 Holland & Holland. But that's not the end of the story. Let's move on.

The 300 H&H was also dubbed the "Super Thirty

Belted Magnum," and it drove a 150-grain pointed bullet in excess of 3000 fps. That was *fast* for 1920. In 1925, the American firm of Western Cartridge Company brought the big 30 to these shores. No factory rifles were chambered for it, but the custom houses like Griffin & Howe did a land-office business. When Winchester replaced the Model 54 turnbolt with the Model 70 in 1937, one of the cartridges catalogued was the Super Thirty, or, as the British called it, the "Super 30 Magnum Rimless" (or the 375/300, due to the fact that the 300 originated from a necked down 375 H&H).

One of the things that likely prompted Winchester to tool up for the round was the Wimbledon Cup Match of 1935. Said contest was won by an American veteran of Camp Perry by the name of Ben Comfort. Mr. Comfort used a 1917 Enfield which had been rebarreled by Griffin & Howe for the 300 H&H. The word of this achievement burned up the wires; everybody hankered for a 300 Magnum.

Winchester was happy to oblige with their Model 70. Some years later, Remington reamed their Models 721 and 700 for the load. American hunters took to the new round, although not exactly in droves. Disputations arose amongst the nimrods as to the merit of the 300 H&H when compared to the 30-06. Some fellows allowed as how the belted number was more sound than fury, doing little that the 30-06 couldn't duplicate when loaded properly. These same worthies berated the in-

Du Pont's IMR 4895 is a good choice for the 300 H&H when it comes to mild, accurate loads. (See the Handloading chart that accompanies this chapter.)

While the recoil with the 300 H&H is greater than the 30-06, it's not so severe that it can't be handled by the average rifleman.

creased recoil as a gift of the devil.

Protagonists acclaimed the 300 H&H the new Queen of the May, citing lofty muzzle velocities and prodigious energy figures. The truth, as always, lay amid stream.

At that time, American 300 Mag. ammo was purported to outrun the 30-06 by about 220 fps, bullet weight for bullet weight. At 400 yards, the advantage was still about 170 fps on the side of the British entry. A real but not earthshaking advantage, in my opinion. Today, the 300 is listed as moving a 180-grain slug at 2880 fps in a 24-inch test barrel; the 30-06 is shown as getting 2700 fps. That's a mere 6.6 percent superiority for the 300 H&H Magnum.

I suspect that if tested in the same barrel length, the 300 H&H has always failed to outdistance the 30-06 by its advertised advantage. According to the Speer Number Nine manual, the 150-grain Winchester factory load (now gone) gave 3094 fps instead of its listed 3190 fps; the 180-grain Remington managed only 2875 fps in lieu of its catalogue number of 2920 fps; and the 180-grain Winchester soft point showed only 2776 fps when plied against an impartial chronograph. And these data were taken in a 26-inch barreled Model 70, not a 24-inch.

Lyman's 45th Handbook backs up the Speer research. The 180-grain Remington actually clocked 2873 fps, while the 180-grain match load showed 2881 fps and the 220-grain Winchester soft point made it to 2550 fps instead of the ballyhooed 2620 fps.

And the 30-06? According to the Speer book, one lot of 150-grain Remington ammunition chronographed 2980 fps (published figure is 2970 fps) from a 24-inch barreled Model 70, although a batch of Winchester ammo of the same weight managed only 2808 fps. The 180-grain Remington loading made it to 2702 fps, the 180-grain Federal to 2696 fps, with the 180-grain Winchester again bringing up the rear at 2589 fps. The only 220-grain load tested was a batch of Winchester that clocked 2294 fps instead of the reported 2410.

As you can see, the 30-06 was not embarrassed. The average across-the-weight range is 181 fps in favor of the 300 H&H, pitting the best 30-06 loads against the fastest 300s. Although that is a demonstrable difference on a chronograph — and at your shoulder — I doubt any game animal would notice the difference.

One of the primary reasons the 300 kicks noticeably more than the 30-06 is that it holds more powder. The

300 H&H Magnum: Deer/Bear

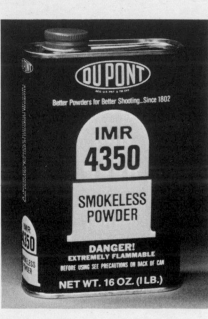

In 1983, Remington made up a special run of 700 Classics in 300 H&H. They sold out fast.

When it comes to maximum, heavy-bullet loads, IMR 4350 usually provides excellent accuracy and velocity in the 300 H&H.

While it's not billed as a varmint rifle, the 300 H&H, with light-bullet loads, will do the job.

more propellant, the more recoil if all else is equal. Add the increased "jet effect" from the larger charge of powder to the additional muzzle speed, and you get a more obvious kick. Of course a heavier rifle would negate some of the recoil.

Let's look at what some of the older gun writers had to say about the Super 30. In the 1952 edition of Jack O'Conner's *The Big-Game Rifle,* we find this:

Since the middle 1920s an increasing number of mountain hunters have carried rifles chambered for the cartridge which in this country has always been known as the 300 Holland & Holland Magnum . . . It was developed before the first World War [note the disagreement here on introduction date; Frank Barnes gives it at 1925. I'll stand by 1920] by the famous London rifle making firm of Holland & Holland, which has made many rifles for it on Magnum Mauser actions. . .

The Hoffman Arms Co. . . . and Griffin & Howe, of New York, pioneered the 300 Magnum cartridge in this country, and during the 1920s they built many rifles in that caliber for the better-heeled sportsmen. . .

For the size of the case the performance of the 300 H&H has always been a disappointment. It has a slight shoulder and great body taper, since it was designed for British Cordite powder, and American powder pressures have run high, velocity low, and barrel life short.

The illustrious Henry Stebbins wrote of the 300 H&H in his tome, *Rifles — A Modern Encyclopedia.* He follows:

Standard factory rifles for the 300 weigh about 8¼ pounds, minus sling and scope. Most custom rifles made for it before the late Winchester 54s [this reference to the Model 54 as being chambered to the 300 is interesting, although none of my other sources corroborates it], the 70s, and the Remington 722s [this is in error; the 722 was too short for the belted 30 Super, being chambered for such as the 222 and 244 Remington] came out were a pound or two heavier.

It is a long-range cartridge, and meant for such use, but at close range it has lots of stopping power when the right bullets are chosen.

. . . the sporting 180-grain is a familiar hunting cartridge, about as heavy as most of us can use with our full accuracy potential. It's hardly an exaggeration to say that it adds 100 yards to 30-06 deadliness, for those who can shoot it that much better.

Elmer Keith used to consider his 300 H&H a long-range pest and pronghorn load, and I suppose he thought it adequate for deer. Hard to say with Elmer.

As far as big game is concerned, the 300 Holland &

Holland should do as well as the 30-06, maybe a tad better on really big animals if loaded to max with heavy premium slugs from makers like Nosler or Bitterroot. According to the *Lyman Reloading Handbook Number 46,* Du Pont IMR 4350 provides the best muzzle velocity, and frequently fine accuracy to go with it. The Hodgdon version of the same propellant should do well also.

In 1983, Remington Arms Company offered a special run of their Model 700 Classic turnbolt chambered for the 300 Magnum. If you can locate one, it might be wise to pick it up. Not only will you be acquiring an instant collector's item, but you will be availing yourself of a cartridge rich in tradition, competitive heritage, and hunting experience. My French amigo, Claude Chauvigné, used a Holland & Holland in Africa in the '50s. I've never heard him complain about the 300's performance.

300 Holland & Holland Magnum

HANDLOAD DATA

Bullet Wt. Grs.	Type	Powder Wt. Grs.	Type	Primer	Case	MV (fps)	ME (fpe)	Rifle/ Bbl. (in.)	Remarks
150	Rem. SP	60.0	IMR 4895	8½-120	Win.	3115	3231	Rem. 721/26	Lym. Hndbk., 46th Ed. (Acc. Ld.)
180	Rem. SP	**67.0**	IMR 4350	8½-120	Win.	**2985**	**3561**	Rem. 721/26	Lym. Hndbk., 46th Ed. (Acc. Ld.)
200	Speer RN	**65.0**	IMR 4350	8½-120	Win.	**2808**	**3500**	Rem. 721/26	Lym. Hndbk., 46th Ed. (Acc. Ld.)
220	Rem. SP	**64.0**	IMR 4350	8½-120	Win.	**2732**	**3645**	Rem. 721/26	Lym. Hndbk., 46th Ed. (Acc. Ld.)

SP—Soft Point; RN—Round Nose.

FACTORY LOAD DATA

Bullet Wt. Grs.	Type	MV (fps)	ME (fpe)	Rifle/ Bbl. (in.)	Remarks
150	Win. SP	3094	3188	Win. M70/26	Speer Manual No. 9
180	Rem. SP	2875	3303	Win. M70/26	Speer Manual No. 9
180	Rem. (M)	2881	3317	Test barrel/26	Lym. Hndbk., 45th Ed.
180	Win. SP	2776	3079	Win. M70/26	Speer Manual No. 9
220	Rem. SP	2550	3176	Test barrel/26	Lym. Hndbk., 45th Ed.

SP—Soft Point; (M)—Match.

SPECIFICATIONS

Shell Holders
RCBS: 4
Bonanza: 2
Lyman: 13
Pacific: 5

Bullet Diameter
Jacketed: .308"

Lengths
Trim: 2.840"
Maximum Case: 2.850"
Maximum Overall: 3.600"

CAUTION:
Loads recommended and suggested herein have been carefully listed, but are intended solely as a guide to readers and neither the publisher nor author accept any responsibility for results of their use.
Maximum loads, listed in bold, should be reduced by 10 percent and worked up to cautiously.

300 Winchester Magnum

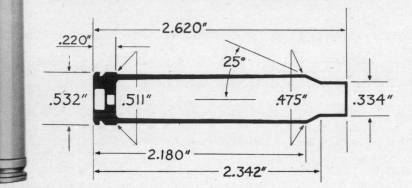

"The 180-grain Sierra slammed into the bear broadside, left a golf-ball-sized exit wound. As if the ground were jerked from beneath its paws, the bear hit the deck."

THIS should be Rick Jamison's chapter. He's the staunchest supporter of the 300 Winchester Magnum I know of, and one of its most experienced users. I've got about as much use for the big belted 300 as a 'possum has for a set of snow tires, but Rick really dotes on his.

Winchester's contribution to dislocated shoulders was inaugurated in 1963. Since then it has gone on to some degree of fame and fortune as a long-range target cartridge, a premier big game round, and a topic of much heated debate as to just what it's good for. Let's jump right in.

Ballistics

Factory-quoted ballistics are pretty impressive. There is a 150-grain bullet at a listed 3290 fps and 3605 fpe, a 180-grain at 2960 fps for 3501 fpe, and a 220-grain Silvertip at 2680 fps and 3508 fpe in case you want to shoot a pilot whale. How close does the stuff that you can buy come to achieving such lofty numbers?

In my Winchester Model 70 with 24-inch barrel, the 150-grain Winchester soft point clocks 3200 fps, for 3412 fpe. That's 90 fps short of the goal line. The 180-grain load from the same firm manages 2867 fps, 93 fps on the slow side. Energy is 3286 fpe. In an Ithaca CF-2 of the same barrel length, the 180-grain Winchester ammo showed 2910 fps on the clock; close but no cigar. My Ruger Model 77, same barrel length as the other two, got 3245 fps with the 150-grain Winchester prod-

uct, for only a 45 fps deficit. I've never chronographed the 220-grain factory loads, but the 200-grain Federal Premium soft point boat-tail reached 2763 fps in the Ithaca, 2768 fps in the Ruger 77. Energy numbers are 3391 and 3403 fpe respectively.

Note that all of the foregoing are in 24-inch tubes, as are the factory ballistics. Switch to a longer spout and naturally things look better for the big 30. In a Ruger Number 1 with 26-inch tube, I clocked the following figures: 150-grain Winchester SP, 3302 fps for 3632 fpe; 150-grain Federal SP, 3278 fps for 3580 fpe; 180-grain Winchester SP, 2914 fps and 3395 fpe; 180-grain Federal SP, 2936 fps and 3446 fpe. Much better, right? The 150-grain Win. even outran the factory specs a little.

The 7mm Remington and Weatherby magnums are in the same energy ballpark as the 300 Win.-Mag. Either of the 7mms can reach from 3350 to 3400 fpe with top loads. The 30-caliber also has the slight advantage of taking heavier bullets, but it is doubtful if *any* .308-inch diameter bullet will outpenetrate the magnificent 175-grain Nosler Partition .284-inch slug. Thus, it seems to me that the 7mm mags. are about equal to the 300 Winchester or 308 Norma Magnums when it comes to effectiveness on big game.

What about the lesser 30s? The 300 Winchester Mag. runs a strong 200-300 fps faster than the 308 Winchester with good handloads in both, perhaps 350-400 fps with factory ammo in barrel lengths common to each. The

The author's friend and hunting companion, gun writer Rick Jamison, has had a long term love affair with the 300 Winchester Magnum. Rick's favorite 300 is this old, well-used, converted Springfield.

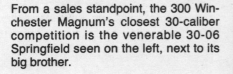

From a sales standpoint, the 300 Winchester Magnum's closest 30-caliber competition is the venerable 30-06 Springfield seen on the left, next to its big brother.

30-06 shades the 308 by about 100 fps across the boards, so the 300 Mag. would outrace the '06 by from 275 to perhaps 325 fps, depending on the exact load and barrel length involved. The old 300 Holland & Holland is within about 100-150 fps of the 300 Win.-Mag. in modern guns, bullet weight for bullet weight. Obviously, the better non-belted 30-calibers are about 10 percent slower in muzzle zip and from 500 to as much as 800 fpe of energy in arrears of the 300 Winchester.

All this has a price. I went to the Speer loading manual and averaged some charge weights for typical handloads in the above-mentioned cartridges. The 308 averaged out at 46.3 grains with all those powders listed under the 180-grain heading. The 30-06 showed an average charge weight of 56.0 grains, 21 percent more than the 308. (The average velocity increase was only 5.2 percent.) Loading 180-grain slugs in the 300 Winchester Magnum, the average charge was 73.5 grains, an increase of 17.5 grains over the 30-06 (31 percent) and 27.2 grains over the 308 (59 percent!). Velocity gain over the 30-06 was 252 fps, which is 9.4 percent. That's *31 percent more* propellant to yield 9.4 percent more velocity! Thought you'd want to know.

But *you're* not concerned with a little extra powder cost. After all, this is an expensive big game hunt you're going on; a trivial matter like loading economy is irrelevant. I agree. Then why the hell did I bring it up? Because you may not be aware of the other penalties you'll be exacting by using a 300 Win.-Mag. instead of 308, 30-06, or whatever. So, what are they? Glad you asked.

Recoil. The 300 Winchester Magnum provides an abundance of recoil. An abundance. We're not speaking here of an unpleasant jolt, an immoderate push; I'm talking hurt. The kind of pain that necessitates tuning it out mentally to accomplish any kind of decent shooting. The kind of pain a boxer accepts on his "beezer" from a left jab so he can get in close and deliver a right hook. Now, you may prefer to use some kind of protection between your shoulder and the buttplate of your rifle, to lessen the blow. Or maybe you just won't shoot much except when you're after game. Perhaps you think you won't notice the kick when the excitement of the hunt has you in its fevered grip. Or you can always load down for practice, stoking up with he-man ammo only when pursuing some large bovine or nasty-tempered bruin. Sure. All those things might work.

Just try getting to know your rifle without shooting it much; try adjusting to the feel of a sandbag against your shoulder instead of a rifle's butt; try shooting jackrabbits all day and see if you notice the kick; try getting off a shot from a hasty position, maybe aiming uphill, with-

Because of the recoil generated by the 300 Winchester, be sure to tie your scope mounts down, firmly. To do the job correctly, thoroughly degrease all receiver mount threads, and screws, and apply LocTite. The extra effort will be well worth it in the long run.

(Below) The now-discontinued Golden Eagle was offered in 300 Winchester Magnum. If you can find an owner of one of these rifles, who is willing to give it up, buy it. The Golden Eagle in 300 Winchester Magnum has an excellent reputation for *superb* accuracy.

out gapping your eyebrow with the scope; try shooting all summer with reduced loads then hitting an elk 350 yards up a mountain with a cartridge in the chamber you *know* is going to belt you a good one when you touch it off. If it works for you, fine. Not for me.

Muzzle blast. I'm not going to belabor this issue. If *you* don't mind a marked deterioration in your hearing, why should I fuss over it? Suffice to say this: the 300 Winchester Magnum is loud. *Real loud.* Of course, a painful bellow is not the exclusive province of the 300 Winchester Magnum. The 264 Winchester, 7mm Remington Magnum, 338 Winchester, and other magnums are equally strident. Which is one of the reasons I am sort of anti-magnum.

On this subject of hearing and muzzle blast, let me quote from Donald Hamilton's article in the 1971 *Gun Digest:*

> Here's where the uninformed layman, firing his souped-up magnum, makes his first mistake. He thinks that when he neglects to protect his ears he is gambling only with his hearing, but he is wrong.
>
> Certainly exposure to loud gunfire can result in some degree of deafness . . . but it's not only the sounds you can't hear that can become troublesome, but the sounds you can hear that aren't there. *Tinnitus,* or ringing of the ears, is no fun . . . it can become permanent, it can do so without warning, and once it does, there's no real cure.
>
> Furthermore, in addition to the hearing mechanism, the human ear also contains the body's balance center. This can also be affected by extremely loud, explosive sounds. Dizziness and vertigo are uncomfortable at best. They can be disabling.
>
> So you're actually risking a certain amount of lifetime discomfort and inconvenience, if not worse, when you step up to the firing line and pull the trigger. The extent of the risk *depends on the gun you use,* the precautions you take, and just how sensitive your ears happen to be.

Mr. Hamilton went on to explain how his problems had started, progressed, and finally led to an ear operation. And he said this: "My downfall was due largely to a 300 Winchester Magnum with muzzle brake."

As I'm certain you realize, a muzzle brake exacerbates the blast problem. The point is, if the shooter wasn't hurt by the recoil, he wouldn't feel the need to put some recoil-reducing device on his rifle.

The final point is that I'm convinced that a magnum rifle kills little if any quicker than a 30-06 or similar gun. Heresy? Perhaps. I have talked to many, many people who hunt virtually year round, folks who have slain many types and sizes of animals and examined the results. The consensus usually is that the game would travel just about as far whether hit with a 7mm Magnum, a 308, a 30-06, or a 375 Holland & Holland. A big mag is needed when a large *dangerous* animal is on the agenda, one which is normally broken down with the first shot to prevent it from deflating the nimrod's ego by slapping him around some. To break heavy bone, you need as much punch and sectional density as you can get. A magnum *does* provide that.

Bear in mind that the shooter's skill is not as critical for such close encounters as it would be on a longer shot, so the effects of recoil are not so pronounced as they would be at long range. As for the old saw about the superior retained energy at 350, 400, even 500 yards, enjoyed by the belted magnums, that is surely

Two popular rifles available in 300 Winchester Magnum are the Weatherby Vanguard (above) and the Ruger 77 (top). The Ruger 77 seen here is the round-top receiver variant that comes with iron sights, a plus for big game hunters who want a back-up sighting system.

Kleinguenther is another gun-making outfit that has a solid reputation for turning out *accurate* rifles. Seen here is that firm's K-15 Instafire.

the case. And largely irrelevant. Not one hunter out of 500, maybe 1000, has any business shooting at big game at distances past 300 yards, and I don't care what he's shooting.

But let's suppose that you can handle recoil; you are a sufficiently fine shot to take game out to 400 yards or so; you always wear ear protection when you shoot; and you want to avail yourself of any advantages the 300 Winchester might offer. Let's suppose further that you don't particularly mind carrying a rifle a bit heavier and longer than need be, and that you are not primarily a whitetail deer hunter, but a pursuer of elk, moose, and similar-size animals. Just what will the 300 Winchester Magnum do for you?

For one thing, it shoots as flat as about anything you can buy. *Anything.* According to the Winchester ballistics sheet, the following cartridges shoot flatter than the 300 Winchester out to 400 yards: the 22-250, the 6mm Remington with 80-grain spitzers, the 25-06 with the 90-grain Positive Expanding Point, and the 125-grain spitzer in the 7mm Remington Magnum. That's all. (I did not include any of the proprietary Weatherby car-

tridges, nor the Federal boat-tail ammo in the comparison.) Since the 22-250, 6mm, and 25-06 are suitable only for varmint hunting *with the loads mentioned,* that means we are left with only the 125-grain load in the Big Seven, which is not the best choice for big game except possibly antelope. The 150-grain soft point is excellent for use on mule deer, pronghorn, caribou, sheep, goat and similar fauna under 400 pounds in heft, just as it is in the 300 Magnum. The kicker is that the 150-grain 7mm slug drops 5 inches more at 400 yards than a 30-caliber bullet of identical weight, again according to the Winchester data. Pretty big difference.

Energy retention is another 300 Winchester strong suit. My Winchester data shows the 180-grain spitzer as having 1859 fpe at 400 yards. What other cartridges are close? Well, the 300 Holland & Holland retains 1584 fpe, and the 375 Holland & Holland carries 1669 fpe with the streamlined 300-grain Silvertip, and the 458 Winchester Magnum hangs onto 1839 fpe of punch. All are close, but none is better. There is only one Winchester factory loading that exceeds the 300 Winchester Magnum in retained energy after covering the length of four football fields, the 225-grain 338 Winchester Magnum, which delivers 2005 fpe. It's the *only* one.

So, what we have is a cartridge that shoots flatter than any non-proprietary big game load commonly available in this country and hits with more energy at 400 yards than all but one, which in turn carries even more flinch-inducing recoil than the 300. That's pretty impressive.

(If I included the Federal Premium line of boat-tail hunting ammo, the 300 would beat the 338 substantially. The 200-grain Federal 300 load shows 2230 foot-pounds of energy left out at 400 yards! This comparison is not kosher, however; the 338 is not loaded with a boat-tail bullet by the factories.)

How about accuracy? I've done a fair amount of shooting with three 300 Win. Mag. turnbolt sporters. With their pet loads, the average for several five-shot strings ran from 1.69 inches in the most accurate, to 1.93 inches in the least precise. I don't recall a single 300 (including a Ruger Number 1) that failed to group inside 2 inches at 100 yards. My experience has been that the average sporter-weight 7mm Magnum (either Weatherby or Remington) will generally outgroup the

that no sooner do you fit a barrel, get some sight data and some practice, and fire a few matches than suddenly the bore is washed out . . . I once kept a careful record of the rounds I put through a 300 Magnum with stainless-steel barrel. The sum total of its accuracy life was a brief *613 rounds!* Some rifles . . . seem to keep going for upwards of 2,000 rounds, but 1,000 seems to be about the average.

Hunting

Forget the barrel life (or lack of it); ignore the paper ballistics; don't worry about intrinsic accuracy. Let's see how good the 300 Winchester is at its forte, dispatching large animals.

Rick Jamison, current hunting editor of *Shooting Times,* bought his 300 Winchester Magnum after he had a 30-06 disappoint him on a smallish black bear. He'd tagged the bruin in the shoulder, the bullet coursing on through lungs and liver to exit the flank. As its shoulder was broken, Rick was shocked that the bear ran 300 or 400 yards before toppling over. "To this day, I don't know why that bear didn't drop in its tracks," says Rick.

Rick swapped an elderly Marlin rimfire for "Old Ugly," his 300 Winchester Mag. (If you saw his rifle,

If you want a clip-fed 300 Winchester, consider the Savage 110-C. It's well built, handsome and has a good reputation for accuracy when chambered for the 300 Winchester Magnum.

run-of-the-mill 300 Winchester Magnum, but that's by no means set in stone. I've worked with more than twice as many Big Sevens as 300 Mags.

So to discuss *real* accuracy, I'll turn the floor over to Jim Carmichel in his book, *The Modern Rifle*. To wit:

> The most accurate long-range rifle I've ever owned, or used, is a 300 Winchester Magnum with Douglas barrel on a Model 70 action. Five-shot test groups fired from a bench rest have measured as small as .300-inch between the center of the two widest shots.

Now Jim is speaking here of pure-bred target guns weighing up to 16 pounds, but the point shouldn't be lost: the 300 Winchester Magnum is intrinsically very accurate. To prove it, Jim provides a photo on page 273 of a five-shot group spanning only .356-inch and fired from a 300 target rifle.

Jim also touches on another 300 Winchester Magnum sore spot in his section devoted to 1000-yard target rifles. Quote:

> Barrels, unfortunately, are always a heartbreaking proposition on the magnum-class target rifle. It seems

you wouldn't wonder where it got its name.) Rick hand-loaded some 180-grain Sierra spitzers ahead of various charges of Hodgdon H4831, then repaired to the range. His first five shots clustered into one ragged hole. And thus was he hooked.

Since the gun was heavy — probably 9½ or 10 pounds dry — the recoil wasn't too bad. He says the kick wasn't as severe as a particularly nasty J.C. Higgins 270 he had used earlier. He settled on a specific charge of H4831 and went hunting.

To date, Rick and Old Ugly have accounted for about a dozen elk, four black bear, a pronghorn, and uncounted deer, coyotes, and jack rabbits. The recoil doesn't bother him much, although he says that most of his shooting is offhand, which takes the sting out somewhat.

Rick's first big game animal was a black bear, shot about 30 yards away. The 180-grain Sierra slammed into the bear broadside, left a golf-ball-sized exit wound. As if the ground were jerked from beneath its paws, the bear hit the deck.

Next up was a fine four-point (Western count) mule deer, then a big six-point bull elk. Rick had been hunting hard for 5 consecutive days without sighting elk hair. On the sixth day he was high atop Anderson Mesa in northern Arizona.

Rick was 200 or 300 feet above a thick stand of junipers when he spied something moving into an opening a long way off. He quickly wriggled out of his sweatshirt, draped it across a boulder for a rest, plopped on his belly, and peered through his scope. From his aerie he checked out a cow elk and her calf. They crossed the opening and disappeared into the junipers. Directly following came the big six-point. The distance was so great, Rick would not have been able to discern the bull's antlers if the sun hadn't reflected from them.

Rick held just above the elk's back and squeezed off. The bull collapsed. Unfortunately, it tried to regain its feet. Rick had to go down and finish him with a head shot from a 357 Magnum revolver. The first shot had broken both front legs; the bull wasn't going anywhere.

That wapiti was a right "fer" piece from Rick's vantage point on the mesa. He told me. "My rifle was sighted in to hit 2¾-inches high at 100 yards. The load I used chronographed 3050 fps. I was holding right over his back and broke both legs at the knees. Check the ballistics charts and you'll have some idea how far away that elk was." I did; my estimate is roughly 500 yards.

Once, while on a "drive" of sorts in Colorado, Rick and Old Ugly teamed up on two big mule deer in just a few hours. Rick had already dropped and gutted an elk that day and was going after help to tote it into camp when he spotted a fine four-point mule deer trotting along in a canyon. Rick fired, the deer hit the deck and bounced back up. Rick was about to lower the boom when another hunter saw the buck and killed it. Rick let it pass; there was plenty of game around.

Shortly after this, he met up with two hunters from his party. They decided to wait for more drivers to come down off the mountain and help bring in the elk. Rick walked off a ways and sat down. A half-hour later, a trophy mule deer wandered out of the timber near Rick's two compadres, who promptly opened up on it. The buck headed for quieter surroundings. Right toward Rick. His 180-grain slug caught the deer in the center of its chest as it plunged through the snow, dumping it base over apex and sending snow cascading in all directions. When the flakes settled, the buck was still kicking; Rick placed another 180-grain Sierra right beside the first. An elk and two buck deer down, and before noon!

And so on. No need to keep going. The 300 Winchester Magnum will indeed fill the larder in capable hands, and I know of none more capable than Rick Jamison's.

Handloading the 300 Winchester Magnum is pretty straightforward except for considerations necessitated by the extremely short neck. My favorite powders are H4831, IMR 4350 and 4831, and Hodgdon's H450 ball. My Model 70 liked 76.0 grains of H4831 under the 180-grain Hornady SP for 3039 fps. Runner-up was 74.0 grains of H450 and the same 180-grain Hornady, getting 2979 fps and 3547 fpe. The loads are equally accurate.

If you can shoulder the recoil and your ears can stand the noise, give the 300 a try. It will do its job if you can handle yours.

Rick Jamison, staunch 300 Mag. supporter, is shown firing an H&S 300 Mag. built on a Remington 700 action and having a Hiberthane stock.

300 Winchester Magnum

HANDLOAD DATA

Bullet Wt. Grs.	Type	Powder Wt. Grs.	Type	Primer	Case	MV, (fps)	ME, (fpe)	Rifle/ Bbl. (in.)	Remarks
180	Hrndy. SP	71.6	IMR 4350	8½-120	Win.	2990	3573	Win. M70/24	Accurate
180	Sierra SP	75.0	H4831	CCI 250	Win.	3050	3718	Cust. Sprngfld./24	Very acc.; R. Jamison load
180	Hrndy. SP	**76.0**	H4831	Fed. 215	Win.	**3039**	**3691**	Win. M70/24	Accurate
180	Hrndy. SP	74.0	H450	Fed. 215	Win.	2979	3547	Win. M70/24	Accurate
180	Hrndy. SP	76.3	MRP	Fed. 215	Win.	2950	3478	Win. M70/24	Accurate

SP—Soft Point.

FACTORY LOAD DATA

Bullet Wt. Grs.	Type	MV, (fps)	ME, (fpe)	Rifle/ Bbl. (in.)	Remarks
150	Win. SP	3200	3404	Win. M70/24	Good velocity
150	Win. SP	3302	3632	Ruger No. 1/26	Very fast
150	Fed. SP	3278	3580	Ruger No. 1/26	_____
180	Win. SP	2910	3384	Ithaca CF-2/24	Good velocity
180	Fed. SP	2936	3446	Ruger No. 1/26	Fast
200	Fed. Prem. SPBT	2763	3391	Ithaca CF-2/24	_____

SP—Soft Point; SPBT—Soft Point Boat-Tail.

SPECIFICATIONS

Shell Holders
RCBS: 4 or 26
Bonanza: 2
Lyman: 13
Pacific: 5

Bullet Diameter
Jacketed: .308″

Lengths
Trim: 2.610″
Maximum Case: 2.620″
Maximum Overall: 3.340″

The 300 Winchester Magnum is well suited for use on the larger species of North American game. With heavy bullets and stiff charges of propellant, the 300 Win. Mag. churns up some impressive energy levels.

CAUTION:
Loads recommended and suggested herein have been carefully listed, but are intended solely as a guide to readers and neither the publisher nor author accept any responsibility for results of their use. **Maximum loads, listed in bold, should be reduced by 10 percent and worked up to cautiously.**

300 Weatherby Magnum

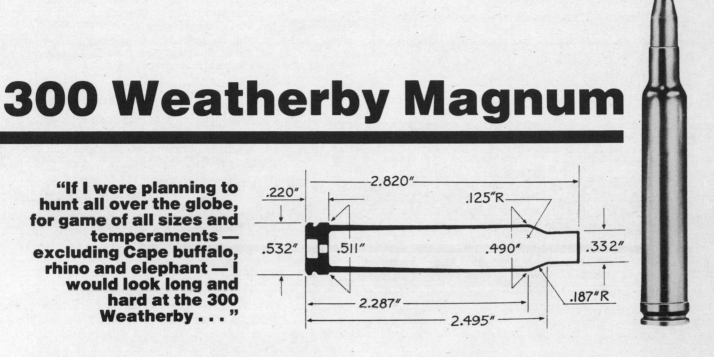

"If I were planning to hunt all over the globe, for game of all sizes and temperaments — excluding Cape buffalo, rhino and elephant — I would look long and hard at the 300 Weatherby . . . "

LET'S begin this chapter with the hypothesis that the 30-06 is the "standard" size among 30-caliber cartridges. With that as a working postulate, we can place such worthies as the 30-30, 300 Savage, 30-40 Krag, and the 308 on the underside of "standard," and cartridges of greater capacity than the ought-six on the "magnum" side. Using such as our criteria, I'm sure you realize that the 300 Weatherby Magnum was not the first 30-caliber magnum, nor even the most popular. It *is* the most powerful, the most widely heralded, the most prestigious, and the flattest shooting. Before analyzing it, let's have a look at some of its predecessors.

The original super-thirty was the 30 Adolph Express, better known as the 30 Newton. Making its appearance in 1913, the 30 Newton was ballyhooed as providing a 180-grain bullet with a 2860 fps start in life. That's good for 3270 fpe. Remember, this was in 1913, when the 30-06 was still getting around 2700 fps from a 150-grain slug. The old Adolph Express was quite a package; it wore no belt and was unencumbered with the "magnum" title.

Aside from being the first high-octane 30-caliber cartridge, the Newton was the first American cartridge to wear the now-common 25-degree shoulder angle. It also boasted a case head similar in size to the later belted magnums, the minimum body taper fashionable today, and an overall length about like the so-called short magnums exemplified by the 7mm Remington Magnum. Quite a trail blazer, the 30 Newton.

Charles Newton's firearms company foundered in unfriendly financial waters, finally sinking sometime in the 1920s. Western Cartridge Company continued to offer the 256, 30, and 35 Newton ammunition until just before World War II. So far as I know, the last batch of 30 Newton cases was fabricated in 1950 by Dick Speer, originator of Cascade Cartridge Company in Lewiston, Idaho.

Even in its heyday, the 30 Newton was not overwhelmingly popular. However, it influenced high-velocity cartridge design for years. The well-known 30/338 wildcat was originally called the 30 Belted Newton, and I've read that the initial version of the 7mm Remington Magnum was dubbed by some the 7mm Belted Newton. The relatively short necks, fat bodies, straight-tapers, and sharp 25-degree shoulders, of modern belted magnums are inherited from the 30 Newton.

Incidentally, when the major loading companies were constructing their bullet jackets of cupro-nickel, Newton surmised that said cupro-nickel was the cause of the severe metal fouling that plagued shooters of that earlier time. He subsequently switched to pure copper-jacketed slugs of a construction similar to Remington's current Core-Lokt, one of the best hunting bullets made by anyone. Smart man, Charles Newton. But unlucky; he died penniless.

The next super thirty was the 300 Holland & Holland

The Colt Sauer (left) is available chambered for the 300 Weatherby Mag., and comes with a detachable magazine (below). The big Colt, like other 300 Weatherby turnbolts, isn't a lightweight. It tips the scale at well over 8 lbs. when fully loaded and scoped.

Assuming you can do your part, excellent accuracy can be had from a 300 Weatherby at the 100-yard line.

(Right) The 300 Weatherby can turn in groups like this if the shooter can handle the recoil. (The black aiming mark is 1 inch square.)

Magnum, or as the British called it, the Super 30 Magnum Rimless (or the 375/300, due to its necked-down 375 H&H Magnum origin). As I wrote in the chapter devoted to it, the 300 was first chambered in this country by such high-roller outfits as Griffin & Howe. In 1937, Winchester poked it into their lineup of Model 70 chamberings.

And then came the 300 Weatherby. Although some amateur ballisticians believe that the 270 Weatherby followed on the successful heels of the 300 Weatherby, such is not the case. According to *Cartridges of the World,* the 300 was one of the last Weatherby loads to be developed around the 300 Holland & Holland case. Weatherby's version amounts to a blown-out or "improved" 300 H&H, with a typical Weatherby double-radius shoulder, scant body taper, and originally was chambered in rifles having considerable free-bore. Combining those features produced a cartridge capable of some pretty giddy velocities for a 30-caliber.

According to Weatherby data, the 300 will give the following numbers with factory ammunition in a 26-inch barrel: 110-grain soft point, 3900 fps and 3716 fpe; 150-grain soft point or Nosler Partition, 3545 fps for 4187 fpe; 180-grain soft point or Nosler Partition, 3245 fps and 4210 fpe; 200-grain Nosler Partition, 3000 fps and 3998 fpe; 220-grain round nose, 2905 fps for 4123 fpe. The best all-around load, which is the 180-grain in my opinion, still yields 2639 fpe at 300 yards in soft point form, according to the Weatherby chart. That's more energy than the 30-40 Krag, the 300 Savage, the 375 Winchester, the 7x57 Mauser, or the 25-06 produce *at the muzzle* in any factory load of any bullet weight. Wow!

And flat! Going by factory figures, a 300 Weatherby zeroed at 300 yards with the 150-grain soft point will drop only 8.1 inches at 400 yards and rise above the line of sight a mere 3.2 inches at half that distance. Wow again! Even the plodding 200-grainer dips only 18 inches at 400 yards from a *200-yard* zero. And it still has 2480 fpe of sting at that lengthy distance. Imagine this: shooting an animal 400 yards away with a 200-grain Nosler Partition fired from a 300 Weatherby is about like sticking the muzzle of a 300 Savage against the hide. If *you're* not impressed, *I* sure as hell am!

I have read that the well-known Californian, Elgin Gates, has slain almost every species of African animal, including elephant, with a 300 Weatherby. I have also seen data claiming that more seekers after Alaska brown and polar bears tote 300 Weatherby Magnums than anything else.

Although the Weatherby Mark V is the most popular rifle made for the 300 Weatherby, I have seen catalogue listings for the Colt-Sauer, Mauser M66S, Kleinguenther K-15, and the Golden Eagle. All are high-ticket items appealing to the jet set, no plebian ordnance these.

Okay, so we know the 300 Weatherby will drive reasonably heavy bullets at head-spinning velocities and provide a striking force greater than 2 tons way out past where anyone should attempt a shot. So what'll she do? There are two schools of thought.

One holds that the 300 Weatherby (and the other modern 300 magnums) cannot be stuffed in rifles light enough to be carried up mountains by anyone other than a Russian weight lifter without kicking you out from under your derby when you touch off a shot. Few men, this group opines, can shoot well a rifle of such recoil and muzzle blast. Finally, say these savants, the 300 Weatherby is too much for any animal smaller than a moose but hasn't enough bullet weight and diameter to be reliable on heavy dangerous game.

The second school says the first is full of prunes and promotes the 300 Weatherby as adequate for anything this side of a brontosaurus, and a big one at that. These fellows have backed up their theories by taking all manner of critters and living to chide the other group.

In *The Hunting Rifle,* Jack O'Conner had this to say about our subject:

I have used a 300 Weatherby in Africa and North America enough to know something about it. If an animal is hit right with a good bullet some very spectacular kills result, but he must be hit right. I'll never forget two very sensational kills with the 300 Weatherby. Onc was a Yukon grizzly. He was walking rapidly and about 100 yards away when I bushwhacked him. The 180-grain Remington bronze point bullet driven by 78 grains of [IMR] 4350 hit him through the lungs. He dropped in his tracks. On the off side was a hole you could stick a fist in and bright against the green grass was a fan-shaped spray of blood and bits of bone and lung.

Another spectacular performance was on a Tanganyika sable. With the same load, I aimed high for a lung shot at about 150 yards. I squeezed off and the next thing I knew I could see all four feet in the air.

Weatherby's Mark V in 300 Weatherby Magnum comes in a number of flavors. At the top is the Mark V Safari Grade rifle; in the middle is the Mark V Lasermark; on the bottom is the Mark V Deluxe. The choice is yours.

One of the benefits of any 30-caliber magnum is the fact that handloaders have a lot to choose from. From left to right: 110-grain Hornady soft point; 110-grain Sierra hollow point; 125-grain Sierra soft point; 130-grain Hornady soft point; 130-grain Speer hollow point and the 150-grain Nosler solid base. The lighter bullets are ideal for off-season varmints; the 150-grain Nosler is a good bet for deer-sized game.

(Right) If you shoot the 300 Weatherby Magnum, the powder of choice is IMR 4350. Of *all* the slow-burners, this is the "best of show" when it comes to loading the big 300.

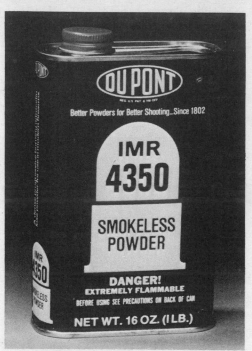

Obviously, if you do your job of directing a good bullet to a vital spot, the 300 is up to its end.

Handloading

Virtually every loading manual except the Hornady shows IMR 4350 to be the undisputed velocity king in the 300 Weatherby. Hornady favors Hodgdon H450, H4831, and Norma MRP as being the best for speed. For my part, I'll go with IMR 4350, ignition by Federal.

If I were planning to hunt all over the globe, for game of all sizes and temperments — excluding Cape buffalo, rhino, and elephant — I would look long and hard at the 300 Weatherby, particularly in the handy, handsome, and hard-working new Fibermark. I'd stoke my brass with the superb 200-grain Nosler Partition and a maximum charge of about 75-76 grains of Du Pont IMR 4350. For long-range elk hunting exclusively, I'd probably choose the 180-grain Sierra boat-tail spitzer and a grain or two more powder. Plains hunting of critters no heavier than 200 pounds or so would find me with max-loaded 150-grain ammunition, if I were to use the 300 Weatherby. (Of course, for such use the 300 is not necessary.)

Despite the fact that some hunters consider the 300 too light for the big, thick-skinned stuff, I have to go along with O'Conner in his summation of the 300 Mags. He wrote: " . . . anything that cannot be knocked off with a 30 magnum with a well-placed 220-grain bullet at about 2,800 or a 200-grain bullet at 3,000 would be hard to bump off with just about anything."

I heard that.

300 Weatherby Magnum

HANDLOAD DATA

Bullet Wt. Grs.	Type	Powder Wt. Grs.	Type	Primer	Case	MV, (fps)	ME, (fpe)	Rifle/ Bbl. (in.)	Remarks
150	Rem. SP	**82.0**	IMR 4350	Fed. 215	Wby.	3401	3852	Wby. Mk. V/26	Lym. Hndbk., 46th Ed.
165	Speer SP	**80.0**	IMR 4350	Fed. 215	Wby.	3285	3953	Wby. Mk. V/26	Lym. Hndbk., 46th Ed.
180	Rem. SP	**79.0**	IMR 4350	Fed. 215	Wby.	3194	4077	Wby. Mk. V/26	Lym. Hndbk., 46th Ed.
200	Speer RN	**76.0**	IMR 4350	Fed. 215	Wby.	3008	4017	Wby. Mk. V/26	Lym. Hndbk., 46th Ed. (Acc. Ld.)
200	Speer RN	**79.0**	H4831	Fed. 215	Wby.	2865	3645	Wby. Mk. V/26	Lym. Hndbk., 46th Ed. (Acc. Ld.)

SP—Soft Point; RN—Round Nose.

FACTORY LOAD DATA

Bullet Wt. Grs.	Type	MV, (fps)	ME, (fpe)	Rifle/ Bbl. (in.)	Remarks
150	Wby. SP	3130	3262	Wby. Mk. V/26	Speer Manual No. 9
150	Wby. SP	3559	4218	Wby. Mk. V/26	Lym. Hndbk., 45th Ed.
180	Wby. SP	3179	4039	Wby. Mk. V/26	Speer Manual No. 9
180	Wby. SP	3164	4000	Wby. Mk. V/26	Lym. Hndbk., 45th Ed.
220	Wby. RN	2906	4125	Wby. Mk. V/26	Lym. Hndbk., 45th Ed.

SP—Soft Point; RN—Round Nose.

SPECIFICATIONS
Shell Holders
RCBS: 4
Bonanza: 2
Lyman: 13
Pacific: 5

Bullet Diameter
Jacketed: .308"

Lengths
Trim: 2.815"
Maximum Case: 2.820"
Maximum Overall: 3.562"

The 300 Weatherby Magnum has more than sufficient punch for North America's larger game. Elk, moose — name it. The big 30-caliber Weatherby can do the job.

CAUTION:
Loads recommended and suggested herein have been carefully listed, but are intended solely as a guide to readers and neither the publisher nor author accept any responsibility for results of their use. **Maximum loads, listed in bold, should be reduced by 10 percent and worked up to cautiously.**

32 Winchester Special

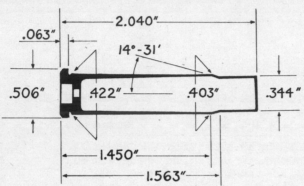

> "But, if you already own a 32 Winchester Special, I'd certainly not recommend you trade the gun off just because of its chambering. Ballistically, it is a capable cartridge for woods hunting of moderate-sized game."

PITY the poor 32 Winchester Special. For more than 80 years it has lived in the shadow of the 30-30, and it probably will for 80 more. I'm not sure just why; in a proper firearm, rifled with the correct twist, the 32 is every bit as good ballistically as the old 30 W.C.F., alias the 30-30. Despite that fact, the 32 Special should have faded away many years ago. That it didn't is cause for considerable head scratching.

Before going into the pros and cons of the 32 Special as a cartridge, let's spin the clock back to the turn of the century. (Incidentally, authorities tend to disagree as to the introduction date for the 32. It is listed variously as 1895 and 1902. In Watrous' book on Winchester rifles, the 32 Special is shown as being first chambered in the Model 1894 lever-action in June of 1902.) Smokeless powder (then called "white powder") had been around for more than a decade, but was not readily available to the handloader. In addition, reactionary reloaders were not entirely convinced that smokeless was here to stay. In consequence, many shooters used black powder to reload such modern smokeless cartridges as the 30-30.

It was soon noted that the relatively fast twist of the 30-caliber, one turn in 12 inches, fouled very badly and very quickly when coupled with the small bore diameter (for that time). The use of cast-lead bullets instead of jacketed ones exacerbated the bore-fouling tendency.

The 32 Special was designed to obviate these difficulties. It had been determined that a slight increase in bore diameter and a slowing of the twist rate to 1-in-16 alleviated much of the problem associated with reloading black powder and lead bullets. That was the *raison d'être* for the 32 Special. By combining the bore diameter of the popular and accurate 32-40 Winchester with the case shape of the new and exciting 30-30, Winchester was creating a new cartridge of obvious virtues for the time. It worked well.

As the century progressed and smokeless propellants settled in to stay, accepted by handloaders, the virtues of the 1-in-16 twist began to wane. Jacketed hunting bullets became more readily available; fewer reloaders messed with bullet casting, especially for big game hunting. The advantage of the slow twist transmogrified into an ogre. Many were the articles that stated flatly that a badly worn or pitted 32 Special bore would not shoot worth beans. Here's an example from Barnes' *Cartridges of the World:* "Once the bore of a 32 Special rifle begins to go, you can't hit a flock of barns with it."

And this from the *Speer Reloading Manual Number Ten:* "The 30-30 has a 1-12 twist and even barrels which are pretty well worn will still provide hunting accuracy. Once the 32 Special barrel, with its 1-16 twist, gets a bit worn or suffers from neglect, it becomes so hopelessly inaccurate that it is useless."

Hmmm. Are there no kind words to be said in the 32 Special's defense? Henry Stebbins had this to say in *Rifles: A Modern Encyclopedia:* "One advantage claimed

Du Pont's IMR 4895 is a good powder choice for the 32 Winchester Special. (Speer and Hornady currently offer 170-grain flat nose bullets .321-inch diameter.)

The 32 Winchester Special was introduced in the Winchester Model 94 carbine over 80 years ago. Complete with 1-in-16 barrel twist, the 32 Special was brought out to help eliminate the bore fouling that handloaders were experiencing with black powder in the 30-30.

for the 30-30 is that a badly rusted barrel will still spin bullets out with fair accuracy. Few of us *have* to hunt with such barrels, and the slow 32 twist makes for a little longer [barrel] life. So it's a toss-up.''

Ken Waters did a "Pet Loads" article on the 32 Special in the July-August, 1978 issue of *Handloader* magazine. Ken was not nearly so acerbic as his contemporaries in his assessment of the cartridge's merits. Let me quote:

> Actually, the slower twist and larger bore accomplished more than just adapting rifle and cartridge for use with blackpowder. A second advantage derived from these same factors is in the heightened suitability of the 32 Special for use with cast bullets, due principally to lessened rotational torque.
>
> Yet a third reason prompting the 32 Special's development may well have been the practicability of equaling 30-30 velocities with lower pressures, made possible by the larger base area of 32 Special bullets and increased expansion ratio of the bore.
>
> If we accept the premise, then, that the 32 Winchester Special as a *caliber* (i.e., rifle and cartridge together)

offered advantages to blackpowder and cast-bullet shooters, doing so at lower pressures, I think we can conclude that it did indeed have a valid reason for being. Granted that today its adaptability to black powder has lost much if not all of its original significance, there still remains its affinity for cast bullets and happy characteristic of lower pressures. Hence, I for one refuse to view it as useless or even inferior to the 30-30.

Well said. However, we still need to address the accusation of abysmal accuracy from worn or rusted 32 Special bores.

Accuracy and Energy

Now I've never owned a 32 Special, and I'm about as interested in obtaining one as I am in house-training a yak. Therefore, I'll take Ken Waters' word on the subject. Using an early Model 1894 Winchester, which had seen much use and had a rough and well-worn bore, Ken had no difficulty in achieving 100-yard, five-shot groups of 2.75 inches, and 15-shot groups of 3.75 inches! If that is an example of a rifle that "won't hit a

Many brush-country cartridges (all chambered in lever-actions, at one time or another) have competed with the 32 Winchester Special. From left to right: 30-30 Winchester; 300 Savage; 308 Winchester; 30-06; (32 Winchester Special, for comparison); 35 Remington; 358 Winchester and 44 Remington Magnum.

Over the years, Winchester also offered the 32 Special chambering in their Model 64 lever-action rifle. While the 32 found its way into some of the most beautiful lever-actions ever made, the cartridge never came close to the 30-30 in popularity.

flock of barns," one that is "hopelessly inaccurate," then I would dearly love to own a *good*-shooting lever-action carbine. (Incidentally, Ken used a tang peep sight, not a scope, to obtain such accuracy.)

Verbal warfare was waged in the shooting press for years regarding alleged differences in killing power between the 30-30 and the 32 Special. Talk about counting the angels on the head of a pin! There is *no* difference in killing power. None. Zero. And you don't have to shoot a carload of animals to prove it to yourself. Look at the ballistics. The 30-30 is shown as kicking a 170-grain soft point out the muzzle at 2200 fps. The 32 will shove a similar bullet at 2250 fps. That's a 50 fps advantage for the 32, big deal. (Assuming of course that the ammo actually reaches such numbers, which it probably doesn't in either cartridge. Regardless, the relationship should remain constant.) At 100 yards, the 30-30 retains 1895 fps, the 32 shows 1921. The 30-30 has failed to gain an advantage despite the superior ballistic properties of the 170-grain 30-caliber slug over its 32-caliber cousin.

Energy figures are similarly close. The 32 Special has the edge at the muzzle with 1911 fpe against the 30-30's 1827. At 100 yards the 30-30 shows 1355 fpe with the 170-grain factory load, the 32 has 1393 fpe. Not much difference is there? Even out at 200 yards, which is stretching it for either cartridge, the 30-30 is still in arrears by 9 foot-pounds.

Drop figures favor the 30-30 slightly. The 170-grain Winchester Power-Point factory ammo drops 4.8 inches at 200 yards from a 150-yard zero. Showing a 5.1-inch dip at the same range with the same zero and bullet weight, the 32 is so close the difference is meaningless.

Some writers cited the superior sectional density of the 170-grain 30-30 bullet as giving it a significant advantage in penetrative ability. Hogwash. Assuming identical bullet construction, penetration should be virtually the same.

Conversely, 32 Special advocates advanced the postulate that their pet's larger bullet diameter endowed it with increased knockdown punch on big game. Horse apples. Again, with equal bullet construction, the expansion qualities of each bullet negate such theoretical nonsense.

The upshot of this is that what the 30-30 will do, the 32 Special will do as well but no better. The two are as alike as a pair of corn muffins. However, the 30-30 does enjoy a considerable advantage over the 32 when it comes to variety of factory ammunition. You can buy 30-30 factory ammo stuffed with 55-grain 22-caliber bullets for varmint shooting, 125-grain hollow points for varminting or predator control, 150- and 170-grain hollow points for the same purpose; there's even a 170-grain Nosler Partition load by Federal for taking a poke at a *big* black bear or an elk. Pretty fair selection.

On the other hand, you can buy 32 Special factory loads in 170-grain soft point persuasion. That's all. (Of course, Winchester offers both the Power Point and the Silvertip, but both are soft points in my lexicon.)

Handloading

When it comes to handloading, the 32 still takes the backseat. For the 30-30 you can purchase 100-grain flat points, 150-grain round nose, and 170-grain flat points from Hornady. From Sierra you can select a 125-grain hollow point, or 150- and 170-grain flat points. From Speer you can buy 100-grain Plinkers, 110-grain hollow points, 130-grain flat points, and the usual 150- and 170-grain flat points. Nosler offers 150- and 170-grain flat points in their Solid Base line, and I wouldn't be surprised to see them add the 170-grain Partition flat point they produce for Federal's Premium lineup of factory ammunition. All in all, quite a selection of bullets for the reloader.

The 32 Winchester Special shell stuffer can buy nothing from Nosler, a 170-grain flat nose from Speer, naught from Sierra, and a 170-grain flat point from Hornady. Not exactly overwhelming, is it? Oh well, the 32 is best used as a moderate-range deer and black bear cartridge anyway.

Cast-bullet shooters can try Lyman mold number 321297 if they can find one. Nominal weight, as-cast, is

When it comes to handloading, Winchester's 748 Ball powder is an excellent choice for the 32 Winchester Special.

181 grains. Bullets should be cast very hard and sized at least .001-inch over bore diameter. Du Pont IMR 4227 and IMR 4198 should give acceptable accuracy if your bore is up to snuff.

Which brings us to proper powders for use with jacketed bullets in the 32 Special. My research tells me that the original 32 factory ammo was loaded with 23.5 grains of the long-defunct Hercules "Lightning" powder. Bullet diameter was .321-inch; average chamber pressures were around 36,000 pounds per square inch. When it comes to powder selection, I would suggest you try Hodgdon's version of 4895, IMR 3031, or Hercules ReLoder 7. Ken Waters found that 34.0 grains of H4895, 31.0 grains of 3031, or 29.0 grains of ReLoder 7 gave the best accuracy, with 170-grain jacketed bullets, in his Winchester Model 64 Deluxe. He reached maximum velocities with 35.0 to 36.0 grains of IMR 4320, or 36.0 to 36.5 grains of Norma N202. With these two, he managed to achieve 2300 fps with 170-grain jacketed bullets.

The loading manuals back Ken up. Lyman, in their Reloading Handbook, 46th Ed., got the highest muzzle speeds with maximum loads of 31.0 grains of ReLoder 7, at 2283 fps, and 35.0 grains of 4320, at 2169—both loads using 170-grain jacketed bullets. Speer managed 2205 fps from 35.0 grains of IMR 4895. (Please note that Ken used a 24-inch-barreled rifle; the manuals used Model 94 carbines with 20-inch tubes.)

And so goes the old 32 Special. Rifles are no longer available on the new-gun market, although a good used one shouldn't be too hard to turn up if you want one. Winchester (U.S. Repeating Arms Co.) made a nonstandard run of Specials in 1983, in the Model 94 Wrangler rendition. This year the Wrangler Angle Eject is chambered for the ancient 38-55; obviously Winchester is viewing the series as a limited edition. If you desire one of the 1983 Wranglers in 32 Special, some dealers may have a few left.

The big question is why should you buy one. In my opinion, you shouldn't. You'd limit yourself significantly in choice of ammunition and component bullets. If you're a deer hunter and you like the Model 94 carbine, the 32 Special is adequate, but no better than the 30-30. The Special offers no real virtues, only liabilities in rifle and ammunition alternatives. But, if you already own a 32 Winchester Special, I'd certainly not recommend you trade the gun off just because of its chambering. Ballistically, it is a capable cartridge for woods hunting of moderate-sized game. It is not outdated and useless, simply *outdated*.

32 Winchester Special

HANDLOAD DATA

Bullet Wt. Grs. Type	Powder Wt. Grs. Type	Primer	Case	MV (fps)	ME (fpe)	Rifle/ Bbl. (in.)	Remarks
170 Rem. HPFN	28.0 Rel. 7	Rem. 9½	Rem.	2123	1702	Win. M94/20	Lyman Hndbk., 46th Ed.; (Acc. Ld.)
170 Rem. HPFN	**31.0** Rel. 7	Rem. 9½	Rem.	**2283**	**1968**	Win. M94/20	Lym. Hndbk., 46th Ed.
170 Speer FN	**35.0** IMR 4895	CCI 200	Win.	**2205**	**1836**	Win. M94/20	Speer Rel. Man., No. 10
170 Speer FN	**36.0** Win. 748	CC1 250	Win.	**2197**	**1822**	Win. M94/20	Speer Rel. Man., No. 10
170 Hrndy. FP	**36.9** IMR 4320	Fed. 210	Rem.	**2200**	**1827**	Win. M94/20	Hrndy. Hndbk., 3rd Ed.
170 Hrndy. FP	**36.2** H380	Fed. 210	Rem.	**2100**	**1665**	Win. M94/20	Hrndy. Hndbk., 3rd Ed.

HPRN—Hollow Point Flat Nose; FN—Flat Nose; FP—Flat Point.

FACTORY LOAD DATA

Bullet Wt. Grs. Type	MV (fps)	ME (fpe)	Rifle/ Bbl. (in.)	Remarks
170 Win. FN	2284	1969	Win. M64/24	Data courtesy Ken Waters

FN—Flat Nose.

SPECIFICATIONS

Shell Holders
RCBS: 2
Bonanza: 4
Lyman: 6
Pacific: 2

Bullet Diameter
Jacketed: .320″ to .321″

Lengths
Trim: 2.030″
Maximum Case: 2.040″
Maximum Overall: 2.565″

The 32 Winchester Special found its place in the wooded areas of the East where the 94 Carbine held sway. As a deer/bear cartridge, the 32 Win. Spl. is as good as, but no better than, the old 30-30.

CAUTION:
Loads recommended and suggested herein have been carefully listed, but are intended solely as a guide to readers and neither the publisher nor author accept any responsibility for results of their use.
Maximum loads, listed in bold, should be reduced by 10 percent and worked up to cautiously.

MEDIUM/HEAVY BIG GAME

Popular Sporting Rifle Cartridges

338 WINCHESTER MAGNUM
340 WEATHERBY MAGNUM
38-55 WINCHESTER
357 MAGNUM (RIFLE)
35 REMINGTON
350 REMINGTON MAGNUM
358 WINCHESTER
358 NORMA MAGNUM
375 WINCHESTER
375 HOLLAND & HOLLAND MAGNUM
378 WEATHERBY
44 REMINGTON MAGNUM
444 MARLIN
45-70 GOVERNMENT
458 WINCHESTER MAGNUM
460 WEATHERBY MAGNUM

338 Winchester Magnum

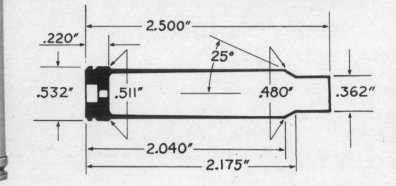

.220" 2.500" 25° .532" .511" .480" .362" 2.040" 2.175"

"So the 338 is a hard-kicking, butt-whipping big game cartridge, right? You bet. Its forte is showing big, mean critters who's boss, and it's just the load that can do it."

WHEN THE 338 Winchester Magnum was still in its gestation phase, the inimitable Charley Askins took one to Africa and punctured a score of animals by way of what used to be called a "field test." Said unfortunates ranged in size from the little Thomson's gazelle (around 50 pounds wearing galoshes and an overcoat) to the eland (about 1500 pounds by Askins' own estimate). Averaging the estimated weights of all 20 animals slain, I came up with 410 pounds.

Charley expended a total of 30 rounds on this assortment of game. Thirteen of the animals required only one shot. I suppose the foregoing rates as a reasonably auspicious beginning for the 338 Magnum, and was reported in the 1959 *Gun Digest*.

Before delving further into the 338's game-downing prowess, let's examine its family tree. Although it has never been uncommonly popular in the United States, the 33-caliber is not without its representatives both here and abroad. The initial 33-caliber cartridge was the American 33 Winchester, introduced in 1902 in the Model 1886 Winchester lever-action and discontinued with the rifle in 1936. It was replaced by the Model 71 rifle and the 348 Winchester cartridge. The old 33 was fairly potent for those days, with a 200-grain flat point at a catalogued 2200 fps. It developed a following as a deer, bear, and elk load.

The British dreamed up a few 33s of their own, but only the 333 Jeffery attained any real distinction. Both rimmed and rimless versions were available, for use in double-barreled and magazine rifles respectively, and the Jeffery made its appearance about 1911. The English 33 calibers used .333-inch bullets, unlike the 33 Winchester which took .338-inch-diameter slugs. The Jeffery, also known as the 333 Rimless Nitro-Express, offered 250-grain bullets at a claimed 2500 fps, and 300-grain slugs at a professed 2200. Energies ranged from 3230 to nearly 3500 fpe. Those are serious numbers, especially for 1911. The cartridge gained wide acceptance in Africa due to the high energy levels (for a small-bore) and the excellent penetration provided by the relatively long, heavy bullets (for the caliber).

In America, the Jeffery inspired the wildcat 333 OKH, based on 30-06 brass and taking .333-inch bullets. The '06 case provided a bit more enthusiasm at the muzzle than the British cartridge, being capable of about 2600 fps with a 250-grain bullet, around 2300 fps with the long 300s.

Later came the 334 OKH made up on 375 Holland & Holland cases. Used in proper length actions, the 334 could boost the 250-grainers along at approximately 2900 fps. It required a 26-inch barrel and a hatful of Hodgdon's old H4831 to achieve such lofty speeds. Also based on Holland & Holland brass, this time the 300 version, the 333 OKH Belted was a foreshortened permutation for use in 30-06-length actions. Muzzle velocity took a dip to about 2750 fps with the 250-grain

The 338 Win. Mag. is impressive when compared to other popular cartridges. From left to right: 6mm Remington; 25-06; 7mm Rem. Mag.; 270 Weatherby Mag.; 30-06 and the 338 Win. Mag. The 338 has a strong following of hunters who use this round on tough, thin-skinned game the world over.

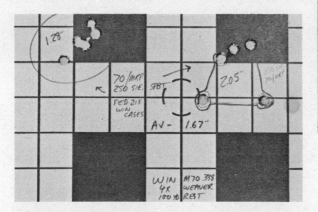

The pair of 5-shot groups seen here were fired from the author's Model 70 in 338 Win. Mag. The load consisted of 70 grains of Norma MRP and the Sierra 250-grain soft point boat-tail. The group on the left measures 1.28 inches while the group on the right measures 2.05 inches. The average for the 10 shots runs 1.67 inches.

bullets, still nothing to take lightly.

The upshot of this brief trip into the past is that it becomes obvious the 338 Magnum was a natural result of the success displayed on large North American game as well as African fauna up through lion in temperament, eland in cubic inches.

The 338 Winchester is a short, belted case based on the 458 Winchester Magnum necked down, which was in turn based on abbreviated 375 Holland & Holland brass. Following current trends, the 338 shows little body taper, which means it has almost as much internal capacity as the longer 334 OKH.

Factory-quoted ballistics are pretty impressive. There is a 200-grain soft point at a listed 2960 fps and 3890 fpe, plus a 225-grain soft point (which replaced an earlier 250-grain load) at 2780 fps for 3862 fpe. A 300-grain loading has long since been abandoned. Federal has added the 338 Magnum to their queue, offering a

nifty 210-grain Nosler Partition bullet at a published 2830 fps, the same velocity they list for their 200-grain 300 Winchester Magnum load. Muzzle energy for the 210-grain Nosler is 3735 fpe.

I have read that the 338 lives up to its specs in most rifles. Not in mine. My Model 70 Winchester showed 2800 fps on the button from the 200-grain Winchester factory load, good for 3482 fpe. The defunct 250-grain Silvertip gave 2593 fps; it was listed at 2700 fps. Maybe my 24-inch barreled Model 70 was unusually slow, or perhaps I had a low-voltage lot of ammo. Maybe both. The *Speer Reloading Manual Number Nine* shows that their test crew achieved much higher speeds from their rifle and batches of ammunition than did I. The Speer contingent clocked the 200-grain Winchester loading at 2959 fps and the 250-grain load at 2711 fps. The defunct 300-grain load failed to achieve its advance notice, getting only 2386 fps instead of 2450 fps. Speer's test gun was a 24-inch barreled M70.

As far as accuracy is concerned — admittedly something not normally given priority with a cartridge so obviously intended to be used on heavy game — my Model 70 would manage groups in the 1⅝-inch neighborhood. Five-shot strings, not three. Such accuracy came via one load: the 250-grain Sierra soft point boat-tail over 70.0 grains of Norma MRP ignited by a Federal 215 cap. Three other loads would print 2 inches or less, but none was really close to the above-mentioned recipe.

338 Winchester Magnum: Medium/Heavy Game

The author's Winchester Model 70 in 338 Win. Mag. will group 1⅝ inches, at 100 yards, with good loads.

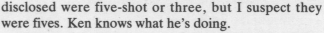

The author's Winchester Model 70 in 338 Win. Mag. will group 1⅝ inches, at 100 yards, with good loads.

(Below) Three of the author's favorite 338-caliber bullets include (from left to right) the 200-grain Speer soft point; the 225-grain Hornady soft point and the 250-grain Sierra soft point boat-tail.

There was a tie for second place, with both loads grouping 1.97 inches for the average. Seventy-five grains of Olin's 785 pushed the 200-grain Speer spitzer to 2826 fps at the muzzle while grouping as mentioned. Norma's MRP, in a 76.0-grain dose, outran the former load by a significant 80 fps. Considering that accuracy was identical, I'd go with the faster load myself.

The only noteworthy performance I could coax out of the streamlined 225-grain Hornady spire point came with 67.0 grains of Hodgdon H205. Groups hovered at 2 inches and the speed was 2680 fps for 3589 fpe.

You may have noticed that my handloads are not as hefty as many of those listed in the various manuals; I remarked that myself. My Model 70 didn't care; it wouldn't accept much more powder in any case without displaying signs of indigestion. Sometimes acute. An individualist, that Model 70.

If you don't find the grouping provided by my rifle praiseworthy, let me mention that Ken Waters tested one of the earliest 338 Model 70s to leave Winchester's bosom. Reporting in the 1961 *Gun Digest*, Ken quoted group sizes of 7/8, 11/16, and 1⅛ inches with three different loads featuring the 275-grain Speer semi-spitzer. He also related that the 200-grain Winchester Power-Point factory stuff stayed in 1⅜ inches. An accurate rifle, Ken's. I don't know for certain whether the groups

disclosed were five-shot or three, but I suspect they were fives. Ken knows what he's doing.

About recoil. Ken wrote the following in the article I mentioned above: "Recoil is noticeably greater than that of a 30-06, but with the solid rubber recoil pad it's not too bad for the shooter used to a light 30-06 sporter." To that I must say a *really* light sporter.

Askins had this to say on kick: "The 338 develops about the push of the 300 H&H, I'd reckon [*demonstrably incorrect*], around 27 f.p. and is not punishing. On the contrary it seems to me on the mild side, for certainly I've been battered a lot more severely by various 30-06s I've shot in the past."

Before you take this at face value, let me apprise you of the fact that Col. Askins is a lefty and by his own admission earlier in the same article ("A southpaw, I've always detested the bolt-action because it is not for me.") had traditionally eschewed turnbolts. The Remington pump and automatic chambered to 30-06 had been around only a few years when the above lines were penned, although the Garand was old hat. (I doubt that *anyone* would claim that the Garand kicked more than a 338!) I therefore submit that the 30-06 firearm that Charley was likely referring to as a "kicker" was the old crooked-stocked Model 1895 Winchester levergun. I don't blame him.

Here's Jon Sundra: "The 338 kicks like hell — about three times what a 270 does — and a lot of gents who shoot infrequently can't handle such guns." (From the September, 1983, *Guns & Ammo* magazine.)

I agree with Jon. The 338 is uncomfortable to shoot. I *can* shoot it, but it takes much more mental control than something on the order of the 30-06 or 7mm magnums. From the bench, it can be downright punishing. Don't let anyone convince you that the 338 is a pussycat. It isn't. It can be handled, but it takes effort, patience, and a lot of ammo. Whether the result is worth the expenditure only you can decide.

So the 338 is a hard-kicking, butt-whipping big game cartridge, right? You bet. Its forte is showing big, mean critters who's boss, and it's just the load that can do it. In *The Hunting Rifle,* Jack O'Conner wrote:

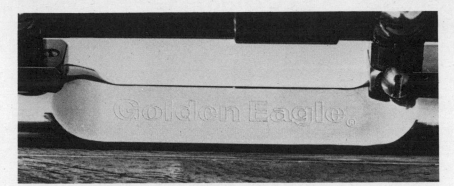

The now defunct Nikko Golden Eagle was available in a number of magnum chamberings, the 338 included. If you can find one of these rifles in the used-gun market, grab it; the Golden Eagle had an excellent reputation for accuracy.

The 338 has been successful but, from what I hear, not as successful as it deserves to be. Theoretically anyway it has some advantages over the 375 [H&H]. It is a shorter cartridge and hence can be used in shorter actions with a shorter and faster bolt-throw. It has somewhat less recoil — about 38 foot-pounds with the 250-grain bullet against 45 foot-pounds with the 270-grain 375 caliber bullet. . . .

Les Bowman, who has seen a lot of game shot and who has shot plenty himself, tells me that the . . . 200-grain Western soft-point . . . was an excellent killer on elk, moose, and grizzly . . .

. . . I have played around with three 338s and own a very fine pre-1964 Model 70 altered and stocked in Circassian walnut by Earl Milliron. I used this rifle in Zambia in 1969. All the 338s I have shot have given good accuracy and Western factory loads are right on the button when checked on a chronograph. I have shot the 250-grain Silvertip and 300-grain Power-Point bullets into wet paper pulp at 100, 200, and 300 yards. All bullets opened perfectly yet held together at all ranges. I have never seen more uniform bullet action.

Jim Carmichel, who took over O'Conner's position as Shooting Editor for *Outdoor Life*, has hunted extensively with the 338 Mag. A few years ago he wrote of an Idaho quest for elk. Jim carried a 338 built on a 1909 Argentine Mauser action by the David Miller company of Tucson, Arizona. Stuffed in that rifle were a handful of cartridges loaded with 210-grain Nosler Partition bullets over 68.0 grains of IMR 4350. From that same batch of cartridges, Jim had taken a record-class Cape buffalo, a charging lion, and a large Alaskan brown bear.

When his chance came, Jim decked a monster bull at about 450 yards. Could a lesser cartridge have dumped that bull? Maybe. Maybe not. I know a lesser man couldn't.

Dave Petzal, hunter extraordinaire and Executive Editor for *Field & Stream* has written of the 338. Thus:

. . . the 338 [and other mediums] are without exception highly specialized tools for skilled shots. If you have a properly stocked rifle . . . and it comes in at 9½ to 10 pounds, it will not kill you [from recoil] . . . the 338 . . . loaded with the 210-grain Nosler spitzer, will perform prodigies at long range. But except for the far-gone elk hunter or chaser after brown bears, they're too much. (September, 1981, *Field & Stream*.)

The author's favorite 338 Win. Mag. load features Norma MRP, an excellent propellant for large-capacity rifle cases.

One further remark from the erudite Mr. Petzal, from the same source and relevant to the 338 and other magnums: "If you think I [make] too much of a thing about portability and recoil, it is because you either have not hunted enough or shot enough." Right on, Dave.

As for me, if I were anticipating becoming a far-gone elk hunter (instead of an occasional one) and a chaser after brown bears, I would choose the 338 as my rifle cartridge and never look back. Why?

I like the fact that it handles slugs a little broader and heavier than you can stuff in the 30s. I like the better choice of bullets than is enjoyed by the 8mm Remington Magnum, not to mention ammo availability and shorter bolt throw. I like the fact that it kicks less than the 340 Weatherby — a *lot* less — and really isn't *that* much shy of achieving similar ballistics. I like the fact that I can load it with the fine 210-grain Nosler and reach way out across a flat to deck whatever I can hit. I like the way it treats my shoulder with more respect than does the 375 Holland & Holland, and that the ammo sags my cartridge belt less obtrusively, and that bolt manipulation is quicker.

For real sizable critters, especially ones that can saunter over and do the rumba on your toupee, the 338 offers manageable life insurance. And who wants insurance you can't control?

338 Winchester Magnum

HANDLOAD DATA

Bullet Wt. Grs.	Type	Powder Wt. Grs.	Type	Primer	Case	MV (fps)	ME (fpe)	Rifle/ Bbl. (in.)	Remarks
200	Speer SP	70.0	H205*	CCI 200	Win.	2840	3583	Win. M70/24	Poor accuracy
200	Speer SP	75.0	Win. 785	Fed. 215	Win.	2826	3548	Win. M70/24	Accurate
200	Speer SP	76.0	MRP	Fed. 215	Win.	2906	3751	Win. M70/24	Accurate
225	Hrndy. SP	67.0	H205*	CCI 200	Win.	2680	3589	Win. M70/24	Accurate & consistent
225	Hrndy. SP	71.5	Win. 785	Fed. 215	Win.	2633	3465	Win. M70/24	Poor accuracy
225	Hrndy. SP	73.0	MRP	Fed. 215	Win.	2746	3768	Win. M70/24	Good vel.; highest energy
250	Sierra SPBT	70.0	Win. 785	Fed. 215	Win.	2553	3619	Win. M70/24	Poor accuracy
250	Sierra SPBT	70.0	MRP	Fed. 215	Win.	2600	3754	Win. M70/24	Most acc., gd. all-around load

*Propellant discontinued
SP—Soft Point; SPBT—Soft Point Boat-Tail.

FACTORY LOAD DATA

Bullet Wt. Grs.	Type	MV (fps)	ME (fpe)	Rifle/ Bbl. (in.)	Remarks
200	Win. SP	2800	3482	Win. M70/24	Fair accuracy
250	Win. ST	2593	3732	Win. M70/24	High energy

SP—Soft Point; ST—Silvertip.

SPECIFICATIONS

Shell Holders
RCBS: 4
Bonanza: 2
Lyman: 13
Pacific: 5

Bullet Diameter
Jacketed: .338"

Lengths
Trim: 2.490"
Maximum Case: 2.500"
Maximum Overall: 3.340"

In 1984, Federal announced a new Premium loading for the 338. It features the 210-grain Nosler Partition bullet.

CAUTION:
Loads recommended and suggested herein have been carefully listed, but are intended solely as a guide to readers and neither the publisher nor author accept any responsibility for results of their use.
Maximum loads, listed in bold, should be reduced by 10 percent and worked up to cautiously.

340 Weatherby Magnum

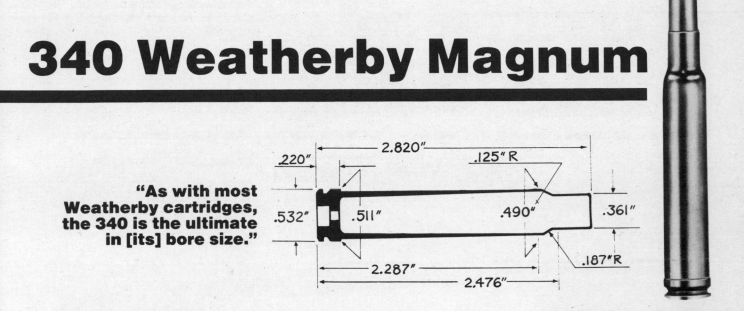

"As with most Weatherby cartridges, the 340 is the ultimate in [its] bore size."

2.820" .220" .125" R .532" .511" .490" .361" .187" R 2.287" 2.476"

THE 340 Weatherby came along in 1962, just a few years after the introduction and public acceptance of the 338 Winchester Magnum. While there are undoubtedly several practical applications for the 340, I believe it's safe to speculate that the big 33-caliber cartridge was intended to upstage the New Haven effort. Considering the ballistics of the 338 Win. Mag., it is doubtful whether another big, belted medium (as cartridges of this bore size are called) was a crying necessity.

Published data on the 340 Weatherby show a 200-grain soft point at 3210 fps, giving 4577 fpe, a 210-grain Nosler Partition at 3180 fps and 4717 fpe, and a 250-grain soft point or Partition at 2850 fps which is good for 4510 fpe. All but the semi-pointed 250-grain load carry more than 2330 fpe way out at 300 yards, and the 210-grain Nosler spitzer Partition retains 2816 fpe at the 300-yard mark. That's more bullet weight and energy than any 308 Winchester factory load carries at the *muzzle!*

Aside from its use on some of the bigger and nastier species of African game, such as lion and Cape buffalo, I'm not quite certain how extensively useful the 340 Weatherby Magnum is. For taking big, trophy elk under adverse conditions and from imprudent angles, and for decking Alaskan brown bears, grizzlies, and the largest moose, I suppose the 340 is in its element. So are the 338 Winchester Magnum, the 300 Winchester Magnum, the 8mm Remington Magnum, the 300 Weath-

The 378 Weatherby (left) is a much larger cartridge than the 340 (right) which is necked up from a 300 Weatherby.

erby Magnum, and perhaps the Big Seven mags and the 375 Holland & Holland. If a fellow wanted a highly specialized rig for such game, and planned to pursue his hobby on a regular basis, then one of these bruisers might just be the ticket.

And now up rears the recoil question. Perhaps some of you are of the opinion that I belabor the issue of rifle kick. I think not. Excessive, punishing recoil takes its

340 Weatherby Magnum: Medium/Heavy Big Game

The 340 Weatherby would feel right at home in a Montana trophy-elk camp. When a horse can do the carrying, a 10-pound rifle (as most 340s tend to be) isn't a deficit.

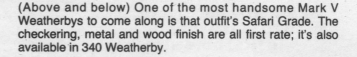

(Above and below) One of the most handsome Mark V Weatherbys to come along is that outfit's Safari Grade. The checkering, metal and wood finish are all first rate; it's also available in 340 Weatherby.

For those hunters interested in a utility-oriented 340, the Weatherby Fibermark should be just the ticket. It features a dull, non-reflective, fiberglass stock and matte-finished metal.

toll on virtually all shooters. One scribe, a confirmed magnum buff, likens the big cartridges to a boxing arena. His thought is that if you can't take it on the chin, you shouldn't climb through the ropes. He is absolutely right! And how many of us climb through those ropes? Not many. The flaw with this analogy is that most of us have a very good idea what it would be like to get socked on the proboscis by a hard right hook. Unfortunately, many shooters have little conception of what it feels like to get slammed in the shoulder and jaw while receiving a simultaneous horrendous assault on tender ear drums. It is not fun. Over the long haul, it can do permanent damage, both to the ears and the nerves of the back.

If it were *provably* necessary to utilize such heavy-kicking loads on herbivorous animals in the 600- to 1200-pound class, then I'd be all for it., Alas, too many elk, moose, and caribou — not to mention grizzlies — have been taken cleanly by less-vigorous cartridges and will continue to be.

So. If you are of the opinion that the medium magnums are requisite on game such as we've been discussing, and you are certain you can stand the gaff, then the 340 Weatherby is perhaps the best cartridge you can buy for your purpose. It skunks the 338 Winchester nicely. Going by factory data, the top 338 loads show 3890 fpe at the muzzle; the 340 manages 4510 fpe from its *worst* factory listing. The 8mm Remington Magnum gets an advertised 3912 fpe from its meanest loading, the 220-grain Core Lokt; the 340 Weatherby shows 4717 fpe from its 210-grain product. Even the big 375 Holland & Holland — slayer of many an elephant, Cape buff, rhino, brown bear, tiger, and similar ill-tempered creatures — manages a mere 4337 fpe from its most powerful factory version; the 340 shades that by nearly 9 percent! If power is what you desire, the 340 Weatherby has it in trumps.

Trajectory is naught to worry about, either. Based on factory material, the 340 Weatherby will drop its 200-

grain bullets 10 inches below the line of sight at 400 yards if zeroed at 300. Bullet rise at 200 yards is shown as 4 inches. For the larger species of game at more reasonable distances, I'd choose the 210-grain Nosler Partition loaded to around 3100 fps. Assuming a 200-yard zero, my bullets would dip only 6.5 inches at 300 yards while retaining 2615 fpe. For *really* big game at spittin' distance, I'd opt for the 250-grain Nosler Partition loaded atop 76.0 grains of IMR 4350 for a tad over 2700 fps.

Since the 340 Weatherby is merely the 300 Weatherby Magnum case necked up for .338-inch bullets, it has a capacious boiler room just like its parent case. As with the 300, most sources agree that IMR 4350 is, if not the best choice of propellants, at least one of them. IMR 4831 and Hodgdon H450 are good too.

The heaviest handloader's bullet you can buy for the 340 is the fine 275-grain Speer semi-spitzer which has a whopping sectional density of .348-inch. For elk and moose in the timber, the 275-grain Speer kicking along at about 2650 fps would be a serious proposition. You can get that speed or a little better from a maximum charge of 78.0 grains of IMR 4831 according to the *Speer Reloading Manual Number 10.*

As with most Weatherby cartridges, the 340 is the ultimate in the 33-caliber bore size. Ballistically, it has no flies on it as a cartridge for the really large species, both on this continent and any other. From a practicality standpoint, the 340 will never equal the popularity of, say, the 22-250. But then try using a 22-250 on an irate polar bear.

340 Weatherby Magnum

HANDLOAD DATA

Bullet Wt. Grs.	Type	Powder Wt. Grs.	Type	Primer	Case	MV (fps)	ME (fpe)	Rifle/ Bbl. (in.)	Remarks
200	Speer SP	84.0	IMR 4350	Fed. 215	Wby.	3144	4391	Wby. Mk.V/26	Lym. Hndbk., 46th Ed. (Acc. Ld.)
225	Hrndy. SP	80.0	IMR 4350	Fed. 215	Wby.	2923	4270	Wby. Mk. V/26	Lym. Hndbk., 46th Ed.
250	Hrndy. RN	77.0	IMR 4350	Fed. 215	Wby.	2739	4166	Wby. Mk. V/26	Lym. Hndbk., 46th Ed. (Acc. Ld.)
275	Speer SP	66.0	IMR 4350	Fed. 215	Wby.	2262	3125	Wby. Mk.V/26	Lym. Hndbk., 46th Ed. (Acc. Ld.)
275	Speer SP	73.0	IMR 4350	Fed. 215	Wby.	2544	3953	Wby. Mk. V/26	Lym. Hndbk., 46th Ed.

SP—Soft Point; RN—Round Nose.

FACTORY LOAD DATA

Bullet Wt. Grs.	Type	MV (fps)	ME (fpe)	Rifle/ Bbl. (in.)	Remarks
200	Wby. SP	3201	4546	Wby. Mk. V/26	Speer Manual No. 9
200	Wby. SP	3115	4308	Wby. Mk. V/26	Lym. Hndbk., 45th Ed.
210	Wby. Part.	3040	4309	Wby. Mk. V/26	Lym. Hndbk., 45th Ed.
250	Wby. SP	2730	4136	Wby. Mk. V/26	Lym. Hndbk., 45th Ed.
250	Wby. SP	2839	4473	Wby. Mk. V/26	Speer Manual No. 9

SP—Soft Point.

SPECIFICATIONS

Shell Holders
RCBS: 4
Bonanza: 2
Lyman: 13
Pacific: 5

Bullet Diameter
Jacketed: .338"

Lengths
Trim: 2.815"
Maximum Case: 2.820"
Maximum Overall: 3.562"

CAUTION:
Loads recommended and suggested herein have been carefully listed, but are intended solely as a guide to readers and neither the publisher nor author accept any responsibility for results of their use.
Maximum loads, listed in bold, should be reduced by 10 percent and worked up to cautiously.

38-55 Winchester

2.129"

.506" .421" .392"

.063"

"... many experienced hunters regard the 38-55 quite highly. And rightly so. Out to 100 yards, the 38-55 should perform on deer about like the best 44 Magnum carbine loadings..."

THE cartridge known today as the 38-55 Winchester was originally a Ballard development. Intended as a target cartridge, the commercial version saw light of day in 1884, chambered in the Ballard Perfection Number 4. (The Union Hill Numbers 8 and 9 were also reamed for the load.) A popular cartridge among handloaders of that distant day was the 38-55 Everlasting, which was nearly identical to the 38-55 Ballard in outside dimensions. The 38-55 Everlasting was simply a slightly lengthened version of the 38-50 Everlasting introduced by Ballard in 1876.

The Marlin Model 1893 was chambered for the 38-55, as might have been expected; the Marlin Fire Arms Co. had taken over the Ballard company in 1881. Winchester offered the cartridge in their Model 1894; the Remington Lee was chambered for it, as was the Colt New Lightning pump, Stevens, Remington, Winchester (in various single shots), and Savage in the Model 99 lever-action. Only commemorative rifles have been available for the 38-55 since about 1940 when Winchester dropped the chambering from their Model 94 lineup.

The 38-55 gained quite a reputation as a target round. In the book, *Complete Guide to Handloading,* Phil Sharpe wrote: "It set a great many records for accuracy which would make some of our modern match rifles blush with shame."

Although originally a blackpowder cartridge, the 38-55 remained popular when the switch to smokeless be-

gan. Winchester, oddly, tried to discourage the handloading of smokeless ammunition. In their 1898 catalogue, there appeared an article entitled, *Reloading Smokeless Powder Cartridges Impractical.* The following year, the new Winchester catalogue proclaimed it was, "... very unsafe to load smokeless powder, unless the means of determining the chamber pressures are at hand." (Sounds about like what the big companies tell us today; only *they* can load ammunition safely.)

The 38-55 Ballard-Winchester, as it should be called, is said to be the last American rifle cartridge to be built around a preconceived bullet diameter. Starting with that diameter, the case was designed backward, being given just enough taper to facilitate extraction and sufficient length to contain the charge of powder necessary to achieve the required ballistics. The resulting cartridge case ended up 2.129 inches long, .42-inch in diameter at its base, and with a .506-inch diameter rim. Overall cartridge length was 2.48 inches, about like the 250-3000 Savage.

A whole raft of modern gunners aren't aware of it, but the 38-55 sired many cartridges, some of which are still with us. Examples are the 22 Savage, 219 Zipper, 25-35 Winchester, and the 30-30, all simply necked-down versions of the basic 38-55 case.

The original Winchester loading of the 38-55 featured a flat-nosed lead bullet weighing 255 grains at a little more than 1300 fps muzzle velocity. That was about par

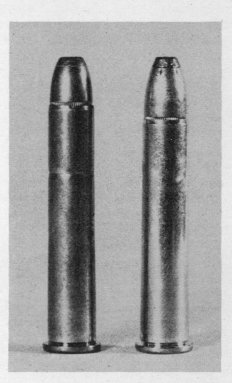

For comparison the 38-55 (center) is flanked by the lever-action competition. From left to right: 348 Winchester, 35 Remington, 38-55, 405 Winchester and the 45-70.

The new 375 Winchester (right) is designed for that outfit's Model 94 lever-action. The cartridge on the left, if you haven't already guessed, is the 38-55. The similarity is a bit more than obvious.

for the blackpowder numbers of the day. Nonetheless, the load gained a wide following as a big game cartridge. It was used on animals large and small, successfully, and was considered a genuine 300-yard (!) cartridge. Despite the relatively low velocity by today's standards, the big blunt bullet killed well due to its heft and excellent sectional density. It penetrated and cut a wide swath.

Some years later a high-speed version was added, using jacketed bullets of the same weight but much higher velocity. With a muzzle speed in the 1700 fps range, the old 38-55 killed better than the 30-30 and 32 Special of the same era. Today we still have the jacketed-bullet loading, but the velocity has been reduced to the century-old level of 1320 fps. Still, that load wouldn't do a buck deer any good. I doubt, however, if it is consid-

ered a 300-yard loading today.

I have read that the 38-55 uses .375-inch diameter jacketed bullets and takes .376-inch cast slugs, even those as girthsome as .3775-inch and .383-inch. Goodness. (But then, just to confuse us further, some old-timers call the cartridge the 38-55 Marlin-Ballard. Trying to find areas of agreement is pretty hard with this load.) If you have an elderly 38-55 lying around that you plan to shoot, better slug and mike the bore.

Aside from the Barnes bullets, which are very, very hard to come across, the only jacketed slug that might work in some 38-55 rifles is the 220-grain Hornady flat point designed around the 375 Winchester. If the rifle in question has a bore diameter larger than .376-inch, maybe even .375-inch, then I doubt that the accuracy provided by the undersized Hornady bullet will win many benchrest matches. May be worth a try. The only feasible alternative is casting your own.

If I had one of the old guns, I'd load up with the Winchester factory load and let it go at that. The Olin outfit will likely keep the 38-55 fodder in production for a while longer; Winchester still catalogues a couple of guns for the load. The shorty Wrangler II Angle Eject carbine is made, and the Chief Crazy Horse Commemorative Model 94. The latter may draw a few horse laughs if taken to the woods, but with its 24-inch barrel and no encircling barrel bands, it might be pretty fair in the accuracy department. The Wrangler II would be the choice as a deer gun, if the cartridge strikes your fancy and you can't find a used one. I have no idea what the bore diameter is on these newer 38-55s, but it might be close to .375-inch which would mean you could use the Hornady bullet.

Ever wonder about the 38-55's ability to down a deer? Let me quote from *Handloader* magazine Number 17, Don Zutz doing the writing:

> Smacked by a 255- or 280-grain 38-caliber slug that expends all its energy in an animal's body, whitetails either go down for keeps on the first shot or immediately become so sick and shocked they can't run. With upwards from [sic] 255 grains of lead sagging in their vitals, even the strongest bucks will generally stand straddle-legged so the telling shot can be made at an easy target. The 45-70s and 45-90s have the same effect on deer, which is quite desirable in this age when red-clad huntsmen abound—and are ready to claim your deer!

And here is Ken Waters from *Handloader* number 61:

> Most authorities apparently believe it was the 30-30 which put the skids under the 38-55, with the 30's higher velocity, longer range and flatter trajectory proving an irresistible selling point. While that's probably so, if forced to choose between the 30-30 and a 38-55 for big game hunting, I would prefer the 38-55, especially in its High Power version or a handloaded equivalent . . . I'd rather take my chances with the big 255-grain 38 slug at 1,800 fps than the 30-caliber 170-grain at 2,100 or 2,200 fps.

Obviously, many experienced hunters regard the 38-55 quite highly. And rightly so. Out to 100 yards, the 38-55 should perform on deer about like the best 44 Magnum carbine loadings, and I hear little complaint about the Maggie's deer-dumping ability at reasonable ranges.

In her day, the 38-55 Marlin-Ballard-Winchester was quite a dish. She won many a target match, set more than her share of records, hung legions of deer, elk, and bear on the meat pole. Today her skin is wrinkled; she's not up to her former match-winning qualifications; new guns are seldom stamped with her name. No matter. She's as good as she ever was; time has merely passed her by. Guys who once had an affair with the old gal still remember her fondly; younger guys like to read about her. And with the new Winchester Wrangler testing the market, she might still have a dance in her yet. We'll see.

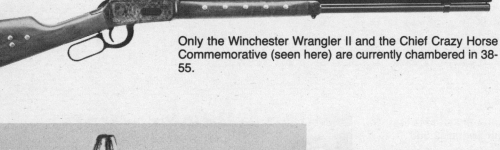

Only the Winchester Wrangler II and the Chief Crazy Horse Commemorative (seen here) are currently chambered in 38-55.

Aside from the hard-to-find Barnes bullets, the only jacketed slug that might work in *some* 38-55s is the 220-grain, .375-inch diameter flat point from Hornady. Before using this, or any other slug in your 38-55, be sure to slug the bore.

38-55 Winchester

HANDLOAD DATA

Bullet Wt. Grs.	Type	Powder Wt. Grs.	Type	Primer	Case	MV, (fps)	ME, (fpe)	Rifle/ Bbl. (in.)	Remarks
255	Win. FP	**30.0**	Rel. 7	Rem. 9½	Rem.	**1543**	**1348**	Win. M94/26	Lym. Hndbk., 46th Ed., (Acc. Ld.)
249	Lym. (375248)*	**9.5**	Unique	Rem. 9½	Rem.	**1170**	757	Stevens M44½/29	Lym. Hndbk., 46th Ed. (Acc. Ld.)
249	Lym. (375248)*	**9.5**	Du Pont PB	Rem. 9½	Rem.	**1140**	718	Stevens M44½/29	Lym. Hndbk., 46th Ed.

*Cast Bullet Load
FP—Flat Point.

FACTORY LOAD DATA

Bullet Wt. Grs.	Type	MV, (fps)	ME, (fpe)	Rifle/ Bbl. (in.)	Remarks
255	Win. FP	1320	987	Test barrel/24	Win. published ballistics

FP—Flat Point.

SPECIFICATIONS

Shell Holders
RCBS: 2
Bonanza: 4
Lyman: 6
Pacific: 2

Bullet Diameter
Jacketed: .376"
Cast: .377"-.380"

Lengths
Trim: 2.118"
Maximum Case: 2.129"
Maximum Overall: 2.550"

The 38-55 had (and still has) a reputation for superb accuracy. Get close, pick your spot, pull the trigger and the 38-55 will put meat on the table.

CAUTION:
Loads recommended and suggested herein have been carefully listed, but are intended solely as a guide to readers and neither the publisher nor author accept any responsibility for results of their use.
Maximum loads, listed in bold, should be reduced by 10 percent and worked up to cautiously.

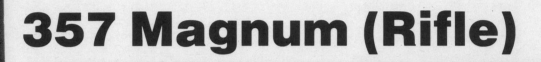

357 Magnum (Rifle)

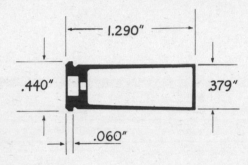

1.290"

.440"

.379"

.060"

"I can hear you saying, 'The 357 Magnum will certainly kill a deer.' You bet it will. So will a 22 Short in the brain."

ONE HUNDRED and ten years ago, Winchester introduced their spanking-new Model 1873 lever-action rifle to a receptive shooting world. With it they offered for the first time the 44-40 WCF cartridge, which was destined to become one of the most popular ever produced. Colt Firearms quickly countered by chambering their equally new Single Action Army revolver for the nascent cartridge. Hunters, law-enforcement officers, frontiersmen, outlaws, collectively took to their bosoms the convenience of carrying six-guns and rifles chambered for the same cartridge. A few years later, the 38-40 saw daylight and was drafted into similar service. The following decade witnessed yet another load being added to the dual-purpose line-up, the little 32-20. Although somewhat sporadic and inconsistent in popularity, the idea of joint rifle/handgun chamberings has remained with us to this day.

Most often seen is the pairing of 44 Magnum revolvers and quick-firing carbines, both semi-auto and lever-actions. The 44 Mag. is adequate for deer-sized animals at close ranges, say 100 yards or so, and makes a viable hunting longarm. Rifles that ignored the fast-working aspects of the game, such as the Remington Model 788 bolt-action and various single shots, fell flat in the market place. Buyers of 44 carbines wanted rapid-fire capabilities, traditional lever-action appeal, or a short, handy repeater as a companion for their 44 revolvers.

A few years ago, Rossi introduced a clone of the

Model '92 Winchester chambered for the 357 Magnum. Directly, Marlin followed suit with their 1894-C. In 1983, Browning entered the arena with their own Model '92 copy, fabricated in Japan. Overnight, it seemed, owners of 357 Magnum revolvers could buy a rifle to complement their handgun, just as users of the 44 Magnum had been able to do for years. The Marlin, for example, sold like calorie counters at a Weight Watchers convention.

I wonder why. Aside from the questionable value of carrying two firearms that use the same cartridge, I can see scant use for a 357 Magnum rifle. As a deer rifle, it is better than a 218 Bee or 25-20, even shades the 32-30 a little. Are any of those loads your idea of a gee-whiz deer cartridge? Not mine. Neither is the 357 Magnum.

I can hear you saying, "The 357 Magnum will certainly kill a deer." You bet it will. So will a 22 Short in the brain. Ah, but you argue that the 357 doesn't have to hit the brain to kill, it will deck a buck with a lung shot. Will it? How far will the deer likely travel after the hit? One hundred yards? A quarter-mile?

With its better loadings, the 357 Magnum carbine offers around 1100 fpe at the muzzle. Some loads do a tad better; many do considerably worse. Thus, at 50 yards the average 357 load hits with about 800 fpe, about like the 30-30 at 250 yards. If you believe that the 30-30 is adequate for deer at 250 yards, then I don't blame you for feeling that the 357 carbine is sufficient at 50 yards. I

Remington offers a wide selection of 357 Magnum ammo in bullet weights ranging from 125 to 158 grains. The choice is yours.

The 357 Magnum, as a rifle cartridge, is commonly confined to the lever-actions. They are fast, light, handy and well suited for animals up to 40 pounds, providing ranges are kept reasonable. The rifle seen here is an Interarms Rossi that's capable of 5-inch groups, at 100 yards, with iron sights.

don't agree with you, but I respect your opinion.

Would you pass up a 100-yard shot at a big 10-pointer, one that was feeding slowly away from you just before dark on the last day of the season? You should. Your 800 pounds of energy have now dwindled to a paltry 550 fpe or so, about what the 30-30 retains at 350 yards. Few hunters of my acquaintance would shoot a deer 350 yards distant with a 30-30 unless they were starving.

I don't mean to belittle the 357 Magnum; I merely wish to keep the load and its usage in perspective. So let's be absolutely frank: the 357 Magnum is no deer cartridge, whether in a rifle or handgun. It will kill a deer, perhaps humanely, if the range is not very long, the shot placement within a very precise area, the load optimum, and the hunter a cool customer, able to pass up risky shots with no inner qualms whatever. For any

other conditions except survival, forget the 357 Magnum.

Consider that we are inundated by articles comparing the deer-slaying qualities of the 270 Winchester to those of the 30-06, questioning the employment of the 6mm rifle cartridges on deer, denigrating the 30-30 class of cartridges as modern buck slayers. All of the foregoing are infinitely better suited, inordinately more powerful, much longer-ranging than the 357 Magnum.

Okay, if the 357 is no deer load, what's it good for? Here's a partial list: woodchuck, badger, opposum, jack-rabbit, porcupine, raccoon, coyote, javelina, turkey, and fox. With suitable lead-bullet loads, it will do yeoman work on edible game such as rabbits and squirrels. It is a fine home-defense gun, an excellent plinker, a superb practice gun as an understudy for a really serious lever-action caliber. Up to animals of around 40 pounds in weight, and for a host of fun-shooting chores, the 357 is one of the best gun/cartridge combinations available. That covers a lot of territory.

Handloading

I have done a fair amount of work with a Marlin Model 1894-C. As with most 357 revolvers I've tested, Winchester 296, Hercules 2400, and Norma R-123 showed the best combination of accuracy and velocity. Hercules Blue Dot, Du Pont 4227, and Hodgdon H110 have fine reputations and work well in some guns, but the foregoing threesome is hard to beat in my experience.

The most accurate load in my Marlin consists of the 158-grain Remington Semi-jacketed Hollow Point (no longer sold as a component bullet) and 16.5 grains of Winchester 296. Five-shot strings at 100 yards run 3.75 inches with open sights, with a muzzle speed of 1747 fps. The same charge kicks the 158-grain Speer soft point along at 1780 fps, for 1112 fpe, but accuracy is inferior to the Remington bullet in my gun.

The runner-up for accuracy in my 1894-C is 14.0 grains of R123 and the 158-grain Remington soft point; groups go 3.87 inches for an average. Muzzle speed is only 1650 fps with that load, but considering the size of the game it is suited for, the drop in energy is not much of a handicap. What is a handicap is the poor availability of Norma propellants in this country.

Tops for energy in my rifle is 16.0 grains of Hercules 2400 behind the 146-grain Speer JHP. Groups are not so hot, but muzzle velocity runs 1880 fps for 1146 fpe. For close-in shooting of tougher game, such as javelina, I'd give this load some thought.

The fastest handload tested was 18.1 grains of 296

animals.

I prefer magnum primers with all of the above loads. Specifically, I like the Winchester 1½M-108 cap; ignition is fine, accuracy good, chronograph readings consistent. In addition, I use a heavy crimp for two very important reasons. First, it keeps the bullet in place in the case, enabling it to withstand heavy spring pressure while in the magazine tube. Second, it gives more uniform ignition.

My choice among factory ammunition is the fine 158-grain Remington SJHP which groups under 4 inches at 100 yards and clocks 1735 fps at the muzzle, for 1055 fpe of punch. Almost as accurate and a mite faster is the 158-grain Remington JSP. The 158-grain Federal JSP is excellent, grouping right on the heels of the hollow-point Remington load while only a bit lighter in muzzle zip.

The speediest factory load I've tested is the 125-grain Winchester JHP. Muzzle velocity of my test lot was 2100 fps, for a whopping 1225 fpe. Accuracy was only fair, groups running in the 5-inch range from 100 yards. Out to 75-80 yards, that load should be extremely destructive on chucks and crows.

I know of no one in my area who has hunted with a 357 carbine. I use a 357 revolver on woodchucks sometimes, but have not hunted with my Marlin. This summer, using my 357 revolver, I poked a chuck through the shoulder at 60 yards with a 125-grain Speer JHP factory load. She flopped over on her back and kicked. Had to shoot her again. I was not happy with that performance. Despite the fact that the hog didn't go any-

Two popular lever-action 357s currently available are the Browning B-92 (above) and the Marlin Model 1894 (top). They are both well made. The author's Marlin 1894 provided 100-yard groups of 3.75 inches with its best handload.

and the 140-grain Speer JHP. The chronograph showed 1900 fps, which is good for 1123 fpe. Like the 146-grain Speer/16.0 grains of 2400 load, accuracy is naught to brag on.

If I planned to hunt squirrels or cottontail rabbits for the pot, I'd likely use a 158-grain Perfecast RN lead bullet ahead of from 10 to 10.7 grains of Du Pont SR-4759. Velocities will run from about 1050 to a bit over 1100 fps, so destruction should be minimal to bite-size

where, I prefer animals I shoot to turn off like flipping a light switch.

Another time, my partner smacked a chuck at 20 yards with my 357 using the super-lethal 145-grain Winchester Silvertip hollow point. The pig took the slug through its ribcage, rolled, then scampered for its den. Backing my partner up with a 22-250, I raked that chuck, the slug going in behind the ribs on the left side as the animal ran quartering away. The chuck rolled again, fetched up at the lip of its den, and kicked itself in. I hate that. Really hate it.

If we had been using a 357 rifle, and those chucks had been out at 120 and 70 yards, respectively, the performance would likely have been comparable. Neither groundhog died instantly; both had to be shot twice. And some folks reckon the 357 is a *deer* cartridge?

The handly little 357 carbines are a ball to shoot,

make a great learner's gun, will roll tin cans with the best of them, provide the makings for a squirrel stew, can serve as an excellent home defender, are fine for close-range hunting of medium-sized pests and vermin. They are light to carry, quick to mount, have negligible recoil, assault your ears with scarcely a harsh note. Used wisely and well, they will perform as intended. Get 'em out of their league and they'll let you down.

357 Magnum

HANDLOAD DATA

Bullet Wt. Grs. Type	Powder Wt. Grs. Type	Primer	Case	MV, (fps)	ME, (fpe)	Rifle/ Bbl. (in.)	Remarks
140 Speer JHP	18.1 Win. 296	1½M-108	Fron.	1900	1123	Mar. 1894-C/18½	Not acc.; gd. velocity
146 Speer JHP	16.0 2400	1½M-108	Fron.	1880	1116	Mar. 1894-C/18½	Max. in test gun
150 Sierra JHC	**16.0** 2400	1½M-108	Fron.	**1775**	**1049**	Mar. 1894-C/18½	50-yd. acc. acceptable
158 Rem. JSP	14.0 R123	1½M-108	Win.	1650	955	Mar. 1894-C/18½	Very accurate
158 Speer JSP	**16.5** Win. 296	1½M-108	Fron.	**1780**	**1112**	Mar. 1894-C/18½	Mediocre acc. at 100 yds.
158 Rem. JSP	14.0 R123	CCI 400	Win.	1655	961	Mar. 1894-c/18½	Note primer; acc. poor
158 Rem. SJHP	16.5 Win. 296	1½M-108	Fron.	1747	1071	Mar. 1894-C/18½	Most accurate load
158 Hrndy. JHP	14.0 R123	1½M-108	Win.	1655	961	Mar. 1894-c/18½	Very accurate

JHP—Jacketed Hollow Point; JHC—Jacketed Hollow Cavity; JSP—Jacketed Soft Point; SJHP—Semi-Jacketed Hollow Point.

FACTORY LOAD DATA

Bullet Wt. Grs. Type	MV, (fps)	ME, (fpe)	Rifle/ Bbl. (in.)	Remarks
125 Hrndy. JHP	1990	1099	Mar. 1894-C/18½	Fair accuracy
125 Win. JHP	2100	1225	Mar. 1894-C/18½	Fair accuracy
158 Rem. SJHP	1735	1055	Mar. 1894-C/18½	Most acc. fact. load
158 Rem. JSP	1740	1062	Mar. 1894-C/18½	Accurate
158 Fron. JHP	1720	1038	Mar. 1894-C/18½	Poor accuracy
158 Fed. JSP	1710	1025	Mar. 1894-C/18½	Extremely accurate

JHP—Jacketed Hollow Point; SJHP—Semi-Jacketed Hollow Point; JSP—Jacketed Soft Point.

SPECIFICATIONS

Shell Holders
RCBS: 6
Bonanza: 3
Lyman: 1
Pacific: 6

Bullet Diameter
Jacketed: .357" to .358"
Lengths
Trim: 1.285"
Maximum Case: 1.290"
Maximum Overall: 1.590"

CAUTION:
Loads recommended and suggested herein have been carefully listed, but are intended solely as a guide to readers and neither the publisher nor author accept any responsibility for results of their use.
Maximum loads, listed in bold, should be reduced by 10 percent and worked up to cautiously.

35 Remington

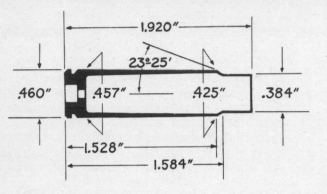

"Taking into account all factors, including energy levels, portability of the rifles, trajectory data, and particularly recoil levels, I can think of no better whitetail cartridge than the old 35 Remington."

IF THERE ever were a lackluster cartridge, the 35 Remington would be it. Despite its age and a long, successful hunting career, the 35 is genuinely nondescript. None of the notoriety that surrounds the 30-30 pervades the 35; none of the Wild-West acclaim of the black-powder holdovers such as the 38-55 and 44-40 envelops it. A lot of folks never heard of it.

The bearded 35 will soon celebrate its 80th birthday. It was introduced in 1906, concurrent with the John Browning-designed Remington Model 8 self-loader. Along with the 35-caliber round, Remington offered the 25 Remington, the 30 Remington, and the 32 Remington. All but the 35 were similar in shape and capacity to existing Winchester cartridges—the 25-35, 30-30, and 32 Special—except that the Remington versions were bereft of rims to facilitate functioning in an autoloader. The 35 Remington was not copied after, or similar to, any Winchester round, although some had said the 35 was designed to compete with the more powerful 33 and 35 Winchester cartridges. Actually, the 35 Remington was a near-twin to the European Mannlicher 9x56mm load, for which the Fabrique Nationale semi-auto Model of 1906 was chambered. Coincidentally, the FN was designed by John Browning and was a virtual clone of the Remington Model 8. Or vice versa.

Over the years many rifles have been sold with ".35 Remington" stamped on their barrels. Some were: the Remington Models 8 and 81 autos; Models 14, 141, and 760 trombone actions; the Standard Arms Models G and M, one of which was a pump-autoloader; the Remington Models 30 and 600 bolt-actions; various Stevens lever-actions; the Savage Model 170; the Mossberg Model 472; and the Winchester Model 70. At this writing it is available only in the Marlin Model 336-C, although a few were produced in the 24-inch barreled 336-A permutation some years ago.

Marlin is indeed the firm to be thanked for keeping the elderly cartridge from drawing Social Security. They've been chambering it since the Second Millennium, or so it seems. The popularity of the little lever-action 336 is largely responsible, but the 336 is also chambered for the immensely popular 30-30 as well as such modern rounds as the 375 Winchester and the proprietary 444 Marlin, as well as the antideluvian bruiser and former government agent, the 45-70. With such popular and potent loads available, one might expect the 35 Remington to go belly up against the onslaught. It isn't happening. The old boy's holding his own, thank you.

Why? Good question. For one thing, many hunters cling to the notion that the old 35 is considerably more potent than the 30-30. The truth is that in factory guise it is only slightly so. Older nimrods similarly clutch to their bosoms the idea that the 35 will mow down acres of timber enroute to an unwary whitetail, deflecting not a tad from the stoutest of limbs. That's cowchips, but lotsa guys out there *believe* it. The 375 Winchester, de-

From left to right: Winchester Model 94, Marlin 336, Browning BAR, Winchester Model 88, Winchester Model 100 and the Ruger 44 Mag. Carbine. All of these rifles have excellent reputations when it comes to deer hunting; however, only the Marlin 336 is currently available in 35 Remington.

spite being a bit more powerful in factory form, is not setting records in the sales department, and likely never will. In addition, the 35 Remington is a more toothy load when handloaded to its potential. The 444 and 45-70 are in a different class from the 35, are bought for bigger game, and in the case of the 45-70, nostalgia. So, among the Marlin lineup just what really competes with the 35? The 30-30, that's all.

Compared to the Winchester cartridge, the 35 offers these ballistics: muzzle velocity, 2080 fps with a 200-grain bullet, and 2300 fps with the strange, semi-pointed 150-grain slug. The 30-30 gets 2200 fps from its 170-grain load, 2390 fps with the 150-grain offering. Muzzle energies for the 35 are 1921 fpe for the 200-grain slug, 1762 fpe for the 150-grain load; the yield is 1827 fpe for the 170-grain 30-30, 1903 fpe for the 150-grain load. As you can see, the 30-30 is about even in energy figures.

But there's an invisible fly in the broth. Most lots of Remington and Winchester 35 ammo come close to, or even exceed, factory specs in 22-inch barreled rifles. The 30-30 will equal or beat factory-quoted data in a 24-inch barreled gun, but in the common 20-inch barreled carbines (such as the Model 94 Winchester), factory loads churn up around 100 fps shy of the published mark. Thus, muzzle energy numbers for the 30-30 in the guns most often used are in the 1600 to 1650 fpe neighborhood. For the 35 Remington, even the slow Federal 200-grain load manages 1680 fpe, and most loads give about 1750 to 1800 fpe in 22-inch tubes.

Handloading really inspires the 35 to lofty heights.

Over the years, the 35 Remington has received some stiff competition from a number of deer hunting cartridges. Here's a lineup (left to right) of some of the old-timers, including the 35 Remington: 348 Winchester, 35 Remington, 38-55, 405 Winchester and the 45-70 Government.

The 180-grain Speer flat point can be driven to exceed 2400 fps very easily in a 22-inch barreled rifle. A 300 Savage can attain equivalent velocities from handloads, roughly 2350 fps with factory 180-grain loads. Both cartridges reach around 2200 to 2300 fpe at the muzzle. At longer ranges, the 180-grain round nose 300 Savage load carries 1184 fpe at 200 yards, 828 fpe at 300 yards. The 180-grain Speer flat point 35 shows 1188 fpe at 200 yards, a concomitant amount at 300. So loaded, the cartridges are virtually identical in punch.

Aha, you say, you can load spitzer-shaped bullets in the 300 Savage and increase downrange performance. And so you can. Admittedly, you can do likewise with the 35 Remington but only in box-magazine rifles. Quite simply, spire point bullets and tubular magazines can lead to a violent explosion of the ammunition stored in the tube. (Here's what happens: When the rifle is fired, the resulting recoil forces the end-to-end ammo supply to compress, violently shoving the nose of the pointed bullet directly against the primer. The resulting explosion can be downright dangerous to one's long-term health. In short, *do not* load pointed slugs into ammo that's to be used in a tube-fed centerfire.) In box-magazine rifles like the Remington Model 760, Winchester Model 70, and the Remington Model 600, pointed bullets pose no problems. Starting the streamlined 200-grain Hornady spire point at 2200 fps, you get 2150 fpe at the muzzle, 1667 fpe at 100 yards, 1281 fpe at 200 yards and 971 fpe at a full 300 yards! Factory-loaded spitzers in the 300 show only 1217 fpe at 300 yards, and with a smaller-diameter bullet of 10 percent less weight.

Using the 200-grain spire point in the 35 Remington the 200-yard drop from a 150-yard zero is 4.6 inches. The 300 Savage factory load shows only 1 inch less drop at 200 yards.

How about accuracy? Since most of the rifles chambered for the 35 Remington are not noted for being tack drivers, many hunters believe that the old cartridge is a mite imprecise. Not so. The Marlin 336-A I used for some of the chronograph data for this chapter provided groups that averaged 2.25 inches at 100 yards with its favored load, groups of 2.32 inches with its runner-up. (These averages are, as are the ones that follow, for several five-shot strings, not three-shotters as are often used.) The Marlin printed under 2¾ inches with nearly every load tried in it.

My Remington 760 pump grouped into 2.50 inches with its pet recipe, 2.59 inches with its next best. It shot well under 3 inches with every factory load tested.

My most accurate 35 Remington to date was a Savage Model 170 slide-action. With 33.0 grains of Hercules ReLoder 7 under the 200-grain Hornady round nose, the little Savage fired a four-group average of 1.33 inches, with a 3x scope! The 200-grain spire point coupled with the same charge averaged 2.29 inches and clocked 2244 fps for 2236 fpe. Inaccurate? Low in power? I think not.

Hunting

An acquaintance of mine has killed a lot of deer, with a lot of cartridges. The quickest he ever saw a whitetail dropped was with his 35 Remington and 200-grain Hornady round-nose bullets.

He was sitting beneath a tree one afternoon, watching a pair of does watching him. A third deer was screened behind some brush; he could make out its outline, but couldn't determine its sex. Since does were legal and his freezer was bare, he drew down on the partially-hidden deer and touched off. The deer reared up and fell over backward. He said it never twitched.

Turned out to be a fat eight-pointer. The postmortem revealed that his slug, directed at the center of the chest as the buck stood facing him, had destroyed the heart

Over the years, the author has found that the 35 Remington, in a Marlin 336, will group into 2½ to 3 inches from a rest at 100 yards. That sort of accuracy is sufficient for deer-sized game, providing you don't extend the range unreasonably.

and messed up a lung. Typical. One shot, one deer.

The same fellow hunts black bear with a group in the North Carolina mountains. He says that the most popular rifle is the Marlin 336 chambered for the 35. One mountain bear slayer swears by his 35, has used it on numerous blacks to complete satisfaction. Once he tried a 30-06; he had to pop the bruin several times and nearly lost a dog and some personal hide. He swore off the ought-six and has been happily reunited with his 35 ever since.

Now, I don't for one moment think that the 35 is better than, or even equal to, the 30-06 for black bear or anything else. My point is, there is one *experienced* bear hunter who *does*. Remember, confidence in your rifle and load is half the story.

Another fellow I know surprised a big whitetail buck napping in a clump of weeds smack in the middle of a field. The hunter was nearly as surprised as the hunted. Knowing he'd been caught, the big seven-point took off like a dragster, no demure hopping along for him. At about 80 yards, and just before the deer would have made it to the woodline, my pal socked him in the ribs with a 200-grain Hornady soft point. The buck disappeared. Hurrying over, the hunter spied a logging road leading off from the corner of the field where the animal had vanished. Blood was everywhere. My buddy took up the trail, found the dead buck 50 yards from where he had been hit. One shot, one deer.

Handloading

Handloading the 35 can be a bit of a nuisance unless you steel yourself mentally. The cartridge's very small shoulder is easily set back from an improperly adjusted full-length sizing die, which increases headspace and does nothing good for accuracy, safety, or case life. Additionally, the low working pressures contribute to relatively poor obturation (gas sealing) for a bottle-necked cartridge. The combination of low obturation and a tiny shoulder to headspace against (remember, the case is rimless) causes primers to back out a little with factory loads. Neck sizing can cure these ills, enabling a fire-formed case to fit snugly in the chamber with the shoulder in the proper position. Some rear-locking guns will accept neck-sized brass grudgingly or not at all, so this approach may not be open to all reloaders.

Case trimming, a particularly onerous chore in my book, is made more frequent by the 35's rimless design, adaptation to rear-locking actions, and use in tubular magazines. A tube magazine demands case crimping; case crimping demands uniform lengths close to those present at the time the bullet crimp-seating die was set up. As the cases lengthen, as they will quite rapidly from one firing to the next, the crimp becomes increasingly more pronounced until case buckling results. I have found it necessary to trim my brass every three fir-

ings for use in tube-magazine rifles. Naturally, loads for box-type magazines such as those used by Remington with their 760 pump need not be crimped at all, alleviating much of the problem.

Aside from the foregoing, loading the 35 is relatively straightforward. Powder choice is somewhat limited because of the modest case capacity, but that is a minor drawback. Well suited are such propellants as Du Pont 4198, 4320, and 3031; Winchester 748; Hodgdon H-4895, and BL-C(2); and last and best Hercules ReLoder 7.

As mentioned before, a superbly accurate maximum load for any 35 Remington in sound condition is 33.0 grains of ReLoder 7 and the 200-grain Hornady round nose. Nearly as good and very fast is 37.0 grains of IMR 3031 and the same 200-grain Hornady round nose. Velocity ran 2240 fps in my Savage Model 170, with a velocity variation of only 13 fps.

Summing up the 35 Remington, we have a cartridge that is no party to reload—from the mechanics standpoint—but one that responds well to being reloaded, both from a ballistic and an accuracy standpoint. We have a cartridge that is capable of fine accuracy, astounding in some instances. All the power you'll ever need for deer of any size is available, and a trajectory useful for normal ranges is included free of charge. Some cartridges hit harder, on both ends. Some shoot flatter, but offer lesser terminal ballistics or increased recoil. Some come in shinier rifles, with platinum inlays and skipline herringbone checkering patterns, but those are too embarrassing to mention, let alone hunt with. Taking into account all factors, including energy levels, portability of the rifles, trajectory data, and particularly recoil levels, I can think of no better whitetail cartridge than the old 35 Remington.

IMR 3031 is one of the best choices for reloading the 35 Remington. A load of 37 grains of 3031 and the Hornady 200-grain round nose bullet provides a muzzle velocity of 2240 fps in the author's Savage 170 pump. That is *very* fast for the 35 Remington.

35 Remington

HANDLOAD DATA

| Bullet | | Powder | | | | MV, | ME, | Rifle/ | |
Wt. Grs.	Type	Wt. Grs.	Type	Primer	Case	(fps)	(fpe)	Bbl. (in.)	Remarks
180	Speer FP	**42.0**	Win. 748	8½-120	Fed.	**2217**	**1965**	Sav. 170/22	Fine deer load
200	Hrndy. RN	**33.0**	Rel. 7	8½-120	Win.	**2182**	**2115**	Mar. 336-A/24	Very accurate
200	Hrndy. RN	**33.0**	Rel. 7	8½-120	Fed.	**2190**	**2130**	Sav. 170/22	Good velocity
200	Hrndy. RN	**33.0**	Rel. 7	Fed. 210	Fed.	**2175**	**2101**	Sav. 170/22	Most acc. ld. in Sav.
200	Hrndy. RN	**33.0**	Rel. 7	Fed. 210	Win.	**2214**	**2177**	Rem. 760/22	Accurate
200	Hrndy. RN	37.0	IMR 3031	8½-120	Win.	2145	2044	Mar. 336-A/24	Good velocity
200	Hrndy. RN	37.0	IMR 3031	Fed. 210	Fed.	2240	2229	Sav. 170/22	Poor acc. in Savage
200	Hrndy. RN	**37.5**	IMR 3031	Fed. 210	Rem.	**2153**	**2059**	Rem. 760/22	Accurate
200	Hrndy. RN	**39.0**	Win. 748	8½-120	Win.	2004	1784	Mar. 336-A/24	Accurate
200	Win. PP	**39.0**	Win. 748	CCI 250	Fed.	1945	1680	Sav. 170/22	Very accurate in Sav.

FP—Flat Point; RN—Round Nose; PP—Power-Point.

FACTORY LOAD DATA

| Bullet | | MV, | ME, | Rifle/ | |
Wt. Grs.	Type	(fps)	(fpe)	Bbl. (in.)	Remarks
150	Rem. SP	2300	1761	Rem. 760/22	Fastest load tested
200	Win. RN	2039	1848	Rem. 760/22	Lot #1, most acc. in M760
200	Win. RN	2178	2106	Sav. 170/22	Lot #2, most acc. in M170
200	Rem. RN	2131	2016	Rem. 760/22	Good velocity
200	Fed. RN	1945	1680	Sav. 170/22	Mediocre acc. in M170

SP—Soft Point; RN—Round Nose.

SPECIFICATIONS

Shell Holders
RCBS: 9
Bonanza: 14
Lyman: 8 or 2
Pacific: 26

Bullet Diameter
Jacketed: .358″

Lengths
Trim: 1.910″
Maximum Case: 1.920″
Maximum Overall: 2.525″

CAUTION:
Loads recommended and suggested herein have been carefully listed, but are intended solely as a guide to readers and neither the publisher nor author accept any responsibility for results of their use. **Maximum loads, listed in bold, should be reduced by 10 percent and worked up to cautiously.**

350 Remington Magnum

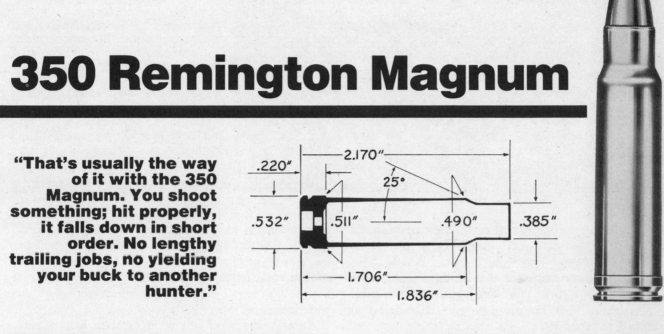

"That's usually the way of it with the 350 Magnum. You shoot something; hit properly, it falls down in short order. No lengthy trailing jobs, no yielding your buck to another hunter."

THIRTY-FIVE-caliber rifle cartridges, as a rule, do not set the woods on fire in the United States. The 35 Remington is relatively popular and durable, although only the Marlin 336 carbine is currently available for it. The 358 Winchester kind of comes and goes; Browning offers it in their BLR levergun; Savage recently discontinued it in the 99 series; and Ruger made some as recently as 1983, according to *Gun Digest*. Nonetheless, it is not really popular. The 358 Norma Magnum is as dead as a Thanksgiving turkey; few shooters mourn its passing. Matter of fact, few ever knew of its existence.

And then we have—or had—the 350 Remington Magnum. Not only is it *not* popular today, it was never popular and never will be. It is homely, not readily adaptable to quick-repeating rifles such as levers and pumps, and at its best is no ballistic marvel. It kicks, despite what you may have read to the contrary. Not excessively, but noticeably. There is a dearth of good bullets available for handloading, and only one factory load. The case is belted, which is never an asset. In short, the 350 Rem. *cartridge* has very little going for it.

However, the 350 Magnum when coupled with the most practical rifle ever made for it was quite an extraordinary package. Like the Model 94 30-30 carbine, the gun/cartridge *combination* should have attained wide and everlasting approbation. That it did not is a travesty and shows what little influence the firearms' press actually wields.

Introduced in 1965 in the Remington Model 600 carbine, the 350 Magnum did not exactly take off like a rocket; it fell over on its side. But not before generating some good press. Hunters of big game, and I mean *big* game, took the potent little guns to their bosoms. For elk, moose, and the big bears, particularly in heavy cover, the new gun had no peer. It still doesn't. Sure, you can lug a long, heavy 338 or 375 Magnum deep into the woods, but you can drive from Duluth to Daytona in a 1903 Peerless; that doesn't make it the ideal machine for the trek. What a lot of gun writers won't admit, particularly those living west of the Mississippi River, is that the shorter and lighter the rifle, the slicker it handles in dense brush. If one of the Western-based scribes does design to discuss ordnance for use in thick terrain, he will ofttimes dismiss such activities as useless, saying that you won't be offered a shot in such tangled vegetation anyway. Such advice should be filed under B-U-L-L and forgotten.

For woods hunting, the short, light rifle is superior. Always. If you can manage to stay on a logging road, or up in a tree stand, or propped on a stump, then maybe you can make do with a longer gun. (Then again, one of my favorite tree stands has so many limbs surrounding it that I doubt I could maneuver a long-barreled rifle.) However, if you actually *leave* the road and go into the woods to hunt, you'll quickly discover the virtues of a stubby firearm. It follows that if you can stuff a car-

Remington's 600 series carbines in 350 Remington Magnum became real favorites with eastern hunters looking for a light handy carbine with plenty of punch. Today, a 600/660 will command a healthy price in the used-gun market.

tridge of significant power into an abbreviated gun, you have a surefire outfit for big critters at spitting distances. If you can combine such a quick-handling rifle with a load that will reach out to smite animals way across a canyon, then you have a pearl beyond price. Such is the 350 Remington Magnum/Remington 600 combo.

Why then did the 350/600 (as I'll hereafter refer to the cartridge/gun pairing, since I consider them inseparable) fail in the marketplace? First and foremost is that the Model 600 carbine was ugly! It had a nylon ventilated rib riding the barrel, a Buck Rogers front sight, a nylon trigger guard/floorplate assembly, the homeliest bolt handle you ever laid eyes on, and a multi-hued laminated stock. I suppose if you hung fender skirts and mudflaps on the thing, you would render it more unsightly, but then maybe not. It was as if the Remington design team set out to shock every rifle shooter in the country. The public's acceptance of plastics as suitable for firearm fabrication, even in lightly-stressed parts, was only beginning to bud. Laminated stocks were viewed with a jaundiced eye. That bolt handle, not even a mother could love. (The fact that the moderately successful Remington XP-100 handgun boasts the identical bolt configuration is insignificant. The XP-100 was not designed to appeal to a broad spectrum of *hunters*, but a limited number of erudite *shooters,* who were only coincidentally hunters. Shooters will put up with function for its own sake; hunters most often will not.)

Overlooked in the ensuing brouhaha was the fact that the nylon rib, which was included on the standard-caliber Model 600s in the first place to disguise the ultra-slim barrel profile, actually did reduce the barrel-marriage effects of long strings of shots. Ignored was the fact that the laminated stock exhibited scant warpage if ze-

roed in Tucson, then transported for a hunt to Anchorage. Unnoticed went the tendency of the bolt handle to be right where you expected it when you triggered a shot and reached for it in a hurry. Unappreciative were the hunters who carried the lissome carbines all day with no fatigue.

Hunters who were serious about their *hunting,* who viewed their firearms as tools, not *objets d'art,* snatched up the 350/600 with glee. From what I read and hear of the used-gun market, they aren't turning loose of many. I suspect a goodly number of 350/600 carbines are alive and working in the northwestern United States, western Canada, and Alaska, and will be for many years to come.

The 350/600 lasted only 3 years. In 1968 Remington announced an "improved" (read "different") version of the Model 600 carbine, dubbing it the Model 660. It was *sans* ventilated rib and carried another 1½ inches of barrel. The only item that actually needed attention, the ridiculous bolt release, went unattended. And thus did the handy, homely Model 600 become the less-handy, heftier, marginally-less-homely Model 660 complete with an increased price and modest improvement in ballistics. Surprise; it still didn't sell.

As a last-ditch effort, Remington chambered the Model 700 bolt-action to 350 Magnum. It lasted about as long as a case of hives and wasn't quite as well-liked. The M700 sported a 24-inch barrel, the same as on the 7mm Remington Magnum and 300 Winchester Magnum. Why purchase a long-spout, belted cartridge of 30-06 case capacity and medium bore? Why indeed. No one did. Remington had come too far afield of the 350's intended bailiwick. The unencumbered Model 600 carbine had grown into a clumsy piece more suited to plains hunting than forested terrain.

Remington's 660 Carbine was the last of the "Short-rifle" 350 Rem. Mags. The Model 600, the forerunner of the 660, differed primarily by the presence of a nylon rib and a rakish front sight.

A pair of popular propellants for the 350 Remington Magnum: Du Pont's IMR 4064 (left) and IMR 4320 (right).

One noted writer was overjoyed upon receiving word that the Model 700 could be had in 350 Magnum. In fact, according to an article penned by him, he'd been barnstorming for just such a marriage for years.

I have never understood this prediliction on the part of some of my colleges to redesign every cartridge or rifle that comes down the pike to their personal specifications. The 350/600 filled a legitimate *need*. The 350 Magnum cartridge housed in such a rifle as the Remington 700 met no such need, either real or imagined. And why in the world would anyone want an elongated action for the 350 Magnum, except as a ballistic exercise? For experimental purposes, it would serve no function that the wildcat 35 Whelen wouldn't perform as well. Ballistically, it would take a backseat to the 338 Winchester Magnum and 358 Norma Magnum, both of which were attainable in heavy, cumbersome rifles if that were your pleasure.

No sir. The 350 Magnum was presented in the right gun, at least from a functional standpoint. There is no way of knowing whether it would have gone over successfully in a more handsome package, such as the current Remington Model 7, but the *concept* was sound.

Aside from the aesthetic difficulties faced by the 350/600, there were other issues contributing to its demise. Deer hunters did not need the power of the 350 Magnum, and many if not most couldn't have handled the recoil if they were convinced they did need the punch. Secondly, the 350 was available only in a turnbolt; many, many nimrods—especially woods hunters—were absolutely certain that they needed a fast-workin' repeater for such enterprise. Those fellows wouldn't have anted up for a boltgun no matter what the caliber.

Elk hunters in the western states, I'm convinced, felt that they required a cartridge with all the range and retained energy they could get. I doubt that a short, squat cartridge like the 350 got much notice from them, regardless of its belted case and pointy bullets.

Nope, the 350/600 was a special-purpose cartridge and rifle. And for the limited spectrum it was intended for, I doubt that a better combination has ever been produced in this country.

One negative I've never seen associated with the 350/600 is poor accuracy. Practically everyone who's ever tried one has raved about the tight groups so easily provided by the little carbines. Groups in the 1-inch class seem reasonably common, and that's for five shots, not three. Several researchers reported accuracy at least as good from the Model 700 rifles, one experimenter quoting ¾-inch clusters.

I've read that the Mossberg Model 800 was produced for a while in 350 Mag., though I've never seen one. Ruger catalogued the 350 in the Model 77 lineup. Ken Waters did a fine write-up in the September-October,

1981, edition of *Handloader* magazine, using a Ruger 77 as his test gun. Ken obtained excellent accuracy from his rifle, reporting several five-shooters well under an inch.

Handloading

Al Miller once wrote of his cast-bullet experiments with a Remington 600. Al's gun averaged around 1½ inches with Remington factory ammo, and from 2 to 3 inches with good cast-bullet loads. Said Al: "The 350's most endearing characteristic, and one that sets it apart from practically every other sporting round ever conceived, is its refusal to distinguish between cast and jacketed bullets. Weight for weight, they can be sent down range with all the energy of jacketed bullets and almost as accurately, too."

Other writers have spoken of the affinity the 350 takes to the use of pistol bullets. A chap by the name of Ray Fitzgerald wrote in the January-February, 1973, *Handloader* that he received ⅝-inch groups with 52.2 grains of IMR 3031 under the 158-grain Hornady hollow point! Muzzle velocity was quoted at 2482 fps in a 24-inch barreled M700. Up to 150 yards or so, that load should disintegrate a crow or woodchuck.

The original factory-quoted ballistics for the 350 Remington Magnum were supposedly taken in a 20-inch barrel. They went as follows: 200-grain Remington soft point, muzzle velocity, 2710 fps—muzzle energy 3260 fpe; 250-grain Remington soft point, muzzle velocity 2410 fps—muzzle energy, 3220 fpe. Actual chronographing by independent testers corroborates the 250 data, but the 200-grain factory load usually falls short.

The best propellants for the 350 Magnum are the medium burners, from IMR 3031 on the fast side to IMR 4320 and Winchester 760 on the slow. IMR 4350 is noted for excellent accuracy, but velocities leave something to be desired for hunting use.

The best currently-available bullets are the 200-grain Hornady spire point and round nose, and the 180-grain Speer flat point if you're after deer-size animals. For bigger game, Speer and Hornady make 250-grain slugs; I like the Speer in pointed form, the Hornady when desiring a round nose. The blunt Hornady bullet has a long ogive and short bearing surface, contributing to lower pressures with normal overall length, or higher speeds with shallow bullet seating. Conversely, the 250-grain Speer spitzer can be seated farther out of the case than the defunct 250-grain Hornady spire point. Barnes makes a nifty 300-grain round nose if you can find some for sale. At 2200 fps, it should make a superlative bruin tranquilizer.

The only fellow I know personally who hunts with a 350 is Layne Simpson, the well-known South Carolina gun writer. Layne has taken eight deer with his Model 600, only two at more than 100 yards. He says his 350 has stay-down power; whatever he hits tends to stay down. Five of the deer he has shot dropped on the spot; the other three covered less than 20 yards after being hit. He uses the 200-grain Remington Pointed Soft-Point Core Lokt bullet exclusively, having a hoarded supply on hand.

One of Layne's best shots on deer came with the 350/600. He had just eaten lunch and was engaged in a post-prandial stroll down a logging road when a juicy four-pointer attempted to cross 40 yards ahead. The buck tried to negotiate the road in one leap; Layne upped his rifle, snapped off a shot as if shot-gunning quail. The deer folded in mid-air; the bullet almost seemed to fling the deer into the ditch. Layne is fond of his 350/600.

That's usually the way of it with the 350 Magnum. You shoot something; hit properly, it falls down in short order. No lengthy trailing jobs, no yielding your buck to another hunter. The cartridge deserves a far better fate than rampant shooter apathy.

350 Remington Magnum

HANDLOAD DATA

Bullet Wt. Grs.	Type	Powder Wt. Grs.	Type	Primer	Case	MV, (fps)	ME, (fpe)	Rifle/ Bbl. (in.)	Remarks
180 Speer	FP	**60.0**	IMR 4895	CCI 200	Rem.	2900	3361	Rug. M77/22	Speer Manual No. 10
180 Speer	SP	**60.0**	BL-C(2)	CCI 250	Rem.	2942	3460	Rug. M77/22	Speer Manual No. 10
200 Hrndy.	RN	**56.0**	IMR 4064	Fed. 210	Rem.	2600	3002	Rem. M600/18½	Hrndy. Hndbk., 3rd Ed.
200 Hrndy.	RN	**60.5**	IMR 4320	Fed. 210	Rem.	2700	3238	Rem. M600/18½	Hrndy. Hndbk., 3rd Ed.
250 Hrndy.	RN	**51.0**	IMR 3031	Fed. 210	Rem.	2400	3195	Rem. M600/18½	Hrndy. Hndbk., 3rd Ed.
250 Hrndy.	RN	**54.9**	IMR 4320	Fed. 210	Rem.	2400	3195	Rem. M600/18½	Hrndy. Hndbk., 3rd Ed.
250 Speer	SP	**53.0**	IMR 4895	CCI 200	Rem.	2353	3073	Rug. M77/22	Speer Manual No. 10

FP—Flat Point; SP—Soft Point; RN—Round Nose.

FACTORY LOAD DATA

Bullet Wt. Grs.	Type	MV, (fps)	ME, (fpe)	Rifle/ Bbl. (in.)	Remarks
200 Rem.	SP	2529	2838	Rem. M600/18½	Well below quoted figures
250 Rem.	SP	2430	3278	Rug. M77/22	Gd. velocity and energy

SP—Soft Point.

SPECIFICATIONS

Shell Holders
RCBS: 4
Bonanza: 2
Lyman: 13
Pacific: 5

Bullet Diameter
Jacketed: .358″

Lengths
Trim: 2.160″
Maximum Case: 2.170″
Maximum Overall: 2.800″

When the ranges are reasonable, and the game large, the 350 Remington Magnum fills the bill nicely.

CAUTION:
Loads recommended and suggested herein have been carefully listed, but are intended solely as a guide to readers and neither the publisher nor author accept any responsibility for results of their use. **Maximum loads, listed in bold, should be reduced by 10 percent and worked up to cautiously.**

358 Winchester

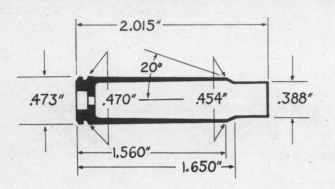

2.015"

20°

.473" .470" .454" .388"

1.560"

1.650"

> "Assuming the correct choice of bullet and powder, [the 358] will do a creditable job on any animal on this continent at reasonable ranges, and do an excellent job on critters up to 400 pounds in heft. . . ."

I HAD never seen so many deer before. It was my first hunt for western mule deer, and the open terrain made spotting deer easy. Just driving in to the campsite was a revelation; we must have seen 40 deer as it neared full dark. I looked forward to the next day with ill-concealed anticipation.

Two California hunters and I were being directed by a pair of seasoned Wyoming guides who knew the Absaroka Mountains like their own dens. Our hunt was to be a 3-day affair. One of my partners dropped a small deer at sunrise of opening day; the other busted a nice buck just after lunchtime with his 300 Weatherby. My guide worked his tail off, but no deer could we find.

Toward evening of that first day, I left the others and strolled back to camp in a circuitous direction. I hadn't been walking more than 15 minutes when I jumped a band of 13 does. I sneaked around a rocky outcropping and squatted down in case an unseen buck was bringing up the rear. No buck. While I crouched waiting, I glanced across a valley and spotted another herd of deer numbering 12 does and an unknown. Climbing to the ridgetop, I put my binoculars on them. They watched me in unison.

It was nearly dusk and squint as I might I couldn't make a single one of them grow horns. They slowly worked their way up their ridge, feeding as they went and taking turns watching me. Finally the lead deer, the one whose sex I was unsure of, skylined himself. *Himself!* It was too far to shoot, and if I tried a stalk, it would be completely dark before I got off my hilltop, let alone made it to theirs. I hurried back to camp and told the guides what I'd seen. They were confident the band would be in the same general location the next morning.

They were right. We parked the pickup on one ridge; the deer were partway up another and acting skittish. My guide estimated the range at 350 yards, which surprised me a little. I had figured it for 300. Deciding that he likely was a better judge of range than I, I held a few inches over the buck's back and touched off. The buck and all his girlfriends took off up the ridge and out of sight. My guide and I tumbled down our mountain and scrambled up the one the deer had vacated. When we topped out, we spotted the herd at the bottom of a draw, at about the same distance I had fired just moments before. I plopped belly-down in the snow, set my hat on a sagebrush, rested my 358 Savage Model 99 on the hat and, since I figured my zero was off, held under the buck. That's right where I hit. He took off again. I led him a bit and let him have another one. This one connected; he hit the ground in a heap.

By the time we negotiated the draw, the buck had recovered enough to curl himself into a big ball. I slipped a finisher into his neck, and he collapsed.

The autopsy revealed that my first slug had taken him in the left hip, smashing the bone and ruining a quarter of meat. The bullet had gone to pieces; we found only a

(Right) The author used his Savage 99 in 358 Winchester to take this four-point mule deer. It was a running shot, about 275 yards distant.

(Below) In taking his four-point mule deer buck, the author used a pre-Interlock Hornady 200-grain slug. That projectile exploded on the buck's hip. What you see is all that was left.

large jacket fragment. My *coup de grace* in the neck had disintegrated, leaving nothing but a smushed spine and tiny copper slivers.

Incidentally, my first slug had grooved a furrow from his back right at the top, not even drawing blood. The indication was that my shot had gone right where it was supposed to, considering the range. If I had held for 300 yards, the slug would have dropped right into the lungs and the buck likely would never have moved.

The load was 47.0 grains of IMR 3031 under the 200-grain Hornady spire point. Muzzle speed in my 22-inch barreled Savage levergun was close to 2500 fps. Out where the buck took the first hit, retained energy was about 1300 fpe.

Rick Jamison used an identical Savage 99 to take a monster black bear in Arizona the following year. Rick

is a dedicated and proficient varmint caller; in fact he wrote a book entitled *Calling Coyotes*. He had never spent much time trying to call up a bear, although some of his friends assured him it was possible to do so. Rick made a few half-hearted efforts, with no result.

Then one fall day he discovered, quite inadvertently, a prime bear spot. On a grassy, mast-covered ledge in a secluded canyon, he discovered profuse bear sign. Droppings were in abundance, and so were round depressions from many padded feet. Everything, in fact, except a neon sign flashing *bear* in scarlet letters.

The terrain was too brushy to still-hunt, so Rick, though long of limb and lung but short on sit-still patience, dug out his predator call to give it a go. He climbed a small knoll and perched on a fallen log. A steep canyon wall heaved itself up directly behind Rick, about 50 yards from his seat, so he didn't expect an approach from that direction. Running along the lip of the canyon about 20 yards to his front was a trail, and along that trail did he anticipate company if it came. A mistake. One should never try to devine the path chosen by an approaching predator. *Rick* taught me *that*.

Surrounded by thick undergrowth, Rick tooted his call and succeeded in nothing except the frightening of various forest denizens. After 20 minutes, nerves less on edge from keen anticipation, Rick's mind began to wander. Thirty minutes. Rick squalled again, then heard a sound he thought was coming from his right, down the trail. The sound was *big,* if you know what I mean, and at first Rick thought it might be a Hereford. Then he remembered that he had seen no cattle sign. He squeaked again with his call and was rewarded by an immediate and urgent increase in noise and activity directly *behind him!* He didn't even have time to stand, merely swiveled his conk and shouldered his Savage.

As he completed the turn, he spotted the source of the commotion. A very large, very angry, very *hungry* black bear burst from the brush so close Rick could have spit in his eye. Reflexively, Rick centered the crosswires on the blocky head and poked a hole in it just under the left eye. The bruin dropped on the spot, its momentum carrying it a ways before it lay still. Since the bear was uphill, and since "dead" bears have a propensity for regaining life with alarming ferocity, Rick let him have two more shots for insurance. Smart guy.

The back up shots proved unnecessary; the first slug had gone on through the skull into the neck, breaking 8 inches of spine where it stopped. As Rick performed his inspection, the reaction began to set in. Undoubtedly, the bear had neither seen nor smelled him and was convinced that Rick was a critter in distress and thus excellent bruin fodder. The thought made Rick's knees a mite rubbery.

Jamison's load was based on a generous portion of IMR 4320 and the 250-grain Speer spitzer. He was getting around 2250 fps at the muzzle, of which the bear absorbed a goodly portion.

That same year, Linda Jamison took a magnificent six-point bull elk with Rick's Savage. The elk were in the rut; Rick had been imitating a horny bull for quite a spell when one ole boy took up the challenge. Rick brought him in to about 80 yards, where the bull stood partially screened by pines and pondered this tiny, antlerless creature with the big mouth and the funny pelage. Linda tossed a 250-grain Speer at him while he was thus engaged. The slug hit left of center as the bull faced them and deflected along the ribcage, never getting inside the chest wall. Deciding that this wicked little filly was not worth fighting over, the big guy attempted to retire from the scene. Having none of that, Linda smacked him in the hip. She fired again and turned him; he ran off to their right heading for a jack pine thicket to seek refuge from the nasty whirring things that stung. Linda slid one into his ribcage and decked him.

Three of Linda's four shots had connected, the final one had negotiated the ribcage, wrecking the lungs and dropping the bull in his tracks. The pointed Speer slug performed satisfactorily.

A whitetail hunter extraordinaire lives in my neck of the woods. For years he used a Winchester Model 88 358 with 200-grain Hornady round-nose bullets. He hunts with dogs, so the bucks he kills are highly adrenalized. Of the 20 or more deer he slew with the 358, only one required more than one shot. That buck, a tremendous plus-200-pounder soaked up four slugs before succumbing.

More typical is the big eight-point Jim decked at about 70 yards. The Hornady bullet found the spine and Jim swears that it looked as if the deer was *thrown* into the creek it was standing beside.

The foregoing hunting yarns illustrate the efficacy of the 358 cartridge on game of varying sizes and temperaments. Assuming the correct choice of bullet and powder, it will do a creditable job on any animal on this continent at reasonable ranges, and do an excellent job on critters up to 400 pounds in heft as far as you should be shooting. Why, then, isn't it more popular? Let's see.

Sprung on an unreceptive public in 1955, along with its sibling the 243 Winchester, the 358 was based on the 308 Winchester case simply necked up to accept 35-caliber bullets. It offered the punch and blunt-profile slugs of the renowned 35 Remington—magnifying the energy of the elderly 35 by a considerable amount—and the relatively flat and useful trajectory of the 300 Savage. What a combination! Woods hunters should have stood in line to embrace the embryonic load, such was its potential. Alas, it was not to be. Ingratiatory nimrods merely greeted the new cartridge with a yawn.

The reasons for this sad state of affairs are many. First, the introductory vehicle was the Winchester Model 70, a long, heavy slow-operating piece of machinery, anethema to a woods hunter. Aware of their folly, Winchester was quick to add the 358 to the line-up of chamberings for the Model 88 lever-action. Now they had a quick-firer housing the load, but to scant avail. The 358 sold like Edsels. The Model 88 was a thoroughly modern, incredibly strong, nicely accurate levergun. Unfortunately, it also was an ugly duckling, did not look "western," had no hammer sticking up where a fellow could grab it, and it was cursed with a really lousy trigger.

Stoeger imported some Mannlicher-Schoenauer carbines for the 358, and Savage Arms tooled up, poking the new load in their Model 99 queue. Nice guns. Accurate, reliable, and powerful. But problem number two reared its loathsome head; the 358 kicked. Hard. The Mannlicher was a pretty light turnbolt, and the gun Savage chose to house the 358 was the slender Featherweight model. Both guns merely exacerbated the recoil inherent in moving massive 250-grain missiles at 2250 fps muzzle speeds. The milksops couldn't cope with the recoil and the cartridge gained a black eye.

Arm-chair theorists postulate that the shooting public was so enamored of high-velocity cartridges when the slow-moving 358 was sired that it virtually escaped notice, thereby sealing its doom. Maybe. But if that were true, why then did the 444 Marlin, introduced a few years later, manage to attain such popularity that Mar-

Bullets for 358-caliber cartridges, with case capacities greater than that of the 35 Remington are, left to right: 150-gr. Remington soft point; 180-gr. Speer flat point; 200-gr. Hornady round nose; 200-gr. Norma soft point; 200-gr. Sierra round nose; 200-gr. Winchester Silvertip; 220-gr. Speer flat point; 250-gr. Hornady soft point; 250-gr. Speer soft point and the 250-gr. Speer round nose.

lin continues to sell them even in this day of light-bullet, Mach III cartridges? I think the roots of the 358's failure go deeper than public apathy to a modest-velocity load.

The main problem was that Winchester failed to follow through a publicity push for the 358. The 243 took off so quickly that the company chiefs may have decided to concentrate advertising ballyhoo on that golden-haired load, leaving the pedestrian 358 to fend for itself. In addition, the 358 has long been thought of as a short-to-medium range cartridge. Gun writers have done little to thwart that misconception, in fact have advanced it themselves through design or ignorance.

In order to pigeonhole a cartridge according to its ranging capabilities, we first must agree on the parameters of the applicable classifications. Load characteristics should include an adequately flat trajectory for minimum holdover, ample retained energy for the game sought, sufficient accuracy in common hunting rifles to enable hits in the killing zone. On game, I would define short range as anything up to 125 yards; a typical short-range rifle would be the 44 Magnum. Medium range should include yardages from 125 to about 250 or so. In this category, we can include the 30-30 (although it is not good enough for the longer distance), the 22 Hornet (which is barely adequate on chucks to 200 yards, crows a bit farther), and the 243 (on deer-sized animals). Long range begins at 250 yards in my opinion, and extends to 400 for an excellent shot using a flat-shooting cartridge in a super-accurate rifle, firing at a standing animal from a solid rest. Shots past 400 yards should be taken rarely by an expert, never by the average hunter.

Let's see how the 358 Winchester stacks up. With factory 200-grain loads providing a muzzle speed of 2490 fps, the 358 shows 9.7 inches of drop at 250 yards, with a 150-yard zero. If you drive a 200-grain Hornady spire point to the same velocity with handloads, and zero at 200 yards instead of 150, the drop is only 8.3 inches at 300 yards. Retained energy is 1280 fpe. Does that sound like short-range ballistics to you?

To make the 358 into a real hairy-chested load, kick a 250-grain Speer spitzer to 2400 fps, which is not difficult with Winchester 748 powder. The 300-yard drop is 11.2

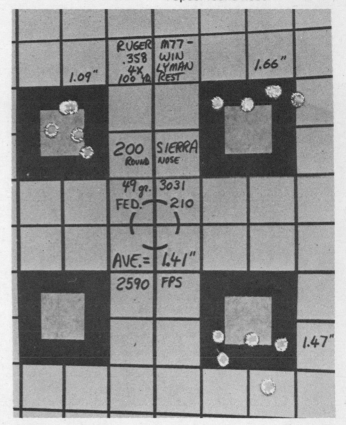

This is a typical target with one of the better loads in the Ruger 77 in 358 Winchester. The load consisted of 49.0 grains of IMR 3031. The three, five-shot 100 yard groups averaged 1.41 inches.

inches and the energy left at that distance is a whopping 1928 fpe! Thus, with a hold just below the backline of a bull elk, you could drive a 250-grain slug carrying nearly a ton of energy into his lungs at 300 yards or a bit better. Short range? Medium? Buffalo chips!

A recent article, penned by a gentleman whose opinions I normally respect, thrust two more assumptions at the public as to why the 358 has languished—deservedly in his view. The first is that the 358 is prone to mysterious misfires, and with less than infrequent occurrence. The reason for these phenomena, he advances, is the combination (not unique to the 358, he reluctantly admits) of a small case shoulder and the accumulation of *ice* on the cartridge. The cure for that problem is simple; keep your ammo supply dry and watch for freezing condensation on your case necks. Then the 358's pitiful little shoulder may prove adequate after all.

Pondering this altruistic behavior, I wondered why the old 35 Remington, veteran of more than 75 years of hunting in the snow, and available in semi-automatic rifles, (which the writer implied exacerbated the situation), was free of this abhorrent condition. The 35 Remington has a shoulder smaller yet than that gracing the 358. Anyhow, the writer concluded by admonishing the 358 user to be sure and keep his chamber and cartridges free of moisture. Remember that.

The other allegation the aforementioned writer aimed at the 358 was that it was not particularly accurate. Let me quote him: "Even when used in a good bolt-action rifle such as the Winchester Model 70 Featherweight, accuracy is seldom better than 2 inches for 5 shots at 100 yards." At this point I will simply state that one of the 358s I used to gather data for this chapter was a Ruger Model 77 sporter. In that rifle I developed 14 different handloads using 10 bullets and seven propellants, and fired each for an average of three or more five-shot strings at 100 yards. *Not one load* failed to average *less* than 2 inches; five grouped under 1½ inches. In addition, my Savage 99 averaged under 2 inches, as did a Browning BLR, both with factory ammunition.

So far as I know, only six rifles have been offered as standard production items in 358 Winchester. They were: Winchester Model 70, Winchester Model 88, Ruger Model 77, Savage Model 99, Browning BLR, and the imported Mannlicher-Schoenauer. Only the BLR is available currently, at least as far as I know. If you want a 358, it's a lever-action or nothing, unless you want a custom or semi-custom such as the Shilen DGA, which just might be obtainable in 358 Winchester on special order. No matter; the BLR is a very nice rifle in most respects, and quite accurate. Certainly amply so for normal big game seeking at ranges permitted by the trajectory.

The Winchester 200-grain Silvertip factory load gave excellent accuracy in both my BLR and my 99 Savage. The Browning grouped into 1.94 inches for an average; the Savage produced an average of 1.96 inches for four, five-shot 100-yard strings. Chronograph readings were in the 2450 fps neighborhood in both guns. Although somewhat faster in my Ruger boltgun, at 2521 fps, accuracy was less than noteworthy at 2.37 inches for three, five-shot strings. The 250-grain Silvertip was both slow and inaccurate in my Ruger.

Favored handloads include the one used on my Wyoming mule deer buck, 47.0 grains of IMR 3031 and the 200-grain Hornady pointed slug, as discussed previously. Were I to use the 358 on varmints, I'd opt for the 180-grain Speer flat point pushed by a maximum charge of 51.0 grains of IMR 3031 for an impressive 2757 fps. For more loads, see the chart accompanying this chapter; give one or two a try, starting low and working up.

Since there are so few 358 factory guns available, and the Browning levergun may not be your cup of tea, you might have to look hard for a new rifle in that chambering. Some good used ones are around if their owners will part with them. I suspect they might not. *Mine* aren't for sale.

The ".358 Winchester" barrel marking on this Ruger 77 is rare. Those who own one are lucky indeed—they're accurate.

358 Winchester

HANDLOAD DATA

Bullet Wt. Grs.	Type	Powder Wt. Grs.	Type	Primer	Case	MV, (fps)	ME, (fpe)	Rifle/ Bbl. (in.)	Remarks
180	Speer FP	**51.0**	IMR 3031	8½-120	Win.	**2757**	**3039**	Rug. M77/22	Fair accuracy
200	Hrndy. SP	47.0	IMR 3031	Fed. 210	Win.	2505	2788	Sav. M99/22	Accurate
200	Sierra RN	**49.0**	IMR 3031	Fed. 210	Win.	2590	2980	Rug. M77/22	Acc. in Rug. 77
250	Hrndy. SP	**42.0**	IMR 3031	Rem. 9½	Win.	**2232**	**2766**	Rug. M77/22	Fair accuracy

FP—Flat Point; SP—Soft Point; RN—Round Nose.

FACTORY LOAD DATA

Bullet Wt. Grs.	Type	MV, (fps)	ME, (fpe)	Rifle/ Bbl. (in.)	Remarks
200	Win. ST	2458	2682	Sav. M99/22	Accurate
200	Win. ST	2433	2608	Brown. BLR/22	Very accurate
200	Win. ST	2521	2822	Rug. 77/22	Fair accuracy
250	Win. ST	2120	2495	Rug. 77/22	Fair accuracy

ST—Silvertip.

SPECIFICATIONS

Shell Holders
RCBS: 3
Bonanza: 1
Lyman: 2
Pacific: 1

Bullet Diameter
Jacketed: .358″
Cast: .358″

Lengths
Trim: 2.005″
Maximum Case: 2.015″
Maximum Overall: 2.780″

CAUTION:
Loads recommended and suggested herein have been carefully listed, but are intended solely as a guide to readers and neither the publisher nor author accept any responsibility for results of their use.
Maximum loads, listed in bold, should be reduced by 10 percent and worked up to cautiously.

358 Norma Magnum

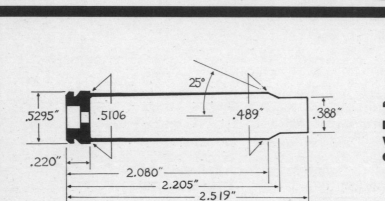

.5295" .5106 25° .489" .388"

.220" 2.080" 2.205" 2.519"

"No, I wouldn't buy a new 358 Norma, but I wouldn't trade a trusted one off, either."

ANOTHER of the medium-bore magnums that has languished in popular acceptance is the Big Swede, Norma's 358 Magnum. The big, belted 35 was introduced to the American market by A.B. Norma Projektilfabrik of Amotfors, Sweden, in 1959, preceding the 308 Norma Magnum by a year. When first presented, there were no rifles produced for it, either here or abroad. Norma Precision, the American marketing arm of the Swedish parent company, supplied Yankee gunsmiths with chambering specs and the shooting public with virgin brass and loaded ammo. A year later, the Danish firm of Schultz & Larsen and Sweden's Husqvarna had tooled up for the load and were exporting rifles to the United States. The big bruiser took off.

Although some American-made rifles may have cropped up from time to time, I've never seen one from a major producer. Since the 358 is a standard-length cartridge—like the 30-06 or the 338 Winchester Magnum—such actions as the Model '98 Mauser, the '03 Springfield, and the Winchester Model 70 were perfectly suited for it. The cash registers of custom gunsmiths rang with joy.

Of the two rifles that were available off the shelf, one was an old-fashioned Mauser derivative, the other a new-fangled gun with its locking lugs on the wrong end of the bolt. Neither was exactly inexpensive. After the initial surge, the big bruiser slowed a mite.

Now, there was nothing in the world wrong with the rear-locking system of the Schultz & Larsen. It closed up tight; it was very strong; and it was silky smooth. No matter, it developed a bad reputation for stretching cases. In fact, I'll bet an oatmeal cookie it was the Schultz & Larsen Model 65 that prompted the following statement, culled from a section devoted to the 358 Norma in a *current* loading manual: "Actions with locking lugs in the rear, however, are a poor choice for use with such powerful cartridges." I expect that's news to Colt Firearms and Golden Eagle, both of whom have chambered such potent numbers as the 338 Winchester, the 300 Weatherby, and the 458 Winchester Magnums in bolt-action rifles having rear lockup. And need I mention Remington, who has produced uncounted thousands of rear-locking Model 788s in such high-pressure cartridges as the 243 and the 7mm-08?

The 358 Norma's fall from grace did not entirely hinge on such matters as limited rifle choice. First, it was basically a proprietary cartridge, similar in concept to the Weatherby line of belted magnums. Neither of the American monoliths of cartridge manufacturers saw fit to tool up for it, and that was two massive strikes against it from the outset. If you were going to have a hard time finding ammo or brass, and were likely to be buying a rifle cobbled up by a custom 'smith anyway, you'd be about as well off having your rifle chambered for a wildcat like the 35 Ackley Short Magnum or the 35-338, both of which were nearly identical to the 358

From left to right: 35 Newton, 358 Norma Magnum, 35 Winchester, 350 Remington Magnum and the 358 Winchester. All five of these cartridges have, unfortunately, seen better times in terms of popularity.

Here's a selection of 358-caliber slugs that are well suited in the 358 Norma Magnum. From left to right: 250-grain Hornady spire point; 250-grain Speer pointed soft point and the 250-grain Speer round nose.

Norma Magnum and were formed from easily obtainable brass.

Handloading

The other big problem confronting Norma was the lack of a good 35-caliber *high-velocity* big game bullet. Up to the advent of the 358 Norma Magnum, such cartridges as the 358 Winchester and the wildcat 35 Whelen represented the upper velocity range of common 35-caliber cartridges, roughly 2600 fps with the 200-grain bullets, 2400 fps with the stouter 250-grain slugs. Along comes the Big Swede, capable of pushing 200-grain slugs to 3100 fps or so, and getting 2800 fps from factory-loaded 250-grain Dual-Cores. Common sense indicated that if a 250-grain round nose bullet was designed for controlled expansion and deep penetration at an impact velocity of from 1800 to 2200 fps, that same slug, in all likelihood, would shred to confetti if it bumped into an elk's shoulder bone at 2600 fps! And that is the fat fly in the *potage:* few, if any, 35-caliber bullets were designed expressly for 358 Norma-class terminal ballistics.

Only the 250-grain Speer spitzer and 250-grain Hornady round nose are suitable, and they only marginally so. The Speer bullet will do quite well at the longer ranges, where its velocity has fallen off somewhat. The Hornady will hang together as well, but its blunt profile hinders it as a long-range load.

Bitterroot is said to produce a premium 35-caliber bullet, and if you can find some, snatch 'em up. Unfortunately, in my experience Bitterroot bullets are as scarce as solid gold bowling balls, and nearly as expensive if you do run across some.

Nosler does not offer a 35-caliber Partition bullet, or even a Solid Base for that matter. I doubt they will. If they did, it would probably be designed for one of the more popular and smaller-cased 35s, like the 35 Remington or the new 356 Winchester, and weigh in the 200-grain neighborhood.

Norma no longer imports bullets (at this writing), so the famous Dual-Core is unobtainable as a reloading component. The current importer of things Norma does not carry 358 Magnum ammunition on his list, according to my local source. Matters are growing even bleaker for the big 35.

For the reloader, this presents no problem; he can fabricate 358 Norma brass from a number of popular cartridge cases. For normal big game usage—black bear, deer, goats, sheep, caribou, and the like—most any of the available 35-caliber bullets will serve if some care is given to velocity levels. A fine and relatively mild load is 70.0 grains of Du Pont's IMR 4350 behind a 250-grain Speer soft point for a little over 2500 fps. Additional below-max handloads can be found, particularly with IMR 4895, a powder noted for its flexibility and accuracy at three-quarters throttle.

Du Pont's IMR 4895 is also an excellent propellant for use in full-power loadings of bullets up to 250 grains. Couple Hornady's 250-grain round nose with 67.5 grains of IMR 4895 for first-rate grouping and factory-load velocities. Sixty-nine grains of IMR 4895 will push the 180-grain Speer flat point to over 3100 fps if you want a flat-shooting load. Use it for non-edible game; it is quite destructive.

Most authorities recommend the use of magnum primers with the 358 Norma, even with the faster-burning powders like IMR 4895 and IMR 4320. Since these propellants are of compact granulation, loading density is less than 100 percent; hot primers reduce the risk of hangfires in a large-capacity case like the 358 Norma. Although you will often have a near 100 percent charge density with such slow powders as H4831, the burning rate itself necessitates a magnum cap.

If I were contemplating the purchase of a new rifle and wanted a brute to handle big elk, dull moose, or mean grizzly bears, I'd cast not a glance at the 358 Norma Magnum. If I already had one, and were scheming a trip to the far north in search of such critters, I'd load up a batch of heavy handloads featuring the 250-grain Speer spitzer and buy a plane ticket. No, I wouldn't buy a new 358 Norma, but I wouldn't trade a trusted one off, either.

Hodgdon's H4895 is a versatile propellant. It's capable of providing some excellent middle-of-the-road muzzle velocities in the big 358 Norma.

Hodgdon's H4831 is a good choice for the 358 Norma Magnum. Considering the large capacity of the 358 Norma case, and the fact that slow burning powders are popular for this cartridge, the reloader should consider the use of magnum primers for such propellants.

358 Norma Magnum

HANDLOAD DATA

Bullet Wt. Grs.	Type	Powder Wt. Grs.	Type	Primer	Case	MV, (fps)	ME, (fpe)	Rifle/ Bbl. (in.)	Remarks
200	Rem. SPCL	79.5	IMR 4350	Rem. 9½	Norm.	**2941**	3842	S&L/24	Lym. Hndbk., 46th Ed. (Acc. Ld.)
200	Hrndy. RN	66.5	IMR 4064	CCI 250	Norm.	2900	3734	Rem. 700/25½	Hrndy. Hndbk., 3rd
250	Rem. SPCL	55.0	IMR 3031	Rem. 9½	Norm.	2358	3087	S&L/24	Lym. Hndbk., 46th Ed.
250	Hrndy. RN	**67.5**	IMR 4895	CCI 250	Norm.	**2800**	**4353**	Custom/24	Accurate
250	Speer SP	70.0	IMR 4350	CCI 250	Norm.	2550	3610	Custom/24	Accurate
275	Hrndy. RN	68.0	IMR 4350	Rem. 9½	Norm.	2409	3544	S&L/24	Lym. Hndbk., 46th Ed. (Acc. Ld.)

RN—Round Nose; SPCL—Soft Point Core Lokt; SP—Soft Point.

FACTORY LOAD DATA

Bullet Wt. Grs.	Type	MV, (fps)	ME, (fpe)	Rifle/ Bbl. (in.)	Remarks
250	Norma SP	2800	4353	Custom/24	Speer No. 9 Data

SP—Soft Point.

COMPARATIVE DATA — MAGNUM MEDIUMS

Cartridge	Bullet Wt. Grs.	Muzzle	VELOCITY (fps) 100 yds.	200 yds.	300 yds.	Muzzle	ENERGY (fpe) 100 yds.	200 yds.	300 yds.	BULLET PATH* 100 yds.	200 yds.	300 yds.
308 Norma Mag.	180	3020	2798	2585	2382	3646	3130	2671	2268	+1.3	0	−6.1
300 Win. Mag.	180	2960	2745	2540	2344	3501	3011	2578	2196	+1.9	0	−7.3
8mm Rem. Mag.	220	2830	2581	2346	2123	3912	3254	2688	2201	+2.2	0	−8.5
338 Win. Mag.	250	2660	2395	2145	1910	3927	3184	2554	2025	+2.6	0	−10.2
340 Wby. Mag.	250	2850	2563	2296	2049	4510	3648	2927	2331	+1.8	0	−8.2
358 Norma Mag.	250	2800	2493	2231	2001	4322	3451	2764	2223	+2.0	0	−8.3
350 Rem. Mag.	200	2710	2410	2130	1870	3261	2579	2014	1553	+2.6	0	−10.3
375 H&H Mag.	270	2690	2420	2166	1928	4337	3510	2812	2228	+2.5	0	−10.0
378 Wby. Mag.	270	3180	2840	2515	2220	6064	4837	3793	2955	+1.5	0	−7.3

*Bullet path based on 200-yd. zero.

SPECIFICATIONS

Shell Holders
RCBS: 4
Bonanza: 2
Lyman: 13
Pacific: 5

Bullet Diameter
Jacketed: .358″

Lengths
Trim: 2.509″
Maximum Case: 2.519″
Maximum Overall: 3.275″

CAUTION:
Loads recommended and suggested herein have been carefully listed, but are intended solely as a guide to readers and neither the publisher nor author accept any responsibility for results of their use. **Maximum loads, listed in bold, should be reduced by 10 percent and worked up to cautiously.**

375 Winchester

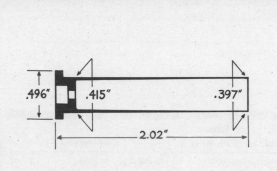

.496" .415" .397" 2.02"

"The 375 is a nice cartridge, easy to load for with no annoying quirks. While I've never fired one that was notably accurate, the accuracy level displayed has been co-incident with that required for deer-sized animals at reasonable ranges."

I'D BEEN propped against a thick pine tree for over an hour. The evening light was dwindling rapidly; I was cold, becoming impatient. Abruptly, a shotgun blast shredded the stillness. Buckshot pellets thwacked into the trees behind me, showering bark and sappy wood chips on the ground. The sodden *BOOM!* of another shot, followed by the angry slap of heavy pellets striking wood. Another. I hunkered more firmly against my protective tree, cocked my head toward the sounds. A heavy animal was coming toward me, rapidly, rattling the leaves, tugging at my nerves.

I eased away from the tree trunk, settled on one knee, bit off my gloves, cocked the hammer of my rifle. And waited. Drawing nearer, *clump-clump!* My heart was doing the rumba inside my ribcage. A moving flash of brown snagged my eye. Still coming straight toward me. Raising my rifle, I peered dimly over the sights. Daylight was but a memory; the gray of twilight blurred the scene.

The deer ran into view. A buck. What a buck! His heavy antlers spread well past his funneled ears; his heaving belly looked as protuberant as a cow's. The next few seconds would eternally hang in my mind's eye just as they transpired, in slow motion, taking forever.

I snapped the gun to my shoulder, only it didn't seem to snap but to drag, heavy, like the anchor of a ponderous ship. The monster buck spotted the movement, but it was too late; I knew I had him. He was 40 feet away,

running directly at me, careening to meet my speeding bullet with his broad chest, my rifle coming into line, reaching for the trigger. . . . Incredibly, he stabbed the ground with both front legs, spraying pine needles, braking, then changed direction so rapidly I could not believe my eyes, switching full-tilt to his left, jumping, putting timber between us. My mind screamed *NO!* as I felt the rifle snug against my shoulder. I searched frantically for the sights, couldn't find them, then the stab of recoil, the orange flash, not hearing the shot, knowing I was *high!* My follow-up shot was merely a gesture of frustration.

My rifle that day was one of the first Winchester Big Bore 94 carbines to leave the factory. It was chambered for the spanking new 375 Winchester, topped with a Lyman receiver sight. I never hunted with it again.

Don't misunderstand; it was not the rifle's fault. It was mine. I'd made several errors, not the least of which was hunting with a peep sight under conditions of fading light. Nonetheless, I've not hunted with a 375 since that day more than 5 years ago.

The Big Bore 94 and the cartridge it housed were introduced during the fall of 1978 as a 1979 model. The gun was an upscaled version of the ubiquitous Model 94, with the addition of cut-checkered walnut, glossy metalwork, lengthened side panels on the receiver, assorted odds and ends. It was a nice rifle, but the *cartridge* drew the most attention.

Winchester's Big Bore 94 lever-action was designed specifically for the deer hunter. It's a short, handy rifle well suited for close, brushy quarters.

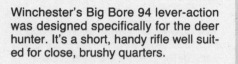

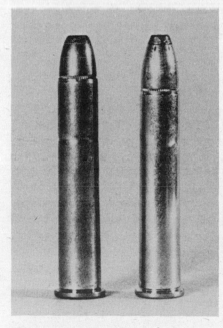

(Left) The 375 Winchester, at right, is shown with its granddaddy, the 38-55 (left). Note that the overall lengths are similar, but the 375 has a shorter case. It is also loaded to much higher chamber pressures.

Winchester's Model 94 Big Bore 375 has distinctive side panels at the rear of the receiver. These panels provide the strength necessary to handle the 375 Winchester.

Resembling the 38-55 Winchester, an ancient Ballard creation, the 375 Winchester evoked memories of high-button shoes and celluloid collars. The 38-55 was first chambered in the Ballard Perfection Number 4 single shot rifle in 1884. Marlin followed suit with the Model 93; Remington tooled up a batch of Remington-Lee turnbolts as well as a modicum of single shots; Colt catalogued the Lightning slide-action for the round; Stevens and Winchester each put one in their single shot lineup. The 38-55 earned quite a reputation as a target cartridge. Phil Sharpe wrote of the 38-55: "It set a great many records for accuracy which would make some of our modern match rifles blush with shame."

Unfortunately, the 375 has not followed in its progenitor's footsteps where accuracy is concerned. The most precise 375 I've fired, out of three, was that first Big Bore 94. With its favorite recipe, it grouped 3.11 inches for three, five-shot strings at 100 yards with iron sights. The bridesmaid load averaged 3.27 inches. Nope, no records there.

Actually, the 375 and the 38-55 are not so similar as it first appears. The 38-55 uses a bullet of from .377- to

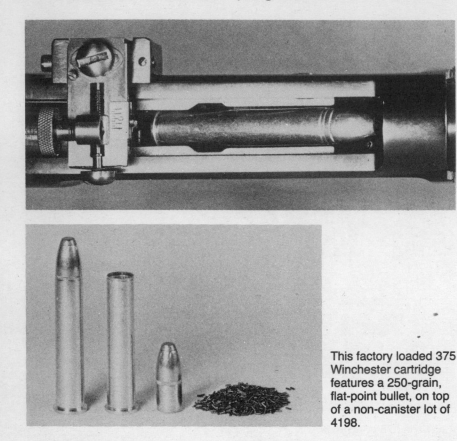

(Left) As you can see, there's little room left over; the Model 94 Big Bore action is *just* long enough to handle the 375.

This factory loaded 375 Winchester cartridge features a 250-grain, flat-point bullet, on top of a non-canister lot of 4198.

The 200-grain Winchester flat point (left) and the 250-grain Winchester flat point (right) are loaded commercially by that company and not available as a component. The 220-grain Hornady flat point is the bullet of choice for reloaders.

.378-inch diameter, depending on your source. The 375 takes a .375-inch slug. The Ballard cartridge sports a case cannelure; the 375 is bereft of such decoration. Although the loaded overall length is similar for each, the 375 boasts a shorter, stronger-headed case that is loaded to *much* higher pressures than is the 20th century holdover. Thus, the cartridges are not interchangeable. A 38-55 chamber will likely accept a 375 cartridge, but the high chamber pressures of the latter would preclude its firing by a sensible person. Conversely, while a 38-55 cartridge would probably fit into a 375-chambered gun, the longer case might jam into the throat, preventing easy release of the bullet upon firing. Couple that hazard with the oversized bullet of the 38-55 and disaster would be imminent.

The 375 is not simply a modified 30-30 case, either. Its head is much stronger than the 30-caliber. It would be foolhardy to use *any* other brass for full-power handloads in the 375 Winchester. Reduced-level handloads might be permissible in blown-out 30-30 cases, but I'm not certain; I haven't tried it. Better stick with brass headstamped ".375 Winchester" to be on the safe side.

Factory ballistics for the 375 are as follows: a 200-grain soft point at a quoted 2200 fps; a 250-grain soft point at 1900 fps. My own tests of my sample Big Bore 94 showed 2110 fps with one lot of 200-grain ammo, 2126 fps with another. The only batch of 250-grain ammo I clocked gave 1855 fps. Considering that the fac-

tory numbers are taken in 24-inch test barrels, my results from a 20-inch barreled carbine aren't bad.

Energy figures run in the 2000 to 2150 fpe range, at least in the published data. Actual numbers are more like 1900 to 2000 fpe. Factory data for the 35 Remington with a 200-grain bullet shows 1920 fpe; the 30-30 carries from 1830 to 1900 fpe or so; the 444 Marlin makes 2940 fpe in factory lists.

Move out to 200 yards and things change a mite. The 375 still totes between 1030 and 1210 fpe, the 30-30 about 940 to 990 fpe, the 35 Remington yields 840 fpe, the 444 only 1010 fpe. Therefore, using factory figures, the 375 shades 'em all. Actually chronographed, the relationship remains about the same.

Trajectory-wise, the 375 beats the 35 Remington and 444 but is less horizontal than the 30-30. Dropping 4.3 inches at 200 yards with the 150-grain load, and 4.8 inches with the 170-grain slug, the 30-30 is the flattest "deer" cartridge extant. The 35 Remington plunges 6.3 inches at the same distance, the 375 a bit less at 5.2 inches with the 200-grain load, and the 444 Marlin dips 5.6 inches. All the foregoing assume a 150-yard zero and sights .9-inch above the boreline.

Handloading

Handloading shifts the positions. The 35 Remington can be goosed up to around 2200 fps with either 33.0 grains of Hercules ReLoder 7 or 37.0 grains of IMR

The 220-grain Hornady flat point is the only *commonly* available component bullet available for the 375 Winchester.

A Lyman receiver sight was used in the author's accuracy test of the 375 Winchester. This Big Bore 94 groups 3⅛ inches at 100 yards with its best handload.

One of the best powders in the 375 Winchester is IMR 4198; 32.0 grains of that propellant clocked 2045 fps in a Winchester Model 94.

3031 under the 200-grain Hornady round nose. Two-hundred-yard retained energy becomes 982 fpe and drop a mere 5.2 inches. Better, but still not good enough. Top handloads in the 375 show 1212 fpe at 200, with a drop of 5.1 inches. The 444 takes the energy sweepstakes at 1260 fpe, but the drop numbers improve little, gaining only .10-inch. Thus, the 35 Remington gains much from handloading, both in energy and trajectory, while both the 375 and 444 show increased punch but little change in trajectory.

Being a straight-walled case, the 375 requires a three-die set for reloading. The proper shell holder is that for the 30-30. Currently, there is only one readily-available bullet for handloading. Let me tell about the bullet.

Shortly after the 375 Winchester's introduction, Olin went out of the component-bullet business. The other 375-caliber bullets on the market were designed for the big magnums, such as the 375 Holland & Holland and the 378 Weatherby. That left an unfortunate state of affairs: no suitable bullets for the reloader. I phoned Speer, Sierra, and Nosler to inquire. None expressed even the slightest interest in building a 375 slug for handloaders.

That left only Steve Hornady. Before calling Steve, I sat down and mulled over the situation, trying to decide just what kind of bullet was needed. The 200-grain Hornady round-nose 35-caliber bullet has achieved one helluva reputation over the years, not only in the 35 Remington, but in the 358 Winchester and the wildcat 35 Whelen as well. Seemed like that was a good place to start. I ascertained the sectional density of the 35-caliber bullet, did a few calculations, arrived at the conclusion that it would take a 220-grain 375 bullet to duplicate the sectional density and businesslike profile of the smaller caliber. I called Steve. We discussed the idea; he wasn't adverse to it. Told me he'd be in touch. A few days later he informed me that the specs had been okayed by his dad and other members of the Hornady research team. The only change was that they had decided on a flat-pointed bullet instead of a round nose.

At the 1979 NRA show in San Antonio, Steve told me, "We have only two bullets in our lineup designed by gun writers, the 140-grain 270 designed by Jon Sundra and the 220-grain 375 slug of yours. If either fails to sell, I'll know who to blame." Actually, the design was purely Hornady's. Only the idea and choice of bullet weight were mine.

The first lots of Winchester factory 375 ammunition were loaded with a non-canister lot of IMR 4198. (I haven't checked any lately.) My preference in propellants is ReLoder 7 for high velocity, and Norma 200 for accuracy. Du Pont 3031 did poorly, grouping large and moving the bullet slowly. IMR 4198 wasn't bad; it grouped under 4 inches and was the second fastest handload tried.

My pet load is 38.0 grains of ReLoder 7 with the 220-grain Hornady, for 2107 fps and 2169 fpe. Thirty-six grains of Norma 200 is most accurate at 3.11 inches, and clocks 2013 fps.

When loading the 375, I use standard-force primers. Magnum caps aren't necessary, but a heavy crimp is, not only for consistent ignition but to prevent the bullets from being moved by magazine spring pressure. A long drop tube is a necessity; even then most charges are compressed.

In my Big Bore 94, handloads were held to a loaded overall length of 2.56 inches with the Hornady bullet. A .002-inch increase over the 2.56 froze the action up tight as the cartridges tried to feed up out of the magazine and jammed their noses against the frame.

During its 5 years of existence, the 375 Winchester has been available in several rifles other than the Winchester Big Bore 94. Savage chambered it in the Model 99; Marlin offered it in the 336 series and still catalogues it in the 336-CS; Ruger ran a bunch of Number 3 single shots for the cartridge. That is a pretty eclectic selection.

The 375 is a nice cartridge, easy to load for with no annoying quirks. While I've never fired one that was notably accurate, the accuracy level displayed has been coincident with that required for deer-sized animals at reasonable ranges. It's no barnstormer, just a good, reliable load in the power range of the 30-30 and 35 Remington that offers heavier bullets of larger diameter for those hunters who view such to be important. Handicapping it are a limited range of suitable powders, only one brand of factory ammunition, and only one component bullet. None of that matters much. Brass is not really hard to find; ReLoder 7 is available and will do all that is needed; and the 220-grain Hornady is an excellent bullet. Not uncommonly versatile for the experimental handloader, the 375 is nonetheless competent at its intended purpose, killing whitetail deer. If you can hit one.

Groups at 100 yards with the Big Bore 94 375 were often spoiled by flyers such as these seen here; the bottom four shots are tight for a lever-action. Group size: 6.73 inches.

375 Winchester

HANDLOAD DATA

Bullet Wt. Grs.	Type	Powder Wt. Grs.	Type	Primer	Case	MV, (fps)	ME, (fpe)	Rifle/ Bbl. (in.)	Remarks
220	Hrndy. FP	32.0	IMR 4198	Fed. 210	Win.	2045	2043	Winchester M94/20	Accurate and fast
220	Hrndy. FP	**36.0**	N200	CCI 200	Win.	**2013**	**1969**	Winchester M94/20	Most accurate load
220	Hrndy. FP	**38.0**	Rel. 7	CCI 200	Win.	**2107**	**2169**	Winchester M94/20	Most powerful load; acc.

FACTORY LOAD DATA

Bullet Wt. Grs.	Type	MV, (fps)	ME, (fpe)	Rifle/ Bbl. (in.)	Remarks
200	Win. FP	2126	2008	Win. M94/20	Accuracy only fair
250	Win. FP	1855	1910	Win. M94/20	Good accuracy

FP—Flat Point.

SPECIFICATIONS

Shell Holders
RCBS: 2
Bonanza: 4
Lyman: 6
Pacific: 2

Bullet Diameter
Jacketed: .375"

Lengths
Trim: 2.010"
Maximum Case: 2.020"
Maximum Overall: 2.560"

The 375 Winchester was designed primarily as a brush-country deer cartridge. Combined with the Winchester Big Bore 94, the 375 is a good choice in cramped quarters.

375 H & H Magnum

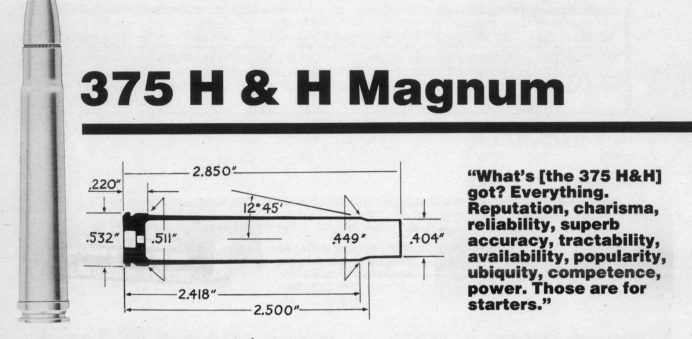

.220" 2.850"

.532" .511" 12°45' .449" .404"

2.418" 2.500"

"What's [the 375 H&H] got? Everything. Reputation, charisma, reliability, superb accuracy, tractability, availability, popularity, ubiquity, competence, power. Those are for starters."

"THE WORLD'S most useful cartridge is no ultra-modern super-duper fresh from the ballistic designer's drawing board, written up by swooning gun editors and ballyhooed with four-color ads. Instead, it is as cartridges go an old-timer born over a half century ago in a cluttered low-pressure shop in London's West End. The cartridge is the famous 375 Magnum."

That opening was lifted intact from Jack O'Conner's memorable tome, *The Hunting Rifle*, where it served to introduce the chapter entitled, "The Wonderful .375 Magnum." I used it here because it is probably the best exordium I have ever read. Since there was no chance of improving on it, I purloined it. Read it again; it's marvelous.

In 1912, the staid firm of Holland & Holland, at the time 77 years old, sprang on the hunting scene the cartridge known variously as the 375 Belted Rimless Nitro Express, 375 Holland & Holland Magnum, 375 H&H Magnum, or simply the 375 H&H. To say that it went on to fame and fortune would be an unforgivable understatement. It has become *the* world-wide, all-purpose cartridge. It has no competitor for the title. Not the 338 Winchester Magnum, not the 340 or 378 Weatherby Magnums, not the 416 Rigby, especially not such outdated and unpopular numbers as the 358 Norma Magnum and the 375 Weatherby. None. The 375 H&H is *king!*

Why? What's it got? Everything. Reputation, charisma, reliability, superb accuracy, tractability, availability, popularity, ubiquity, competence, power. Those are for starters.

Back to England. Holland & Holland, for all their British conservatism, has long been a bold pioneer in the field of cartridge development. It sired, for example, the 275 Holland & Holland—the first belted 7mm Magnum—which kicked along a 175-grain bullet at close to 2700 fps, about what some lots of 7mm Remington Magnum factory ammo give today. Then there was the 240 Apex, a hot 6mm that pushed a 100-grain slug to a claimed 3000 fps long before the 243 Winchester or 6mm Remington were ever dreamed of. Holland of course fathered the 300 Holland & Holland Magnum—called the Super 30 over there—which went on to win at Wimbledon, although in the hands of an American. The renowned 465 Nitro Express, slayer of more elephants than the greediest ivory hunter ever imagined, was a Holland invention. Their most recent hotshot, I believe, is the 244 Magnum, which does its best to drive a 100-grain projectile to 3500 fps.

Of course, the most heralded of the Holland creations is the good old 375. It can and has been used on game from the tiny African dik-dik through the mightiest pachyderm. And such diversity doesn't necessitate much of a compromise in either instance, merely a change in bullet type and weight. According to those who have used the 375 enough to know it, the big car-

(Left, right and below) All of these propellants are well suited for use in the 375 H&H: IMR 4320, IMR 4895 and IMR 3031.

tridge is a one-shot killer on African lion and Indian tiger. And those cats are not only tenacious of life, but are quick to take umbrage if they are plinked with a marginal caliber or in a non-vital spot.

African hunter Finn Aagaard initiated his 375 on a pair of cattle-killing lions. Said felines were at the time engaged in polishing off the remains of an elephant, feeding at night. Aagaard and a couple of cronies slipped to within 30 yards of the smelly carcass and commenced a vigil. Directly, sounds of supper came from the rotting bull; the tracker switched on a flashlight, illuminating a large lion atop the elephant jerking at the tender meat behind an ear. Startled by the light, *simba* evaporated without giving Finn time to shoot. Off went the light and up went the blood pressure.

Presently, the sounds of soft padding circled the trio,

evidence that the lion was investigating the course of its discomfiture. The air grew uncommonly tense. The hunters remained still; with the lion so close, things could become lively right sudden.

Directly the lion moved away, back toward its odoriferous delicatessen to renew its refection. After about 10 minutes of crunching and thumping, on flicked the light. This time the big cat stood its ground; so did a second one. Aagaard centered the first lion in his scope and touched off. Old Leo abandoned the carcass with much coughing and grunting, doubtless miffed at this second and more painful interruption of its repast. After a discreet wait, during which the growling and muttering tapered off, our threesome advanced on the elephant with the tracker oscillating the light in search of the second lion.

And there it was! Sneaking back to the elephant. As it slunk between two trees, Finn let it have a slug in the chest, whereupon it abandoned the field. From the bushes emanated no groans of remorse, no angry growling, no nothing. A once-over with the torch revealed foliage, shadows, and a partially decomposed elephant. Quoting Finn: "To have gone stumbling around in the dark looking for possibly wounded and angry lions with a fading flashlight would have been more than a little stupid, it might have been terminal."

They went for the Land Rover.

Both lions were later found dead, lying within 20 feet of each other. Good medicine, the 375.

Alaskan brown bear guides also think highly of the 375. So do many stateside hunters. Jack O'Conner took both of his brownies with a 375. The first one he had to tackle alone because the tide was going out and his guide had to stay with the skiff.

Jack waded ashore to set up an ambush. He stalked the bear to within 250 yards and suddenly found no vestige of cover between himself and yon bruin. Lying down in the muck—it was raining—Jack slithered into a tight sling, placing his left hand hard against the front sling swivel of his old 375 Model 70.

Jack wiggled around a bit, waited for the bear to turn broadside, then let the big fellow have one in the shoulder. At the shot, the bear dropped, both shoulders kibbled by the heavy Silvertip slug. Despite such a devastating wound, the brown was trying to regain his feet, so Jack poured in two more. That was the ballgame. Wrote Jack: "Old Betsy, my beat-up 375, had become one of the few rifles in the world that had taken all the three great predators—African lion, Indian tiger, and Alaskan brown bear."

Jack paced off the distance and came up with 290 yards. He said that he doubted the bear was that far, more like 250 or 260 yards. Long range for a big bruiser like the 375.

Nor is the 375 overmatched on game as large as gaur or Cape buffalo. In the January, 1984, *American Rifleman,* Finn Aagaard had this to say:

> . . . there exists some controversy concerning [the 375's] use on elephant and buffalo. My own experience is that, given suitable bullets, it kills buffalo about as quickly as anything in the 450 to 500 Nitro Express

class, particularly as the majority of hunters are apt to place their shots better with it than with a "heavy."

Finn went on to discuss the various bullets he had used on buff. He wrote of using a soft point bullet for the first shot, then backing it up with "solids" in the magazine. He abandoned this idea:

> . . . after I had three different soft-points blow up in buffalo shoulder joints or on the upper leg bone, and fail to penetrate, I quit doing that. Since then I have never used anything but solid bullets on buffalo, which is fine except that one must take care not to wound a second animal, as they will go through on broadside shots as often as not.

My good friend, Claude Chauvigné, a transplanted Frenchman who spent many years in Africa after the war, disagrees with Aagaard on the subject of soft point ammunition on Cape buffalo. Claude used a 375 to take many buffs, borrowing the rifle from a missionary who didn't get as much opportunity to hunt as he would have liked. Of the bulls Claude slew with the 375, all were taken with soft points. Monsieur Chauvigné always tried for a brain or spine shot; he never complained of poor bullet performance. Of course Claude used the 375 on comparatively few buffalo. His favorite rifle was an 8mm Mauser (called the 7.92 at that time and place). He used the little 8mm for most African game, including I believe, rhino as well as *m'bogo*. Small man, great heart, Claude Chauvigné.

How about American big game? Surely, aside from an occasional foray after the likes of brown or polar bear, the 375 is not needed on this continent. Right. In the above mentioned article, Aagaard had this to say, ". . . we probably do not *need* anything more powerful than a 30-06, while cartridges such as the 338, 8mm Rem. Mag. or 300 Magnums are undoubtedly ample for anything we have on this side of the pond."

Furthermore, he wrote:

> Under normal conditions, with chest shots from reasonably fair angles and decent ranges, I have never been able to ascertain that the 375 Mag. killed game of this class [African plains game such as zebra, antelope, etc.] any better than lesser cartridges such as the 30-06.
>
> I well remember shooting a 150-lb. impala solidly through the lungs with a 270-gr. soft-point only to have it run 90 paces before dropping. Actually, I believe the 270 Win. with 130-gr. bullets, for one, will give a higher percentage of spectacularly sudden kills on animals of up to about 350 lbs. in weight.

Jack O'Conner opined in *The Hunting Rifle:*

> As much as I love the 375, I must admit that in the United States the big-game hunter can get along very nicely without one. The big magnum will kill deer very neatly, of course, but no better than many smaller cali-

bers. With elk one is beginning to get into 375 territory. This is not to say that lighter cartridges like the 30-06, 280, 308 and 270 aren't adequate for elk. They are—with well-placed shots. Even the 375, or for that matter a cannon like the 465, is not adequate with poorly placed shots.

Jack went on to say that despite the adequacy of the 30-06 and similar cartridges, he felt that an elk was likely to make fewer tracks after being hit with a 375, assuming good placement with each. Perhaps. Many years ago, I read of a very tightly controlled test wherein an oversized herd of wapiti was pruned by a game warden. He used both a 30-06 with 180-grain bullets and a 375 (I can't recall which slug in the magnum). Careful shot placement was undertaken, and a detailed record of reaction to the shot, distance traveled, destructiveness of the bullet, and similar germane aspects was kept. Somewhere around 20 elk were taken with each cartridge unless my memory fails me. As I recall, animals shot with the 30-06 covered 50 or 60 additional yards than the elk busted with the 375.

O'Conner was also of the opinion that the 375 was

ly where intended, entering just behind the foreleg, taking the top off the heart and punching a hole in the lungs you could stick your head in, and what was left of it was lodged against the ribs on the far side.

Did that bull moose make many tracks before passing away? Would he have made *six* trips to the dam and back instead of three if he'd been poked with a 308 or 7x57? What do you think? I'm inclined to doubt it.

Let's leave the question of killing power. If ever a cartridge used on North American game had aplenty, it is the 375 H&H. Let's take a look at *measurable* power. According to Remington's ballistics sheet, the 375 offers a 270-grain soft point at a quoted 2690 fps for 4337 fpe of muzzle whump. A 300-grain slug gets 2530 fps and 4263 fpe. Winchester's data mirror these numbers, although Olin offers the 300-weight in both Silvertip Expanding and full-jacketed form.

Will the average 375 actually meet these figures? Well, my Interarms Alaskan came pretty close. Out of its 24-inch barrel the 270 Winchester Power-Point managed 2687 fps, only three shy of notices. The 300-grain Silvertip showed 2525 fps on the chronograph, just 5 fps

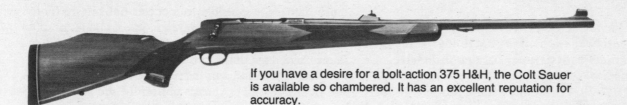

If you have a desire for a bolt-action 375 H&H, the Colt Sauer is available so chambered. It has an excellent reputation for accuracy.

unnecessary for moose, even the gigantic species of the northern Canada and Alaska. However, he believed that, as with elk, there would be fewer moose tracks from a 375-hit bull than one decked with a 30-06 or 270. I wonder.

In his book, *Game Loads and Practical Ballistics for the American Hunter,* Bob Hagel told this tale of a moose and the 375 H&H:

The bull [one of the smaller Shiras specimens] I decided to take was below me and about 175 yards away, belly-deep in a big beaver pond. I figured this load [a 285-grain Speer soft point at 2745 fps] should flatten the old boy . . . When he stepped up on the edge of the beaver dam, his big nose hanging over, I held for his heart and touched it off. That bull didn't do more than shudder a little, and slowly backed out into the middle of that big ice-covered mud pie. I was sitting down with a beautiful rest over a log and knew within an inch of where that bullet had landed, so there was nothing to do but wait and pray that he'd come out of the drink before he collapsed. He made three trips backing to the center of the pond and back to the dam before he finally realized he was dead, and expired with his head hanging over the dam . . . The 285 gr. 375 bullet had gone exact-

on the short side. That is very close indeed, and most unusual for a magnum, the makers of which generally tend toward optimism in published charts.

The 375 is renowned as an all-around load not only because of its prodigious punch, but because it shoots quite flat in the bargain. Zero your 375 at 200 yards, load up some 270-grain pointed factory loads, and you're ready for anything within 30-06/180-grain range. The 250-yard drop is only 3.9 inches, and the plunge is a mere 10 inches out at 300 yards. The 180-grain Winchester Power-Point drops only .7-inch less at 300 yards when fired from a 30-06. It's hard to imagine a stretched-string trajectory from such a bruiser isn't it?

As I'm sure you realize by now, I am no fan of recoil. I'm nonetheless going to skip over the problem of kick as it is associated with the 375. Why? First, the 375 is not advocated as an elk, moose, or grizzly cartridge by even its more ardent admirers, as we've seen earlier. Therefore, since its usefulness on this continent is limited, I see no reason to belabor the issue. The 375 kicks a lot. So what. Don't hunt with one here.

Secondly, since the 375 is generally considered the

minimum caliber on dangerous foreign game, it follows that whatever is deemed *adequate* will belt you much harder yet. Therefore, the 375 wins by default. No lesser load will see you through a touchy situation like a 375; anything more will boot you harder. Under those conditions, the 375's comeback at the buttplate is of little import.

The 375 H&H is famed for its accuracy. Jack O'Conner claimed that his 375 would put five 270-grain bullets and five 300-grain slugs into a common 100-yard group of about 2 inches. The two 375s I have fired—a Ruger Number 1 and the Interarms Alaskan mentioned earlier—would both print five-shot strings well under 2 inches with Winchester factory ammo of both bullet weights. (I don't know how they'd have done if I'd mixed the bullet weights like O'Conner did.)

The Number 1 preferred the 270-grain load, averaging 1.61 inches for several five-shot strings. Groups with the heavier load ran 1.83 for an average. My Alaskan liked the 300-grain Silvertip best, printing 1.69 inches for five, five-shot clusters. First rate accuracy, especially from a hard-kicker. (A heavy-recoiling rifle makes bag technique both more critical and tougher to handle consistently from shot to shot.)

Handloading

Many sources seem to think IMR 4064 is the only powder for the 375. My Lyman handbook disagrees. Of the four bullet weights they tested, two were most accurate with IMR 3031, and one each did best with IMR 4320 and IMR 4895. From the velocity standpoint, I doubt there's much to be gained by going to a powder slower than IMR 4350.

The Hornady book shows such slow burners as Norma 204 (about like IMR 4350 in burning rate) and Hodgdon H4831 as giving highest muzzle speeds with the 300-grain round nose. With the 270-grain spire point, even such relative quick-burners as IMR 3031 and H4895 equaled the speed of Winchester 760, the slowest number listed with that slug.

Sierra makes only the streamlined and heavy 300-grain soft point boat-tail. According to their data, IMR 4350 gets 2600 fps with a 78.7-grain maximum charge. No other propellant exceeds 2550 fps, and such disparate powders as IMR 4064 and Norma MRP both achieve that figure.

Speer's Number Ten manual shows H380 (a medium-slow burner) as getting the most speed from the 235-grain semi-spitzer, with the much quicker burning IMR 4064 just 15 fps off the pace. Moving up to the 285-grain Grand Slam, IMR 4350 triumphs as the velocity leader, getting a tidy 2756 fps from a maximum 84.0-grain dollop. What we find is that the 375 is pretty cosmopolitan about its powder selection. Unfinicky, the old H&H.

About bullets. Since the 375 is the kind of load you rely on when the going is tough and your adversaries are not only able but liable to either gore, chew, claw, puncture, or simply pummel you to death, you need good bullets on your team. Finn Aagaard and Rick Jamison do a lot of bullet testing, in both media and meat. So far as I know, neither fellow is acquainted with the other, but I've read of Finn's results, and Rick and I have spoked often of his. For the price of admission, here is the consensus: if you want to shoot something mean with a soft point, maybe negotiating a few heavy bones, buy the Speer Grand Slam. If you plan to do as much damage as possible to a critter unlikely to try to trample you in return, and intend to avoid bones of substance, and might possibly have to take a shot at long range, load up with the beautiful 300-grain Sierra boat-tail. The big Sierra gives the least penetration of all the soft point 375s, but expands uniformly and impressively. All the time. The tough Speer will dig from here to China, expand acceptably and uniformly. All the time. A bonus: if you need as much bone-breaking, meat-cleaving penetration as you can get, go to the 300-grain Hornady full-metal-jacket.

Jack O'Conner opened this treatise. Let's let him have the last word. ". . . the 375 . . . is primarily a rifle for thin-skinned game, dangerous and nondangerous. And for that stuff it has no rival. It is a big *high-velocity* rifle, a super 30/06, an ultra 270. With its heavy bullets, its flat trajectory, its high velocity, its enormous power, it is in a class by itself."

Ruger's No. 1 Tropical Rifle is available in 375 H&H. It comes with a 24-inch barrel and weighs 8¼ pounds.

375 Holland & Holland Magnum

HANDLOAD DATA

Bullet Wt. Grs. Type	Powder Wt. Grs. Type	Primer	Case	MV, (fps)	ME, (fpe)	Rifle/ Bbl. (in.)	Remarks
235 Speer SP	71.0 IMR 3031	Rem. 9½M	Win.	2849	4235	Win. M70/24	Lym. Hndbk., 46th Ed. (Acc. Ld.)
270 Rem. SP	66.5 IMR 3031	Rem. 9½M	Win.	2631	4149	Win. M70/24	Lym. Hndbk., 46th Ed. (Acc. Ld.)
285 Speer SP	70.5 IMR 4320	Rem. 9½M	Win.	2525	4034	Win. M70/24	Lym. Hndbk., 46th Ed. (Acc. Ld.)
300 Hrndy. RN	82.0 IMR 4350	Rem. 9½M	Win.	2617	4561	Win. M70/24	Lym. Hndbk., 46th Ed. (Acc. Ld.)

SP—Soft Point; RN—Round Nose.

FACTORY LOAD DATA

Bullet Wt. Grs. Type	MV, (fps)	ME, (fpe)	Rifle/ Bbl. (in.)	Remarks
270 Win. PP	2687	4328	Intrms. Alas./24	Accurate
300 Win. ST	2525	4245	Intrms. Alas./24	Very accurate

PP—Power Point; ST—Silvertip.

SPECIFICATIONS

Shell Holders
RCBS: 4
Bonanza: 2
Lyman: 13
Pacific: 5

Bullet Diameter
Jacketed: .375″

Lengths
Trim: 2.840″
Maximum Case: 2.850″
Maximum Overall: 3.600″

When it comes to thin-skinned dangerous game, the 375 Holland & Holland is hard to beat.

CAUTION:
Loads recommended and suggested herein have been carefully listed, but are intended solely as a guide to readers and neither the publisher nor author accept any responsibility for results of their use. **Maximum loads, listed in bold, should be reduced by 10 percent and worked up to cautiously.**

378 Weatherby Magnum

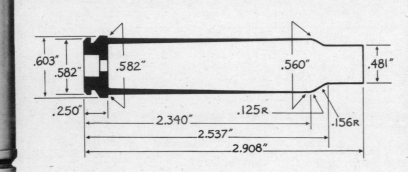

" . . . the 378 Weatherby is a big, powerful, hard-kicking, hungry, expensive 'sonuvagun.' . . . a cartridge that is tougher than anything on your block. Unless you live near a missile base."

IDAHO gun scribe Bob Hagel once penned an article in which he referred to the 378 Weatherby Magnum as, "The Magnum's Magnum." That's a fitting description of the big belted Weatherby, which dwarfs such potent shoulder-bruising numbers as the 300, 340, and the discontinued 375 Weatherby Magnums significantly.

The cavernous 378 case is 2.908 inches long. Standing alongside the burly 375 Holland & Holland, the 378 looks like a pro lineman compared to a high school quarterback. The shoulder of the 378 measures .560-inch, bigger than the 375 H&H mikes at the *belt!* The body diameter ahead of the belt is .582-inch, the belt goes .603-inch, and the rim reads .582-inch in diameter. Note that the rim is rebated, something to remember when you read that the 284 Winchester is the only American cartridge sporting such a feature.

The 378 is based on no other existing case, but is a Weatherby original. It was developed in 1953 or thereabouts by Roy Weatherby, who took one to Africa and made things tough on an elephant or two. I have read that the excellent Federal 215 magnum primer was developed for use in this cartridge; caps available at the time would not ignite the prodigious charges of slow-burning powders used in the 378. I don't doubt it; the big case digests powder in up to 119-grain gulps! Consider that the 375 H&H, itself no cartridge for the faint-hearted, takes only (only!) 87.0 grains of H4831 when filled to its mouth and packed down. (This is *not* a load.) An unfired 378 case will swallow 127 grains of the same powder before dribbling over its side. (Again, that is not a load but only an indication of case *capacity*.)

The 375 H&H can drive a 300-grain bullet at 2550 fps and a 270-grain slug at 2740 fps. Pretty impressive. The defunct 375 Weatherby Magnum, simply a blown-out 375 H&H, would add a couple hundred fps to that. Really impressive. The 378 Weatherby will kick 300-grain slugs out at 2900 fps; the little-bitty 270s in excess of 3100 fps. Awesome! These numbers are for hand-loads, of course.

What the foregoing means is that the 378 will blow 270-grain bullets out its spout faster than the 270 Winchester will move 130-grain slugs. That's *more* speed and more than *double* the bullet weight. Incredible.

Energy figures run in the 5600 to 6000 fpe range with the top reloads. The puny 458 Winchester Magnum shows a mere 5000 or so from most loads: the runty 375 H&H only 4300-4500 fpe. Pshaw! Milksops.

Reckon the 378 Weatherby kicks much? Knew a farmer once who used one on a chicken-stealing fox. Missed the fox. Hens wouldn't lay for a week, cows went off their feed, the old man himself couldn't hear anything ceptin' a train whistle for several days after. His shoulder healed up quick though, and directly he got the feeling back in his right hand.

Factory-quoted ballistics are 3180 fps for the 270-

Speer's 285-grain Grand Slam is a fine bullet for soft skinned dangerous game.

Naturally, Hodgdon's slow burning H4831 is an excellent choice for the 378 Weatherby. If you like your numbers "Large" try this load on for size: 118.0 grains of H4831 and a 270-grain bullet—see the chart if you don't believe it.

grain bullets, both soft point and partition, and 2925 fps with the 300-grainers. Hagel's test rifle, as mentioned in *Handloader* number 42, got 2803 fps from the 300-grain load.

According to Weatherby data, the 378 shows this trajectory with the 270-grain soft point: 1.5 inches high at 100 yards; zero at 200; 7.3 inches low at 300; 22.3 inches down at 400 yards. That's as flat as the 25-06 shooting 120-grain spitzers. Amazing.

So, assuming you can hit anything with a rifle that belts you like a leading heavyweight contender, it should certainly keel right over. Correct? Maybe.

Quoting from Hagel's article in the aforementioned *Handloader* magazine:

> . . . for whatever it's worth, I did clobber a pretty husky bull [moose] with it and a 270-grain Nosler that started on its way at 3,130 fps. The huge old bull was standing quartering to the gun at what proved to be 175 yards, and had no idea anyone was around. I laid the

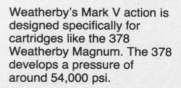

Weatherby's Mark V action is designed specifically for cartridges like the 378 Weatherby Magnum. The 378 develops a pressure of around 54,000 psi.

crosshair on the big shoulder joint and touched the 378 off. The slap of the bullet came back almost as loud as the rifle shot. The bull shuddered from the end of his big nose to the tip of his stubby tail, but he didn't even sag. [!] He just stood there as though he had suddenly frozen solid. I could see that the bullet had landed exactly where it should have gone, so there was no reason to give him another. It took that moose about the usual 1 minute and 53 seconds to discover he was dead, and he didn't know it then until he tried to take a step.

Hmmm. A lot of food for thought about cartridge effectiveness there. Hagel went on to say that the Nosler had pulverized the shoulder, gone on through the ribs and the top of the lungs, stopping somewhere in the paunch. Excellent bullet, perfect shot placement, a load giving nearly 5900 fpe at the muzzle from a bullet weighing 270 grains, and the moose stood around as if he were waiting for a bus. What would he have done with an identical hit from a 280 Remington firing a 175-grain Nosler at 2700 fps? The same thing?

Well anyway, you can see that the 378 Weatherby is a big, powerful, hard-kicking, hungry, expensive "sonuvagun." It dotes on massive doses of slow-burning powders, requires thick-jacketed bullets (lest they shred like confetti on impact with anything stouter than an emu). In return, you get a cartridge that is tougher than anything on your block. Unless you live near a missile base.

378 Weatherby Magnum

HANDLOAD DATA

Bullet Wt. Grs.	Type	Powder Wt. Grs.	Type	Primer	Case	MV, (fps)	,ME (fpe)	Rifle/ Bbl. (in.)	Remarks
270 Rem. SP		118.0 H4831		Fed. 215	Wby.	3086	5709	Wby. Mk. V/26	Lym. Hndbk., 46th Ed.
300 Hrndy. RN		103.0 IMR 4350		Fed. 215	Wby.	2832	5342	Wby. Mk. V/26	Lym. Hndbk., 46th Ed. (Acc. Ld.)
300 Hrndy. RN		112.0 H4831		Fed. 215	Wby.	2923	5690	Wby. Mk. V/26	Lym. Hndbk., 46th Ed.

SP—Soft Point; RN—Round Nose.

FACTORY LOAD DATA

Bullet Wt. Grs.	Type	MV, (fps)	ME, (fpe)	Rifle/ Bbl. (in.)	Remarks
270 Wby. SP		3180	6064	Wby. Mk. V/26	Wby. factory data
300 Wby. SP		2925	5700	Wby. Mk. V/26	Wby. factory data

SP—Soft Point.

SPECIFICATIONS

Shell Holders
RCBS: 14
Bonanza: 16
Lyman: 17
Pacific: 14

Bullet Diameter
Jacketed: .375"

Lengths
Trim: 2.898"
Maximum Case: 2.908"
Maximum Overall: 3.635"

CAUTION:
Loads recommended and suggested herein have been carefully listed, but are intended solely as a guide to readers and neither the publisher nor author accept any responsibility for results of their use.
Maximum loads, listed in bold, should be reduced by 10 percent and worked up to cautiously.

44 Remington Magnum

"The 44 Magnum is an acceptable rifle cartridge for specific tasks at moderate ranges. For game in deer-sized hides to 125 yards or so, it works well."

1.285"
.514"
.456"
.060"

I'VE BEEN intrigued by the 44 Remington Magnum since my adolescence. Goodness knows why; it's certainly no paragon as a rifle cartridge. Admittedly, it *is* one of the premier handgun rounds. In a six-gun it is incredibly accurate, as potent as any handgun cartridge needs to be, is easy to reload and amenable to many different powder/bullet combinations, is available in a satisfying array of revolvers—both single- and double-action, foreign and domestic—and at least three single shot pistols, and a plethora of factory-loaded ammunition is catalogued.

As a rifle cartridge, the ease of handloading and profusion of factory ammo remains a virtue, but the other assets begin to pale. Accuracy in every 44 carbine or rifle I've ever shot was so-so. The energy levels reached by the best of loads is only in the 30-30 class, which isn't little league but it's not 30-06 level either. To make matters worse, the selection of available long guns is underwhelming in scope.

Available Rifles

Let's look at what's around. The first shoulder arm that comes to mind is the Ruger 44 carbine, which used to wear the title "Deerstalker." Having been around since 1961 in various iterations, including a nifty and extremely rare Mannlicher-stocked version, the Ruger is the epitome of 44 rifles. Short, light, quick-handling and fast-shooting, the little Ruger is a fine gun for

woods hunting of deer-sized game.

Next most common, at least in my area, is the excellent Marlin Model 1894. It has a straight-grip stock, 20-inch barrel, tubular magazine, and a smooth-working lever-action. At one time, Marlin chambered the 44 Magnum in their Model 336 series. I once owned one. Accuracy was not too shabby for a levergun, but functioning was below par. Which, I suppose, is why we now have the resurrected Model 1894.

Winchester made a few Model 94s chambered to 44 Magnum, but these are now collector's items. In 1984, they added the 44 to the new lineup of Angle Eject 94 carbines, so you can again corral a Winchester without haunting gun shows and paying a collector's price.

Browning offers a modern rendition of the ancient Winchester 1892, cataloguing it as the B-92. The Browning has a lot going for it, but it has several serious drawbacks. The barrel bands are aluminum, which is inexcusable. The front sight not only is *not* drift-adjustable, it is not removable. It has no bead, thus is too small to pick up quickly for rapid shooting. The rear sight is an abominable semi-buckhorn; fortunately, it *is* replaceable. (Before you excuse the Browning's sights by saying that they duplicate the originals, which they don't exactly, the point is irrelevant. If perfect authenticity was desired, why did they opt for aluminum barrel bands?) In all other respects, the Browning is first rate. It is well-finished, amply accurate, and has the slickest

One of the most popular 44 Magnum carbines is Marlin's Model 1894S. Accuracy is usually quite good in this short-barreled carbine.

Ruger's Model 44 Carbine was the first rifle chambered for the 44 Magnum. It's light, fast and accurate.

action of the crop of 44 carbines.

Ruger makes up some Number 3 single shots chambered to 44 Magnum. For the untimorous handloader, this is the gun to choose. The stout action will digest heavier loads than are prudent in other action types currently available. Of course, that is not a carte blanche excuse for ladling immoderate portions of powder beneath your favorite bullet and stuffing the works into your Number 3. It merely suggests that if you are after top muzzle speeds from *responsible* handloads, the Ruger single shot is the proper vehicle.

Harrington & Richardson at one time listed the Topper single shot in 44 Magnum. That rifle, catalogue number 158, is currently shown as being chambered for the 22 Hornet and 30-30 only. The H & R Handy-Gun II, a nickel-finished single shot with both a rifle and shotgun tube included in the asking price, furnished with a dandy carrying case, is available in 44 Magnum. It has a straight-grip buttstock, an exposed hammer, and open sights on the rifle barrel. For hiking, camping, or fishing, it's a pretty good idea.

According to the latest *Gun Digest,* that's it for 44 Magnum long guns. It wasn't always so. In the late 1960s Remington offered their excellent Model 788—a bargain-basement, rear-locking, turnbolt—for the round. The bolt was fabricated in two pieces, with only the rear section rotating as you lifted the bolt knob, and boasted dual extractors like a 22 rimfire unless my memory fails me. I've owned two and wish I still had one. They made very few; those are now commanding exorbitant chunks of money.

Universal once assembled a pump-action carbine dubbed the Vulcan 440. It was sort of a beefed-up 30-Carbine action, modified to manual function of course, and utilized a nylon box-type magazine. The gun weighed around 6½ pounds, shot acceptably, and was reputed to function reliably. It did not, alas, overload Universal cash registers; it was dropped subsequent to the fall of 1968.

Except for some rechambered ordnance such as the Remington Model 14 pump, the Model 92 Winchester (which was particularly popular for this conversion), and the petite 310 Martini, that about covers it for the 44 Magnum as far as I can recollect.

Accuracy

Back to the question of accuracy. During the years I was most infatuated by the 44 Magnum as a rifle load, I tried several different guns. Included were the aforementioned Marlin 336 and a pair of Remington 788s, two or three Ruger semi-autos, and most recently a Marlin 1894. Since most of these guns were acquired and traded off without more than a perfunctory accuracy test, I'm not certain of the levels attained. My impression is that the Marlin 336 and the Rugers all grouped five-shot averages in the 3- to 4-inch range. As I recall, my 788s clustered their shots around 2½ inches.

The only rifle I have a target file on is the Marlin 1894. With its favorite load, 28.4 grains of Winchester 296 and the 200-grain Hornady hollow point, that little gun averaged 3.80 inches for six, five-shot strings. The best group was 2.44 inches; the worst went 5.63 inches. All groups were shot with open iron sights at 100 yards from benchrest. Interestingly, I fired two, five-shot strings offhand one afternoon that averaged tighter than the gun would group from the bench. The two strings went 2.93 and 4.03, for a 3½-inch average! (No, I can't hold that well consistently. My norm is about 6 inches with a gun that fits me and has a decent trigger.)

Another interesting fact about that Marlin is that the 3.80-inch average was obtained using the Winchester 7M111F magnum pistol primer. Switching to the Federal 150 standard-brisance cap opened the average to 4.40 inches for seven strings. It's not often a rifle is so primer-sensitive.

The runner-up load in that rifle was the fine Federal 240-grain jacketed hollow point factory number. It grouped 4.30 inches for three strings.

My experience has been that such accuracy levels as displayed by the 1894 Marlin are about par for most 44

Hercules 2400 is an old favorite with 44 Magnum shooters. It provides plenty of velocity.

Factory loads from left: Federal 180-grain hollow point; Norma 240-grain power cavity; Remington 240-grain hollow point; Remington 240-grain soft point; Remington 240-grain lead-gas-check. It's all but impossible to exceed factory load velocities with handloads because factory ammo is loaded to high pressures. (Photo courtesy Layne Simpson)

(Left) One of the best factory loads available in 44 Magnum is Federal's 240-grain hollow soft point. The author has found this ammo to be extremely accurate in most 44 Magnum rifles.

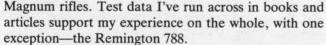

Magnum rifles. Test data I've run across in books and articles support my experience on the whole, with one exception—the Remington 788.

In the December, 1968 issue of *Gunfacts,* an excellent gun magazine that unfortunately failed to last, a gentleman by the name of Frank Marshall gave an account of his experiences with a 788 in 44 Magnum. Mr. Marshall's rifle proved capable of grouping 2 minutes-of-angle with the Remington 240-grain jacketed soft point, from the bench at 100 yards. Even the lead-bullet factory load stayed close to the 2-inch mark. Mr. Marshall's handload of 24.0 grains of Hercules 2400 (which is over handbook maximum, and *not recommended* but reprinted here for information only) under the 236-grain Norma jacketed hollow point did even better, printing *inside* the 2-inch 10 ring of a 100-yard smallbore target. One group is depicted actual size in the article; it measures just under 1½ inches for the five shots. I wish I could find a 44 that would shoot so well.

In the sixth edition of *Handloader's Digest,* a fellow by the name of Gene West tested a 788. He reported that most of his groups, from both handloads and factory fodder, were around 1½ inches. That would be pretty amazing, but certainly possible. But that's not all; he quoted ⅞-inch spreads from the jacketed Rem-

ington factory load! All shots in one ragged hole! He didn't say just how many groups were included in the average, but if true, that is the most accurate 44 Magnum I've encountered in years of reading and research. Of course, the Remington 788 is fully capable of that level of accuracy and better. I'm just not sure about the 44 Magnum cartridge. . . .

Ballistics

We've covered accuracy; let's discuss ballistics. Factory tables show the 240-grain jacketed loads as having a 1760 fps muzzle velocity, for 1650 fpe. Remington and Federal both make a 180-grain jacketed hollow point, but don't list it under "rifle loads." In my Marlin 1894, the Federal 180-grain gave 2146 fps at the muzzle, for 1840 fpe. On the other hand, the 240-grain Federal hollow point failed to live up to its advance notice, reaching only 1623 fps in the same 20-inch-barreled Marlin. Another Model 1894 showed 1761 fps and 1653 fpe with the Winchester 240-grain hollow soft point. An old lot of 180-grain Super Vel clocked a whopping 2331 fps in the Marlin, for 2172 fpe. Let's settle on about 2150-2200 fps as normal for 180-grain hollow points, and the factory-quoted 1760 fps as par for the 240-grain slugs.

The 30-30 Winchester is quoted at 2200 fps with a 170-grain factory load, for 1830 fpe. The 150-grain 30-30 gets credit for 2390 and 1900 fpe. In the real world, the 170-grain load will achieve only about 2100 fps in a 20-inch barreled carbine, much less with some loads. That's good for about 1665 fpe. The 150-grain loads show around 2250 fps and 1687 fpe.

As far as "woods" cartridges go, the 44 has a bit of competition. From left to right: 35 Remington; 375 Winchester; 44 Magnum; 444 Marlin; and the 45-70 Government.

The 35 Remington is listed at 2080 fps with the 200-grain soft point, for 1920 fpe. Actually chronographed, it will reach these figures in 22-inch barrels and get about 2000 fps in 20-inchers. The latter is good for about 1777 fpe.

From the foregoing, you can see that the 44 Magnum holds its own, as far as muzzle energy is concerned, with cartridges of the 30-30 class. All of them run from about 1650 to a maximum of 1880 fpe, with rare exceptions. Actually, the 180-grain 44 Magnum factory ammo leads the parade. At the muzzle.

Moving out to 100 yards stirs things up a mite. The hot 180-grain load has dropped off to about 1630 fps and 1062 fpe. The 240-grain hollow point retains 1380 fps, 1015 fpe. The 170-grain 30-30 carries about 1700 fps and 1091 fpe; the 150-grain load gets about 1750 fps for a little over 1000 fpe. Doing a bit better, the 200-grain 35-caliber shows around 1650 fps and 1209 fpe. The 44 is starting to wane. As the range increases, the smaller calibers rapidly outdistance the stubby 44 Magnum.

The above data were taken from the Hornady and Sierra loading manuals. Factory ballistics tables show a more marked superiority for the 30-30 and the 35, but the muzzle velocities shown are not attainable in 20-inch barrels as a rule.

Trajectory considerations rule against the 44 Mag.'s use as much or more than potency numbers. Zeroed at 100 yards, the 240-grain hollow point factory load is down more than 6 inches at 150 yards, assuming the use of a scope sight. The 30-30 170-grain load starting at 2100 fps drops only 3.9 inches at 150 yards from a 100-yard zero, and the 150-grainer dips about 3½ inches when kicked along at close to 2300 fps. A 200-grain Hornady round nose pushed to 2000 fps from a 35 Remington plunges a mere 4.0 inches at the 150-yard mark. As you can see, the 44 Magnum is a decided third best.

The 44 as a Hunting Round

Despite such dry statistics, the 44-caliber carbine is a serious hunting tool out to 125 yards or so, perhaps 150 in experienced hands. Bailey Simpson, father of well-known gun scribe Layne Simpson, used a Ruger 44 carbine to take a half-dozen deer. Most if not all of his shots were under 60 yards, and he seldom had to trail a buck very far. The one deer that managed to cover several hundred yards after being hit left a blood trail a drunk man could have followed. In fact, one endearing trait of the 44 Magnum is its ability to bore on through deer to leave a gaping hole in the offside to drain off blood.

Keith Campbell, an acquaintance of Layne's, has slain perhaps 25 deer with a Ruger carbine. Campbell has nearly worn out his rifle, knows it intimately, and keeps the trajectory in his head like a computer. He has taken deer out to 150-175 yards, and as far as I know, has never had one get away.

John Leigh is a professional bear hunter. John uses dogs—very expensive dogs—to hunt bear, and he had taken around 100 the last I heard. The rifle he used for about half of them was a Marlin 1894 that has had the barrel cut back to make it handier in a scrap. Some time ago, Layne gave John a mess of Remington 240-grain semi-jacketed hollow point factory ammo to try. John has used that load ever since, claims it drops bear as if they swallowed a hand grenade. To John, the most important aspect of the Remington load, aside from its adroitness at decking an irate bruin, is its tendency to *stay inside* a bear rather than zipping on out the offside to wound a dog.

Which brings up the question of a specific bullet for use on big game. For smallish Southern whitetail, I'd opt for the 180-grain Sierra, the 200-grain Speer, or the 200-grain Hornady hollow points. Kicked along at 2000 fps and up, these three bullets will usually expand on relatively light resistance. As noted, the 240-grain Remington semi-jacketed hollow point will, as Layne Simpson puts it, "expand on a marshmallow." Unfortunately, they are no longer available as a component bullet. No matter; Remington gets pretty good velocity out of them in factory-loaded guise.

For game requiring deeper penetration, like wild boar and monster bucks, the 240-grain soft points are okay. Perhaps best is the 265-grain Hornady flat point. Its increased sectional density should aid penetration when you need it. Like when a mean old Russian boar is bearing down on you, aimin' to slit your hide from ankle to Adam's apple. Or when a whitetail buck is thumbing his tail at you as he bounces off through the scrub oaks.

My choice of powder is Winchester 296, first, second, and third. However, Hodgdon H110 is so similar it can usually be substituted charge for charge. Either requires a magnum pistol primer or hot rifle cap and a very tight crimp. I decant 24.0 grains of 296, then stuff atop it a 240-grain Sierra hollow cavity for a very accurate load, giving about the same muzzle speed as factory-loaded 240-grain ammo. The load my Marlin prefers, 28.4 grains of 296 and the 200-grain Hornady, gets 2008 fps for 1791 fpe.

Hercules 2400 is a traditional propellant for use in the 44 Magnum. A maximum 23.0-grain dose of 2400 pumps a 240-grain slug to about the same speed as the above-listed 296 load, roughly 1750-1780 fps in 20 inches of barrel. IMR 4227 at a maximum 25.0-grain level gets excellent accuracy and comparable speed. Variations on any of these recipes may work well in your rifle. For my use, I'll stick with the two loads utiliz-

ing Winchester 296 and be content with the performance those loads provide.

The 44 Magnum is an acceptable rifle cartridge for specific tasks at moderate ranges. For game in deer-sized hides to 125 yards or so, it works well. For black bear and other evil-tempered critters in the same weight class, I'd shorten the range by half and have no qualms. On close-in javelina and coyotes, I doubt you'll find a better outfit than a quick-handling repeater chambered to 44 Magnum. A side benefit is that the little carbine makes a dandy household defense gun, especially one of the large-capacity leverguns. No, the rifle/cartridge combination is no all-rounder, but a highly specialized rig. But the fact that a brain surgeon is not a general practitioner makes him no less competent. The 44 Mag.'ll do.

44 Remington Magnum

HANDLOAD DATA

Bullet Wt. Grs. Type	Powder Wt. Grs. Type	Primer	Case	MV (fps)	ME (fpe)	Rifle/ Bbl. (in.)	Remarks
200 Hrndy. JHP	28.0 Win. 296	7M111F	Fed.	1983	1747	Mar. 1894/20	Accurate
200 Hrndy. JHP	28.4 Win. 296	7M111F	Fed.	2008	1791	Mar. 1894/20	Note charge increase
200 Hrndy. JHP	28.4 Win. 296	Fed. 150	Fed.	2020	1812	Mar. 1894/20	Note primer change
240 Sierra JHC	24.0 Win. 296	7M111F	Fed.	1740	1613	Mar. 1894/20	Accurate
240 Sierra JHC	24.0 Win. 296	CCI 350	Rem.	1772	1674	Mar. 1894/20	Note primer/ case change

JHP—Jacketed Hollow Point; JHC—Jacketed Hollow Cavity.

FACTORY LOAD DATA

Bullet Wt. Grs. Type	MV (fps)	ME (fpe)	Rifle/ Bbl. (in.)	Remarks
180 Fed. JHP	2146	1840	Mar. 1894/20	Good velocity
180 Super-Vel. JHP	2331	2172	Mar. 1894/20	Incredibly fast
200 Hrndy. JHP	1620	1164	Mar. 1894/20	Accurate
240 Fed. JHP	1623	1402	Mar. 1894/20	Very accurate
240 Fed. JHP	1637	1428	Rug. Carb./18½	Fair accuracy
240 Win. JHP	1761	1653	Mar. 1894/20	Good velocity

JHP—Jacketed Hollow Point.

SPECIFICATIONS

Shell Holders
RCBS: 18
Bonanza: 9
Lyman: 7
Pacific: 30

Bullet Diameter
Jacketed: .429″ to .430″
Lengths
Trim: 1.275″
Maximum Case: 1.285″
Maximum Overall: 1.610″

CAUTION:
Loads recommended and suggested herein have been carefully listed, but are intended solely as a guide to readers and neither the publisher nor author accept any responsibility for results of their use.
Maximum loads, listed in bold, should be reduced by 10 percent and worked up to cautiously.

444 Marlin

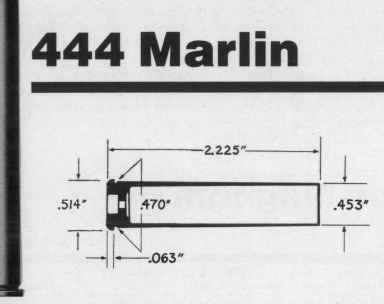

2.225"

.514" .470" .453"

.063"

"Aside from the fact that a properly-directed 444 will deck a deer or black bear like lightning, and perform tolerably on elk . . . the thing about it that impresses me most is its accuracy."

ACCORDING to Barnes' *Cartridges of the World,* the 444 Marlin was introduced in June of 1964, although it took some months for guns and ammo to appear on dealers' shelves. The 444 cartridge was nothing more or less than an elongated 44 Remington Magnum, using a similar rimmed case of about 1 inch greater length, and pushing the exact same 240-grain jacketed bullet as loaded in the 44 Mag. but at a 550 fps increase in muzzle speed. The primary criticism aimed at the 444 was the use of the light-jacketed revolver bullet; it was said to come apart on any serious resistance. Reams of prose were devoted to the subject of bullets for the big 444, with every gun writer stumping for a pet weight or nose design. Meanwhile, the 444 went merrily on its way.

Original factory ballistics for the 444 were a 240-grainer at 2400 fps, for 3069 fpe. That was a pretty potent package for a levergun. Those early Marlins were graced with a 24-inch barrel; frequently they would indeed achieve factory-quoted ballistics. The *Speer Reloading Manual Number Nine* shows their test gun as reaching 2442 fps from a typical Marlin rifle. The 45th edition of Lyman's handbook shows that the lot and rifle they tested managed 2415 fps. It seems that the good old 444 is one cartridge that can be relied on to produce as advertised.

Currently, the 240-grain load is listed at 2350 fps. Why, you ask, did they lower the numbers if the factory ammo was having no trouble achieving them. The an-

swer is that Marlin cut their barrel length back to 22 inches in response to the pleas of woods hunters who, rightly, consider 24 inches a bit much, especially on a rifle meant for timber hunting. Lose a couple inches of barrel, you lose a few fps. In this case, about 50. Some years ago, Remington added a 265-grain bullet (made for them by Hornady, I believe) to the 444's meager lineup of bullet availability. The heavier bullet is catalogued at 2120 fps for 2644 fpe. Since the 240-grain shows an energy of 2942 fpe, even at its reduced muzzle speed, I'd rather have the lighter slug for use on deer. Of course, the 265-grain bullet has caught up to the light slug in energy by the time each passes 100 yards, due to its superior ballistic coefficient. Since most deer are taken under 100 yards, I doubt this fact holds much significance.

Actually, such energy levels as we're referring to here are more than sufficient for deer. The reason I would prefer the lightweight bullet over its bulkier brother is the quick expansion of the former. My personal feeling is that the quicker the bullet expands (without actually blowing up), the more instantly effective it is on deer. Naturally, on black bear I'd opt for the deeper penetration and bone-cracking qualities of the 265-grain slug.

The 444 is no long-range wonder. Zeroed at 100 yards, both bullet weights plunge about 10 inches at 200 yards. Switch to a 150-yard zero and the 200-yard drop is around 6 inches, but the 100-yard rise becomes about

The old Model 71 Winchester in 348 Winchester once filled the role that the 444 serves today, that of a big-bore bruiser for heavy animals or deer in close cover. The M71/348 shown here is nowhere near as accurate as the average 444.

The 444's competition in the woods includes, from left to right: 35 Remington, 375 Winchester, 44 Magnum, 444 Marlin and the 45-70 Government.

2¼ inches. If I were zeroing a 444, I'd compromise at a 125-yard zero; then a hold on the spine at 200 yards would still provide table meat. Bear in mind that bullet energy has dropped off to from 1000 to 1150 fpe out at 200 yards, about the minimum for clean kills on deer at such a distance.

Aside from the fact that a properly-directed 444 will deck a deer or black bear like lightning, and perform tolerably on elk if you don't try to drive through too much meat or heavy bone, the thing about it that impresses me most is its accuracy. Ever since it first came out, the 444 has been bedecked with accolades regarding its tight grouping skills. I've owned a couple of 444s. Unfortunately, I long ago lost my target files so I don't remember specific group sizes. My *impression* is that both would put factory ammo in 2 inches or less all day, with iron sights.

A young fellow used to bring a 444 out to the range

When first introduced, the Marlin 444 generated a lot of press as to which style and weight of bullet worked best. Current 240-grain factory loads exit the muzzle at 2350 fps.

where I went to shoot nearly every Sunday. He was not a hunter, but an accuracy buff of the first magnitude. He showed me group after group fired from his 444 that were in the 1¼- to 1½-inch range, for five-shot strings. I recall being particularly impressed by the close proximity of those huge, 44-caliber holes, all fired from the bench at 100 yards. I believe he used a receiver-mounted micrometer sight.

Let me quote the knowledgeable and forthright Ken Waters, from the 1966 edition of *Gun Digest:*

> . . . the 444 has had field as well as bench testing, and I can attest to both its power and accuracy. Let's not mince words; it is the most accurate *big bore* lever-action rifle the author has ever tested, our particular rifle turning in 5-shot groups at 100 yards with 3X scope measuring from .75″ to 2″, (averaging 1¼″), and it will drive a bullet which has expanded to 70-caliber clear through to the hide on the far side of large bucks, breaking any bone it hits.

Seems like Ken was impressed with the 444 and the Model 336 permutation that housed it. On the subject of barrel length, which I discussed earlier, Ken wrote this:

> It was gratifying to see the 444 with a 24-inch barrel. Already the cries are being heard for a 20-inch carbine, but unless you do your hunting on horseback, a shorter barrel will exact too great a sacrifice in velocity and energy; this straight-case cartridge needs a fairly long bore

for complete powder burning. Marlin knew what they were doing in selecting a 24″ barrel.

Although I personally would rather have portability than a few extra foot-seconds, that's what makes a horse race. Ken summed up thusly:

> For the big game hunter who prefers a lever-action and takes his shots inside 200 yards, I can't think of a better choice, especially if his quarry is one of the really big species or the cover is thick.

The 45-70, 375 Winchester, 307 Winchester, and 356 Winchester were not available at the time Ken wrote those lines. (I *know* the 45-70 was around in 1966, but not in new lever-action rifles. Don't nitpick.) I'm not certain whether Ken would stand by the foregoing opinion today, what with the wider choice of cartridges.

If I were going after deer or black bear only, I would support Ken's choice, despite the other loads mentioned. For elk or moose I'd rather a heavy-loaded 45-70 Marlin, or perhaps a 356 Model 94 (or perhaps not). But for most of my hunting the 444 would do just fine.

The 444 is almost a one-powder cartridge, that propellant being IMR 4198. It has been so since its debut. With the 265-grain Hornady soft point, such powders as Hodgdon's H322 and Du Pont IMR 3031 work about as well, but I see no pressing need to abandon the use of IMR 4198. So I won't, when I get another 444. And I will.

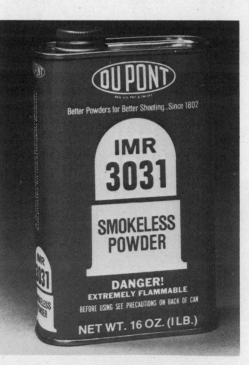

Du Pont's IMR 4198 is, in the eyes of many handloaders, *the* powder for the 444 Marlin.

Du Pont's IMR 3031 is a good choice for the 444 when using the 265-grain Hornady flat point.

444 Marlin

HANDLOAD DATA

Bullet Wt. Grs.	Type	Powder Wt. Grs.	Type	Primer	Case	MV, (fps)	ME, (fpe)	Rifle/ Bbl. (in.)	Remarks
225	Speer JHP	**49.0**	IMR 4198	Rem. 9½	Rem.	**2409**	**2899**	Mar. 444/22	Lym. Hndbk., 46th Ed., (Acc. Ld.)
240	Rem. JSP	**47.0**	IMR 4198	Rem. 9½	Rem.	**2341**	**2920**	Mar. 444/22	Lym. Hndbk., 46th Ed., (Acc. Ld.)
265	Hrndy. FP	**52.8**	IMR 3031	Alcan	Rem.	**2200**	**2847**	Mar. 336/24	Hrndy. Hndbk., 3rd Ed.

JHP—Jacketed Hollow Point; JSP—Jacketed Soft Point; FP—Flat Point.

FACTORY LOAD DATA

Bullet Wt. Grs.	Type	MV, (fps)	ME, (fpe)	Rifle/ Bbl. (in.)	Remarks
240	Rem. SP	2442	3177	Marlin 336/24	Speer No. 9 Manual

SP—Soft Point.

SPECIFICATIONS

Shell Holders
RCBS: 28
Bonanza: 27
Lyman: 14B
Pacific: 27

Bullet Diameter
Jacketed: .429″ to .430″

Lengths
Trim: 2.220″
Maximum Case: 2.225″
Maximum Overall: 2.570″

The 444 Marlin, left, is nothing more than an elongated 44 Magnum, right. What you get is a 600 fps increase in muzzle velocity from the same grain slug.

CAUTION:
Loads recommended and suggested herein have been carefully listed, but are intended solely as a guide to readers and neither the publisher nor author accept any responsibility for results of their use.
Maximum loads, listed in bold, should be reduced by 10 percent and worked up to cautiously.

45-70 Government

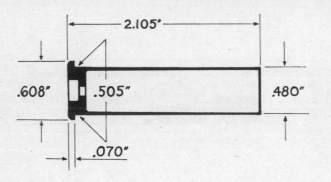

"... within 100 yards or so [the 45-70] will do ... as well as anything you can buy. It's a useful cartridge with a proud tradition, historical past, and secure future."

THE 45-70 Government, often called the 45-70 Springfield, is 111 years old in this, George Orwell's year. It is the oldest military rifle cartridge still in common usage. It is tied with the 44-40 Winchester Centerfire as the oldest centerfire rifle cartridge still factory-loaded in the United States. The old warhorse has won many a target match, including those held at ranges out to 1000 yards. It established its reputation fighting Indians and was with General Custer at his ill-fated donnybrook with the Sioux. The isle called Cuba resounded to its deep-throated roar during the Spanish-American fracas. Tons of bison have grazed their last thanks to fat, slow-moving slugs belched from rifles so chambered.

So many different firearms have been produced for the 45-70 it would take several pages just to list them all. Here are a few: Trapdoor Springfield (from which the cartridge acquired one of its *nom de plumes*), Remington Rolling-Block, Remington-Keene, Sharps-Borchardt, Sharps 1874 Side-Hammer, Marlin 1881, Colt Lightning, Ballard single shots, Maynard, Peabody, Whitney Rolling-Blocks, Whitney-Burgess, Phoenix, Harrington & Richardson Springfield replicas, Winchester 1886, Winchester High-Wall, Winchester-Hotchkiss, Marlin 1895 (original and current version), Peabody-Martini, Kropatschek, Bullard, Remington-Lee, Siamese Mauser, Browning 78, Clerke Hi-Wall, Riedl, and more. Some date from the last century, some from last week; they were all reamed for the 45-70.

Currently you can purchase a 45-70 in the Ruger Number 1 single shot, the modern version of the Marlin 1895 (which is little more than a cosmetic permutation of the basic Model 336), the various Harrington & Richardson Springfield iterations, the Ruger Number 3, the Sharps "Old Reliable," the Navy Arms Rolling Block, and perhaps one or two I missed.

I've owned a couple of Marlins, and fired a Ruger Number 1. The former would be my first choice as a hunting rifle, not because it is superior to any of the others but because I am not enamored of a single shot rifle as a big game getter. I like the looks of the Sharps, and the Number 1 just might be the most accurate of the bunch if a vehicle for testing your handloading skills is what you're after. The Harrington & Richardson is the traditional 45-70; for non-serious use I would seriously consider it.

Okay, forget the guns. Just how good is the old government load as a hunting round? It depends. If you are using one of the older, weaker actions, then the factory specs are about all you can hope for in ballistics. Those are either a 300-grain jacketed hollow point at a listed 1880 fps muzzle speed, or a 405-grain bruiser at 1330 fps. The former is good for 2355 fpe, the latter gets only 1590.

Moving to 100 yards, the heavy slug retains 1227 fpe, the lightweight 1815 fpe. At 200 yards, a very long shot for a 45-70 with such loads, the 300-grainer shows 1355

Although primarily a rifle round, the 45-70 is sometimes chambered in pistols like this modified Thompson-Center. Such a gun/cartridge is great on close-in boars, as shown here.

(Left) The old 45-70 Government (at right) is shown with some of its contemporaries such as, from left to right: 38-40, 38-55 and the 44-40 WCF. The only one as old as the 45-70 is the 44-40.

From the bench, with stout loads, the 45-70 generates a good deal of recoil. Heavy reloads in rifles like the Ruger No. 1 add a new dimension to the old war horse. Those same heavy reloads, however, are not suitable for Trapdoor actions.

fpe; the 405-grain soft point keeps 1001 fpe of its initial thrust. Naturally, either of these loads retains more than enough for deer and black bear clear out to 200 yards. The problem is hitting said fauna. From a 100-yard zero, the 405-grain soft point drops a whopping 24.6 inches at 200; the 300-grain hollow point dives only 12.8 inches.

For comparison, the 30-30 dips a mere 8.2 inches at 200 yards, assuming a 100-yard zero and the 150-grain Remington factory load. The 180-grain 300 Savage drops a paltry 6.7 inches. Neither of these is considered the last word in long-range wonders.

Certainly, a careful shot who can judge range like a professional golfer, has a rifle capable of sufficient accuracy, and is offered a shot at a standing animal 200 yards distant, might connect with a hold just above the backline of an animal. But then again he might not. Heck, the 30-30 is often considered to be a 150-yard cartridge, with some old-timers allowing as how it's okay to 175. The 30-30 shoots *more than twice* as flat covering 200 yards as does the 45-70 with factory ammo. Far as I'm concerned, the 45-70 is a 125-yard cartridge with factory fodder.

277

The author considers the Marlin 1895 lever-action, in 45-70, to be among the best of the bunch. It's strong, well made and sufficiently accurate to bring home the bacon, any day.

Bullets useful in the 45-70 range from the 300-grain Sierra at left to the 405 Winchester soft point on the right.

The 45-70 is versatile. This custom Thompson Center Contender single shot (in 45-70) would be well suited for handgunning deer at reasonable ranges.

On really big animals like elk and moose, I would prefer to keep my shots under 100 yards with the factory loads, if possible. For such work I would want the 405-grain load in my chamber. The energy of that bullet has plunged to just a little more than 1200 fpe at 100 yards, which is meager enough on such game. The lighter-weight bullet has more retained energy at this football-field length, but the sectional density of the short slug is suspect for the deep penetration often required on large animals.

In such strong modern ordnance as the 1895 Marlin, factory ballistics can be boosted considerably. The handloading manuals are chock full of pertinent data. If you feed a really stout 45-70, such as one of the Ruger single shots, you can reach very stiff numbers if your shoulder can stand the gaff. I'll pass. I have no elephants cavorting on my front lawn, and I don't care

enough about the biggest elk that walks to put up with the recoil generated by such fearsome loads.

Handloading

I once penned an article on handloading the strong, modern 45-70. My test gun was one of the now-defunct Browning 78 single shots. The rifle had a hellacious drop to its stock, replicating 19th century styling. The buttplate was crescent-shaped steel. Ouch! I want no more of such treatment. If I plan to hunt big critters, I'll opt for more modern armament, meaning a smaller bore, lighter bullet, higher speed. If I'm caught lugging a 45-70 around, you can bet it will be stoked with factory-equivalent ammo or thereabouts. And I will more likely be after deer, boar, or black bear than heftier stuff.

When handloading the 45-70, I lean toward the clas-

One Federal 45-70 factory load is topped with a 300-grain jacketed hollow point that exits the muzzle at 1810 fps.

sic powder—IMR 3031. Dumping 43.0 grains of it into a Remington case, priming with a Federal 210, and seating the Sierra 300-grain flat point atop the whole thing, my Browning 78 did its part by grouping well under 3¾ inches from the bench at 100 yards. With iron sights. Muzzle speed: a comfortable 1482 fps, for 1463 fpe. Plenty for close-in whitetails; balm for my shoulder.

Most accurate load in the B-78 consisted of 60.0 grains of Hodgdon H322 under the 300-grain Hornady hollow point. Grouping was super at 2.20 inches for three, five-shot strings, again with open sights. Muzzle speed: 2127 fps. Muzzle energy: 3014 fpe. If you want an elk load, that one should do the trick unless you have to go through heavy bone or quarter through the paunch. Need a heavier bullet for that. Incidentally, this load of 60.0 grains of H322 and a 300-grain slug is safe for use in one of the strong 45-70s like the Marlin, Ruger, or Browning. *Don't use it in one of the weaker actions*.

Another good reload for the stronger 45-70s is 56.0 grains of H322 behind the 350-grain Hornady round nose for nearly 2000 fps at the nozzle and 3100 fpe. Now there is an elk, moose, or abominable snowman load if ever there were one. Accuracy is fine at 2.80 inches. This load kicks.

Factory Remington and Winchester 405-grain soft points averaged 2.61 inches (both loads) while chronographing 1303 fps (both loads!). I'd unhesitatingly use either for anything I wanted to hunt.

One potential area for frustration is achieving a proper zero with a 45-70. I once repaired to the range with a new Marlin 1895 and a box each of Remington and Winchester factory loads weighing 405 grains. I zeroed with the Winchester ammo then switched to the Remington to compare accuracy. No new holes appeared on the target. I was puzzled. I walked downrange, peered at the target board, found my second group. It was centered off the bottom of my target, *18 inches* from the group center of the first load fired! With the same bullet weight at virtually identical velocity!

Aside from such minor problems, the 45-70 is pretty well clear of blemishes. Sure, it kicks a bit, especially with heavy loads in a stout rifle. So don't load heavy. Accuracy is just fine for any hunting purpose I can think of within its normal range, which is dictated by trajectory. It may not be modern, but it's efficient. And it will still bring home the venison. In fact, within 100 yards or so, it will do so as well as anything you can buy. It's a useful cartridge with a proud tradition, historical past, and a secure future. I should do so well when I get to be 111 years old.

When it comes to elk, or other large big game animals, the 45-70 can handle the job, providing you keep the range under 100 yards.

45-70 Government

HANDLOAD DATA

Bullet Wt. Grs.	Type	Powder Wt. Grs.	Type	Primer	Case	MV, (fps)	ME, (fpe)	Rifle/ Bbl. (in.)	Remarks
300	Sierra FP	43.0	IMR 3031	Fed. 210	Rem.	1482	1463	Browning 78 (24)	Pleasant load
300	Sierra FP*	56.0	H322	Fed. 210	Rem.	1898	2400	Browning 78 (24)	Mediocre accuracy
300	Hrndy. JHP*	60.0	H322	CCI 200	Rem.	2127	3014	Browning 78 (24)	Most accurate load tested
350	Hrndy. SP*	56.0	H322	Fed.210	Rem.	1997	3100	Browning 78 (24)	Exc. ld.; high energy

*This load *not* to be used in Trapdoor, single shot rifles.
FP—Flat Point; JHP—Jacketed Hollow Point; SP—Soft Point.

FACTORY LOAD DATA

Bullet Wt. Grs.	Type	MV, (fps)	ME, (fpe)	Rifle/ Bbl. (in.)	Remarks
405	Remington SP	1303	1526	Browning 78 (24)	Very acc.; consistent
405	Winchester SP	1303	1526	Browning 78 (24)	Very accurate

SP—Soft Point.

SPECIFICATIONS

Shell Holders
RCBS: 14
Bonanza: 16
Lyman: 17
Pacific: 14

Bullet Diameter
Jacketed: .457″ to .458″

Lengths
Trim: 2.100″
Maximum Case: 2.105″
Maximum Overall: 2.550″

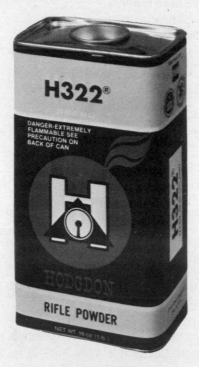

Hodgdon's H322 is an excellent propellant for handloading the big 45-70. The most accurate load in the author's Browning B-78, 45-70 consisted of 60.0 grains of H322 under a 300-grain Hornady hollow point.

CAUTION:
Loads recommended and suggested herein have been carefully listed, but are intended solely as a guide to readers and neither the publisher nor author accept any responsibility for results of their use. **Maximum loads, listed in bold, should be reduced by 10 percent and worked up to cautiously.**

458 Winchester Magnum

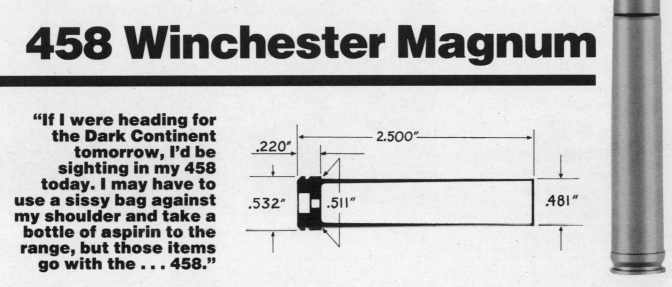

"If I were heading for the Dark Continent tomorrow, I'd be sighting in my 458 today. I may have to use a sissy bag against my shoulder and take a bottle of aspirin to the range, but those items go with the . . . 458."

THE 458 Winchester Magnum debuted in 1956, housed in a gussied-up permutation of the Model 70 Winchester turnbolt dubbed the "African." The geographical sobriquet was unnecessary; published data on the new cartridge spoke most eloquently of the intended area of usage.

Factory ballistics show a 500-grain full-metal jacketed slug and a 510-grain soft point starting at 2040 fps. Muzzle energies run 4620 and 4712 fpe respectively. Recoil is in the 65 foot-pound neighborhood, in a 9-pound rifle, which is a tough neighborhood. Considering the foregoing, using the 458 Magnum on North American game is akin to employing a 12-pound sledge to crack walnuts: it's fun unless somebody sees you.

Adding to the recoil problem is a decidedly arched trajectory. Even the 30-30 shoots flatter than the 458. What we have here is a gun/cartridge combination that is not only ludicrous but unsuitable for 99.99 percent of the hunting situations found on this continent. Of course, it might be comforting to have a 458 along if you plan to dig an Alaskan brown bear out of the alders with the end of your gun barrel, but even for that purpose there are guns and loads I'd rather use. And things I'd rather do. Suffice to say that the 458 has virtually no *practical* hunting application in this hemisphere and let it go at that.

If the 458 has no hunting value in the United States, why then does it sell so well? Good question. There are several reasons: the typical American penchant for the biggest or best of anything; a fascination for big-bore rifles, and cartridges housing bullets heavy enough to use as a paper weight in an 80-mile-per-hour gale; a nostalgia for the golden days of African hunting (the best of which expired long before the 458 saw the light of day); something fun to play with. Likely some 458 buyers harbor a hope of one day visiting Africa; some perhaps entertain the thought of becoming a brown bear guide; a few may even subscribe to Elmer Keith's theories regarding such loads as the 458 to be about right for elk.

Of those justifications mentioned, I suspect that one carries the most weight: a lot of fellows simply enjoy playing with the big bores. Sure, they may tote their 458 after deer or elk, but that's just for fun. No one takes it serious. I suspect that most times said 458s are loaded down—*way* down—to more manageable levels. As corroboration, I offer the resurgence of interest in the 45-70 Government, which, when loaded properly in a stout modern rifle, approximates watered-down 458 Magnum ballistics.

My pal Layne Simpson uses a Ruger Number 1 45-70 for deer hunting on occasion. He once examined a couple of whitetails that had each absorbed a 300-grain jacketed hollow point through the ribcage. The deer were very dead indeed, with lungs he described as appearing to have spent time in a food blender. What bothered Layne was the bloodshot quarters, the worst

Remington Model 700 Safari in 458 Win. Mag. is a beautifully made rifle. Note the heavy barrel and butt pad.

The working end of any 458 Win. Mag. is, in a word, impressive.

(Left) Misfires are often a problem when loading-down a 458 to moderate velocity and pressure levels. This 400-grain Speer slug stuck in the bore from an improperly ignited powder charge. The slug was driven out with a cleaning rod from the muzzle. Note the land markings on the ogive.

he'd ever seen and Layne has seen a *lot* of downed bucks. He decided then that if he used 45-caliber rifle bullets on deer, he was either going to cut the velocity or increase the weight. I'll buy that.

It is doubtful that many gunners burn up much factory ammo in their 458s. I recently tested a borrowed Ruger Number 1 in 458 for a magazine article. I had little time to develop reduced handloads (it isn't easy, with a 458) so I fired three, five-shot strings from the bench with 510-grain factory loads, to see if the gun would shoot well. Big mistake. I won't make it again. (An 11-pound Colt-Sauer once pounded me into submission in short order; the lighter Ruger was murder.) I want no more truck with a 458 Magnum and factory ammo, thanks just the same, at least in the United States.

Incidentally, despite the brutal recoil and resulting poor bag technique at the bench, both the Ruger and the Colt-Sauer shot quite well with factory stuff. The Colt averaged 1.84 inches for three, five-shotters, the Ruger, 1.76 inches. The final group fired in the Ruger measured just .75-inch, with all shots in one oblong hole. Pretty good.

Don't let me mislead you, the 458 is a great hunting cartridge for areas where crocodiles and Cape buffalo roam, where pachyderms putter in the sweetpeas and

rhinos view everything through a red mist of malice. If I were heading for the Dark Continent tomorrow, I'd be sighting my 458 in today. I may have to use a sissy bag against my shoulder and take a bottle of aspirin to the range, but those items go with the territory with a bruiser like the 458. The effort certainly pays large dividends when lions roar in the night. African game is the forte of the 458, and from what I read and hear, it has few peers.

Hunting

Finn Aagaard once flushed a slightly wounded lion from its hidey hole, whereupon it burst from the thorn bush intent on mangling a tracker. Aagaard swung his 458 through the cat, like pass-shooting a duck, and fired in one continuous movement, shooting instinctively. The shot dumped the big lion as if it were a dove taking a load of sixes.

John Buhmiller has written long and eloquently about the 458. Buhmiller hunted much in Africa, long before the 458 came out. When it did, he went over to it almost exclusively. He had been using a cartridge similar to the 450 Nitro Express, but loaded with blackpowder. Although many of the old-time African hunters used ponderous doubles that shot huge, heavy bullets, Buhmiller and a few others discovered that such loads often failed to penetrate according to the script. Too fat and too short, and sometimes not stoutly constructed. On the other hand, hunters like Buhmiller found that a hard, 500-grain, lead, 45-caliber bullet would penetrate broadside through an elephant's skull, which is good penetration indeed.

Of course, it took a *good* 45-caliber bullet to smash so much bone and sinew. Buhmiller saw a Cape buffalo absorb three slugs from a 450 Nitro, all impacting at the back of the head. The buff's head and neck were pulped but no bullet broke the spine; the bull had to be followed up and finished in the thick bush. The bullets, Kynoch soft points, were too frangible for such heavy-duty work.

The 458 was a godsend. The 500-grain solid was one of the toughest bullets ever made, and still is. The jacket material was steel, covered with a thin wash of copper to ease passage down the bore, and was thick and tough as a harlot's heart. Buhmiller performed many autopsies on Cape buff and elephant; he wrote that he never saw one of the Winchester solids deformed in any way. He also wrote that if you poked one of those bullets in a buffalo's shoulder, it would often turn and run at the shot. Then, he advised, you could leisurely plant two or three more into its retreating fanny and deck it. Only excellent solids would do this, Buhmiller said.

While the solid bullet was recommended for the big stuff, lions and leopards required less penetration but more meat-rending expansion. That is the province of the 510-grain soft point. Stories abound of the effectiveness of the big soft nose on thin-skinned dangerous game; there's no need to repeat them here.

Some years after the 458's introduction, Buhmiller began to experiment with two bigger numbers, both wildcats. One utilized 570-grain bullets of .510-inch diameter, the other was a 470 Magnum using .474-inch slugs. He claimed that either of these two cartridges was superior to the factory-loaded 458, citing as evidence the tendency for shoulder-shot elephants to wander off or require additional hits before succumbing. Buhmiller said that his wildcat cartridges more often dropped *tembo* on the spot.

On the subject of recoil, Buhmiller wrote the following, in the May-June, 1968, issue of *Handloader:*

This particular individual procured a 45-caliber Farquharson rifle and used it for the next 20 years. He stated that if he'd used it when he started hunting, he'd have killed three times as many elephants. This man would also have averted the permanent injury he suffered from the murderous recoil of his four-bore cannon.

One hunter, doing buffalo control work, shot heavily for two days, and was laid up for three weeks due to recoil damage to his shoulder. No matter how tough you think you are, the big guns are really punishing if shot more than a few rounds a day.

Amen.

Buhmiller was of the opinion that many people load the 458 Magnum far too heavily. Not only is recoil a factor, but so are the mechanical aspects of feeding and extraction. Buhmiller stated that on dangerous game, particularly in a tropical climate, he'd opt for easy extraction over a few extra foot-pounds any time. Prudent.

John Buhmiller summed up the cartridge thus, from the same issue of *Handloader:* " . . . the standard 458 with solids is all you need for the biggest game Africa has to offer. Learn how to use this cartridge properly and it should never let you down."

The 458 Winchester Magnum is not a particularly versatile cartridge; it was never meant to be. It was designed to replace the girthsome and expensive British elephant cartridges and the double rifles that housed them. Such American wildcats as the 450 Watts, 450 Ackley, and 450 Mashburn came and went with little effect on the market. Not so the 458. Not only did it revolutionize African hunting cartridges, it was available and affordable to the average Joe who had worked long and hard to save enough money for a safari. (Before the advent of the 458 in the Model 70, a fine British double cost nearly as much as a safari!) It is inherently quite accurate, at least in the three guns I've used. It's tricky to load for, but so what? It's a specialist.

Good 458 bullets, left to right: the 300-grain Hornady JHP, 300-grain Sierra FP, 350-grain Hornady SP, 400-grain Speer FP, 405-grain Remington FP and the 405-grain Winchester FP.

458 Winchester Magnum

HANDLOAD DATA

Bullet Wt. Grs.	Type	Powder Wt. Grs.	Type	Primer	Case	MV, (fps)	ME, (fpe)	Rifle/ Bbl. (in.)	Remarks
405 Rem.	FP	71.0	IMR 3031	8½-120	Win.	**2237**	**4501**	Win. 70/22	Lym. Rld. Hndbk., 46th Ed. (Acc. Ld.)
500 Rem.	FMJ	73.0	IMR 4895	8½-120	Win.	**2066**	**4740**	Win. 70/22	Lym. Rld. Hndbk., 46th Ed. (Acc. Ld.)

FP—Flat Point; FMJ—Full Metal Jacket.

FACTORY LOAD DATA

Bullet Wt. Grs.	Type	MV, (fps)	ME, (fpe)	Rifle/ Bbl. (in.)	Remarks
510 Winchester	SP	2020	4621	Ruger Number 1-H/24	Very accurate
510 Winchester	SP	2040	4712	Colt-Sauer/24	Accurate

SP—Soft Point.

SPECIFICATIONS

Shell Holders
RCBS: 4
Bonanza: 2
Lyman: 13
Pacific: 5

Bullet Diameter
Jacketed: .457" to .458"

Lengths
Trim: 2.495"
Maximum Case: 2.500"
Maximum Overall: 3.340"

The Colt-Sauer Grand African is a fine 458, accurate too. It groups 1⅝ inches, with pet loads, at 100 yards.

CAUTION:
Loads recommended and suggested herein have been carefully listed, but are intended solely as a guide to readers and neither the publisher nor author accept any responsibility for results of their use. **Maximum loads, listed in bold, should be reduced by 10 percent and worked up to cautiously.**

460 Weatherby Magnum

"If one day I hie off to The Dark Continent . . . I'll likely tote some heavy ordnance. I will, however, have to think long and hard about the 460 Weatherby Magnum. It's a lot of gun."

IF I were troubled with elephants trampling my begonias, I would grab a 460 Weatherby Magnum to rid myself of the nuisance. Then again, I might not. The current *Hornady Handbook* has a section of load data pertaining to the 460. In the remarks section that serves as a preamble to each cartridge division, we find this:

> . . . for those who shot the data, a 25-pound bag of lead shot between the shoulder and the buttstock was necessary to prevent badly bruised shoulders. Our test rifle also had a muzzle brake, which is intended to limit muzzle jump; however, with anything having as much recoil as the 460 Weatherby Magnum and considering the amount of shooting necessary, the shoulder protection was still necessary.

Perhaps I'll have none of the 460 after all. I could simply annoy the irksome pachyderms with a 458 Winchester Magnum.

The fearsome 460 Weatherby was proffered to the public in 1958, its *raison d' etre* simply to be the world's most powerful cartridge. A matter of prestige, you understand. The former holder of the most-potent title was the piddling 600 Nitro Express, which propelled a 900-grain bullet at a claimed 1950 fps, for a mere 7600 fpe of rhinoceros-pulping energy. The 460 Weatherby Magnum, on the other hand, provides some serious juice to its paltry 500-grain slug. Listed muzzle speed is 2700 fps, about the same as the 30-06 gets with a bullet

The awesome 460 Weatherby Magnum, right, dwarfs the elephant-getting 458 Winchester Magnum, left.

The 300- and 350-grain Hornady bullets shown here can be loaded in the 460 Magnum, although the lighter hollow point might not hold together on big game.

Three of Weatherby's biggest bruisers, left to right: the 340 Weatherby Magnum, 378 Weatherby Magnum, and the 460 Weatherby Magnum. The 460 boasts a 500-grain slug at 2700 fps and more than 8000 pounds of energy!

one-third the weight. Muzzle energy is advertised at 8095 fpe. For my part, I'll take Roy Weatherby's word; the chance of my ever chronographing a 460 factory load is about the same as my being elected mayor of Pawtucket, Rhode Island.

In Barnes' *Cartridges of the World,* it is written that the 460 Weatherby Magnum, " . . . has no sensible use for any North American big game. . . " I'll append that by stating that I doubt there is a pressing need for the 460 on any game anywhere. No matter.

I have read that you can shoot an elephant in the head with a 458 Winchester and have him trundle off if the hit isn't quite right. I have also read that if you sock old tembo in the noggin with a 460, he'll just topple right over. No mention was made as to what happens to the guy who turned loose the shot.

If you did find yourself in Africa accompanied by a 460 Weatherby, long-range shooting would not be entirely out of the question. Assuming you could get off a careful shot without flinching, and that's a hell of an assumption, animals as far away as 300 yards or a little more would be well within range. Zero your 460 at 200 yards (or better yet, have your brother-in-law zero it), and the 300-yard drop will be less than 10 inches. That information might come in handy if you plan to have a go at woodchucks in the off season.

Since you'll probably reload your 460, the best powders appear to be the medium-slow numbers like Hodgdon's H380 or Winchester 760 with the 350-grain bullets. You might try IMR 4350 with the heavy 500-grain round nose slug. If going after the soft-skinned dangerous game is your bag, you may want to try the 350-grain Hornady soft point booted along at close to 3000 fps. I

suspect if you poked a lion or grizzly with such medicine, you could carry home the remains in a number-10 can.

For ole jumbo, you'll likely feel more secure if your magazine is stuffed with ammo containing 500-grain warheads. Nail even the heftiest elephant with one of those missiles and I'm sure you will ruin his day. After your head clears and your eyes uncross, you can meander on over and examine the carcass. Better you than me.

If you are taken aback by my levity, it's merely because of my lack of grasp. I know the 460 Weatherby Magnum is a serious cartridge. The 460 is the most devastating load to be launched from something other than a missile silo; it is put up in a beautifully crafted rifle of unimpeachable strength; it costs a wad of dough; it is impressive to look at.

It will warm your heart cockles to know that according to the Hornady manual aforementioned, the 460 is *very* accurate. Stuff a 25-pound bag of shot under your shirt and you just might duplicate the sub-1-inch three-shot strings produced by the Hornady contingent.

If one day I hie off to the Dark Continent in search of fauna the size of several sofas and having the temperment of a politician who just lost an election, I'll likely tote some heavy ordnance. I will, however, have to think long and hard about the 460 Weatherby Magnum. It's a lot of gun.

I *would* like to stoke up a batch of 300-grain Hornady hollow points to around 3200 fps. I'd like for someone to sight-in the rifle for me, then I'd wander off in search of a woodchuck within a reasonable range. Now *that* might be interesting.

460 Weatherby Magnum

HANDLOAD DATA

Bullet Wt. Grs.	Type	Powder Wt. Grs.	Type	Primer	Case	MV, (fps)	ME, (fpe)	Rifle/ Bbl. (in.)	Remarks
500	Rem. FMJ	**121.0**	IMR 4350	Fed. 215	Wby.	**2624**	**7643**	Wby. Mk. V/26	Lym. Hndbk., 46th Ed.
500	Rem. FMJ	**112.0**	H380	Fed. 215	Wby.	**2481**	**6833**	Wby. Mk. V/26	Lym. Hndbk., 46th Ed.
500	Rem. FMJ	**128.0**	H4831	Fed.215	Wby.	**2481**	**6833**	Wby. Mk. V/26	Lym. Hndbk., 46th Ed. (Acc. Ld.)

FACTORY LOAD DATA

Bullet Wt. Grs.	Type	MV, (fps)	ME, (fpe)	Rifle/ Bbl. (in.)	Remarks
500	Wby. FMJ	2700	8095	Wby. Mk. V/26	Wby. Factory Data

FMJ—Full Metal Jacket.

SPECIFICATIONS

Shell Holders
RCBS: 14
Bonanza: 16
Lyman: 17
Pacific: 14

Bullet Diameter
Jacketed: .458″

Lengths
Trim: 2.898″
Maximum Case: 2.908″
Maximum Overall: 3.710″

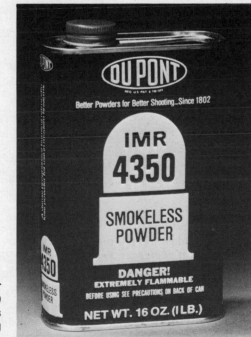

IMR 4350 is perhaps the best powder for use with heavy bullets in the 460 Weatherby. IMR 4831 or Hodgdon's H380 are also good choices for the big 460.

CAUTION:
Loads recommended and suggested herein have been carefully listed, but are intended solely as a guide to readers and neither the publisher nor author accept any responsibility for results of their use.
Maximum loads, listed in bold, should be reduced by 10 percent and worked up to cautiously.

Choosing a Varmint Cartridge

The 250-3000 (center) serves up a trajectory similar to a medium-range varmint round, like the 222 Remington (left), and offers the energy of the long-range varmint cartridges, like the 220 Swift (right).

VARMINT cartridges mean different things to different people. If you have a pachyderm prowling your petunias, then he constitutes a varmint, and you'll do well to rid yourself of his presence, although a 222 Remington is probably not the load for the job. If on the other hand, a flock of crows is wreaking havoc with your roasting ears, a 458 Winchester Magnum is not the ideal armament for their discouragement. The idea is to fit the cartridge to the varmint and the circumstance.

And so we discover that there are varying kinds of vermin, just as there are diverse varmint cartridges. Let's look at the animals first.

In the eastern United States, the traditional varmints are woodchucks, crows, foxes, and perhaps gophers. Out West vermin are more abundant. There they have several species of chucks (marmots), prairie dogs and ground squirrels, jackrabbits, coyotes, armadillos, badgers, porcupines, crows and magpies, bobcats, and goodness knows what all. Now some of these critters are also found east of the Mississippi, but most cannot be classed as vermin per se.

Now, for coyote, fox, bobcat, and similar predator hunting, a quick-handling firearm is apropos. Such game is most often called in with some type of sneaky device designed to imitate the distress signal of a coyote's dinner. The shooting is fun, fast, and furious. While it's handy to have a far-reaching rifle/cartridge combo, it is not a requirement. I know for a fact that

friend Rick Jamison, for example, has taken a *shotgun* on a coyote-calling foray. (Some fellows have no self-respect!)

The point is that out West, the *hunt* seems to be the focal point of predator-calling. That, and the acquisition of the game. (For prairie dog and rockchuck gathering, a different aspect is stressed, as we shall see.) Jackrabbits offer a similar line of thought. Actually, jacks more often are used as a dress rehearsal for big game season. Hunters frequently use whatever armament they carry during their fall excursion after wapiti, mule deer, and suchlike. The lowly jackson bunny is the premier teacher of how to miss running game.

I submit that much western varmint hunting is not of

Jimmy Michael took this chuck with the author's Ruger International 250-3000, a fine combination varmint/deer cartridge.

Good bullets for a 243, 6mm Rem. or 240 Weatherby are, left to right: the 70-grain Sierra M-JHPBT, the 85-grain Sierra JHPBT, the 95-grain Nosler Partition, the 100-grain Hornady SP, and the 100-grain Nosler Solid Base. Such a wide range of bullets is what makes the 6mm cartridges both varmint and deer loads. The 224s as a rule do not have such range, although the 70-grain Speer SP 224 is considered a deer bullet, not a varmint slug.

the purest nature as is practiced back East. Along the Atlantic Seaboard, the *equipment* is the key. A bag of two or three woodchucks for a day's work is completely satisfying, even if it means far more rodents shot at than collected. A chuck hunter doesn't strive to lure a groundhog into range by imitating the sound of ripe alfalfa. In fact the farther the pig is from the hunter, the better. The dedicated woodchucker, in commonality with his soul-mate, the western seeker after rockchuck and prairie pups, is a *rifleman* first, a hunter second.

Thus, whereas a western coyote cajoler, jackrabbit buster, or bobcat chaser will often use whatever armament is handy (unless of course he's a pelt hunter, which is another ball game altogether), the serious chuck hunter or prairie-poodle taker will, nine times out of eight, have a carefully considered and selected battery. So let's leave the coyote crowd to their own devices and concentrate the rest of this chapter on suitable weaponry for use on small critters taken at longish yardage. Which brings us back to varmint cartridges.

There are varmint cartridges; then there are cartridges used for varmints. I suspect that groundhogs and prairie dogs have been slain with most everything that holds a bullet in one end and a primer in the other. That doesn't make them all varmint cartridges. So let's get specific; name some names. I'll delete from consideration such antediluvian members of the clan as the 2R-Lovell, 218 Bee, 219 Zipper, and other oldies and not especially goodies. This chapter is on how to choose a varmint cartridge, not how to identify them in a lineup.

The varmint cartridges are (fanfare): the 17 Remington, 22 Hornet, 222 Remington, 222 Remington Magnum, 223 Remington, 224 Weatherby Magnum, 225 Winchester, 22-250 Remington, and the 220 Swift. That's the lot, folks.

Before one of you raises his hand to point out that I have neglected the 243 Winchester or some other pet cartridge, let me hasten to agree. The 243 is not a varmint cartridge. It instead belongs to one of the most useful cartridge classifications ever developed, the combination varmint/deer loads. Its brethren include the 6mm Remington, 250-3000 Savage, 257 Remington

As the author shows here, the 243 will work fine on varmints, although it is not purely a varmint cartridge.

The 17 is limited in scope, and thus usefulness, and bullets made for it are scarce as Martian women. However, if you shoot largely in settled areas but want more range than the equally quiet 22 Hornet offers, you might take a look at the little 17 Remington. With its exceedingly fragile bullets, which will break up from a hard look, it is probably the safest varmint load extant. Limit yourself to crows, prairie dogs, and woodchucks at the top end with the 17; even its staunchest admirers

The 22-250 came out about the same time as the 225 Win. and virtually killed the Winchester cartridge at the start. The 22-250 had its years as a successful wildcat in its corner.

Roberts, and some might say the 25-06 Remington and 240 Weatherby. These last two are much more specialized than the first four combination cartridges, but we will include them out of respect for their many admirers.

Once we get into the area of the 257 Weatherby, 6.5 Remington Magnum, 270 Winchester, and even larger cartridges, we leave behind any varmint denotation. Certainly these loads can and do slay many varmints annually, but that doesn't make them varmint cartridges, nor yet combination cartridges. They are big game loads *used* for varmint hunting, and we'll discuss them later.

Now, out of our list of varmint cartridges—nine of them—just which ones are worth consideration? All of them. Well, almost all. Some are not especially noteworthy in any regard; one or two are obsolete or easily outdistanced by one or more of the others. We shall expunge those at the outset, leaving the cream of the crop. Let's begin the elimination.

The 17 Remington has several things in its favor such as a very light report, high muzzle velocity, and recoil so mild as to be nonexistent. It also has a few black marks; it has a reputation as being tricky to reload, unreliable in bullet performance on game, and is said to be a severe bore fouler. Additionally, the 17 seems to be abnormally wind-sensitive.

draw the line at game of bobcat size and tenacity.

The 22 Hornet. For use in heavily-populated areas, or regions where shots past 175 yards or so are uncommon, or just for the fun of it, the Hornet is adequate and pleasant. Aside from its low noise factor, I can think of no overwhelming reason to carry a Hornet. It's sort of like driving a Model A Ford; if you understand and accept its limitations, it'll not disappoint you. Unfortunately, its limitations outweigh its allure. For a serious chuck or crow rifle, pass up the Hornet. Not enough voltage.

The 222 Remington is a grand cartridge, bedecked with countless world records, responsible for the demise of several trainloads of chucks, crows, ground squirrels, ad infinitum. It created a dynasty of cartridges, both in factory and wildcat form. Its popularity is legion, its ballistics (a 50-grain bullet at about 3140 fps) adequate for most varminting needs, and its bark is merely authoritative, not hostile. Nonetheless, if I were preparing to purchase a varmint rifle, the 222 would not head my list. Or even appear on it.

The 222 Remington Magnum, slightly bigger brother to the 222, offers a smidgen more speed (3240 fps) from a bullet 5 grains heavier than that of the lesser load. While that is no earthshaking advantage, it does enable the magnum version to shoot 1.3 inches flatter at 300 yards (assuming both to be zeroed at 200) and carry a 35 percent increase in retained energy at the same range. That is not paltry. Additionally, the 222 Magnum exhibits a 2¼-inch advantage in wind drift out at 300 yards, about 22 percent. Again, not paltry.

The problem with the 222 Magnum is that no one makes rifles for it anymore, ammo is hard to find, and neither of these situations is likely to improve. And since the 222 Magnum is matched by the next cartridge we will cover, which is more readily available and in an

Three high-speed varmint 22s are the 220 Swift (left), 22-250 (center), and the now-dead but still-good 225 Win.

(Left) The author's favorite components for his 223 rifles are: Fed. 205 primers, Rem. brass, H4895 powder, and the fine 52-grain Sierra JHPBT-Match. Two of his 223s will group about ⅝-inch with these components.

ever-increasing array of rifles, I'll pass on the 222 Remington Magnum, as most folks have.

Remington's blue-eyed 22 centerfire is the 223 Remington, the civilian version of Uncle Sam's strong right hand. Ballistically, it is indistinguishable from the 222 Magnum. In precision, it will do virtually anything its smaller brother—the 222—will do, unless you put both in full-fledged benchrest rifles. And then I'm not so sure the 223 wouldn't hold its own. The 223 comes in rifles of all shapes and sizes, and every action type except pump and lever. In my opinion, it's the best choice of the 222-head-sized cartridges: stronger, flatter, less wind-sensitive, and equal in accuracy to the 222; the equal in every way of the 222 Magnum plus much cheaper (in military form) to obtain, more popular, and offered in many strong, modern guns. From my seat, it's no contest.

Moving up a notch in power, trajectory, noise, and recoil, we come to the proprietary 224 Weatherby. Available only in the Weatherby Varmintmaster, admittedly a superb but expensive rifle, the 224 Magnum suffers a lack of notoriety. Few people know of its existence. It is not available in a true varmint-weight rifle, at least from the factory, which further limits it. While the ballistic equal of the 225 Winchester, it is more expensive to purchase. The 22-250 shades it in punch and trajectory, and is available in many more rifles, not to mention the Weatherby Varmintmaster. If I desired a

long-barreled walk-around varmint rifle, and could afford the Weatherby, this is the cartridge I would choose in that gun.

The 225 Winchester is dead. Defunct. Deceased. It is no great loss. Some day I'd like to play with one, but so far as this confabulation is concerned, I'd recommend to no one the 225 Winchester. Its ballistics are not unusually bodacious, simply a 55-grain spitzer at an unremarkable 3570 fps according to the Winchester sheet. Both the 22-250 and the 224 Weatherby will better that nicely. Eschew the 225 Winchester except as an investment.

Now we hit a vein of gold, the 22-250 Remington. Although I have never felt an overwhelming urge to spend much time at the loading bench or range with a 22-250, I have owned a few. They all performed adequately, thank you. My pal Rick Jamison is a fan of the hottest Remington 224-bore, and has shot enough groups and taken enough game to fill three books this size with tales. Local gunner Ed White simply dotes on his 22-250s (he has three or four), one of which will average just under ½-inch for several five-shot groups. And it's no target gun, just a garden-variety Ruger M77 Varmint that's had a bit of work.

The 22-250 tosses a 55-grain bullet at 3680 fps according to the factory data. Some lots and brands of ammo will manage that; alas, some won't. I'd peg the norm at

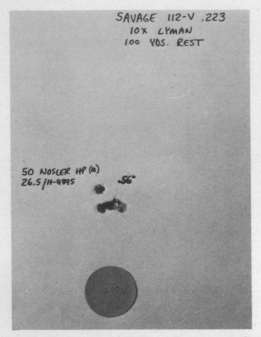

SAVAGE 112-V .223
10X LYMAN
100 YDS. REST

50 NOSLER HP (M)
26.5/H-4895   .56"

A good varmint 22 centerfire, like the author's 223 Savage 112-V will group like this, consistently.

The superb Remington 788, now defunct, makes a super-accurate rig that is not too heavy. The author has one that will stay in ⅝-inch, another that groups around ¾-inch. Lewis Dawkins owns a 22-250 that will group .58-inch on the average, and Ed White's 22-250 is nigh as good as Lewis'. The pictured gun, a 243, will group .70-inch for an average of more than a dozen five-shot strings!

(Right) Even a lever-action chambered for one of the combination varmint/deer loads can take chucks at *reasonable* ranges. While accuracy as is shown here was mediocre for the 250-3000 Savage M99 owned by the author, it is still plenty good for 200-yard shooting at vermin.

The 243 Win. (left) and the 250-3000 are examples of good combination varmint/deer cartridges.

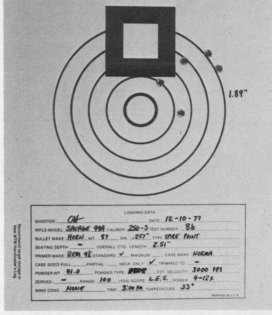

1.89"

about 3700 fps for select factory ammo and good handloads, but that's nothing to sneeze at. Four-hundred-yard drop from a 250-yard zero is only 14.1 inches if Remington's computer hasn't gone haywire. The rise at 150 yards is only 2.5 inches with the above zero. That's pretty flat, folks.

My interest in the 22-250 is increasing of late. Old buddy Lewis "Hawkeye" Dawkins recently acquired one of the excellent and unfortuitously discontinued Remington Model 788 turnbolts. He lapped the locking lugs until all nine of them bear in the receiver and performed one of the sloppiest-looking glass-bedding jobs

you ever saw. While he had the rifle out of the stock, he misplaced the front guard screw, which he replaced with a carriage bolt and washer. That is one ugly rifle.

Hawkeye took that gun to the range one afternoon, late so nobody would see it and mistake it for a tire iron. Next day he showed me the groups it fired. Shooting 37.0 grains of Hodgdon H380 behind the 53-grain Hornady match hollow point, he fired a four-group average of .58-inch! One of those five-shot strings measured .2656-inch; from a sporter! No, he won't sell the rifle, the cantankerous so-and-so.

The hottest of the factory-loaded 22 centerfires is the

good old 220 Swift. I've owned Swifts that would group under ¾-inch with almost no load development at all, and boot 45-grain spitzers to 4100 fps or more while doing so. The Swift will reach out and kill a chuck so sudden you'll think he's playin' possum. Loaded with 55-grain spitzers, the Swift will shoot 1-inch flatter at 400 yards than the hotshot 22-250 Remington when both are zeroed at 300 yards, and will hit with 14 percent more enthusiasm. Not earthshaking, but not trifling either. The 22-250 is close, but the 220 Swift is King.

And now to separate the *crème de la crème*. I can narrow it down easily for you. We can keep the Hornet both to placate Layne Simpson and leave a quiet-spoken alternative for days when our nerves are frayed and the chucks are not spooked. That also takes care of all shots up to perhaps 200 yards.

The 223 is the wise choice for a mid-range 22, one not overly loud-mouthed, but miserly with powder and mild of nudge at the rear end. The 222 Magnum is dying. The 222, while still healthy, offers no discernible advantage over the 223. The reverse is not true; the 223 is demonstrably flatter-shooting and harder hitting, and there is

the availability of arsenal brass as a bonus. For distances up to a long 275 yards, maybe 300 for a good wind-doper and range estimator, the 223 is all you need.

For the longest shots feasible with the hot 224s the 22-250 and 220 Swift are in their own class. The Swift is the faster, more potent, less wind-sensitive of the duo. The 22-250 has the edge in ammo and brass availability, barrel life, tractability, and gun choice. I'd go with the Swift unless I coveted a rifle it wasn't reamed for, like the Browning BLR or the Remington 700-V. Then I'd likely find bliss in the arms of the 22-250.

Ideally, I'd own one each from the three distinct classifications above mentioned. If restricted to one rifle for come-what-may varminting (clear the throat, toe the ground), I'd buy the 22-250, all factors considered. However . . .

Getting into the realm of the combination cartridges mentioned earlier, if I wanted one strictly for varmints I'd grab a 6mm Remington, preferably in a heavy-tubed version. If I owned a 6mm—or 243, 250-3000, or 25-06—I would pass up the 22-250 or Swift as redundant and opt for the 223 Remington as my one 22-bore. The

If you have a combination varmint/deer gun, a good variable scope like this Bausch & Lomb 3-9x is a necessity for chucks past 300 yards. Up to 250 yards or a little more, a 4x will do.

Pictured is a typical heavy-barreled varmint rifle, this one a Winchester M70-V. Such rifles are commonly available in most popular 224 chamberings plus some of the combination varmint/deer cartridges.

Choosing a Varmint Rifle

223 would then handle all my varminting chores at the medium ranges and I'd switch to the heavier bore for true long-range work.

I like that idea. The bore sizes larger than .224-inch have distinct advantages way out yonder: greater weight, diameter, and bullet energy. Whether they buck the wind better is not all that important to me; my first consideration is for a clean kill. The heavier cartridges have it on the hot 22s in that regard. Recoil is not a factor at this level, at least for me. Since I wear ear protection when I hunt vermin, neither is muzzle blast. If my rifle is a good heavy-barrel 6mm or 25-06, I'll yield so little in ultimate accuracy to a comparable 22 centerfire that it's meaningless. That's fact, not opinion.

If choosing a cartridge to be used for both varmints and deer, I would pick a medium-weight sporter along the lines of the Ruger M77, the Remington 700 Classic, or the handsome new short-action Winchester M70. Depending on exactly which rifle I wanted, my caliber choice would be 6mm Remington first, 250-3000 second, 243 closely tied for third, the 25-06 right on the heels of the 243. I wouldn't choose a Roberts at all unless someone had already tested it and found it capable of 1-inch grouping, something I'll have to see. All four of the other loads mentioned will easily group in the 1-inch range, even in a sporter. Fact, not opinion.

I have and will continue to use many other cartridges for varmint hunting. One of my favorites is a particularly accurate Kleinguenther 30-06. Another is a fine Model 70 Featherweight 270, with a terrific trigger and accuracy to spare. But those are big game rifles chambered to big game cartridges. They are rifles I use for varminting; they are *not* varmint rifles.

My Remington 788 223 is. Ed White's Ruger 77-V 22-250 is also, and Lewis Dawkins' Hart-barreled 6mm Remington. And Rick Jamison's lightweight 222. Yes, even Layne Simpson's 22 Hornet is a bonafide varmint rifle. But don't tell him I said so.

Doctor Bill Barry is shown with a typical lightweight vermin/deer rifle, this one a 243 Ruger Ultra Light. Such guns will not only take the wind out of a buck's sails, it'll reach out for a chuck at 300 yards, with ease.

(Above) The 22 Hornet is one of the oldest 22-caliber centerfire cartridges available to varmint hunters. In recent years the Hornet has seen a resurgence of interest, mainly as a result of the availability of high-quality rifles like the Kimber Hornet seen here.

Cartridges
for
Heavy Game

These two 7mm Magnums, Weatherby at right, Remington at left, are considered the bottom row of take-em-as-they-come elk cartridges.

IF I were a brown bear guide in Alaska, serving not only to direct my clients within shooting distance of one of the big bruins, but as a backup in case the scenario went awry, I'd carry a big rifle. Were I a well-heeled nimrod given to global excursions for animals of imposing size and uneven temperament, I'd carry a big rifle. Should I find myself hieing after trophy elk or monster moose or nasty grizzlies on a regular basis, taking whatever shot presented itself, I'd carry a big rifle.

But I am none of these things. And if I were I'd have a pretty good idea what type of armament was best suited to my avocation or pursuit.

Similarly, the native of an area harboring such game as mentioned above needs no advice. He can saunter off into the bush on a regular basis, knows where the game is likely to be found, can pass up risky shots knowing he's not out a wad of dough and that there is always tomorrow. He doesn't need a big rifle, although he sometimes carries one.

The fellows who want the wicked, hard-hitting guns are those who save for years for one big hunt, maybe a mixed-bag sojourn, and who will take whatever shot comes their way. If it's at the caboose of a moose hellbent on vacating the area, so be it. If it's at a barely-seen portion of some big critter's anatomy that the hunter is not sure of, I suppose the bigger and more potent the load the better.

This chapter is based on the proposition that those who read it are entertaining a hope of one day making a trip out West, or up North, or across the pond in search of really large, possibly dangerous game, and are wondering just what to "graduate" to. Okay, let's talk about it.

Africa first. For large dangerous game like rhino and elephant, some countries have laws establishing a minimum caliber, usually the 375. Therefore, since you will undoubtedly have a guide to assist you if you muff your shot, I'll suggest the 375 Holland & Holland or 458 Winchester Magnum. Ammo is said to be plentiful, a definite plus. If you're not worried about your ammunition supply, then you can add the 378 Weatherby and 460 Weatherby Magnums, assuming you can take the recoil. If you want to try something esoteric, like the 416 Rigby, the hot-loaded 45-70 Government, the 475

Although the 30-06 Jimmy Michael is shown here with is sometimes considered to be a suitable rifle for really big game, the magnums are better.

The Whitworth Express shown here comes in several potent big game calibers. It's a well-made turnbolt.

Nitro-Express, or the 505 Gibbs, far be it from me to suggest you shouldn't.

On the big cattle of Africa and Asia, as well as the big cats like lion and tiger, the 375 is generally considered about perfect. The 338 Winchester Magnum, 340 Weatherby, and 378 Weatherby Magnum all have their adherents. Fine with me. All will do the job in business-like fashion if you put a proper bullet in a tender spot. The key word here is bullet. On the feline spectrum, plus all the large antelope like eland, a soft point bullet is considered best. On gaur and Cape buffalo you run into some disputation. Bullet choice is beyond the scope of this discussion, so I'll leave you to your conundrum.

Back on this continent is where all the uproar begins. Basically, about the only fauna we can lay claim to that is likely to gobble you up, or at least slap you around a lot, are the large bears of the north. Certainly a moose or bull elk, or even a buck deer for that matter, can gore or stomp you a little if they're in the rut or you've shot them around the edges. But the chances of it happening are probably a good deal less than of your winning the Irish Sweepstakes. Wound a bull elk in the guts, and he doesn't lay for you in a tenuous copse like a Cape buffalo. Plink a cougar in a non-vital but irritating spot, and he is unlikely to await your coming, crouched on a tree limb leopard-fashion.

So why all the concern about cartridge potency; why does everyone want to tote a load with enough punch to set a ¾-ton truck back on its axles? Well, in addition to the tendency of the one-expensive-hunt-a-year nimrod to shoot at *something* for his money, there is the very

Lewis Dawkins is shown with a Weatherby Mk.V Magnum. In 300, 340, or 378 Weatherby Magnum, this rifle would be fine for elk.

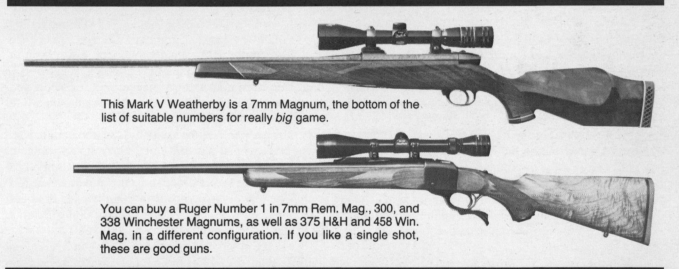

This Mark V Weatherby is a 7mm Magnum, the bottom of the list of suitable numbers for really *big* game.

You can buy a Ruger Number 1 in 7mm Rem. Mag., 300, and 338 Winchester Magnums, as well as 375 H&H and 458 Win. Mag. in a different configuration. If you like a single shot, these are good guns.

real possibility that an elk you wound right *here* might be claimed by another hunter if the elk manages to walk over *there* after being hit. With such poaching abroad in the land, the feeling is that said elk should pitch forward on his nose the instant he takes a hit. I'll buy that.

The rub is that the really large herbivores like elk and moose usually just don't topple over like a deer. Their displacement is so great that it normally takes a minute or two for the machinery to shut down completely. Unfortunately, while this is going on the animal tends to cover some acreage. My opinion is that it doesn't make much difference what you hit them with if you wreck their vitals, but some very knowledgeable hunters feel that the number of tracks made after a solid hit (and especially a hit that is not *quite* where it should be) is directly proportional to the power of the load.

With that theory as the base for our speculation (although not stating that I agree with it), let's see what cartridges should be considered adequate for the bigger big game. I would start with the 7mm Magnums, both Remington and Weatherby versions, but that alone will start an argument. I include the Seven because all the elk guides I have spoken with on the subject value it highly. From there we proceed through the 300 Winchester Magnum, 300 Weatherby Magnum, (and you can include the 30/338 and 308 Norma if you like) the 8mm Remington Magnum, the 338 Winchester Magnum, the 340 Weatherby Magnum, the 375 H&H Magnum, the 378 Weatherby Magnum, the 45-70 Government if: a) it's handloaded *up* in modern rifles with bullets of at least 350 grains weight; and b) it is limited to 150 yards, preferably less. I'll also include the 458 Winchester Magnum if it is loaded *down* to hot 45-70 ballistics and limited to similar ranges.

I deleted a few good numbers. The 358 Norma is a fine load but scarce as giraffes in Cleveland, and good

The Mark V Weatherby comes in many different calibers suitable for elk, moose, big bears, lions, and even elephant.

The Golden Eagle was chambered in 7mm Remington Magnum, 300 Winchester Magnum, and the 300 Weatherby, good loads all.

bullets are not exactly common. The 375 Weatherby is just fine if you own one; if you don't, you're unlikely ever to see one so forget I mentioned it. The 444 Marlin just might have sufficient close-in punch if a really good bullet for deep, bone-snappin' penetration could be had. Alas, such is not the case.

Now let's narrow the field. First the 7mm Mags. Although Warren Page hunted all over the world with Old Betsy, his 7mm Mashburn Magnum, and obviously considered it a suitable elk rifle since there is a photo in the 1959 *Gun Digest* of him with a fine bull he decked at 425 yards, I'm still not convinced that the 7mm is the ultimate big game thumper. It's a good one, no doubt of that. But the ultimate? I think not.

For rear-end shots on elk, moose, and whatnot, I'd load naught but the 175-grain Nosler, which will penetrate as well as any soft point bullet fired from any caliber rifle. However, the Nosler gets its supreme penetrative powers because of its relatively small frontal area, which also contributes to a wound channel that is not all it might be. If I were planning to pick my shots carefully, I wouldn't need a big bruiser like the Nosler and would more likely choose a "softer" 150- or 160-grain slug. But this chapter is about taking shots as they come, not carefully placing your bullets.

Despite the fact that Rick Jamison dotes on his 300 Winchester Magnum, just as Elgin Gates used to write of his favorite 300 Weatherby, Rick tells me that for a simon-pure elk and moose gun he'd choose nothing less than a 338 Winchester Magnum. I agree with that in *theory,* being a fan of the 338, but it's pretty hard to convince myself that a mere .03-inch of bullet diameter can make the 338 so much better than, say, the 300 Weath-

erby. Rick tells me that many of his Colorado elk-hunting buddies rely on the 210-grain Nosler Partition as their preferred elk medicine. Several of these very experienced hunters have tried the 250-grain Nosler and abandoned it for the 210-grain version.

Now, the 300 Weatherby will drive the superb 200-grain Nosler Partition to a full 2960 fps in 24 inches of barrel, according to the Nosler manual. That's good for 3892 fpe from a bullet having a sectional density of .301-inch. The Nosler book shows the 300 Winchester as getting nearly 3000 fps from a 26-inch barreled rifle, so in 24 inches it should be close to the 300 Weatherby.

The same source shows the 338 Magnum as giving 2909 fps from the 210-grain Nosler Partition with its sectional density of only .263-inch. (I mention the sectional density because, all things equal, the bullet having a higher s.d. will outpenetrate another showing a lower number.) That's good for 3947 fpe of muzzle thump, an increase of less than 1½ percent over that of the 300 Weatherby. So what some folks are saying is that there is a *demonstrable* difference between the two cartridges, one of which carries 98.6 percent of the energy, slightly higher velocity, much superior bullet sectional density, and only .03-inch less bullet diameter. Maybe. I doubt it. If I were using a 338 I'd want more bullet weight than I can get from a 30-caliber, say a 250-grainer. If, as some guys claim, the 200- and 210-grain 338 bullets deck elk quicker than the slower 250s, then I say why not simply drop to a 300 Mag. and a good 200-grain slug? I'd gain a flatter trajectory and likely greater penetration. You decide.

Back to the 338. I'll admit my gut feeling is that the 338 *should* be more potent than the 300s, at least with

The author is shown with an Interarms 300 Winchester Magnum, a good elk and moose load with 180- or 200-grain Noslers.

the heavier bullets. I'll also admit that if I were to purchase a rifle *just for elk and moose,* it would probably be a 338 Magnum. It's just that my head can't back up my decision with cold, hard facts. Maybe if I could buy a good 250-grain spitzer that I *knew* I could rely on for raking shots . . . The streamlined 250-grain Sierra soft point boat-tail might do it, if the core and jacket would stay together. And, as Rick Jamison says, there is more to bullet performance—even on elk and moose—than penetration. I agree, but remember we are talking about cartridges for come-what-may shooting, not "picturebook broadside shots." With perfect shot placement, we could use the 7mm Magnums, or even the 270 or 30-06.

The 8mm Remington Magnum looks good on paper. The 200-grain Nosler Partition can be driven to about 3000 fps and gives energy in the same neighborhood as the 210-grain 338 Magnum and the 200-grain 300 Magnum, and retains it all the way out to as far as elk should be shot. The problem is that the 8mm requires the full-length 375 H&H casing, which means a long bolt throw. In return, you merely get 300/338 Magnum ballistics in a longer cartridge. No advantage I can see. Additionally, Remington is said to be dropping the 8mm rifles, so soon there will be another cartridge without a home. Unless you already own one, better let the 8mm Remington Magnum slide.

The fine 340 Weatherby is plenty powerful and kicks plenty hard. If a hunter can stand the recoil, it would be a good choice. However, if a guy can take the shoulder punishment dished out by the 340, he can jump to a really serious elk buster, the 375 Holland & Holland. This is Jamison's number one choice, although he has

In factory persuasion, this is one of the best 7mm Remington Magnum load from an accuracy standpoint; plus, the heavy bullet should give good penetration on big game.

seen only one elk killed with the big cartridge. He himself has slain about a dozen with a 300 Winchester Magnum and is just not satisfied with how far elk travel despite being poked with enough energy to derail a train. Hence, his intent to go to the 375.

I won't argue the logic of the 375 H&H on elk; the cartridge belts me about as badly as the 338, not terribly worse. (Actually, once I get to the 300 Magnum level, recoil starts to get to me. I can shoot the big maggies okay, but it's no fun.) What bothers me about the 375 H&H is the lengthy bolt throw. Let me quote W.D.M. Bell from his book, *The Wanderings of an Elephant Hunter,* circa 1923:

At right is an old '50s vintage Weatherby built on an FN Mauser action. At left is a new Fibermark Mk.V; the center gun is a standard Weatherby. The Mk.V comes in several elk calibers. (Photo courtesy Layne Simpson.)

For those who like their actions "Mauser," the old Interarms Cavalier was once available in 7mm Rem. Mag. or 300 Win. Mag. Currently the Mark X Interarms Classic is offered in those chamberings.

[A] *point in favor of the [7x57] is the shortness of the motions required to reload. This is most important in thick stuff. If one develops the habit by constant practice of pushing the rifle forward with the left hand while the right hand pulls back the bolt and then* vice versa *draws the rifle towards one while closing it, the rapidity of fire becomes quite extraordinary. With a long cartridge, necessitating long bolt movements, there is a danger that on occasions requiring great speed the bolt may not be drawn back quite sufficiently far to reject [sic] the fired case, and it may become re-entered into the chamber. This once happened to me with a 350 Mauser at very close quarters with a rhino . . . At a very few paces distance the grass showed where he was and I fired into it, reloading almost instantaneously. At the shot he swerved across, almost within kicking range, showing a wonderful chance at his neck. I fired, but there was only a click. I opened the bolt and there was my empty case.*

I'm kind of a nut on action length myself, thinking the 308 Winchester-length about right. The 30-06/short-magnum actions are about as long as I care to use for hunting, and often the 375 H&H is longer yet. For *that* reason, I would pass up the 375 in favor of the 338.

The 378 Weatherby is way too much for me, and I suspect for most, but there is no doubt it will kill an elk or moose from any angle if a good bullet is used. Since Nosler quit producing the .375-inch Partition, the 285-grain Speer Grand Slam is the premium soft point, with the 300-grain Sierra boat-tail a good choice for cross-canyon shooting and where the deepest penetration is not needed. In the 378 Weatherby, the 300-grain Sierra may be a trifle frangible.

For elk and moose up close, a Marlin 45-70 filled with

ammo featuring the 350-grain Hornady soft point would be good medicine. Assuming a 1900 fps muzzle speed, we'd have 2805 fpe, a healthy portion of which would be from bullet weight, not velocity. For deep digging, you could stoke up some 500-grain round nose slugs. The energy level is not high, but it would offer ample penetration and make a pretty big hole. The 458 Winchester Magnum can add 200 fps to the above without running into recoil too stiff to handle.

And now for the decision. My first choice would be the 338 Winchester Magnum with 250-grain Sierra soft point boat-tails unless that bullet proved unreliable on raking angles. If so, I suppose I could go to the semi-pointed Nosler Partition, but that would certainly limit me on long shots. I could compromise, as many do, by using the pointy 210-grain Nosler and be prepared for chances at any distance, but the nagging thought that I would really not be outclassing the 300 Magnums would always bug me.

As runner-up, I'm undecided. I strongly suspect that the supreme elk and moose load is the 340 Weatherby. My reservations revolve around the lack of a bullet I consider both suitable for long distance and heavy enough to convince me I'm not toting a 300 Weatherby with an oversized bore. Also there is the matter of recoil; I remain unconvinced that I can toss a 340 to my shoulder and get off a shot without maiming myself for life if the gun isn't snuggled into my torso *just so*. And then there's the price . . .

In third slot would be a toss-up between the hoary 375 H&H and the 300 Weatherby. Against the 375 is its long cartridge, action, and bolt throw. Aside from that, it is fine, although I could never learn to love the boot it gives me. On the debit side of the 300 is that all I'd be doing to an elk at 400 yards is what I'd be doing to him at 250 yards with a 30-06 and 200 yards with a 308. No more, no less.

To make it indelible: If I had to choose a rifle cartridge purely for really big game such as trophy elk, Alaska moose, and the big bears, I'd take the 338 Winchester Magnum and run. It has the right blend of power, trajectory, bullet weight, sectional density, and diameter, all with an amount of recoil I can live with if not delight in.

Although suitable for elk and moose under normal conditions, the 7x57 Mauser (left) and 280 Remington (second from left) are not as potent for adverse shots as the 7mm Remington Mag. next to them. The same goes for the 308 Winchester (third from right) and the 30-06 (second from right) when compared to the 300 Win. Mag. (right).

Selecting the All Around Centerfire Cartridge

ABOUT THE quickest way I know to start an argument is to disparage someone's notion of a real gee-whiz cartridge for all types of hunting, from moles to musk oxen. You'd be surprised just how much mail can be generated when an article on that subject appears in one of the firearms periodicals. For economic reasons, many fellows have to limit their batteries to maybe a shotgun for birds or rabbits, a 22 rimfire for squirrels and general pleasure shooting, and just one big game rifle to serve all their needs. To a shooting writer who is provided with the latest ordnance every time something new turns the corner, such circumstance seems far-fetched. After all, we don't have to purchase every gun we play with. Similarly, the died-in-the-wool shooting hobbiest often spends all his extra money on shooting and ancillary accoutrements, and maybe his wife's dough as well.

Alas, such is not usually the case. For every hunter who owns a half-dozen centerfire rifles, I'd wager there are 500 who have only one. The ratio of gun buffs who boast maybe a dozen rifled longarms in their closets to those with but one standing in the corner is likely 1000 to one. Unfortunately, or so it seems to us avid gunners, the children have to be fed, clothed, and the rent kept up to date; the car also runs better when it's full of gas and serviced regularly. And as hard as it is for some of us to believe, there are actually guys out there who have more than one abiding interest, who think of their

Although the 243 (left) is marginal as an all-purpose load, these others are okay: (left to right): 308 Win., 7mm-08 Rem., 358 Win., and 350 Rem. Magnum. All but the 350 Mag. are built on the same case. (Photo courtesy Layne Simpson)

(Right) The 30-06 is the king of the all-purpose cartridges; it can be loaded with round-nosed slugs (left) for use on big, heavy game or in brush and with pointed slugs (right) for longer ranges.

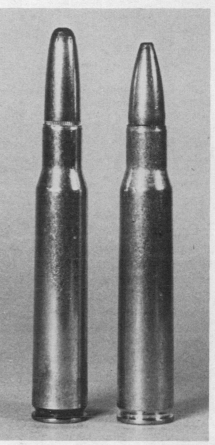

All these cartridges could be considered as all-round numbers under some circumstances, although the 243 and 25-06 are more specialized. The 30-06 is the all-purpose king.

trusty deer rifle only once a year, during the open season. Some of these wayward chaps actually elect to spend a portion of their paychecks on such needless items as motorcycles, or model airplanes, or dune buggies, or sail boats, or potted plants. Thus, the subject of what rifle caliber performs the most services for the money is one that wants answering. So let's address it.

First, let's clean the air of some old wives' tales. There is really no cartridge that will serve all functions from long-range crow shooting to busting big brown bears on an Alaskan tidal flat. A 375 Holland & Holland Magnum will take care of the bruin, but it also slaps backward a mite roughly for real precision at long range, not to mention its too-curved trajectory and non-frangible bullets. Conversely, while a 22-250 Remington will let the starch out of a black bandit at unseemly ranges, such is not the load with which to annoy a bear. Therefore, let us consider these as our extremes, affairs for special-purpose armament only.

So what *should* serve as reasonable parameters? I'd put woodchucks on the bottom end, along with long-range sniping at jack rabbits or rockchucks out West. (Prairie dogs belong in the category with crows; they are very small and require extreme precision to hit consistently at long distance.) As the ceiling let's agree on normal-sized elk and moose of average moosely proportions, not the bull-of-the-woods. (Actually, a really large elk or moose can be fully as hard to put down as the biggest brown bear or grizzly, it's just that they don't have quite the same propensity for restructuring your framework while expiring.)

Now, with chucks as our smallest target and elk or moose as our most prodigious, where do we go from there? To where you live. Should you reside in one of our elk-hunting states, then you'll likely hunt elk as often as you do deer, although the odds are you won't be

Selecting The All Around Centerfire Cartridge

For long-range deer and antelope out on the prairie, the 6mm works fine, though it is overmatched on elk. Gunner is Rick Jamison.

Such 6.5mm loads as these (three of which are wildcats) would make good all-purpose loads for many conditions. They are (left to right): the 264 Win. Magnum, the 6.5 Rem. Magnum, the wildcat 6.5-06, the wildcat 6.5-284, and the wildcat 6.5-257 Roberts. (Photo courtesy Layne Simpson.)

as successful. If you live in the Midwest, chances are that most of your targets are going to be deer-sized and smaller. Plains dwellers might expend a large portion of their time afield in pursuit (at long range) of mule deer, antelope, and coyotes. The Southern nimrod would more likely seek turkey, deer, boar, or black bear, none of which requires a cannon. Up North, the game is of similar ilk as down South, and requires similar armament. Beginning to see the problem?

Let's look at the cartridges. Arbitrarily, I am going to place the 22 centerfires out of the running, despite the fact that Rick Jamison corresponds with a man in Montana who does all his hunting—for elk, deer, moose, everything—with a 22-250, and disregarding the pal of mine who thinks the 220 Swift is the ultimate whitetail cartridge. I will (with two exceptions) draw the line at 30-caliber—that's as big as we need to go. The larger bores are either simon-pure moose/elk/bear loads, elephant fodder, or close-range stuff unsuitable for varmints unless you shoot them in your barn. All are too specialized. I will further dismiss from consideration such low-speed numbers as the 30-30 and 35 Remington, although I realize the 30-30 is available in two factory loads that are intended for varmints and will do a good job at moderate range. Neither of these cartridges, nor others of the same class, is really suited for elk-sized fauna.

So what does that leave us? Before further elimination, let's list the batch: 243 Winchester, 6mm Remington, 240 Weatherby, 250-3000 Savage, 257 Roberts, 25-06 Remington, 257 Weatherby Magnum, 6.5 Remington Magnum, 264 Winchester Magnum, 270 Winchester, 270 Weatherby Magnum, 7x57 Mauser, 7mm-08 Remington, 284 Winchester, 280 Remington, 7mm Remington Magnum, 7mm Weatherby Magnum, 300 Savage, 308 Winchester, 30-06 Springfield, 300 Holland & Holland Magnum, 300 Winchester Magnum, 300 Weatherby Magnum, 307 Winchester, 358 Winchester, and the 350 Remington Magnum. (The 358 and 350 being the above-mentioned exceptions).

I'm aware that I have omitted several suitable calibers from this list, most notably the 308 Norma Magnum, the 8x57 Mauser, and the many good but thoroughly obsolete 6.5mm cartridges. The reason is that

The old 6.5x54 Mannlicher (second from left) would be considered a good all-around load today with good bullets in a modern gun, but it's no longer commonly available. The 250-3000 (far left) is still around and often used by the experienced hunter for both varmints and deer; some even take elk and moose with it. The 243 (second from right) serves the same uses as the 250-3000. The 308 Win. (far right) is one of the top five all-purpose loads extant. (Photo courtesy Layne Simpson.)

The 307 Winchester (left) and the Improved 307 (second from left) would make acceptable all-purpose loads if spitzer bullets could be safely used in tube-fed firearms. Ditto for the 356 Winchester (third from left). The wildcat 370 Winchester (right) is too limited in purpose for all-round use. (Photo courtesy Layne Simpson.)

very few rifles were made for them (excluding military arms), and you can't buy a new one today, to my knowledge.

Let's eliminate some more. While the 6.5 Remington Magnum, the 300 Savage, the 300 H&H, and the 350 Remington Magnum are all fine loads, few guns are or ever were chambered for them. If you own one, fine; this chapter is for the fellow who is contemplating a purchase, not obtaining corroborative evidence for his past selection. Besides, none of these loads is noteworthy in any respect when viewed by itself instead of as a gun/cartridge entity.

Before cutting further, let's discuss purpose and geography once again as they relate to each other. For the guy—like my buddy and hunting partner Mike Holloway—who might never leave the southern states for the purpose of hunting, such calibers as the little 250-3000 are all that is necessary. But the guy residing in Idaho just might need something bigger if he goes after all game indigenous to his location. For him, a 300 Winchester Magnum might be a good choice.

Of course, there are plenty of hunters out there who will hunt only deer and turkey at moderate range, in which case a 30-30 will do just fine thank you. And then there's the gentleman who lives in prime antelope country, with a few mule deer sprinkled in for spice; his gun should be a real long-range number.

Due to such considerations, we must devise a "typical" hunter and from here forward consider only his needs. Our average nimrod will not live in a prime elk state and will therefore seek elk only on an occasional basis. Ditto moose. Most of his chances at game will be on such common critters as deer, black bear, turkey, antelope, and perhaps boar (or javelina). As our pal in-

tends to take at least a biannual foray into varying North American locales, he might one year find himself in the Yukon looking down his barrel at a sheep while the next year finds him deep in the Arizona wilds after a bull elk. As a consequence, he will need a rifle/cartridge combo that will shoot flat, hit hard, and not belt him so badly that he'll develop a flinch. Additionally, our friend will pursue whatever varmints frequent his bailiwick, and on a regular basis.

With this to guide us, we can eliminate some more

Even out West, as shooter Rick Jamison shows, the new 307 Win. is an acceptable all-purpose cartridge, but it would do better with pointed bullets, which *cannot* be safely used in a tube-magazine gun.

The author took this mule deer at close to 300 yards with the Savage 99 in 358 Win., proving that both the Savage lever-action and the 358 Win. are suitable for longish distances.

cartridges from consideration. All the 6mms can go. Many experienced hunters view them as marginal for deer; nearly everyone views them as inadequate elk loads. The smaller 25-calibers can be excluded along with the 6mms, since they are virtually identical ballistically. The 25-06, 257 Weatherby Magnum, and 264 Winchester are pretty specialized rigs, in my opinion. For picking off a pronghorn at 400 yards, they are without peer. As long-range varminters, they are superb; they also kick too much, make too much noise, and go through barrels as if they belonged to a gunsmiths' union.

The new 307 Winchester can be deep-sixed because of its flat-pointed bullets. For moderate ranges it would do all right, and you could use any lightweight 30-caliber slug you wanted on varmints so long as you single-loaded the chamber. But all that is too limiting for an all-rounder.

The 358 Winchester can go, much as I like the little rascal. It's a fine 300-yard load for most anything, and you can stoke it with lightweight handgun bullets for vermin at moderate distances. Still, it doesn't have the versatility for a true all-purpose load.

Our list has thus been pared to the following: 270 Winchester, 270 Weatherby, 7x57, 7mm-08, 284 Winchester, 280 Remington, 7mm Remington and Weatherby Magnums, 308 Winchester, 30-06, 300 Winchester and Weatherby Magnums. An even dozen. Shall we cut further?

Actually, you could choose any one of these loads, hunt with it for 50 years, and never be presented with an alibi that could be laid at the cartridge's feet. That's assuming of course that you put a good, suitable bullet (for the game and conditions) in the proper spot. However, I believe that we can make a few additional dismissals without creating much of a hole in our fabric of choices.

Let's dump the 270 Weatherby because it will do nothing that the 7mm Mags won't do and doesn't offer the bullet selection of the 28-calibers. Also, as good as the 160-grain Nosler Partition is in the 270 Weatherby Mag., it isn't *quite* up to the 175-grain Nosler 7mm in penetration. Admittedly, we're nit-picking. We have to; as I said above, all the cartridges we have left are darned good. Of course, the 270 Weatherby will more than hold its own for long-range gunning of animals under 500 pounds in weight, and it does kick a bit less, but then it's tougher on barrel steel . . . aw, forget it.

We'll cashier the 284 because you can scarcely find

If you like the 308 Winchester, and your taste runs toward autoloaders, the H&K 770 is an excellent choice. The 770 has an excellent reputation for remarkable accuracy.

Although the 284 Winchester is an excellent all around cartridge, it can be currently had only in the Shilen DGA, a well made, semi-custom rifle. The lack of rifle selection is what hurts.

The 30-06 is *versatile*. As can be seen here, the old ought-six can even do a fair job on varmints.

one except from such semi-custom makers as Shilen, more's the pity. It would be my first choice except for that one minor detail. Ballistically, it's all you need.

So is the 280 Remington, but I'm dumping it as well and for the same reason: not enough guns made for it. Like the 284, which it mirrors in range and punch, it has what it takes in the field. But not in the marketplace.

I'm going to let the 300 Magnums slide. For most of us they simply kick too much and assault our ears and wallets with a vengeance. If *you* can stand the recoil and don't mind toting a 9½- or 10-pound rifle around the whitetail woods, it's fine with me. Our mythical hero

does; he passes on the super thirties.

What's left now? The little 7x57, darling of W.D.M. Bell of African fame; its ballistic twin, the handy 7mm-08, which offers identical punch in a shorter, more accurate, less noisy package; the 270 Winchester, Jack O'Conner's cartridge, favorite of Townsend Whelen; the 7mm Remington Magnum, offspring of the cartridge the great Warren Page carried all over the world, dropping game with finality; the 7mm Weatherby Magnum, slightly more potent brother of the 7mm Remington; the 308 Winchester, accuracy expert, former darling of the benchrest crowd, now wowing the silhouette

The new Winchester Model 70 Featherweight is light, handy and is available in chamberings such as 308, 270, 30-06 and more — caliber choice is yours.

If you like lever guns, the Savage Model 99 in 308 Winchester is an excellent all around choice. In fact it's the best cartridge choice when it comes to lever-actions.

shooters and over-the-course target panners; and the 30-06, grandaddy of them all, wielded by Grancil Fitz to slay virtually all species of North American game. Those are our finalists.

More eliminations. The Big Seven mags will outpenetrate anything left on our list when fed the 175-grain Nosler Partition, which makes them the berries for game on the heavy end of our spectrum. However, for varmint hunting they are pretty grim. If necessary, one could hold down the powder charge a bit, and go to a faster number, but then trajectory and likely accuracy would suffer. The 7mm mags require a long action (compared to the 308 class), but so do the 270, 30-06 and 7x57, so we can't hold that against them. Instead, let's hold their recoil, muzzle blast, and barrel wear in disregard and kiss them good-bye. Remember, our mythical nimrod is going to be hunting *primarily* animals of less than 450 pounds in weight; on such game, the extra punch and penetration of the Big Sevens is not needed. Also bear in mind that regular varmint hunting is part of the plan; I would not want to spend a summer hunting chucks or crows with a 7mm magnum!

The 7mm-08 and 308 Winchester are dear to my heart. Unfortunately, they do not offer quite as much zip and slap as the longer 270 or 30-06. Thus, even for varmints, their range limitations are *slightly* inferior to the two larger cartridges, and we're trying to come up with a winner here. With a great sense of loss but in the interest of impartiality, I will suggest passing up these two worthies.

The 7x57 offers no more than the 308 or 7mm-08 and necessitates a longer action to house it. It is not as accurate as most of the cartridges we started with, particu-

larly with its fast twist. Thus, as a varmint round it would contribute to a woodchuck population explosion unless the hunter were adept at sneaking through the clover. No to the old 7mm Mauser.

The Finalists

Down to two, the good old 270 and the good older 30-06. Believe it or not, both are excellent varmint cartridges clear out to as far as you can hit 'em. Both cartridges are exceptionally accurate in good rifles, although no more so than many rounds we've eliminated. For varminting alone, the nod goes to the 270. Fas-

A good 270, like this Remington Model 700 Classic, makes an excellent all around gun for vermin, deer and elk.

ter, flatter, kicks a bit less.

On plains game like pronghorn, the 130-grain 270 at about 3050 fps is a classic. It drops only 19½ inches at 400 yards from a 200-yard zero if one of the boat-tail bullets is used. Retained energy is a healthy 1420 fpe, give or take a pound. That's a lot flatter than the 30-06, right? Nope. Kick a 150-grain Nosler soft point boat-tail along at 3000 fps from your 30-06 and 400-yard drop is 20.3 inches, with a retained energy reading of nearly 1500 fpe. Sounds like the old ought-six is holding its own.

But the 270 kicks less. Yep. If our hunter is recoil-sensitive, it might make a difference. But then the 270 is a little tougher on barrels, and our hero will be using his rifle on lots of varmints. If our hunter is money-sensitive, it might make a difference.

The 270 is loud. So's the 30-06. The 270 requires a

Load a modern 308 Winchester with these components and you'll get a real all-purpose load capable of taking deer, elk, caribou, and sheep at any reasonable range.

Layne Simpson is shown with his pet Ruger International. Chambered for the 243, 250-3000, or 308, the Ruger will perform many jobs well. (Photo by Layne Simpson.)

Shooter Mike Holloway works out a Savage M111 in 30-06. The old ought-six is, all things considered, the supreme all around cartridge.

A good 30-06 will often group like this with select handloads. Think that's good enough for chucks?!

.3125"

165 FRONTIER SPBT
FACTORY LOAD

KLEINGUENTHER
K-15 .30-06
10X ZEISS
100 YDS. REST

long action, and some of them run a little heavy. Ditto the 30-06. Inexpensive military brass is readily available for the 30-06. Bullets are cheaper for the 270.

Sounds like a draw doesn't it. It isn't. Up until now, each cartridge displays a very slight advantage over its fellow in some category or other. The big tie-breaker is the 200-grain Nosler Partition 30-caliber bullet. For use on elk and moose the 270 offers nothing to equal it. *Nothing*. Ignore the increased penetration the 200-grain Nosler .30-inch slug has over the 160-grain 270 Nosler; just look at down-range ballistics. Start the 200-grainer at 2650 fps in the 30-06 and you show 1894 fpe out at 400 yards. Goose the 160-grain 270 to 2750 fps and the retained energy out at 400 will be only 1373 fpe, 28 percent less for the 270. You say I cheated because the 160-grain Nosler is semi-pointed whereas the 200-grain is a spitzer? That's not my fault. But let's use the heaviest pointed slug in the 270, the 150-grain Partition. Started at 2900 fps (which takes a *hot* load), the 150-grain 270 bullet reaches 400 yards carrying a 1549 fpe payload, still 18 percent below the 30-06. That is a significant difference.

The Winner

It's no contest. The 30-06 beats all the rest when you look at it objectively. If you take into account that you can buy an ought-six chambered in any action type, that ammo is available everywhere ammo is sold, that you can buy match-grade bullets and enter a hunter-rifle benchrest match and not embarrass yourself, the aging but hale 30-06 looks all the better.

For a little cerebral stimulation, let's see what it would take to shade the ought-six if we were to design

No matter what the terrain, whether out West or back East, the 30-06 is at home. Hunter Glenn Barnes is shown with his pet M70 Winchester.

our own cartridge. The 30-284 would equal it and be adaptable to short actions, always a plus. But it wouldn't *beat* it.

How about taking the 6.5 Remington Magnum case and necking it up to 7mm? Then you could probably kick the 160-grain Nosler Partition out the muzzle at about 3000 fps, which brings with it nearly 3200 fpe at the muzzle and retains a serious 1839 fpe out at 400 yards. That is within less than 3 percent of the 30-06 and its 200-grain Nosler. Trajectory would favor the 7mm/6.5 Magnum: our wildcat would dip a mere 18.8 inches at 400 yards from a 200-yards zero compared to 23.8 inches for the 30-06. Five inches is a lot.

So here we would have a load that should burn powder in similar amounts to the 30-06, and recoil about the same, or so close no one could tell the difference. Energy levels would be comparable, although the 200-grain Nosler would likely outpenetrate the lighter 7mm bullet, making it preferable on the really big stuff. Our wildcat would shoot flatter with the best bullets in each, and serve at least as well on varmints.

Better than the 30-06? Perhaps a little. Enough to warrant the exercise? I doubt it. The 30-06 is tough to beat, just as it has been for nearly eight decades.

Choosing a Rifle and Cartridge for Deer

ANY RIFLE cartridge is a good deer cartridge. That is unarguable. Absolute. If you are the type of hunter who can sneak up to within 10 yards of a buck, wait patiently and motionlessly until his head is turned just right, then shoot him in his left eye, a 22 Short will serve you well. If you know of a water hole frequented by deer, and can sit idly for days at a time until one comes to drink, and can slip a bullet anywhere you want it at the 25-yard distance separating you from the deer, then a 22 Hornet bullet legally placed between the ear and the eye will gain you venison. If you can abide hour after chilling hour perched in a tree stand, awaiting the crunch of a feeding buck in the cornfield 50 yards to your front, a 243 slug applied to his ribcage will put steaks in your freezer. If you have the ability to lie belly-down in the snow while scanning yonder ridge with your binoculars, spot a bedded mule deer buck two football fields away, poke a quick-expanding 270 bullet through his neck or lungs, you'll need search no longer.

On the other hand, if you run deer with dogs until the quarry is processing gallons of adrenalin through their systems, you'll need stouter ordnance. If you like to push through the woods, jumping deer like rabbits, taking shots as they come at whatever portion of the deer's anatomy presents itself, the more cartridge you shoot the better. If you feel no qualms about drawing a bead on a buck making tracks 400 yards away across a sage flat, what you need is a heavy cartridge throwing a sizable chunk of lead at a 3000 fps muzzle speed. In short, the kind of *hunter* you are dictates the kind of cartridge you need.

Most hunters can't consistently sneak up to within 30 or 40 yards of a deer, particularly a buck. However, most can and do get shots at less than 100. I have never had a shot at a whitetail *past* 100 yards, but a few of my field-watching hunting cronies have. (I've watched plenty of fields. I just never saw a buck in one.) Taken nationwide, I'd expect the average whitetail to be taken under the 100-yard mark.

A list of cartridges that have the wherewithal to take bucks cleanly at such distances would include the 30-30 class (32 Winchester Special, 35 Remington, 44 Magnum and 375 Winchester); the 30-06 class (7x57 Mauser, 7mm-08 Remington, 270 Winchester, 300 Savage, 308 Winchester, and 8mm Mauser); the 6mm class (243 Winchester, 6mm Remington, 250-3000, 257 Roberts); and those that defy classification such as the 25-06, the 444 Marlin, and the 45-70. Of course, most of these cartridges are more potent than necessary for close-in deer shooting, and many offer sufficient ballistics for greater distances. Nonetheless, all of these loads have their following among the stump-sitting, let-the-deer-come-to-them clan.

For the guys who like to oversee large tracts of turf, whether an eastern soybean field, a midwestern cornrow, or a southwestern mesquite flat, where ranges run from 150 to 400 yards or so, the following are apropos: the 25-06, 270 Winchester, 7x57, 284 Winchester, 7mm-08, 280 Remington, 308 Winchester, 30-06, 8mm Mauser, and such magnums as the 264 Winchester, 6.5 Remington, 7mm Remington, 300 Holland & Holland, 300 Winchester, and the host of Weatherby magnums below 30-caliber.

If your taste in hunting runs to deeply-forested ter-

Hugh Brodie took this super-fine eight-point whitetail at less than 100 yards with a 30-06 Browning. The 30-06 is the most popular deer cartridge made, although it offers more power than needed.

(Left) If the hunter sits on a stand all day, a long, heavy turn-bolt will do fine on whitetails. For moving through the timber, such ordnance can get in the way.

rain, or if you dote on *proper* still-hunting, here's the list: 308 Winchester, 358 Winchester, 350 Remington Magnum, 444 Marlin, and 45-70 Government.

Let's begin our specifics with the average deer hunter who climbs a tree or straddles a log. Aside from adequate killing power, which all the loads on the above list contain, his most important cartridge attribute is moderate recoil. Why? Well, the most obvious reason is that

he doesn't want to get booted out of his stand, particularly one high in an oak tree. This happens far more frequently than you might think. A friend of a friend, hunting during blackpowder season, got belted out of his tree stand, fell a couple of dozen feet, broke both his sternum and his spine. No fun.

Another case for moderate recoil is a fast follow-up shot. When hunting in densely-wooded terrain, your

The Heckler & Koch M770 308 is a good deer gun, but a bit heavy to be ideal, plus the safety is awkward. Good but not perfect.

This Shilen DGA 284 makes a crackerjack deer gun for any kind of terrain, although its barrel would do better in brush if it were 4 inches shorter.

deer is never more than a jump or two from cover. If your hit is not a good one, you may trail your buck to another man's pickup truck. Moderate kick enables you to smack your deer again if your first shot is a poor one, or is deflected by brush.

Rifle Selection

A specific choice of cartridge depends on several factors. Will you use the rifle for another purpose, such as off-season varminting or turkey hunting? What type of rifle will you be using? One of my hunting buddies, Grady Shields, hunts year-round with one rifle, a Remington Model 788 in 308 Winchester. It's his only centerfire rifle; he shoots it well; it drops deer. He's satisfied.

Mike Holloway carries a Ruger 77 chambered to 250-3000. Like Grady, Mike owns only one centerfire rifle. He never shot a buck with his 250 that got away. Dave Coffee likes a Remington 788 243 and a Winchester Model 94 30-30. Which gun he chooses depends on the weather; he uses the scoped 243 on clear days, the iron-sighted 30-30 when it rains. The last buck Dave shot with his 243 took not a step. Jimmy Michael owns one deer gun, a Remington 788 in 308.

Note that all the above hunters use bolt-action rifles. From choice. None of these hunters is much concerned with follow-up speed since not one of them has had to shoot a deer twice. They are all careful hunters, good game shots, and are knowledgeable about a buck's anatomy. They all hunt from a stand. They are all satisfied with their armament. All their rifles offer moderate recoil.

My case is a bit different; I have trouble sitting still for long spells. I tend to go to sleep. (In fact, I once had a deer cross right in front of me as I dozed against a comfortable pine tree. I found its tracks when I got up for lunch.) I'm a still-hunter by nature. I do sit down at dawn and dusk, but during the middle of the day I stay

The Savage M99-E in 250-3000 is a fine deer rifle and cartridge for ranges up to 250-300 yards. This outfit can double on chucks in summer; it's very accurate.

(Below) Hunter Bill Barry claims that a whitetail hunter in such terrain as this can do nicely with a longer bolt-action, like this Model 70 Featherweight in 7x57.

on the move. My movin' gun is a Marlin Model 336 in 35 Remington. Why a 35? Because you can't get a Marlin 336 in 7mm-08 or 308 Winchester, and I like the Marlin. In this instance, the gun virtually dictates the cartridge.

When I am on a stand I use either a Ruger M77 Ultra Light in 243 Winchester, or a Remington Model Seven 7mm-08. The 243 wears a Bausch & Lomb 4x scope; the Model Seven sports a Leupold 1.5x5 in Leupold mounts. Both rifles are light, accurate, and I have confidence in them. Of course, sometimes I hunt with a rifle on which I'm preparing an article, but these three guns are my standbys.

You might decide to hunt with a 7mm-08 or a 35 Remington because I like them, or your Uncle Fudd does. Further, since your cousin Cletus dotes on his Remington Model Four autoloader, you may want one of those. Sorry, doesn't come in either caliber. Here you must decide whether you want the *cartridge* of your choice, or the *rifle*.

This Smith & Wesson Classic Hunter would be a nice deer rifle both in the East and out West if chambered for the 308 or 270 or 30-06. Dave Coffee is the guy behind the gun.

If it's accuracy you're after, a quality turnbolt like the Browning BBR seen here, can fill the bill nicely. A quality variable power scope — this BBR is wearing a Bushnell — can be a decided plus, especially if the terrain is varied.

Lewis Dawkins with the author's Remington Model Six pump, a fine deer gun. Recoil is light, the action is fast-working, but the gun is too long and heavy to be ideal.

Such decisions are often dictated when choosing a hunting rifle. If you are enamored of the traditional deer loads, like the 35 Remington or 32 Special, you can pick a lever-action, period. Ditto if you plan to utilize one of the big thumpers like the 444 Marlin or 375 Winchester. The 45-70 comes in both levers and single shots, as does the 30-30, and the 44 Magnum in lever, autoloading, and single shot persuasion, so there you have a modicum of preference.

The 7x57 Mauser is available in the Ruger Number 1 and various boltguns, the 300 Savage only in the Savage Model 99, the 7mm-08 in bolts and levers, the 8mm Mauser not in anything new. Only when you get into the realm of the truly popular cartridges do you begin to get a real selection. The 243 and 308 come in the Savage 99 and Browning BLR, the Remington Model Six pump, the Browning BAR and Remington Model Four semi-autos, and too many turnbolts to list. The 243 is offered in the Number 1; both are chambered by Heckler & Koch for the Model 770 self-loader. The 30-06 is chambered in all types of actions, the 270 all but the le-

vers. And so on.

My point is that if you are content to use one of the revered cartridges mentioned here, you can just about pick your action type and be done with it. It is only when you venture into less-familiar waters—like those in which the 250-3000 or 280 Remington eddy—that the choice of rifles becomes limited.

The magnum fanciers are pretty much wed to the Ruger Number 1 or the many bolt-actions that are produced in the belted numbers. Only Browning offers an alternative, chambering the BAR semi-automatic for the 7mm Remington Magnum and the 300 Winchester Magnum. Such useful but unpopular loads as the 6.5 and the 350 Remington Magnums have been relegated to the used-gun rack.

Assuming you to be a rugged individualist, not content merely to purchase your deer rifle based solely on the opinions of your hunting club, just what *should* you buy? If you're convinced that firepower is the best way to go, as obviously many are, then I suppose you need a self-loader. There are a plenitude of calibers for you to

Fred Ritter has taken more than a few whitetails with this Marlin 336 in 30-30. He says under 100 yards the 30-30 will deck 'em as quick as anything.

survey and four brands of rifles cater to your needs.

If a tad less speed will satisfy you, a Remington Model Six, or one of its less-expensive siblings, will serve as a willing and faithful servant. And the average Remington slide-action will reward you with accuracy most semi-automatics can only dream of. Not to mention better reliability and a broader taste in ammunition.

For the traditionalist, the Marlin and Winchester leverguns are chambered in an ever-increasing plethora of deer cartridges. Contrary to what you may have heard, such guns as these are plenty accurate at the ranges for which their cartridges are suited. Now that Winchester has introduced the Angle Eject, the Model 94 can be scoped centrally over the bore, relieving a complaint that has harried the gun for years. Of course, the Marlin has never been hounded by this problem; it ejects to the side.

The less-traditional minded—and more pragmatic and demanding of gilt-edged accuracy from their fast-firing ordnance—will find happiness in the arms of Sav-

(Right) Shooter Dave Coffee and the author's Remington M700 Classic; in 270, 30-06, or 6mm, this would do okay for deer, although it is longer and heavier than need be.

This Marlin 336 in 35 Remington will handle any whitetail that hunter Dave Coffee will come across in the type of area he hunts.

The 35 Rem., left, and the 30-30, right, are both suitable deer loads for most deer hunting in brushy country.

Glenn Barnes has set up a whitetail "blind"; from such a position it makes little difference what kind of rifle you use. One shot will usually do the job from a good 308, 270, 7mm-08, 7x57, or 30-06.

age and Browning. The Savage M99 can be had in several modern deer loads, as can the BLR. In my experience, either of these rifles can be counted on to group nearly as well as the average boltgun of comparable caliber.

The bolt-action and single shot rifles are for the connoisseur, the gentleman deer hunter who is more interested in a clean, quick kill than in blowing multiple holes in a deer's carcass, filling the woods with flying lead, or playing soldier of fortune in the off season. After years of interviewing hunters, I have noted one interesting fact: Most bolt-action users somehow manage to deck their bucks with one shot. The wielders of quick-shooting smokepoles, most particularly the self-shuckers, seem to require more ammunition to bring their venison to bag. If they do.

Take your pick. But it's my book and I'm supposed to offer my opinion, right? I already did. I hunt with a lever-action and two turnbolts, and I'd not kick if I were forced to use a Remington Model Six if its barrel were shortened and the weight slimmed down.

Caliber Selection

Now for caliber. Here, the plot thickens and the water begets the consistency of pea soup. If I were satisfied with stump-sitting or limb-perching, and my ranges would be confined to the length of a football field, I would be happy with nearly any cartridge from the 243 up through the 30-06. You could shoot thousands of deer with all of them and never notice any difference, assuming a good bullet and proper shot placement.

Unconvinced? I know a policeman who has slain 25 deer with 25 shots from an ancient Savage 99 in 300 Savage. No deer went as far as 90 yards from where it was hit; none was farther than 50 yards at the shot; all were taken with factory ammunition.

Another friend has dropped nine deer with his Winchester 30-30 with factory 170-grain soft points. None ever got away; only one traveled more than a few yards; all were shot at under 100 yards.

Fred Ritter and Gary Wade have between them killed around 50 deer with the 243 and 6mm Remington. Only one was ever lost, and that one because of swampy conditions that failed to reveal a blood trail. They have also taken a similar number with the 270 Winchester and no failures. Gary believes that the 243 drops deer closer to where they're standing than does the 270. Fred likes the 308, claims it really mows 'em down.

Troy Pickett used to hunt with a Remington 30-06 until a lung-shot buck, hit at close range, escaped. (He found the deer next day, spoiled.) He switched to the 6mm Remington and the 44 Magnum. Last time I saw him, he'd just killed a buck with each, both one-shot kills.

This buck and rifle belong to Layne Simpson. The gun is the Remington M7 in 7mm-08. The author believes that this rifle/cartridge combo is the ultimate deer outfit currently produced.

And so on. You're perfectly welcome to read all you want, talk to as many hunters as you can find, gain as much experience as you can. If you do, and the folks you read and talk to are honest, impartial observers, you'll discover one undeniable fact: at ranges up to 100 yards or a little more, it matters little what you hit 'em with.

Move the range out to 150 yards and more, and such classics as the 30-30 and 35 Remington begin to lose their *oomph*. Add another 100 yards or so and the 6mm cartridges and small-case 25s begin to run out of steam. (Actually, bullet performance becomes undependable, which is not the fault of the cartridge, but is still an undeniable limitation.) So, for true 300-yard shooting, we are left with the 25-06, 6.5 Remington Mag., 270, 7x57, 7mm-08, 284 Winchester, 280 Remington, 308 Winchester, 30-06, 8mm Mauser, 358 Winchester, and the 350 Remington Magnum. (Of course, you have the bigger-cased magnums such as the 264 and the 7mm, but these are not really necessary for deer at any reasonable range.) Of these, we can eliminate the 6.5 Mag., the

8mm Mauser, and the two 35s from our list of ideals. Rifles in these calibers are either limited to one model or are discontinued altogether, and ammunition for them is not always available at Elmo's Shooting Emporium. If you have a stout, modern rifle chambered for the 30-40 Krag or the 300 Savage, feel free to add either to this list.

If I planned to hunt from a stand most of the time, I'd opt for the 25-06, the 270, the 280 Remington, the 30-06, or the 284 if I could locate one. All but the 284 are put up in long-actioned turnbolts (the action type I'd pick), which is no disadvantage to the sit-and-watch nimrod.

On the other hand, if I intended to divide my hunting day between watching the wide, open spaces and pussyfooting through the blowdowns, I'd insist on a handier bolt-action. Like a Ruger Ultra light or a Remington Model Seven or one of the new abbreviated Model 70 Featherweights. Caliber choice would be either 308 Winchester or 7mm-08, depending on the rifle. The difference in handling qualities between these marvelous rifles and their longer, heavier brethren is unbelievable. Try one for yourself.

Back in the woods, jump-shooting anything that moved, most likely in its rear end, I'd want to tote a Marlin 444 or 45-70 with heavy Hornady bullets of 265 and 350 grains respectively. The chance of having to fire a follow-up shot at a departing whitetail would be very real under such conditions, which is why I would choose a levergun if I had my druthers. Why not an auto? Too long of limb and broad of beam, ungainly things that handle like fire hydrants. Whoever heard of a sweet-handling self-loader chambered for a cartridge delivering around 2500 fpe at the muzzle? (You need this kind of punch to drive a slug lengthwise through an excited buck.) As runner-up choices, I could make do with a Browning BLR or Savage 99 in 7mm-08, 308, or 358 Winchester, but the BLR is too long in the buttstock for me and the Model 99 has too much barrel and no exposed hammer.

One of the discontinued Remington Model 760 pump-action carbines would do okay, just a little heavy. Any caliber from 270 Winchester up should do just fine.

Finally, such bolt-action carbines as the Remington Model Seven and Ruger International chambered to 7mm-08 or 308 would work out. They'd be a bit slow on repeat shots, but probably not enough to matter much. All things considered, the Marlin levers or possibly the new Winchester Angle Eject 444 would be first choice.

One final exercise before leaving this matter of deer guns and loads. I have often read that there is no ideal deer rifle or cartridge. I'll agree as far as the rifle is concerned; there's simply too much room for personal preference and prejudice. Let's beg the question of the perfect rifle and concentrate on the possibility of an

The new 307 and 356 Winchester cartridges make fine deer loads, and the Angle-Eject Model 94 is a fine, short, fairly light deer gun.

indefectible deer cartridge. Pretend we have a computer at our disposal into which we can feed all the theoretical attributes of an ideal deer load. Hmm, what should they be?

We'll need ample killing power; let's say a bullet of at least 6mm caliber and 100 grains in weight with a retained energy of at least 1355 fpe at 300 yards. These were chosen not arbitrarily; the 243 is generally considered to be of minimum caliber, the 100-grain bullet the lightest for use on deer, and the 30-30's 100-yard energy level is usually considered about par. If we settled on the 30-06 as having a useful and near-optimum trajectory when stoked with the popular 180-grain pointed soft point, then our mythical cartridge should equal or better 9.3 inches of drop at 300 yards from a 200-yard zero.

Our cartridge should work through true short-action rifles, for several reasons. First, it should fit as many different types and brands of rifles as possible, to enable hunters to have a wide choice of guns. Second, I believe even the most hardened 30-06 or 7mm Magnum fan will grudgingly concede that the shorter the rifle the better for handling, the shorter the cartridge the quicker a bolt or lever can be manipulated, and the smaller a cartridge the more efficient it is. Additionally, a small-cased cartridge is easier on the ears, caresses the shoulder more lovingly, and is almost always potentially more accurate. So long as our computer cartridge provides adequate (but not excessive) killing power along with a useful trajectory, the smaller and milder it is, the better. We needn't even go into the economic factors or ease of handloading or conserving of powder, right? No need gilding the lily.

Our computer has taken the information we've fed into it, boiled it in a seething caldron, muttered secret imprecations, and spewed forth a readout. On it is printed the specifications for the perfect deer cartridge. The joke's on us. It's been with us in commercial form for several years: the 7mm-08 Remington. Don't believe me? Check it out for yourself.

The standard 140-grain factory load shows nearly 1500 fpe at 300 yards, still carries more than 1000 fpe way out at 500 yards. Three-hundred-yard drop is only 8.1 inches, flatter than *any* deer-weight bullet Remington stuffs in the 30-06 save the 150-grain bronze point at 8.0 inches. The cartridge is short enough to work through the Savage 99 and Browning BLR (both of which offer it), the Remington trombone action, such short-action autos as the Heckler & Koch, and the whole clan of petite turnbolts exemplified by the Remington Model Seven (which also chambers it). It is mild of voice, accurate (it's a very popular cartridge in the demanding game of metallic silhouette competition), and recoil is managable even by neophytes. Is it perfect? Can you come up with anything else that fits *all* the criteria?

So there you have it, as good a way as any to settle on a rifle and cartridge for *your* type of deer hunting. Of course, there may be overriding circumstances that could nullify the preceding discussion. You might, for example, have 3000 rounds of surplus 30-06 military ammunition in your attic, which would have some influence on your choice of cartridge. It's possible that you grew up quail hunting with an elderly Model 12, 20-gauge pump; you might prefer to stick with that action type when selecting your deer rifle, thus limiting your selection of cartridge candidates. For various health reasons, you might require a very light-recoiling rifle/cartridge combination such as the 250-3000. Or you may plan to hunt deer in an area where you are likely to be attacked by wild boars, et by vicious grizzlies, treed by packs of marauding feral dogs. The point is that elements beyond your control could very well dictate your choice of armament. Aside from such esoteric influences, this chapter should at least point you in the right direction.